business **solutions**

# Formulas **and** Functions with Microsoft® Excel 2003

*Paul McFedries*

# Contents at a Glance

800 E. 96th Street
Indianapolis, Indiana 46240

# Formulas and Functions with Microsoft® Excel 2003

## Copyright © 2005 by Sams Publishing

International Standard Book Number: 0-7897-3153-3

Library of Congress Catalog Card Number: 2004102248

Printed in the United States of America

First Printing: July 2004

07　06　05　04　　　　　4　3　2　1

## Trademarks

## Warning and Disclaimer

## Bulk Sales

Sams Publishing offers excellent discounts on this book when ordered in quantity for bulk purchases or special sales. For more information, please contact

**U.S. Corporate and Government Sales**
**1-800-382-3419**
corpsales@pearsontechgroup.com

For sales outside the U.S., please contact

**International Sales**
**1-317-428-3341**
international@pearsontechgroup.com

**Associate Publisher**
Michael Stephens

**Acquisitions Editor**
Loretta Yates

**Development Editor**
Sean Dixon

**Managing Editor**
Charlotte Clapp

**Project Editor**
Tonya Simpson

**Copy Editor**
Krista Hansing

**Indexer**
Erika Millen

**Proofreader**
Jennifer Timpe

**Technical Editor**
Greg Perry

**Publishing Coordinator**
Cindy Teeters

**Book Designer**
Anne Jones

# Contents

## III BUILDING BUSINESS MODELS

# About the Author

**Paul McFedries** is the president of Logophilia Limited, a technical writing company. Now primarily a writer, Paul has worked as a programmer, consultant, spreadsheet developer, and Web site developer. He has written more than 40 books that have sold nearly three million copies worldwide. These books include *Access 2003 Forms, Reports, and Queries* (Sams, 2004), *The Absolute Beginner's Guide to VBA* (Que, 2004), and *The Complete Idiot's Guide to Windows XP* (Alpha, 2001).

# Dedication

*To Karen and Gypsy.*

# Acknowledgments

Being an author is the most wonderful vocation (I don't think of it as a job) I can imagine. I get to play with words, I get to talk about things I'm intensely interested in, and I get some big-time warm, fuzzy feelings when people write to me to tell me that, in some small way, something I've written has helped them.

However, just because my name is the only one that appears on the cover, don't think that this book is solely my creation. Any book is the result of the efforts of many hard-working people. The Que editorial staff, in particular, never fail to impress me with their dedication, work ethic, and commitment to quality. You'll find a list of all the people who worked on this book near the front, but there are a few I'd like to thank personally: acquisitions editor Loretta Yates, development editor Sean Dixon, project editor Tonya Simpson, copy editor Krista Hansing, and tech editor Greg Perry.

# We Want to Hear from You!

As the reader of this book, *you* are our most important critic and commentator. We value your opinion and want to know what we're doing right, what we could do better, what areas you'd like to see us publish in, and any other words of wisdom you're willing to pass our way.

As an associate publisher for Que Publishing, I welcome your comments. You can email or write me directly to let me know what you did or didn't like about this book—as well as what we can do to make our books better.

*Please note that I cannot help you with technical problems related to the topic of this book. We do have a User Services group, however, where I will forward specific technical questions related to the book.*

When you write, please be sure to include this book's title and author as well as your name, email address, and phone number. I will carefully review your comments and share them with the author and editors who worked on the book.

Email:    feedback@quepublishing.com

Mail:     Michael Stephens
          Associate Publisher
          Que Publishing
          800 East 96th Street
          Indianapolis, IN 46240 USA

For more information about this book or another Que title, visit our Web site at www.quepublishing.com. Type the ISBN (0789731533) or the title of a book in the Search field to find the page you're looking for.

# INTRODUCTION

The old 80/20 rule for software—that 80% of a program's users use only 20% of a program's features—doesn't apply to Microsoft Excel. Instead, this program probably operates under what could be called the 95/5 rule: 95% of Excel users use a mere 5% of the program's power. On the other hand, most people *know* that they could be getting more out of Excel if they could only get a leg up on building formulas and using functions. Unfortunately, this side of Excel appears complex and intimidating to the uninitiated, shrouded as it is in the mysteries of mathematics, finance, and impenetrable spreadsheet jargon.

If this sounds like the situation you find yourself in, and if you're a businessperson who *needs* to use Excel as an everyday part of your job, then you've come to the right book. In *Formulas and Functions with Microsoft Excel 2003*, I demystify the building of worksheet formulas and present the most useful of Excel's many functions in an accessible, jargon-free way. This book not only takes you through Excel's intermediate and advanced formula-building features, but it also tells you *why* these features are useful to you and shows you *how* to use them in everyday situations and real-world models. This book does all this with no-nonsense, step-by-step tutorials and lots of practical, useful examples aimed directly at business users.

Even if you've never been able to get Excel to do much beyond storing data and adding a couple of numbers, you'll find this book to your liking. I show you how to build useful, powerful formulas from the ground up, so no experience with Excel formulas and functions is necessary.

## What's in the Book

This book isn't meant to be read from cover to cover, although you're certainly free to do just that if the mood strikes you. Instead, most of the chapters are set up as self-contained units that you can dip into at will to extract whatever nuggets of information you need. However, if you're a relatively new Excel user, I suggest starting with Chapters 1, "Getting the Most Out of Ranges"; 2, "Using Range Names"; 3, "Building Basic Formulas"; and 6, "Using Functions" to ensure that you have a thorough grounding in the fundamentals of Excel ranges, formulas, and functions.

The book is divided into four main parts. To give you the big picture before diving in, here's a summary of what you'll find in each part:

- **Part I, "Mastering Excel Ranges and Formulas"**—The five chapters in Part 1 tell you just about everything you need to know about building formulas in Excel. Starting with a thorough look at ranges (crucial for mastering formulas), this part also discusses operators, expressions, advanced formula features, and formula-troubleshooting techniques.

- **Part II, "Harnessing the Power of Functions"**—Functions take your formulas to the next level, and you'll learn all about them in Part 2. After you see how to use functions in your formulas, you examine the eight main function categories—text, logical, information, lookup, date, time, math, and statistical. In each case, I tell you how to use the functions and give you lots of practical examples that show you how you can use the functions in everyday business situations.

- **Part III, "Building Business Models"**—The four chapters in Part 3 are all business as they examine various facets of building useful and robust business models. You learn how to analyze data with Excel lists, how to use what-if analysis and Excel's Goal Seek and scenarios features, how to use powerful regression-analysis techniques to track trends and make forecasts, and how to use the amazing Solver feature to solve complex problems.

- **Part IV, "Building Financial Formulas"**—The book finishes with more business goodies related to performing financial wizardry with Excel. You learn techniques and functions for amortizing loans, analyzing investments, dealing with bonds, and using discounting for business case and cash-flow analysis.

## This Book's Special Features

*Formulas and Functions with Microsoft Excel 2003* is designed to give you the information you need without making you wade through ponderous explanations and interminable technical background. To make your life easier, this book includes various features and conventions that help you get the most out of the book and Excel itself.

- **Steps**—Throughout the book, each Excel task is summarized in step-by-step procedures.

- **Things you type**—Whenever I suggest that you type something, what you type appears in a **bold** font.

- **Commands**—I use the following style for Excel menu commands: File, Open. This means that you pull down the File menu and select the Open command.
- **Dialog box controls**—Dialog box controls have underlined accelerator keys: Close.
- **Functions**—Excel worksheet functions appear in capital letters and are followed by parentheses: SUM(). When I list the arguments you can use with a function, optional arguments appear surrounded by square brackets: CELL(*info_type*, [*reference*]).
- **Code-continuation character (➥)**—When a formula is too long to fit on one line of this book, it's broken at a convenient place, and the code-continuation character appears at the beginning of the next line.

This book also uses the following boxes to draw your attention to important (or merely interesting) information.

> **NOTE**
> The Note box presents asides that give you more information about the topic under discussion. These tidbits provide extra insights that give you a better understanding of the task at hand.

> **TIP**
> The Tip box tells you about Excel methods that are easier, faster, or more efficient than the standard methods.

> **CAUTION**
> The all-important Caution box tells you about potential accidents waiting to happen. There are always ways to mess things up when you're working with computers. These boxes help you avoid at least some of the pitfalls.

➔ These cross-reference elements point you to related material elsewhere in the book.

## CASE STUDY

You'll find these case studies throughout the book, designed to apply what you've learned to projects and real-world examples.

# Mastering Excel Ranges and Formulas

# Getting the Most Out of Ranges

**1**

Other than performing data-entry chores, you probably spend most of your Excel life working with ranges in some way. Whether you're copying, moving, formatting, naming, or filling them, ranges are a big part of Excel's day-to-day operations. And why not? After all, working with a range of cells is a lot easier than working with each cell individually. For example, suppose that you want to know the average of a column of numbers running from B1 to B30. You *could* enter all 30 cells as arguments in the AVERAGE function, but I'm assuming that you have a life to lead away from your computer screen. Typing =AVERAGE(B1:B30) is decidedly quicker (and probably more accurate).

In other words, ranges save time and they save wear and tear on your typing fingers. But there's more to ranges than that. Ranges are powerful tools that can unlock the hidden power of Excel. So, the more you know about ranges, the more you'll get out of your Excel investment. This chapter reviews some range basics and then takes you beyond the range routine and shows you some techniques for taking full advantage of Excel's range capabilities.

## A Review of Excel's Range-Selection Techniques

As you work with Excel, you'll come across three situations in which you'll select a cell range:

- When a dialog box field requires a range input
- While entering a function argument
- Before selecting a command that uses a range input

In a dialog box field or function argument, the most straightforward way to select a range is to enter the range coordinates by hand. Just type the address of the upper-left cell (called the *anchor cell*), followed by a colon and then the address of the lower-right cell. To use this method, either you must be able to see the range you want to select or you must know in advance the range coordinates you want. Because often this is not the case, most people don't type the range coordinates directly; instead, they select ranges using either the mouse or the keyboard.

## Selecting a Range with the Mouse

Although you can use either the mouse or the keyboard to select a range, you'll find that the mouse makes the job much easier. The following sections take you through several methods you can use to select a range with the mouse.

### Selecting a Contiguous Range with the Mouse

A rectangular, contiguous (without gaps) grouping of cells is the most common type of range. To use the mouse to select such a range, follow these steps:

1. Point the mouse at the upper-left cell of the range (this cell is called the *anchor*); then press and hold down the left mouse button.

2. With the left mouse button still pressed, drag the mouse pointer to the lower-right cell of the range. The cell selector remains around the anchor cell, and Excel highlights the other cells in the range in reverse video. The formula bar's Name box shows the number of rows and columns you've selected, as shown in Figure 1.1.

> **NOTE**
> These steps show you how to select the range from the top left to the lower right. However, no rule says you have to do it this way. That is, you're free to select the range by clicking and dragging from the lower-right cell to the upper-left cell. This is particularly useful if the lower-right cell is onscreen but the upper-left cell is not. Dragging the selection up scrolls the top of the range into view.

3. Release the mouse button. The cells remain selected to show the range you've defined, and the Name box shows the address of the anchor cell.

### Selecting a Row or Column with the Mouse

Using the worksheet row and column headings, you can quickly select a range that consists of an entire row or column. For a row, click the row's heading; for a column, click the column's heading. If you need to select adjacent rows or columns, click and drag the mouse pointer across the appropriate headings.

What if you want to select every row and every column (or, in other words, the entire worksheet)? Easy: Click the Select All button near the upper-left corner of the sheet, as shown in Figure 1.2. (You can also press Ctrl+A.)

The Name box shows the number
of rows and columns selected

Five rows are selected

**Figure 1.1**

As you select a range, the
Name box shows the
number of rows and
columns you've selected.

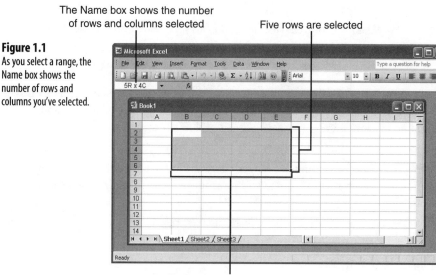

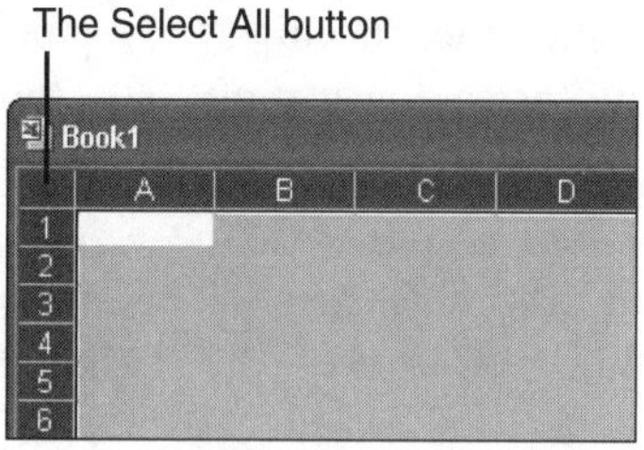

Four columns are selected

The Select All button

**Figure 1.2**

Click the Select All but-
ton to select the entire
worksheet.

## Selecting a Range in Extend Mode with the Mouse

An alternative method for using the mouse to select a rectangular, contiguous range uses
Excel's Extend mode. When you activate this mode, Excel extends the current selection to
whatever cell you click. Here's how it works:

1. Click the upper-left cell of the range you want to select.
2. Press F8. Excel enters Extend mode (you see EXT in the status bar).
3. Click the lower-right cell of the range. Excel selects the entire range.
4. Press F8 again to turn off Extend mode.

## Selecting a Noncontiguous Range with the Mouse

If the cells you want to work with are scattered willy-nilly throughout the sheet, you need
to combine them into a noncontiguous range. The secret to defining a noncontiguous
range is to hold down the Ctrl key while selecting the cells. The following steps give you
the details:

**1**

> **CAUTION**
>
> Be careful when selecting cells with this method. After you've selected a cell, the only way to dese-
> lect it is by starting over.

1. Select the first cell or the first rectangular range you want to include in the noncontiguous range. If you're selecting a rectangular range, you can use any of the methods
   described previously.

2. Press and hold down the Ctrl key.

3. Select the other cells or rectangular ranges you want to include in the noncontiguous
   range. Note, however, that for subsequent rectangular ranges, you can't use the Extend
   mode procedure.

4. When you've finished selecting cells, release the Ctrl key.

### Mouse Range-Selection Tricks

Bear in mind these handy techniques when using a mouse to select a range:

- When selecting a rectangular, contiguous range, you might find that you select the
  wrong lower-right corner and your range ends up either too big or too small. To fix it,
  hold down the Shift key and click the correct lower-right cell. The range adjusts automatically.

- After selecting a large range, you'll often no longer see the active cell because you've
  scrolled it off the screen. If you need to see the active cell before continuing, you can
  either use the scrollbars to bring it into view or press Ctrl+backspace.

> **CAUTION**
>
> When selecting a noncontiguous range, always press and hold down the Ctrl key *after* you've
> selected your first cell or range. Otherwise, Excel includes the currently selected cell or range as part
> of the noncontiguous range. This action could create a circular reference in a function if you were
> defining the range as one of the function's arguments.

→ If you're not sure what a "circular reference" is, **see** "Fixing Circular References," **p. 113**.

## Selecting Cell Ranges with the Keyboard

If your mouse is buried under paperwork, or if you just prefer to use your keyboard, you
still have plenty of range-selection methods at your disposal. In fact, you have no fewer
than three methods to choose from, as described in the next few sections.

## Selecting a Contiguous Range with the Keyboard

If the cells you want to work with form a rectangular, contiguous block, here's how to select them from the keyboard:

1. Use the arrow keys to select the upper-left cell of the range (this is the anchor cell).
2. Press and hold down the Shift key.
3. Use the arrow keys (or Page Up and Page Down, if the range is a large one) to highlight the rest of the cells.
4. Release Shift.

## Selecting a Row or a Column with the Keyboard

Selecting an entire row or column from the keyboard is a snap. Just select a cell in the row or column you want, and then press either Ctrl+spacebar to select the current column or Shift+spacebar to select the current row.

If you want to select the entire worksheet, press Ctrl+A.

## Selecting a Noncontiguous Range with the Keyboard

If you need to select a noncontiguous range with the keyboard, follow these steps:

1. Select the first cell or range you want to include in the noncontiguous range.
2. Press Shift+F8 to enter Add mode. (ADD appears in the status line.)
3. Select the next cell or range you want to include in the noncontiguous range.
4. Repeat steps 2 and 3 until you've selected the entire range.

## Keyboard Range-Selection Tricks

Excel also comes with a couple of tricks to make selecting a range via the keyboard easier or more efficient:

- If you want to select a contiguous range that contains data, there's an easier way to select the entire range. First, move to the upper-left cell of the range. To select the contiguous cells below the upper-left cell, press Ctrl+Shift+down arrow; to select the contiguous cells to the right of the selected cells, press Ctrl+Shift+right arrow.
- If you select a range large enough that all the cells don't fit on the screen, you can scroll through the selected cells by activating the Scroll Lock key. When Scroll Lock is on, pressing the arrow keys (or Page Up and Page Down) scrolls you through the cells while keeping the selection intact.

## Working with 3D Ranges

A *3D range* is a range selected on multiple worksheets. This is a powerful concept because it means that you can select a range on two or more sheets and then enter data, apply formatting, or give a command, and the operation will affect all the ranges at once.

To create a 3D range, you first need to group the worksheets you want to work with. To select multiple sheets, use any of the following techniques:

- To select adjacent sheets, click the tab of the first sheet, hold down the Shift key, and click the tab of the last sheet.
- To select nonadjacent sheets, hold down the Ctrl key and click the tab of each sheet you want to include in the group.
- To select all the sheets in a workbook, right-click any sheet tab and click the Select All Sheets command.

When you've selected your sheets, each tab is highlighted and [Group] appears in the workbook title bar. To ungroup the sheets, click a tab that isn't in the group. Alternatively, you can right-click one of the group's tabs and select the Ungroup Sheets command from the shortcut menu.

With the sheets now grouped, you create your 3D range by activating any of the grouped sheets and then selecting a range using any of the techniques you just learned. Excel selects the same cells in all the other sheets in the group.

You can also type in a 3D range by hand when, say, entering a formula. Here's the general format for a 3-D reference:

`FirstSheet:LastSheet!ULCorner:LRCorner`

Here, `FirstSheet` is the name of the first sheet in the 3D range, `LastSheet` is the name of the last sheet, and `ULCorner` and `LRCorner` define the cell range you want to work with on each sheet. For example, to specify the range A1:E10 on worksheets Sheet1, Sheet2, and Sheet3, use the following reference:

`Sheet1:Sheet3!A1:E10`

> **CAUTION**
>
> If one or both of the sheet names used in the 3D reference contains a space, be sure to enclose the sheet names in single quotation marks, as in this example:
>
> `'First Quarter:Fourth Quarter'!A1:F16`

You normally use 3D references in worksheet functions that accept them. These functions include AVERAGE(), COUNT(), COUNTA(), MAX(), MIN(), PRODUCT(), STDEV(), STDEVP(), SUM(), VAR(), and VARP(). (You'll learn about all of these functions and many more in Part 2, "Harnessing the Power of Functions."

# Advanced Range-Selection Techniques

So much for the basic, garden-variety range-selection techniques. Now you'll learn a few advanced techniques that can make your selection chores faster and easier.

## Selecting a Range Using Go To

For very large ranges, Excel's Go To command comes in handy. You normally use the Go To command to jump quickly to a specific cell address or range name. The following steps show you how to exploit this power to select a range:

1. Select the upper-left cell of the range.

2. Choose <u>E</u>dit, <u>G</u>o To, or press Ctrl+G. The Go To dialog box appears, as shown in Figure 1.3.

**Figure 1.3**
You can use the Go To dialog box to easily select a large range.

3. Use the <u>R</u>eference text box to enter the cell address of the lower-right corner of the range.

> **TIP**
> You also can select a range using Go To by entering the range coordinates in the <u>R</u>eference text box.

4. Hold down the Shift key and click OK. Excel selects the range.

> **TIP**
> Another way to select very large ranges is to choose <u>V</u>iew, <u>Z</u>oom and click a reduced magnification in the Zoom dialog box (say, 50% or 25%). You can then use this "big picture" view to select your range.

## Using the Go To Special Dialog Box

You normally select cells according to their position within a worksheet, but Excel includes a powerful feature that enables you to select cells according to their contents or other special properties. If you choose Edit, Go To and then click the Special button in the Go To dialog box, the Go To Special dialog box appears, as shown in Figure 1.4.

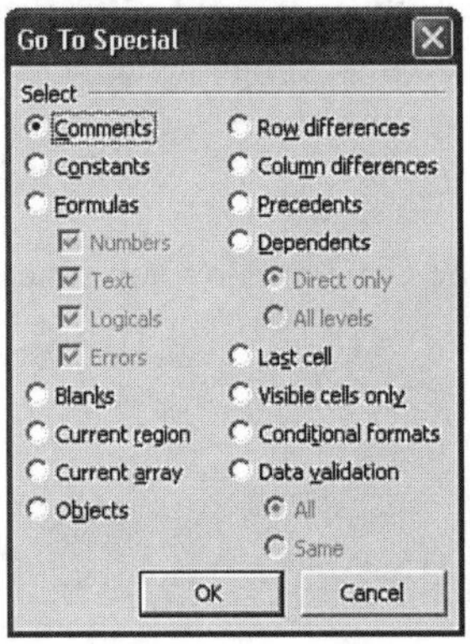

**Figure 1.4**
Use the Go To Special dialog box to select cells according to their contents, formula relationships, and more.

### Selecting Cells By Type

The Go To Special dialog box contains many options, but only four of them enable you to select cells according to the type of contents they contain. Table 1.1 summarizes these four options. (The next few sections discuss the other Go To Special options.)

| **Table 1.1** | **Options for Selecting a Cell By Type** |
|---|---|
| **Option** | **Description** |
| Comments | Selects all cells that contain a comment |
| Constants | Selects all cells that contain constants of the types specified in one or more of the check boxes listed under the Formulas option |
| Formulas | Selects all cells containing formulas that produce results of the types specified in one or more of the following four check boxes:<br>Numbers—Selects all cells that contain numbers<br>Text—Selects all cells that contain text<br>Logicals—Selects all cells that contain logical values<br>Errors—Selects all cells that contain errors |
| Blanks | Selects all cells that are blank |

### Selecting Adjacent Cells

If you need to select cells adjacent to the active cell, the Go To Special dialog box gives you two options. Click the Current Region option to select a rectangular range that includes all the nonblank cells that touch the active cell.

If the active cell is part of an array, click the Current <u>A</u>rray option to select all the cells in the array.

→ For an in-depth discussion of Excel arrays, **see** "Working with Arrays," **p. 85**.

## Selecting Cells By Differences

Excel also enables you to select cells by comparing rows or columns of data and selecting only those cells that are different. The following steps show you how it's done:

1. Select the rows or columns you want to compare. (Make sure that the active cell is in the row or column with the comparison values you want to use.)

2. Display the Go To Special dialog box, and click one of the following options:

   Ro<u>w</u> Differences
   : This option uses the data in the active cell's column as the comparison values. Excel selects the cells in the corresponding rows that are different.

   Colu<u>mn</u> Differences
   : This option uses the data in the active cell's row as the comparison values. Excel selects the cells in the corresponding columns that are different.

3. Click OK.

For example, Figure 1.5 shows a selected range of numbers. The values in column B are the budget numbers assigned to all a company's divisions; the values in columns C and D are the actual numbers achieved by the East Division and the West Division, respectively. Suppose you want to know the items for which a division ended up either under or over the budget. In other words, you want to compare the numbers in columns C and D with those in column B, and select the ones in C and D that are different. Because you're comparing rows of data, you would select the Ro<u>w</u> Differences option from the Select Special dialog box. Figure 1.6 shows the results.

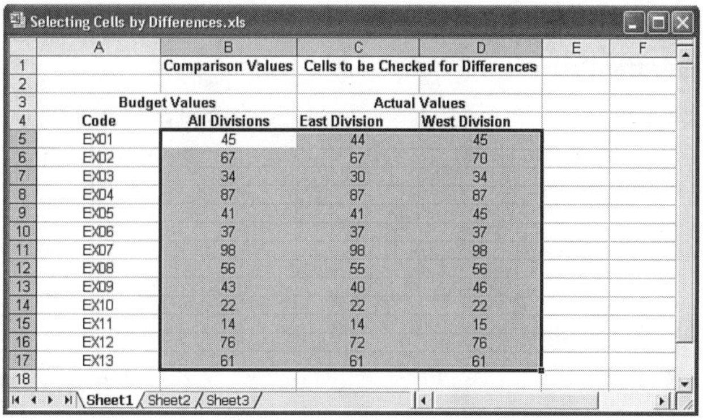

**Figure 1.5**
Before using the Go To Special feature that compares rows (or columns) of data, select the entire range of cells involved in the comparison.

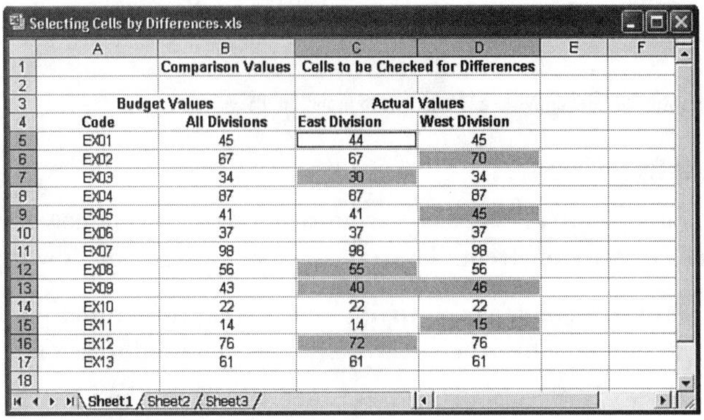


| | A | B | C | D | E | F |
|---|---|---|---|---|---|---|
| 1 | | Comparison Values | Cells to be Checked for Differences | | | |
| 2 | | | | | | |
| 3 | Budget Values | | Actual Values | | | |
| 4 | Code | All Divisions | East Division | West Division | | |
| 5 | EX01 | 45 | 44 | 45 | | |
| 6 | EX02 | 67 | 67 | 70 | | |
| 7 | EX03 | 34 | 30 | 34 | | |
| 8 | EX04 | 87 | 87 | 87 | | |
| 9 | EX05 | 41 | 41 | 45 | | |
| 10 | EX06 | 37 | 37 | 37 | | |
| 11 | EX07 | 98 | 98 | 98 | | |
| 12 | EX08 | 56 | 55 | 56 | | |
| 13 | EX09 | 43 | 40 | 46 | | |
| 14 | EX10 | 22 | 22 | 22 | | |
| 15 | EX11 | 14 | 14 | 15 | | |
| 16 | EX12 | 76 | 72 | 76 | | |
| 17 | EX13 | 61 | 61 | 61 | | |
| 18 | | | | | | |

**Figure 1.6**
After running the Row Differences option, Excel shows those rows in columns C and D that are different than the value in column B.

## Selecting Cells By Reference

If a cell contains a formula, Excel defines the cell's *precedents* as those cells that the formula refers to. For example, if cell A4 contains the formula `=SUM(A1:A3)`, then cells A1, A2, and A3 are the precedents of A4. A *direct* precedent is a cell referred to explicitly in the formula. In the preceding example, A1, A2, and A3 are direct precedents of A4. An *indirect* precedent is a cell referred to by a precedent. For example, if cell A1 contains the formula `=B3*2`, cell B3 is an indirect precedent of cell A4.

Excel also defines a cell's *dependents* as those cells with a formula that refers to the cell. In the preceding example, cell A4 would be a dependent of cell A1. (Think of it this way: The value that appears in cell A4 *depends on* the value that's entered into cell A1.) Like precedents, dependents can be direct or indirect.

The Go To Special dialog box enables you to select precedents and dependents as described in these steps:

1. Select the range you want to work with.
2. Display the Go To Special dialog box.
3. Click either the Precedents or the Dependents option.
4. Click the Direct Only option to select only direct precedents or dependents. If you need to select both the direct and the indirect precedents or dependents, click the All Levels option.
5. Click OK.

## Other Go To Special Options

The Go To Special dialog box includes a few more options to help you in your range-selection chores:

| Option | Description |
|---|---|
| La̱st Cell | Selects the last cell in the worksheet (that is, the lower-right corner) that contains data or formatting. |
| Visible Cells Onl̲y | Selects only cells that are unhidden. |
| Condi̲tional formats | Selects only cells that contain conditional formatting. |
| Data V̲alidation | Selects cells that contains data-validation rules. If you click A̲ll, Excel selects every cell with a data-validation rule; if you click Sam̲e, Excel selects every cell that has the same validation rule as the current cell. |

→ To learn about data validation, **see** "Applying Data Validation Rules to Cells," **p. 98**.

### Shortcut Keys for Selecting Via Go To

Table 1.2 lists the shortcut keys you can use to run many of the Go To Special operations.

| Table 1.2 | Shortcut Keys for Selecting Precedents and Dependents |
|---|---|
| **Shortcut Key** | **Selects** |
| Ctrl+* | Current region |
| Ctrl+/ | Current array |
| Ctrl+\ | Row differences |
| Ctrl+I | Column differences |
| Ctrl+[ | Direct precedents |
| Ctrl+] | Direct dependents |
| Ctrl+{ | All levels of precedents |
| Ctrl+} | All levels of dependents |
| Ctrl+End | The last cell |
| Alt+; | Visible cells |

# Data Entry in a Range

If you know in advance the range you'll use for data entry, you can save yourself some time and keystrokes by selecting the range before you begin. As you enter your data in each cell, use the keys listed in Table 1.3 to navigate the range.

**Table 1.3   Navigation Keys for a Selected Range**

| Key | Result |
| --- | --- |
| Enter | Moves down one row |
| Shift+Enter | Moves up one row |
| Tab | Moves right one column |
| Shift+Tab | Moves left one column |
| Ctrl+. (period) | Moves from corner to corner in the range |
| Ctrl+Alt+right arrow | Moves to the next range in a noncontiguous selection |
| Ctrl+Alt+left arrow | Moves to the preceding range in a noncontiguous selection |

The advantage of this technique is that the active cell never leaves the range. For example, if you press Enter after adding data to a cell in the last row of the range, the active cell moves back to the top row and over one column.

# Filling a Range

If you need to fill a range with a particular value or formula, Excel gives you two methods:

- Select the range you want to fill, type the value or formula, and press Ctrl+Enter. Excel fills the entire range with whatever you entered in the formula bar.

- Enter the initial value or formula, select the range you want to fill (including the initial cell), and choose Edit, Fill. Then choose the appropriate command from the submenu that appears. For example, if you're filling a range down from the initial cell, choose the Down command. If you've selected multiple sheets, use Edit, Fill, Across Worksheets to fill the range in each worksheet.

> **TIP**
>
> Press Ctrl+D to choose Edit, Fill, Down; press Ctrl+R to choose Edit, Fill, Right.

# Using the Fill Handle

The *fill handle* is the small black square in the bottom-right corner of the active cell or range. This versatile little tool can do many useful things, including creating a series of text or numeric values and filling, clearing, inserting, and deleting ranges. The next few sections show you how to use the fill handle to perform each of these operations.

## Using AutoFill to Create Text and Numeric Series

Worksheets often use text series (such as January, February, March; or Sunday, Monday, Tuesday) and numeric series (such as 1, 3, 5; or 2003, 2004, 2005). Instead of entering these series by hand, you can use the fill handle to create them automatically. This handy feature is called *AutoFill*. The following steps show you how it works:

1. For a text series, select the first cell of the range you want to use, and enter the initial value. For a numeric series, enter the first two values and then select both cells.

2. Position the mouse pointer over the fill handle. The pointer changes to a plus sign (+).

3. Click and drag the mouse pointer until the gray border encompasses the range you want to fill. If you're not sure where to stop, keep your eye on the pop-up value that appears near the mouse pointer and shows you the series value of the last selected cell.

4. Release the mouse button. Excel fills in the range with the series.

When you release the mouse button after using AutoFill, Excel not only fills in the series, but it also displays the Auto Fill Options Smart Tag. To see the options, move your mouse pointer over the Smart Tag and then click the downward-pointing arrow to drop down the list. The options you see depend on the type of series you created. (See "Creating a Series," later in this chapter, for details on some of the options you might see.) However, you'll usually see at least the following four:

- **Copy Cells**—Click this option to fill the range by copying the original cell or cells.

- **Fill Series**—Click this option to get the default series fill.

- **Fill Formatting Only**—Click this option to apply only the original cell's formatting to the selected range.

- **Fill Without Formatting**—Click this option to fill the range with the series data but without the formatting of the original cell.

Figure 1.7 shows several series created with the fill handle (the shaded cells are the initial fill values). Notice, in particular, that Excel increments any text value that includes a numeric component (such as Quarter 1 and Customer 1001).

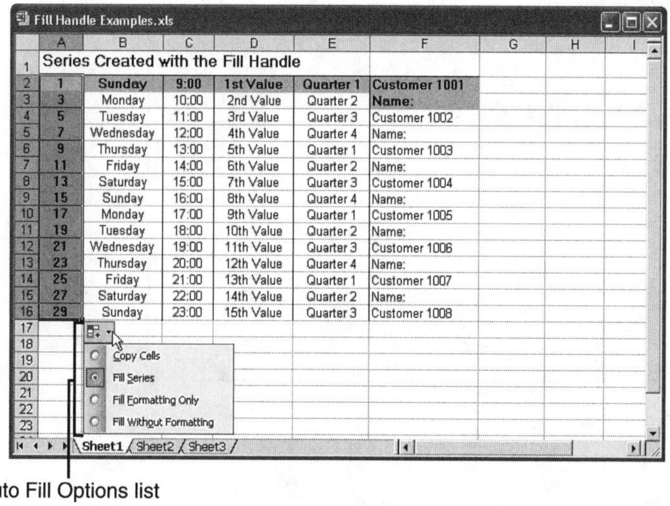

**Figure 1.7**
Some sample series created with the fill handle. Shaded entries are the initial fill values.

Auto Fill Options list

Keep a few guidelines in mind when using the fill handle to create series:

- Clicking and dragging the handle down or to the right increments the values. Clicking and dragging up or to the left decrements the values.

- The fill handle recognizes standard abbreviations, such as Jan (January) and Sun (Sunday).

- To vary the series interval for a text series, enter the first two values of the series and then select both of them before clicking and dragging. For example, entering 1st and 3rd produces the series 1st, 3rd, 5th, and so on.

- If you use three or more numbers as the initial values for the fill handle series, Excel creates a "best fit" or "trend" line.

→ To learn more about using Excel for trend analysis, **see** "Using Regression to Track Trends and Make Forecasts," **p. 339**.

## Creating a Custom AutoFill List

As you've seen, Excel recognizes certain values (for example, January, Sunday, 1st Quarter) as part of a larger list. When you drag the fill handle from a cell containing one of these values, Excel fills the cells with the appropriate series. However, you're not stuck with just the few lists that Excel recognized out of the box. You're free to define your own AutoFill lists, as described in the following steps:

1. Choose Tools, Options to display the Options dialog box.

2. Click the Custom Lists tab.

3. In the Custom Lists box, click New List. An insertion point appears in the List Entries box.

4. Type an item from your list into the List Entries box and press Enter. Repeat this step for each item. (Make sure that you add the items in the order in which you want them to appear in the series.) Figure 1.8 shows an example.

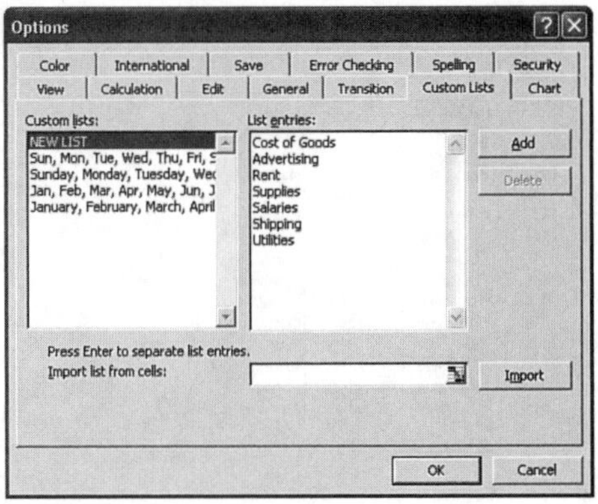

**Figure 1.8**
Use the Custom Lists tab to create your own lists that Excel can fill in automatically using the AutoFill feature.

5. Click <u>A</u>dd to add the list to the Custom <u>L</u>ists box.

6. Click OK to return to the worksheet.

> **TIP**
>
> If you already have the list in a worksheet range, don't bother entering each item by hand. Instead, activate the <u>I</u>mport List from Cells edit box and enter a reference to the range (you can either type the reference or select the cells directly on the worksheet). Click the <u>I</u>mport button to add the list to the Custom <u>L</u>ists box.

> **NOTE**
>
> If you need to delete a custom list, highlight it in the Custom <u>L</u>ists box and then click <u>D</u>elete.

## Filling a Range

You can use the fill handle to fill a range with a value or formula. To do this, enter your initial values or formulas, select them, and then click and drag the fill handle over the destination range. (I'm assuming here that the data you're copying won't create a series.) When you release the mouse button, Excel fills the range.

Note that if the initial cell contains a formula with relative references, Excel adjusts the references accordingly. For example, suppose the initial cell contains the formula =A1. If you fill down, the next cell will contain the formula =A2, the next will contain =A3, and so on.

→ For information on relative references, **see** "Understanding Relative Reference Format," **p. 62**.

# Creating a Series

Instead of using the fill handle to create a series, you can use Excel's Series command to gain a little more control over the whole process. Follow these steps:

1. Select the first cell you want to use for the series, and enter the starting value. If you want to create a series out of a particular pattern (such as 2, 4, 6, and so on), fill in enough cells to define the pattern.

2. Select the entire range you want to fill.

3. Choose <u>E</u>dit, F<u>i</u>ll, <u>S</u>eries. Excel displays the Series dialog box, shown in Figure 1.9.

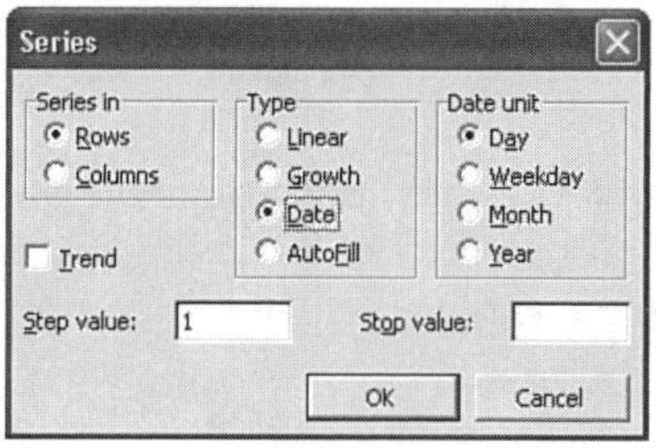

**Figure 1.9**
Use the Series dialog box to define the series you want to create.

4. Either click Rows to create the series in rows starting from the active cell, or click Columns to create the series in columns.
5. Use the Type group to click the type of series you want. You have the following options:

| | |
|---|---|
| Linear | This option finds the next series value by adding the step value (see step 7) to the preceding value in the series. |
| Growth | This option finds the next series value by multiplying the preceding value by the step value. |
| Date | This option creates a series of dates based on the option you select in the Date Unit group (Day, Weekday, Month, or Year). |
| AutoFill | This option works much like the fill handle does. You can use it to extend a numeric pattern or a text series (for example, Qtr1, Qtr2, Qtr3). |

6. If you want to extend a series trend, activate the Trend check box. You can use this option only with the Linear or Growth series types.
7. If you chose a Linear, Growth, or Date series type, enter a number in the Step Value box. This number is what Excel uses to increment each value in the series.
8. To place a limit on the series, enter the appropriate number in the Stop Value box.
9. Click OK. Excel fills in the series and returns you to the worksheet.

Figure 1.10 shows some sample column series. Note that the Growth series stops at cell C12 (value 128) because the next term in the series (256) is greater than the stop value of 250. The Day series fills the range with every second date (because the step value is 2). The Weekday series is slightly different: The dates are sequential, but weekends are skipped.

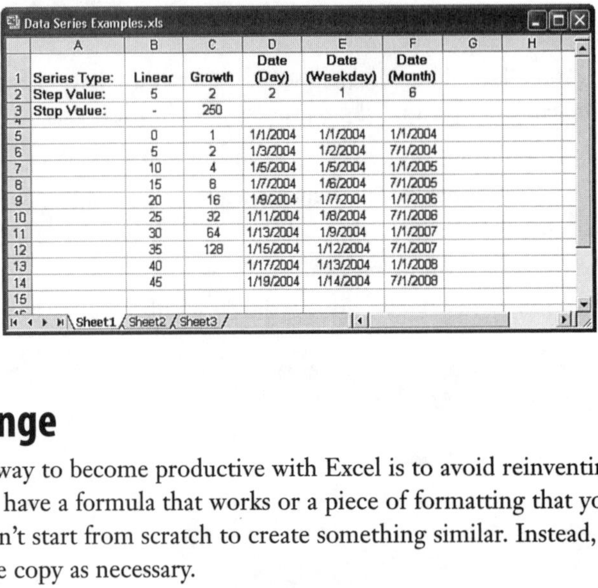

Data Series Examples.xls

| | A | B | C | D | E | F | G | H |
|---|---|---|---|---|---|---|---|---|
| 1 | Series Type: | Linear | Growth | Date (Day) | Date (Weekday) | Date (Month) | | |
| 2 | Step Value: | 5 | 2 | 2 | 1 | 6 | | |
| 3 | Stop Value: | - | 250 | | | | | |
| 5 | | 0 | 1 | 1/1/2004 | 1/1/2004 | 1/1/2004 | | |
| 6 | | 5 | 2 | 1/3/2004 | 1/2/2004 | 7/1/2004 | | |
| 7 | | 10 | 4 | 1/5/2004 | 1/5/2004 | 1/1/2005 | | |
| 8 | | 15 | 8 | 1/7/2004 | 1/6/2004 | 7/1/2005 | | |
| 9 | | 20 | 16 | 1/9/2004 | 1/7/2004 | 1/1/2006 | | |
| 10 | | 25 | 32 | 1/11/2004 | 1/8/2004 | 7/1/2006 | | |
| 11 | | 30 | 64 | 1/13/2004 | 1/9/2004 | 1/1/2007 | | |
| 12 | | 35 | 128 | 1/15/2004 | 1/12/2004 | 7/1/2007 | | |
| 13 | | 40 | | 1/17/2004 | 1/13/2004 | 1/1/2008 | | |
| 14 | | 45 | | 1/19/2004 | 1/14/2004 | 7/1/2008 | | |
| 15 | | | | | | | | |

Sheet1 / Sheet2 / Sheet3

**Figure 1.10**
Some sample column series generated with the Series command.

# Copying a Range

The quickest way to become productive with Excel is to avoid reinventing your worksheet wheels. If you have a formula that works or a piece of formatting that you've put a lot of effort into, don't start from scratch to create something similar. Instead, make a copy and then adjust the copy as necessary.

Fortunately, Excel offers all kinds of ways to make copies of your worksheet ranges. Most of these methods involve the Copy command, but I'll begin by showing you the very handy drag-and-drop method.

## Using Drag-and-Drop to Copy a Range

If you have a mouse, you can use it to copy a range by selecting the range and then clicking and dragging it to the appropriate destination. There are no menus to maneuver and no risks of accidentally overwriting data because you can see exactly where the copied range will go. The following steps show you how to copy a range:

1. Select the range you want to copy.

2. Hold down the Ctrl key.

3. Move the mouse pointer over any edge of the selection (except the fill handle!). You'll know you've positioned the mouse pointer correctly when it changes to an arrow with a plus sign (+).

4. Click and drag the mouse pointer to the destination range. Excel displays a gray outline that shows you the border of the copy.

5. When you've positioned the range border properly in the destination area, release the mouse button and then the Ctrl key (in that order). Excel pastes a copy of the original range.

> **NOTE** If you can't get drag-and-drop to work, you need to turn it on. Choose Tools, Options; click the Edit tab; and then activate the Allow Cell Drag and Drop check box.

## Copying a Range with the Copy Command

If you don't have a mouse kicking around, or if you prefer the pull-down menu approach, you can copy a range using the Copy command.

> **CAUTION**
> Before copying a range, look at the destination area and make sure that you won't be overwriting any nonblank cells. Remember that you can use the Undo command if you accidentally destroy some data. If you want to insert the range among some existing cells, see the section later in this chapter titled "Inserting a Copy of a Range."

Follow these steps to copy a range using the Copy command:

1. Select the range you want to copy.

2. Choose Edit, Copy. (You can also either press Ctrl+C or right-click any cell in the range and then choose Copy). Excel copies the contents of the range to the Clipboard and displays a moving border around the range.

3. Select the upper-left cell of the destination range.

4. Choose Edit, Paste. (You can also either press Ctrl+V or right-click any cell in the range and then choose Paste.) Excel pastes the range to your destination.

When you use this method, Excel displays the Paste Options Smart Tag in the lower-right corner of the cell or range you pasted. The list of options displayed by the Smart Tag more or less corresponds to the options in the Paste Special dialog box. See "Copying Selected Cell Attributes," later in this chapter.

## Making Multiple Copies of a Range

If you need to make multiple copies of a range, you *could* execute a separate Paste command for each destination, but Excel offers an easier way. The following procedure gives the steps:

1. Select the range you want to copy.

2. Copy the range.

3. Select the upper-left cell for each destination range (see Figure 1.11). The cells you select can be contiguous or noncontiguous.

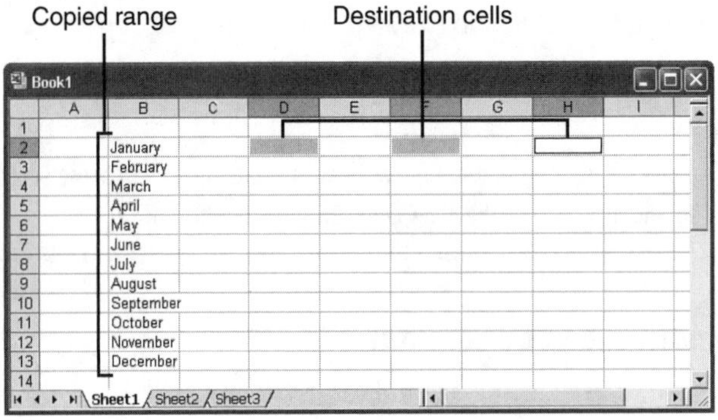

Copied range                Destination cells

**Figure 1.11**
To paste multiple copies, select the upper-left cell for each destination range.

4. Choose Edit, Paste. Excel pastes the range to each destination, as shown in Figure 1.12.

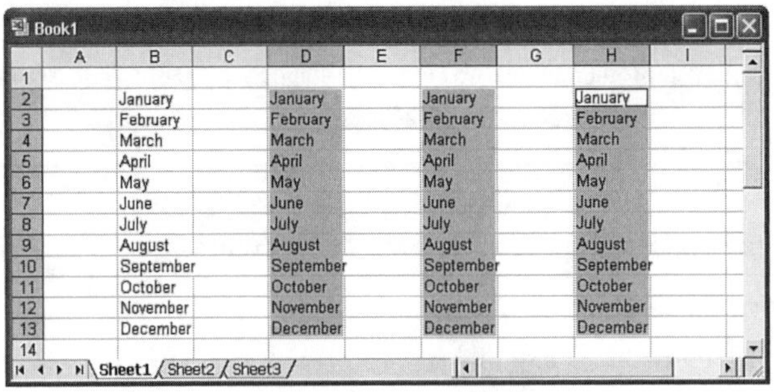

**Figure 1.12**
When you execute the Paste command, Excel copies the range to each destination.

## Inserting a Copy of a Range

If you don't want a pasted range to overwrite existing cells, you can tell Excel to *insert* the range. In this case, Excel moves the existing cells out of harm's way before pasting the range. (As you'll see, you have control over where Excel moves the existing cells.) Follow these steps to insert a copy of a range:

**1.** Select the range you want to copy.

**2.** Use any of the methods described earlier in this chapter to copy the range.

**3.** Select the upper-left cell of the destination range.

**4.** Choose Insert, Copied Cells. Excel displays the Insert Paste dialog box to enable you to choose where to move the existing cells that would otherwise be overwritten (see Figure 1.13).

**Figure 1.13**
Use the Insert Paste dialog box to tell Excel which direction to move the existing cells.

**TIP**
You also can insert a copied range by right-clicking the destination cell and choosing Insert Copied Cells from the shortcut menu.

**5.** Either click Shift Cells Right to move the cells to the right, or click Shift Cells Down to move them down.

**6.** Click OK. Excel shifts the existing cells and then pastes the range.

## Advanced Range Copying

The copying techniques we've looked at so far normally copy the entire contents of each cell in the range: the value or formula, the formatting, and any attached cell comments. If you like, you can tell Excel to copy only some of these attributes, you can transpose rows and columns, or you can combine the source and destination ranges arithmetically. All this is possible with Excel's Paste Special command. These techniques are outlined in the next three sections.

### Copying Selected Cell Attributes

When rearranging a worksheet, you can save time by combining cell attributes. For example, if you need to copy several formulas to a range but you don't want to disturb the existing formatting, you can tell Excel to copy only the formulas.

If you want to copy only selected cell attributes, follow these steps:

1. Select and then copy the range you want to work with.

2. Select the destination range.

3. Choose Edit, Paste Special. Excel displays the Paste Special dialog box, shown in Figure 1.14.

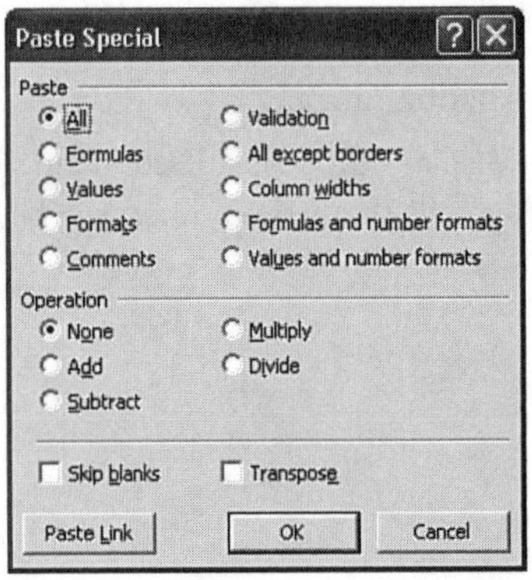

**Figure 1.14**
Use the Paste Special dialog box to select the cell attributes you want to copy.

> **TIP**
>
> You also can display the Paste Special dialog box by right-clicking the destination range and choosing Paste Special from the shortcut menu.

4. In the Paste group, click the attribute you want to paste into the destination range:

   - **All**—Pastes all of the source range's cell attributes.
   - **Formulas**—Pastes only the cell formulas.
   - **Values**—Converts the cell formulas to values and pastes only the values.
   - **Formats**—Pastes only the cell formatting.
   - **Comments**—Pastes only the cell comments.
   - **Validation**—Pastes only the cell-validation rules.
   - **All Except Borders**—Pastes all the cell attributes except the cell's border formatting.
   - **Column Widths**—Changes the width of the destination columns to match the widths of the source columns. No data is pasted.
   - **Formulas and Number Formats**—Pastes the cell formulas and numeric formatting.
   - **Values and Number Formats**—Converts the cell formulas to values and pastes only the values and the numeric formats.

5. If you don't want Excel to paste any blank cells included in the selection, activate the Skip <u>B</u>lanks check box.

6. If you want to paste only formulas that set the destination cells equal to the values of the source cells, click Paste <u>L</u>ink. (For example, if the source cell is A1, the value of the destination cell is set to the formula =$A$1.) Otherwise, click OK to paste the range.

## Combining the Source and Destination Arithmetically

Excel enables you to combine two ranges arithmetically. For example, suppose that you have a range of constants that you want to double. Instead of creating formulas that multiply each cell by 2 (or, even worse, doubling each cell by hand), you can create a range of the same size that consists of nothing but 2s. You then combine this new range with the old one and tell Excel to multiply them. The following steps show you what to do:

1. Select the destination range. (Make sure that it's the same shape as the source range.)

2. Type the constant you want to use, and then press Ctrl+Enter. Excel fills the destination range with the number you entered.

3. Select and copy the source range.

4. Select the destination range again.

5. Choose <u>E</u>dit, Paste <u>S</u>pecial to display the Paste Special dialog box.

6. Use the following options in the Operation group to click the arithmetic operator you want to use:

   - **N<u>o</u>ne**—Performs no operation
   - **A<u>d</u>d**—Adds the destination cells to the source cells
   - **<u>S</u>ubtract**—Subtracts the source cells from the destination cells
   - **<u>M</u>ultiply**—Multiplies the source cells by the destination cells
   - **D<u>i</u>vide**—Divides the destination cells by the source cells

7. If you don't want Excel to include any blank cells in the operation, activate the Skip <u>B</u>lanks check box.

8. Click OK. Excel pastes the results of the operation into the destination range.

## Transposing Rows and Columns

If you have row data that you would prefer to see in columns (or vice versa), you can use the Paste Special command to transpose the data. Follow these steps:

1. Select and copy the source cells.

2. Select the upper-left corner of the destination range.

3. Choose <u>E</u>dit, Paste <u>S</u>pecial to display the Paste Special dialog box.

4. Activate the Transpos<u>e</u> check box.

5. Click OK. Excel transposes the source range, as shown in Figure 1.15.

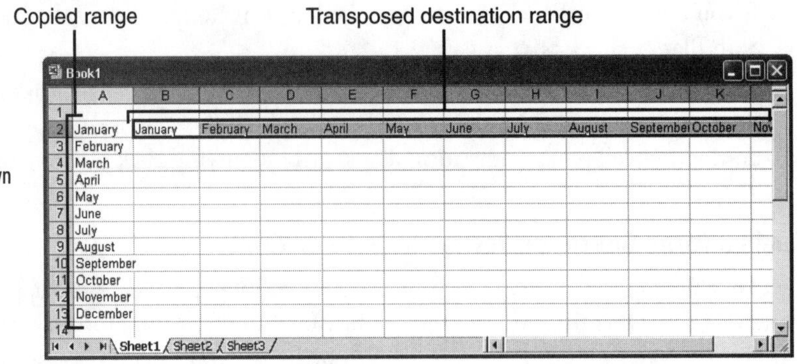

Copied range                    Transposed destination range

**Figure 1.15**
You can use the Paste
Special command to
transpose a column of
data into a row (as shown
here), or vice versa.

## Moving a Range

Moving a range is very similar to copying a range, except that the source range gets deleted when all is said and done. You also have the choice of using drag-and-drop or the menu commands.

### Using Drag-and-Drop to Move a Range

The drag-and-drop method for moving a range is identical to the one you learned for copying a range, except that you don't have to hold down the Ctrl key. Follow these steps:

1. Select the range you want to move.
2. Move the mouse pointer over any edge of the selection until you see a four-pointed arrow added to the regular pointer.
3. Click and drag the mouse pointer to the destination range. Excel displays a gray outline that shows the border of the copy.
4. When you've positioned the range border properly in the destination area, release the mouse button.
5. If your moved range will paste over any nonblank cells, Excel asks whether you want to replace the contents of the destination cells. If everything looks reasonable, click OK to continue. Excel deletes the original range and pastes it in the destination.

### Using the Menu Commands to Move a Range

To move a range with the menu commands, you need to cut the range and then paste it. The following procedure details the steps involved.

> **CAUTION**
>
> As with copying, you need to be careful when moving ranges so that you don't write over any exist-ing data. If necessary, you can always insert the range by choosing the Insert, Cut Cells command. If you do make a mistake, be sure to choose the Edit, Undo command right away.

1. Select the range you want to move.

2. Choose <u>E</u>dit, Cu<u>t</u>. (You can also either press Ctrl+X or right-click any cell in the range and then choose Cu<u>t</u>.) Excel cuts the contents of the range to the Clipboard and displays a moving border around the range.

3. Select the upper-left cell of the destination range.

4. Choose <u>E</u>dit, <u>P</u>aste. Excel pastes the range to your destination.

# Inserting and Deleting a Range

When you begin a worksheet, you generally use rows and columns sequentially as you add data, labels, and formulas. More often than not, however, you need to go back and add some values or text that you forgot or that you need for another part of the worksheet. When this happens, you need to insert ranges into your spreadsheet to make room for your new information. Conversely, you often have to remove old or unnecessary data from a spreadsheet, which requires you to delete ranges. The next couple of sections describe various methods for inserting and deleting ranges in Excel.

## Inserting an Entire Row or Column

The easiest way to insert a range into a worksheet is to insert an entire row or column. The following steps show you how it's done:

1. Select the row or column before which you want to insert the new row or column. If you want to insert multiple rows or columns, select the appropriate number of rows or columns, as shown in Figure 1.16.

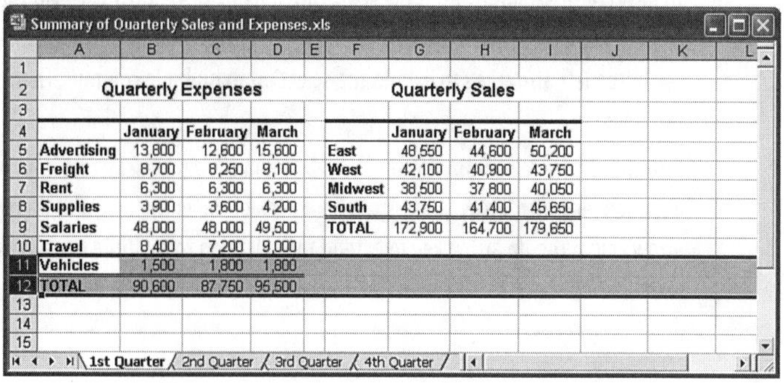

**Figure 1.16**
Two rows have been selected at the point where two new rows are to be inserted.

2. If you're inserting rows, choose <u>I</u>nsert, <u>R</u>ows. Excel shifts the selected rows down, as shown in Figure 1.17. If you're inserting columns, choose <u>I</u>nsert, <u>C</u>olumns instead. In this case, Excel shifts the selected columns to the right.

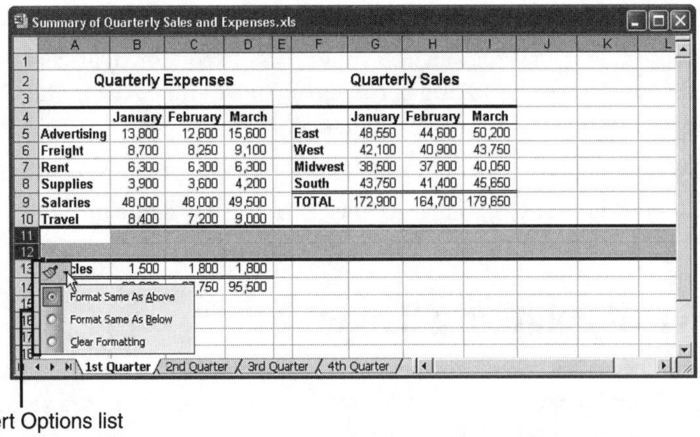

**Figure 1.17**
When you insert rows, Excel shifts the existing cells down.

The Insert Options list

3. After inserting the row or column, Excel displays the Insert Options control. Click the arrow to display the list (shown in Figure 1.17), and then click the formatting option you prefer (the choices are slightly different if you inserted columns instead of rows):

- **Format Same As Above**—Click this option to format the new rows using the same formatting as the row directly above them.

- **Format Same As Below**—Click this option to format the new rows using the same formatting as the row directly below them.

- **Clear Formatting**—Click this option to insert the new rows without any formatting.

> **TIP**
>
> To insert entire columns from the keyboard, start by selecting any cell in the first column you want to work with. Press Ctrl+spacebar to select the entire column, and then press either the right arrow key or the left arrow key to extend the selection to multiple columns. Then press Ctrl++ to insert the columns.
>
> Inserting entire rows from the keyboard is similar. Begin by selecting any cell in the first row you want to work with. Press Shift+spacebar to select the entire row, and then press either the down arrow key or the up arrow key to extend the selection to multiple rows. Press Ctrl++ to insert the rows.

## Inserting a Row or Column with the Fill Handle

You can use the fill handle we looked at earlier to insert entire rows and columns effortlessly. Here's how it works:

1. Select the row or column where you want to perform the insertion. Notice that the first cell in the row or column contains the fill handle. (If you selected multiple rows or columns, the fill handle appears in the first cell of the last row or column you selected.)

**2.** Hold down the Shift key, and click and drag the fill handle in the direction in which you want to insert the rows or columns. The number of rows or columns you drag across determines the number of rows or columns that get inserted.

**3.** Release both the mouse button and the Shift key. Excel performs the insertion.

## Inserting a Cell or Range

In some worksheets, you might need to insert only a single cell or a range of cells, so as not to disturb the arrangement of surrounding data. For example, suppose that you want to add a Repair line between Rent and Supplies in the Quarterly Expenses table in Figure 1.16. You don't want to add an entire row because it would create a gap in the Quarterly Sales table. Instead, you can insert a range that covers just the area you need. Follow these steps to see how this works:

**1.** Select the range where you want the new range to appear. In the Quarterly Expenses example, you would select the range A8:D8 (see Figure 1.18).

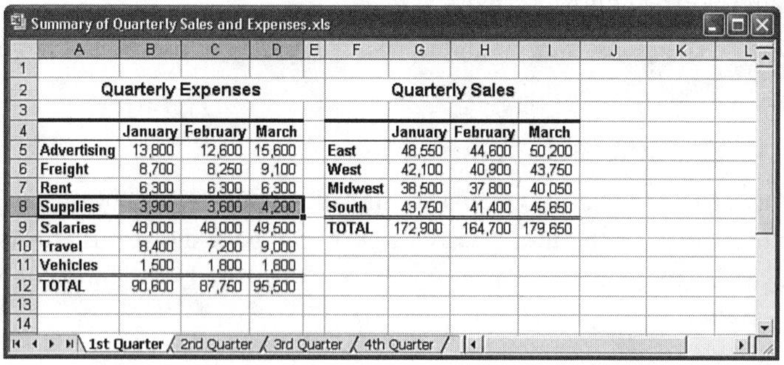

**Figure 1.18**
When inserting a range, first select only the range that you want moved to accommodate the new cells. In this example, only the appropriate cells in the Quarterly Expenses table have been selected.

**2.** Choose Insert, Cells. Excel displays the Insert dialog box, shown in Figure 1.19.

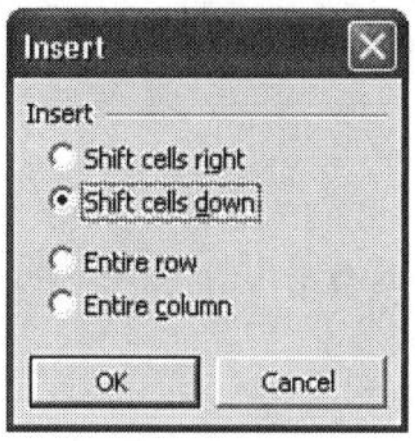

**Figure 1.19**
Use the Insert dialog box to tell Excel which way to shift the existing cells.

**3.** Click either Shift Cells Right or Shift Cells Down, as appropriate.

**4.** Click OK. Excel inserts the range.

**5.** (Optional) Use the Insert Options control (shown in Figure 1.20) to click the formatting option you want to apply to the inserted cells.

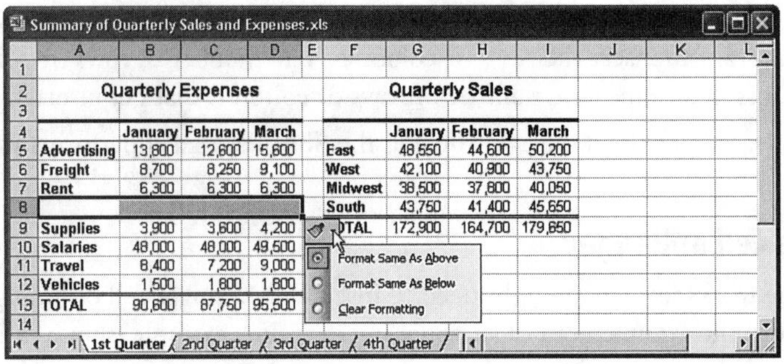

**Figure 1.20**
Excel has shifted the existing cells down to create room for the new range.

## Inserting a Range with the Fill Handle

The fill handle also comes in handy when you are inserting a range:

1. Select the range in which you want the insertion to occur.

2. Hold down the Shift key, and click and drag the fill handle over the area where you want the new range inserted.

3. Release the mouse button and the Shift key. Excel inserts the range.

## Deleting an Entire Row or Column

Deleting a row or column is similar to inserting. In this case, however, you need to exercise a little more caution because a hasty deletion can have disastrous effects on your worksheet. (However, keep in mind that you can always select the Edit, Undo command if you make any mistakes.)

The following procedure shows you how to delete a row or column:

1. Select the row or column you want to delete.

2. Choose Edit, Delete, or press Ctrl+– (minus sign). Excel deletes the row or column and shifts the remaining data appropriately.

## Deleting a Cell or Range

If you need to delete only one cell or a range to avoid trashing any surrounding data, follow these steps:

1. Select the cell or range you want to delete.

2. Choose Edit, Delete. Excel displays the Delete dialog box, as shown in Figure 1.21.

3. Click either Shift Cells Left or Shift Cells Up, as appropriate.

4. Click OK. Excel deletes the range.

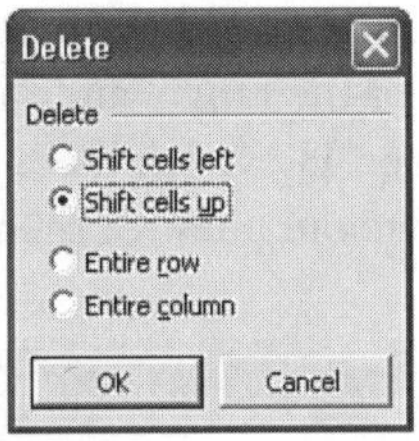

**Figure 1.21**
Use the Delete dialog box to let Excel know which way to adjust the remaining cells after it has performed the deletion.

# Clearing a Range

As you've seen, deleting a range actually removes the cells from the worksheet. What if you want the cells to remain, but you want their contents or formats cleared? For that, you can use Excel's Clear command, as described in the following steps:

1. Select the range you want to clear.

2. Choose Edit, Clear. Excel displays a submenu of Clear commands.

3. Select either All, Formats, Contents, or Comments, as appropriate.

## Clearing a Range with the Fill Handle

To clear the values and formulas in a range with the fill handle, you can use either of the following two techniques:

- If you want to clear only the values and formulas in a range, select the range and then click and drag the fill handle into the range and over the cells you want to clear. Excel grays out the cells as you select them. When you release the mouse button, Excel clears the cells' values and formulas.

- If you want to scrub everything from the range (values, formulas, formats, and comments), select the range and then hold down the Ctrl key. Next, click and drag the fill handle into the range and over each cell you want to clear. Excel clears the cells when you release the mouse button.

# Using Excel's Reference Operators

As you probably know, Excel has various operators that you use for building formulas (such as +, *, and &). You'll learn all about them in Chapter 3, "Building Basic Formulas," but I'd like to close your look at ranges by talking about Excel's three *reference operators*. You use these operators when working with cell references, as discussed in the next three sections.

## Using the Range Operator

The *range* operator is just the familiar colon (:) that you've been using all along. All you do is insert a colon between two references, and Excel creates a range (for example, A1:C5).

Until now, though, you've probably been creating your ranges by using the reference on the left side of the colon to define the upper-left corner of the range, and the reference on the right side of the colon to define the lower-right corner. However, there are other ways to create ranges with the range operator. Table 1.4 points out a few of them.

**Table 1.4   Sample Ranges Created with the Range Operator**

| Range | What It Refers To |
| --- | --- |
| A:A | Column A (that is, the entire column) |
| A:C | Columns A through C |
| 1:1 | Row 1 |
| 1:5 | Rows 1 through 5 |

## Using the Intersection Operator

If you have ranges that overlap, you can use the *intersection* operator (a space) to refer to the overlapping cells. For example, Figure 1.22 shows two ranges: C4:E9 and D8:G11. To refer to the overlapping cells (D8:E9), you would use the following notation: C4:E9 D8:G11.

C4:E9

**Figure 1.22**
The intersection operator returns the intersecting cells of two ranges.

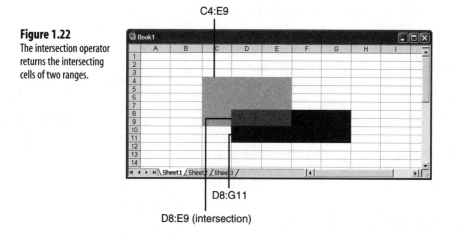

D8:G11

D8:E9 (intersection)

➔ To learn how to use range names with the range operator and intersection operators, **see** "Range Names and the Reference Operators," **p. 50**.

## Using the Union Operator

To create a reference that combines two or more ranges, use the *union* operator (,). For example, Figure 1.23 shows the range C4:E9,D8:G11, which is the union of C4:E9 and D8:G11.

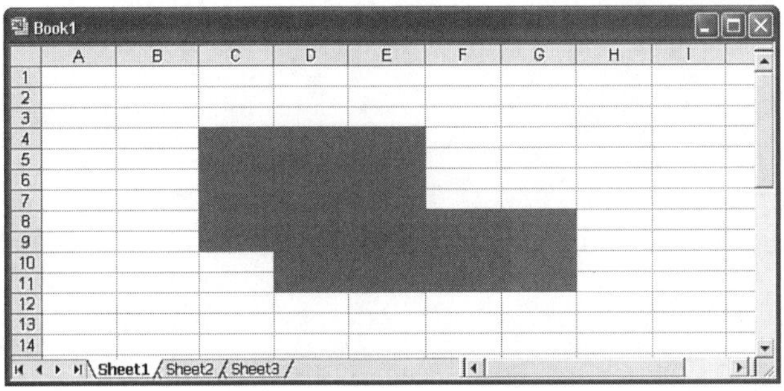

**Figure 1.23**
Use the union operator to create a single reference that combines two or more ranges.

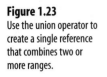

**1**

## From Here

- To learn how to use range names with the range operator and intersection operators, **see** "Range Names and the Reference Operators," **p. 50**.

- For information on relative references, **see** "Understanding Relative Reference Format," **p. 62**.

- If you're not sure what a circular reference is, **see** "Fixing Circular References," **p. 113**.

- For an in-depth discussion of Excel arrays, **see** "Working with Arrays," **p. 85**.

- To learn about data validation, **see** "Applying Data Validation Rules to Cells," **p. 98**.

- To learn more about using Excel for trend analysis, **see** "Using Regression to Track Trends and Make Forecasts," **p. 339**.

# Using Range Names

**2**

Although ranges enable you to work efficiently with large groups of cells, there are some disadvantages to using range coordinates:

- You can't work with more than one set of range coordinates at a time. Each time you want to use a range, you have to redefine its coordinates.

- Range notation is not intuitive. To know what a formula such as =SUM(E6:E10) is adding, you have to look at the range itself.

- A slight mistake in defining the range coordinates can lead to disastrous results, especially when you're erasing a range.

You can overcome these problems by using *range names*, which are labels applied to a single cell or to a range of cells. With a name defined, you can use it in place of the range coordinates. For example, to include the range in a formula or range command, you use the name instead of selecting the range or typing in its coordinates. You can create as many range names as you like, and you can even assign multiple names to the same range.

Range names also make your formulas intuitive and easy to read. For example, assigning the name AugustSales to a range such as E6:E10 immediately clarifies the purpose of a formula such as =SUM(AugustSales). Range names also increase the accuracy of your range operations because you don't have to specify range coordinates.

Besides overcoming these problems, range names bring several advantages to the table:

- Names are easier to remember than range coordinates.

- Names don't change when you move a range to another part of the worksheet.

- Named ranges adjust automatically whenever you insert or delete rows or columns within the range.

- Names make it easier to navigate a worksheet. You can use the Go To command to jump to a named range quickly.

- You can use worksheet labels to create range names quickly.

This chapter shows you how to define and work with range names, but I also hope to show you the power and flexibility that range names bring to your worksheet chores.

# Defining a Range Name

Range names can be quite flexible, but you need to follow a few restrictions and guidelines:

- The name can be a maximum of 255 characters.

- The name must begin with either a letter or the underscore character (_). For the rest of the name, you can use any combination of characters, numbers, or symbols, except spaces. For multiple-word names, separate the words by using the underscore character or by mixing case (for example, Cost_Of_Goods or CostOfGoods). Excel doesn't distinguish between uppercase and lowercase letters in range names.

- Don't use cell addresses (such as Q1) or any of the operator symbols (such as +, –, *, /, <, >, and &) because these could cause confusion if you use the name in a formula.

- To make typing easier, try to keep your names as short as possible while still retaining their meaning. TotalProfit04 is faster to type than Total_Profit_For_Fiscal_Year_2004, and it's certainly clearer than the more cryptic TotPft04.

- Don't use any of Excel's built-in names: Auto_Activate, Auto_Close, Auto_Deactivate, Auto_Open, Consolidate_Area, Criteria, Data_Form, Database, Extract, FilterDatabase, Print_Area, Print_Titles, Recorder, and Sheet_Title.

With these guidelines in mind, the next few sections show you various methods for defining range names.

## Working with the Name Box

The Name box in Excel's formula bar usually just shows you the address of the active cell. However, the Name box also comes with a couple of extra features that make it easier to work with range names:

- After you've defined a name, it appears in the Name box whenever you select the range, as shown in Figure 2.1.

- The Name box doubles as a drop-down list. To select a named range quickly, drop the list down and select the name you want. Excel moves to the range and selects the cells.

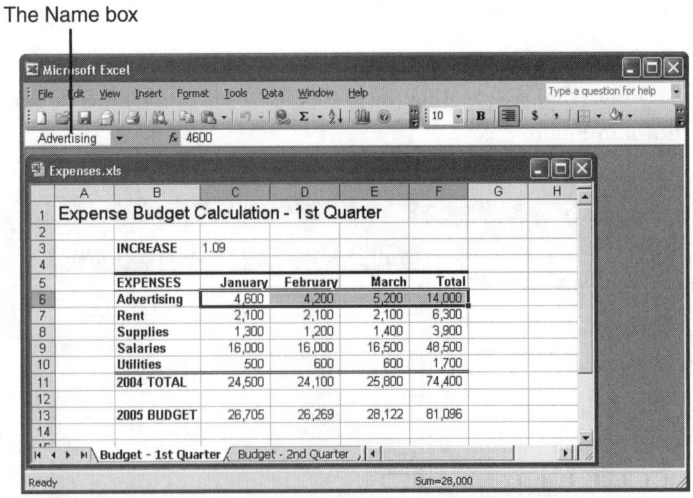

The Name box

**Figure 2.1**
When you select a range with a defined name, the name appears in Excel's Name box.

The Name box also happens to be the easiest way to define a range name. Here's what you do:

1. Select the range you want to name.

2. Click inside the Name box to display the insertion point.

3. Type the name you want to use, and then press Enter. Excel defines the new name automatically.

## Using the Define Name Dialog Box

Using the Name box to define a range name is fast and intuitive. However, it suffers from two minor but annoying drawbacks:

- If you try to define a name that already exists, Excel collapses the current selection and then selects the range corresponding to the existing name. This means you have to reselect your range and try again with a new name.

- If you select the range incorrectly and then name it, Excel doesn't give you any direct way to either fix the range or delete it and start again.

To solve both of these problems, you need to use the Define Name dialog box, which offers the following advantages:

- It shows a list of all the defined names, so there's less chance of trying to define a duplicate name.

- It's easy to fix the range coordinates if you make a mistake.

- You can delete a range name.

Follow these steps to define a range name using the Define Name dialog box:

1. Select the range you want to name.

2. Choose Insert, Name, Define (or press Ctrl+F3). The Define Name dialog box appears, as shown in Figure 2.2.

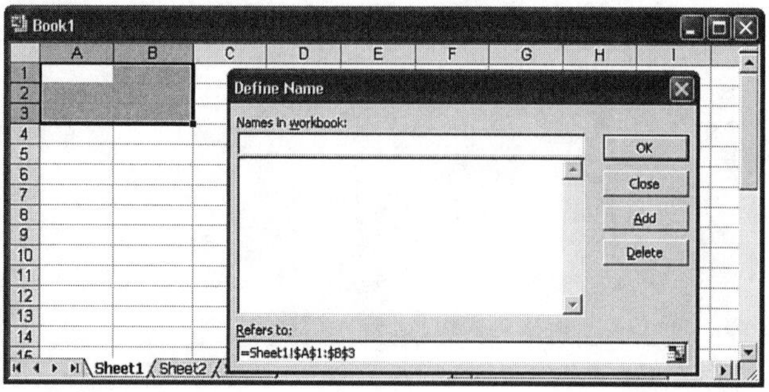

**Figure 2.2**
When you display the Define Name dialog box to define a range name, the coordinates of the selected range appear automatically in the Refers To box.

3. Enter the range name in the Names in Workbook text box.

> **TIP**
>
> When defining a range name, always enter at least the first letter of the name in uppercase. Why? It will prove invaluable later when you need to troubleshoot your formulas. The idea is that you type the range name entirely in lowercase letters when you insert it into a formula. When you accept the formula, Excel then converts the name to the case you used when you first defined it. If the name remains in lowercase letters, Excel doesn't recognize the name, so it's likely that you misspelled the name when typing it.

4. If the range displayed in the Refers To box is incorrect, you can use one of two methods to change it:

   • Type the correct range address (be sure to begin the address with an equals sign).

   • Click inside the Refers To box, and then use the mouse or keyboard to select a new range on the worksheet.

> **CAUTION**
>
> If you need to move around inside the Refers To box with the arrow keys (say, to edit the existing range address), first press F2 to put Excel into Edit mode. If you don't, Excel remains in Point mode, and the program assumes that you're trying to select a cell on the worksheet.

5. Click Add. Excel adds the name to the Names in Workbook list.

6. Repeat steps 3–5 for any other ranges you want to name.

7. When you're done, click Close to return to the worksheet.

## Defining Sheet-Level Range Names

Range names are available to all the sheets in a workbook. (These are called *workbook-level names*.) This means, for example, that a formula in Sheet1 can refer to a named range in Sheet3 simply by using the name directly. This can be a problem, however, if you need to use the same name in different worksheets. For example, you might have four sheets—First Quarter, Second Quarter, Third Quarter, and Fourth Quarter—and you might need to define an Expenses range name in each sheet.

If you need to use the same name in different sheets, you can create *sheet-level* names. This means that the name will refer only to the range on the sheet in which it was defined.

You create a sheet-level name by displaying the Define Name dialog box and then entering into the Names in <u>W</u>orkbook text box a name with the following general format:

*SheetName!RangeName*

Here, *SheetName* is the name of the worksheet and *RangeName* is the range name you want to use. For example, Sheet1!Sales refers to a range named Sales in Sheet1, and Sheet2!Sales refers to a range named Sales in Sheet2. If the worksheet name contains a space, surround the sheet name with single quotation marks, as in this example:

`'First Quarter'!Expenses`

## Assigning a Name to a 3D Range

In Chapter 1, "Getting the Most Out of Ranges," you learned how to work with 3D ranges, which are ranges that extend across multiple worksheets. Recall the general format for a 3D reference:

*FirstSheet:LastSheet!ULCorner:LRCorner*

Here, *FirstSheet* is the name of the first sheet in the 3D range, *LastSheet* is the name of the last sheet, and *ULCorner* and *LRCorner* define the cell range you want to work with on each sheet.

→ To get the details of Excel's 3D ranges, **see** "Working with 3D Ranges," **p. 12**.

Excel also enables you to define a range name on a 3D range. You can't use the Name box to define a 3D range name, but you can use the Define Name dialog box, as described in the next two sections.

### Entering a 3D Range Name Manually

Follow these steps to define a 3D range name by entering the range coordinates by hand:

1. Choose <u>I</u>nsert, <u>N</u>ame, <u>D</u>efine (or press Ctrl+F3) to display the Define Name dialog box.

2. Enter the range name in the Names in <u>W</u>orkbook text box.

3. In the <u>R</u>efers To text box, delete the existing text and enter the 3-D range coordinates.

4. Click <u>A</u>dd. Excel adds the name to the Names in <u>W</u>orkbook list.

5. Click Close.

### Entering a 3D Range Name By Selecting the Range

You can also define a 3D range name by using your mouse to select the 3D range. Here are the steps to follow:

1. Choose <u>I</u>nsert, <u>N</u>ame, <u>D</u>efine (or press Ctrl+F3) to display the Define Name dialog box.

2. Enter the range name in the Names in <u>W</u>orkbook text box.

3. In the <u>R</u>efers To text box, delete the existing text.

4. In the workbook, group the sheets you want to include in the 3D range.

5. Select the range. You should now see the proper 3D range coordinates in the <u>R</u>efers To text box.

6. Click <u>A</u>dd. Excel adds the name to the Names in <u>W</u>orkbook list.

7. Click Close.

## Using Worksheet Text to Define Names

When you use the Define Name dialog box, Excel sometimes suggests a name for the selected range. For example, Figure 2.3 shows that Excel has suggested the name Rent for the range C7:F7. As you can see, Rent is the row heading of the selected range, so Excel has used an adjacent text entry to make an educated guess about what you'll want to use as a name. (Note, too, that the <u>R</u>efers To formula specifies the worksheet name, so Excel also assumes that you want to create a sheet-level name.)

**Figure 2.3**
Excel uses adjacent text to guess the range name you want to use.

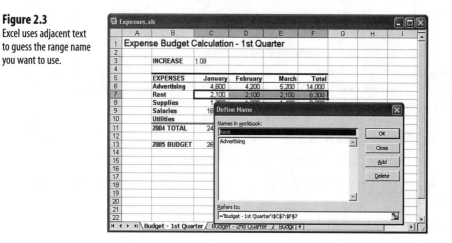

Instead of waiting for Excel to guess, you can tell the program explicitly to use adjacent text as a range name. The following procedure shows you the appropriate steps:

1. Select the range of cells you want to name, including the appropriate text cells that you want to use as the range names (see Figure 2.4).

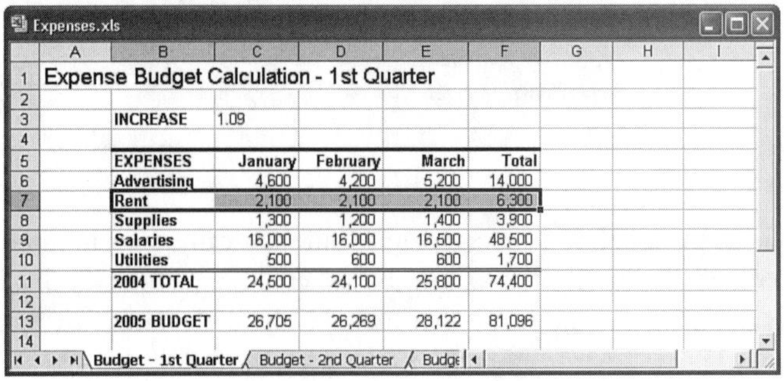

**Figure 2.4**
Include the text you want to use as names when you select the range.

2. Choose Insert, Name, Create, or press Ctrl+Shift+F3. Excel displays the Create Names dialog box, shown in Figure 2.5.

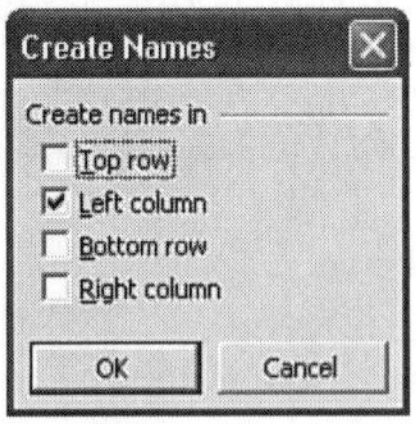

**Figure 2.5**
Use the Create Names dialog box to specify the location of the text to use as a range name.

3. Excel guesses where the text for the range name is located and activates the appropriate check box (Left Column, in the preceding example). If this isn't the check box you want, clear it and then activate the appropriate one.

4. Click OK.

> **NOTE**
> If the text you want to use as a range name contains any illegal characters (such as a space), Excel replaces those characters with an underscore (_).

When naming ranges from text, you're not restricted to working with just columns or rows. You can select ranges that include both row and column headings, and Excel will happily assign names to each row and column. For example, in Figure 2.6, the Create Names dialog box appears with both the Top Row and Left Column check boxes activated.

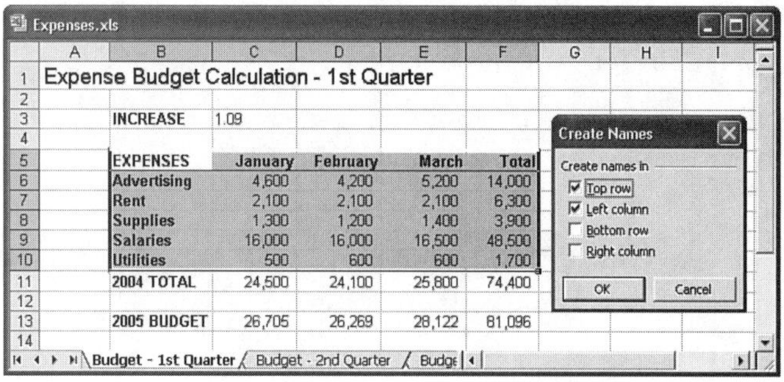

**Figure 2.6**
Excel can create names
for rows and columns at
the same time.

When you use this method to create names automatically, bear in mind that Excel gives special treatment to the top-left cell in the selected range. Specifically, it uses the text in that cell as the name for the range that includes the table data (that is, the table without the headings). In Figure 2.6, for example, the top-left corner of the selected range is cell B5, which contains the label Expenses. After creating the names, the table data—the range C6:F10—is given the name Expenses, as shown in Figure 2.7.

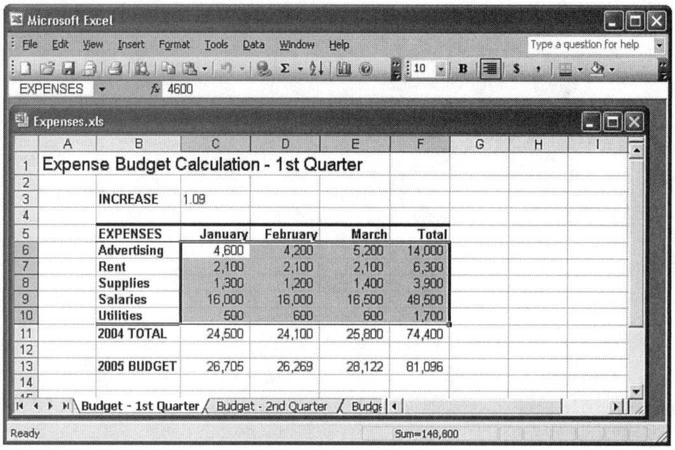

**Figure 2.7**
When creating names
from rows and columns
at the same time, Excel
uses the label in the top-
left corner as the name
of the range that
includes the table data.

## Naming Constants

One of the best ways to make your worksheets comprehensible is to define names for every constant value. For example, if your worksheet uses an interest rate variable in several formulas, you can define a constant named Rate and use the name in your formulas to make them more readable. You can do this in two ways:

- Set aside an area of your worksheet for constants, and name the individual cells. For example, Figure 2.8 shows a worksheet with three named constants: Rate (cell B5), Term (Cell B6), and Amount (cell B7). Notice how the formula in cell E5 refers to each constant by name.

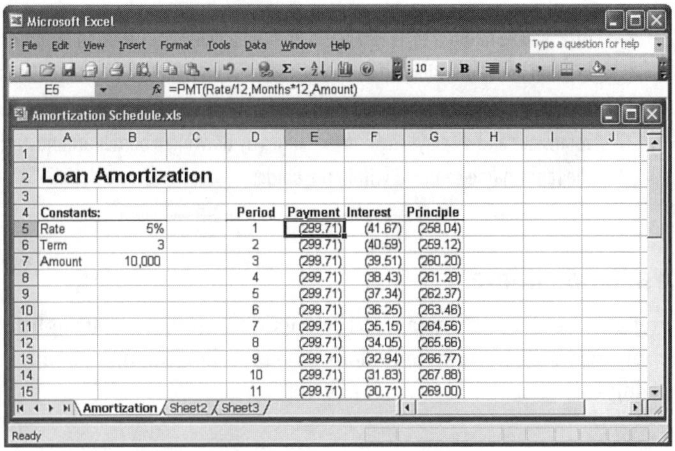

**Figure 2.8**
Grouping formula constants and naming them makes worksheets easy to read.

- If you don't want to clutter a worksheet, you can name constants without entering them in the worksheet. Choose Insert, Name, Define to display the Define Name dialog box. Enter a name for the constant in the Names in Workbook text box, and enter an equals sign (=) and the constant's value in the Refers To text box. Figure 2.9 shows an example.

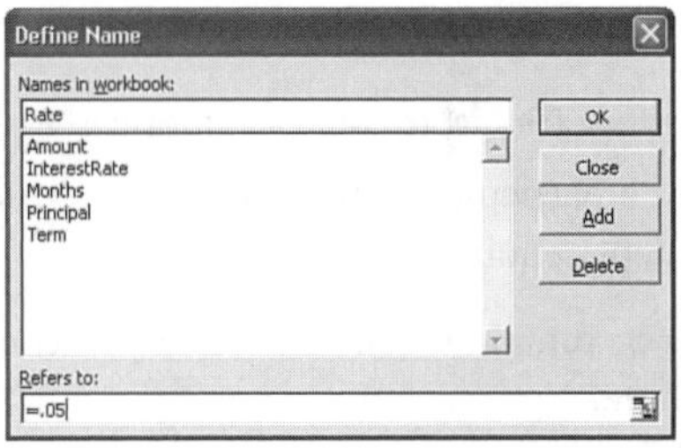

**Figure 2.9**
You can create and name constants in the Define Name dialog box.

> **TIP**
>
> When naming a constant, you're not restricted to the usual constant values of numbers and text strings. Excel also allows you to assign a worksheet function to a name. For example, you could enter =YEAR(NOW()) in the Refers To text box to create a name that always returns the current year. However, this feature is better suited to assigning a name to a long and complex formula that you need to use in different places.

# Working with Range Names

After you've defined a name, you can use it in formulas or functions, navigate with it, edit it, and delete it. The next few sections take you through these techniques and more.

> **TIP**
>
> After you've defined several range names on a worksheet, it often becomes difficult to visualize the location and dimensions of the ranges. Excel's Zoom feature can help. Choose View, Zoom to display the Zoom dialog box. In the Custom text box, enter a value of 39% or less, and then click OK. Excel zooms out and displays the named ranges by drawing a border around each one and by displaying the range name centered within the border.

## Referring to a Range Name

Using a range name in a formula or as a function argument is straightforward: Just replace a range's coordinates with the range's defined name. For example, suppose that a cell contains the following formula:

`=G1`

This formula sets the cell's value to the current value of cell G1. However, if cell G1 is named TotalExpenses, then the following formula is equivalent:

`=TotalExpenses`

Similarly, consider the following function:

`SUM(E3:E10)`

If the range E3:E10 is named Sales, then the following is equivalent:

`SUM(Sales)`

→ For more information on using names in your Excel formulas, **see** "Working with Range Names in Formulas," **p. 66**.

If you're not sure about a particular name, you can get Excel to paste it into the worksheet for you. Here are the steps required:

1.  Start your formula or function, and stop when you come to the spot where you need to insert the range name.
2.  Choose Insert, Name, Paste, or press F3. Excel displays the Paste Name dialog box.
3.  In the Paste Name list, click the name you want to use.
4.  Click OK. Excel pastes the name.

If you're working with sheet-level names, how you use a name depends on where you use it:

-   If you're using the sheet-level name on the sheet in which it was defined, you can just use the range name part. (That is, you don't need to specify the sheet name.)
-   If you're using the sheet-level name on any other sheet, you must use the full name (*SheetName!RangeName*).

If the named range exists in a different workbook, you must precede the name with the name of the file in single quotation marks. For example, if the Mortgage Amortization workbook contains a range named Rate, you use the following to refer to this range in a different workbook:

```
'Mortgage Amortization.xls'!Rate
```

> **CAUTION**
>
> Excel doesn't mind if you create a sheet-level name that's the same as a workbook-level name. In all the other sheets, if you use the range name by itself, Excel assumes that you're talking about the workbook-level name. However, if you use only the range name on the sheet in which the sheet-level name was defined, Excel assumes that you're talking about the sheet level name.
>
> So how do you refer to the workbook-level name from the sheet in which the sheet-level name was defined? You precede the range name with the workbook filename and an exclamation mark. For example, in a workbook named Expenses.xls, suppose that the current worksheet has a sheet-level range named Total and that there's also a workbook-level range named Total. To refer to the latter in the current worksheet, you use the following:
>
> ```
> Expenses.xls!Total
> ```

## Navigating Using Range Names

Ranges that have defined names are easy to select. Excel gives you two methods:

- The Name box doubles as a drop-down list. To select a named range quickly, drop the list down and select the name you want.
- Choose Edit, Go To to display the Go To dialog box. Click the range name in the Go To list and then click OK.

## Pasting a List of Range Names in a Worksheet

If you need to document a worksheet for others to read (or figure out the worksheet yourself a few months from now), you can paste a list of the worksheet's range names. This list includes the name and the range it represents (or the value it represents, if the name refers to a constant). Follow these steps to paste a list of range names:

1. Move the cell pointer to an empty area of the worksheet that's large enough to accept the list without overwriting any other data. (Note that the list uses up two columns: one for the names and one for the corresponding range coordinates.)
2. Choose Insert, Name, Paste, or press F3. Excel displays the Paste Name dialog box.
3. Click Paste List. Excel pastes the worksheet's names and range coordinates.

## Editing a Range Name's Coordinates

If you want an existing name to refer to a different set of range coordinates, Excel offers a couple of ways to edit the name:

- Move the range. When you do this, Excel moves the range name right along with it.
- If you want to adjust the existing coordinates or associate the name with a completely different range, choose Insert, Name, Define to display the Define Name dialog box. In the Names in Workbook list, click the name you want to change, and then edit the range coordinates using the Refers To text box.

## Adjusting Range Name Coordinates Automatically

It's common in spreadsheet work to have a row or column of data that you add to constantly. For example, you might have to keep a list of ongoing expenses in a project, or you might want to track the number of units that a product sells each day. From the perspective of range names, this isn't a problem if you always insert the new data within the existing range. In this case, Excel automatically adjusts the range coordinates to compensate for the new data. However, that doesn't happen if you always add the new data to the end of the range. In this case, you need to manually adjust the range coordinates to include the new data. The more data you enter, the bigger the pain this can be. To avoid this time-consuming drudgery, this section offers two solutions.

### Solution 1: Include a Blank Cell at the End of the Range

The first solution is to define the range and include an extra blank cell at the end, if possible. For example, in the worksheet shown in Figure 2.10, the Amount name has been applied to the range C4:C11, where C11 is a blank cell.

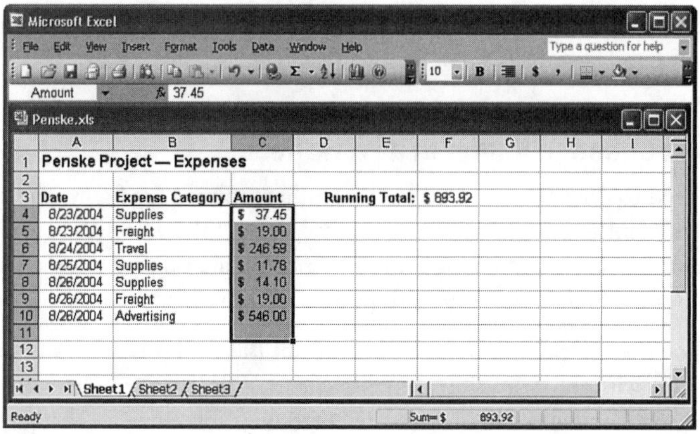

**Figure 2.10**
To get Excel to adjust a range name's coordinates automatically, include a blank cell at the end of the range, if possible.

The advantage here is that you can get Excel to adjust the Amount name's range coordinates automatically by inserting new data *above* (in this case) the blank line immediately below the table. Because you're inserting the new data within the existing range, Excel adjusts the name's range coordinates automatically, as shown in Figure 2.11.

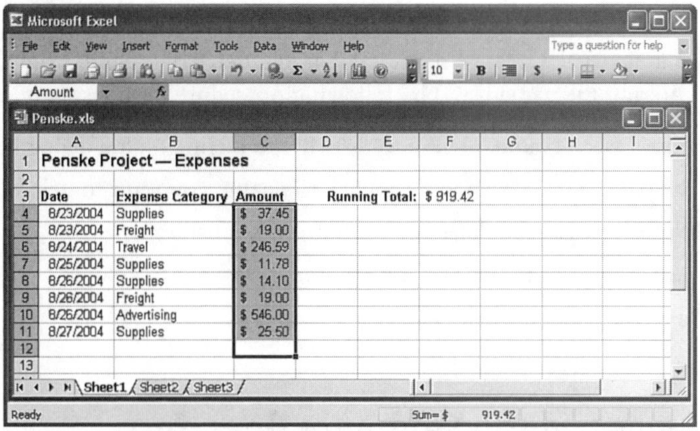

**Figure 2.11**
The Amount name now refers to the range C3:C12.

| | A | B | C | D | E | F | G | H | I |
|---|---|---|---|---|---|---|---|---|---|
| 1 | Penske Project — Expenses | | | | | | | | |
| 2 | | | | | | | | | |
| 3 | Date | Expense Category | Amount | | Running Total: | $ 919.42 | | | |
| 4 | 8/23/2004 | Supplies | $ 37.45 | | | | | | |
| 5 | 8/23/2004 | Freight | $ 19.00 | | | | | | |
| 6 | 8/24/2004 | Travel | $ 246.59 | | | | | | |
| 7 | 8/25/2004 | Supplies | $ 11.78 | | | | | | |
| 8 | 8/26/2004 | Supplies | $ 14.10 | | | | | | |
| 9 | 8/26/2004 | Freight | $ 19.00 | | | | | | |
| 10 | 8/26/2004 | Advertising | $ 546.00 | | | | | | |
| 11 | 8/27/2004 | Supplies | $ 25.50 | | | | | | |
| 12 | | | | | | | | | |
| 13 | | | | | | | | | |

### Solution 2: Name the Entire Row or Column

An even easier solution is to name the entire row or column to which you're adding data. You do this by selecting the row or column, entering the name in the Name box, and pressing Enter. With this method, any data you add to the row or column automatically becomes part of the range name.

> **CAUTION**
>
> Use this method only if the row or column to which you're adding data contains no other conflicting data. For example, if you're adding numbers to a column and that column has other, unrelated numbers above or below, those numbers will be included in the range name you define for the entire column. This would prevent you from using the name in a formula because the formula would also include the extraneous data.

## Changing a Range Name

If you need to change the name of one or more ranges, you can use one of two methods:

- If you've changed some row or column labels, just redefine the range names based on the new text, and delete the old names (as described in the next section).
- Choose Insert, Name, Define. Click the name you want to change in the Names in Workbook list, make your changes in the Refers To text box, and click Add.

> **CAUTION**
>
> Note that these methods don't actually change the name of the range. They just define a new name for the range while leaving the old name intact. This also means that any formulas that refer to the original range name won't get changed.

## Deleting a Range Name

If you no longer need a range name, you should delete the name from the worksheet to avoid cluttering the name list. The following procedure outlines the necessary steps:

1. Choose Insert, Name, Define to display the Define Name dialog box.
2. In the Names in Workbook list, click the name you want to delete.
3. Click Delete. Excel deletes the name from the list.
4. Repeat steps 2 and 3 for any other names you want to delete.
5. When you're done, click OK.

# Range Names and the Reference Operators

In Chapter 1, you learned about Excel reference operators. As you'll see in the next two sections, these useful operators also work with range names.

➜ For the details on these operators, **see** "Using Excel's Reference Operators," **p. 33**.

## Using Names with the Range Operator

When using the range operator (:), you normally surround it with cell addresses. However, you also can use a range name on either side of the colon. In this case, the named range becomes a *corner* for the larger range. For example, Figure 2.12 shows a worksheet with the named range Rent that refers to B7:D7. Table 2.1 shows some sample ranges you can create with Rent as one corner.

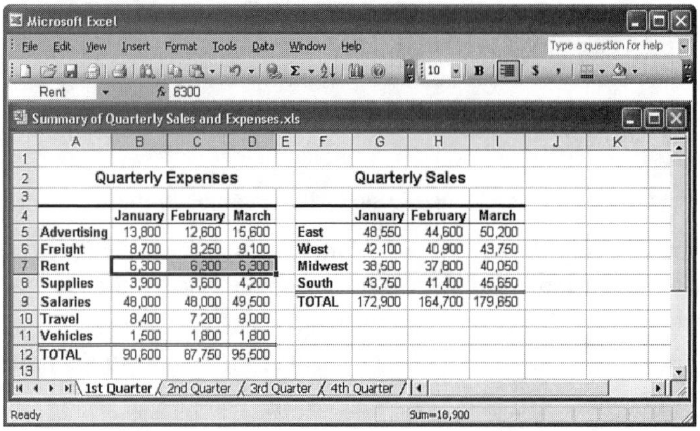

**Figure 2.12**
The named range Rent used in Table 2.1.

**Table 2.1    Sample Ranges Created with a Range Name**

| Range | What It Refers To |
|-------|-------------------|
| Rent:A1 | A1:D7 |
| Rent:G2 | B2:G7 |
| Rent:E10 | B7:E10 |
| Rent:A13 | A7:D13 |

## Using Names with the Intersection Operator

If you've named the ranges on your worksheet, the intersection operator can make things much easier to read because you can refer to individual cells by using the names of the cell's row and column. For example, in Figure 2.13, the range B5:B12 is named January and the range B7:D7 is named Rent. This means that you can refer to cell B7 as January Rent (see cell H11).

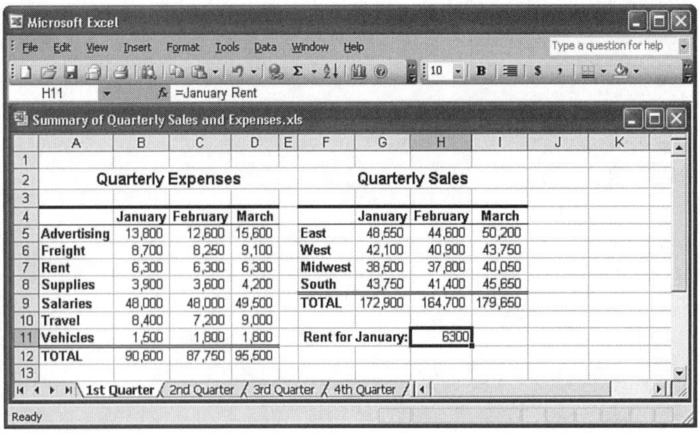

**Figure 2.13**
After you name ranges, you can combine row and column headings to create intersecting names for individual cells.

---

**CAUTION**

If you try to define an intersection name and Excel displays #NULL! in the cell, it means that the two ranges don't have any overlapping cells.

---

## From Here

- To get the details of Excel's 3D ranges, **see** "Working with 3D Ranges," **p. 12**.
- For the details on these operators, **see** "Using Excel's Reference Operators," **p. 33**.
- For more information on using names in your Excel formulas, **see** "Working with Range Names in Formulas," **p. 66**.

# Building Basic Formulas

**3**

A worksheet is merely a lifeless collection of numbers and text until you define some kind of relationship among the various entries. You do this by creating *formulas* that perform calculations and produce results. This chapter takes you through some formula basics, including constructing simple arithmetic and text formulas, understanding the all-important topic of operator precedence, copying and moving worksheet formulas, and making formulas easier to build and read by taking advantage of range names.

## Understanding Formula Basics

Most worksheets are created to provide answers to specific questions: What is the company's profit? Are expenses over or under budget, and by how much? What is the future value of an investment? How big will an employee bonus be this year? You can answer these questions, and an infinite variety of others, by using Excel formulas.

All Excel formulas have the same general structure: an equals sign (=) followed by one or more *operands*—which can be a value, a cell reference, a range, a range name, or a function name—separated by one or more *operators*—the symbols that combine the operands in some way, such as the plus sign (+) and the greater-than sign (>). Although it's unlikely that you'll ever reach it, the maximum number of characters that Excel allows within a single formula is 1,024.

> **NOTE**
> Excel won't object if you use spaces between operators and operands in your formulas. This is actually a good practice to get into because separating the elements of a formula in this way can make them much easier to read. Note, too, that Excel also accepts line breaks in formulas. This is handy if you have a very long formula because it enables you to "break up" the formula so that it appears on multiple lines. To create a line break within a formula, press Alt+Enter.

## Entering and Editing Formulas

Entering a new formula into a worksheet appears to be a straightforward process:

1. Select the cell in which you want to enter the formula.
2. Type an equals sign (=) to tell Excel that you're entering a formula.
3. Type the formula's operands and operators.
4. Press Enter to confirm the formula.

However, Excel has three different *input modes* that determine how Excel interprets certain keystrokes and mouse actions:

- When you type the equals sign to begin the formula, Excel goes into *Enter mode*, which is the mode you use to enter text (such as the formula's operands and operators).
- If you press any keyboard navigation key (such as Page Up, Page Down, or any arrow key), or if you click any other cell in the worksheet, Excel enters *Point mode*. This is the mode you use to select a cell or range as a formula operand. When you're in Point mode, you can use any of the range-selection techniques that you learned in Chapter 1, "Getting the Most Out of Ranges." Note that Excel returns to Enter mode as soon as you type an operator or any character.
- If you press F2, Excel enters *Edit mode*, which is the mode you use to make changes to the formula. For example, when you're in Edit mode, you can use the left and right arrow keys to move the cursor to another part of the formula for deleting or inserting characters. You can also enter Edit mode by clicking anywhere within the formula. Press F2 to return to Enter mode.

> **TIP**
> You can tell which mode Excel is currently in by looking at the status bar. On the left side, you'll see one of the following: Enter, Point, or Edit.

After you've entered a formula, you might need to return to it to make changes. Excel gives you three ways to enter Edit mode and make changes to a formula in the selected cell:

- Press F2.
- Double-click the cell.
- Use the formula bar to click anywhere inside the formula text.

Excel divides formulas into four groups: arithmetic, comparison, text, and reference. Each group has its own set of operators, and you use each group in different ways. In the next few sections, I'll show you how to use each type of formula.

## Using Arithmetic Formulas

*Arithmetic formulas* are by far the most common type of formula. They combine numbers, cell addresses, and function results with mathematical operators to perform calculations. Table 3.1 summarizes the mathematical operators used in arithmetic formulas.

**Table 3.1  The Arithmetic Operators**

| Operator | Name | Example | Result |
|---|---|---|---|
| + | Addition | =10+5 | 15 |
| – | Subtraction | =10-5 | 5 |
| – | Negation | =-10 | –10 |
| * | Multiplication | =10*5 | 50 |
| / | Division | =10/5 | 2 |
| % | Percentage | =10% | 0.1 |
| ^ | Exponentiation | =10^5 | 100000 |

Most of these operators are straightforward, but the exponentiation operator might require further explanation. The formula =x^y means that the value x is raised to the power y. For example, the formula =3^2 produces the result 9 (that is, 3*3=9). Similarly, the formula =2^4 produces 16 (that is, 2*2*2*2=16).

## Using Comparison Formulas

A *comparison formula* is a statement that compares two or more numbers, text strings, cell contents, or function results. If the statement is true, the result of the formula is given the logical value TRUE (which is equivalent to any nonzero value). If the statement is false, the formula returns the logical value FALSE (which is equivalent to 0). Table 3.2 summarizes the operators you can use in comparison formulas.

**Table 3.2  Comparison Formula Operators**

| Operator | Name | Example | Result |
|---|---|---|---|
| = | Equal to | =10=5 | FALSE |
| > | Greater than | =10>5 | TRUE |
| < | Less than | =10<5 | FALSE |

*continues*

| Table 3.2 | Continued | | |
|---|---|---|---|
| **Operator** | **Name** | **Example** | **Result** |
| >= | Greater than or equal to | ="a">="b" | FALSE |
| <= | Less than or equal to | ="a"<="b" | TRUE |
| <> | Not equal to | ="a"<>"b" | TRUE |

Comparison formulas have many uses. For example, you can determine whether to pay a salesperson a bonus by using a comparison formula to compare actual sales with a predetermined quota. If the sales are greater than the quota, the rep is awarded the bonus. You also can monitor credit collection. For example, if the amount a customer owes is more than 150 days past due, you might send the invoice to a collection agency.

→ Comparison formulas also make use of Excel's logical functions, so **see** "Adding Intelligence with Logical Functions," **p. 155**.

## Using Text Formulas

So far, I've discussed formulas that calculate or make comparisons and return values. A *text formula* is a formula that returns text. Text formulas use the ampersand (&) operator to work with text cells, text strings enclosed in quotation marks, and text function results.

One way to use text formulas is to concatenate text strings. For example, if you enter the formula ="soft"&"ware" into a cell, Excel displays software. Note that the quotation marks and the ampersand are not shown in the result. You also can use & to combine cells that contain text. For example, if A1 contains the text Ben and A2 contains Jerry, then entering the formula =A1&" and " &A2 returns Ben and Jerry.

→ For other uses of text formulas, **see** "Working with Text Functions," **p. 133**.

## Using Reference Formulas

The reference operators combine two cell references or ranges to create a single joint reference. I discussed reference formulas in detail in Chapter 1, but Table 3.3 gives you a quick summary.

| Table 3.3 | Reference Formula Operators | |
|---|---|---|
| **Operator** | **Name** | **Description** |
| : (colon) | Range | Produces a range from two cell references (for example, A1:C5) |
| (space) | Intersection | Produces a range that is the intersection of two ranges (for example, A1:C5 B2:E8) |
| , (comma) | Union | Produces a range that is the union of two ranges (for example, A1:C5,B2:E8) |

# Understanding Operator Precedence

You'll often use simple formulas that contain just two values and a single operator. In practice, however, most formulas you use will have a number of values and operators. In these mo s crucial. For example, consider the formula =3+5^2. If you calculate from left to right, the answer you get is 64 (3+5 equals 8, and 8^2 equals 64). However, if you perform the exponentiation first and then the addition, the result is 28 (5^2 equals 25, and 3+25 equals 28). As this example shows, a single formula can produce multiple answers, depending on the order in which you perform the calculations.

To control this problem, Excel evaluates a formula according to a predefined *order of precedence*. This order of precedence enables Excel to calculate a formula unambiguously by determining which part of the formula it calculates first, which part second, and so on.

## The Order of Precedence

Excel's order of precedence is determined by the various formula operators outlined earlier. Table 3.4 summarizes the complete order of precedence used by Excel.

**3**

| Table 3.4  The Excel Order of Precedence | | |
|---|---|---|
| **Operator** | **Operation** | **Order of Precedence** |
| : | Range | 1st |
| \<space\> | Intersection | 2nd |
| , | Union | 3rd |
| -- | Negation | 4th |
| % | Percentage | 5th |
| ^ | Exponentiation | 6th |
| * and / | Multiplication and division | 7th |
| + and -- | Addition and subtraction | 8th |
| & | Concatenation | 9th |
| = < > <= >= <> | Comparison | 10th |

From this table, you can see that Excel performs exponentiation before addition. Therefore, the correct answer for the formula =3+5^2, given previously, is 28. Notice also that some operators in Table 3.4 have the same order of precedence (for example, multiplication and division). This means that it usually doesn't matter in which order these operators are evaluated. For example, consider the formula =5*10/2. If you perform the multiplication first, the answer you get is 25 (5*10 equals 50, and 50/2 equals 25). If you perform the division first, you also get an answer of 25 (10/2 equals 5, and 5*5 equals 25). By convention, Excel evaluates operators with the same order of precedence from left to right, so you should assume that's how your formulas will be evaluated.

## Controlling the Order of Precedence

Sometimes you want to override the order of precedence. For example, suppose that you want to create a formula that calculates the pre-tax cost of an item. If you bought something for $10.65, including 7% sales tax, and you want to find the cost of the item minus the tax, you use the formula =10.65/1.07, which gives you the correct answer of $9.95. In general, this is the formula:

Figure 3.1 shows how you might implement such a formula. Cell B5 displays the Total Cost variable, and cell B6 displays the Tax Rate variable. Given these parameters, your first instinct might be to use the formula =B5/1+B6 to calculate the original cost. This formula is shown (as text) in cell E9, and the result is given in cell D9. As you can see, this answer is incorrect. What happened? Well, according to the rules of precedence, Excel performs division before addition, so the value in B5 first is divided by 1 and then is added to the value in B6. To get the correct answer, you must override the order of precedence so that the addition 1+B6 is performed first. You do this by surrounding that part of the formula with parentheses, as shown in cell E10. When this is done, you get the correct answer (cell D10).

> **TIP**
>
> In Figure 3,1. how did I convince Excel to show the formulas in cells E9 and E10 as text? I preceded each formula with an apostrophe, as in this example:
>
>     ' =B5/1+B6

**Figure 3.1**
Use parentheses to control the order of precedence in your formulas.

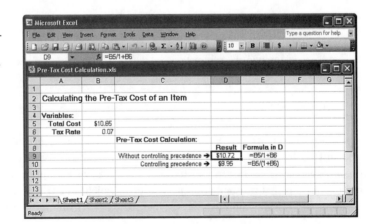

In general, you can use parentheses to control the order that Excel uses to calculate formulas. Terms inside parentheses are always calculated first; terms outside parentheses are calculated sequentially (according to the order of precedence).

> **TIP**
>
> Another good use for parentheses is raising a number to a fractional power. For example, if you want to take the *n*th root of a number, you use the following general formula:
>
> `=number ^ (1 / n)`
>
> For example, to take the cube root of the value in cell A1, use this:
>
> `=A1 ^ (1 / 3)`

To gain even more control over your formulas, you can place parentheses inside one another; this is called *nesting* parentheses. Excel always evaluates the innermost set of parentheses first. Here are a few sample formulas:

| Formula | 1st Step | 2nd Step | 3rd Step | Result |
|---------|----------|----------|----------|--------|
| 3^(15/5)*2-5 | 3^3*2–5 | 27*2–5 | 54–5 | 49 |
| 3^((15/5)*2-5) | 3^(3*2–5) | 3^(6–5) | 3^1 | 3 |
| 3^(15/(5*2-5)) | 3^(15/(10-5)) | 3^(15/5) | 3^3 | 27 |

Notice that the order of precedence rules also hold within parentheses. For example, in the expression (5*2–5), the term 5*2 is calculated before 5 is subtracted.

Using parentheses to determine the order of calculations enables you to gain full control over your Excel formulas. This way, you can make sure that the answer given by a formula is the one you want.

> **CAUTION**
>
> One of the most common mistakes when using parentheses in formulas is to forget to close a parenthetic term with a right parenthesis. If you do this, Excel generates an error message (and offers a solution to the problem). To make sure that you've closed each parenthetic term, count all the left and right parentheses. If these totals don't match, you know you've left out a parenthesis.

# Controlling Worksheet Calculation

Excel always calculates a formula when you confirm its entry, and the program normally recalculates existing formulas automatically whenever their data changes. This behavior is fine for small worksheets, but it can slow you down if you have a complex model that takes several seconds or even several minutes to recalculate. To turn off this automatic recalculation, follow these steps:

1. Choose Tools, Options. The Options dialog box appears.
2. Select the Calculation tab to display the Calculation options (see Figure 3.2).
3. To disable automatic recalculation, choose Manual. If you'd prefer to leave automatic calculation on except for data tables, select the Automatic Except Tables option instead.

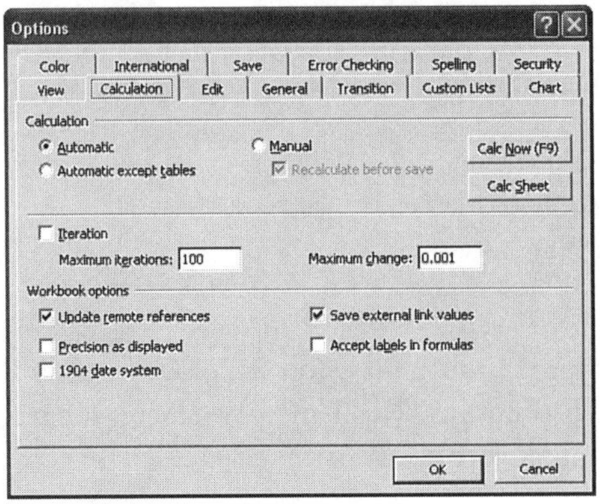

**Figure 3.2**
Select the Calculation tab in the Options dialog box to control worksheet calculations.

→ To learn how to set up data tables, **see** "Using What-If Analysis," **p. 315**.

   **4.** If you chose <u>M</u>anual, you also can tell Excel not to recalculate before saving the worksheet by clearing the Recalcu̲late Before Save check box.

   **5.** Click OK.

With manual calculation turned on, you'll see a `Calculate` message appear in the status bar whenever your worksheet data changes and your formula results need to be updated. When you want to recalculate, choose <u>T</u>ools, <u>O</u>ptions; select the Calculation tab; and then click one of the following buttons:

■ Click Calc <u>N</u>ow to recalculate every open worksheet.

■ Click Calc <u>S</u>heet to recalculate only the active worksheet.

> **TIP**
>
> Excel offers the following shortcut keys for recalculating without bothering with the Options dialog box:
>
> ■ F9—Recalculates the changed formulas in all open worksheets
>
> ■ Shift+F9—Recalculates the changed formulas in the current worksheet
>
> ■ Ctrl+Alt+F9—Recalculates every formula (even those that are unchanged) in all open worksheets

If you want to recalculate only part of your worksheet while manual calculation is turned on, you have two options:

■ To recalculate a single formula, select the cell containing the formula, activate the formula bar, and then confirm the cell (by pressing Enter or clicking the Enter button).

■ To recalculate a range, select the range; choose <u>E</u>dit, <u>R</u>eplace (or press Ctrl+H); and enter an equals sign (=) in both the Fi̲nd What and Re̲place With boxes. Click Replace

All. Excel "replaces" the equals sign in each formula with another equals sign. This doesn't change anything, but it forces Excel to recalculate each formula.

# Copying and Moving Formulas

In Chapter 1, I showed you various techniques for copying and moving ranges. The procedures for copying and moving ranges that contain formulas are identical, but the results are not always straightforward.

For an example, check out Figure 3.3, which shows a list of expense data for a company. The formula in cell C11 uses the SUM() function to total the January expenses (range C6:C10). The idea behind this worksheet is to calculate a new expense budget number for 2005 as a percentage increase of the actual 2004 total. Cell C3 displays the INCREASE variable (in this case, the increase being used is 3%). The formula that calculates the 2005 BUDGET number (cell C13 for the month of January) multiplies the 2004 TOTAL by the INCREASE (that is, =C11*C3).

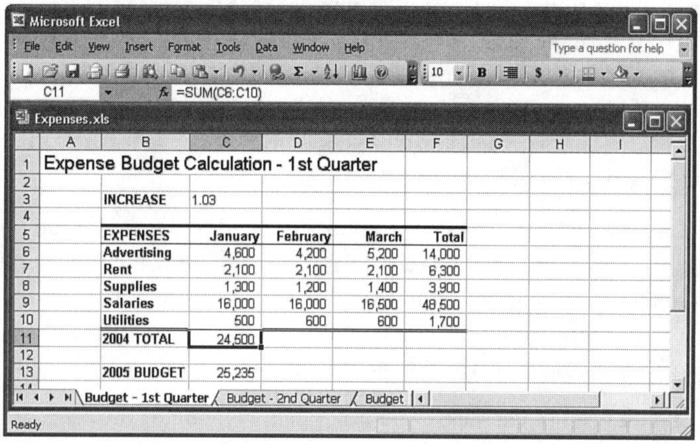

**Figure 3.3**
A budget expenses worksheet with two calculations for the January numbers: the total (cell C11) and a percentage increase for next year (cell C13).

The next step is to calculate the 2004 TOTAL expenses and the 2005 BUDGET figure for February. You could just type each new formula, but you learned in Chapter 1 that you can copy a cell much more quickly. Figure 3.4 shows the results when you copy the contents of cell C11 into cell D11. As you can see, Excel adjusts the range in the formula's SUM() function so that only the February expenses (D6:D10) are totaled. How did Excel know to do this? To answer this question, you need to know about Excel's relative reference format.

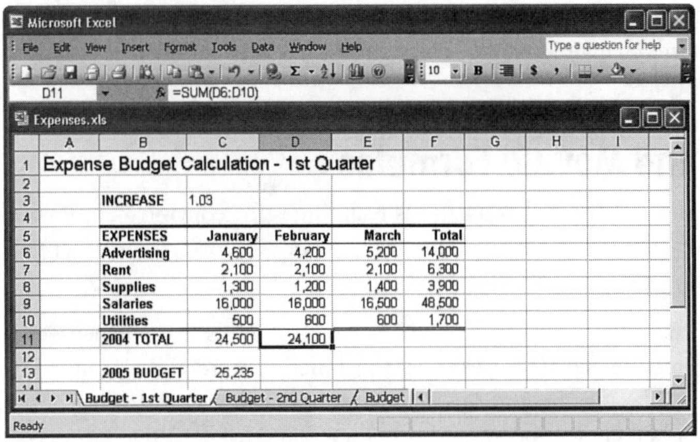

**Figure 3.4**
When you copy the January 2004 TOTAL formula to February, Excel automatically adjusts the range reference.

## Understanding Relative Reference Format

When you use a cell reference in a formula, Excel looks at the cell address relative to the location of the formula. For example, suppose that you have the formula =A1*2 in cell A3. To Excel, this formula says, "Multiply the contents of the cell two rows above this one by 2." This is called the *relative reference format*, and it's the default format for Excel. This means that if you copy this formula to cell A4, the relative reference is still "Multiply the contents of the cell two rows above this one by 2," but the formula changes to =A2*2 because A2 is two rows above A4.

Figure 3.4 shows why this format is useful. You had to copy only the formula in cell C11 to cell D11 and, thanks to relative referencing, everything comes out perfectly. To get the expense total for March, you would just have to paste the same formula into cell E11. You'll find that this way of handling copy operations will save you incredible amounts of time when you're building your worksheet models.

However, you need to exercise some care when copying or moving formulas. Let's see what happens if you return to the budget expense worksheet and try copying the 2005 BUDGET formula in cell C13 to cell D13. Figure 3.5 shows that the result is 0!

What happened? The formula bar shows the problem: The new formula is =D11*D3. Cell D11 is the February 2004 TOTAL, and that's fine, but instead of the INCREASE cell (C3), the formula refers to a blank cell (D3). Excel treats blank cells as 0, so the formula result is 0. The problem is the relative reference format. When the formula was copied, Excel assumed that the new formula should refer to cell D3. To see how you can correct this problem, you need to learn about another format: the *absolute reference format*.

> **NOTE**
> The relative reference format problem doesn't occur when you move a formula. When you move a formula, Excel assumes that you want to keep the same cell references.

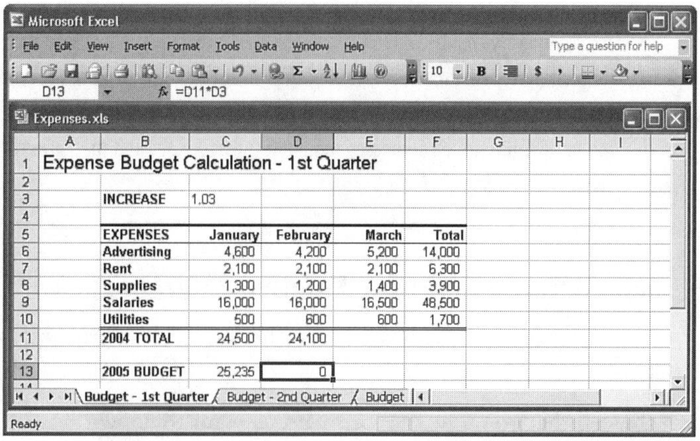

**Figure 3.5**
Copying the January 2004 BUDGET formula to February creates a problem.

| | A | B | C | D | E | F | G | H | I |
|---|---|---|---|---|---|---|---|---|---|
| 1 | Expense Budget Calculation - 1st Quarter | | | | | | | | |
| 2 | | | | | | | | | |
| 3 | | INCREASE | 1.03 | | | | | | |
| 4 | | | | | | | | | |
| 5 | | EXPENSES | January | February | March | Total | | | |
| 6 | | Advertising | 4,600 | 4,200 | 5,200 | 14,000 | | | |
| 7 | | Rent | 2,100 | 2,100 | 2,100 | 6,300 | | | |
| 8 | | Supplies | 1,300 | 1,200 | 1,400 | 3,900 | | | |
| 9 | | Salaries | 16,000 | 16,000 | 16,500 | 48,500 | | | |
| 10 | | Utilities | 500 | 600 | 600 | 1,700 | | | |
| 11 | | 2004 TOTAL | 24,500 | 24,100 | | | | | |
| 12 | | | | | | | | | |
| 13 | | 2005 BUDGET | 25,235 | 0 | | | | | |

D13 ▾ ƒx =D11*D3

Expenses.xls

Budget - 1st Quarter / Budget - 2nd Quarter / Budget

Ready

## Understanding Absolute Reference Format

When you refer to a cell in a formula using the absolute reference format, Excel uses the physical address of the cell. You tell the program that you want to use an absolute reference by placing dollar signs ($) before the row and column of the cell address. To return to the example in the preceding section, Excel interprets the formula =$A$1*2 as "Multiply the contents of cell A1 by 2." No matter where you copy or move this formula, the cell reference doesn't change. The cell address is said to be *anchored*.

To fix the budget expense worksheet, we need to anchor the INCREASE variable. To do this, we first change the January 2005 BUDGET formula in cell C13 to read =C11*$C$3. After making this change, copying the formula to the February 2005 BUDGET column gives the new formula =D11*$C$3, which produces the correct result.

> **CAUTION**
>
> Most range names refer to absolute cell references. This means that when you copy a formula that uses a range name, the copied formula will use the same range name as the original. This might produce errors in your worksheet.

You also should know that you can enter a cell reference using a mixed-reference format. In this format, you anchor either the cell's row (by placing the dollar sign in front of the row address only—for example, B$6) or its column (by placing the dollar sign in front of the column address only—for example, $B6).

**TIP**

You can quickly change the reference format of a cell address by using the F4 key. When editing a formula, place the cursor to the left of the cell address (or between the row and column values), and keep pressing F4. Excel cycles through the various formats. If you want to apply the new reference format to multiple cell addresses, highlight the addresses and then press F4 until you get the format you want.

## Copying a Formula Without Adjusting Relative References

If you need to copy a formula but don't want the formula's relative references to change, follow these steps:

1. Select the cell that contains the formula you want to copy.
2. Click inside the formula bar to activate it.
3. Use the mouse or keyboard to highlight the entire formula.
4. Copy the highlighted formula.
5. Press Esc to deactivate the formula bar.
6. Select the cell in which you want the copy of the formula to appear.
7. Paste the formula.

**NOTE**

Here are two other methods you can use to copy a formula without adjusting its relative cell references:

- To copy a formula from the cell above, select the lower cell and press Ctrl+' (apostrophe).
- Activate the formula bar and type an apostrophe (') at the beginning of the formula (that is, to the left of the equals sign) to convert it to text. Press Enter to confirm the edit, copy the cell, and then paste it in the desired location. Now delete the apostrophe from both the source and destination cells to convert the text back to a formula.

# Displaying Worksheet Formulas

By default, Excel displays the results of a formula in cells instead of the formula. If you need to see a formula, you can simply choose the appropriate cell and look at the formula bar. However, sometimes you'll want to see all the formulas in a worksheet (such as when you're troubleshooting your work). To display your worksheet's formulas, follow these steps:

→  For more information about solving formula problems, **see** "Troubleshooting Formulas," **p. 107**.

1. Choose Tools, Options to display the Options dialog box.
2. Choose the View tab.
3. Activate the Formulas check box.
4. Click OK. Excel displays the worksheet formulas.

**TIP** You can also press Ctrl+` (backquote) to toggle a worksheet between values and formulas.

# Converting a Formula to a Value

If a cell contains a formula whose value will never change, you can convert the formula to that value. This speeds up large worksheet recalculations, and it frees up memory for your worksheet because values use much less memory than formulas do. For example, you might have formulas in part of your worksheet that use values from a previous fiscal year. Because these numbers aren't likely to change, you can safely convert the formulas to their values. To do this, follow these steps:

1. Select the cell containing the formula you want to convert.
2. Double-click the cell or press F2 to activate in-cell editing.
3. Press F9. The formula changes to its value.
4. Press Enter or click the Enter button. Excel changes the cell to the value.

You'll often need to use the result of a formula in several places. If a formula is in cell C5, for example, you can display its result in other cells by entering =C5 in each of the cells. This is the best method if you think the formula result might change because, if it does, Excel updates the other cells automatically. However, if you're sure that the result won't change, you can copy only the value of the formula into the other cells. Use the following procedure to do this:

**CAUTION**

If your worksheet is set to manual calculation, make sure that you update your formulas (by pressing F9) before copying the values of your formulas.

1. Select the cell that contains the formula.
2. Copy the cell.
3. Select the cell or cells to which you want to copy the value.
4. Choose Edit, Paste Special. The Paste Special dialog box appears.
5. Activate the Values option button in the Paste group.
6. Click OK. Excel pastes the cell's value to each cell you selected.

Remember, too, that in Excel 2003, you can paste the cell into the destination, drop down the Paste Options list, and then choose Values Only.

# Working with Range Names in Formulas

Chapter 2, "Using Range Names," showed you how to define and use range names in your worksheets. You probably use range names often in your formulas. After all, a cell that contains the formula =Sales-Expenses is much more comprehensible than one that contains the more cryptic formula =F12-F3. The next few sections show you some techniques that make it easier for you to use range names in formulas.

## Pasting a Name into a Formula

One way to enter a range name in a formula is to type the name in the formula bar. But what if you can't remember the name? Or what if the name is long and you've got a deadline looming? For these kinds of situations, Excel has a feature that enables you to select the name you want from a list and paste it right into the formula. The following procedure gives you the details:

1. In the formula bar, place the insertion point where you want the name to appear.
2. Choose Insert, Name, Paste (or press F3). Excel displays the Paste Name dialog box, shown in Figure 3.6.

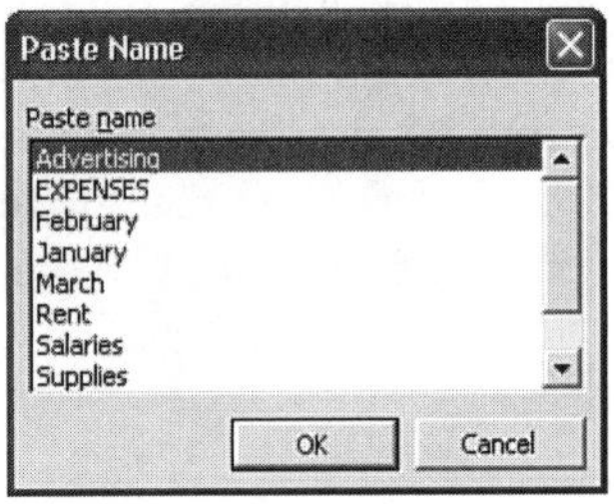

**Figure 3.6**
Use the Paste Name dialog box to paste a range name into a formula.

3. Use the Paste Name list to highlight the range name you want to use.
4. Click OK. Excel pastes the name in the formula bar.

## Applying Names to Formulas

If you've been using ranges in your formulas and you name those ranges later, Excel doesn't automatically apply the new names to the formulas. Instead of substituting the appropriate names by hand, you can get Excel to do the hard work for you. Follow these steps to apply the new range names to your existing formulas:

1. Select the range in which you want to apply the names, or select a single cell if you want to apply the names to the entire worksheet.
2. Choose Insert, Name, Apply. Excel displays the Apply Names dialog box, shown in Figure 3.7.

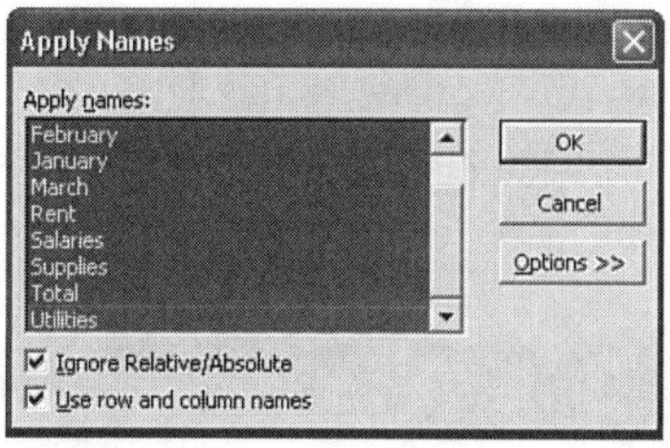

**Figure 3.7**
Use the Apply Names dialog box to select the names you want to apply to your formula ranges.

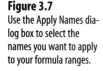

3. Choose the name or names you want applied from the Apply Names list.

4. Activate the Ignore Relative/Absolute check box to ignore relative and absolute references when applying names. (See the next section for more information on this option.)

5. The Use Row and Column Names check box tells Excel whether to use the worksheet's row and column names when applying names. If you activate this check box, you also can click the Options button to see more choices. (See the section in this chapter titled "Using Row and Column Names When Applying Names" for details.)

6. Click OK to apply the names.

### Ignoring Relative and Absolute References When Applying Names

If you clear the Ignore Relative/Absolute option in the Apply Names dialog box, Excel replaces relative range references only with names that refer to relative references, and it replaces absolute range references only with names that refer to absolute references. If you leave this option activated, Excel ignores relative and absolute reference formats when applying names to a formula.

For example, suppose that you have a formula such as =SUM(A1:A10) and a range named Sales that refers to $A$1:$A$10. With the Ignore Relative/Absolute option turned off, Excel will not apply the name Sales to the range in the formula; Sales refers to an absolute range, and the formula contains a relative range. Unless you think you'll be moving your formulas around, you should leave the Ignore Relative/Absolute option activated.

### Using Row and Column Names When Applying Names

For extra clarity in your formulas, leave the Use Row and Column Names check box activated in the Apply Names dialog box. This option tells Excel to rename all cell references that can be described as the intersection of a named row and a named column. In Figure 3.8, for example, the range C6:C13 is named January, and the range C7:E7 is named Rent. This means that cell C7—the intersection of these two ranges—can be referenced as January Rent.

→ The space character is Excel's intersection operator. For more information, **see** "Using the Intersection Operator," **p. 34.**

As shown in Figure 3.8, the Total for the Rent row (cell F7) currently contains the formula =C7+D7+E7. If you applied range names to this worksheet and activated the <u>U</u>se Row and Column Names option, you'd think this formula would be changed to this:

```
=January Rent + February Rent + March Rent
```

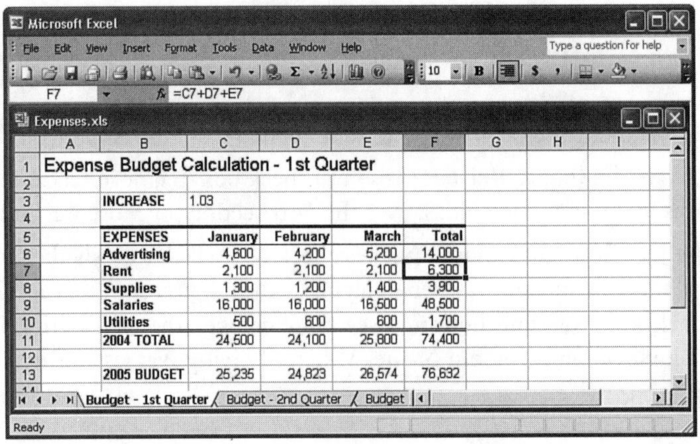

**Figure 3.8**

Before applying range names to the formulas, cell F7 (Total Rent) contains the formula =C7+D7+E7.

If you try this, however, you'll get a slightly different formula, as shown in Figure 3.9.

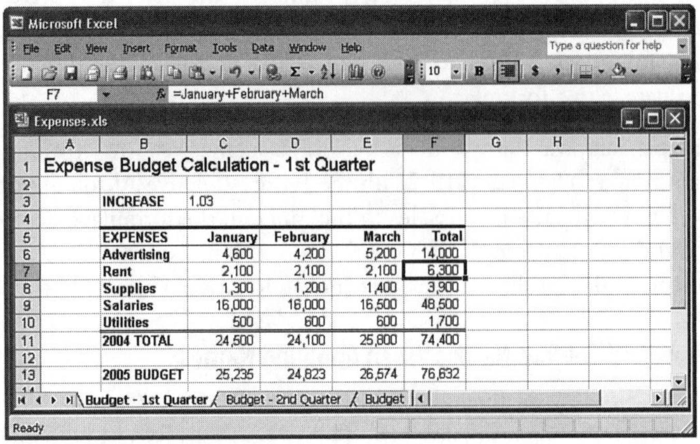

**Figure 3.9**

After applying range names, the Total Rent cell contains the formula =January+ February+March.

The reason for this is that when Excel is applying names, it omits the row name if the formula is in the same row. (It also omits the column name if the formula is in the same column.) In cell F7, for example, Excel omits Rent in each term because F7 is in the Rent row.

Omitting row headings isn't a problem in a small model, but it can be confusing in a large worksheet, where you might not be able to see the names of the rows. Therefore, if you're applying names to a large worksheet, you'll probably prefer to include the row names when applying names.

Choosing the <u>O</u>ptions button in the Apply Names dialog box displays the expanded dialog box shown in Figure 3.10. This includes extra options that enable you to include column (and row) headings:

- **Omit <u>C</u>olumn Name If Same Column**—Clear this check box to include column names when applying names.

- **Omit <u>R</u>ow Name If Same Row**—Clear this check box to include row names.

- **Name Order**—Use these options to choose the order of names in the reference (Ro<u>w</u> Column or Col<u>u</u>mn Row).

**Figure 3.10**
The expanded Apply Names dialog box.

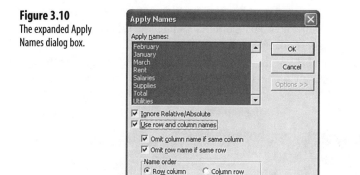

## Naming Formulas

In Chapter 1, you learned how to set up names for often-used constants. You can apply a similar naming concept for frequently used formulas. As with the constants, the formula doesn't physically have to appear in a cell. This not only saves memory, but it often makes your worksheets easier to read as well. Follow these steps to name a formula:

1. Choose <u>I</u>nsert, <u>N</u>ame, <u>D</u>efine to display the Define Name dialog box.

2. Enter the name you want to use for the formula in the Names in <u>W</u>orkbook edit box.

3. In the <u>R</u>efers To box, enter the formula exactly as you would if you were entering it in a worksheet.

4. Click OK.

Now you can enter the formula name in your worksheet cells (instead of the formula itself). For example, the following is the formula for the volume of a sphere (r is the radius of the sphere):

$4\pi r^3/3$

So, assuming that you have a cell named Radius somewhere in the workbook, you could create a formula named, say, SphereVolume, and make the following entry in the <u>R</u>efers To box of the Define Name dialog box (where `PI()` is the Excel worksheet function that returns the value of Pi):

```
=(4 * PI() * Radius ^ 3) / 3
```

# Working with Links in Formulas

If you have data in one workbook that you want to use in another, you can set up a link between them. This action enables your formulas to use references to cells or ranges in the other workbook. When the other data changes, Excel automatically updates the link.

For example, Figure 3.11 shows two linked workbooks. The Budget Summary sheet in the 2005 Budget—Summary workbook includes data from the Details worksheet in the 2005 Budget workbook. Specifically, the formula shown for cell B2 in 2005 Budget—Summary contains an external reference to cell R7 in the Details worksheet of 2005 Budget. If the value in R7 changes, Excel immediately updates the 2005 Budget—Summary workbook.

**Figure 3.11**

These two workbooks are linked because the formula in cell B2 of the 2005 Budget— Summary workbook references cell R7 in the 2005 Budget workbook.

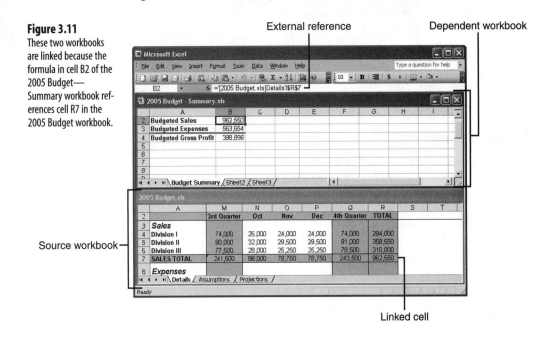

External reference

Dependent workbook

Source workbook

Linked cell

> **NOTE**
> The workbook that contains the external reference is called the *dependent* workbook (or the *client* workbook). The workbook that contains the original data is called the *source* workbook (or the *server* workbook).

## Understanding External References

There's no big mystery behind these links. You set up links by including an external reference to a cell or range in another workbook (or in another worksheet from the same workbook). In the example shown in Figure 3.11, all I did was enter an equals sign in cell B2 of the Budget Summary worksheet, and then click cell R7 in the Details worksheet.

The only thing you need to be comfortable with is the structure of an external reference. Here's the syntax:

```
'path[workbookname]sheetname'!reference
```

| | |
|---|---|
| path | The drive and directory in which the workbook is located. You need to include the path only when the workbook is closed. |
| workbookname | The name of the workbook, including an extension. Always enclose the workbook name in square brackets ([ ]). You can omit *workbookname* if you're referencing a cell or range in another sheet of the same workbook. |
| sheetname | The name of the worksheet's tab. You can omit *sheetname* if *reference* is a defined name in the same workbook. |
| reference | A cell or range reference, or a defined name. |

For example, if you close the 2005 Budget workbook, Excel automatically changes the external reference shown in Figure 3.11 to this (depending on the actual path of the file):

```
='C:\My Documents\Worksheets\[2005 Budget.xls]Details'!$R$7
```

> **NOTE**
> You need the single quotation marks around the path, workbook name, and sheet name only if the workbook is closed or if the path, workbook, or sheet name contains spaces. If in doubt, include the single quotation marks anyway; Excel happily ignores them if they're not required.

## Updating Links

The purpose of a link is to avoid duplicating formulas and data in multiple worksheets. If one workbook contains the information you need, you can use a link to reference the data without re-creating it in another workbook.

To be useful, however, the data in the dependent workbook should always reflect what actually is in the source workbook. You can make sure of this by updating the link, as explained here:

- If both the source and the dependent workbooks are open, Excel automatically updates the link whenever the data in the source file changes.
- If the source workbook is open when you open the dependent workbook, Excel automatically updates the links again.

- If the source workbook is closed when you open the dependent workbook, Excel displays a dialog box asking whether you want to update the links. Click Yes to update or No to cancel.

- If you didn't update a link when you opened the dependent document, you can update it any time by selecting the Edit, Links command. In the Edit Links dialog box that appears (see Figure 3.12), highlight the link and then click Update Values.

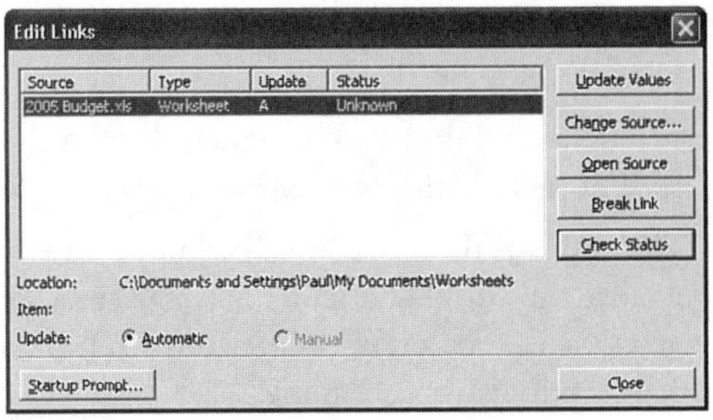

**Figure 3.12**
Use the Edit Links dialog box to update the linked data in the source workbook.

### Editing Links

If the name of the source document changes, you'll need to edit the link to keep the data up-to-date. You can edit the external reference directly, or you can change the source by following these steps:

1. With the dependent workbook active, choose Edit, Links to display the Edit Links dialog box.

2. Select the link you want to change.

3. Click Change Source. Excel displays the Change Source dialog box.

4. Find and then choose the new source document, and then click OK to return to the Edit Links dialog box.

5. Click Close to return to the workbook.

# Formatting Numbers, Dates, and Times

One of the best ways to improve the readability of your worksheets is to display your data in a format that is logical, consistent, and straightforward. Formatting currency amounts with leading dollar signs, percentages with trailing percent signs, and large numbers with commas are a few of the ways you can improve your spreadsheet style.

This section shows you how to format numbers, dates, and times using Excel's built-in formatting options. You'll also learn how to create your own formats to gain maximum control over the appearance of your data.

## Numeric Display Formats

When you enter numbers in a worksheet, Excel removes any leading or trailing zeros. For example, if you enter 0123.4500, Excel displays 123.45. The exception to this rule occurs when you enter a number that is wider than the cell. In this case, Excel usually expands the width of the column to fit the number. However, in some cases, Excel tailors the number to fit the cell by rounding off some decimal places. For example, a number such as 123.45678 is displayed as 123.4568. Note that, in this case, the number is changed for display purposes only; Excel still retains the original number internally.

When you create a worksheet, each cell uses this format, known as the *General* number format, by default. If you want your numbers to appear differently, you can choose from among Excel's seven categories of numeric formats: Number, Currency, Accounting, Percentage, Fraction, Scientific, and Special:

- **Number formats**—The number formats have three components: the number of decimal places (0–30), whether the thousands separator (,) is used, and how negative numbers are displayed. For negative numbers, you can display the number with a leading minus sign, in red, surrounded by parentheses, or in red surrounded by parentheses.

- **Currency formats**—The currency formats are similar to the number formats, except that the thousands separator is always used, and you have the option of displaying the numbers with a leading dollar sign ($) or some other currency symbol.

- **Accounting formats**—With the accounting formats, you can select the number of decimal places and whether to display a leading dollar sign (or other currency symbol). If you do use a dollar sign, Excel displays it flush left in the cell. All negative entries are displayed surrounded by parentheses.

- **Percentage formats**—The percentage formats display the number multiplied by 100 with a percent sign (%) to the right of the number. For example, .506 is displayed as 50.6%. You can display 0–30 decimal places.

- **Fraction formats**—The fraction formats enable you to express decimal quantities as fractions. There are nine fraction formats in all, including displaying the number as halves, quarters, eighths, sixteenths, tenths, and hundredths.

- **Scientific formats**—The scientific formats display the most significant number to the left of the decimal, 2–30 decimal places to the right of the decimal, and then the exponent. So, 123000 is displayed as 1.23E+05.

- **Special formats**—The special formats are a collection designed to take care of special cases. Here's a list of the special formats, with some examples:

| Format | Enter This | It Displays As This |
| --- | --- | --- |
| ZIP code | 1234 | 01234 |
| ZIP code + 4 | 123456789 | 12345-6789 |
| Phone number | 1234567890 | (123) 456-7890 |
| Social Security number | 123456789 | 123-45-6789 |

**3**

## Changing Numeric Formats

The quickest way to format numbers is to specify the format as you enter your data. For example, if you begin a dollar amount with a dollar sign ($), Excel automatically formats the number as currency. Similarly, if you type a percent sign (%) after a number, Excel automatically formats the number as a percentage. Here are a few more examples of this technique. Note that you can enter a negative value using either the negative sign (–) or parentheses.

| Number Entered | Number Displayed | Format Used |
|---|---|---|
| $1234.567 | $1,234.57 | Currency |
| ($1234.5) | ($1,234.50) | Currency |
| 10% | 10% | Percentage |
| 123E+02 | 1.23E+04 | Scientific |
| 5 3/4 | 5 3/4 | Fraction |
| 0 3/4 | 3/4 | Fraction |
| 3/4 | 4–Mar | Date |

> **NOTE**  Excel interprets a simple fraction such as 3/4 as a date (March 4, in this case). Always include a leading zero, followed by a space, if you want to enter a simple fraction from the formula bar.

Specifying the numeric format as you enter a number is fast and efficient because Excel guesses the format you want to use. Unfortunately, Excel sometimes guesses wrong (for example, interpreting a simple fraction as a date). In any case, you don't have access to all the available formats (for example, displaying negative dollar amounts in red). To overcome these limitations, you can select your numeric formats from a list. Here are the steps to follow:

1. Select the cell or range of cells to which you want to apply the new format.
2. Choose Format, Cells (or press Ctrl+1). The Format Cells dialog box appears.
3. Choose the Number tab, if it's not already displayed.
4. Select the format you want to use in the Category list box. Excel displays the various options available for the category you choose. For example, Figure 3.13 shows the options that appear when you choose the Number format.
5. Choose the formatting options you want to use. The Sample information box shows a sample of the format applied to the current cell's contents.
6. Click OK. Excel returns you to the worksheet with the new formatting applied.

As an alternative to the Format Cells dialog box, Excel offers several keyboard shortcuts for setting the numeric format. Select the cell or range you want to format, and use one of the key combinations listed in Table 3.5.

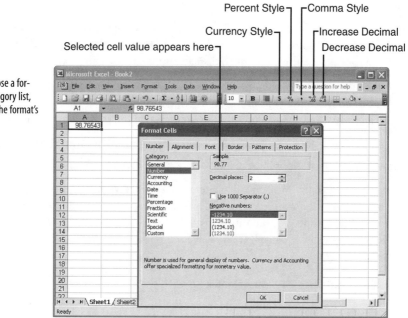

**Figure 3.13**
When you choose a format in the Category list, Excel displays the format's options.

| Table 3.5 | Shortcut Keys for Selecting Numeric Formats |
|---|---|
| **Shortcut Key** | **Format** |
| Ctrl+~ | General |
| Ctrl+! | Number (two decimal places; using thousands separator) |
| Ctrl+$ | Currency (two decimal places; using dollar sign; negative numbers surrounded by parentheses) |
| Ctrl+% | Percentage (zero decimal places) |
| Ctrl+^ | Scientific (two decimal places) |

If your mouse is nearby, you can use the tools in the Formatting toolbar as another method of selecting numeric formats. Here are the four available tools (see Figure 3.13):

| **Button** | **Format** |
|---|---|
| Currency Style | Accounting (two decimal places; using dollar sign) |
| Percent Style | Percentage (zero decimal places) |
| Comma Style | Number (two decimal places; using thousands separator) |
| Increase Decimal | Increases the number of decimal places in the current format |
| Decrease Decimal | Decreases the number of decimal places in the current format |

## Customizing Numeric Formats

Excel numeric formats give you lots of control over how your numbers are displayed, but they have their limitations. For example, no built-in format enables you to display a number such 0.5 without the leading zero, or to display temperatures using, say, the degree symbol.

To overcome these and other limitations, you need to create your own custom numeric formats. You can do this either by editing an existing format or by entering your own from scratch. The formatting syntax and symbols are explained in detail later in this section.

Every Excel numeric format, whether built-in or customized, has the following syntax:

`positive format;negative format;zero format;text format`

The four parts, separated by semicolons, determine how various numbers are presented. The first part defines how a positive number is displayed, the second part defines how a negative number is displayed, the third part defines how zero is displayed, and the fourth part defines how text is displayed. If you leave out one or more of these parts, numbers are controlled as shown here:

| Number of Parts Used | Format Syntax |
|---|---|
| Three | `positive format;negative format;zero format` |
| Two | `positive and zero format; negative format` |
| One | `positive, negative, and zero format` |

Table 3.6 lists the special symbols you use to define each of these parts.

### Table 3.6  Numeric Formatting Symbols

| Symbol | Description |
|---|---|
| General | Displays the number with the General format. |
| # | Holds a place for a digit and displays the digit exactly as typed. Displays nothing if no number is entered. |
| 0 | Holds a place for a digit and displays the digit exactly as typed. Displays 0 if no number is entered. |
| ? | Holds a place for a digit and displays the digit exactly as typed. Displays a space if no number is entered. |
| . (period) | Sets the location of the decimal point. |
| , (comma) | Sets the location of the thousands separator. Marks only the location of the first thousand. |
| % | Multiplies the number by 100 (for display only) and adds the percent (%) character. |
| E+ e+ E- e- | Displays the number in scientific format. E- and e- place a minus sign in the exponent; E+ and e+ place a plus sign in the exponent. |
| / (slash) | Sets the location of the fraction separator. |

| Symbol | Description |
|---|---|
| $ ( ) : – + <space> | Displays the character. |
| * | Repeats whatever character immediately follows the asterisk until the cell is full. Doesn't replace other symbols or numbers. |
| _ (underscore) | Inserts a blank space the width of whatever character follows the underscore. |
| \ (backslash) | Inserts the character that follows the backslash. |
| "*text*" | Inserts the *text* that appears within the quotation marks. |
| @ | Holds a place for text. |
| [*COLOR*] | Displays the cell contents in the specified color. |
| [*condition value*] | Uses conditional statements to specify when the format is to be used. |



Before looking at some examples, let's run through the basic procedure. To customize a numeric format, select the cell or range you want to format and then follow these steps:

1. Choose Format, Cells (or press Ctrl+1) and select the Number tab, if it's not already displayed.
2. In the Category list, choose Custom.
3. If you're editing an existing format, choose it in the Type list box.
4. Edit or enter your format code.
5. Click OK. Excel returns you to the worksheet with the custom format applied.

Excel stores each new format definition in the Custom category. If you edited an existing format, the original format is left intact and the new format is added to the list. You can select the custom formats the same way you select the built-in formats. To use your custom format in other workbooks, you copy a cell containing the format to that workbook. Figure 3.14 shows a dozen examples of custom formats.

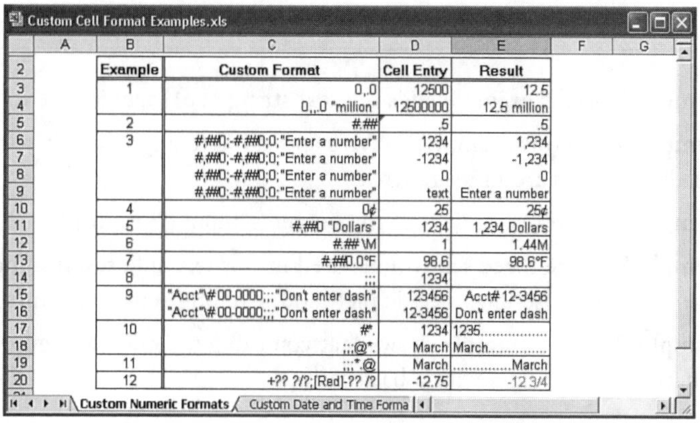


| Example | Custom Format | Cell Entry | Result |
|---|---|---|---|
| 1 | 0,.0 | 12500 | 12.5 |
| | 0,,.0 "million" | 12500000 | 12.5 million |
| 2 | #.## | .5 | .5 |
| 3 | #,##0;-#,##0;0;"Enter a number" | 1234 | 1,234 |
| | #,##0;-#,##0;0;"Enter a number" | -1234 | -1,234 |
| | #,##0;-#,##0;0;"Enter a number" | 0 | 0 |
| | #,##0;-#,##0;0;"Enter a number" | text | Enter a number |
| 4 | 0¢ | 25 | 25¢ |
| 5 | #,##0 "Dollars" | 1234 | 1,234 Dollars |
| 6 | #.## \M | 1 | 1.44M |
| 7 | #,##0.0°F | 98.6 | 98.6°F |
| 8 | ;;; | 1234 | |
| 9 | "Acct"\#00-0000;;;"Don't enter dash" | 123456 | Acct#12-3456 |
| | "Acct"\#00-0000;;;"Don't enter dash" | 12-3456 | Don't enter dash |
| 10 | #*. | 1234 | 1235................ |
| | ;;;@*. | March | March.............. |
| 11 | ;;;*.@ | March | ...............March |
| 12 | +?? ?/?;[Red]-?? /? | -12.75 | -12 3/4 |

**Figure 3.14**
Sample custom numeric formats.

Here's a quick explanation for each example:

- **Example 1**—These formats show how you can reduce a large number to a smaller, more readable one by using the thousands separator. A format such as 0,000.0 would display, say, 12300 as 12,300.0. If you remove the three zeros between the comma and the decimal (to get the format 0,.0), Excel displays the number as 12.3 (although it still uses the original number in calculations). In essence, you've told Excel to express the number in thousands. To express a larger number in millions, you just add a second thousands separator.

- **Example 2**—Use this format when you don't want to display any leading or trailing zeros.

- **Example 3**—These are examples of four-part formats. The first three parts define how Excel should display positive numbers, negative numbers, and zero. The fourth part displays the message Enter a number if the user enters text in the cell.

- **Example 4**—In this example, the cents sign (¢) is used after the value. To enter the cents sign, press Alt+0162 on your keyboard's numeric keypad. (This won't work if you use the numbers along the top of the keyboard.) Table 3.7 shows some common ANSI characters you can use.

**Table 3.7   ANSI Character Key Combinations**

| Key Combination | ANSI Character |
|---|---|
| Alt+0163 | £ |
| Alt+0162 | ¢ |
| Alt+0165 | ¥ |
| Alt+0169 | © |
| Alt+0174 | ® |
| Alt+0176 | ° |

- **Example 5**—This example adds the text string "Dollars" to the format.

- **Example 6**—In this example, an M is appended to any number, which is useful if your spreadsheet units are in megabytes.

- **Example 7**—This example uses the degree symbol (°) to display temperatures.

- **Example 8**—The three semicolons used in this example result in no number being displayed (which is useful as a basic method for hiding sensitive values).

- **Example 9**—This example shows that you can get a number sign (#) to display in your formats by preceding # with a backslash (\).

- **Example 10**—In this example, you see a trick for creating dot trailers. Recall that the asterisk (*) symbol fills the cell with whatever character follows it. So, creating a dot trailer is a simple matter of adding "*." to the end of the format.

- **Example 11**—This example shows a similar technique that creates a dot leader. Here the first three semicolons display nothing; then comes "*.", which runs dots from the beginning of the cell up to the text (represented by the @ sign).

- **Example 12**—This example shows a format that's useful for entering stock quotations.

## Hiding Zeros

Worksheets look less cluttered and are easier to read if you hide unnecessary zeros. Excel enables you to hide zeros either throughout the entire worksheet or only in selected cells.

To hide all zeros, choose Tools, Options; choose the View tab in the Options dialog box; and clear the Zero Values check box.

To hide zeros in selected cells, create a custom format that uses the following format syntax:

*positive format*;*negative format*;

The extra semicolon at the end acts as a placeholder for the zero format. Because there's no definition for a zero value, nothing is displayed. For example, the format $#,##0.00_);($#,##0.00); displays standard dollar values, but it leaves the cell blank if it contains zero.

> **TIP**
> If your worksheet contains only integers (no fractions or decimal places), you can use the format #,### to hide zeros.

## Using Condition Values

The action of the formats you've seen so far have depended on whether the cell contents were positive, negative, zero, or text. Although this is fine for most applications, sometimes you need to format a cell based on different conditions. For example, you might want only specific numbers, or numbers within a certain range, to take on a particular format. You can achieve this effect by using the [*condition value*] format symbol. With this symbol, you set up conditional statements using the logical operators =, <, >, <=, >=, and <>, and the appropriate numbers. You then assign these conditions to each part of your format definition.

For example, suppose that you have a worksheet for which the data must be within the range –1,000 and 1,000. To flag numbers outside this range, you set up the following format:

```
[>=1000]"Error: Value >= 1,000";[<=-1000]"Error: Value <= -1,000";0.00
```

The first part defines the format for numbers greater than or equal to 1,000 (an error message). The second part defines the format for numbers less than or equal to –1,000 (also an error message). The third part defines the format for all other numbers (0.00).

> **NOTE**
> Excel also enables you to apply a particular font automatically when a cell meets a specified condition. This is called *conditional formatting*, and you apply it by choosing Format, Conditional Formatting. To construct the condition for a value, choose Cell Value Is in the first list, and then select a comparison operator (such as Between or Less Than) in the second list. You then enter one or two values (depending on the operator). Finally, click Format to select the font formatting to apply to the cell when the condition is met.

## Date and Time Display Formats

If you include dates or times in your worksheets, you need to make sure that they're presented in a readable, unambiguous format. For example, most people would interpret the date 8/5/04 as August 5, 2004. However, in some countries, this date would mean May 8, 2004. Similarly, if you use the time 2:45, do you mean a.m. or p.m.? To avoid these kinds of problems, you can use Excel's built-in date and time formats, listed in Table 3.8.

**Table 3.8   Excel's Date and Time Formats**

| Format | Display |
| --- | --- |
| m/d | 8/3 |
| m/d/yy | 8/3/05 |
| mm/dd/yy | 08/03/05 |
| d-mmm | 3-Aug |
| d-mmm-yy | 3-Aug-05 |
| dd-mmm-yy | 03-Aug-05 |
| mmm-yy | Aug-05 |
| mmmm-yy | August-05 |
| mmmm d, yyyy | August 3, 2005 |
| h:mm AM/PM | 3:10 PM |
| h:mm:ss AM/PM | 3:10:45 PM |
| h:mm | 15:10 |
| h:mm:ss | 15:10:45 |
| mm:ss.0 | 10:45.7 |
| [h]:[mm]:[ss] | 25:61:61 |
| m/d/yy h:mm AM/PM | 8/23/94 3:10 PM |
| m/d/yy h:mm | 8/23/94 15:10 |

The [h]:[mm]:[ss] format requires a bit more explanation. You use this format when you want to display hours greater than 24 or minutes and seconds greater than 60. For example, suppose that you have an application in which you need to sum several time values (such as the time you've spent working on a project). If you add, say, 10:00 and 15:00, Excel normally shows the total as 1:00 (because, by default, Excel restarts times at 0 when they hit 24:00). To display the result properly (that is, as 25:00), use the format [h]:00.

You use the same methods you used for numeric formats to select date and time formats. In particular, you can specify the date and time format as you input your data. For example, entering Jan-04 automatically formats the cell with the mmm-yy format. Also, you can use the following shortcut keys:

| Shortcut Key | Format |
|---|---|
| Ctrl+# | d-mmm-yy |
| Ctrl+@ | h:mm AM/PM |
| Ctrl+; | Current date (m/d/yy) |
| Ctrl+: | Current time (h:mm AM/PM) |

> **TIP**
>
> Excel for the Macintosh uses a different date system than Excel for Windows uses. If you share files between these environments, you need to use Macintosh dates in your Excel for Windows worksheets to maintain the correct dates when you move from one system to another. Select Tools, Options; choose the Calculation tab; and activate the 1904 Date System check box.

### Customizing Date and Time Formats

Although the built-in date and time formats are fine for most applications, you might need to create your own custom formats. For example, you might want to display the day of the week (for example, Friday). Custom date and time formats generally are simpler to create than custom numeric formats. There are fewer formatting symbols, and you usually don't need to specify different formats for different conditions. Table 3.9 lists the date and time formatting symbols.

**Table 3.9   The Date and Time Formatting Symbols**

| Symbol | Description |
|---|---|
| *Date Formats* | |
| d | Day number without a leading zero (1–31) |
| dd | Day number with a leading zero (01–31) |
| ddd | Three-letter day abbreviation (Mon, for example) |
| dddd | Full day name (Monday, for example) |
| m | Month number without a leading zero (1–12) |

*continues*

**Table 3.9 Continued**

| Symbol | Description |
|---|---|
| *Date Formats* | |
| mm | Month number with a leading zero (01–12) |
| mmm | Three-letter month abbreviation (`Aug`, for example) |
| mmmm | Full month name (`August`, for example) |
| yy | Two-digit year (00–99) |
| yyyy | Full year (1900–2078) |
| *Time Formats* | |
| h | Hour without a leading zero (0–24) |
| hh | Hour with a leading zero (00–24) |
| m | Minute without a leading zero (0–59) |
| mm | Minute with a leading zero (00–59) |
| s | Second without a leading zero (0–59) |
| ss | Second with a leading zero (00–59) |
| AM/PM, am/pm, A/P | Displays the time using a 12-hour clock |
| / : . – | Symbols used to separate parts of dates or times |
| [*COLOR*] | Displays the date or time in the color specified |
| [*condition value*] | Uses conditional statements to specify when the format is to be used |



Figure 3.15 shows some examples of custom date and time formats.

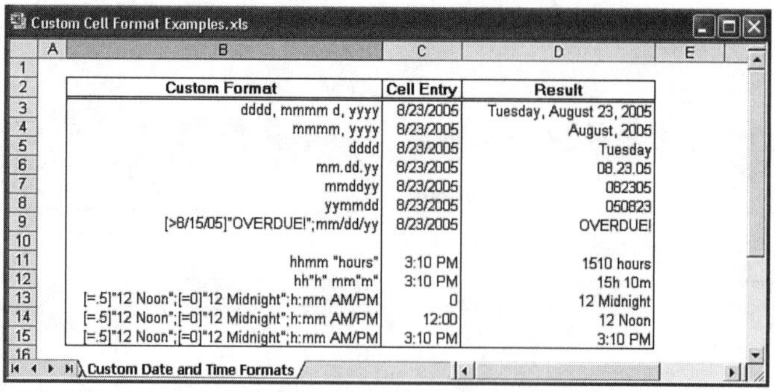


| Custom Format | Cell Entry | Result |
|---|---|---|
| dddd, mmmm d, yyyy | 8/23/2005 | Tuesday, August 23, 2005 |
| mmmm, yyyy | 8/23/2005 | August, 2005 |
| dddd | 8/23/2005 | Tuesday |
| mm.dd.yy | 8/23/2005 | 08.23.05 |
| mmddyy | 8/23/2005 | 082305 |
| yymmdd | 8/23/2005 | 050823 |
| [>8/15/05]"OVERDUE!";mm/dd/yy | 8/23/2005 | OVERDUE! |
| | | |
| hhmm "hours" | 3:10 PM | 1510 hours |
| hh"h" mm"m" | 3:10 PM | 15h 10m |
| [=.5]"12 Noon";[=0]"12 Midnight";h:mm AM/PM | 0 | 12 Midnight |
| [=.5]"12 Noon";[=0]"12 Midnight";h:mm AM/PM | 12:00 | 12 Noon |
| [=.5]"12 Noon";[=0]"12 Midnight";h:mm AM/PM | 3:10 PM | 3:10 PM |

**Figure 3.15**
Sample custom date and time formats.

## Deleting Custom Formats

The best way to become familiar with custom formats is to try your own experiments. Just remember that Excel stores each format you try. If you find that your list of custom formats is getting a bit unwieldy or that it's cluttered with unused formats, you can delete formats by following the steps outlined here:

1. Choose F<u>o</u>rmat, C<u>e</u>lls, and then choose the Number tab in the Options dialog box.

2. Choose the Custom category.

3. Select the format in the <u>T</u>ype list box. (Note that you can delete only the formats you've created yourself.)

4. Click <u>D</u>elete. Excel removes the format from the list.

5. To delete other formats, repeat steps 2–4.

6. Click OK. Excel returns you to the spreadsheet.

## From Here

- For more information on using Excel's intersection operator, **see** "Using the Intersection Operator," **p. 34**.

- To learn how to solve formula problems, **see** "Troubleshooting Formulas," **p. 107**.

- To get the details on text formulas and functions, **see** "Working with Text Functions," **p.133**.

- If you want to use logical worksheet functions in your comparison formulas, **see** "Adding Intelligence with Logical Functions," **p. 155**.

- To learn how to create and use data tables, **see** "Using What-If Analysis," **p. 315**.

**3**

# Creating Advanced Formulas

Excel is a versatile program with many uses, from acting as a checkbook to a flat-file database-management system, to an equation solver, to a glorified calculator. For most business users, however, Excel's forte is building models that enable them to quantify particular aspects of the business. The skeleton of the business model is made up of the chunks of data entered, imported, or copied into the worksheets. But the lifeblood of the model and the animating force behind it is the collection of formulas that summarize data, answer questions, and make predictions.

You saw in Chapter 3, "Building Basic Formulas," that, armed with the humble equals sign and a set of operators and operands, you can cobble together useful, robust formulas. But Excel has many other tricks up its digital sleeve, and these techniques enable you to create muscular formulas that can take your business models to the next level.

## Working with Arrays

When you work with a range of cells, it might appear as though you're working with a single thing. In reality, however, Excel treats the range as a number of discrete units.

This is in contrast with the subject of this section: the array. An *array* is a group of cells or values that Excel treats as a unit. You create arrays either by running a function that returns an array result (such as DOCUMENTS( )—see the section in this chapter titled "Functions That Use or Return Arrays") or by entering an *array formula*, which is a single formula that either uses an array as an argument or enters its results in multiple cells.

## Using Array Formulas

Here's a simple example that illustrates how array formulas work. In the Expenses workbook shown in Figure 4.1, the 2005 BUDGET totals are calculated using a separate formula for each month, as shown here:

| | |
|---|---|
| January 2005 BUDGET | =C11*$C$3 |
| February 2005 BUDGET | =D11*$C$3 |
| March 2005 BUDGET | =E11*$C$3 |

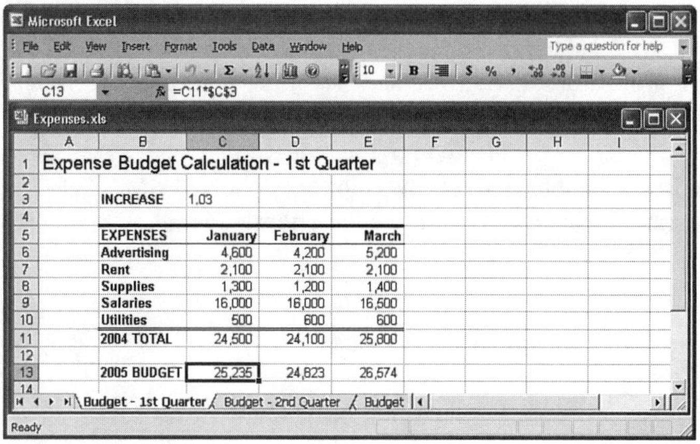

**Figure 4.1**
This worksheet uses three separate formulas to calculate the 2005 BUDGET figures.

You can replace all three formulas with a single array formula by following these steps:

1. Select the range that you want to use for the array formula. In the 2005 BUDGET example, you'd select C13:E13.

2. Type the formula and, in the places where you would normally enter a cell reference, type a range reference that includes the cells you want to use. *Don't*—I repeat, *don't*—press Enter when you're done. In the example, you'd enter =C11:E11*$C$3.

3. To enter the formula as an array, press Ctrl+Shift+Enter.

The 2005 BUDGET cells (C13, D13, and E13) now all contain the same formula:

`{=C11:E11*$C$3}`

Notice that the formula is surrounded by braces ({ }). This identifies the formula as an array formula. (When you enter array formulas, you never need to enter these braces yourself; Excel adds them automatically.)

Because Excel treats arrays as a unit, you can't move or delete part of an array. If you need to work with an array, you must select the whole thing. If you want to reduce the size of an array, select it, activate the formula bar, and then press Ctrl+Enter to change the entry to a normal formula. You can then select the smaller range and re-enter the array formula.

Note that you can select an array quickly by activating one of its cells and pressing Ctrl+/.

## Understanding Array Formulas

To understand how Excel processes an array, you need to keep in mind that Excel always sets up a correspondence between the array cells and the cells of whatever range you entered into the array formula. In the 2005 BUDGET example, the array consists of cells C13, D13, and E13, and the range used in the formula consists of cells C11, D11, and E11. Excel sets up a correspondence between array cell C13 and input cell C11, D13 and D11, and E13 and E11. To calculate the value of cell C13 (the January 2005 BUDGET), for example, Excel just grabs the input value from cell C11 and substitutes that in the formula. Figure 4.2 shows a diagram of this process.

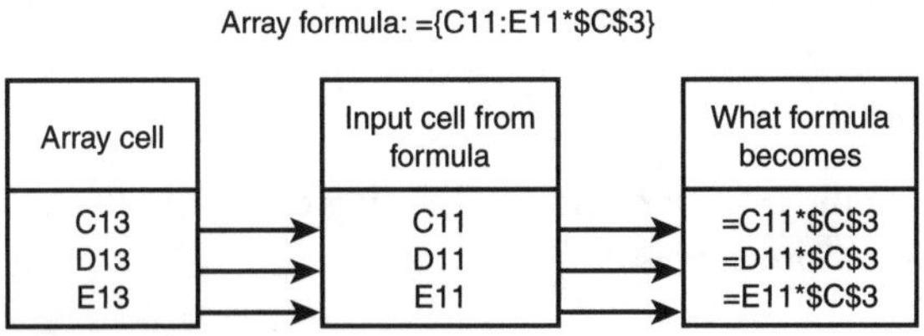

**Figure 4.2**
When processing an array formula, Excel sets up a correspondence between the array cells and the range used in the formula.

Array formula: ={C11:E11*$C$3}

| Array cell | Input cell from formula | What formula becomes |
|---|---|---|
| C13 | C11 | =C11*$C$3 |
| D13 | D11 | =D11*$C$3 |
| E13 | E11 | =E11*$C$3 |

Array formulas can be confusing, but if you keep these correspondences in mind, you should have no trouble figuring out what's going on.

## Array Formulas That Operate on Multiple Ranges

In the preceding example, the array formula operated on a single range, but array formulas also can operate on multiple ranges. For example, consider the Invoice Template worksheet shown in Figure 4.3. The totals in the Extension column (cells F12–F16) are generated by a series of formulas that multiply the item's price by the quantity ordered:

| Cell | Formula |
|---|---|
| F12 | =B12*E12 |
| F13 | =B13*E13 |
| F14 | =B14*E14 |
| F15 | =B15*E15 |
| F16 | =B16*E16 |

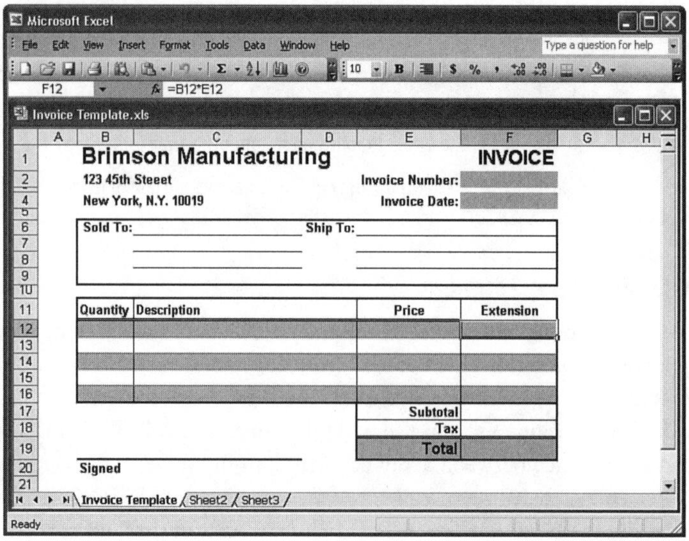

**Figure 4.3**
This worksheet uses several formulas to calculate the extended totals for each line.

You can replace all these formulas by making the following entry as an array formula into the range F12:F16:

`=B12:B16*E12:E16`

Again, you've created the array formula by replacing each cell reference with the corresponding range (and by pressing Ctrl+Shift+Enter).

> **NOTE** You don't have to enter array formulas in multiple cells. For example, if you don't need the Extended totals in the Invoice Template worksheet, you can still calculate the Subtotal by making the following entry as an array formula in cell F17:
>
> `=SUM(B12:B16*E12:E16)`

## Using Array Constants

In the array formulas you've seen so far, the array arguments have been cell ranges. You also can use constant values as array arguments. This procedure enables you to input values into a formula without having them clutter your worksheet.

To enter an array constant in a formula, enter the values right in the formula and observe the following guidelines:

- Enclose the values in braces ({}).
- If you want Excel to treat the values as a row, separate each value with a semicolon.
- If you want Excel to treat the values as a column, separate each value with a comma.

For example, the following array constant is the equivalent of entering the individual values in a column on your worksheet:

{1;2;3;4}

Similarly, the following array constant is equivalent to entering the values in a worksheet range of three columns and two rows:

{1,2,3;4,5,6}

As a practical example, Figure 4.4 shows two different array formulas. The one on the left (used in the range E4:E7) calculates various loan payments, given the different interest rates in the range C5:C8. The array formula on the right (used in the range F4:F7) does the same thing, but the interest rate values are entered as an array constant directly in the formula.

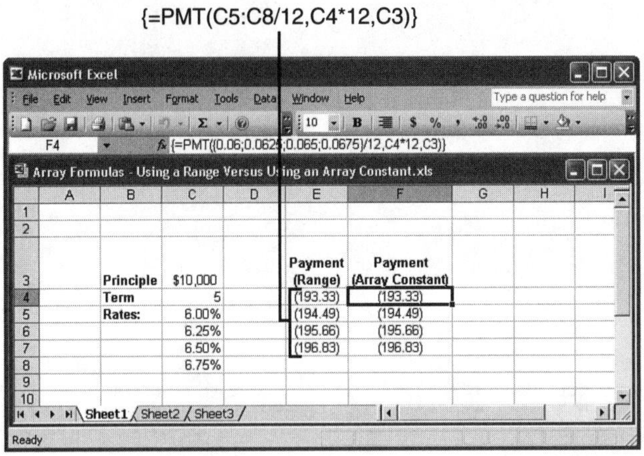

{=PMT(C5:C8/12,C4*12,C3)}

**Figure 4.4**
Using array constants in your array formulas means you don't have to clutter your worksheet with the input values.

→   To learn how the PMT ( ) function works, **see** "Calculating the Loan Payment," **p. 400**.

## Functions That Use or Return Arrays

Many of Excel's worksheet functions either require an array argument or return an array result (or both). Table 4.1 lists several of these functions and explains how each one uses arrays. (See Part 2, "Harnessing the Power of Functions," for explanations of these functions.)

**Table 4.1   Some Excel Functions That Use Arrays**

| Function Uses | Array Argument? | Returns Array Result? |
|---|---|---|
| COLUMN ( ) | No | Yes, if the argument is a range |
| COLUMNS ( ) | Yes | No |
| GROWTH ( ) | Yes | Yes |

*continues*

**Table 4.1    Continued**

| Function Uses | Array Argument? | Returns Array Result? |
| --- | --- | --- |
| HLOOKUP() | Yes | No |
| INDEX() | Yes | Yes |
| LINEST() | No | Yes |
| LOGEST() | No | Yes |
| LOOKUP() | Yes | No |
| MATCH() | Yes | No |
| MDETERM() | Yes | No |
| MINVERSE() | No | Yes |
| MMULT() | No | Yes |
| ROW() | No | Yes, if the argument is a range |
| ROWS() | Yes | No |
| SUMPRODUCT() | Yes | No |
| TRANSPOSE() | Yes | Yes |
| TREND() | Yes | Yes |
| VLOOKUP() | Yes | No |

When you use functions that return arrays, be sure to select a range large enough to hold the resulting array, and then enter the function as an array formula.

→ Arrays become truly powerful weapons in your Excel arsenal when you combine them with worksheet functions such as IF() and SUM(). I'll provide you with many examples of array formulas as I introduce you to Excel's worksheet functions throughout Part 3, "Building Business Models." In particular, **see** "Combining Logical Functions with Arrays," **p. 162**.

# Using Iteration and Circular References

A common business problem involves calculating a profit-sharing plan contribution as a percentage of a company's net profits. This isn't a simple multiplication problem because the net profit is determined partly by the profit-sharing figure. For example, suppose that a company has a gross margin of $1,000,000 and expenses of $900,000, which leaves a gross profit of $100,000. The company also sets aside 10% of net profits for profit sharing. The net profit is calculated with the following formula:

```
Net Profit = Gross Profit - Profit Sharing Contribution
```

This is called a *circular reference formula* because there are terms on the left and right sides of the equals sign that depend on each other. Specifically, the Profit Sharing Contribution is derived with the following formula:

```
Profit Sharing Contribution = (Net Profit)*0.1
```

→ Circular references are usually a bad thing to have in a spreadsheet model. To learn how to combat the bad kind, **see** "Fixing Circular References," **p. 113**.

One way to solve such a formula is to guess at an answer and see how close you come. For example, because profit sharing should be 10% of net profits, a good first guess might be 10% of *gross* profits, or $10,000. If you plug this number into the formula, you end up with a net profit of $90,000. This isn't right, however, because 10% of $90,000 is $9,000. Therefore, the profit-sharing guess is off by $1,000.

So, you can try again. This time, use $9,000 as the profit-sharing number. Plugging this new value into the formula gives a net profit of $91,000. This number translates into a profit-sharing contribution of $9,100—which is off by only $100.

If you continue this process, your profit-sharing guesses will get closer to the calculated value (this process is called *convergence*). When the guesses are close enough (for example, within a dollar), you can stop and pat yourself on the back for finding the solution. This process is called *iteration*.

Of course, you didn't spend your (or your company's) hard-earned money on a computer so that you could do this sort of thing by hand. Excel makes iterative calculations a breeze, as you'll see in the following procedure:

1. Set up your worksheet and enter your circular reference formula. Figure 4.5 shows a worksheet for the example discussed previously. If Excel displays a dialog box telling you that it can't resolve circular references, click OK.

**Figure 4.5**
A worksheet with a circular reference formula.

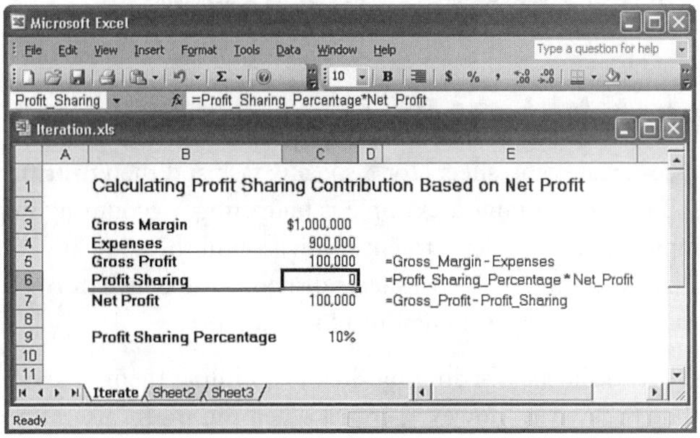

2. Choose Tools, Options to display the Options dialog box.
3. Choose the Calculation tab.
4. Activate the Iteration check box.
5. Use the Maximum Iterations text box to specify the number of iterations you need. In most cases, the default figure of 100 is more than enough.

6. Use the Maximum Change text box to tell Excel how accurate you want your results to be. The smaller the number is, the longer the iteration takes and the more accurate the calculation will be. Again, the default value is probably a reasonable compromise.

7. Click OK. Excel begins the iteration and stops when it has found a solution (see Figure 4.6).

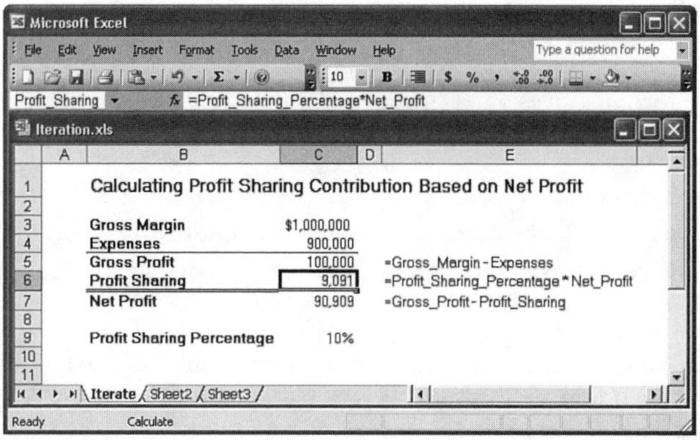

**Figure 4.6**
The solution to the iterative profit-sharing problem.

> **TIP**
>
> If you want to watch the progress of the iteration, activate the Manual check box in the Calculation tab, and enter **1** in the Maximum Iterations text box. When you return to your worksheet, each time you press F9, Excel performs a single pass of the iteration.

## Consolidating Multisheet Data

Many businesses create worksheets for a specific task and then distribute them to various departments. The most common example is budgeting. Accounting might create a generic "budget" template that each department or division in the company must fill out and return. Similarly, you often see worksheets distributed for inventory requirements, sales forecasting, survey data, experimental results, and more.

Creating these worksheets, distributing them, and filling them in are all straightforward operations. The tricky part, however, comes when the sheets are returned to the originating department, and all the new data must be combined into a summary report showing company-wide totals. This task is called *consolidating* the data, and it's often no picnic, especially for large worksheets. However, as you'll soon see, Excel has some powerful features that can take the drudgery out of consolidation.

Excel can consolidate your data using one of the following two methods:

■ **Consolidating by position**—With this method, Excel consolidates the data from several worksheets using the same range coordinates on each sheet. You would use this method if the worksheets you're consolidating have an identical layout.

■ **Consolidating by category**—This method tells Excel to consolidate the data by look-ing for identical row and column labels in each sheet. So, for example, if one worksheet lists monthly Gizmo sales in row 1 and another lists monthly Gizmo sales in row 5, you can still consolidate as long as both sheets have a "Gizmo" label at the beginning of these rows.

In both cases, you specify one or more *source ranges* (the ranges that contain the data you want to consolidate) and a *destination range* (the range where the consolidated data will appear). The next couple of sections take you through the details for both consolidation methods.

## Consolidating by Position

If the sheets you're working with have the same layout, consolidating by position is the easi-est way to go. For example, check out the three workbooks—Division I Budget, Division II Budget, and Division III Budget—shown in Figure 4.7. As you can see, each sheet uses the same row and column labels, so they're perfect candidates for consolidation by position.

**Figure 4.7**
When your worksheets are laid out identically, use consolidation by position.

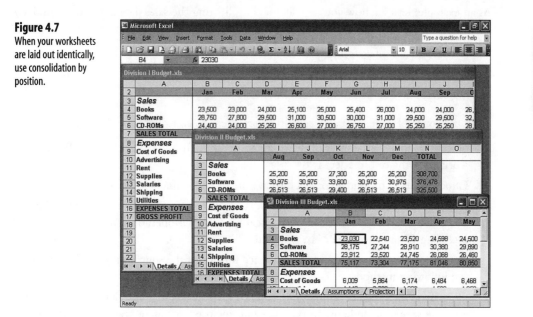

Begin by creating a new worksheet that has the same layout as the sheets you're consolidat-ing. Figure 4.8 shows a new Consolidation workbook that I'll use to consolidate the three budget sheets.

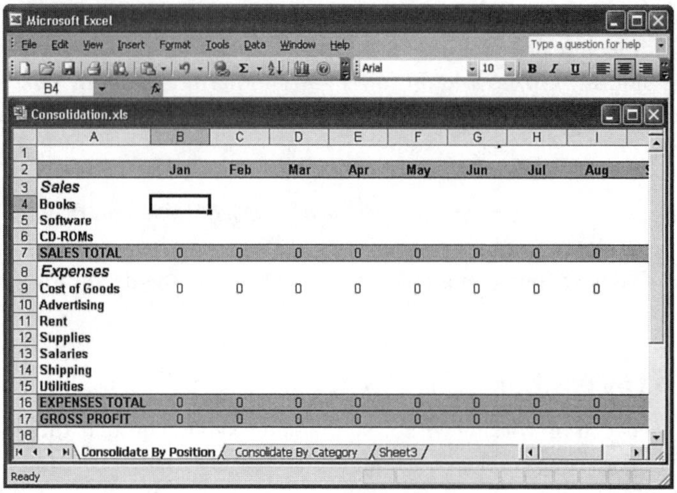

**Figure 4.8**
When consolidating by position, create a separate consolidation worksheet that uses the same layout as the sheets you're consolidating.

As an example, let's see how you'd go about consolidating the sales data in the three budget worksheets shown in Figure 4.7. We're dealing with three source ranges:

```
'[Division I Budget]Details'!B4:M6

'[Division II Budget]Details'!B4:M6

'[Division III Budget]Details'!B4:M6
```

With the consolidation sheet active, follow these steps to consolidate by position:

1. Select the upper-left corner of the destination range. In the Consolidate By Position worksheet, the cell to select is B4.

2. Choose Data, Consolidate. Excel displays the Consolidate dialog box.

3. In the Function drop-down list, select the operation to use during the consolidation. You'll use Sum most of the time, but Excel has 10 other operations to choose from, including Count, Average, Max, and Min.

4. In the Reference text box, enter a reference for one of the source ranges. Use one of the following methods:

   • Type the range coordinates by hand. If the source range is in another workbook, be sure to include the workbook name enclosed in square brackets. If the workbook is in a different drive or folder, include the full path to the workbook as well.

   • If the sheet is open, activate it (either by clicking on it or by clicking it in the Window menu), and then use your mouse to highlight the range.

   • If the workbook isn't open, choose Browse, highlight the file in the Browse dialog box, and then choose OK. Excel adds the workbook path to the Reference box. Fill in the sheet name and the range coordinates.

5. Click Add. Excel adds the range to the All References box (see Figure 4.9).

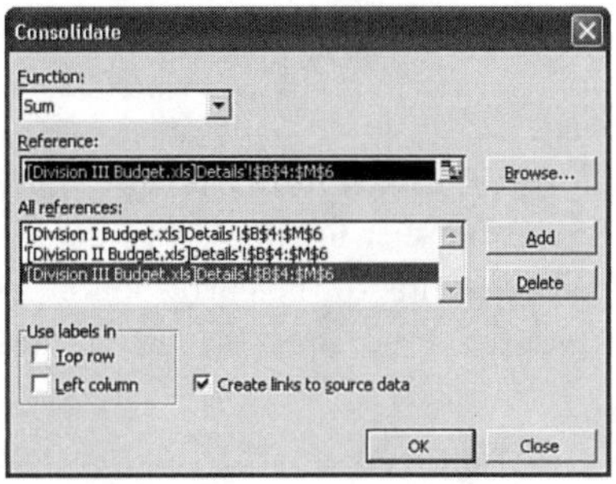

**Figure 4.9**
The Consolidate dialog box, with several source ranges added.

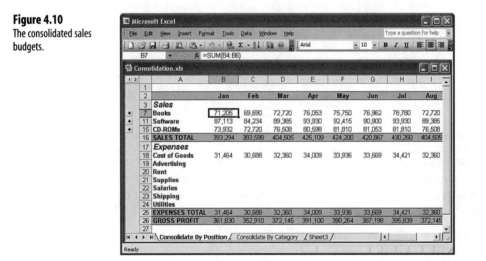

6. Repeat steps 4 and 5 to add all the source ranges.

7. If you want the consolidated data to change whenever you make changes to the source data, leave the Create Links to Source Data check box activated.

8. Click OK. Excel gathers the data, consolidates it, and then adds it to the destination range (see Figure 4.10).

**Figure 4.10**
The consolidated sales budgets.

If you chose not to create links to the source data in step 7, Excel just fills the destination range with the consolidation totals. If you did create links, however, Excel does three things:

■ Adds link formulas to the destination range for each cell in the source ranges you selected

→ To get the details on link formulas, **see** "Working with Links in Formulas," **p. 70.**

■ Consolidates the data by adding SUM() functions (or whatever operation you selected in the Function list) that total the results of the link formulas

- Outlines the consolidation worksheet and hides the link formulas, as you can see in Figure 4.10

If you display the Level 1 data, you'll see the linked formulas. For example, Figure 4.11 shows the detail for the consolidated sales number for Books in January (cell B7). The detail in cells B4, B5, and B6 contain formulas that link to the corresponding cells in the three budget worksheets (for example, `'[Division I Budget.xls]Details'!$B$4`).

**Figure 4.11**
The detail (linked formulas) for the consolidated data.

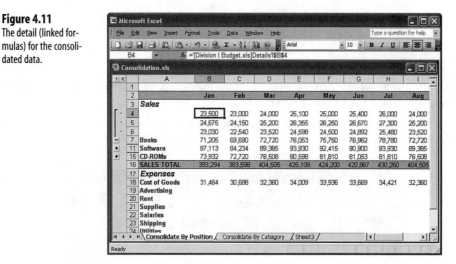

## Consolidating by Category

If your worksheets don't use the same layout, you need to tell Excel to consolidate the data *by category*. In this case, Excel examines each of your source ranges and consolidates data that uses the same row or column labels. For example, take a look at the Sales rows in the three worksheets shown in Figure 4.12.

As you can see, Division C sells books, software, videos, and CD-ROMs; Division B sells books and CD-ROMs; and Division A sells software, books, and videos. Here's how you go about consolidating these numbers (note that I'm skipping over some of the details given in the preceding section):

1. Create or select a new worksheet for the consolidation, and select the upper-left corner of the destination range. It isn't necessary to enter labels for the consolidated data because Excel does it for you automatically. However, if you want to see the labels in a particular order, it's okay to enter them yourself. (Just make sure, however, that you spell the labels exactly as they're spelled in the source worksheets.)

2. Choose <u>D</u>ata, Co<u>n</u>solidate to display the Consolidate dialog box.

3. In the <u>F</u>unction drop-down list, choose the operation to use during the consolidation.

4. In the <u>R</u>eference text box, enter a reference for one of the source ranges. In this case, make sure that you include in each range the row and column labels for the data.

5. Click <u>A</u>dd to add the range to the All R<u>e</u>ferences box.

6. Repeat steps 4 and 5 to add all the source ranges.

7. If you want the consolidated data to change whenever you make changes to the source data, leave the Create Links to <u>S</u>ource Data check box activated.

8. If you want Excel to use the data labels in the top row of the selected ranges, activate the <u>T</u>op Row check box. If you want Excel to use the data labels in the left column of the source ranges, activate the <u>L</u>eft Column check box.

9. Click OK. Excel gathers the data according to the row and column labels, consolidates it, and then adds it to the destination range (see Figure 4.13).

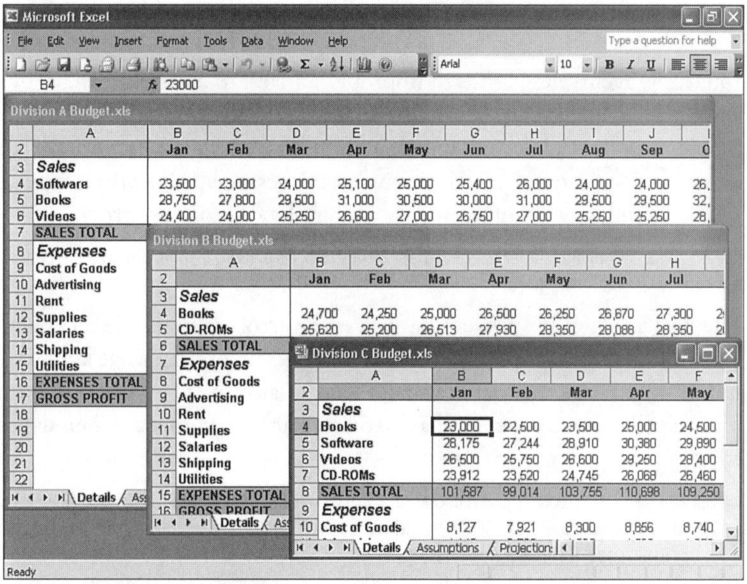

**Figure 4.12**
Each division sells a different mix of products, so we need to consolidate by category.

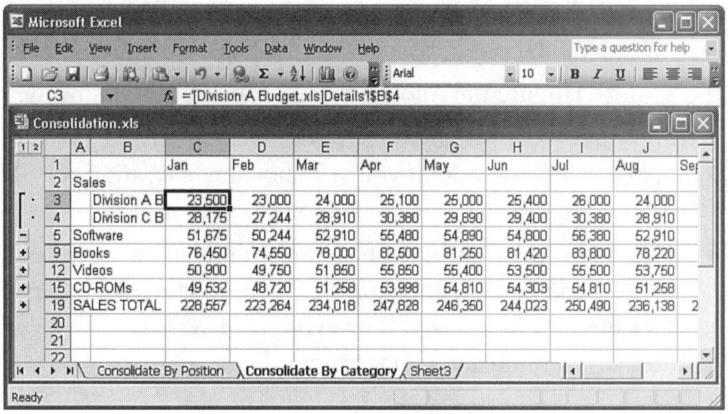

**Figure 4.13**
The sales numbers consolidated by category.

# Applying Data-Validation Rules to Cells

It's an unfortunate fact of spreadsheet life that your formulas are only as good as the data they're given. It's the GIGO effect, as the programmers say: garbage in, garbage out. In worksheet terms, "garbage in" means entering erroneous or improper data into a formula's input cells. For basic data errors (for example, entering the wrong date or transposing a number's digits), there's not a lot you can do other than exhorting yourself or the people who use your worksheets to enter data carefully. Fortunately, you have a bit more control when it comes to preventing improper data entry. By "improper," I mean data that falls in either of the following categories:

- Data that is the wrong type—for example, entering a text string in a cell that requires a number

- Data that falls outside of an allowable range—for example, entering 200 in a cell that requires a number between 1 and 100

You can prevent these kinds of improper entries, to a certain extent, by adding comments that provide details on what is allowable inside a particular cell. However, this requires other people to both read *and* act on the comment text. Another solution is to use custom numeric formatting to "format" a cell with an error message if the wrong type of data is entered. This is useful, but it works only for certain kinds of input errors.

→ To learn about custom numeric formats and to see some examples of using them to display input error messages, **see** "Formatting Numbers, Dates, and Times," **p. 72**.

The best solution for preventing data entry errors is to use Excel's data-validation feature. With data validation, you create *rules* that specify exactly what kind of data can be entered and in what range that data can fall. You can also specify pop-up input messages that appear when a cell is selected, as well as error messages that appear when data is entered improperly.

→ You can also ask Excel to "circle" those cells that contain data-validation errors (which is handy when you import data into a list that contains data-validation rules). You do this by clicking the Circle Invalid Data button on the Formula Auditing toolbar. To learn more about this toolbar, **see** "Auditing a Worksheet," **p. 117**.

Follow these steps to define the settings for a data-validation rule:

1. Select the cell or range to which you want to apply the data validation rule.

2. Choose Data, Validation. Excel displays the Data Validation dialog box.

3. In the Settings tab, use the Allow list to click one of the following validation types:
   - **Any Value**—Allows any value in the range. (That is, it removes any previously applied validation rule. If you're removing an existing rule, be sure to also clear the input message, if you created one as shown in step 7.)
   - **Whole Number**—Allows only whole numbers (integers). Use the Data list to choose a comparison operator (between, equal to, less than, and so on), and then enter the specific criteria. (For example, if you click the Between option, you must enter a Minimum and a Maximum value.)

- **Decimal**—Allows decimal numbers or whole numbers. Use the <u>D</u>ata list to choose a comparison operator, and then enter the specific numeric criteria.

- **List**—Allows only values specified in a list. Use the <u>S</u>ource box to specify either a range on the same sheet or a range name on any sheet that contains the list of allowable values. (Precede the range or range name with an equals sign.) Alternatively, you can enter the allowable values directly into the <u>S</u>ource box (separated by commas). If you want the user to be able to select from the allowable values using a drop-down list, leave the <u>I</u>n-Cell Drop-Down check box activated.

- **Date**—Allows only dates. (If the user includes a time value, the entry is invalid.) Use the <u>D</u>ata list to choose a comparison operator, and then enter the specific date criteria (such as a <u>S</u>tart Date and an E<u>n</u>d Date).

- **Times**—Allows only times. (If the user includes a date value, the entry is invalid.) Use the <u>D</u>ata list to choose a comparison operator, and then enter the specific time criteria (such as a <u>S</u>tart Time and an E<u>n</u>d Time).

- **Text Length**—Allows only alphanumeric strings of a specified length. Use the <u>D</u>ata list to choose a comparison operator, and then enter the specific length criteria (such as a <u>M</u>inimum and a Ma<u>x</u>imum length).

- **Custom**—Use this option to enter a formula that specifies the validation criteria. You can either enter the formula directly into the <u>F</u>ormula box (be sure to precede the formula with an equals sign) or enter a reference to a cell that contains the formula. For example, if you're restricting cell A2 and you want to be sure the entered value is not the same as what's in cell A1, you'd enter the formula =A2<>A1.

**4.** To allow blank entries, either in the cell itself or in other cells specified as part of the validation settings, leave the Ignore <u>B</u>lank check box activated. If you clear this check box, Excel treats blank entries as zero and applies the validation rule accordingly.

**5.** If the range had an existing validation rule that also applied to other cells, you can apply the new rule to those other cells by activating the App<u>l</u>y These Changes to All Other Cells with the Same Settings check box.

**6.** Click the Input Message tab.

**7.** If you want a pop-up box to appear when the user selects the restricted cell or any cell within the restricted range, leave the <u>S</u>how Message When Cell Is Selected check box activated. Use the <u>T</u>itle and <u>I</u>nput Message boxes to specify the message that appears. For example, you could use the message to give the user information on the type and range of allowable values.

**8.** Click the Error Alert tab.

**9.** If you want a dialog box to appear when the user enters invalid data, leave the <u>S</u>how Error Alert After Invalid Data Is Entered check box activated. In the St<u>y</u>le list, click the error style you want: Stop, Warning, or Information. Use the <u>T</u>itle and <u>E</u>rror Message boxes to specify the message that appears.

4

> **CAUTION**
>
> Only the Stop style can prevent the user from ignoring the error and entering the invalid data anyway.

**10.** Click OK to apply the data-validation rule.

# Using Dialog Box Controls on a Worksheet

In the previous section, you saw how choosing List for the type of validation enabled you to supply yourself or the user with an in-cell drop-down list of allowable choices. This is good data-entry practice because it reduces the uncertainly about the allowable values.

One of Excel's slickest features is that it enables you to extend this idea and place not only lists, but other dialog box controls such as spinners and check boxes, directly on a worksheet. You can then link the values returned by these controls to a cell to create an elegant method for entering data.

## Using the Forms Toolbar

You add the dialog box controls by selecting tools from the Forms toolbar, shown in Figure 4.14. (To display the Forms toolbar, choose View, Toolbars, Forms.) Note that only some of the controls are available for worksheet duty. I'll discuss the controls in detail a bit later in this section.

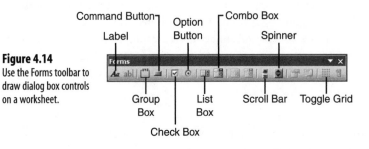

**Figure 4.14**
Use the Forms toolbar to draw dialog box controls on a worksheet.

> **NOTE**　You can add a command button to a worksheet, but you have to assign a Visual Basic for Applications (VBA) macro to it. To learn how to create macros, see my book *The Absolute Beginner's Guide to VBA* (Que, 2004).

## Adding a Control to a Worksheet

You add controls to a worksheet using the same steps you use to create any graphic object. Here's the basic procedure:

1. In the Forms toolbar, click the control you want to create. The mouse pointer changes to a crosshair.

2. Move the pointer onto the worksheet at the point where you want the control to appear.

3. Click and drag the mouse pointer to create the control.

Excel assigns a default caption to group boxes, check boxes, and option buttons. To edit this caption, you have two ways to get started:

- Right-click the control and choose Edit Te<u>x</u>t.
- Hold down Ctrl and click the control to select it. Then click inside the control.

Edit the text accordingly and, when you're done, click outside the control.

## Linking a Control to a Cell Value

To use the dialog box controls for inputting data, you need to associate each control with a worksheet cell. The following procedure shows you how it's done:

1. Select the control you want to work with. (Again, remember to hold down the Ctrl key before you click the control.)

2. Choose F<u>o</u>rmat, <u>C</u>ontrol (or press Ctrl+1) to display the Format Control dialog box.

3. Click the Control tab and then use the Cell <u>L</u>ink box to enter the cell's reference. You can either type the reference or select it directly on the worksheet.

4. Choose OK to return to the worksheet.

> **TIP**
> Another way to link a control to a cell is to select the control and enter a formula in the formula bar of the form =`cell`. Here, `cell` is a reference to the cell you want to use. For example, to link a control to cell A1, you enter the formula =A1.

> **NOTE**
> When working with option buttons, you have to enter only the linked cell for one of the buttons in a group. Excel automatically adds the reference to the rest.

## Understanding the Worksheet Controls

To get the most out of worksheet controls, you need to know the specifics of how each control works and how you can use each one for data entry. To that end, the next few sections take you through detailed accounts of each control.

## Group Boxes

Group boxes don't do much on their own. Instead, you use them to create a grouping of two or more option buttons. The user can then select only one option from the group. For this to work, you must proceed as follows:

1. Select the Group Box tool in the Forms toolbar.
2. Click and drag to draw the group box on the worksheet.
3. Choose the Option Button tool.
4. Click and drag within the group box to create an option button.
5. Repeat steps 3 and 4 as often as needed to create the other option buttons.

Remember, it's important that you create the group box first and then draw your option buttons within the group box.

> **NOTE** If you have one (and only one) option button outside of a grouping, you can still include it in a group box. (If you have multiple option buttons outside of a group box, this technique won't work.) To do this, first hold down Ctrl and click the option button to select it. Release Ctrl, click and drag an edge of the option button, and then drop it within the group box.

## Option Buttons

Option buttons are controls that usually appear in groups of two or more, and the user can activate only one of the options. As I said in the previous section, option buttons work in tandem with group boxes, in which the user can activate only one of the option buttons within a group box.

> **NOTE** All the option buttons that don't lie within a group box are treated as a de facto group. (That is, Excel allows you to select only one of these nongroup options at a time.) This means that a group box isn't strictly necessary when using option buttons on a worksheet. Most people do use them because it gives the user a visual clue for which options are related.

By default, Excel draws each option button in the unchecked state. Therefore, you should specify in advance which of the option buttons is checked:

1. Hold down Ctrl and click the option button you want to display as checked.
2. Choose Format, Control (or press Ctrl+1) to display the Format Control dialog box.
3. In the Control tab, activate the Checked option.
4. Click OK.

On the worksheet, activating a particular option button changes the value stored in the linked cell. The value stored depends on the option button, where the first button added to the group box has the value 1, the second button has the value 2, and so on. The advantage of this is that it enables you to translate a text option into a numeric value. For example, Figure 4.15 shows a worksheet in which the option buttons give the user three freight choices: Surface Mail, Air Mail, and Courier. The value of the chosen option is stored in the linked cell, which is E4. So, for example, if Air Mail is selected, the value 2 is stored in E4. In a production model, the worksheet would use this value to, say, look up the corresponding freight charges and adjust an invoice accordingly.

➔ To learn how to look up values in a worksheet, **see** "Working with Lookup Functions," **p. 181**.

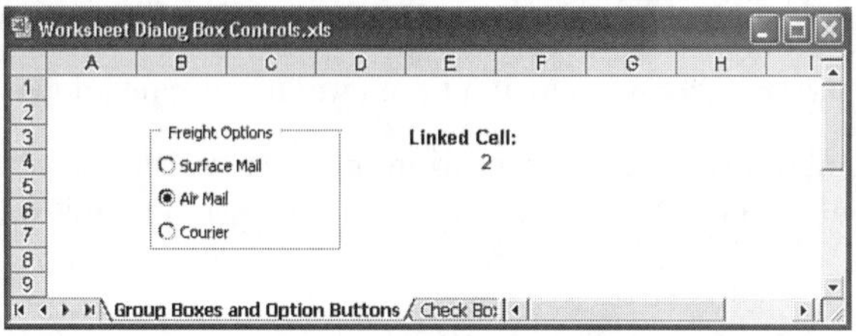

**Figure 4.15**
For option buttons, the value stored in the linked cell is given by the order in which each button was added to the group box.

**Check Boxes**

Check boxes enable you to include options that the user can toggle on or off. As with option buttons, Excel draws each check box in the unchecked state. If you prefer that a particular check box start in the checked state, use the Format Control dialog box to activate the control's <u>C</u>hecked option, as described in the previous section.

On the worksheet, an activated check box stores the value TRUE in its linked cell; if the check box is cleared, it stores the value FALSE. This is handy because it enables you to add a bit of logic to your formulas. That is, you can test whether a check box is activated and adjust a formula accordingly. Figure 4.16 shows a couple of examples:

- **Use End-Of-Period Payments**—This check box could be used to determine whether a formula that determines the monthly payments on a loan assumes that those payments are made at the end of each period (TRUE) or at the beginning of each period (FALSE).

- **Include Extra Monthly Payments**—This check box could be used to determine whether a model that builds a loan amortization schedule formula includes an extra principal repayment each month.

In both cases, and in most formulas that take check box results into account, you would use the IF() worksheet function to read the current value of the linked cell and branch accordingly.

➔ To learn how to use the IF() worksheet function, **see** "Using the IF() Function," **p. 156**. To learn how to build a loan amortization, **see** "Building a Loan Amortization Schedule," **p. 406**.

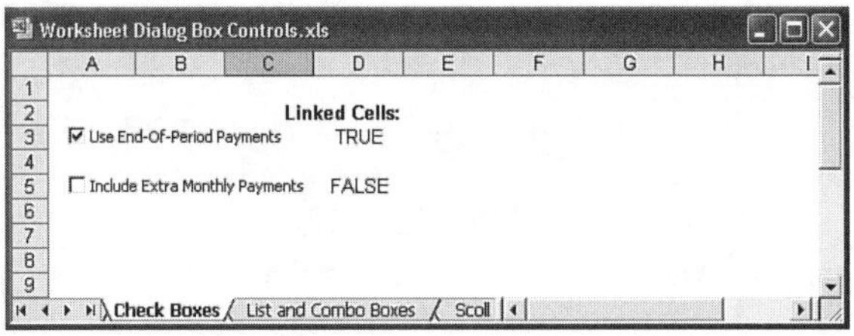

**Figure 4.16**
For check boxes, the value stored in the linked cell is TRUE when the check box is activated and FALSE when it is cleared.

## List Boxes and Combo Boxes

The list box control creates a list box from which the user can select an item. The items in the list are defined by the values in a specified worksheet range, and the value returned to the linked cell is the number of the item chosen. A combo box is similar to a list box; however, the control shows only one item at a time until it's dropped down.

List boxes and combo boxes are different from other controls because you also have to specify a range that contains the items to appear in the list. The following steps show you how it's done:

1. Enter the list items in a range. (The items must be listed in a single row or a single column.)

2. Add the list control to the sheet (if you haven't done so already), and then select it.

3. Choose Format, Control to display the Format Object dialog box.

4. Select the Control tab, and then use the Input Range box to enter a reference to the range of items. You can either type in the reference or select it directly on the worksheet.

5. Click OK to return to the worksheet.

Figure 4.17 shows a worksheet with a list box and a drop-down list.

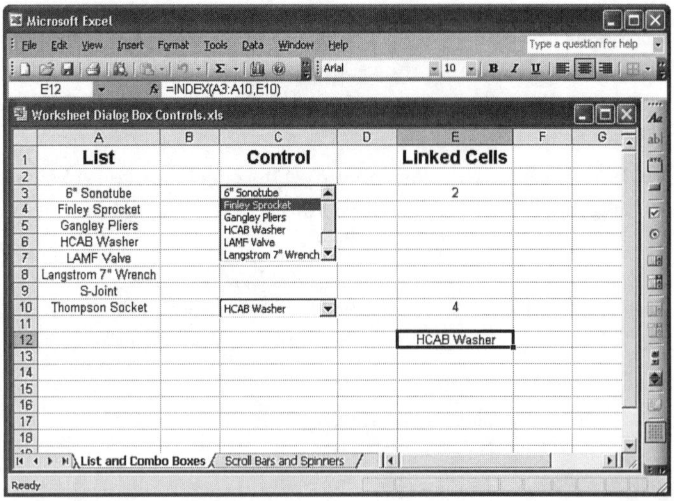

**Figure 4.17**
For list boxes and combo boxes, the value stored in the linked cell is the number of the selected list item. To get the item text, use the INDEX() function.

The list used by both controls is in the range A3:A10. Notice that the linked cells display the number of the list selection, not the selection itself. To get the selected list item, you can use the INDEX() function with the following syntax:

INDEX(*list_range, list_selection*)

| | |
|---|---|
| *list_range* | The range used in the list box or drop-down list |
| *list_selection* | The number of the item selected in the list |

For example, to find the item that's currently selected in the combo box in Figure 4.17, you use the following formula (as shown in cell E12):

=INDEX(A3:A10,E10)

➔ To learn more about the INDEX() function, **see** "Working with Lookup Functions," **p. 181**.

## Scrollbars and Spinners

The Scrollbar tool creates a control that resembles a window scrollbar. You use this type of scrollbar to select a number from a range of values. Clicking on the arrows or dragging the scroll box changes the value of the control. This value is what gets returned to the linked cell. Note that you can create either a horizontal or a vertical scrollbar.

In the Format Control dialog box for a scrollbar, the Control tab includes the following options:

- **Current Value**—The initial value of the scrollbar
- **Minimum Value**—The value of the scrollbar when the scroll box is at its leftmost position (for a horizontal scrollbar) or its topmost position (for a vertical scrollbar)
- **Maximum Value**—The value of the scrollbar when the scroll box is at its rightmost position (for a horizontal scrollbar) or its bottommost position (for a vertical scrollbar)
- **Incremental Change**—The amount that the scrollbar's value changes when the user clicks on a scroll arrow
- **Page Change**—The amount that the scrollbar's value changes when the user clicks between the scroll box and a scroll arrow

The Spinner tool creates a control that is similar to a scrollbar; that is, you can use a spinner to select a number between a maximum and a minimum value by clicking on the arrows. The number is returned to the linked cell. A spinner's options are also identical to those of a scrollbar, except that you can't set a Page Change value.

Figure 4.18 shows an example scrollbar and spinner. Note that the numbers above the scrollbar giving the minimum and maximum values are extra labels that I added by hand. This is usually a good idea because it gives the user the numeric limits of the control.

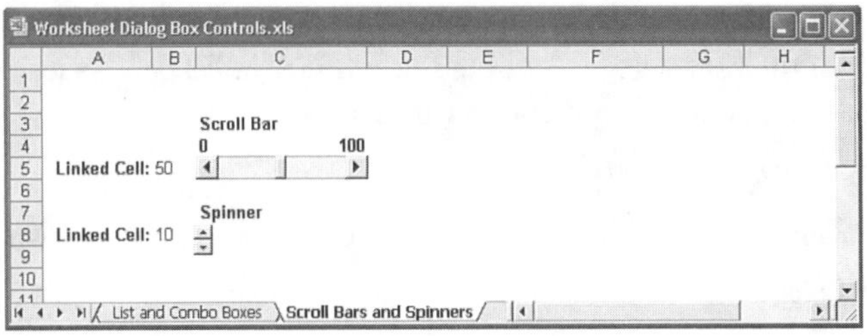

**Figure 4.18**
For scrollbars and spinners, the value stored in the linked cell is the current numeric value of the control.

## From Here

- To get the details on link formulas, **see** "Working with Links in Formulas," **p. 70**.

- To learn about custom numeric formats, and to see some examples of using them to display input error messages, **see** "Formatting Numbers, Dates, and Times," **p. 72**.

- Circular references are usually a bad thing to have in a spreadsheet model. To learn how to combat the bad kind, **see** "Fixing Circular References," **p. 113**.

- To learn how to get Excel to circle cells that contain data-validation errors, **see** "Auditing a Worksheet," **p. 117**.

- To learn how to use the IF() worksheet function, **see** "Using the IF() Function," **p. 156**.

- To learn how to look up values in a worksheet, **see** "Working with Lookup Functions," **p. 181**.

- To learn more about the INDEX() function, **see** "The MATCH() and INDEX() Functions," **p. 192**.

- To learn how the PMT() function works, **see** "Calculating the Loan Payment," **p. 400**.

- To learn how to build a loan amortization, **see** "Building a Loan Amortization Schedule," **p. 406**.

# Troubleshooting Formulas

Despite your best efforts, the odd error might appear in your formulas from time to time. These errors can be mathematical (for example, dividing by zero), or Excel might simply be incapable of interpreting the formula. In the latter case, problems can be caught while you're entering the formula. For example, if you try to enter a formula that has unbalanced parentheses, Excel won't accept the entry; it displays an error message instead. Other errors are more insidious. For example, your formula might *appear* to be working—that is, it returns a value—but the result is incorrect because the data is flawed or because your formula has referenced the wrong cell or range.

Whatever the error and whatever the cause, formula woes need to be worked out because you or someone else in your company is likely, depending on your models, to produce inaccurate results. But don't fall into the trap of thinking that *your* spreadsheets are problem free. A recent University of Hawaii study found that 50% of spreadsheets contain errors that led to "significant miscalculations." And the more complex the model is, the greater the chance is that errors can creep in. A 1999 KPMG study found that a staggering 90% of spreadsheets used for tax calculations contained errors.

The good news is that fixing formula flaws need not be drudgery. With a bit of know-how and Excel's top-notch troubleshooting tools, sniffing out and repairing model maladies isn't hard. This chapter tells you everything you need to know.

> **TIP**  If you try to enter an incorrect formula, Excel won't enable you to do anything else until you either fix the problem or cancel the operation (which means you lose your formula). If the formula is complex, you might not be able to see the problem right away. Instead of deleting all your work, place an apostrophe (') at the beginning of the formula to convert it to text. This way, you can save your work while you try to figure out the problem.

## Understanding Excel's Error Values

When you enter or edit a formula or change one of the formula's input values, Excel might show an error value as the formula "result." Excel has seven different error values: #DIV/0!, #N/A, #NAME?, #NULL!, #NUM!, #REF!, and #VALUE!. The next few sections give you a detailed look these values and offer suggestions for solving them.

### #DIV/0!

The #DIV/0! error almost always means that the cell's formula is trying to divide by zero, a mathematical no-no. The cause is usually a reference to a cell that either is blank or contains the value 0. Check the cell's precedents to look for possible culprits. You'll also see #DIV/0! if you enter an inappropriate argument in some functions. MOD(), for example, returns #DIV/0! if the second argument is 0.

> **NOTE**  To check items such as cell precedents and dependents, see the section later in this chapter titled "Auditing a Worksheet."

That Excel treats blank cells as the value 0 can pose problems in a worksheet that requires the user to fill in the data. If your formula requires division by one of the temporarily blank cells, it will show #DIV/0! as the result, possibly causing confusion for the user. You can get around this by telling Excel not to perform the calculation if the cell used as the divisor is 0. This is done with the IF() worksheet function, which is discussed in detail in Chapter 8, "Working with Logical and Information Functions." For example, consider the following formula that uses named cells to calculate gross margin:

```
=GrossProfit/Sales
```

To prevent the #DIV/0! error from appearing if the Sales cell is blank (or 0), you would modify the formula as follows:

```
=IF(Sales=0, "", GrossProfit/Sales)
```

If the value of the Sales cell is 0, the formula returns the empty string; otherwise, it performs the calculation.

## #N/A

The #N/A error value is short for "not available," and it means that the formula couldn't return a legitimate result. You usually see #N/A when you use an inappropriate argument (or if you omit a required argument) in a function. HLOOKUP() and VLOOKUP(), for example, return #N/A if the lookup value is smaller than the first value in the lookup range.

To solve the problem, first check the formula's input cells to see if any of them are displaying the #N/A error. If so, that's why your formula is returning the same error; the problem actually lies in the input cell. When you've found where the error originates, examine the formula's operands to look for inappropriate data types. In particular, check the arguments used in each function to ensure that they make sense for the function and that no required arguments are missing.

> **NOTE**
> It's common in spreadsheet work to purposely generate an #N/A! error to show that a particular cell value isn't currently available. For example, you might be waiting for budget figures from one or more divisions, or for the final numbers from month- or year-end. This is done by entering =NA() into the cell. In this case, you fix the "problem" by replacing the NA() function with the appropriate data when it arrives.

## #NAME?

You see the #NAME? error when Excel doesn't recognize a name you used in a formula, or when it interprets text within the formula as an undefined name. This means that the #NAME? error pops up in a wide variety of circumstances:

- You spelled a range name incorrectly.
- You used a range name that you haven't yet defined.
- You spelled a function name incorrectly.
- You used a function that is part of an uninstalled add-in.
- You used a string value without surrounding it with quotation marks.
- You entered a range reference and accidentally omitted the colon.
- You entered a reference to a range on another worksheet and didn't enclose the sheet name in single quotation marks.

> **TIP**
> When entering function names and defined names, use all lowercase letters. If Excel recognizes a name, it converts the function to all upper case and the defined name to its original case. If no conversion occurs, you misspelled the name, you haven't defined it yet, or you're using a function from an add-in that isn't loaded.
>
> Remember that you also can use the Insert, Function (shortcut key Shift+F3) or Insert, Name, Paste (shortcut F3) commands to enter functions and names safely.

5

These are mostly syntax errors, so fixing them means double-checking your formula and correcting range name or function name misspellings, or inserting missing quotation marks or colons. Also, be sure to define any range names you use and to install the appropriate add-in modules for functions you use.

---

**CASE STUDY**

## Avoiding #NAME? Errors When Deleting Range Names

If you've used a range name in a formula and then you delete that name, Excel generates the #NAME? error. Wouldn't it be better if Excel just converted the name to its appropriate cell reference in each formula, the way Lotus 1-2-3 does? Possibly, but there is an advantage to Excel's seemingly inconvenient approach. By generating an error, Excel enables you to catch range names that you delete by accident. Because Excel leaves the names in the formula, you can recover by simply redefining the original range name.

> **NOTE**
> Redefining the original range name becomes problematic if you can't remember the appropriate range coordinates. This is why it's always a good idea to paste a list of range names and their references into each of your worksheets. (I showed you how to do this back in Chapter 2, "Using Range Names"; see the section titled "Pasting a List of Range Names in a Worksheet.")

If you don't need this safety net, there *is* a way to make Excel convert deleted range names into their cell references. Here are the steps to follow:

1. Choose Tools, Options to display the Options dialog box.
2. Click the Transition tab.
3. Activate the Transition Formula Entry check box.
4. Choose OK.

This tells Excel to treat your formula entries the same way Lotus 1-2-3 does. Specifically, in formulas that use a deleted range name, the name automatically gets converted to its appropriate range reference. As an added bonus, Excel also performs the following automatic conversions:

- If you enter a range reference in a formula, the reference gets converted to a range name (provided, of course, that a name exists).
- If you define a name for a range, Excel converts any existing range references into the new name. This enables you to avoid the Apply Names feature, discussed in Chapter 2.

---

#NULL!

Excel displays the #NULL! error in a very specific case: When you use the intersection operator on two ranges that have no cells in common. Check your range coordinates to ensure that they're accurate. In addition, check to see if one of the ranges has been moved so that the two ranges in your formula no longer intersect.

### #NUM!

The `#NUM!` error means there's a problem with a number in your formula. This almost always means that you entered an invalid argument in a math or trig function. For example, you entered a negative number as the argument for the `SQRT()` or `LOG()` function. Check the formula's input cells—particularly those cells used as arguments for mathematical functions—to make sure the values are appropriate.

The `#NUM!` error also appears if you're using iteration (or a function that uses iteration) and Excel can't calculate a result. There could be no solution to the problem, or you might need to adjust the iteration parameters.

→ To learn more about iteration, **see** "Using Iteration and Circular References," **p. 90**.

### #REF!

The `#REF!` error means that your formula contains an invalid cell reference, which is usually caused by one of the following actions:

- You deleted a cell to which the formula refers. You need to add the cell back in or adjust the formula reference.

- You cut a cell and then pasted it in a cell used by the formula. You need to undo the cut and paste the cell elsewhere. (Note that it's okay to *copy* a cell and paste it on a cell used by the formula.)

- Your formula references a nonexistent cell address, such as B0. This can happen if you cut or copy a formula that uses relative references and paste it in such a way that the invalid cell address is created. For example, suppose that your formula references cell B1. If you cut or copy the cell containing the formula and paste it one row higher, the reference to B1 becomes invalid because Excel can't move the cell reference up one row.

### #VALUE!

When Excel generates a `#VALUE!` error, it means you've used an inappropriate argument in a function. This is most often caused by using the wrong data type. For example, you might have entered or referenced a string value instead of a numeric value. Similarly, you might have used a range reference in a function argument that requires a single cell or value. Excel also generates this error if you use a value that's larger or smaller than Excel can handle. (Excel can work with values between −1E–307 and 1E+307.) In all these cases, you solve the problem by double-checking your function arguments to find and edit the inappropriate arguments.

# Fixing Other Formula Errors

Not all formula errors generate one of Excel's seven error values. Instead, you might see a warning dialog box from Excel (for example, if you try to enter a function without including a required argument). Or, you might not see any indication that something is wrong. To help you in these situations, the following sections cover some of the most common formula errors.

## Missing or Mismatched Parentheses

If you miss a parenthesis when typing a formula, or if you place a parenthesis in the wrong location, Excel usually displays a dialog box like the one shown in Figure 5.1 when you attempt to confirm the formula. If the edited formula is what you want, choose Yes to have Excel enter the corrected formula automatically; if the edited formula is not correct, choose No and edit the formula by hand.

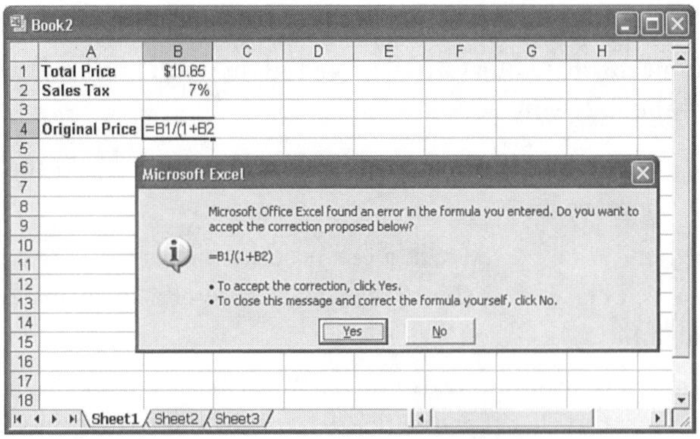

**Figure 5.1**
If you miss a parenthesis, Excel attempts to fix the problem and displays this dialog box to ask if you want to accept the correction.

**5**

---

**CAUTION**

Excel doesn't always fix missing parentheses correctly. It tends to add the missing parenthesis to the end of the formula, which is often not what you want. Therefore, always check Excel's proposed solution carefully before accepting it.

---

To help you avoid missing or mismatched parentheses, Excel provides two visual clues in the formula itself when you're editing it:

- The first clue occurs when you type a right parenthesis. Excel highlights both the right parenthesis and its corresponding left parenthesis. If you type what you think is the last right parenthesis and Excel doesn't highlight the first left parenthesis, your parentheses are unbalanced.

- The second clue occurs when you use the left and right arrow keys to navigate a formula. When you cross over a parenthesis, Excel highlights the other parenthesis in the pair.

## Erroneous Formula Results

If a formula produces no warnings or error values, the result might still be in error. If the result of a formula is incorrect, here are a few techniques that can help you understand and fix the problem:

- **Calculate complex formulas one term at a time**—In the formula bar, highlight the term you want to calculate, and then press F9. Excel converts the highlighted section into its value. Make sure that you press the Esc key when you're done, to avoid entering the formula with just the calculated values.

- **Evaluate the formula**—This feature enables you to step through the various parts of a formula. See "Evaluating Formulas," later in this chapter.

- **Break up long or complex formulas**—One of the most complicated aspects of formula troubleshooting is making sense out of long formulas. The previous techniques can help (by enabling you to evaluate parts of the formula), but it's usually best to keep your formulas as short as you can at first. When you get things working properly, you often can recombine formulas for a more efficient model.

- **Recalculate all formulas**—A particular formula might display the wrong result because other formulas on which it depends need to be recalculated. This is particularly true if one or more of those formulas uses custom VBA functions. Press Ctrl+Alt+F9 to recalculate all worksheet formulas.

- **Pay attention to operator precedence**—As explained in Chapter 3, "Building Basic Formulas," Excel's operator precedence means that certain operations are performed before others. An erroneous formula result could therefore be caused by Excel's precedence order. To control precedence, use parentheses.

- **Watch out for nonblank "blank" cells**—A cell might appear to be blank, but it might actually contain data or even a formula. For example, some users "clear" a cell by pressing the spacebar, which Excel then treats as a nonblank cell. Similarly, some formulas return the empty string instead of a value (see, for example, the IF() function formula I showed you earlier in this chapter for avoiding the #DIV/0! error).

- **Watch unseen values**—For a large model, your formula could be using cells that you can't see because they're offscreen or on another sheet. Excel's Watch Window enables you to keep an eye on the current value of one or more cells. See "Watching Cell Values," later in this chapter.

## Fixing Circular References

A *circular reference* occurs when a formula refers to its own cell. This can happen in one of two ways:

- **Directly**—The formula explicitly references its own cell. For example, a circular reference would result if the following formula were entered into cell A1:

=A1+A2

■ **Indirectly**—The formula references a cell or function that, in turn, references the formula's cell. For example, suppose that cell A1 contains the following formula:

`=A5*10`

A circular reference would result if cell A5 referred to cell A1, as in this example:

`=SUM(A1:D1)`

When Excel detects a circular reference, it displays the dialog box shown in Figure 5.2.

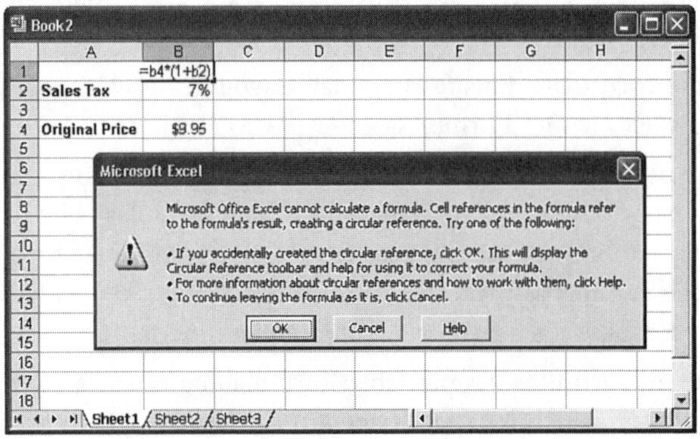

**Figure 5.2**
If you attempt to confirm a formula that contains a circular reference, Excel displays this dialog box.

When you choose OK, Excel displays *tracer* arrows that connect the cells involved in the circular reference. (Tracers are discussed in detail later in this chapter; see "Auditing a Worksheet.") Knowing which cells are involved enables you to correct the formula in one of them to solve the problem. Note, too, that Excel displays the Circular Reference toolbar, which helps you navigate the circular reference by selecting a cell address from its drop-down list.

# Using the Formula Error Checker

If you use Microsoft Word, you're probably familiar with the wavy green lines that appear under words and phrases that the Grammar Checker has flagged as being incorrect. The Grammar Checker operates by using a set of rules that determine correct grammar and syntax. As you type, the Grammar Checker operates in the background and constantly monitors your writing. If something you write goes against one of the Grammar Checker's rules, the wavy line appears to let you know there's a problem.

Excel has a similar feature: the Formula Error Checker. It's similar to the Grammar Checker, in that it uses a set of rules to determine correctness, and it operates in the background to monitor your formulas. If it detects something amiss, it displays an *error indicator*—a green triangle—in the upper-left corner of the cell containing the formula, as shown in Figure 5.3.

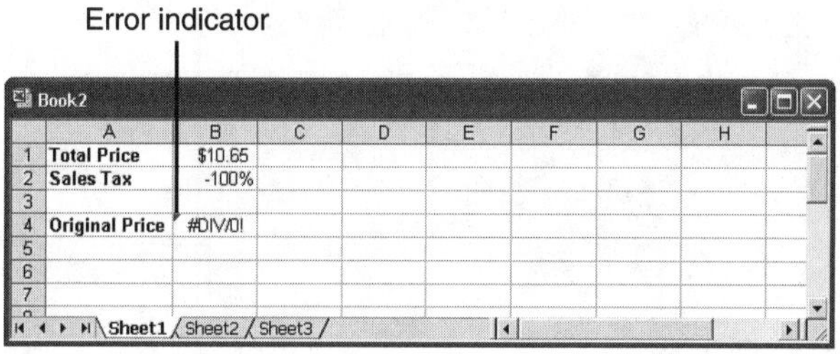

**Figure 5.3**
If Excel's Formula Error Checker detects a problem, it displays a green triangle in the upper-left corner of the formula's cell.

Error indicator

## Choosing an Error Action

When you select the cell, Excel displays a Smart Tag beside it. If you hover your mouse pointer over the icon, a pop-up message describes the error, as shown in Figure 5.4. The Smart Tag doubles as a drop-down list with the following actions:

- **Help on this Error**—Choose this option to get information on the error via the Excel Help system.

- **Show Calculation Steps**—Choose this option to run the Evaluate Formula feature. See "Evaluating Formulas," later in this chapter.

- **Ignore Error**—Choose this option to leave the formula as is.

- **Edit in Formula Bar**—Choose this option to display the formula in Edit mode in the formula bar. This enables you to fix the problem by editing the formula.

- **Error-Checking Options**—Choose this option to display the Error Checking tab of the Options dialog box (discussed next).

- **Show Formula Auditing Toolbar**—Choose this option to display the Formula Auditing toolbar. See "Auditing a Worksheet," later in this chapter.

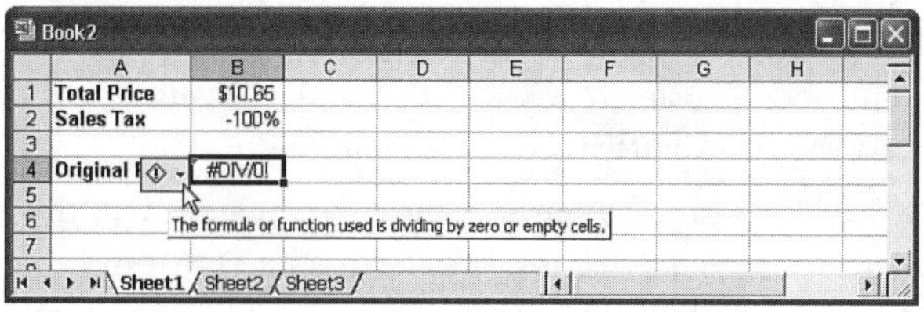

**Figure 5.4**
Select the cell containing the error, and then move the mouse pointer over the Smart Tag to see a description of the error.

## Setting Error Checker Options

Like the Grammar Checker, the Formula Error Checker has a number of options that control how it works and which errors it flags. To see these options, you have two choices:

- Choose Tools, Options to display the Options dialog box, and then click the Error Checking tab, shown in Figure 5.5.

- Choose Error-Checking Options in the Smart Tag's drop-down list (as described in the previous section).

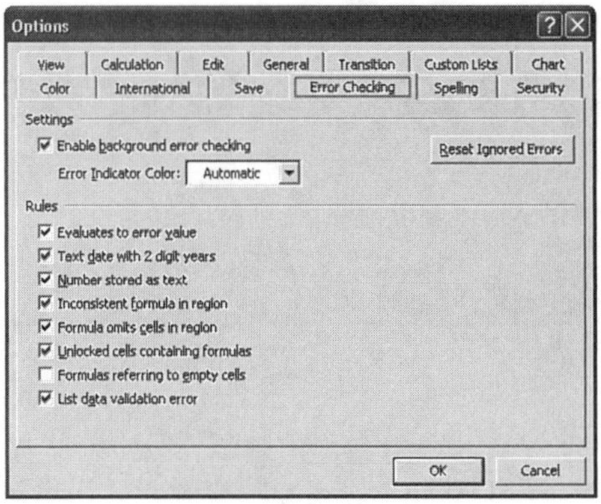

**Figure 5.5**
The Error Checking tab contains the options that govern the workings of the Formula Error Checking feature.

Here's a rundown of the available options:

- **Enable Background Error Checking**—This check box toggles the Error Checker's background operation on and off. If you turn off the background checking, you can run a check at any time by choosing Tools, Error Checking.

- **Error Indicator Color**—Use this color palette to click the color of the error indicator.

- **Reset Ignored Errors**—If you've ignored one or more errors, you can redisplay the error indicators by choosing this button.

- **Evaluates to Error Value**—When this check box is activated, the Error Checker flags formulas that evaluate to #DIV/0!, #NAME?, or any of the other error values discussed earlier.

- **Text Date with 2 Digit Years**—When this check box is activated, the Error Checker flags formulas that contain date text strings in which the year contains only two digits (a possibly ambiguous situation because the string could refer to a date in either the 1900s or the 2000s). In such a case, the list of options supplied in the Smart Tag contains two commands—Convert XX to 19XX and Convert XX to 20XX—that enable you to convert the two-digit year to a four-digit year.

- **Number Stored as Text**—When this check box is activated, the Error Checker flags cells that contain a number that is either formatted as text or preceded by an apostrophe. In such a case, the list of options supplied in the Smart Tag contains the Convert to Number command to convert the test to its numeric equivalent.

- **Inconsistent Formula in Region**—When this check box is activated, the Error Checker flags formulas that are structured differently from similar formulas in the surrounding area. For example, consider the worksheet shown in Figure 5.6. In the SALES TOTAL row (row 7), the totals for Jan, Feb, and Mar (cells B7, C7, and D7) are all derived by summing the cells above. For example, the formula in cell D7 is =SUM(D4:D6). This is also true of the sums in cells F7, G7, and H7. However, the formula in cell E7 is =SUM(B7:D7). In other words, this cell sums the row values instead of the column values. This isn't incorrect, but it is inconsistent and could lead to problems (for example, if someone tried to AutoFill cell E7 to the left or right). In such a case, the list of options supplied in the Smart Tag contain a command such as Copy Formula from <u>L</u>eft to bring the formula into consistency with the surrounding cells.

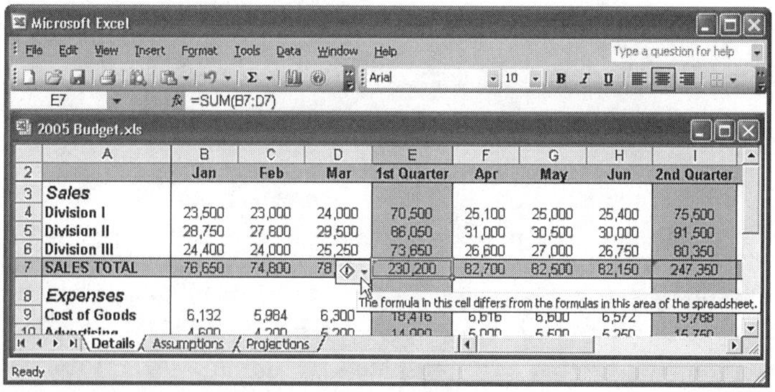

**Figure 5.6**
The Error Checker can flag formulas that aren't consistent with the surrounding formulas. In this case, the formula in E7 sums row values, while the surrounding formulas sum column values.

- **Formula Omits Cells in Region**—When this check box is activated, the Error Checker flags formulas that omit cells that are adjacent to a range referenced in the formula. For example, suppose that the formula is =AVERAGE(A2:A10), where A2:A10 is a range of numeric values. If cell A1 also contains a numeric value, the Error Checker will flag the formula to alert you to the possibility that you missed including cell A1 in the formula. In such a case, the list of options supplied in the Smart Tag will contain the command <u>U</u>pdate Formula to Include Cells to adjust the formula automatically.

- **Unlocked Cells Containing Formulas**—When this check box is activated, the Error Checker flags formulas that reside in unlocked cells. This isn't an error so much as a warning that other people could tamper with the formula even after you have protected the sheet. In such a case, the list of options supplied in the Smart Tag will contain the command <u>L</u>ock Cell to lock the cell and prevent users from changing the formula after you protect the sheet.

- **Formulas Referring to Empty Cells**—When this check box is activated, the Error Checker flags formulas that reference empty cells. In such a case, the list of options supplied in the Smart Tag will contain the command <u>T</u>race Empty Cell to enable you to find the empty cell. (At this point, you can either enter data into the cell or adjust the formula so that it doesn't reference the cell.)

- **List Data Validation Error**—When this check box is activated, the Error Checker enables data validation to apply to lists. (Chapter 13, "Analyzing Data with Lists," discusses lists in detail.)

# Auditing a Worksheet

As you've seen, some formula errors are the result of referencing other cells that contain errors or inappropriate values. The first step in troubleshooting these kinds of formula problems is to determine which cell or cells is causing the error. This is straightforward if the formula references only a single cell, but it gets progressively more difficult as the number of references increases. (Another complicating factor is the use of range names because it won't be obvious which range each name is referencing.)

To determine which cells are wreaking havoc on your formulas, you can use Excel's auditing features to visualize and trace a formula's input values and error sources.

## Understanding Auditing

Excel's formula-auditing features operate by creating *tracers*—arrows that literally point out the cells involved in a formula. You can use tracers to find three kinds of cells:

- **Precedents**—These are cells that are directly or indirectly referenced in a formula. For example, suppose that cell B4 contains the formula =B2; then B2 is a direct precedent of B4. Now suppose that cell B2 contains the formula =A2/2; this makes A2 a direct precedent of B2, but it's also an *indirect* precedent of cell B4.

- **Dependents**—These are cells that are directly or indirectly referenced by a formula in another cell. In the preceding example, cell B2 is a direct dependent of A2, and B4 is an indirect dependent of A2.

- **Errors**—These are cells that contain an error value and are directly or indirectly referenced in a formula (and, therefore, cause the same error to appear in the formula).

Figure 5.7 shows a worksheet with three examples of tracer arrows:

- Cell B4 contains the formula =B2, and B2 contains =A2/2. The arrows (they're blue onscreen) point out the precedents (direct and indirect) of B4.

- Cell D4 contains the formula =D2, and D2 contains =D1/0. The latter produces the #DIV/0! error. Therefore, the same error appears in cell D4. The arrow (it's red onscreen) is pointing out the source of the error.

- Cell G4 contains the formula =Sheet2!A1. Excel displays the dashed arrow with the worksheet icon whenever the precedent or dependent exists on a different worksheet.

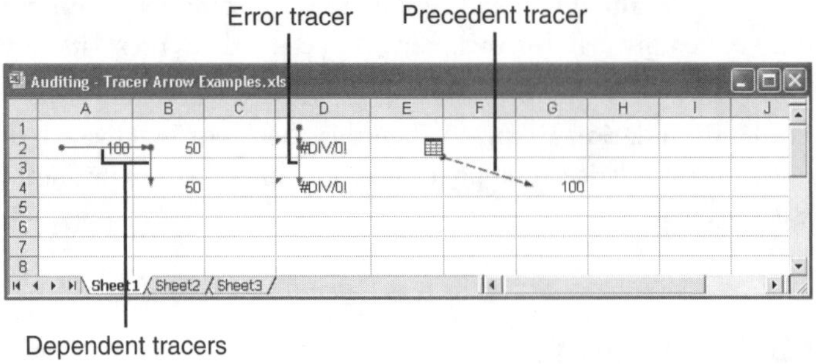

**Figure 5.7**
The three types of tracer arrows.

Error tracer    Precedent tracer

Dependent tracers

As you'll see in the next few sections, Excel's auditing features are available via the Tools, Formula Auditing command. However, you can also access these features using the handy Formula Auditing toolbar, shown in Figure 5.8. (Choose Activate Tools, Formula Auditing, Show Formula Auditing Toolbar.)

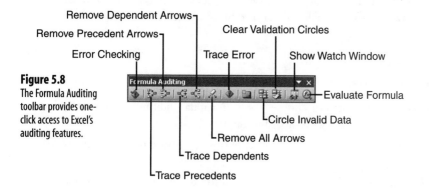

**Figure 5.8**
The Formula Auditing toolbar provides one-click access to Excel's auditing features.

## Tracing Cell Precedents

To trace cell precedents, follow these steps:

1.  Select the cell containing the formula whose precedents you want to trace.

2.  Choose Tools, Formula Auditing, Trace Precedents, or click the Trace Precedents toolbar button. Excel adds a tracer arrow to each direct precedent.

3.  Keep repeating step 2 to see more levels of precedents.

> **TIP**
> You also can trace precedents by double-clicking the cell, provided that you turn off in-cell editing. You do this by choosing Tools, Options to display the Options dialog box, and then deactivating the Edit Directly in Cell check box in the Edit tab. Now when you double-click a cell, Excel selects the formula's precedents.

## Tracing Cell Dependents

Here are the steps to follow to trace cell dependents:

1.  Select the cell whose dependents you want to trace.

2.  Choose Tools, Formula Auditing, Trace Dependents, or click the Trace Dependents toolbar button. Excel adds a tracer arrow to each direct dependent.

3.  Keep repeating step 2 to see more levels of dependents.

# Tracing Cell Errors

To trace cell errors, follow these steps:

1.  Select the cell containing the error you want to trace.

2.  Choose Tools, Formula Auditing, Trace Error, or click the Trace Error toolbar button. Excel adds a tracer arrow to each cell that produced the error.

# Removing Tracer Arrows

To remove the tracer arrows, you have three choices:

- To remove all the tracer arrows, choose Tools, Formula Auditing, Remove All Arrows, or click the Remove All Arrows toolbar button.

- Click the Remove Precedent Arrows toolbar button to remove precedent arrows one level at a time.

- Click the Remove Dependent Arrows toolbar button to remove dependent arrows one level at a time.

# Evaluating Formulas

Earlier you learned that you can troubleshoot a wonky formula by evaluating parts of the formula. This is done by highlighting the part of the formula you want to evaluate and then pressing F9. This works fine, but it can be tedious in a long or complex formula, and there's always the danger that you might accidentally confirm a partially evaluated formula and lose your work.

A better solution is Excel's Evaluate Formula feature. It does the same thing as the F9 technique, but it's easier and safer. Here's how it works:

1.  Select the cell that contains the formula you want to evaluate.

2.  Choose Tools, Formula Auditing, Evaluate Formula, or click the Evaluate Formula toolbar button. Excel displays the Evaluate Formula dialog box.

3.  The current term in the formula is underlined in the Evaluation box. At each step, you choose from one or more of the following buttons:

    - **Evaluate**—Choose this button to display the current value of the underlined term.

    - **Step In**—Choose this button to display the first dependent of the underlined term. If that dependent also has a dependent, choose this button again to see it (see Figure 5.9).

    - **Step Out**—Choose this button to hide a dependent and evaluate its precedent.

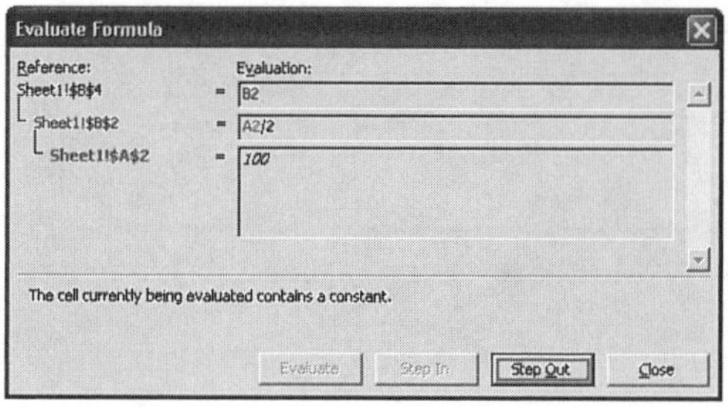

**Figure 5.9**
With the Evaluate
Formula feature, you can
"step in" to the formula to
display its dependent
cells.

**4.** Repeat step 3 until you've completed your evaluation.

**5.** Choose Close.

## Watching Cell Values

In the precedent tracer example shown in Figure 5.7, the formula in cell G4 refers to a cell in another worksheet, which is represented in the trace by a worksheet icon. In other words, you can't see the formula cell and the precedent cell at the same time. This could also happen if the precedent existed on another workbook or even elsewhere on the same sheet if you're working with a large model.

This is a problem because there's no easy way to determine the current contents or value of the unseen precedent. If you're having a problem, troubleshooting requires that you track down the far-off precedent to see if it might be the culprit. That's bad enough with a single unseen cell, but what if your formula refers to 5 or 10 such cells? And what if those cells are scattered in different worksheets and workbooks?

This level of hassle—not at all uncommon in the spreadsheet world—was no doubt the inspiration behind an elegant solution: the Watch Window. This window enables you to keep tabs on both the value and the formula in any cell in any worksheet in any open workbook. Here's how you set up a watch:

**1.** Activate the workbook that contains the cell or cells you want to watch.

**2.** Choose Tools, Formula Auditing, Show Watch Window, or click the Show Watch Window toolbar button. Excel displays the Watch Window.

**3.** Click Add Watch. Excel displays the Add Watch dialog box.

**4.** Either select the cell you want to watch, or type in a reference formula for the cell (for example, =A1). Note that you can select a range to add multiple cells to the Watch Window.

**5.** Choose Add. Excel adds the cell or cells to the Watch Window, as shown in Figure 5.10.

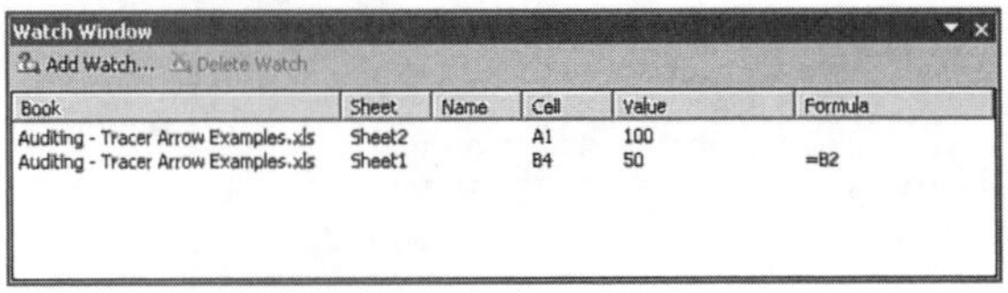
Watch Window
Add Watch... Delete Watch
Book Sheet Name Cell Value Formula
Auditing - Tracer Arrow Examples.xls Sheet2 A1 100
Auditing - Tracer Arrow Examples.xls Sheet1 B4 50 =B2

**Figure 5.10**
Use the Watch Window to keep an eye on the values and formulas of unseen cells that reside in other worksheets or workbooks.

## From Here


- For the details of Excel's operator precedence rules, **see** "Understanding Operator Precedence," **p. 57.**
- To learn more about iteration, **see** "Using Iteration and Circular References," **p. 90.**
- To learn how to paste range names, **see** "Pasting a List of Range Names in a Worksheet," **p. 47.**
- To learn about the `IF()` worksheet function, **see** "Using the `IF()` Function," **p. 156.**
- For the details of Excel's list features, **see** "Analyzing Data with Lists," **p. 283.**

# Harnessing the Power of Functions

II

# Using Functions

**6**

The formulas that you can construct based on the information presented in Part I, "Mastering Excel Ranges and Formulas," can range from simple additions and subtractions to powerful iteration-based solutions to otherwise difficult problems. Formulas that combine Excel's operators with basic operands such as numeric and string values are the bread and butter of any spreadsheet.

But to get to the real meat of a spreadsheet model, you need to expand your formula repertoire to include Excel's worksheet functions. Dozens of these functions exist, and they're an essential part of making your worksheet work easier and more powerful. Excel has various function categories, including the following:

- Text
- Logical
- Information
- Lookup and reference
- Date and time
- Math and trigonometry
- Statistical
- Financial
- Database and list

You can even create your own custom functions if Excel's built-in functions aren't up to the task in certain situations. You build these functions using the Visual Basic for Applications (VBA) macro language, and it's easier than you think.

This chapter gives you a short introduction to Excel's built-in worksheet functions. You'll learn what the functions are, what they can do, and how to use them. The next six chapters give you detailed descriptions of the functions in the categories listed earlier. (The exception is the database and list category, which I cover in Chapter 13, "Analyzing Data with Lists.")

## About Excel's Functions

*Functions* are formulas that Excel has predefined. They're designed to take you beyond the basic arithmetic and text formulas you've seen so far. They do this in three ways:

- Functions make simple but cumbersome formulas easier to use. For example, suppose that you want to add a list of 100 numbers in a column starting at cell A1 and finishing at cell A100. Even if you wanted to, you wouldn't be able to enter 100 separate additions in a cell because you would run out of room (recall that cells are limited to 255 characters). Luckily, there's an alternative: the SUM() function. With this function, you would simply enter =SUM(A1:A100).

- Functions enable you to include complex mathematical expressions in your worksheets that otherwise would be difficult or impossible to construct using simple arithmetic operators. For example, determining a mortgage payment given the principal, interest, and term is a complicated matter, at best, but you can do it with Excel's PMT() function just by entering a few parameters.

- Functions enable you to include data in your applications that you couldn't access otherwise. For example, the INFO() function can tell you how much memory is available on your system, what operating system you're using, what version number it is, and more. Similarly, the powerful IF() function enables you to test the contents of a cell—for example, to see whether it contains a particular value or an error—and then perform an action accordingly, depending on the result.

As you can see, functions are a powerful addition to your worksheet-building arsenal. With proper use of these tools, there is no practical limit to the kinds of models you can create.

## The Structure of a Function

Every function has the same basic form:

```
FUNCTION(argument1, argument2, ...)
```

The *FUNCTION* part is just the name of the function, which always appears in uppercase letters (such as SUM or PMT). Note, however, that you don't need to type in the function name using uppercase letters. Whatever case you use, Excel automatically converts the name to all upper case. In fact, it's good practice to enter function names using only lowercase letters. That way, if Excel doesn't convert the function name to upper case, you know that it doesn't recognize the name, which means you probably misspelled it.

The items that appear within the parentheses and separated by commas are the function *arguments*. The arguments are the function's inputs—the data it uses to perform its calculations. With respect to arguments, functions come in two flavors:

- **No arguments**—Many functions don't require any arguments. For example, the NOW() function returns the current date and time, and doesn't require arguments.

- **One or more arguments**—Most functions accept at least 1 argument, and some accept as many as 9 or 10 arguments. These arguments fall into two categories: required and optional. The required arguments must appear between the parentheses, or the formula will generate an error. You use the optional arguments only if your formula needs them.

Let's look at an example. The FV() function determines the future value of a regular investment based on three required arguments and two optional ones:

FV(*rate*, *nper*, *pmt*, [*pv*], [*type*])

| | |
|---|---|
| *rate* | The fixed rate of interest over the term of the investment. |
| *nper* | The number of deposits over the term of the investment. |
| *pmt* | The amount deposited each period. |
| *pv* | The present value of the investment. The default value is 0. |
| *type* | When the deposits are due (0 for the beginning of the period; 1 for the end of the period, which is the default). |

This is called the function *syntax*. Three conventions are at work here and throughout the rest of this book:

- *Italic type* indicates a placeholder. That is, when you use the function, you replace the placeholder with an actual value.

- Arguments surrounded by square brackets are optional.

- All other arguments are required.

> **CAUTION**
>
> Be careful when using commas in functions that have optional arguments. In general, if you omit an optional argument, you must leave out the comma that precedes the argument. For example, if you omit just the *type* argument from FV(), you write the function like so:
>
>     FV(*rate*, *nper*, *pmt*, *pv*)
>
> However, if you omit just the *pv* argument, you need to include all the commas so that there is no ambiguity about which value refers to which argument:
>
>     FV(*rate*, *nper*, *pmt*, , *type*)

**6**

For each argument placeholder, you substitute an appropriate value. For example, in the FV() function, you substitute *rate* with a decimal value between 0 and 1, *nper* with an integer, and *pmt* with a dollar amount. Arguments can take any of the following forms:

- Literal alphanumeric values
- Expressions

- Cell or range references
- Range names
- Arrays
- The result of another function

The function operates by processing the inputs and then returning a result. For example, the FV() function returns the total value of the investment at the end of the term. Figure 6.1 shows a simple future-value calculator that uses this function. (In case you're wondering, I entered the Payment value in cell B4 as negative because Excel always treats any money you have to pay as a negative number.)

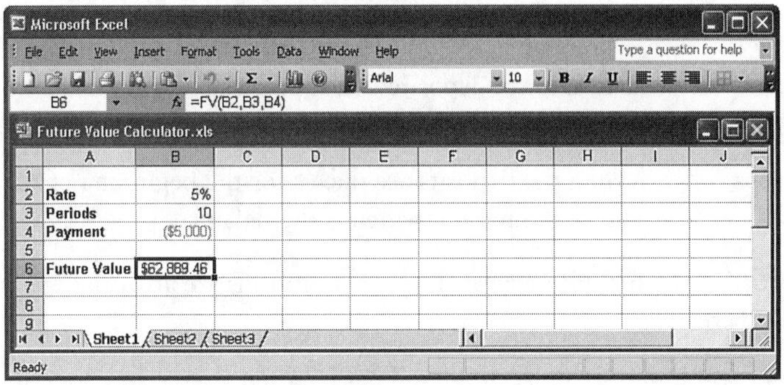

**Figure 6.1**
This example of the FV() function uses the values in cells B2, B3, and B4 as inputs for calculating the future value of an investment.

**NOTE** You can download the workbook that contains this chapter's examples here: www.mcfedries.com/ExcelFormulas/.

# Typing a Function into a Formula

You always use a function as part of a cell formula. So, even if you're using the function by itself, you still need to precede it with an equals sign. Whether you use a function on its own or as part of a larger formula, here are a few rules and guidelines to follow:

- You can enter the function name in either uppercase or lowercase letters. Excel always converts function names to upper case.
- Always enclose function arguments in parentheses.
- Always separate multiple arguments with commas. (You might want to add a space after each comma to make the function more readable. Excel ignores the extra spaces.)
- You can use a function as an argument for another function. This is called *nesting* functions. For example, the function AVERAGE(SUM(A1:A10), SUM(B1:B15)) sums two columns of numbers and returns the average of the two sums.

When you type a function name followed by the left parenthesis, Excel recognizes that you're entering a function (assuming, of course, that you spelled the function name correctly). It then displays a pop-up banner that shows the function syntax. The current argument is displayed in bold type. In the example shown in Figure 6.2, the *nper* argument is shown in bold, so the next value (or cell reference, or whatever) entered will apply to that argument. When you type a comma, Excel bolds the next argument in the list.

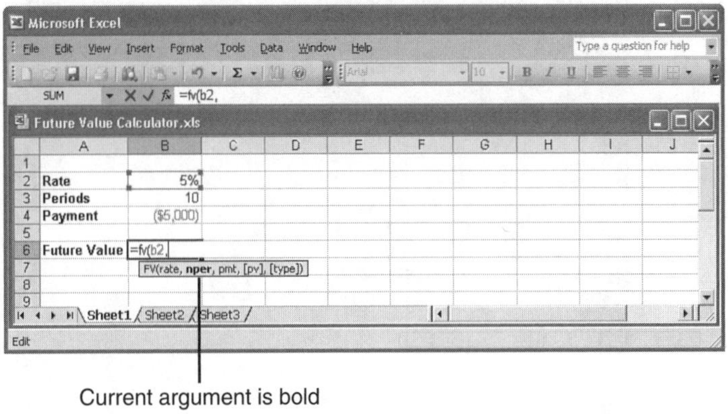

**Figure 6.2**
After you type the function name and the left parenthesis, Excel displays the function syntax, with the current argument shown in bold type.

Current argument is bold

# Using the Insert Function Feature

Although you'll usually type your functions by hand, sometimes you might prefer to get a helping hand from Excel if

- You're not sure which function to use.
- You want to see the syntax of a function before using it.
- You want to examine similar functions in a particular category before choosing the function that best suits your needs.
- You want to see the effect that different argument values have on the function result.

For these situations, Excel offers two tools: the Insert Function feature and the Function Wizard.

You use the Insert Function feature to choose the function you want from a dialog box. Here's how it works:

1. Select the cell in which you want to use the function.
2. Enter the formula up to the point where you want to insert the function.
3. You now have two choices:
   - If the function you want is one you inserted recently, it might appear on the list of recent functions in the Name box. Drop down the Name box list (see Figure 6.3); if you see the name of the function you want, click it. Skip to step 6.

6

- To pick any function, choose Insert, Function, or click the Insert Function button in the formula bar (see Figure 6.3). In this case, the Insert Function dialog box appears, as shown in Figure 6.3.

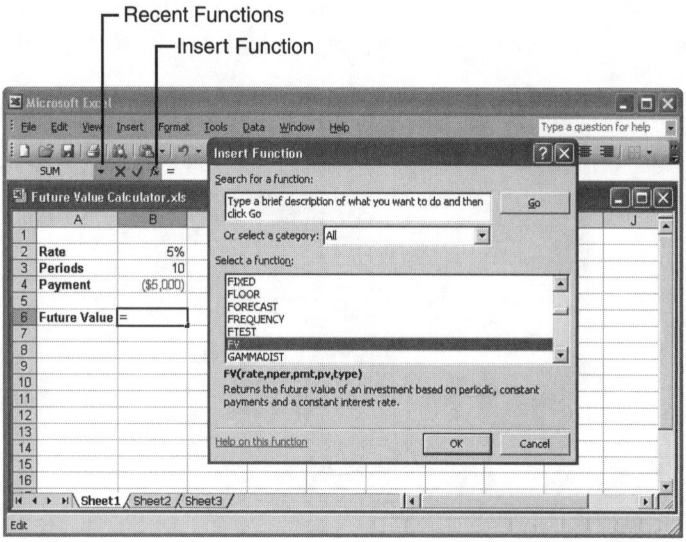

**Figure 6.3**
Choose Insert, Function, or click the Insert Function button to display the Insert Function dialog box.

4. (Optional) In the Or Select a Category list, click the type of function you need. If you're not sure, click All.

5. In the Select a Function list, click the function you want to use. (Note that after you click inside the Select a Function list, pressing a letter moves the selection down to the first function that begins with that letter.)

6. Choose OK. Excel displays the Function Arguments dialog box.

> **TIP**
> To skip the first six steps and go directly to the Function Arguments dialog box, enter the name of the function in the cell, and then either select the Insert Function button or press Ctrl+A. Alternatively, press equals (=) and then click the function from the list of recent functions in the Name box.

7. For each required argument and each optional argument you want to use, enter a value, expression, or cell reference in the appropriate text box. Here are some notes to bear in mind when you're working in this dialog box (see Figure 6.4):

- The names of the required arguments are shown in bold type.
- When you move the cursor to an argument text box, Excel displays a description of the argument.

- After you fill in an argument text box, Excel shows the current value of the argument to the right of the box.

- After you fill in the text boxes for all the required arguments, Excel displays the current value of the function value.

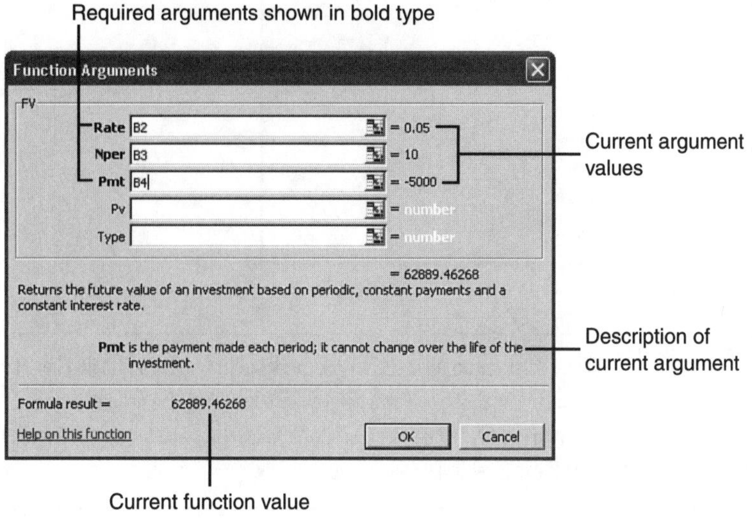

**Figure 6.4**
Use the Function
Arguments dialog box to
enter values for the
function's arguments.

Required arguments shown in bold type

Current argument values

Description of current argument

Current function value

8. When you're done, choose OK. Excel pastes the function and its arguments into the cell.

# Loading the Analysis ToolPak Functions

Excel's Analysis ToolPak is a large collection of powerful statistical functions and commands. Some of these tools use advanced statistical techniques and were designed with only a limited number of technical users in mind. However, many of them have general applications and can be amazingly useful. I go through these more useful functions throughout the next half a dozen chapters.

To use the functions in the Analysis ToolPak, you need to load the add-in that makes them available to Excel. The following procedure takes you through the steps:

1. Choose Tools, Add-Ins. Excel displays the Add-Ins dialog box.

2. Activate the Analysis ToolPak check box, as shown in Figure 6.5.

**Figure 6.5**
Activate the Analysis
ToolPak check box to load
this add-in's functions
into Excel.

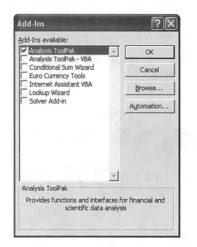

**NOTE** If you don't see an Analysis ToolPak check box in the Add-Ins dialog box, it means that you didn't install the Analysis ToolPak when you installed Excel. You need to run the Excel setup program and use it to install the Analysis ToolPak. Alternatively, if you set up this feature to be installed when you first use it, Excel will install it automatically.

3. Choose OK. Excel loads the add-in.

## From Here

6

# Working with Text Functions

In Excel, *text* is any collection of alphanumeric characters that isn't a numeric value, a date or time value, or a formula. Words, names, and labels are all obviously text values, but so are cell values preceded by an apostrophe (') or formatted as Text. Text values are also called *strings*, and I'll use both terms interchangeably in this chapter.

In Chapter 3, "Building Basic Formulas," you learned about building text formulas in Excel—not that there was much to learn. Text formulas consist only of the concatenation operator (&) used to combine two or more strings into a larger string.

Excel's text functions enable you to take text formulas to a more useful level by giving you numerous ways to manipulate strings. With these functions, you can convert numbers to strings, change lower-case letters to upper case (and vice versa), compare two strings, and more. Table 7.1 summarizes Excel's text functions, and this chapter gives you the details and example uses for most of them.

## Table 7.1   Excel's Text Functions

| Function | Description |
|---|---|
| BAHTTEXT(*number*) | Converts *number* to baht text. |
| CHAR(*number*) | Returns the character that corresponds to the ANSI code given by *number*. |
| CLEAN(*text*) | Removes all nonprintable characters from *text*. |
| CODE(*text*) | Returns the ANSI code for the first character in *text*. |
| CONCATENATE(*text1*,[*text2*],...) | Joins the specified strings into a single string. |
| DOLLAR(*number*,[*decimals*]) | Converts *number* to a string that uses the Currency format. |
| EXACT(*text1*,*text2*) | Compares two strings to see whether they are identical. |
| FIND(*find*,*within*,[*start*]) | Returns the character position of the text *find* within the text *within*. FIND() is case–sensitive. |
| FIXED(*number*,[*decimals*],[*no_commas*]) | Converts *number* to a string that uses the Number format. |
| LEFT(*text*,[*number*]) | Returns the leftmost *number* characters from *text*. |
| LEN(*text*) | Returns the length of *text*. |
| LOWER(*text*) | Converts *text* to lower case. |
| MID(*text*,*start*,*number*) | Returns a *number* of characters from *text* starting at *start*. |
| PROPER(*text*) | Converts *text* to proper case (first letter of each word is capitalized). |
| REPLACE(*old*,*start*,*chars*,*new*) | Replaces the *old* string with the *new* string. |
| REPT(*text*,*number*) | Repeats *text* *number* times. |
| RIGHT(*text*,[*number*]) | Returns the rightmost *number* characters from *text*. |
| SEARCH(*find*,*within*,[*start_num*]) | Returns the character position of the text *find* within the text *within*. SEARCH() is not case-sensitive. |
| SUBSTITUTE(*text*,*old*,*new*,[*num*]) | In *text*, substitutes the *new* string for the *old* string *num* times. |
| T(*value*) | Converts *value* to text. |
| TEXT(*value*,*format*) | Formats *value* and converts it to text. |
| TRIM(*text*) | Removes excess spaces from *text*. |
| UPPER(*text*) | Converts *text* to upper case. |
| VALUE(*text*) | Converts *text* to a number. |

**7**

# Working with Characters and Codes

Every character that you can display on your screen has its own underlying numeric code. For example, the code for the uppercase letter *A* is 65, while the code for the ampersand (&) is 38. These codes apply not only to the alphanumeric characters accessible via your keyboard, but also to "extra" characters that you can display by entering the appropriate code. The collection of these characters is called the ANSI character set, and the numbers assigned to each character are called the ANSI codes.

For example, the ANSI code for the copyright character (©) is 169. To display this character, press Alt+0169, where you use your keyboard's numeric keypad to enter the digits (always including the leading zero for codes higher than 127).

The ANSI codes run from 1 to 255, although the first 31 codes are nonprinting codes that define "characters" such as carriage returns and line feeds.

## The CHAR() Function

Excel enables you to determine the character represented by an ANSI code using the CHAR() function:

CHAR(*number*)

> *number*        The ANSI code, which must be a number between 1 and 255

For example, the following formula displays the copyright symbol (ANSI code 169):

=CHAR(169)

### Generating the ANSI Character Set

Figure 7.1 shows a worksheet that displays the entire ANSI character set (excluding the first 31 nonprinting characters—note, too, that ANSI code 32 represents the space character). In each case, the character is displayed by applying the CHAR() function to the value in the cell to the left.

> **NOTE** The actual character displayed by an ANSI code depends on the font applied to the cell. The characters shown in Figure 7.1 are the ones you see with normal text fonts, such as Arial. However, if you apply a font such as Symbol or Wingdings to the worksheet, you'll see a different set of characters.

> **NOTE** You can download this chapter's example workbooks here:
> www.mcfedries.com/ExcelFormulas/

7

**Figure 7.1**
This worksheet uses the CHAR() function to display each printing member of the ANSI character set.

| Code | CHAR() | Code | CHAR() | Code | CHAR() | Code | CHAR() | Code | CHAR() | Code | CHAR() | Code | CHAR() | Code | CHAR() | Code | CHAR() |
|------|--------|------|--------|------|--------|------|--------|------|--------|------|--------|------|--------|------|--------|------|--------|
| 32 |   | 57 | 9 | 82 | R | 107 | k | 132 | „ | 157 |   | 182 | ¶ | 207 | Ï | 232 | è |
| 33 | ! | 58 | : | 83 | S | 108 | l | 133 | … | 158 | ž | 183 | · | 208 | Đ | 233 | é |
| 34 | " | 59 | ; | 84 | T | 109 | m | 134 | † | 159 | Ÿ | 184 |   | 209 | Ñ | 234 | ê |
| 35 | # | 60 | < | 85 | U | 110 | n | 135 | ‡ | 160 |   | 185 | ¹ | 210 | Ò | 235 | ë |
| 36 | $ | 61 | = | 86 | V | 111 | o | 136 | ˆ | 161 | ¡ | 186 | º | 211 | Ó | 236 | ì |
| 37 | % | 62 | > | 87 | W | 112 | p | 137 | ‰ | 162 | ¢ | 187 | » | 212 | Ô | 237 | í |
| 38 | & | 63 | ? | 88 | X | 113 | q | 138 | Š | 163 | £ | 188 | ¼ | 213 | Õ | 238 | î |
| 39 | ' | 64 | @ | 89 | Y | 114 | r | 139 | ‹ | 164 | ¤ | 189 | ½ | 214 | Ö | 239 | ï |
| 40 | ( | 65 | A | 90 | Z | 115 | s | 140 | Œ | 165 | ¥ | 190 | ¾ | 215 | × | 240 | ð |
| 41 | ) | 66 | B | 91 | [ | 116 | t | 141 |   | 166 | ¦ | 191 | ¿ | 216 | Ø | 241 | ñ |
| 42 | * | 67 | C | 92 | \ | 117 | u | 142 | Ž | 167 | § | 192 | À | 217 | Ù | 242 | ò |
| 43 | + | 68 | D | 93 | ] | 118 | v | 143 |   | 168 | ¨ | 193 | Á | 218 | Ú | 243 | ó |
| 44 | , | 69 | E | 94 | ^ | 119 | w | 144 |   | 169 | © | 194 | Â | 219 | Û | 244 | ô |
| 45 | - | 70 | F | 95 | _ | 120 | x | 145 | ' | 170 | ª | 195 | Ã | 220 | Ü | 245 | õ |
| 46 | . | 71 | G | 96 | ` | 121 | y | 146 | ' | 171 | « | 196 | Ä | 221 | Ý | 246 | ö |
| 47 | / | 72 | H | 97 | a | 122 | z | 147 | " | 172 | ¬ | 197 | Å | 222 | Þ | 247 | ÷ |
| 48 | 0 | 73 | I | 98 | b | 123 | { | 148 | " | 173 | - | 198 | Æ | 223 | ß | 248 | ø |
| 49 | 1 | 74 | J | 99 | c | 124 | \| | 149 | • | 174 | ® | 199 | Ç | 224 | à | 249 | ù |
| 50 | 2 | 75 | K | 100 | d | 125 | } | 150 | – | 175 | ¯ | 200 | È | 225 | á | 250 | ú |
| 51 | 3 | 76 | L | 101 | e | 126 | ~ | 151 | — | 176 | ° | 201 | É | 226 | â | 251 | û |
| 52 | 4 | 77 | M | 102 | f | 127 |   | 152 | ˜ | 177 | ± | 202 | Ê | 227 | ã | 252 | ü |
| 53 | 5 | 78 | N | 103 | g | 128 | € | 153 | ™ | 178 | ² | 203 | Ë | 228 | ä | 253 | ý |
| 54 | 6 | 79 | O | 104 | h | 129 |   | 154 | š | 179 | ³ | 204 | Ì | 229 | å | 254 | þ |
| 55 | 7 | 80 | P | 105 | i | 130 | ‚ | 155 | › | 180 | ´ | 205 | Í | 230 | æ | 255 | ÿ |
| 56 | 8 | 81 | Q | 106 | j | 131 | ƒ | 156 | œ | 181 | µ | 206 | Î | 231 | ç |   |   |

To build the character set shown in Figure 7.1, I entered the ANSI code and CHAR() function at the top of each column, and then filled down to generate the rest of the column. A less tedious method (albeit one with a less useful display) takes advantage of the ROW() function, which returns the row number of the current cell. Assuming that you want to start your table in row 2, you can generate any ANSI character by using the following formula:

```
=CHAR(ROW() + 30)
```

Figure 7.2 shows the results. (The values in column A are generated using the formula =ROW() + 30.)

**Figure 7.2**
This worksheet uses =CHAR(ROW() + 30) to generate the ANSI character set automatically.

| Code | CHAR() |
|------|--------|
| 32 |   |
| 33 | ! |
| 34 | " |
| 35 | # |
| 36 | $ |
| 37 | % |
| 38 | & |
| 39 | ' |
| 40 | ( |
| 41 | ) |
| 42 | * |
| 43 | + |
| 44 | , |
| 45 | - |
| 46 | . |

## Generating a Series of Letters

Excel's Fill handle and <u>D</u>ata, <u>S</u>eries command are great for generating a series of numbers or dates, but they don't do the job when you need a series of letters (such as a, b, c, and so on). However, you can use the CHAR() function in an array formula to generate such a series.

We're concerned with the characters a through z (which correspond to ANSI codes 97 to 122), and A through Z (codes 65 to 90). To generate a series of these letters, follow these steps:

1. Select the range you want to use for the series.

2. Activate in-cell editing by pressing F2.

3. Type the following formula:

   ```
   =CHAR(97 + ROW(range) - ROW(first_cell))
   ```

   In this formula, *range* is the range you selected in step 1, and *first_cell* is a reference to the first cell in *range*. For example, if the selected range is B10:B20, you would type this:

   ```
   =CHAR(97 + ROW(B10:B20) - ROW(B10))
   ```

> **NOTE**
> I'm assuming that you've selected a column for your series. If you've selected a row, replace the ROW() functions in the formula with COLUMN().

4. Press Ctrl+Shift+Enter to enter the formula as an array.

Because you entered this as an array formula, the ROW(*range*) - ROW(*first_cell*) calculation generates a series of numbers (0, 1, 2, and so on) that represent the offset of each cell in the range from the first cell. These offsets are added to 97 to produce the appropriate ANSI codes for the lowercase letters, as shown in Figure 7.3. If you want uppercase letters, replace the 97 with 65 (in Figure 7.3, see the series in row 12).

**Figure 7.3**
Combining the CHAR() and ROW() functions into an array formula to produce a series of letters.

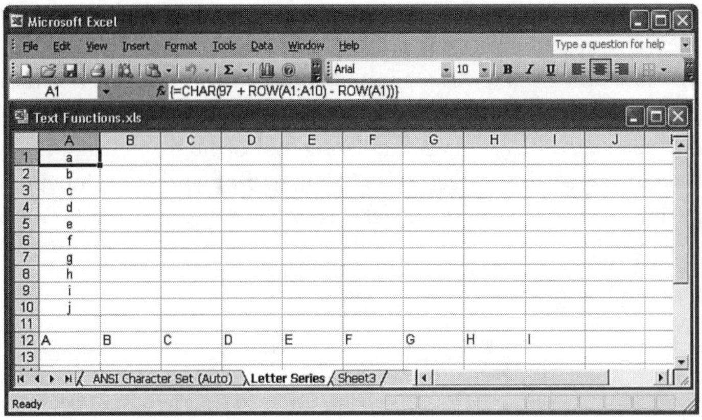

## The CODE() Function

The CODE() function is the opposite of CHAR(). That is, given a text character, CODE() returns its ANSI code value:

CODE(*text*)

> *text*    A character or text string. Note that if you enter a multicharacter string, CODE() returns the ANSI code of the first character in the string.

For example, the following formulas both return 83, the ANSI code of the uppercase letter *S*:

```
=CODE("S")
=CODE("Spacely Sprockets")
```

### Generating a Series of Letters Starting from Any Letter

Earlier in this section, you learned how to combine CHAR() and ROW() in an array formula to generate a series of letters beginning with the letters *a* or *A*. What if you prefer a different starting letter? You can do that by changing the initial value that plugged into the CHAR() function before the offsets are calculated. I used 97 in the previous example to begin the series with the letter *a*, but you could use 98 to start with *b*, 99 to start with *c*, and so on.

Instead of looking up the ANSI code of the character you prefer, however, use the CODE() function to have Excel do it for you:

```
=CHAR(CODE("letter") + ROW(range) - ROW(first_cell))
```

Here, replace *letter* with the letter you want to start the series with. For example, the following formula begins the series with uppercase N (remember to enter this as an array formula in the specified range):

```
=CHAR(CODE("N") + ROW(A1:A13) - ROW(A1))
```

# Converting Text

Excel's forte is number-crunching, so it often seems to give short shrift to strings, particularly when it comes to displaying strings in the worksheet. For example, concatenating a numeric value into a string results in the number being displayed without any formatting, even if the original cell had a numeric format applied to it. Similarly, strings imported from the database or text file can have the wrong case or no formatting. However, as you'll see over the next few sections, Excel offers a number of worksheet functions that enable you to convert strings to a more suitable text format, or for converting between text and numeric values.

## The LOWER() **Function**

The LOWER() function converts a specified string to all-lowercase letters:

LOWER(*text*)

> *text*  The string you want to convert to lower case

For example, the following formula converts the text in cell B10 to lower case:

=LOWER(B10)

The LOWER() function is often used to convert imported data, particularly data imported from a mainframe computer, which often arrives in all-uppercase characters.

## The UPPER() **Function**

The UPPER() function converts a specified string to all-uppercase letters:

UPPER(*text*)

> *text*  The string you want to convert to upper case

For example, the following formula converts the text in cells A5 and B5 to upper case and concatenates the results with a space between them:

=UPPER(A5) & " " & UPPER(B5)

## The PROPER() **Function**

The PROPER() function converts a specified string to proper case, which means the first letter of each word appears in upper case and the rest of the letters appear in lower case:

PROPER(*text*)

> *text*  The string you want to convert to proper case

For example, the following formula, entered as an array, converts the text in the range A1:A10 to proper case:

=PROPER(A1:A10)

# Formatting Text

You learned in Chapter 3 that you can enhance the results of your formulas by using built-in or custom numeric formats to control things such as commas, decimal places, currency symbols, and more. That's fine for cell results, but what about if you want to incorporate a result within a string? For example, consider the following text formula:

="The expense total for this quarter in 2004 is " & F11

No matter how you've formatted the result in F11, the number appears in the string using Excel's General number format. For example, if cell F11 contains $74,400, the previous formula will appear in the cell as follows:

The expense total for this quarter in 2004 is 74400

7

You need some way to format the number within the string. The next three sections show you some Excel functions that let you do just that.

### The DOLLAR() Function

The DOLLAR() function converts a numeric value into a string value that uses the Currency format:

DOLLAR(*number*, [*decimals*])

    *number*      The number you want to convert

    *decimals*      The number of decimals to display (the default is 2)

To fix the string example from the previous section, you need to apply the DOLLAR() function to cell F11:

```
="The expense total for this quarter in 2004 is " & DOLLAR(F11, 0)
```

In this case, the number is formatted with no decimal places. Figure 7.4 shows a variation of this formula in action in cell B16. (The original formula is shown in cell B15.)

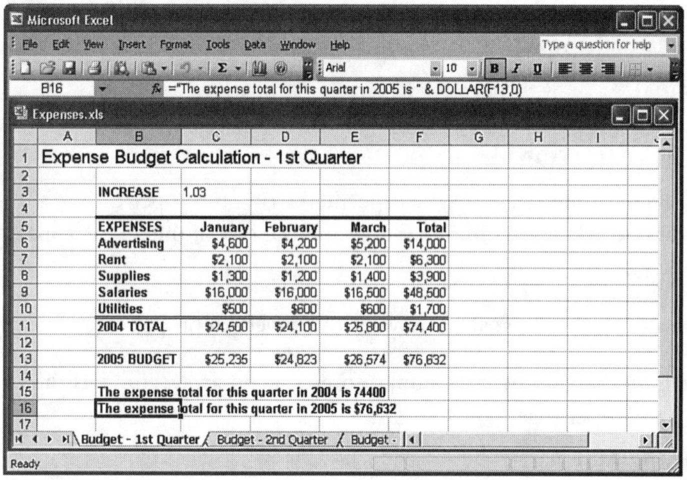

**Figure 7.4**
Use the DOLLAR() function to display a number as a string with the Currency format.

### The FIXED() Function

For other kinds of numbers, you can control the number of decimals and whether commas are inserted as the thousands separator by using the FIXED() function:

FIXED(*number*, [*decimals*], [*no_commas*])

    *number*      The number you want to convert to a string.

    *decimals*      The number of decimals to display (the default is 2).

    *no_commas*      A logical value that determines whether commas are inserted into the string. Use TRUE to suppress commas; use FALSE to include commas (this is the default).

For example, the following formula uses the SUM() function to take a sum over a range and applies the FIXED() function to the result so that it is displayed as a string with commas and no decimal places:

```
="Total show attendance: " & FIXED(SUM(A1:A8), 0, FALSE) & " people."
```

## The TEXT() Function

DOLLAR() and FIXED() are useful functions in specific circumstances. However, if you want total control over the way a number is formatted within a string, or if you want to include dates and times within strings, then the powerful TEXT() function is what you need:

```
TEXT(number, format)
```

| | |
|---|---|
| number | The number, date, or time you want to convert |
| format | The numeric or date/time format you want to apply to number |

The power of the TEXT() function lies in its *format* argument, which is a custom format that specifies exactly how you want the number to appear. You learned about building custom numeric, date, and time formats back in Chapter 3.

→ For the details on custom formatting, **see** "Formatting Numbers, Dates, and Times," **p. 72**.

For example, the following formula uses the AVERAGE() function to take an average over the range A1:A31, and then uses the TEXT() function to apply the custom format #,##0.00°F to the result:

```
="The average temperature was " & TEXT(AVERAGE(A1:A31), "#,##0.00°F")
```

## Displaying When a Workbook Was Last Updated

Many people like to annotate their workbooks by setting Excel in manual calculation mode and entering a NOW() function into a cell (which returns the current date and time). The NOW() function won't update unless you save or recalculate the sheet, so you always know when the sheet was last updated.

Instead of just entering NOW() by itself, you might find it better to preface the date with an explanatory string, such as This workbook last updated:. To do this, you can enter the following formula:

```
="This workbook last updated: " & NOW()
```

Unfortunately, your output will look something like this:

```
This workbook last updated: 38572.51001
```

The number 38572.51001 is Excel's internal representation of a date and time (the number to the left of the decimal is the date, and the number to the right of the decimal is the time). To get a properly formatted date and time, use the TEXT() function. For example, to format the results of the NOW() function in the MM/DD/YY HH:MM format, use the following formula:

```
="This workbook last updated: " & TEXT(NOW(), "mm/dd/yy hh:mm")
```

7

# Manipulating Text

The rest of this chapter takes you into the real heart of Excel's text-manipulation tricks. The functions you'll learn about over the next few pages will all be useful, to be sure, but you'll see that, by combining two or more of these functions into a single formula, you can bring out the amazing versatility of Excel's text-manipulation prowess.

## Removing Unwanted Characters from a String

Characters imported from databases and text files often come with all kinds of string baggage in the form of extra characters that you don't need. These could be extra spaces in the string, or line feeds, carriage returns, and other nonprintable characters embedded in the string. To fix these problems, Excel offers a couple of functions: TRIM() and CLEAN().

### The TRIM() Function

You use the TRIM() function to remove excess spaces within a string:

TRIM(*text*)

    *text*        The string from which you want the excess spaces removed

Here, "excess" means all spaces before and after the string, as well as two or more consecutive spaces within the string. In the latter case, TRIM() removes all but one of the consecutive spaces.

Figure 7.5 shows the TRIM() function at work. Each string in the range A2:A7 contains a number of excess spaces before, within, or after the name. The TRIM() functions appear in column C. To help confirm the TRIM() function's operation, I use the LEN() text function in columns B and D. LEN() returns the number of characters in a specified string, using the following syntax:

LEN(*text*)

    *text*        The string for which you want to know the number of characters

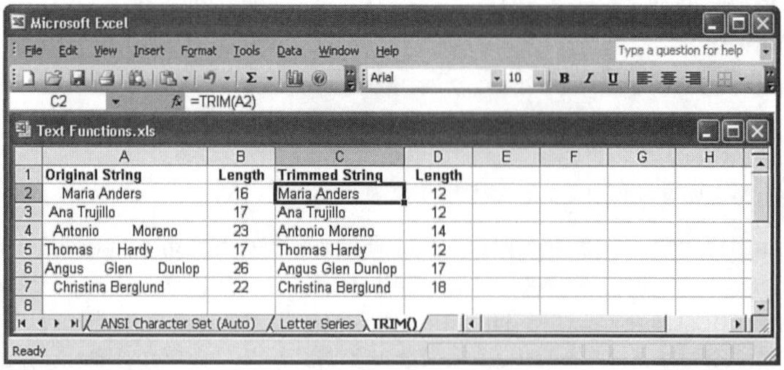

**Figure 7.5**
Use the TRIM() function to remove extra spaces from a string.

### The CLEAN() **Function**

You use the CLEAN() function to remove nonprintable characters from a string:

CLEAN(*text*)

> *text*        The string from which you want the nonprintable characters removed

Recall that the nonprintable characters are the codes 1 through 31 of the ANSI character set. The CLEAN() function is most often used to remove line feeds (ANSI 10) or carriage returns (ANSI 13) from multiline data. Figure 7.6 shows an example.

**Figure 7.6**
Use the CLEAN() function to remove nonprintable characters such as line feeds from a string.

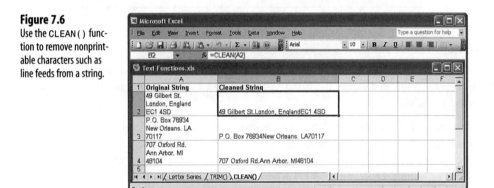

## The REPT() **Function: Repeating a Character**

The REPT() function repeats a string a specified number of times:

REPT(*text*, *number*)

> *text*        The character or string you want to repeat
>
> *number*   The number of times to repeat *text*

### Padding a Cell

The REPT() function is sometimes used to pad a cell with characters. For example, you can use it to add leading or trailing dots in a cell. Here's a formula that creates trailing dots after a string:

```
="Advertising" & REPT(".", 20 - LEN("Advertising"))
```

This formula writes the string Advertising and then uses REPT() to repeat the dot character according to the following expression: 20 - LEN("Advertising"). This expression ensures that a total of 20 characters is written to the cell. Because Advertising is 11 characters, the expression result is 9, which means that nine dots are added to the right of the string. If the string was "Rent" instead (4 characters), 16 dots would be padded. Figure 7.7 shows how this technique creates a "dot follower" effect. Note that, for best results, the cells need to be formatted in a monotype font, such as Courier New.

**7**

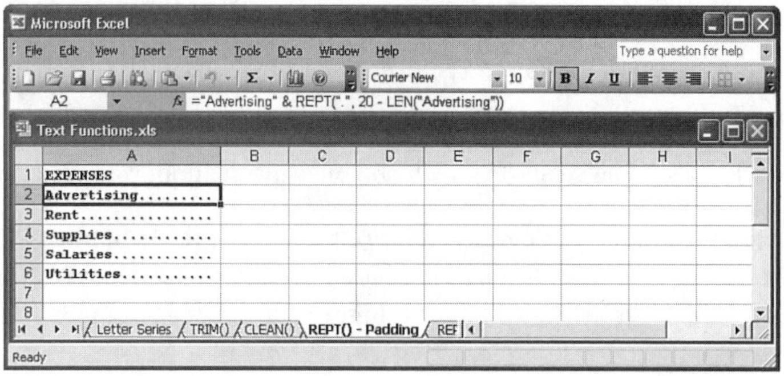

**Figure 7.7**
Use the REPT() function to pad a cell with characters, such as the dot followers shown here.

## Building Text Charts

A more common use for the REPT() function is to build text-based charts. In this case, you use a numeric result in a cell as the REPT() function's *number* argument, and the repeated character then "charts" the result.

A simple example is a basic histogram, which shows the frequency of a sample over an interval. Figure 7.8 shows a text histogram in which the intervals are listed in column A and the frequencies are listed in column B. The REPT() function creates the histogram in column C by repeating the vertical bar (|) according to each frequency, as in this example formula:

```
=REPT("|", B4)
```

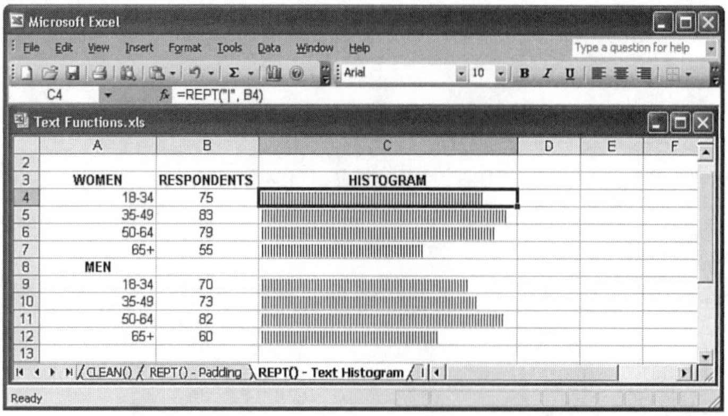

**Figure 7.8**
Using the REPT() function to create a text-based histogram.

With a simple trick, you can turn the histogram into a text-based bar chart, as shown in Figure 7.9. The trick here is to format the "chart" cells with the Webdings font. In this font, the letter *g* is represented by a block character, and repeating that character produces a solid bar. (To get the repeat value, I multiplied the percentages in column B by 100 to get a whole number. To keep the bars relatively short, I divided the result by 5.)

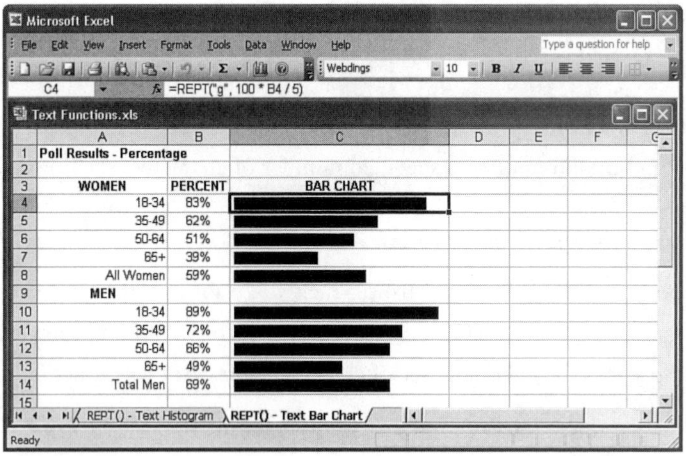

**Figure 7.9**
Using the REPT() function to create a text-based bar chart.

## Extracting a Substring

String values often contain smaller strings, or *substrings*, that you need to work with. In a column of full names, for example, you might want to deal with only the last names so that you can sort the data. Similarly, you might want to extract the first few letters of a company name to include in an account number for that company.

Excel gives you three functions for extracting substrings, as described in the next three sections.

### The LEFT() Function

The LEFT() function returns a specified number of characters starting from the left of a string:

```
LEFT(text, [num_chars])
```

| | |
|---|---|
| *text* | The string from which you want to extract the substring |
| *num_chars* | The number of characters you want to extract from the left (the default value is 1) |

For example, the following formula returns the substring Karen:

```
=LEFT("Karen Elizabeth Hammond", 5)
```

### The RIGHT() Function

The RIGHT() function returns a specified number of characters starting from the right of a string:

```
RIGHT(text, [num_chars])
```

| | |
|---|---|
| *text* | The string from which you want to extract the substring |
| *num_chars* | The number of characters you want to extract from the right (the default value is 1) |

7

For example, the following formula returns the substring Hammond:

```
=RIGHT("Karen Elizabeth Hammond", 7)
```

## The MID() Function

The MID() function returns a specified number of characters starting from any point within a string:

```
MID(text, start_num, num_chars)
```

| | |
|---|---|
| *text* | The string from which you want to extract the substring |
| *start_num* | The character position at which you want to start extracting the substring |
| *num_chars* | The number of characters you want to extract |

For example, the following formula returns the substring Elizabeth:

```
=MID("Karen Elizabeth Hammond", 7, 9)
```

## Converting Text to Sentence Case

Microsoft Word's Change Case command has a "sentence case" option that converts a string to all-lowercase letters, except for the first letter, which is converted to upper case (just as the letters would appear in a normal sentence). You saw earlier that Excel has LOWER(), UPPER(), and PROPER() functions, but nothing that can produce sentence case directly. However, it's possible to construct a formula that does this using the LOWER() and UPPER() functions combined with the LEFT() and RIGHT() functions.

You begin by extracting the leftmost letter and converting it to uppercase (assume that the string is in cell A1):

```
UPPER(LEFT(A1))
```

Then you extract everything to the right of the first letter and convert it to lower case:

```
LOWER(RIGHT(A1, LEN(A1) - 1))
```

Finally, you concatenate these two expressions into the complete formula:

```
=UPPER(LEFT(A1)) & LOWER(RIGHT(A1, LEN(A1) - 1))
```

Figure 7.10 shows a worksheet that puts this formula through its paces.

## A Date-Conversion Formula

If you import mainframe or server data into your worksheets, or if you import online service data such as stock market quotes, you'll often end up with date formats that Excel can't handle. One common example is the YYMMDD format (for example, 20040823).

To convert this value into a date that Excel can work with, you can use the LEFT(), MID(), and RIGHT() functions. If the unrecognized date is in cell A1, LEFT(A1, 4) extracts the year, MID(A1,3,2) extracts the month, and RIGHT(A1,2) extracts the day. Plugging these functions into a DATE() function gives Excel a date it can handle:

```
=DATE(LEFT(A1,2), MID(A1,3,2), RIGHT(A1,2))
```

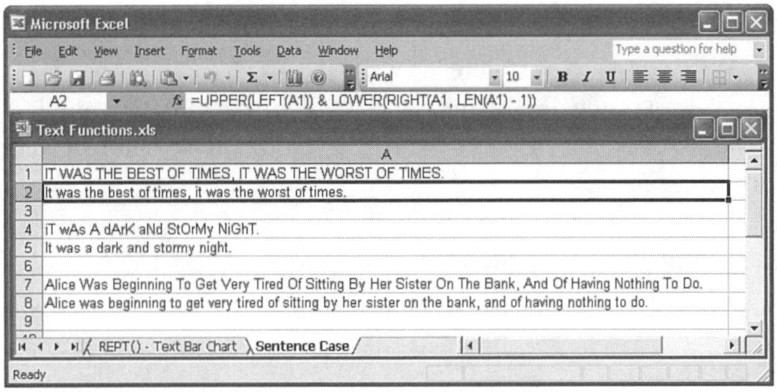

**Figure 7.10**
The LEFT ( ) and RIGHT ( ) functions combine with the UPPER ( ) and LOWER ( ) functions to produce a formula that converts text to sentence case.

→   To learn more about the DATE ( ) function, **see** "DATE ( ): Returning Any Date," **p. 205**.

## CASE STUDY

### Generating Account Numbers

Many companies generate supplier or customer account numbers by combining part of the account's name with a numeric value. Excel's text functions make it easy to generate such account numbers automatically.

To begin, let's extract the first three letters of the company name and convert them to upper case for easier reading (assume that the name is in cell A2):

```
UPPER(LEFT(A2, 3))
```

Next, we'll generate the numeric portion of the account number by grabbing the row number: ROW(A2). However, it's best to keep all account numbers a uniform length, so we'll use the TEXT ( ) function to pad the row number with zeroes:

```
TEXT(ROW(A2), "0000")
```

Here's the complete formula, and Figure 7.11 shows some examples:

```
=UPPER(LEFT(A2, 3)) & TEXT(ROW(A2), "0000")
```

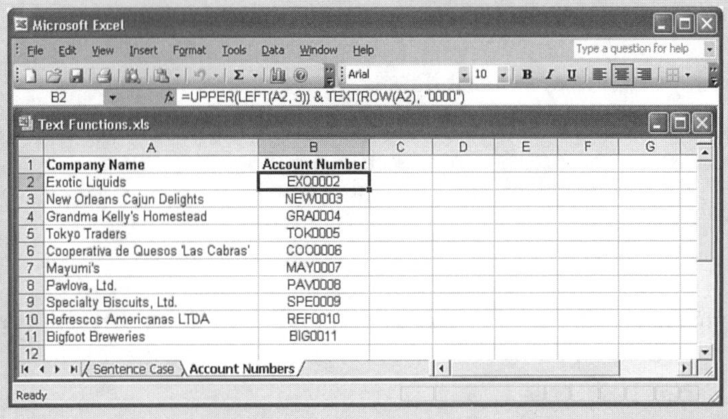

**Figure 7.11**
This worksheet uses the UPPER(), LEFT(), and TEXT() functions to automatically generate account numbers from company names.

## Searching for Substrings

You can take Excel's text functions up a notch or two by searching for substrings within a given text. For example, in a string that includes a person's first and last name, you can find out where the space falls between the names and then use that fact to extract either the first name or the last name.

### The FIND() and SEARCH() Functions

Searching for substrings is handled by the FIND() and SEARCH() functions:

FIND(*find_text, within_text,* [*start_num*])

SEARCH(*find_text, within_text,* [*start_num*])

| | |
|---|---|
| *find_text* | The substring you want to look for |
| *within_text* | The string in which you want to look |
| *start_num* | The character position at which you want to start looking (the default is 1) |

Here are some notes to bear in mind when using these functions:

- These functions return the character position of the first instance (after the *start_num* character position) of *find_text* in *within_text*.
- Use SEARCH() for non–case-sensitive searches. For example, SEARCH("e", "Expenses") returns 1.
- Use FIND() for case-sensitive searches. For example, FIND("e", "Expenses") returns 4.
- These functions return the #VALUE! error if *find_text* is not in *within_text*.
- In the *find_text* argument of SEARCH(), use a question mark (?) to match any single character.
- In the *find_text* argument of SEARCH(), use an asterisk (*) to match any number of characters.
- To include the characters ? or * in a SEARCH() operation, precede each one in the *find_text* argument with a tilde (~).

### Extracting a First Name or Last Name

If you have a range of cells containing people's first and last names, it can often be advantageous to extract these names from each string. For example, you might want to store the first and last names in separate ranges for later importing into a database table. Or perhaps you need to construct a new range using a *Last Name, First Name* structure for sorting the names.

The solution is to use the FIND() function to find the space that separates the first and last names, and then use either the LEFT() function to extract the first name or the RIGHT() function to extract the last name.

For the first name, you would use the following formula (assuming that the full name is in cell A2):

```
=LEFT(A2, FIND(" ", A2) - 1)
```

Notice how the formula subtracts 1 from the `FIND(" ", A2)` result, to avoid including the space in the extracted substring. You can use this formula in more general circumstances to extract the first word of any multiword string.

For the last name, you need to build a similar formula using the `RIGHT()` function:

```
=RIGHT(A3, LEN(A3) - FIND(" ", A3))
```

To extract the correct number of letters, the formula takes the length of the original string and subtracts the position of the space. You can use this formula in more general circumstances to extract the second word in any two-word string.

Figure 7.12 shows a worksheet that puts both formulas to work.

**Figure 7.12**
Use the `LEFT()` and `FIND()` functions to extract the first name; use the `RIGHT()` and `FIND()` functions to extract the last name.

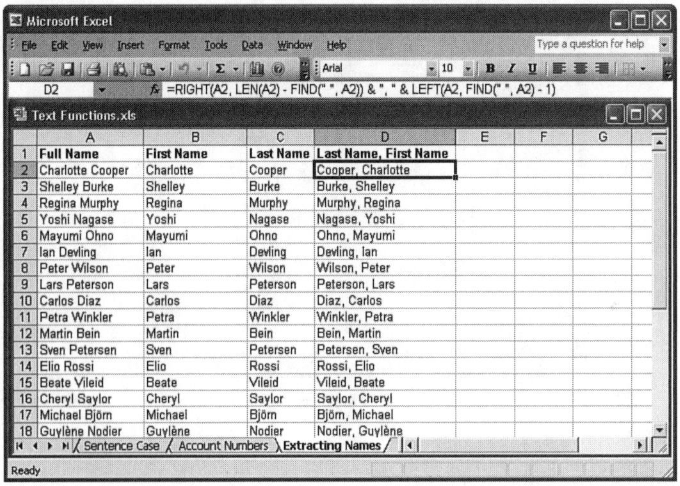

→ These formulas cause an error in any string that contains only a single word. To learn how to allow for this, **see** "Avoiding Text Formula Errors," **p. 179**.

## Extracting First Name, Last Name, and Middle Initial

If the full name you have to work with includes the person's middle initial, the formula for extracting the first name remains the same. However, you need to adjust the formula for finding the last name. There are a couple of ways to go about this, but the method I'll show you utilizes a useful `FIND()` and `SEARCH()` trick. Specifically, if you want to find the *second* instance of a substring, start the search one character position after the *first* instance of the substring. Here's an example string:

```
Karen E. Hammond
```

Assuming that this string is in A2, the formula =FIND(" ", A2) returns 6, the position of the first space. If you want to find the position of the second space, instead set the FIND() function's *start_num* argument to 7—or, more generally, to the location of the first space, plus 1:

```
=FIND(" ", A2, FIND(" ",A32) + 1)
```

You can then apply this result within the RIGHT() function to extract the last name:

```
=RIGHT(A2, LEN(A2) - FIND(" ", A2, FIND(" ", A2) +1))
```

To extract the middle initial, search for the period (.) and use MID() to extract the letter before it:

```
=MID(A2, FIND(".", A2) - 1, 1)
```

Figure 7.13 shows a worksheet that demonstrates these techniques.

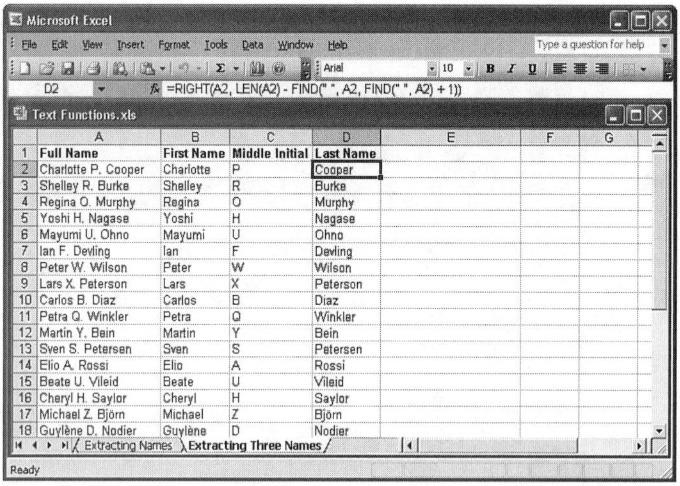

**Figure 7.13**
Apply FIND() after the first instance of a substring to find the second instance of the substring.

## Determining the Column Letter

Excel's COLUMN() function returns the column number of a specified cell. For example, for a cell in column A, COLUMN() returns 1. This is handy, as you saw earlier in this chapter ("Generating a Series of Letters"), but in some cases you might prefer to know the actual column letter.

This is a tricky proposition because the letters run from *A* to *Z*, then *AA* to *AZ*, and so on. However, Excel's CELL() function can return (among other things) the address of a specified cell in absolute format—for example, $A$2 or $AB$10. To get the column letter, you need to extract the substring between the two dollar signs. It's clear to begin with that the substring will always start at the second character position, so we can begin with the following formula:

```
=MID(CELL("Address", A2), 2, num_chars)
```

→ To learn more about the CELL() function, **see** "The CELL() Function," **p. 172**.

The *num_chars* value will be either 1 or 2, depending on the column. Notice, however, that the position of the second dollar will either be 3 or 4, depending on the column. In other words, the length of the substring will always be two less than the position of the second dollar sign. So, the following expression will give the *num_chars* value:

```
FIND("$", CELL("address",A2), 3) - 2
```

Here, then, is the full formula:

```
=MID(CELL("Address", A2), 2, FIND("$", CELL("address", A2), 3) - 2)
```

Getting the column letter of the current cell is slightly shorter:

```
=MID(CELL("Address"), 2, FIND("$", CELL("address"), 3) - 2)
```

## Substituting One Substring for Another

The Office programs (and, indeed, most Windows programs) come with a Replace command that enables you to search for some text and then replace it with some other string. Excel's collection of worksheet functions also comes with such a feature in the guise of the REPLACE() and SUBSTITUTE() functions.

### The REPLACE() Function

Here's the syntax of the REPLACE() function:

```
REPLACE(old_text, start_num, num_chars, new_text)
```

| | |
|---|---|
| *old_text* | The original string that contains the substring you want to replace |
| *start_num* | The character position at which you want to start replacing |
| *num_chars* | The number of characters to replace |
| *new_text* | The substring you want to use as the replacement |

The tricky parts of this function are the *start_num* and *num_chars* arguments. How do you know where to start and how much to replace? This isn't hard if you know the original string in which the replacement is going to take place and if you know the replacement string. For example, consider the following string:

```
Expense Budget for 2004
```

To replace 2004 with 2005, and assuming that the string is in cell A1, the following formula does the job:

```
=REPLACE(A1, 20, 4, "2005")
```

However, it's a pain to have to calculate by hand the *start_num* and *num_chars* arguments. And in more general situations, you might not even know these values. Therefore, you need to calculate them:

- To determine the *start_num* value, use the FIND() or SEARCH() functions to locate the substring you want to replace.
- To determine the *num_chars* value, use the LEN() function to get the length of the replacement text.

**7**

The revised formula then looks something like this (assuming that the original string is in A1 and the replacement string is in A2):

```
=REPLACE(A1, FIND("2004", A1), LEN("2004"), A2)
```

## The SUBSTITUTE() Function

These extra steps make the REPLACE() function unwieldy, so most people use the more straightforward SUBSTITUTE() function:

```
SUBSTITUTE(text, old_text, new_text, [instance_num])
```

| | |
|---|---|
| *text* | The original string that contains the substring you want to replace |
| *old_text* | The substring you want to replace |
| *new_text* | The substring you want to use as the replacement |
| *instance_num* | The number of replacements to make within the string (the default is all instances) |

In the example from the previous section, the following simpler formula does the same thing:

```
=SUBSTITUTE(A1, "2004", "2005")
```

## Removing a Character from a String

Earlier you learned about the CLEAN() function, which removes nonprintable characters from a string, as well as the TRIM() function, which removes excess spaces from a string. A common text scenario involves removing all instances of a particular character from a string. For example, you might want to remove spaces from a string or apostrophes from a name.

Here's a generic formula that does this:

```
=SUBSTITUTE(text, character, "")
```

Here, replace *text* with the original string and *character* with the character you want to remove. For example, the following formula removes all the spaces from the string in cell A1:

```
=SUBSTITUTE(A1, " ", "")
```

> **NOTE**
> One surprising use of the SUBSTITUTE() function is to count the number of characters that appear in a string. The trick here is that if you remove a particular character from a string, the difference in length between the original string and the resulting string is the same as the number of times the character appeared in the original string. For example, the string expenses has eight characters. If you remove all the e's, the resulting string is xpnss, which has five characters. The difference is 3, which is how many e's there were in the original string.
>
> To calculate this in a formula, use the LEN() function and subtract the length of a string with the character removed from the length of the original string. Here's the formula that counts the number of e's for a string in cell A1:
> ```
> =LEN(A1) - LEN(SUBSTITUTE(A1, "i", ""))
> ```

## Removing Two Different Characters from a String

It's possible to nest one SUBSTITUTE() function inside another to remove two different characters from a string. For example, first consider the following expression, which uses SUBSTITUTE() to remove periods from a string:

```
SUBSTITUTE(A1, ".", "")
```

Because this expression returns a string, you can use that result as the *text* argument in another SUBSTITUTE() function. Here, then, is a formula that removes both periods and spaces from a string in cell A1:

```
=SUBSTITUTE(SUBSTITUTE(A1, ".", ""), " ", "")
```

## CASE STUDY

## Generating Account Numbers, Part 2

The formula I showed you earlier for automatically generating account numbers from an account name produces valid numbers only if the first three letters of the name are letters. If you have names in which characters other than letters appear, you need to remove those characters before generating the account number. For example, if you have account names such as J.D. BigBelly, you need to remove periods and spaces before generating the account name. You can do this by adding the expression from the previous section to the formula for generating an account name from earlier in this chapter. Specifically, you replace the cell address in the LEFT() with the nested SUBSTITUTE() functions, as shown in Figure 7.14. Notice that the formula still works on account names that begin with three letters.

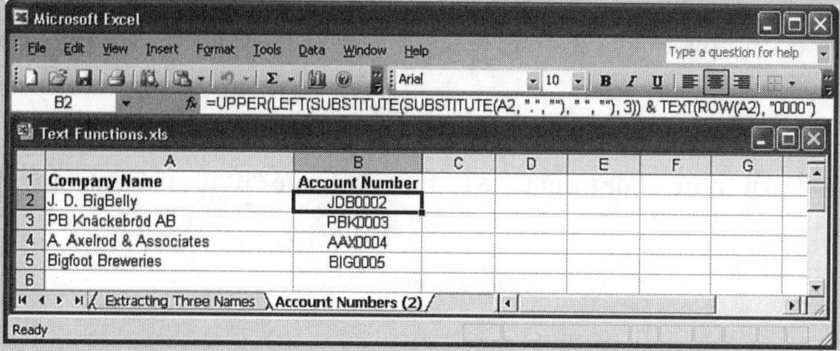

**Figure 7.14**
This worksheet uses nested SUBSTITUTE() functions to remove periods and spaces from account names before generating the account numbers.

## Removing Line Feeds

Earlier in this chapter, you learned about the CLEAN() function, which removes nonprintable characters from a string. In the example, I used CLEAN() to remove the line feeds from a multiline cell entry. However, you might have noticed a small problem with the result: There was no space between the end of one line and the beginning of the next line (see Figure 7.6).

7

If all you're worried about is line feeds, use the following SUBSTITUTE() formula instead of the CLEAN() function:

```
=SUBSTITUTE(A2, CHAR(10), " ")
```

This formula replaces the line feed character (ANSI code 10) with a space, resulting in a proper string, as shown in Figure 7.15.

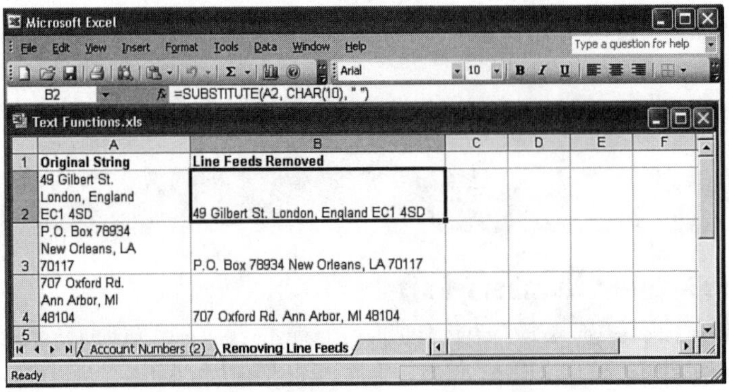

**Figure 7.15**
This worksheet uses SUBSTITUTE() to replace each line feed character with a space.

## From Here

- For the details on custom formatting, **see** "Formatting Numbers, Dates, and Times," **p. 72**.
- For a general discuss of function syntax, **see** "The Structure of a Function," **p. 126**.
- To learn how to avoid some text formula pitfalls, **see** "Avoiding Text Formula Errors," **p. 179**.
- To learn more about the CELL() function, **see** "The CELL() Function," **p. 172**.
- To learn more about the DATE() function, **see** "DATE(): Returning Any Date," **p. 205**.

7

# Working with Logical and Information Functions

I mentioned back in Chapter 6, "Using Functions," that one of the advantages to using Excel's worksheet functions is that they enable you to build formulas that perform actions that are simply not possible with the standard operators and operands.

This idea becomes readily apparent when you learn about those functions that can add to your worksheet models the two cornerstones of good business analysis—intelligence and knowledge. You get these via Excel's logical and information functions, which I describe in detail in this chapter.

## Adding Intelligence with Logical Functions

In the computer world, we *very* loosely define something as *intelligent* if it can perform tests on its environment and act in accordance with the results of those tests. However, computers are binary beasts, so "acting in accordance with the results of a test" means that the machine can do only one of two things. Still, even with this limited range of options, you'll be amazed at how much intelligence you can bring to your worksheets. Your formulas will actually be able to test the values in cells and ranges, and then return results based on those tests.

This is all done with Excel's logical functions, which are designed to create decision-making formulas. For example, you can test cell contents to see whether they're numbers or labels, or you can test formula results for errors. Table 8.1 summarizes Excel's logical functions.

8

### Table 8.1  Excel's Logical Functions

| Function | Description |
|---|---|
| AND(logical1,[logical2],...) | Returns TRUE if all the arguments are true |
| FALSE() | Returns FALSE |
| IF(logical_test,true_expr,[false_expr]) | Performs a logical test and returns a value based on the result |
| NOT(logical) | Reverses the logical value of the argument |
| OR(logical1,[logical2],...) | Returns TRUE if any argument is true |
| TRUE() | Returns TRUE |

## Using the IF() Function

I don't think I'm exaggerating even the slightest when I tell you that the royal road to becoming an accomplished Excel formula builder involves mastering the IF() function. If you become comfortable wielding this function, a whole new world of formula prowess and convenience opens up to you. Yes, IF() is *that* powerful.

To help you master this crucial Excel feature, I'm going to spend a lot of time on it in this chapter. You'll get copious examples that show you how to use it in real-world situations.

### IF(): The Simplest Case

Let's start with the simplest version of the IF() function:

```
IF(logical_test, value_if_true)
```

| | |
|---|---|
| logical_test | A logical expression—that is, an expression that returns TRUE or FALSE (or their equivalent numeric values: 0 for FALSE and any other number for TRUE) |
| value_if_true | The value returned by the function if *logical_test* evaluates to TRUE |

For example, consider the following formula:

```
=IF(A1 >= 1000, "It's big!")
```

The logical expression A1 >= 1000 is used as the test. If this proves to be true (that is, if the value in cell A1 is greater than or equal to 1,000), the function returns the string It's big!. (If A1 is less than 1,000, the formula returns FALSE.)

Another common use for the simple IF() test is to flag values that meet a specific condition. For example, suppose you have a worksheet that shows the percentage increase or decrease in the sales of a long list of products. It would be useful to be able to flag just those products that had a sales decrease. A basic formula for doing this would look something like this:

```
=IF(cell < 0, flag)
```

Here, *cell* is the cell you want to test, and *flag* is some sort of text that you use to point out a negative value. Here's an example:

```
=IF(B2 < 0, "<<<<<")
```

A slightly more sophisticated version of this formula would vary the flag, depending on the negative value. That is, the larger the negative number was, the more less-than signs (in this case) the formula would display. This can be done using the REPT() function discussed in Chapter 7, "Working with Text Functions":

```
REPT("<", B2 * -100)
```

→ For the details on the REPT() function, **see** "The REPT() Function: Repeating a Character," **p. 143**.

This expression multiplies the percentage value by –100 and then uses the result as the number of times the less-than sign is repeated. Here's the revised IF() formula:

```
=IF(B2 < 0, REPT("<", B2 * -100))
```

Figure 8.1 shows how it works in practice.

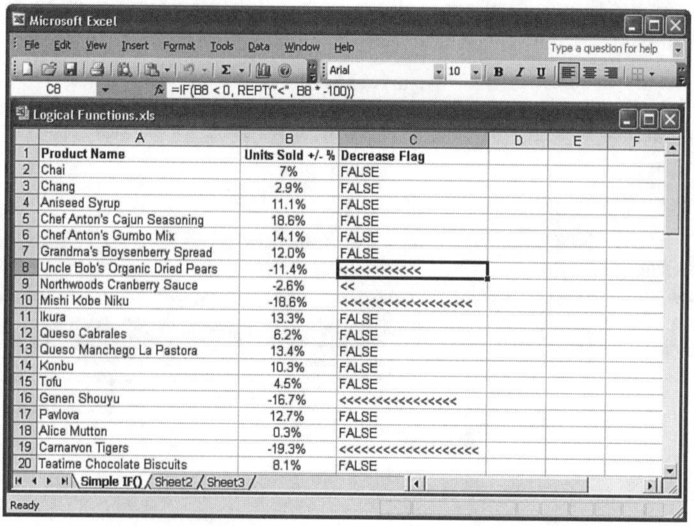

**Figure 8.1**
This worksheet uses the IF() function to test for negative values and then uses REPT() to display a flag for those values.

**NOTE**  You can download this chapter's example workbooks here:
www.mcfedries.com/ExcelFormulas/

## Handling a FALSE Result

As you can see in Figure 8.1, if the result of the IF() condition calculates to FALSE, the function returns FALSE as its result. That's not inherently bad, but our worksheet would look tidier (and, hence, be more useful) if the formula returned the null string (" ") instead.

To do this, you need to use the full IF() function syntax:

```
IF(logical_test, value_if_true, value_if_falsee)
```

| | |
|---|---|
| *logical_test* | A logical expression—that is, an expression that returns TRUE or FALSE (or their equivalent numeric values: 0 for FALSE and any other number for TRUE) |
| *value_if_true* | The value returned by the function if *logical_test* evaluates to TRUE |
| *value_if_false* | The value returned by the function if *logical_test* evaluates to FALSE |

For example, consider the following formula:

```
=IF(A1 >= 1000, "It's big!", "It's not big!")
```

This time, if cell A1 contains a value that's less than 1,000, the formula returns the string It's not big!.

For the negative value flag example, use the following revised version of the formula to return no value if the cell contains a non-negative number:

```
=IF(B2 < 0, REPT("<", B2 * -100), "")
```

As you can see in Figure 8.2, the resulting worksheet looks much tidier than the first version.

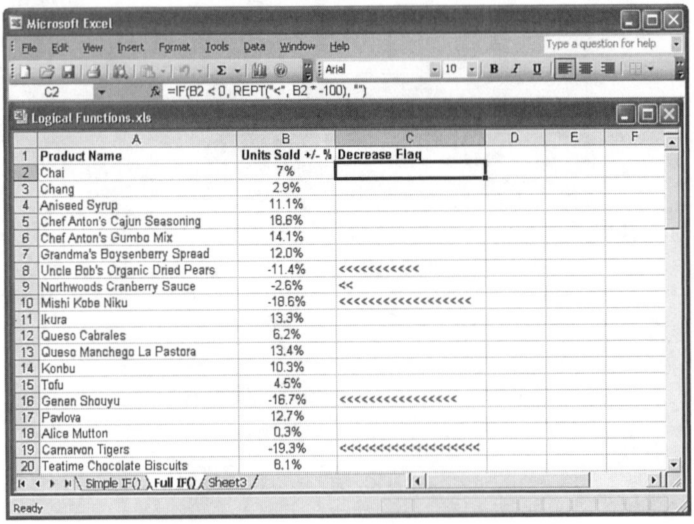

**Figure 8.2**
This worksheet uses the full IF() syntax to return no value if the cell being tested contains a non-negative number.

### Avoiding Division by Zero

As you saw in Chapter 5, "Troubleshooting Formulas," Excel displays the #DIV/0! error if a formula tries to divide a quantity by 0. To avoid this error, you can use IF() to test the divisor and ensure that it's nonzero before performing your division.

→ To learn about the #DIV/0! error, **see** "#DIV/0!," **p. 108**.

For example, the basic equation for calculating gross margin is (Sales – Expenses)/Sales. To make sure that Sales isn't zero, use the following formula (I'm assuming here that you have cells named Sales and Expenses that contain the appropriate values):

```
=IF(Sales <> 0, (Sales - Expenses)/Sales, "Sales are zero!")
```

If the logical expression Sales <> 0 is true, that means Sales is nonzero, so the gross margin calculation can proceed. If Sales <> 0 is false, the Sales value is 0, so the message Sales are zero! is displayed instead.

## Performing Multiple Logical Tests

The capability to perform a logical test on a cell is a powerful weapon, indeed. You'll find endless uses for the basic IF() function in your everyday worksheets. The problem, however, is that the everyday world often presents us with situations that are more complicated than can be handled in a basic IF() function's logical expression. It's often the case that you have to test two or more conditions before you can make a decision.

To handle these more complex scenarios, Excel offers several techniques for performing two or more logical tests: nesting IF() functions, the AND() function, and the OR() function. You learn about these techniques over the next few sections.

### Nesting IF() Functions

When building models using IF(), it's common to come upon a *second* fork in the road when evaluating either the *value_if_true* or *value_if_false* arguments.

For example, consider the variation of our formula that outputs a description based on the value in cell A1:

```
=IF(A1 >= 1000, "Big!", "Not big")
```

What if you wanted to return a different string for values greater than, say, 10,000? In other words, if the condition A1 > 1000 proves to be true, you want to run another test that checks to see if A1 > 10000. You can handle this scenario by nesting a *second* IF() function inside the first as the *value_if_true* argument:

```
=IF(A1 >= 1000, IF(A1 >= 10000, "Really big!!", "Big!"), "Not big")
```

If A1 > 1000 returns TRUE, the formula evaluates the nested IF(), which returns Really big!! if A1 > 10000 is TRUE, and returns Big! if it's FALSE; if A1 > 1000 returns FALSE, the formula returns Not big.

Note, too, that you can nest the IF() function in the *value_if_false* argument. For example, if you wanted to return the description Small for a cell value less than 100, you would use this version of the formula:

```
=IF(A1 >= 1000, "Big!", IF(A1 < 100, "Small", "Not big"))
```

## Calculating Tiered Bonuses

A good time to use nested IF() functions arises when you need to calculate a "tiered" payment or charge. That is, if a certain value is X, you want one result; if the value is Y, you want a second result; and if the value is Z, you want a third result.

For example, suppose you want to calculate tiered bonuses for a sales team as follows:

- If the salesperson did not meet the sales target, no bonus is given.
- If the salesperson exceeded the sales target by less than 10%, a bonus of $1,000 is awarded.
- If the salesperson exceeded the sales target by 10% or more, a bonus of $10,000 is awarded.

Here's a formula that handles these rules:

```
=IF(D2 < 0, "", IF(D2 < 0.1, 1000, 10000))
```

If the value in D2 is negative, nothing is returned; if the value in D2 is less than 10%, 1000 is returned; if the value in D2 is greater than or equal to 10%, 10000 is returned. Figure 8.3 shows this formula in action.

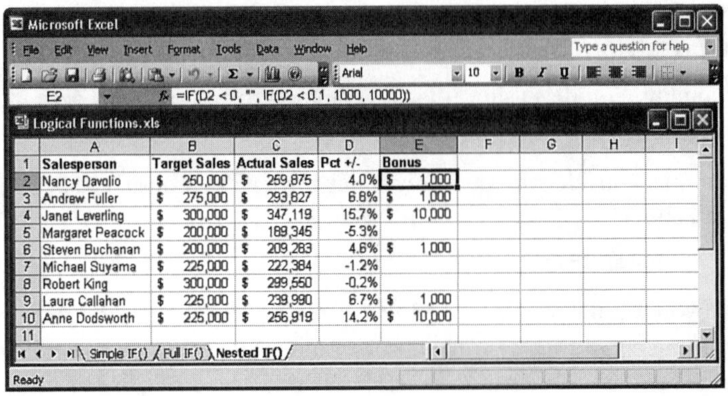

**Figure 8.3**
This worksheet uses nested IF() functions to calculate a tiered bonus payment.

## The AND() Function

It's often necessary to perform an action if and only if two conditions are true. For example, you might want to pay a salesperson a bonus if and only if dollar sales exceeded the budget *and* unit sales also exceeded the budget. If either the dollar sales or the unit sales fell below budget (or if they both fell below budget), no bonus is paid. In Boolean logic, this is called an *And* condition because one expression *and* another must be true for a positive result.

In Excel, And conditions are handled, appropriately enough, by the AND() logical function:

```
AND(logical1, [logical2,...])
```

| | |
|---|---|
| logical1 | The first logical condition to test. |
| logical2,... | The second logical condition to test. You can enter as many conditions as you need. |

The AND() result is calculated as follows:

- If *all* the arguments return TRUE (or any nonzero number), AND() returns TRUE.
- If one or more of the arguments return FALSE (or 0), AND() returns FALSE.

You can use the AND() function anywhere you would use a logical formula, but it's most often pressed into service as the logical condition in an IF() function. In other words, if all the logical conditions in the AND() function are TRUE, then IF() returns its *value_if_true* result; if one or more of the logical conditions in the AND() function are FALSE, then IF() returns its *value_if_false* result. Here's an example:

```
=IF(AND(B2 > 0, C2 > 0), "1000", "No bonus")
```

If the value in B2 is greater than 0 and the value in C2 is greater than 0, the formula returns 1000; otherwise, it returns No bonus.

## Slotting Values into Categories

A good use for the AND() function is to slot items into categories that consist of a range of values. For example, suppose you have a set of poll or survey results, and you want to categorize these results based on the following age ranges: 18–34, 35–49, 50–64, and 65+. Assuming that each respondent's age is in cell B9, the following AND() function can serve as the logical test for entry into the 18–34 category:

```
AND(B9 >= 18, B9 <= 34)
```

If the response is in C9, the following formula will display it if the respondent is in the 18–34 age group:

```
=IF(AND(B9 >= 18, B9 <= 34), C9, "")
```

Figure 8.4 tries this on some data. Here are the formulas used for the other age groups:

```
35-49: =IF(AND(B9 >= 35, B9 <= 49), C9, "")
50-64: =IF(AND(B9 >= 50, B9 <= 64), C9, "")
65+: =IF(B9 >= 65, C9, "")
```

## The OR() Function

Similar to an And condition is the situation when you need to take an action if one thing *or* another is true. For example, you might want to pay a salesperson a bonus if he or she exceeded the dollar sales budget *or* if he or she exceeded the unit sales budget. In Boolean logic, this is called an *Or* condition.

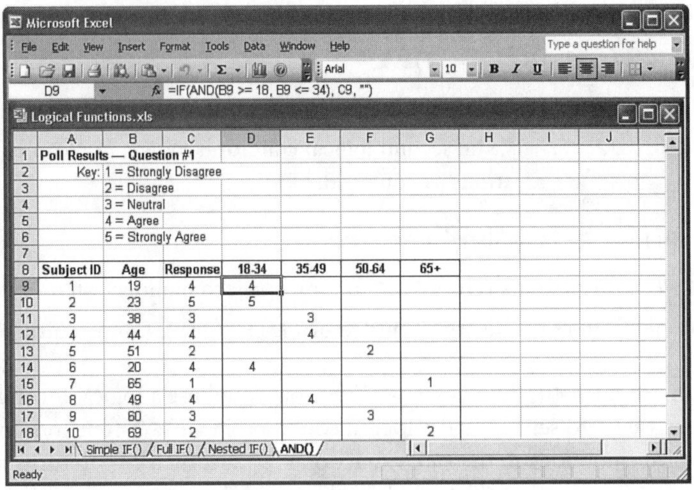

**Figure 8.4**
This worksheet uses the
AND() function as the
logical condition for an
IF() function to slot
poll results into age
groups.

You won't be surprised to hear that Or conditions are handled in Excel by the OR() function:

OR(*logical1*, [*logical2*,...])

> *logical1*            The first logical condition to test.
>
> *logical2*,...       The second logical condition to test. You can enter as many conditions as you need.

The OR() result is calculated as follows:

- If one or more of the arguments return TRUE (or any nonzero number), OR() returns TRUE.

- If *all* of the arguments return FALSE (or 0), OR() returns FALSE.

As with AND(), you use OR() wherever a logical expression is called for, most often within an IF() function. This means that if one or more of the logical conditions in the OR() function are TRUE, then IF() returns its *value_if_true* result; if all of the logical conditions in the OR() function are FALSE, then IF() returns its *value_if_false* result. Here's an example:

=IF(OR(B2 > 0, C2 > 0), "1000", "No bonus")

If the value in B2 is greater than 0 or the value in C2 is greater than 0, the formula returns 1000; otherwise, it returns No bonus.

## Combining Logical Functions with Arrays

When you combine the array formulas that you learned about in Chapter 4, "Creating Advanced Formulas," with IF(), you can perform some remarkably sophisticated operations. Arrays enable you to do things such as apply the IF() logical condition across a range, or sum only those cells in a range that meet the IF() condition.

→ To learn about array formulas, **see** "Working with Arrays," **p. 85**.

## Applying a Condition Across a Range

Using AND() as the logical condition in an IF() function is useful for perhaps three or four expressions. After that, it just gets too unwieldy to enter all those logical expressions. If you're essentially running the same logical test on a number of different cells, a better solution is to apply AND() to a range and enter the formula as an array.

For example, suppose that you want to sum the cells in the range B3:B7, but only if all of those cells contain values greater than 0. Here's an array formula that does this:

```
{=IF(AND(B3:B7 > 0), SUM(B3:B7), "")}
```

> **NOTE**
> Recall from Chapter 4 that you don't include the braces—{ and }—when you enter an array formula. Just type the formula without the braces and then press Ctrl+Shift+Enter.

This is useful in a worksheet in which you might not have all the numbers yet, and you don't want a total entered until the data is complete. Figure 8.5 shows an example. The array formula in B8 is the same as the previous one. The array formula in B16 returns nothing because cell B14 is blank.

**Figure 8.5**
This worksheet uses IF(), AND(), and SUM() in two array formulas (B8 and B16) to total a range only if all the cells have nonzero values.

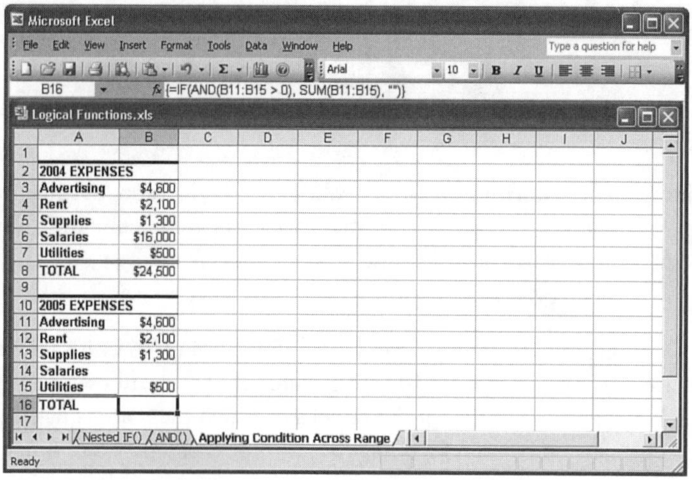

## Operating Only on Cells That Meet a Condition

In the previous section, you saw how to use an array formula to perform an action only if a certain condition is met across a range of cells. A related scenario arises when you want to perform an action on a range, but only on cells that meet a certain condition. For example, you might want to sum only those values that are positive.

To do this, you need to move the operation outside of the IF() function. For example, here's an array formula that sums only those values in the range B3:B7 that contain positive values:

```
{=SUM(IF(B3:B7 > 0, B3:B7, 0))}
```

The IF() function returns an array of values based on the condition (the cell value if it's positive, 0 otherwise), and the SUM() function adds those returned values.

For example, suppose you have a series of investments that mature in various years. It would be nice to set up a table that lists these years and tells you the total value of the investments that mature in each year. Figure 8.6 shows a worksheet set up to do just that.

**Figure 8.6**
This worksheet uses array formulas to sum the yearly maturity values of various investments.

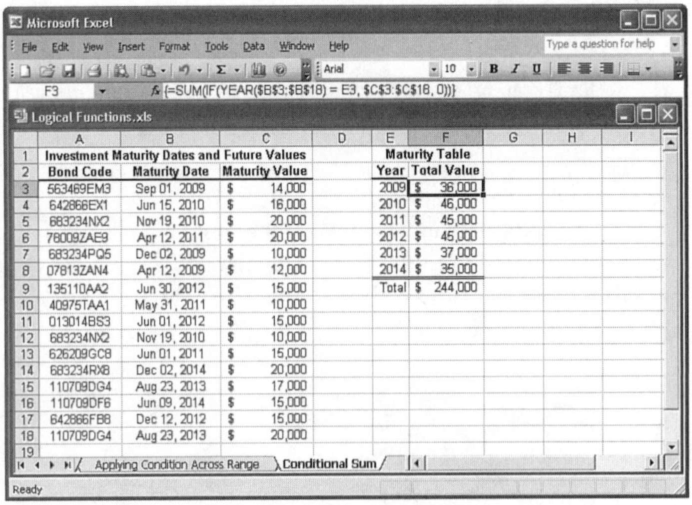

The investment maturity dates are in column B, the investment values at maturity are shown in column C, and the various maturity years are in column E. To calculate the maturity total for, say, 2009, the following array formula is used:

```
{=SUM(IF(YEAR($B$3:$B$18) = E3, $C$3:$C$18, 0))}
```

The IF() function compares the year value in cell E3 (2009) with the year component of the maturity dates in range B3:B18. (Absolute references are used so that the formula can be filled down to the other years.) For cells in which these are equal, IF() returns the corresponding value in column C; otherwise, it returns 0. The SUM() function then adds these returned values.

## Determining Whether a Value Appears in a List

Many spreadsheet applications require you to look up a value in a list. For example, you might have a table of customer discounts in which the percentage discount is based on the number of units ordered. For each customer order, you need to look up the appropriate discount, based on the total units in the order. Similarly, a teacher might convert a raw test score into a letter grade by referring to a table of conversions.

You'll see some sophisticated tools for looking up values in Chapter 9, "Working with Lookup Functions." However, array formulas combined with logical functions also offer some tricks for looking up values.

For example, suppose that you want to know whether a certain value exists in an array. You can use the following general formula, entered into a single cell as an array:

`{=OR(value = range)}`

Here, `value` is the value you want to search for, and `range` is the range of cells in which to search. For example, Figure 8.7 shows a list of customers with overdue accounts. You enter the account number of the customer in cell B1, and cell B2 tells you whether the number appears in the list.

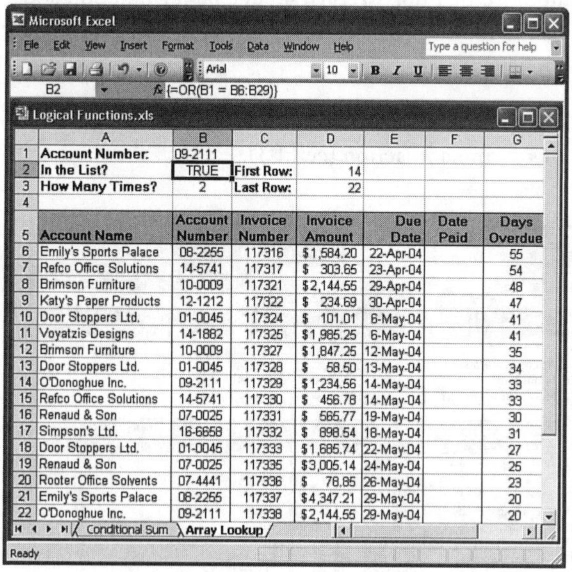

**Figure 8.7**

This worksheet uses the OR() function in an array formula to determine whether a value appears in a list.

Here's the array formula in cell B2:

`{=OR(B1 = B6:B29)}`

The array formula checks each value in the range B6:B29 to see whether it equals the value in cell B1. If any one of those comparisons is true, OR() returns TRUE, which means that the value is in the list.

> **TIP**
>
> As a similar example, here's an array formula that returns TRUE if a particular account number is *not* in the list:
>
> `{=AND(B1 <> B6:B29)}`
>
> The formula checks each value in B6:B29 to see whether it does not equal the value in B1. If all of those comparisons are true, AND() returns TRUE, which means that the value is not in the list.

## Counting Occurrences in a Range

Now you know how to find out whether a value appears in a list, but what if you need to know how many times the value appears? The following formula does the job:

`{=SUM(IF(value = range, 1, 0))}`

Again, *value* is the value you want to look up, and *range* is the range for searching. In this array formula, the IF() function compares *value* with every cell in *range*. The values that match return 1, and those that don't return 0. The SUM() function adds these return values, and the final total is the number of occurrences of *value*. Here's a formula that does this for our list of overdue invoices:

`=SUM(IF(B1 = B6:B29, 1, 0))`

Figure 8.8 shows this formula in action (cell B3).

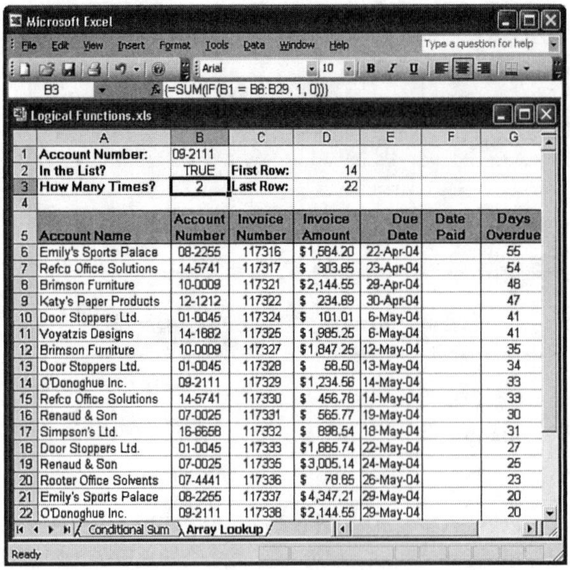

**Figure 8.8**
This worksheet uses SUM() and IF() in an array formula to count the number of occurrences of a value in a list.

> **NOTE** The generic array formula {=SUM(IF(*condition*, 1, 0))} is useful in any context when you need to count the number of occurrences in which *condition* returns TRUE. The *condition* argument is normally a logical formula that compares a single value with each cell in a range of values. However, it's also possible to compare two ranges, as long as they're the same shape (that is, they have the same number of rows and columns). For example, suppose that you want to compare the values in two ranges named Range1 and Range2 to see if any of the values are different. Here's an array formula that does this:
>
> ```
> {=SUM(IF(Range1 <> Range2, 1, 0))}
> ```
>
> This formula compares the first cell in Range1 with the first cell in Range2, the second cell in Range1 with the second cell in Range2, and so on. Each time the values don't match, the comparison returns 1; otherwise, it returns 0. The sum of these comparisons is the number of different values between the two ranges.

## Determining Where a Value Appears in a List

What if you want to know not just whether a value appears in a list, but *where* it appears in the list? You can do this by getting the IF() function to return the row number for a positive result:

```
IF(value = range, ROW(range), "")
```

Whenever *value* equals one of the cells in *range*, the IF() function uses ROW() to return the row number; otherwise, it returns the empty string.

To return that row number, we use either the MIN() function or the MAX() function, which return the minimum and maximum, respectively, in a collection of values. The trick here is that both functions ignore null values, so applying that to the array that results from the previous IF() expression tells us where the matching values are:

- To get the first instance of the value, use the MIN() function in an array formula, like so:
  ```
  {=MIN(IF(value = range, ROW(range), ""))}
  ```
- To get the last instance of the value, use the MAX() function in an array formula, as shown here:
  ```
  {=MAX(IF(value = range, ROW(range), ""))}
  ```

Here are the formulas you would use to find the first and last occurrences in the previous list of overdue invoices:

```
=MIN(IF(B1 = B6:B29, ROW(B6:B29), ""))
=MAX(IF(B1 = B6:B29, ROW(B6:B29), ""))
```

Figure 8.9 shows the results (the row of the first occurrence is in cell D2, and the row of the last occurrence is in cell D3).

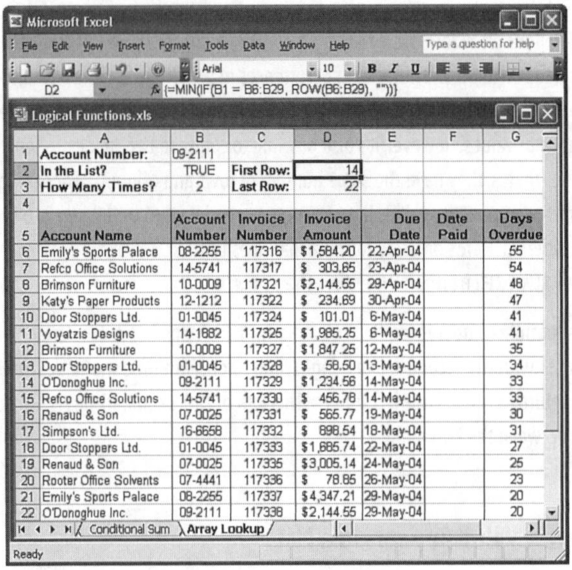


| | A | B | C | D | E | F | G |
|---|---|---|---|---|---|---|---|
| 1 | Account Number: | 09-2111 | | | | | |
| 2 | In the List? | TRUE | First Row: | 14 | | | |
| 3 | How Many Times? | 2 | Last Row: | 22 | | | |
| 4 | | | | | | | |
| 5 | Account Name | Account Number | Invoice Number | Invoice Amount | Due Date | Date Paid | Days Overdue |
| 6 | Emily's Sports Palace | 08-2255 | 117316 | $1,584.20 | 22-Apr-04 | | 55 |
| 7 | Refco Office Solutions | 14-5741 | 117317 | $ 303.65 | 23-Apr-04 | | 54 |
| 8 | Brimson Furniture | 10-0009 | 117321 | $2,144.55 | 29-Apr-04 | | 48 |
| 9 | Katy's Paper Products | 12-1212 | 117322 | $ 234.69 | 30-Apr-04 | | 47 |
| 10 | Door Stoppers Ltd. | 01-0045 | 117324 | $ 101.01 | 6-May-04 | | 41 |
| 11 | Voyatzis Designs | 14-1882 | 117325 | $1,985.25 | 6-May-04 | | 41 |
| 12 | Brimson Furniture | 10-0009 | 117327 | $1,847.25 | 12-May-04 | | 35 |
| 13 | Door Stoppers Ltd. | 01-0045 | 117328 | $ 58.50 | 13-May-04 | | 34 |
| 14 | O'Donoghue Inc. | 09-2111 | 117329 | $1,234.56 | 14-May-04 | | 33 |
| 15 | Refco Office Solutions | 14-5741 | 117330 | $ 456.78 | 14-May-04 | | 33 |
| 16 | Renaud & Son | 07-0025 | 117331 | $ 565.77 | 19-May-04 | | 30 |
| 17 | Simpson's Ltd. | 16-6658 | 117332 | $ 898.54 | 18-May-04 | | 31 |
| 18 | Door Stoppers Ltd. | 01-0045 | 117333 | $1,685.74 | 22-May-04 | | 27 |
| 19 | Renaud & Son | 07-0025 | 117335 | $3,005.14 | 24-May-04 | | 25 |
| 20 | Rooter Office Solvents | 07-4441 | 117336 | $ 78.85 | 26-May-04 | | 23 |
| 21 | Emily's Sports Palace | 08-2255 | 117337 | $4,347.21 | 29-May-04 | | 20 |
| 22 | O'Donoghue Inc. | 09-2111 | 117338 | $2,144.55 | 29-May-04 | | 20 |

**Figure 8.9**
This worksheet uses `MIN()`, `MAX()`, and `IF()` in array formulas to return the row numbers of the first (cell D2) and last (cell D3) occurrences of a value in a list.

8

**TIP**

It's also possible to determine the address of the cell containing the first or last occurrence of a value in a list. To do this, use the `ADDRESS()` function, which returns an absolute address, given a row and column number:

```
{=ADDRESS(MIN(IF(B1 = B6:B29, ROW(B6:B29), "")), COLUMN(B6:B29))}
{=ADDRESS(MAX(IF(B1 = B6:B29, ROW(B6:B29), "")), COLUMN(B6:B29))}
```

**CASE STUDY**

# Building an Accounts Receivable Aging Worksheet

If you use Excel to store accounts receivable data, it's a good idea to set up an aging worksheet that shows past-due invoices, calculates the number of days past due, and groups the invoices into past-due categories (1–30 days, 31–60 days, and so on).

Figure 8.10 shows a simple implementation of an accounts receivable database. For each invoice, the due date (column D) is calculated by adding 30 to the invoice date (column C). Column E uses the `TODAY()` function to calculate the number of days each invoice is past due.

## Calculating a Smarter Due Date

You might have noticed a couple of problems with the due dates in Figure 8.10: The dates in cells D7 and D12 both fall on a weekend. The problem here is that the due date calculation just adds 30 to the invoice date. To avoid weekend due dates, you need to test whether the invoice date plus 30 falls on a Saturday or Sunday. The `WEEKDAY()` function helps because it returns `7` if the date is a Saturday, and `1` if the date is a Sunday.

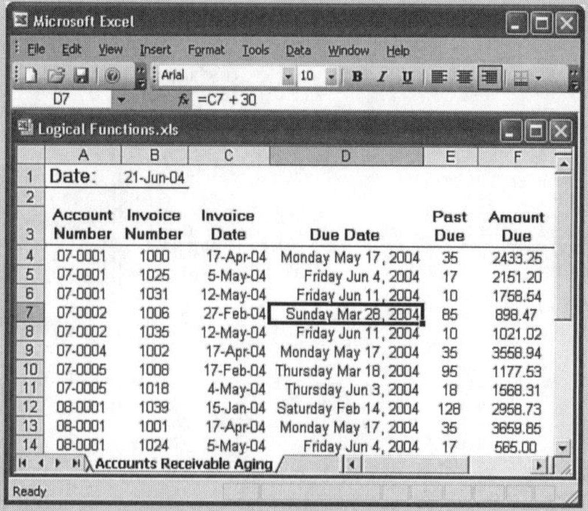

| | A | B | C | D | E | F |
|---|---|---|---|---|---|---|
| 1 | Date: | 21-Jun-04 | | | | |
| 2 | | | | | | |
| 3 | Account Number | Invoice Number | Invoice Date | Due Date | Past Due | Amount Due |
| 4 | 07-0001 | 1000 | 17-Apr-04 | Monday May 17, 2004 | 35 | 2433.25 |
| 5 | 07-0001 | 1025 | 5-May-04 | Friday Jun 4, 2004 | 17 | 2151.20 |
| 6 | 07-0001 | 1031 | 12-May-04 | Friday Jun 11, 2004 | 10 | 1758.54 |
| 7 | 07-0002 | 1006 | 27-Feb-04 | Sunday Mar 28, 2004 | 85 | 898.47 |
| 8 | 07-0002 | 1035 | 12-May-04 | Friday Jun 11, 2004 | 10 | 1021.02 |
| 9 | 07-0004 | 1002 | 17-Apr-04 | Monday May 17, 2004 | 35 | 3558.94 |
| 10 | 07-0005 | 1008 | 17-Feb-04 | Thursday Mar 18, 2004 | 95 | 1177.53 |
| 11 | 07-0005 | 1018 | 4-May-04 | Thursday Jun 3, 2004 | 18 | 1568.31 |
| 12 | 08-0001 | 1039 | 15-Jan-04 | Saturday Feb 14, 2004 | 128 | 2958.73 |
| 13 | 08-0001 | 1001 | 17-Apr-04 | Monday May 17, 2004 | 35 | 3659.85 |
| 14 | 08-0001 | 1024 | 5-May-04 | Friday Jun 4, 2004 | 17 | 565.00 |

**Figure 8.10**
A simple accounts receivable database.

So, to check for a Saturday, you could use the following formula:

```
=IF(WEEKDAY(C4 + 30) = 7, C4 + 32, C4 + 30)
```

Here, I'm assuming that the invoice date resides in cell C4. If `WEEKDAY(C4 + 30)` returns `7`, the date is a Saturday, so you add 32 to C4 instead (this makes the due date the following Monday). Otherwise, you just add 30 days as usual.

Checking for a Sunday is similar:

```
=IF(WEEKDAY(C4 + 30) = 1, C4 + 31, C4 + 30)
```

The problem, though, is that you need to combine these two tests into a single formula. To do that, you can nest one `IF()` function inside another. Here's how it works:

```
=IF(WEEKDAY(C4+30) = 7, C4+32, IF(WEEKDAY(C4+30) = 1, C4+31, C4+30))
```

The main `IF()` checks to see whether the date is a Saturday. If it is, you add 32 days to C4; otherwise, the formula runs the second `IF()`, which checks for Sunday. Figure 8.11 shows the revised aging sheet with the nonweekend due dates in cells D7 and D12.

→ If you calculate due dates based on workdays (that is, excluding weekends and holidays), the Analysis ToolPak has a function named `WORKDAY()` that handles this calculation with ease; **see** "A Workday Alternative: the `WORKDAY()` Function," **p. 208**.

## Aging Overdue Invoices

For cash-flow purposes, you also need to correlate the invoice amounts with the number of days past due. Ideally, you'd like to see a list of invoice amounts that are between 1 and 30 days past due, between 31 and 60 days past due, and so on. Figure 8.12 shows one way to set up accounts receivable aging.

→ The worksheet in Figure 8.12 uses ledger shading for easier reading. To learn how to apply ledger shading automatically, **see** "Creating Ledger Shading," **p. 243**.

→ The aging worksheet calculates the number of days past due by subtracting the due date from the date shown in cell B1. If you calculate days past due using only workdays (weekends and holidays excluded), a better choice is the Analysis ToolPak's `NETWORKDAYS()` function; **see** "`NETWORKDAYS()`: Calculating the Number of Workdays Between Two Dates," **p. 217**.

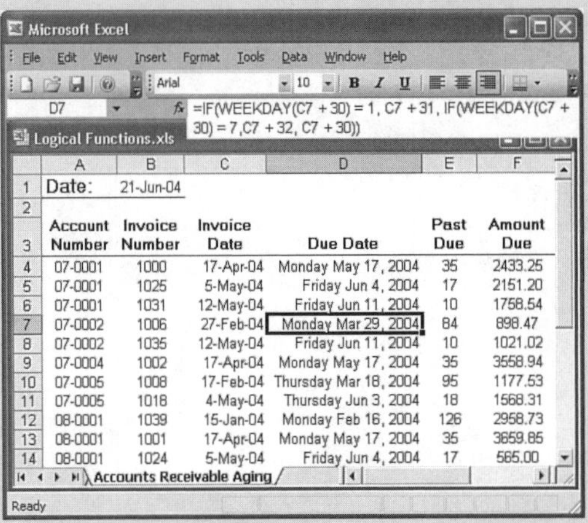

8

**Figure 8.11**
The revised worksheet uses the IF() and WEEKDAY() functions to ensure that due dates don't fall on weekends.

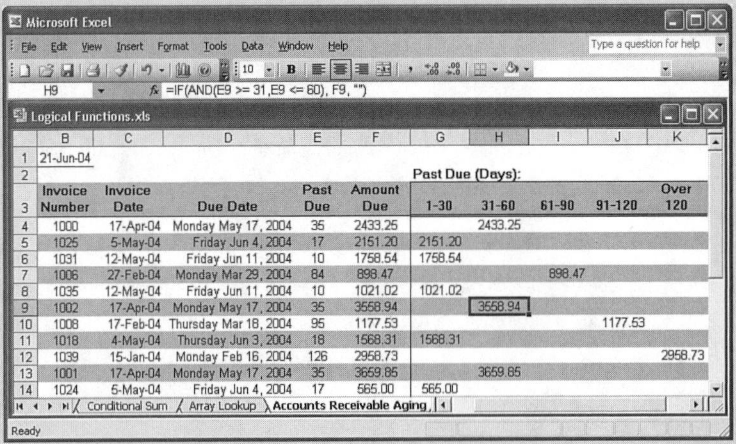

**Figure 8.12**
Using IF() and AND() to categorize past-due invoices for aging purposes.

For the invoice amounts shown in column G (1–30 days), the sheet uses the following formula (this is the formula that appears in G4):

```
=IF(E4 <= 30, F4, "")
```

If the number of days the invoice is past due (cell E4) is less than or equal to 30, the formula displays the amount (cell F4); otherwise, it displays a blank.

The amounts in column H (31–60 days) are a little trickier. Here, you need to check whether the number of days past due is greater than or equal to 31 days *and* less than or equal to 60 days. To accomplish this, you can press the AND() function into service:

```
=IF(AND(E4 >= 31, E4 <= 60), F4, "")
```

The AND() function checks two logical expressions: E4> = 31 and E4 <= 60. If both are true, AND() returns TRUE, and the IF() function displays the invoice amount. If one of the logical expressions isn't true (or if they're both not true), AND() returns FALSE, and the IF() function displays a blank. Similar formulas appear in column I (61–90 days) and column J (91–120 days). Column K (Over 120) looks for past-due values that are greater than 120.

# Getting Data with Information Functions

Excel's information functions return data concerning cells, worksheets, and formula results. Table 8.2 lists all the information functions.

**Table 8.2   Excel's Information Functions**

| Function | Description |
| --- | --- |
| CELL(*info_type*,[*reference*]) | Returns information about various cell attributes, including formatting, contents, and location |
| ERROR.TYPE(*error_val*) | Returns a number corresponding to an error type |
| INFO(*type_text*) | Returns information about the operating system and environment |
| ISBLANK(*value*) | Returns TRUE if the *value* is blank |
| ISERR(*value*) | Returns TRUE if the *value* is any error value except #NA |
| ISERROR(*value*) | Returns TRUE if the *value* is any error value |
| ISEVEN(*number*) | Returns TRUE if the *value* is any error value |
| ISEVEN(*number*) | Returns TRUE if the *number* is even (this is an Analysis ToolPak function) |
| ISLOGICAL(*value*) | Returns TRUE if the *value* is a logical value |
| ISNA(*value*) | Returns TRUE if the *value* is the #NA error value |
| ISNONTEXT(*value*) | Returns TRUE if the *value* is not text |
| ISNUMBER(*value*) | Returns TRUE if the *value* is a number |
| ISODD(*number*) | Returns TRUE if the *number* is odd (this is an Analysis ToolPak function) |
| ISREF(*value*) | Returns TRUE if the *value* is a reference |
| ISTEXT(*value*) | Returns TRUE if the *value* is text |
| N(*value*) | Returns the *value* converted to a number (a serial number if *value* is a date, 1 if *value* is TRUE, 0 if *value* is any other non-numeric; note that N() exists only for compatibility with other spreadsheets and is rarely used in Excel) |

*continues*

**8**

| Table 8.2 | Continued |
| --- | --- |
| **Function** | **Description** |
| NA() | Returns the error value #NA |
| TYPE(value) | Returns a number that indicates the data type of the value: 1 for a number, 2 for text, 4 for a logical value, 8 for a formula, 16 for an error, or 64 for an array |

The rest of this chapter takes you through the details of these functions.

## The CELL() Function

CELL() is one of the most useful information functions. Its job is to return information about a particular cell:

CELL(info_type, [reference])

| | |
| --- | --- |
| info_type | A string that specifies the type of information you want. |
| reference | The cell you want to use (the default is the cell that contains the CELL() function). If reference is a range, CELL() applies to the cell in the upper-left corner of the range. |

Table 8.3 lists the various possibilities for the info_type argument.

| Table 8.3 | The CELL() Function's info_type Argument |
| --- | --- |
| **Info_type Value** | **What CELL() Returns** |
| address | The absolute address, as text, of the reference cell. |
| col | The column number of reference. |
| color | 1 if reference has a custom cell format that displays negative values in a color; returns 0 otherwise. |
| contents | The contents of reference. |
| filename | The full path and filename of the file that contains reference, as text. Returns the null string ("") if the workbook that contains reference hasn't been saved for the first time. |
| format | A string that corresponds to the built-in Excel numeric format applied to reference. Here are the possible return values: |

| **Built-in Format** | **CELL() Returns** |
| --- | --- |
| General | G |
| 0 | F0 |

8

| **Built-in Format** | *CELL( )* **Returns** | |
|---|---|---|
| #,##0 | ,0 | |
| 0.00 | F2 | |
| #,##0.00 | ,2 | |
| $#,##0_);($#,##0) | C0 | |
| $#,##0_);[Red]($#,##0) | C0- | |
| $#,##0.00_);($#,##0.00) | C2 | |
| $#,##0.00_);[Red]($#,##0.00) | C2- | |
| 0% | P0 | |
| 0.00% | P2 | |
| 0.00E+00 | S2 | |
| # ?/? or # ??/?? | G | |
| d-mmm-yy or dd-mmm-yy | D1 | |
| d-mmm or dd-mmm | D2 | |
| mmm-yy | D3 | |
| m/d/yy or m/d/yy h:mm or mm/dd/yy | D4 | |
| mm/dd | D5 | |
| h:mm:ss AM/PM | D6 | |
| h:mm AM/PM | D7 | |
| h:mm:ss | D8 | |
| h:mm | D9 | |

| | |
|---|---|
| parentheses | 1 if *reference* has a custom cell format that uses parentheses for positive or all values; returns 0 otherwise. |
| prefix | A character that represents the text alignment used by *reference*. Here are the possible return values: |

| **Alignment** | *CELL( )* **Returns** |
|---|---|
| Left | ' |
| Center | ^ |
| Right | " |
| Fill | \ |

| | |
|---|---|
| protect | 0 if *reference* isn't locked; 1 otherwise. |
| row | The row number of *reference*. |

*continues*

**Table 8.3    Continued**

| *Info_type* Value | What CELL() Returns |
|---|---|
| type | A letter that represents the type of data in the *reference*. Here are the possible return values: |

| Data Type | CELL() Returns |
|---|---|
| Text | l |
| Blank | b |
| All others | v |

| width | The column width of *reference*, rounded to the nearest integer, where one unit equals the width of one character in the default font size. |
|---|---|

Figure 8.13 puts the CELL() function through some of its paces.

**Figure 8.13**
Some examples of the CELL() function.

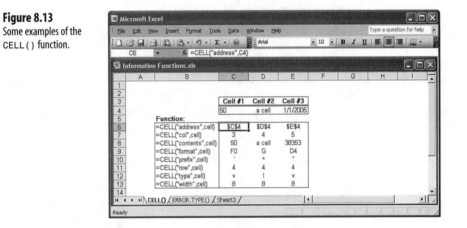

## The ERROR.TYPE() Function

The ERROR.TYPE() function returns a value that corresponds to a specific Excel error value:

ERROR.TYPE(*error_val*)

    *error_val*    A reference to a cell containing a formula that you want to check for the error value. Here are the possible return values:

| *Error_val* Value | ERROR.TYPE() Returns |
|---|---|
| #NULL! | 1 |
| #DIV/0! | 2 |
| #VALUE! | 3 |
| #REF! | 4 |

| *Error_val* **Value** | **ERROR.TYPE() Returns** |
|---|---|
| #NAME? | 5 |
| #NUM! | 6 |
| #N/A! | 7 |
| All others | #NA |

The ERROR.TYPE() function is most often used to intercept an error and then display a more useful or friendly message. You do this by using the IF() function to see if ERROR.TYPE() returns a value less than or equal to 7; if so, the cell in question contains an error value. Because the ERROR.TYPE() return value ranges from 1 to 7, you can apply the return value to the CHOOSE() function to display the error message.

→ For the details of the CHOOSE() function, **see** "The CHOOSE() Function," **p. 183**.

Here's a formula that does all that (I've split the formula so that different parts appear on different lines to make it easier for you to see what's going on):

```
=IF(ERROR.TYPE(D8) <= 7,
➥"***ERROR IN " & CELL("address",D8) & ": " &
➥CHOOSE(ERROR.TYPE(D8),"The ranges do not intersect",
➥"The divisor is 0",
➥"Wrong data type in function argument",
➥"Invalid cell reference",
➥"Unrecognized range or function name",
➥"Number error in formula",
➥"Inappropriate function argument"))
```

Figure 8.14 shows this formula in an example. (Note that the formula displays #N/A when there is no error; this is the return value of ERROR.TYPE() when there is no error.)

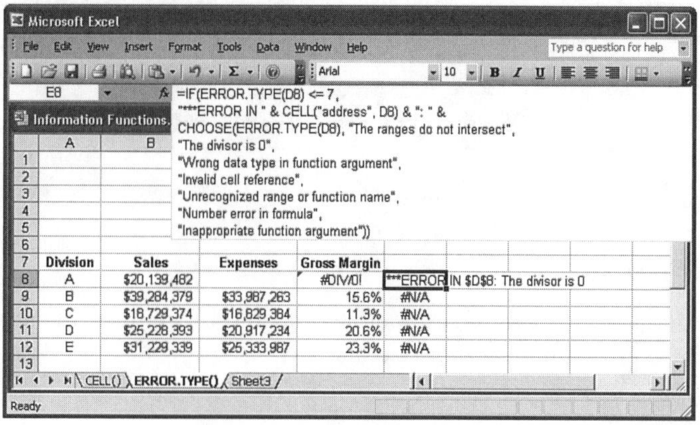

**Figure 8.14**
A formula that uses IF() and ERROR_TYPE() to return a more descriptive error message to the user.

## The INFO() Function

The INFO() function is seldom used, but it's handy when you do need it because it gives you information about the current operating environment:

INFO(*type_text*)

> *type_text*    A string that specifies the type of information you want

Table 8.4 lists the possible values for the *info_type* argument.

| Table 8.4   The INFO() Function's info_type Argument | |
| --- | --- |
| ***Type_text* Value** | **What INFO() Returns** |
| directory | The full pathname of the current folder. (That is, the folder that will appear the next time you display the Open or Save As dialog boxes.) |
| memavail | The amount of system memory available, in bytes. This refers to the DOS memory below 1MB. |
| memused | The amount of memory used for data, in bytes. |
| numfile | The number of worksheets in all the open workbooks. |
| origin | The address of the upper-left cell that is visible in the current worksheet. In Figure 8.15, for example, cell A3 is the visible cell in the upper-left corner. The absolute address begins with $A: for Lotus 1-2-3 release 3.*x* compatibility. |
| osversion | A string containing the current operating system version. |
| recalc | A string containing the current recalculation mode: Automatic or Manual. |
| release | A string containing the version of Microsoft Excel. |
| system | A string containing a code representing the current operating environment: pcdos for Windows or mac for Macintosh. |
| totmem | The sum of the memavail and memused values, in bytes. |

Figure 8.15 shows the INFO() function at work.

## The IS Functions

Excel's so-called IS functions are Boolean functions that return either TRUE or FALSE, depending on the argument they're evaluating:

ISBLANK(*value*)
ISERR(*value*)
ISERROR(*value*)
ISEVEN(*number*)
ISLOGICAL(*value*)
ISNA(*value*)
ISNONTEXT(*value*)
ISNUMBER(*value*)
ISODD(*number*)

```
ISREF(value)
ISTEXT(value)
```

| value | A cell reference, function return value, or formula result |
| number | A numeric value |

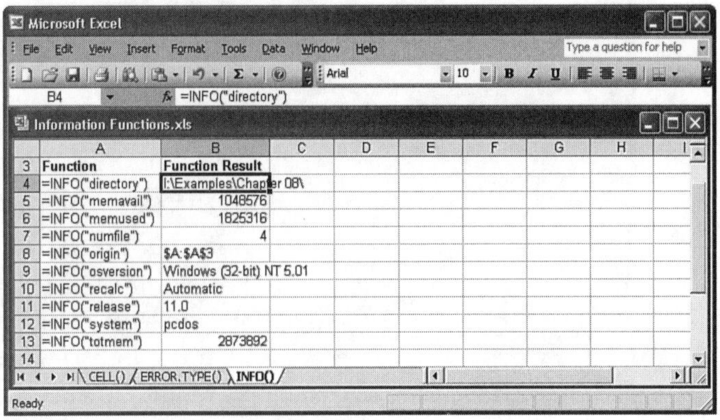

**8**

**Figure 8.15**
The INFO() function in action.

The operation of these functions is straightforward, so rather than run through the specifics of all 11 functions, the next few sections show you some interesting and useful techniques that make use of these functions.

### Counting the Number of Blanks in a Range

When putting together the data for a worksheet model, it's common to pull the data from various sources. Unfortunately, this often means that the data arrives at different times and you end up with an incomplete model. If you're working with a big list, you might want to keep a running total of the number of pieces of data that you're still missing.

This is the perfect opportunity to break out the ISBLANK() function and plug it into the array formula for counting that you learned earlier:

```
{=SUM(IF(ISBLANK(range), 1, 0))}
```

The IF() function runs through the *range* looking for blank cells. Each time it comes across a blank cell, it returns 1; otherwise, it returns 0. The SUM() function adds the results to give the total number of blank cells. Figure 8.16 shows an example (see cell G1).

### Checking a Range for Non-numeric Values

A similar idea is to check a range upon which you'll be performing a mathematical operation to see if it holds any cells that contain non-numeric values. In this case, you plug the ISNUMBER() function into the array counting formula, and return 0 for each TRUE result and 1 for each FALSE result. Here's the general formula:

```
{=SUM(IF(ISNUMBER(range), 0, 1))}
```

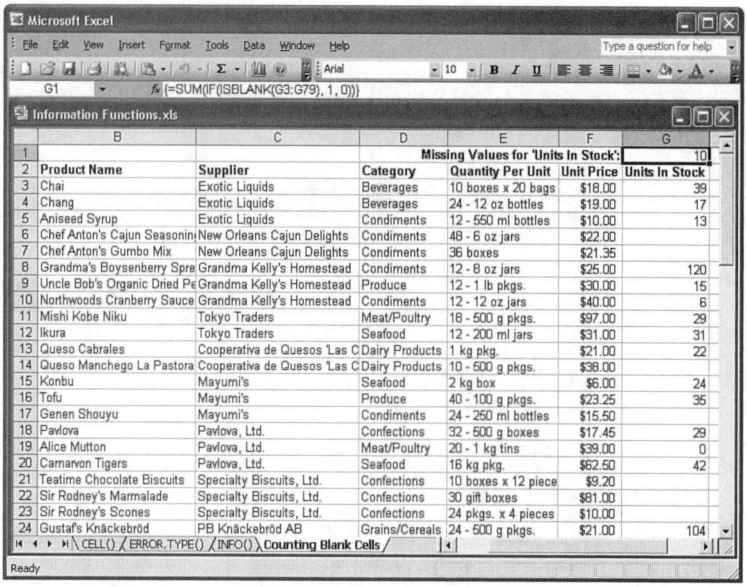

**Figure 8.16**
As shown in cell G1, you can plug ISBLANK() into the array counting formula to count the number of blank cells in a range.

## Counting the Number of Errors in a Range

For the final counting example, it's often nice to know not only whether a range contains an error value, but also how many such values it contains. This is easily done using the ISERROR() function and the array counting formula:

```
{=SUM(IF(ISERROR(range), 1, 0))}
```

## Ignoring Errors When Working with a Range

Sometimes you have to work with ranges that contain error values. For example, suppose that you have a column of gross margin results (which require division), but one or more of the cells are showing the #DIV/0! error because you're missing data. You could wait until the missing data is added to the model, but it's often necessary to perform preliminary calculations. For example, you might want to take the average of the results that you *do* have.

To do this efficiently, you need some way of bypassing the error values. Again, this is possible by using the ISERROR() function plugged into an array formula. For example, here's a general formula for taking an average across a range while ignoring any error values:

```
{=AVERAGE(IF(ISERROR(range), " ", range))}
```

Figure 18.17 provides an example.

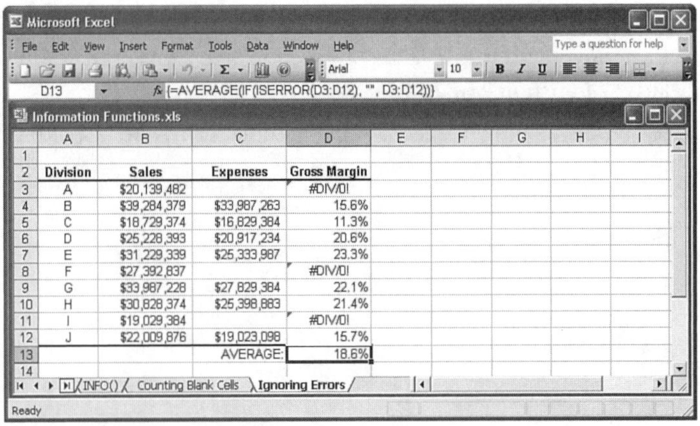


| | A | B | C | D |
|---|---|---|---|---|
| 1 | | | | |
| 2 | Division | Sales | Expenses | Gross Margin |
| 3 | A | $20,139,482 | | #DIV/0! |
| 4 | B | $39,284,379 | $33,987,263 | 15.6% |
| 5 | C | $18,729,374 | $16,829,384 | 11.3% |
| 6 | D | $25,228,393 | $20,917,234 | 20.6% |
| 7 | E | $31,229,339 | $25,333,987 | 23.3% |
| 8 | F | $27,392,837 | | #DIV/0! |
| 9 | G | $33,987,228 | $27,829,384 | 22.1% |
| 10 | H | $30,828,374 | $25,398,883 | 21.4% |
| 11 | I | $19,029,384 | | #DIV/0! |
| 12 | J | $22,009,876 | $19,023,098 | 15.7% |
| 13 | | | AVERAGE: | 18.6% |
| 14 | | | | |

**Figure 8.17**
As shown in cell D13, you can use `ISERROR()` in an array formula to run an operation on a range while ignoring any errors in the range.

## Avoiding Text Formula Errors

In Chapter 7, "Working with Text Functions," you learned how to use the `FIND()` function to extract either the first word from a multiword string or the last word from a two-word string. To refresh your memory, here's the formula for extracting the first word:

```
=LEFT(A2, FIND(" ", A2) - 1)
```

➔ To learn about extracting a name from a string, **see** "Extracting a First Name or Last Name," **p. 148**.

This works fine as long as the string contains multiple words. If it contains just a single word, the `FIND()` function fails and returns a `#VALUE!` error. To avoid this error, use the `ISERROR()` function (or the `ISERR()` function) to check for the error in advance:

```
=IF(ISERROR(FIND(" ", A2)), A2, LEFT(A1, FIND(" ", A2) - 1))
```

The `IF()` function uses `ISERROR()` as its logical condition. `ISERROR()` checks the `FIND()` expression: If that expression returns an error, the formula returns just the contents of the cell; otherwise, the formula safely extracts the first word.

Here's the formula for safely extracting the last word in a two-word string (using `ISERR()` this time):

```
=IF(ISERR(FIND(" ", A2)), A2, RIGHT(A2, LEN(A2) - FIND(" ", A2)))
```

# From Here

- To learn about array formulas, **see** "Working with Arrays," **p. 85**.
- To learn about the `#DIV/0!` error, **see** "`#DIV/0!`," **p. 108**.
- For a general discussion of function syntax, **see** "The Structure of a Function," **p. 126**.
- For the details on the `REPT()` function, **see** "The `REPT()` Function: Repeating a Character," **p. 143**.
- To learn about extracting a name from a string, **see** "Extracting a First Name or Last Name," **p. 148**.

- For the details of the CHOOSE() function, **see** "The CHOOSE() Function," **p. 183**.
- To learn how to use the WORKDAY() function, **see** "A Workday Alternative: The WORKDAY() Function," **p. 208**.
- To learn how to apply ledger shading automatically, **see** "Creating Ledger Shading," **p. 243**.

# Working with Lookup Functions

9

Getting the meaning of a word in the dictionary is always a two-step process: First you look up the word itself, and then you read its definition.

This idea of looking something up to retrieve some related information is at the heart of many spreadsheet operations. For example, you saw in Chapter 4, "Creating Advanced Formulas," that you can add option buttons and list boxes to a worksheet. Unfortunately, these controls return only the number of the item the user has chosen. To find out the actual value of the item, you need to use the returned number to look up the value in a table.

→ For the specifics of adding option buttons and list boxes to a worksheet, **see** "Understanding the Worksheet Controls," **p. 101**.

In many worksheet formulas, the value of one argument often depends on the value of another. Here are some examples:

- In a formula that calculates an invoice total, the customer's discount might depend on the number of units purchased.
- In a formula that charges interest on overdue accounts, the interest percentage might depend on the number of days each invoice is overdue.
- In a formula that calculates employee bonuses as a percentage of salary, the percentage might depend on how much the employee improved upon the given budget.

The usual way to handle these kinds of problems is to look up the appropriate value. This chapter introduces you to a number of functions that enable you to perform lookup operations in your worksheet models. Table 9.1 lists Excel's lookup functions.

9

**Table 9.1  Excel's Lookup Functions**

| Function | Description |
|---|---|
| CHOOSE(*num*,*value1*,[*value2*,...]) | Uses *num* to select one of the list of arguments given by *value1*, *value2*, and so on |
| GETPIVOTDATA(*data*,*table*,*field1*,*item1*,...) | Extracts data from a PivotTable |
| HLOOKUP(*value*,*table*,*row*,[*range*]) | Searches for *value* in *table* and returns the value in the specified *row* |
| INDEX(*ref*,*row*,[*col*],[*area*]) | Looks in *ref* and returns the value of the cell at the intersection of *row* and, optionally, *col* |
| LOOKUP(*lookup_value*,...) | Looks up a value in a range or array (this function has been replaced by the HLOOKUP() and VLOOKUP() functions) |
| MATCH(*value*,*array*,[*match_type*]) | Searches *range* for *value* and, if found, returns the relative position of *value* in *range* |
| RTD(*progID*,*server*,*topic1*,[*topic2*,...]) | Retrieves data in real time from an automation server (not covered in this chapter) |
| VLOOKUP(*value*,*table*,*col*,[*range*]) | Searches for *value* in *table* and returns the value in the specified *col* |

# Understanding Lookup Tables

The table—more properly referred to as a *lookup table*—is the key to performing lookup operations in Excel. The most straightforward lookup table structure is one that consists of two columns (or two rows):

- **Lookup column**—This column contains the values that you look up. For example, if you were constructing a lookup table for a dictionary, this column would contain the words.

- **Data column**—This column contains the data associated with each lookup value. In the dictionary example, this column would contain the definitions.

In most lookup operations, you supply a value that the function locates in the designated lookup column. It then retrieves the corresponding value in the data column.

As you'll see in this chapter, there are many variations on the lookup table theme. The lookup table can be one of these:

- A single column (or a single row). In this case, the lookup operation consists of finding the *n*th value in the column.

- A range with multiple data columns. For example, in the dictionary example, you might have a second column for each word's part of speech (noun, verb, and so on), and perhaps a third column for its pronunciation. In this case, the lookup operation must also specify which of the data columns contains the value required.

■ An array. In this case, the table doesn't exist on a worksheet but is either an array of literal values or the result of a function that returns an array. The lookup operation finds a particular position within the array and returns the data value at that position.

# The CHOOSE ( ) **Function**

The simplest of the lookup functions is CHOOSE(), which enables you to select a value from a list. Specifically, given an integer $n$, CHOOSE() returns the $n$th item from the list. Here's the function's syntax:

```
CHOOSE(num, value1, [value2,...])
```

| | |
|---|---|
| *num* | Determines which of the values in the list is returned. If *num* is 1, *value1* is returned; if *num* is 2, *value2* is returned (and so on). *num* must be an integer (or a formula or function that returns an integer) between 1 and 29. |
| *value1, value2...* | The list of up to 29 values from which CHOOSE() selects the return value. The values can be numbers, strings, references, names, formulas, or functions. |

For example, consider the following formula:

```
=CHOOSE(2,"Surface Mail", "Air Mail", "Courier")
```

The *num* argument is 2, so CHOOSE() returns the second value in the list, which is the string value Air Mail.

> **NOTE**
> If you use range references as the list of values, CHOOSE ( ) returns the entire range as the result. For example, consider the following:
>
>     CHOOSE(1, A1:D1, A2:D2, A3:D3)
>
> This function returns the range A1:D1. This enables you to perform conditional operations on a set of ranges, where the "condition" is the lookup value used by CHOOSE ( ). For example, the follow formula returns the sum of the range A1:D1:
>
>     =SUM(CHOOSE(1, A1:D1, A2:D2, A3:D3))

## Determining the Name of the Day of the Week

As you'll see in Chapter 10, "Working with Date and Time Functions," Excel's WEEKDAY() function returns a number that corresponds to the day of the week, in which Sunday is 1, Monday is 2, and so on.

→ To learn about the WEEKDAY ( ) function, **see** "The WEEKDAY ( ) Function," **p. 206**.

What if you want to know the actual day (not the number) of the week? If you need only to display the day of the week, you can format the cell as dddd. If you need to use the day of the week as a string value in a formula, you need a way to convert the WEEKDAY() result into the appropriate string. Fortunately, the CHOOSE() function makes this process easy. For example, suppose that cell B5 contains a date. You can find the day of the week it represents with the following formula:

```
=CHOOSE(WEEKDAY(B5), "Sun", "Mon", "Tue", "Wed", "Thu", "Fri", "Sat")
```

I've used abbreviated day names to save space, but you're free to use any form of the day names that suits your purposes.

> **TIP**
>
> Here's a similar formula for returning the name of the month, given the integer month number returned by the MONTH() function:
>
> ```
> =CHOOSE(MONTH(date), "Jan", "Feb", "Mar", "Apr", "May", "Jun",
> ➥"Jul", "Aug", "Sep", "Oct", "Nov", "Dec")
> ```

## Determining the Month of the Fiscal Year

For many businesses, the fiscal year does not coincide with the calendar year. For example, the fiscal year might run from April 1 to March 31. In this case, month 1 of the fiscal year is April, month 2 is May, and so on. It's often handy to be able to determine the fiscal month given the calendar month.

To see how you'd set this up, first consider the following table, which compares the calendar month and the fiscal month for a fiscal year beginning April 1:

| Month | Calendar Month | Fiscal Month |
|---|---|---|
| January | 1 | 10 |
| February | 2 | 11 |
| March | 3 | 12 |
| April | 4 | 1 |
| May | 5 | 2 |
| June | 6 | 3 |
| July | 7 | 4 |
| August | 8 | 5 |
| September | 9 | 6 |
| October | 10 | 7 |
| November | 11 | 8 |
| December | 12 | 9 |

So, what you need to do is use the calendar month as the lookup value, and the fiscal months as the data values. Here's the result:

```
=CHOOSE(CalendarMonth, 10, 11, 12, 1, 2, 3, 4, 5, 6, 7, 8, 9)
```

Figure 9.1 shows an example.

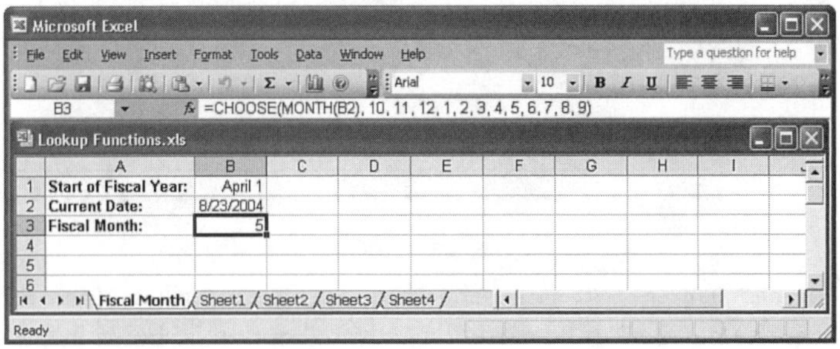

**Figure 9.1**
This worksheet uses the CHOOSE ( ) function to determine the fiscal month (B3), given the start of the fiscal year (B1) and the current date (B2).

---

> **NOTE**
> You can download this chapter's example workbooks here:
> www.mcfedries.com/ExcelFormulas/

## Calculating Weighted Questionnaire Results

One common use for CHOOSE() is to calculate weighted questionnaire responses. For example, suppose that you just completed a survey in which the respondents had to enter a value between 1 and 5 for each question. Some questions and answers are more important than others, so each question is assigned a set of weights. You use these weighted responses for your data. How do you assign the weights? The easiest way is to set up a CHOOSE() function for each question. For instance, suppose that question 1 uses the following weights for answers 1 through 5: 1.5, 2.3, 1.0, 1.8, and 0.5. If so, the following formula can be used to derive the weighted response:

```
=CHOOSE(Question1, 1.5, 2.3, 1.0, 1.8, 0.5)
```

(Assume that the answer for question 1 is in a cell named Question1.)

## Integrating CHOOSE ( ) and Worksheet Option Buttons

The CHOOSE() function is ideal for lookup situations in which you have a small number of data values and you have a formula or function that generates sequential integer values beginning with 1. A good example of this is the use of worksheet option buttons that I mentioned at the beginning of this chapter. The option buttons in a group return integer values in the linked cell: 1 if the first option is clicked, 2 if the second option is clicked, and so on. Therefore, you can use the value in the linked cell as the lookup value in the CHOOSE() function. Figure 9.2 shows a worksheet that does this.

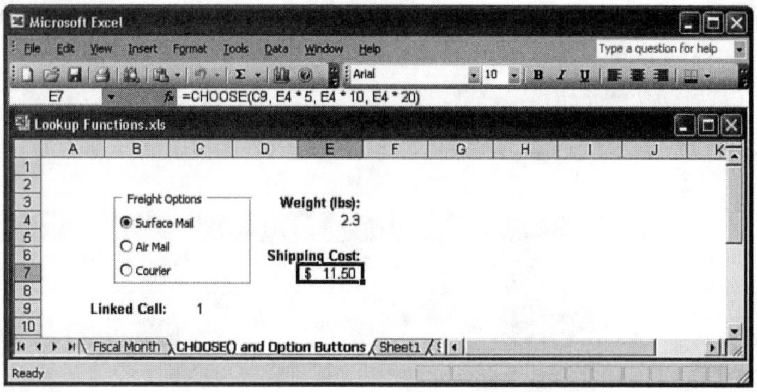

**Figure 9.2**
This worksheet uses the
CHOOSE() function to
calculate the shipping
cost based on the option
clicked in the Freight
Options group.

The Freight Options group presents three option buttons: Surface Mail, Air Mail, and Courier. The number of the currently activated option is shown in the linked cell, C9. A weight, in pounds, is entered into cell E4. Given the linked cell and the weight, cell E7 calculates the shipping cost by using CHOOSE() to select a formula that multiplies the weight by a constant:

```
=CHOOSE(C9, E4 * 5, E4 * 10, E4 * 20)
```

# Looking Up Values in Tables

As you've seen, the CHOOSE() function is a handy and useful addition to your formula toolkit, and it's a function you'll turn to quite often if you build a lot of worksheet models. However, CHOOSE() does have its drawbacks:

- The lookup values must be positive integers.
- The maximum number of data values is 29.
- Only one set of data values is allowed per function.

You'll trip over these limitations eventually, and you'll wonder if Excel has more flexible lookup capabilities. That is, can it use a wider variety of lookup values (negative or real numbers, strings, and so on), and can it accommodate multiple data sets that each can have any number of values (subject, of course, to the worksheet's inherent size limitations)? The answer to both questions is "yes"; in fact, Excel has two functions that meet these criteria: VLOOKUP() and HLOOKUP().

## The VLOOKUP() Function

The VLOOKUP() function works by looking in the first column of a table for the value you specify. (The *V* in VLOOKUP() stands for *vertical*.) It then looks across the appropriate number of columns (which you specify) and returns whatever value it finds there.

Here's the full syntax for VLOOKUP():

```
VLOOKUP(lookup_value, table_array, col_index_num, [range_lookup])
```

| | |
|---|---|
| *lookup_value* | This is the value you want to find in the first column of *table_array*. You can enter a number, a string, or a reference. |
| *table_array* | This is the table to use for the lookup. You can use a range reference or a name. |
| *col_index_num* | If VLOOKUP() finds a match, *col_index_num* is the column number in the table that contains the data you want returned (the first column—that is, the lookup column—is 1, the second column is 2, and so on). |
| *range_lookup* | This is a Boolean value that determines how Excel searches for *lookup_value* in the first column: |
| | TRUE—VLOOKUP() searches for the first exact match for *lookup_value*. If no exact match is found, the function looks for the largest value that is less than *lookup_value* (this is the default). |
| | FALSE—VLOOKUP() searches only for the first exact match for *lookup_value*. |

Here are some notes to keep in mind when you work with VLOOKUP():

- If *range_lookup* is TRUE or omitted, you must sort the values in the first column in ascending order.

- If the first column of the table is text, you can use the standard wildcard characters in the *lookup_value* argument (use ? to substitute for individual characters; use * to substitute for multiple characters).

- If *lookup_value* is less than any value in the lookup column, VLOOKUP() returns the #N/A error value.

- If VLOOKUP() doesn't find a match in the lookup column, it returns #N/A.

- If *col_index_num* is less than 1, VLOOKUP() returns #VALUE!; if *col_index_num* is greater than the number of columns in *table*, VLOOKUP() returns #REF!.

## The HLOOKUP() **Function**

The HLOOKUP() function is similar to VLOOKUP(), except that it searches for the lookup value in the first row of a table. (The *H* in HLOOKUP() stands for *horizontal*.) If successful, this function then looks down the specified number of rows and returns the value it finds there. Here's the syntax for HLOOKUP():

HLOOKUP(*lookup_value*, *table_array*, *row_index_num*, [*range_lookup*])

| | |
|---|---|
| *lookup_value* | This is the value you want to find in the first row of *table_array*. You can enter a number, a string, or a reference. |
| *table_array* | This is the table to use for the lookup. You can use a range reference or a name. |

| | |
|---|---|
| *row_index_num* | If HLOOKUP() finds a match, *row_index_num* is the row number in the table that contains the data you want returned (the first row—that is, the lookup row—is 1, the second row is 2, and so on). |
| *range_lookup* | This is a Boolean value that determines how Excel searches for *lookup_value* in the first column: |

TRUE—VLOOKUP() searches for the first exact match for *lookup_value*. If no exact match is found, the function looks for the largest value that is less than *lookup_value* (this is the default).

FALSE—VLOOKUP() searches only for the first exact match for *lookup_value*.

## Performing Range Lookups

The most common use for VLOOKUP() and HLOOKUP() is to look for a match that falls within a range of values. This section takes you through a few examples of this range-lookup technique.

### Looking Up a Customer Discount Rate

In business-to-business transactions, the cost of an item is often calculated as a percentage of the retail price. For example, a publisher might sell books to a bookstore at half the suggested list price. The percentage that the seller takes off the list price for the buyer is called the *discount*. Often the size of the discount is a function of the number of units ordered. For example, ordering 1–3 items might result in a 20% discount, ordering 4–24 items might result in a 40% discount, and so on.

Figure 9.3 shows a worksheet that uses VLOOKUP() to determine the discount a customer gets on an order, based on the number of units purchased.

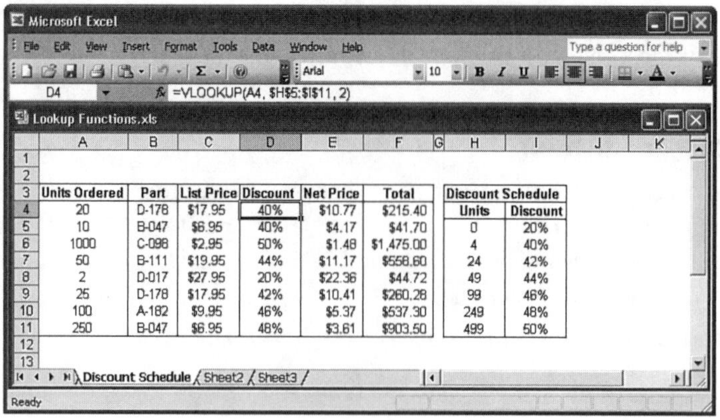

**Figure 9.3**
A worksheet that uses VLOOKUP() to look up a customer's discount in a discount schedule.

For example, cell D4 uses the following formula:

```
=VLOOKUP(A4, $H$5:$I$11, 2)
```

The *range_lookup* argument is omitted, which means VLOOKUP() searches for the largest value that is less than or equal to the lookup value; in this case, this is the value in cell A4. Cell A4 contains the number of units purchased (20, in this case), and the range $H$5:$I$11 is the discount schedule table. VLOOKUP() searches down the first column (H5:H11) for the largest value that is less than or equal to 20. The first such cell is H6 (because the value in H7—24—is larger than 20). VLOOKUP() therefore moves to the second column (because we specified *col_num* to be 2) of the table (cell I6) and grabs the value there (40%).

**9**

> **TIP**
>
> As mentioned earlier in this section, both VLOOKUP() and HLOOKUP() return #N/A if no match is found in the lookup range. If you would prefer to return a friendlier or more useful message, use the IF() function and the ISNA() function to test whether the lookup will fail. Here's the general idea:
>
> ```
> =IF(ISNA(LookupExpression), "LookupValue not found",
> LookupExpression))
> ```
>
> Here, *LookupExpression* is the VLOOKUP() or HLOOKUP() function, and *LookupValue* is the same as the *lookup_value* argument used in VLOOKUP() or HLOOKUP(). If ISNA() returns TRUE, the lookup will fail, so the formula returns the "*LookupValue* not found" string; otherwise, it runs the lookup normally.

## Looking Up a Tax Rate

Tax rates are perfect candidates for a range lookup because a given rate always applies to any income that is greater than some minimum amount and less than or equal to some maximum amount. For example, a rate of 25% might be applied to annual incomes over $28,400 and less than or equal to $68,800. Figure 9.4 shows a worksheet that uses VLOOKUP() to return the marginal tax rate given a specified income.

The lookup table is C9:F14, and the lookup value is cell B16, which contains the annual income. VLOOKUP() finds in column C the largest income that is less than or equal to the value in B16, which is $30,000. In this case, the matching value is $28,400 in cell C11. VLOOKUP() then looks in column 4 to get the marginal rate in row F, which, in this case, is 25%.

> **TIP**
>
> You might find that you have multiple lookup tables in your model. For example, you might have multiple tax rate tables that apply to different types of taxpayers (single versus married, for example). You can use the IF() function to choose which lookup table is used in a lookup formula. Here's the general formula:
>
> ```
> =VLOOKUP(lookup_value, IF(condition, table1, table2),
> col_index_num)
> ```
>
> If *condition* returns TRUE, a reference to *table1* is returned, and that table is used as the lookup table; otherwise, *table2* is used.

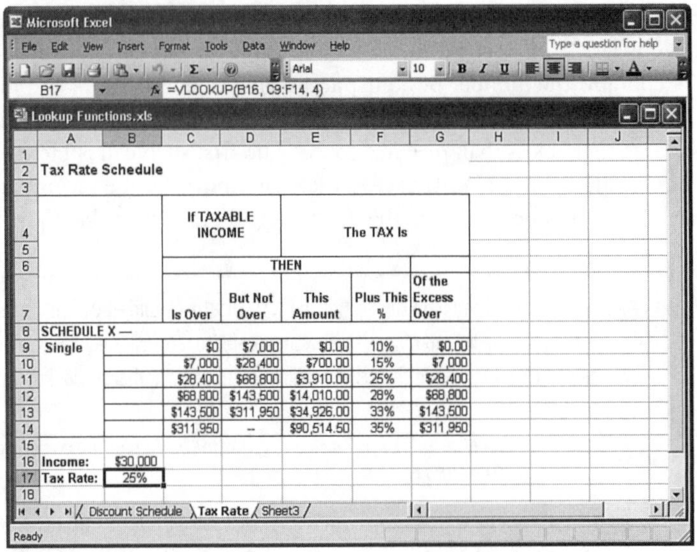

**Figure 9.4**
A worksheet that uses VLOOKUP( ) to look up a marginal income tax rate.

## Finding Exact Matches

In many situations, a range lookup isn't what you want. This is particularly true in lookup tables that contain a set of unique lookup values that represent discrete values instead of ranges. For example, if you need to look up a customer account number, a part code, or an employee ID, you want to be sure that your formula matches the value exactly. You can perform exact-match lookups with VLOOKUP( ) and HLOOKUP( ) by including the *range_lookup* argument with the value FALSE. The next couple of sections demonstrate this technique.

### Looking Up a Customer Account Number

A table of customer account numbers and names is a good example of a lookup table that contains discrete lookup values. In such a case, you want to use VLOOKUP( ) or HLOOKUP( ) to find an exact match for an account number you specify, and then return the corresponding account name. Figure 9.5 shows a simple data-entry screen that automatically adds a customer name after the user enters the account number in cell B2.

The function that accomplishes this is in cell B4:

```
=VLOOKUP(B2, D3:E15, 2, FALSE)
```

The value in B2 is looked up in column D, and because the *range_lookup* argument is set to FALSE, VLOOKUP( ) searches for an exact match. If it finds one, it returns the text from column E.

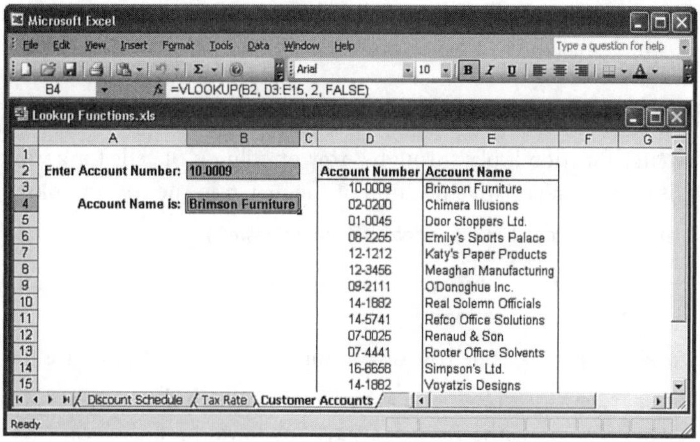

**Figure 9.5**
A simple data-entry worksheet that uses the exact-match version of VLOOKUP ( ) to look up a customer's name based on the entered account number.

## Combining Exact-Match Lookups with In-Cell Drop-Down Lists

In Chapter 4, you learned how to use data validation to set up an in-cell drop-down list. Whatever value the user selects from the list is the value that's stored in the cell. This technique becomes even more powerful when you combine it with exact-match lookups that use the current list selection as the lookup value.

→ To learn how to use data validation to set up an in-cell drop-down list, **see** "Applying Data Validation Rules to Cells," **p. 98**.

Figure 9.6 shows an example. Cell C9 contains a drop-down list that uses as its source the header values in row 1 (C1:N1). The formula in cell C10 uses HLOOKUP ( ) to perform an exact-match lookup using the currently selected list value from C9:

```
=HLOOKUP(C9, C1:N7, 7, FALSE)
```

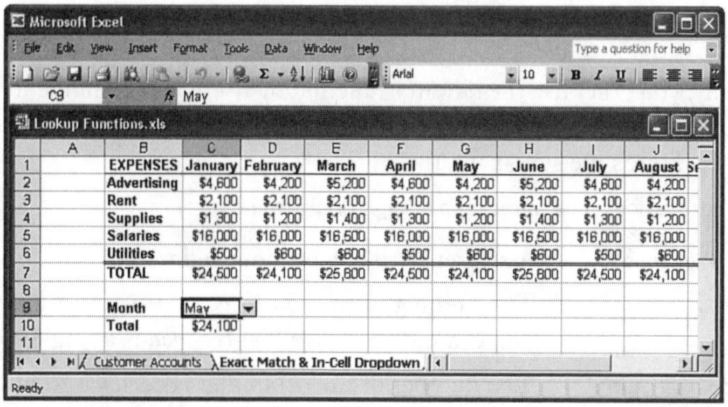

**Figure 9.6**
An HLOOKUP ( ) formula in C10 performs an exact-match lookup in row 1 based on the current selection in C9's in-cell drop-down list.

## Advanced Lookup Operations

The basic lookup procedure—looking up a value in a column or row and then returning an offset value—will satisfy most of your needs. However, a few operations require a more sophisticated approach. The rest of this chapter examines these more advanced lookups, most of which make use of two more lookup functions: MATCH() and INDEX().

### The MATCH() and INDEX() Functions

The MATCH() function looks through a row or column of cells for a value. If MATCH() finds a match, it returns the relative position of the match in the row or column. Here's the syntax:

MATCH(*lookup_value*, *lookup_array*, [*match_type*])

| | |
|---|---|
| *lookup_value* | The value you want to find. You can use a number, string, reference, or logical value. |
| *lookup_array* | The row or column of cells you want to use for the lookup. |
| *match_type* | How you want Excel to match the *lookup_value* with the entries in the *lookup_array*. You have three choices: |

| | |
|---|---|
| 0 | Finds the first value that exactly matches *lookup_value*. The *lookup_array* can be in any order. |
| 1 | Finds the largest value that's less than or equal to *lookup_value* (this is the default value). The *lookup_array* must be in ascending order. |
| −1 | Finds the smallest value that is greater than or equal to *lookup_value*. The *lookup_array* must be in descending order. |

> **TIP**
> You can use the usual wildcard characters within the *lookup_value* argument (provided that *match_type* is 0 and *lookup_value* is text). You can use the question mark (?) for single characters and the asterisk (*) for multiple characters.

Normally, you don't use the MATCH() function by itself; you combine it with the INDEX() function. INDEX() returns the value of a cell at the intersection of a row and column inside a reference. Here's the syntax for INDEX():

INDEX(*reference*, *row_num*, [*column_num*], [*area_num*])

| | |
|---|---|
| *reference* | A reference to one or more cell ranges. |
| *row_num* | The number of the row in *reference* from which to return a value. You can omit *row_num* if *reference* is a single row. |
| *column_num* | The number of the column in *reference* from which to return a value. You can omit *column_num* if *reference* is a single column. |
| *area_num* | If you entered more than one range for *reference*, *area_num* is the range you want to use. The first range you entered is 1 (this is the default), the second is 2, and so on. |

The idea is that you use MATCH() to get *row_num* or *column_num* (depending on how your table is laid out), and then use INDEX() to return the value you need.

To give you the flavor of using these two functions, let's duplicate our earlier effort of looking up a customer name, given the account number. Figure 9.7 shows the result.

**Figure 9.7**

A worksheet that uses INDEX() and MATCH() to look up a customer's name based on the entered account number.

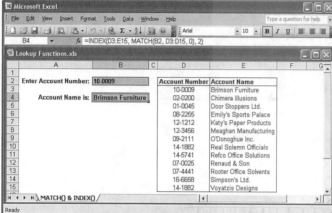

In particular, notice the new formula in cell B4:

```
=INDEX(D3:E15, MATCH(B2, D3:D15, 0), 2)
```

The MATCH() function looks up the value in cell B2 in the range D3:D15. That value is then used as the *row_num* argument for the INDEX() function. That value is 1 in the example, so the INDEX() function reduces to this:

```
=INDEX(D3:E15, 1, 2)
```

This returns the value in the first row and the second column of the range D3:E15.

## Looking Up a Value Using Worksheet List Boxes

If you use a worksheet list box or combo box as explained in Chapter 4, the linked cell contains the number of the selected item, not the item itself. Figure 9.8 shows a worksheet with a list box and a drop-down list. The list used by both controls is the range A3:A10. Notice that the linked cells (E3 and E10) display the number of the list selection, not the selection itself.

To get the selected list item, you can use the INDEX() function with the following modified syntax:

```
INDEX(list_range, list_selection)
```

| | |
|---|---|
| *list_range* | The range used in the list box or drop-down list |
| *list_selection* | The number of the item selected in the list |

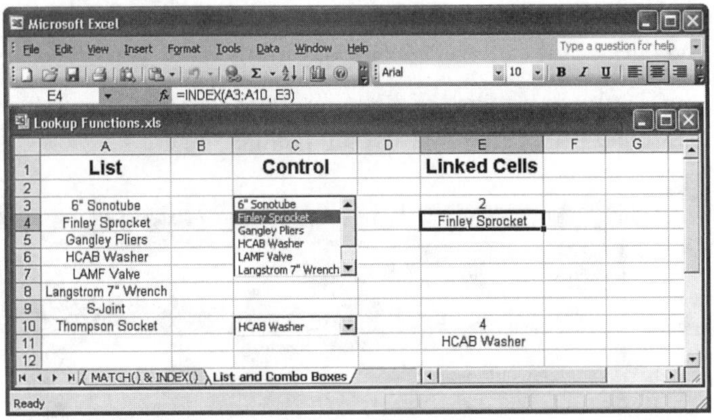

**Figure 9.8**
This worksheet uses
INDEX() to get the
selected item from a list
box and a combo box.

For example, to find the item selected from the list box in Figure 9.8, you use the following formula:

`=INDEX(A3:A10, E3)`

## Using Any Column as the Lookup Column

One of the major disadvantages of the VLOOKUP() function is that you must use the table's leftmost column as the lookup column. (HLOOKUP() suffers from a similar problem: It must use the table's topmost row as the lookup row.) This isn't a problem if you remember to structure your lookup table accordingly, but that might not be possible in some cases, particularly if you inherit the data from someone else.

Fortunately, you can use the MATCH() and INDEX() combination to use *any* table column as the lookup column. For example, consider the parts database shown in Figure 9.9.

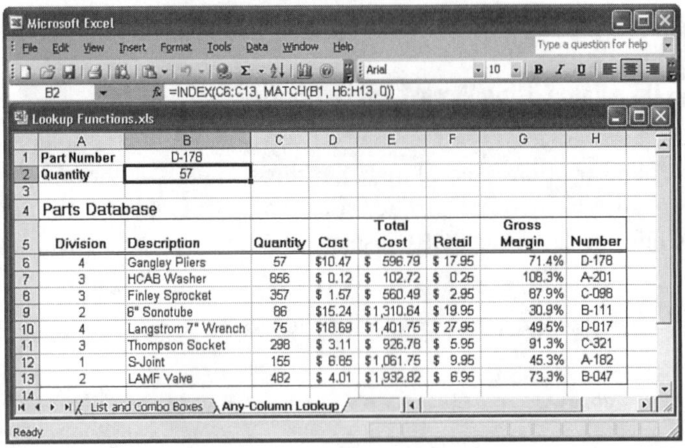

**Figure 9.9**
In this lookup table, the
lookup values are in col-
umn H and the value
you want to find is in
column C.

Column H contains the unique part numbers, so that's what you want to use as the lookup column. The data you need is the quantity in column C. To accomplish this, you first find the part number (as given by the value in B1) in column H using MATCH():

```
MATCH(B1, H6:H13, 0)
```

When you know which row contains the part, you plug this result into an INDEX() function that operates only on the column that contains the data you want (column C):

```
=INDEX(C6:C13, MATCH(B1, H6:H13, 0))
```

## Creating Row-and-Column Lookups

So far, all of the lookups you've seen have been one-dimensional, meaning they searched for a lookup value in a single column or row. However, in many situations you need a two-dimensional approach. This means that you need to look up a value in a column *and* a value in a row, and then return the data value at the intersection of the two. I call this a *row-and-column lookup*.

You do this by using *two* MATCH() functions: one to calculate the INDEX() function's *row_num* argument, and the other to calculate the INDEX() function's *column_num* argument. Figure 9.10 shows an example.

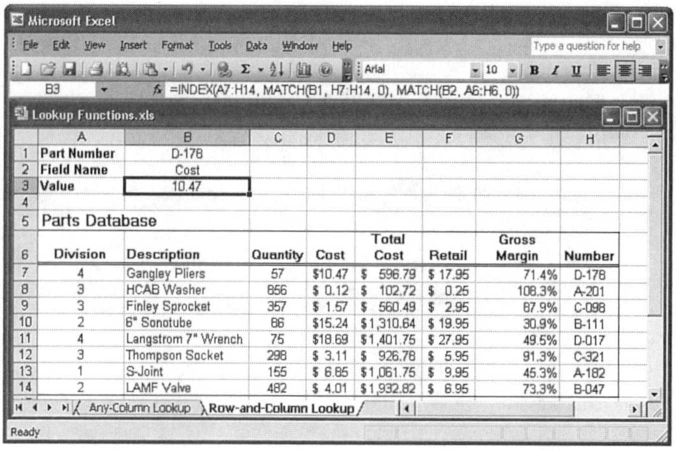

**Figure 9.10**
To perform a two-dimensional row-and-column lookup, use MATCH() functions to calculate both the row and column values for the INDEX() function.

The idea here is to use both the part numbers (column H) and the field names (row 6) to return specific values from the parts database.

The part number is entered in cell B1, and getting the corresponding row in the parts table is no different than what you did in the previous section:

```
MATCH(B1, H7:H14, 0)
```

The field name is entered in cell B2. Getting the corresponding column number requires the following `MATCH()` expression:

```
MATCH(B2, A6:H6, 0)
```

These provide the `INDEX()` function's *`row_num`* and *`column_num`* arguments (see cell B3):

```
=INDEX(A7:H14, MATCH(B1, H7:H14, 0), MATCH(B2, A6:H6, 0))
```

## Creating Multiple-Column Lookups

Sometimes it's not enough to look up a value in a single column. For example, in a list of employee names, you might need to look up both the first name and the last name if they're in separate fields. One way to handle this is to create a new field that concatenates all the lookup values into a single item. However, it's possible to do this without going to the trouble of creating a new concatenated field.

The secret is to perform the concatenation within the `MATCH()` function, as in this generic expression:

```
MATCH(value1 & value2, array1 & array2, match_type)
```

Here, *`value1`* and *`value2`* are the lookup values you want to work with, and *`array1`* and *`array2`* are the lookup columns. You can then plug the results into an array formula that uses `INDEX()` to get the needed data:

```
{=INDEX(reference, MATCH(value1 & value2, array1 & array2, match_type))}
```

For example, Figure 9.11 shows a database of employees, with separate fields for the first name, last name, title, and more.

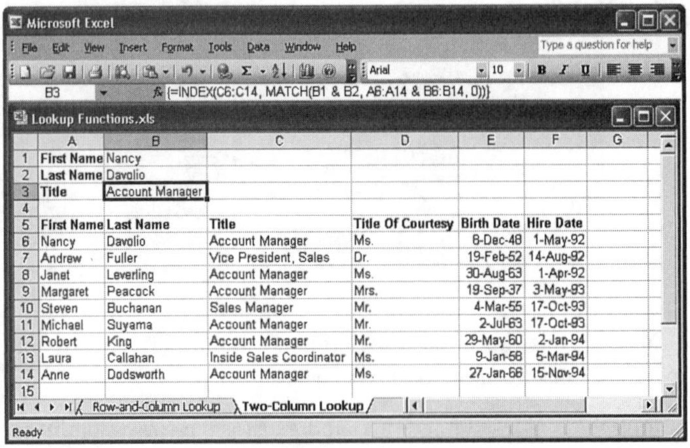


| | A | B | C | D | E | F | G |
|---|---|---|---|---|---|---|---|
| 1 | First Name | Nancy | | | | | |
| 2 | Last Name | Davolio | | | | | |
| 3 | Title | Account Manager | | | | | |
| 4 | | | | | | | |
| 5 | First Name | Last Name | Title | Title Of Courtesy | Birth Date | Hire Date | |
| 6 | Nancy | Davolio | Account Manager | Ms. | 8-Dec-48 | 1-May-92 | |
| 7 | Andrew | Fuller | Vice President, Sales | Dr. | 19-Feb-52 | 14-Aug-92 | |
| 8 | Janet | Leverling | Account Manager | Ms. | 30-Aug-63 | 1-Apr-92 | |
| 9 | Margaret | Peacock | Account Manager | Mrs. | 19-Sep-37 | 3-May-93 | |
| 10 | Steven | Buchanan | Sales Manager | Mr. | 4-Mar-55 | 17-Oct-93 | |
| 11 | Michael | Suyama | Account Manager | Mr. | 2-Jul-63 | 17-Oct-93 | |
| 12 | Robert | King | Account Manager | Mr. | 29-May-60 | 2-Jan-94 | |
| 13 | Laura | Callahan | Inside Sales Coordinator | Ms. | 9-Jan-58 | 5-Mar-94 | |
| 14 | Anne | Dodsworth | Account Manager | Ms. | 27-Jan-66 | 15-Nov-94 | |
| 15 | | | | | | | |

**Figure 9.11**
To perform a two-column lookup, use `MATCH()` to find a row based on the concatenated values of two or more columns.

The lookup values are in B1 (first name) and B2 (last name), and the lookup columns are A6:A14 (the First Name field) and B6:B14 (the Last Name field). Here's the `MATCH()` function that looks up the required column:

```
MATCH(B1 & B2, A6:A14 & B6:B14, 0)
```

We want the specified employee's title, so the INDEX() function looks in C6:C14 (the Title field). Here's the array formula in cell B3:

```
{=INDEX(C6:C14, MATCH(B1 & B2, A6:A14 & B6:B14, 0))}
```

## From Here

- To learn how to use data validation to set up an in-cell drop-down list, **see** "Applying Data Validation Rules to Cells," **p. 98**.

- For the specifics of adding option buttons and list boxes to a worksheet, **see** "Understanding the Worksheet Controls," **p. 101**.

- For a general discussion of function syntax, **see** "The Structure of a Function," **p. 126**.

- To learn about the WEEKDAY() function, **see** "The WEEKDAY() Function," **p. 206**.

9

# Working with Date and Time Functions

**10**

The date and time functions enable you to convert dates and times to serial numbers and perform operations on those numbers. This capability is useful for such things as accounts receivable aging, project scheduling, time-management applications, and much more. This chapter introduces you to Excel's date and time functions and puts them through their paces with many practical examples.

## How Excel Deals with Dates and Times

Excel uses *serial numbers* to represent specific dates and times. To get a date serial number, Excel uses December 31, 1899, as an arbitrary starting point and then counts the number of days that have passed since then. So, for example, the date serial number for January 1, 1900, is 1; for January 2, 1900, is 2; and so on. Table 10.1 displays some example date serial numbers.

**Table 10.1 Examples of Date Serial Numbers**

| Serial Number | Date |
| --- | --- |
| 366 | December 31, 1900 |
| 16229 | June 6, 1944 |
| 38352 | December 31, 2004 |

To get a time serial number, Excel expresses time as a decimal fraction of the 24-hour day to get a number between 0 and 1. The starting point, midnight, is given the value 0, so noon—halfway through the day—has a serial number of 0.5. Table 10.2 displays some example time serial numbers.

**Table 10.2 Examples of Time Serial Numbers**

| Serial Number | Time |
| --- | --- |
| 0.25 | 6:00:00 AM |
| 0.375 | 9:00:00 AM |
| 0.70833 | 5:00:00 PM |
| .99999 | 11:59:59 PM |

You can combine the two types of serial numbers. For example, 38352.5 represents noon on December 31, 2004.

The advantage of using serial numbers in this way is that it makes calculations involving dates and times very easy. A date or time is really just a number, so any mathematical operation you can perform on a number can also be performed on a date. This is invaluable for worksheets that track delivery times, monitor accounts receivable or accounts payable aging, calculate invoice discount dates, and so on.

## Entering Dates and Times

Although it's true that the serial numbers make it easier for the computer to manipulate dates and times, it's not the best format for humans to comprehend. For example, the number 25,404.95555 is meaningless, but the moment it represents (July 20, 1969, at 10:56 p.m. EDT) is one of the great moments in history (the Apollo 11 moon landing). Fortunately, Excel takes care of the conversion between these formats so that you never have to worry about it. To enter a date or time, use any of the formats outlined in Table 10.3.

**Table 10.3 Excel Date and Time Formats**

| Format | Example |
| --- | --- |
| m/d/yyyy | 8/23/2004 |
| d-mmm-yy | 23-Aug-04 |

| Format | Example |
|---|---|
| d-mmm | 23-Aug (Excel assumes the current year) |
| mmm-yy | Aug-04 (Excel assumes the first day of the month) |
| h:mm:ss AM/PM | 10:35:10 PM |
| h:mm AM/PM | 10:35 PM |
| h:mm:ss | 22:35:10 |
| h:mm | 22:35 |
| m/d/y h:mm | 8/23/04 22:35 |

> **TIP**
>
> Here are a couple of shortcuts that will let you enter dates and times quickly. To enter the current date in a cell, press Ctrl+; (semicolon). To enter the current time, press Ctrl+: (colon).

Table 10.3 represents Excel's built-in formats, but these are not set in stone. You're free to mix and match these formats, as long as you observe the following rules:

- You can use either the forward slash (/) or the hyphen (-) as a date separator. Always use a colon (:) as a time separator.
- You can combine any date and time format, as long as you separate them with a space.
- You can enter date and time values using either uppercase or lowercase letters. Excel automatically adjusts the capitalization to its standard format.
- To display times using the 12-hour clock, include either am (or just a) or pm (or just p). If you leave these off, Excel uses the 24-hour clock.

→ For more information on formatting dates and times, **see** "Formatting Numbers, Dates, and Times," **p. 72**.

## Excel and Two-Digit Years

Entering two-digit years (such as 04 for 2004 and 99 for 1999) is problematic in Excel because various versions of the program treat them differently. In versions since Excel 97, the two-digit years 00 through 29 are interpreted as the years 2000 through 2029, while 30 through 99 are interpreted as the years 1930 through 1999. Earlier versions treated the two-digit years 00 through 19 as 2000 through 2019, and 20 through 99 as 1920 through 1999.

Two problems arise here: One is that using a two-digit year such as 25 will cause havoc if the worksheet will ever be loaded into Excel 95 or some earlier version. The second is that you could throw a monkey wrench into your calculations by using a date such as 8/23/30 to mean August 23, 2030, because Excel treats it as August 23, 1930.

The easiest solution to both problems is to always use four-digit years to avoid ambiguity. Alternatively, you can put off the second problem by changing how Excel and Windows interpret two-digit years. Here are the steps to following in Windows XP (Windows 98 and later have similar options):

1. Open the Windows Control Panel and double-click the Regional and Language Options icon.

2. In the Regional Options tab, choose Customize. The Customize Regional Options dialog box appears.

3. Select the Date tab.

4. Use the When a Two-Digit Year Is Entered, Interpret It As a Year Between spinner to adjust the maximum year in which a two-digit year is interpreted as a 21st-century date (see Figure 10.1)

5. Click OK to return to the Regional and Language Options dialog box.

6. Click OK to put the new setting into effect.

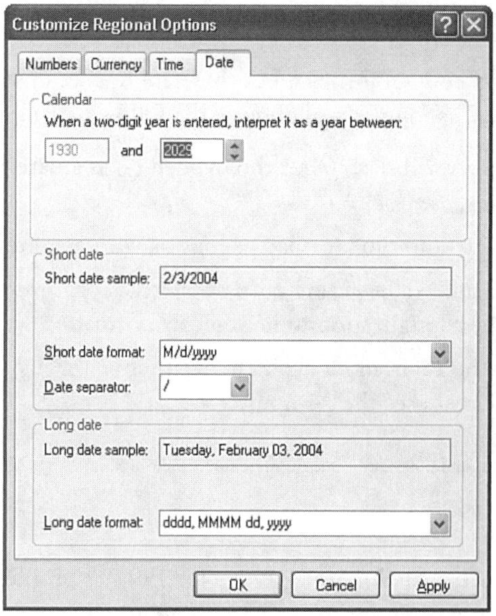

**Figure 10.1**
Use the Date tab to adjust how Windows (and, therefore, Excel) interprets two-digit years.

## Using Excel's Date Functions

Excel's date functions work with or return date serial numbers. All of Excel's date-related functions are listed in Table 10.4. (For the *serial_number* arguments, you can use any valid Excel date.)

**Table 10.4    Excel's Date Functions**

| Function | Description |
|---|---|
| DATE(*year*,*month*,*day*) | Returns the serial number of a date, in which *year* is a number from 1900 to 2078, *month* is a number representing the month of the year, and *day* is a number representing the day of the month |
| DATEDIF(*start_date*, *end_date*, [*unit*]) | Returns the difference between *start_date* and *end_date*, based on the specified *unit* |
| DATEVALUE(*date_text*) | Converts a date from text to a serial number |
| DAY(*serial_number*) | Extracts the day component from the date given by *serial_number* |
| DAYS360(*start_date*, *end_date*, [*method*]) | Returns the number of days between *start_date* and *end_date*, based on a 360-day year |
| EDATE(*start_date*, *months*) | Returns the serial number of a date that is the specified number of *months* before or after *start_date* (this is an Analysis ToolPak function) |
| EOMONTH(*start_date*, *months*) | Returns the serial number of the last day of the month that is the specified number of *months* before or after *start_date* (this is an Analysis ToolPak function) |
| MONTH(*serial_number*) | Extracts the month component from the date given by *serial_number* (January = 1) |
| NETWORKDAYS(*start_date*, *end_date*, [*holidays*]) | Returns the number of working days between *start_date* and *end_date*; doesn't include weekends and any dates specified by *holidays* (this is an Analysis ToolPak function) |
| TODAY() | Returns the serial number of the current date |
| WEEKDAY(*serial_number*) | Converts a serial number to a day of the week (Sunday = 1) |

*continues*

**Table 10.4  Continued**

| Function | Description |
|---|---|
| WEEKNUM(*serial_number*, [*return_type*]) | Returns a number that corresponds to where the week that includes *serial_number* falls numerically during the year (this is an Analysis ToolPak function) |
| WORKDAY(*start_date*, *days*, [*holidays*]) | Returns the serial number of the day that is *days* working days from *start_date*; weekends and *holidays* are excluded (this is an Analysis ToolPak function) |
| YEAR(*serial_number*) | Extracts the year component from the date given by *serial_number* |
| YEARFRAC(*start_date*, *end_date*, *basis*) | Converts the number of days between *start_date* and *end_date* into a fraction of a year (this is an Analysis ToolPak function) |

## Returning a Date

If you need a date for an expression operand or a function argument, you can always enter it by hand if you have a specific date in mind. Much of the time, however, you need more flexibility, such as always entering the current date or building a date from day, month, and year components. Excel offers three functions that can help: TODAY(), DATE(), and DATEVALUE().

### TODAY(): Returning the Current Date

When you need to use the current date in a formula, function, or expression, use the TODAY() function, which doesn't take any arguments:

```
TODAY()
```

This function returns the serial number of the current date, with midnight as the assumed time. For example, if today's date is December 31, 2004, the TODAY() function returns the following serial number:

```
38352.0
```

Note that TODAY() is a dynamic function that doesn't always return the same value. Each time you edit the formula, enter another formula, recalculate the worksheet, or reopen the workbook, TODAY() updates its value to return the current system date.

### DATE(): **Returning Any Date**

A date consists of three components: the year, the month, and the day. It often happens that a worksheet generates one or more of these components, and you need some way of building a proper date out of them. You can do that by using Excel's DATE() function:

DATE(*year, month, day*)

| | |
|---|---|
| *year* | The year component of the date (a number between 1900 and 9999) |
| *month* | The month component of the date |
| *day* | The day component of the date |

> **CAUTION**
>
> Excel's date inconsistencies rear up again with the DATE() function. That's because, if you enter a two-digit year (or even a three-digit year), Excel converts the number into a year value by adding 1900. So, entering 5 as the *year* argument gives you 1905, not 2005. To avoid problems, *always* use a four-digit year when entering the DATE() function's *year* argument.

For example, the following expression returns the serial number of Christmas Day in 2004:

DATE(2004, 12, 25)

Note, too, that DATE() adjusts for "wrong" month and day values. For example, the following expression returns the serial number of January 1, 2005:

DATE(2004, 12, 32)

Here, DATE() adds the extra day (there are 31 days in December) to return the date of the next day. Similarly, the following expression returns January 25, 2005:

DATE(2004, 13, 25)

### DATEVALUE(): **Converting a String to a Date**

If you have a date value in string form, you can convert it to a date serial number by using the DATEVALUE() function:

DATEVALUE(*date_text*)

| | |
|---|---|
| *date_text* | The string containing the date |

For example, the following expression returns the date serial number for the string August 23, 2004:

DATEVALUE("August 23, 2004")

→ To learn how to convert nonstandard date strings to dates, **see** "A Date-Conversion Formula," **p. 146**.

## Returning Parts of a Date

The three components of a date—year, month, and day—can also be extracted individually from a given date. This might not seem all that interesting at first, but actually many useful techniques arise out of working with a date's component parts. A date's components are extracted using Excel's YEAR(), MONTH(), and DAY() functions.

### The YEAR() Function

The YEAR() function returns a four-digit number that corresponds to the year component of a specified date:

YEAR(*serial_number*)

> *serial_number*    The date (or a string representation of the date) you want to work with

For example, if today is August 23, 2004, the following expression will return 2004:

YEAR(TODAY())

### The MONTH() Function

The MONTH() function returns a number between 1 and 12 that corresponds to the month component of a specified date:

MONTH(*serial_number*)

> *serial_number*    The date (or a string representation of the date) you want to work with

For example, the following expression returns 8:

MONTH("August 23, 2004")

### The DAY() Function

The DAY() function returns a number between 1 and 31 that corresponds to the day component of a specified date:

DAY(*serial_number*)

> *serial_number*    The date (or a string representation of the date) you want to work with

For example, the following expression returns 23:

DAY("8/23/2004")

### The WEEKDAY() Function

The WEEKDAY() function returns a number that corresponds to the day of the week upon which a specified date falls:

WEEKDAY(*serial_number*, [*return_type*])

> *serial_number*    The date (or a string representation of the date) you want to work with

| | |
|---|---|
| *return_type* | An integer that determines how the value returned by WEEKDAY() corresponds to the days of the week: |

| | |
|---|---|
| 1 | The return values are 1 (Sunday) through 7 (Saturday); this is the default. |
| 2 | The return values are 1 (Monday) through 7 (Sunday). |
| 3 | The return values are 0 (Monday) through 6 (Sunday). |

For example, the following expression returns 2 because August 23, 2004, is a Monday:

```
WEEKDAY("8/23/2004")
```

→ To learn how to use CHOOSE() to convert the WEEKDAY() return value into a day name, **see** "Determining the Name of the Day of the Week," **p. 183**.

## The WEEKNUM() **Function**

The WEEKNUM() function returns a number that corresponds to where the week that includes a specified date falls numerically during the year:

```
WEEKDAY(serial_number, [return_type])
```

| | |
|---|---|
| *serial_number* | The date (or a string representation of the date) you want to work with |
| *return_type* | An integer that determines how WEEKNUM() interprets the start of the week: |

| | |
|---|---|
| 1 | The week begins on Sunday; this is the default. |
| 2 | The week begins on Monday. |

For example, the following expression returns 35 because August 23, 2004, falls in the 35th week of 2004:

```
WEEKNUM("August 23, 2004")
```

→ WEEKNUM() is available only with the Analysis ToolPak loaded; **see** "Loading the Analysis ToolPak Functions," **p. 131**.

## Returning a Date *X* Years, Months, or Days from Now

You can take advantage of the fact that, as I mentioned earlier, DATE() automatically adjusts "wrong" month and day values by applying formulas to one or more of the DATE() function's arguments. The most common use for this is returning a date that occurs *X* number of years, months, or days from now (or from any date).

For example, suppose that you want to know which day of the week the 4th of July falls on next year. Here's a formula that figures it out:

```
=WEEKDAY(DATE(YEAR(TODAY)) + 1, 7, 4)
```

As another example, if you want to work with whatever date it is six months from now, you would use the following expression:

```
DATE(YEAR(TODAY()), MONTH(TODAY()) + 6, DAY(TODAY()))
```

Given this technique, you've probably figured out that you can return a date that is *X* days from now (or whenever) by adding to the day component of the DATE() function. For example, here's an expression that returns a date 30 days from now:

```
DATE(YEAR(TODAY()), MONTH(TODAY()), DAY(TODAY() + 30))
```

This is overkill, however, because date addition and subtraction works at the day level in Excel. That is, if you simply add or subtract a number to or from a date, Excel adds or subtracts that number of days. For example, to return a date 30 days from now, you need only use the following expression:

```
TODAY() + 30
```

## A Workday Alternative: the WORKDAY() Function

Adding days to or subtracting days from a date is straightforward, but the basic calculation includes *all* days: workdays, weekends, and holidays. In many cases, you might need to ignore weekends and holidays and return a date that is a specified number of workdays from some original date.

You can do this by using the Analysis ToolPak's WORKDAY() function, which returns a date that is a specified number of working days from some starting date:

```
WORKDAY(start_date, days, [holidays])
```

| | |
|---|---|
| start_date | The original date (or a string representation of the date). |
| days | The number of workdays before or after start_date. Use a positive number to return a later date; use a negative number to return an earlier date. Noninteger values are truncated (that is, the decimal part is ignored). |
| holidays | A list of dates to exclude from the calculation. This can be a range of dates or an array constant (that is, a series of date serial numbers or date strings, separated by commas and surrounded by braces {}). |

For example, the following expression returns a date that is 30 workdays from today:

```
WORKDAY(TODAY(), 30)
```

Here's another expression that returns the date that is 30 workdays from December 1, 2003, excluding December 25, 2003, and January 1, 2004:

```
=WORKDAY("12/1/2003", 30, {"12/25/2003","1/1/2004"})
```

→ It's possible to calculate the various holidays that occur within a year and place the dates within a range for use as the WORKDAY() function's *holidays* argument. **See** "Calculating Holiday Dates, **p. 213**.

## Adding *X* Months: A Problem

You should be aware that simply adding *X* months to a specified date's month component won't always return the result you expect. The problem is that the months have a varying number of days. So, if you add a certain number of months to a date that falls on or near the end of a month, the future month might not have the same number of days. Excel adjusts the day component accordingly.

For example, suppose that A1 contains the date 1/31/2005, and consider the following formula:

```
=DATE(YEAR(A1), MONTH(A1) + 3, DAY(A1))
```

You might expect this formula to return the last date in April as the result. Unfortunately, adding three months returns the "wrong" date 4/31/2005, which Excel automatically converts to 5/1/2005.

You can avoid this problem by using two of Excel's Analysis ToolPak functions: EDATE() and EOMONTH().

## The EDATE() Function

The Analysis ToolPak's EDATE() function returns a date that is the specified number of months before or after a starting date:

```
EDATE(start_date, months)
```

| | |
|---|---|
| *start_date* | The original date (or a string representation of the date). |
| *months* | The number of months before or after *start_date*. Use a positive number to return a later date; use a negative number to return an earlier date. Noninteger values are truncated (that is, the decimal part is ignored). |

The nice thing about the EDATE() function is that it performs a "smart" calculation when working with dates at or near the end of the month: If the day component of the returned date doesn't exist (for example, February 31), EDATE() returns the last day of the month (February 28).

The EDATE() function is useful for calculating the coupon payment dates for bond issues. Given the bond's maturity date, you can first calculate the bond's first payment as follows (assuming that the bond was issued this year and that the maturity date is in a cell named MaturityDate):

```
=DATE(YEAR(TODAY()), MONTH(MaturityDate), DAY(MaturityDate))
```

If this result is in cell A1, the following formula will return the date of the next coupon payment:

```
=EDATE(A1, 6)
```

### The EOMONTH() **Function**

The Analysis ToolPak's EOMONTH() function returns the date of the last day of the month that is the specified number of months before or after a starting date:

EOMONTH(*start_date, months*)

| | |
|---|---|
| *start_date* | The original date (or a string representation of the date). |
| *months* | The number of months before or after *start_date*. Use a positive number to return a later date; use a negative number to return an earlier date. Noninteger values are truncated (that is, the decimal part is ignored). |

For example, the following formula returns the last day of the month three months from now:

=EOMONTH(TODAY(), 3)

## Returning the Last Day of Any Month

The EOMONTH() function returns the last date of some month in the future or the past. However, what if you have a date and you want to know the last day of the month in which that date appears?

You can calculate this by using yet another trick involving the DATE() function's capability to adjust "wrong" values for date components. You want a formula that returns the last day of a particular month. You can't specify the *day* argument in the DATE() function directly because the months can have 28, 29, 30, or 31 days. Instead, you can take advantage of an apparently trivial fact: the last day of any month is always the day *before* the first day of the next month. The number before 1 is 0, so you can plug 0 into the DATE() function as the *day* argument:

=DATE(YEAR(MyDate), MONTH(MyDate) + 1, 0)

Here, assume that MyDate is the date you want to work with.

## Determining a Person's Birthday Given the Birth Date

If you know a person's birth date, determining that person's birthday is easy: Just keep the month and day the same, and substitute the current year for the year of birth. To accomplish this in a formula, you could use the following:

=DATE(YEAR(NOW()), MONTH(Birthdate), DAY(Birthdate))

Here, I'm assuming that the person's date of birth is in a cell named BirthDate. The YEAR(NOW()) component extracts the current year, and MONTH(BirthDate) and DAY(BirthDate) extract the month and day, respectively, from the person's date of birth. Combine these into the DATE() function, and you have the birthday.

## Returning the Date of the *N*th Occurrence of a Weekday in a Month

It's a common date task to have to figure out the *n*th weekday in a given month. For example, you might need to schedule a budget meeting for the first Monday in each month, or you might want to plan the annual company picnic for the third Sunday in June. These are tricky calculations, to be sure, but Excel's date functions are up to the task.

As with many complex formulas, the best place to start is with what you know for sure. In this case, we always know for sure the date of the first day of whatever month we're dealing with. For example, Labor Day always occurs on the first Monday in September, so you would begin with September 1 and know that the date you seek is some number of days after that. The formula begins like this:

```
=DATE(Year, Month, 1) + days
```

Here, *Year* is the year in which you want the date to fall, and *Month* is the number of the month you want to work with. The *days* value is what you need to calculate.

To simplify things for now, let's assume that you're trying to find a date that is the first occurrence of a particular weekday in a month (such as Labor Day, the first Monday in September).

Using the first of the month as your starting point, you need to ask whether the weekday you're working with is less than the weekday of the first of the month. (By "less than," I mean that the WEEKDAY() value of the day of the week you're working with is numerically smaller than the WEEKDAY() value the first of the month.) In the Labor Day example, September 1, 2004, falls on a Wednesday (WEEKDAY() equals 4), which is greater than Monday (WEEKDAY() equals 2). The result of this comparison determines how many days you add to the 1st to get the date you seek:

- If the day of the week you're working with is less than the first of the month, the date you seek is the first plus the result of the following expression:
  ```
  7 - WEEKDAY(DATE(Year, Month, 1)) + Weekday
  ```
  Here, *Weekday* is the WEEKDAY() value of the day of the week you're working with. Here's the expression for the Labor Day example:
  ```
  7 - WEEKDAY(DATE(2004, 9, 1)) + 2
  ```

- If the day of the week you're working with is greater than or equal to the first of the month, the date you seek is the first plus the result of the following expression:
  ```
  Weekday - WEEKDAY(DATE(Year, Month, 1))
  ```
  Again, *Weekday* is the WEEKDAY() value of the day of the week you're working with. Here's the expression for the Labor Day example:
  ```
  2 - WEEKDAY(DATE(2004, 9, 1))
  ```

These conditions can be handled by a basic IF() function. Here, then, is the generic formula for calculating the first occurrence of a *Weekday* in a given *Year* and *Month*:

```
=DATE(Year, Month, 1) +
IF(Weekday < WEEKDAY(DATE(Year, Month, 1)),
7 - WEEKDAY(DATE(Year, Month, 1)) + Weekday,
Weekday - WEEKDAY(DATE(Year, Month, 1)))
```

Here's the formula for calculating the date of Labor Day in 2004:

```
=DATE(2004, 9, 1) +
IF(2 < WEEKDAY(DATE(2004, 9, 1)),
7 - WEEKDAY(DATE(2004, 9, 1)) + 2,
2 - WEEKDAY(DATE(2004, 9, 1)))
```

Generalizing this formula for the *n*th occurrence of a weekday is straightforward: The second occurrence comes one week after the first, the third occurrence comes two weeks after the first, and so on. Here's a generic expression to calculate the extra number of days to add (where *n* is an integer that represents the *n*th occurrence):

```
(n - 1) * 7
```

Here, then, in generic form, is the final formula for calculating the *n*th occurrence of a *Weekday* in a given *Year* and *Month*:

```
=DATE(Year, Month, 1) +
IF(Weekday < WEEKDAY(DATE(Year, Month, 1)),
7 - WEEKDAY(DATE(Year, Month, 1)) + Weekday,
Weekday - WEEKDAY(DATE(Year, Month, 1))) +
(n - 1) * 7
```

For example, the following formula calculates the date of the third Sunday (WEEKDAY() equals 1) in June for 2005:

```
=DATE(2005, 6, 1) +
IF(1 < WEEKDAY(DATE(2005, 6, 1)),
7 - WEEKDAY(DATE(2005, 6, 1)) + 1,
1 - WEEKDAY(DATE(2005, 6, 1))) +
(3 - 1) * 7
```

Figure 10.2 shows a worksheet used for calculating the *n*th occurrence of a weekday.

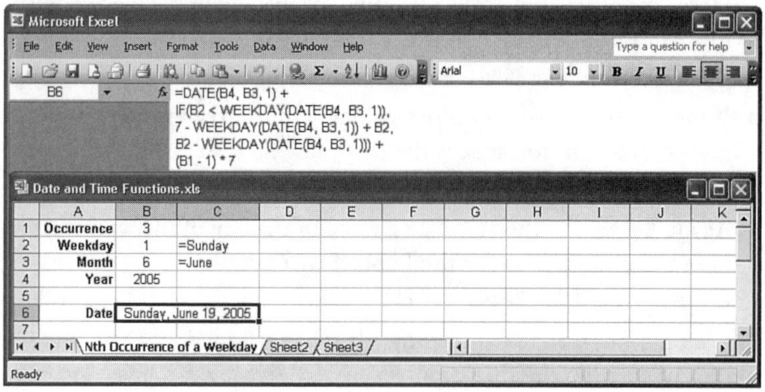

**Figure 10.2**
This worksheet calculates the *n*th occurrence of a specified weekday in a given year and month.

NOTE: You can download the workbook that contains this chapter's examples here:
www.mcfedries.com/ExcelFormulas/

The input cells are as follows:

- **B1**—The number of the occurrence
- **B2**—The number of the weekday (the formula in C2 shows the name of the entered weekday)
- **B3**—The number of the month (the formula in C3 shows the name of the entered month)
- **B4**—The year

The date calculation appears in cell B6. Here's the formula:

```
=DATE(B4, B3, 1) +
IF(B2 < WEEKDAY(DATE(B4, B3, 1)),
7 - WEEKDAY(DATE(B4, B3, 1)) + B2,
B2 - WEEKDAY(DATE(B4, B3, 1))) +
(B1 - 1) * 7
```

## Calculating Holiday Dates

Given the formula from the previous section, it becomes a relative breeze to calculate the dates for most floating holidays (that is, holidays that occur on the *n*th weekday of a month instead of on a specific date each year, as do holidays such as Christmas, Independence Day, and Canada Day).

Here are the standard statutory floating holidays in the United States:

- **Martin Luther King Jr. Day**—Third Monday in January
- **Presidents Day**—Third Monday in February
- **Memorial Day**—Last Monday in May
- **Labor Day**—First Monday in September
- **Columbus Day**—Second Monday in October
- **Thanksgiving Day**—Fourth Thursday in November

Here's the list for Canada:

- **Victoria Day**—Monday on or before May 24
- **Easter Monday**—Monday after Easter Sunday
- **Labor Day**—First Monday in September
- **Thanksgiving Day**—Second Monday in October

Figure 10.3 shows a worksheet used to calculate the holiday dates in a specified year.

Column A holds the name of the holiday; column B holds the occurrence within the month or, for fixed holidays, the actual date within the month; column C holds the days of the week; and column D holds the number of the month.

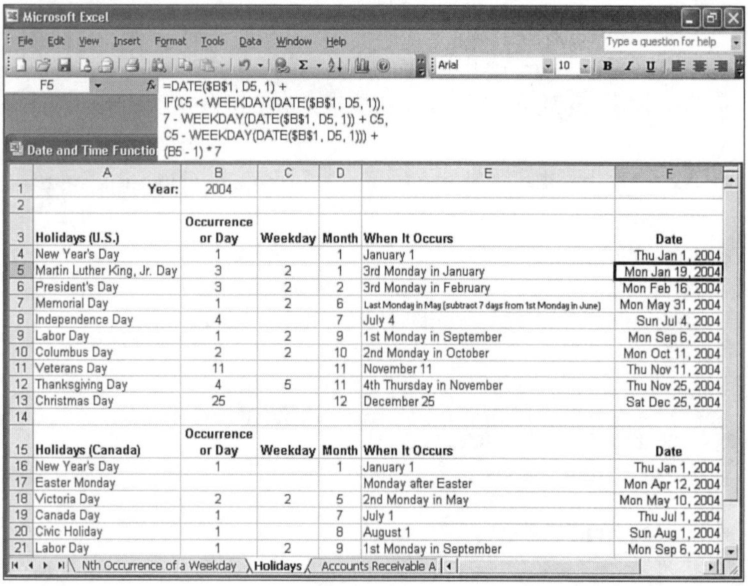


| | A | B | C | D | E | F |
|---|---|---|---|---|---|---|
| 1 | Year: | 2004 | | | | |
| 2 | | | | | | |
| 3 | Holidays (U.S.) | Occurrence or Day | Weekday | Month | When It Occurs | Date |
| 4 | New Year's Day | 1 | | 1 | January 1 | Thu Jan 1, 2004 |
| 5 | Martin Luther King, Jr. Day | 3 | 2 | 1 | 3rd Monday in January | Mon Jan 19, 2004 |
| 6 | President's Day | 3 | 2 | 2 | 3rd Monday in February | Mon Feb 16, 2004 |
| 7 | Memorial Day | 1 | 2 | 6 | Last Monday in May (subtract 7 days from 1st Monday in June) | Mon May 31, 2004 |
| 8 | Independence Day | 4 | | 7 | July 4 | Sun Jul 4, 2004 |
| 9 | Labor Day | 1 | 2 | 9 | 1st Monday in September | Mon Sep 6, 2004 |
| 10 | Columbus Day | 2 | 2 | 10 | 2nd Monday in October | Mon Oct 11, 2004 |
| 11 | Veterans Day | 11 | | 11 | November 11 | Thu Nov 11, 2004 |
| 12 | Thanksgiving Day | 4 | 5 | 11 | 4th Thursday in November | Thu Nov 25, 2004 |
| 13 | Christmas Day | 25 | | 12 | December 25 | Sat Dec 25, 2004 |
| 14 | | | | | | |
| 15 | Holidays (Canada) | Occurrence or Day | Weekday | Month | When It Occurs | Date |
| 16 | New Year's Day | 1 | | 1 | January 1 | Thu Jan 1, 2004 |
| 17 | Easter Monday | | | | Monday after Easter | Mon Apr 12, 2004 |
| 18 | Victoria Day | 2 | 2 | 5 | 2nd Monday in May | Mon May 10, 2004 |
| 19 | Canada Day | 1 | | 7 | July 1 | Thu Jul 1, 2004 |
| 20 | Civic Holiday | 1 | | 8 | August 1 | Sun Aug 1, 2004 |
| 21 | Labor Day | 1 | 2 | 9 | 1st Monday in September | Mon Sep 6, 2004 |

**Figure 10.3**
This worksheet calculates the dates of numerous holidays in a given year.

Most of the values in column E are calculated. For the floating holidays, for example, several `CHOOSE()` functions are used to construct the description. Here's an example for Martin Luther King Jr. Day:

```
=B5 & CHOOSE(B5, "st", "nd", "rd", "th", "th") & " " & CHOOSE(C5,
➥"Sunday", "Monday", "Tuesday", "Wednesday", "Thursday", "Friday",
➥"Saturday") & " in " &  CHOOSE(D5, "January", "February", "March",
➥"April", "May", "June", "July", "August", "September", "October",
➥"November", "December")
```

Finally, column F contains the formulas for calculating the date of each holiday based on the year entered in cell B1.

**NOTE**

Two exceptions exist in column F. The first is the formula for Memorial Day (cell F7), which occurs on the last Monday in May. To derive this date, you first calculate the first Monday in June and then subtract 7 days.

The second exception is the formula for Easter Monday (cell F17). This occurs the day after Easter Sunday, which is a floating holiday, but its date is based on the phase of the moon, of all things. (Officially, Easter Sunday falls on the first Sunday after the first ecclesiastical full moon after the spring equinox.) There are no simple formulas for calculating when Easter Sunday occurs in a given year. The formula in the Holidays worksheet is a complex bit of business that uses the `FLOOR()` function, so I discuss it when I discuss that function in Chapter 11, "Working with Math Functions."

### Calculating the Julian Date

Excel has built-in functions that convert a given date into a numerical day of the week (the WEEKDAY() function) and that return the numerical ranking of the week in which a given date falls (the WEEKNUM() function). However, Excel doesn't have a function that calculates the Julian date for a given date—the numerical ranking of the date for the year in which it falls. For example, the Julian date of January 1 is 1, January 2 is 2, and February 1 is 32.

If you need to use Julian dates in your business, here's a formula that will do the job:

```
=MyDate - DATE(YEAR(MyDate) - 1, 12, 31)
```

This formula assumes that the date you want to work with is in a cell named MyDate. The expression DATE(YEAR(MyDate) - 1, 12, 31) returns the date serial number for December 31 of the preceding year. Subtracting this number from MyDate gives you the Julian number.

## Calculating the Difference Between Two Dates

In the previous section, you saw that Excel enables you to subtract one date from another. Here's an example:

```
=Date1 - Date2
```

Here, Date1 and Date2 must be actual date values, not just date strings. When you create such a formula, Excel returns a value equal to the number of days between the two dates. This date-difference formula returns a positive number if Date1 is larger than Date2; it returns a negative number if Date1 is less than Date2. Calculating the difference between two dates is useful in many business scenarios, including receivables aging, interest calculations, benefits payments, and more.

> **NOTE**
> If you enter a simple date-difference formula in a cell, Excel automatically formats that cell as a date. For example, if the difference between the two days is 30 days, you'll see 1/30/1900 as the result. (If the result is negative, you'll see the cell filled with # symbols.) To see the result properly, you need to format the cell with the General format or some numeric format.

Besides the basic date-difference formula, you can use the date functions from earlier in this chapter to perform date-difference calculations. Also, Excel boasts a number of worksheet functions that enable you to perform more sophisticated operations to determine the difference between two dates. The rest of this section runs through a number of these date-difference formulas and functions.

### Calculating a Person's Age

If you have a person's birth date entered into a cell named Birthdate and you need to calculate how old the person is, you might think that the following formula would do the job:

```
=YEAR(TODAY()) - YEAR(Birthdate)
```

This works, but only if the person's birthday has already passed this year. If he or she hasn't had a birthday yet, this formula reports the age as being one year greater than it really is.

To solve this problem, you need to take into account whether the person's birthday has passed. To see how to do this, check out the following logical expression:

```
=DATE(YEAR(NOW()), MONTH(Birthdate), DAY(Birthdate)) > TODAY()
```

This expression asks whether the person's birthday for this year (which uses the formula from earlier in this chapter—see "Determining a Person's Birthday Given the Birth Date") is greater than today's date. If it is, the expression returns logical TRUE, which is equivalent to 1; if it isn't, the expression returns logical FALSE, which is equivalent to 0. In other words, you can get the person's true age by subtracting the result of the logical expression from the original formula, like so:

```
=YEAR(NOW()) - YEAR(Birthdate) - (DATE(YEAR(NOW()), MONTH(Birthdate),
➥DAY(Birthdate)) > NOW())
```

### The DATEDIF() **Function**

Perhaps the easiest way to perform date-difference calculations in Excel is to use the DATEDIF() function, which returns the difference between two specified dates based on a specified unit:

```
DATEDIF(start_date, end_date, [unit])
```

| | |
|---|---|
| *start_date* | The starting date |
| *end date* | The ending date |
| *unit* | The date unit used in the result: |

| unit | What It Returns |
|---|---|
| y | The number of years between *start_date* and *end_date* |
| m | The number of months between *start_date* and *end_date* |
| d | The number of days between *start_date* and *end_date* |
| md | The difference in the day components between *start_date* and *end_date* (that is, the years and months are not included in the calculation) |
| ym | The difference in the month components between *start_date* and *end_date* (that is, the years and days are not included in the calculation) |
| yd | The number of days between *start_date* and *end_date*, with the year components excluded from the calculation) |

For example, the following formula calculates the number of days between the current date and Christmas:

```
=DATEDIF(TODAY(), DATE(YEAR(TODAY()), 12, 25), "d")
```

You can also use the DATEDIF() function to calculate a Julian date calculation, as explained earlier in this chapter (see "Calculating the Julian Date"). If the date you want to work with is in a cell named MyDate, the following formula calculates its Julian date using DATEDIF():

```
=DATEDIF(DATE(YEAR(MyDate) - 1, 12, 31), MyDate, "d")
```

## Calculating a Person's Age, Part 2

The DATEDIF() function can greatly simplify the formula for calculating a person age (see "Calculating a Person's Age," earlier in this chapter). If the person's date of birth is in a cell named Birthdate, the following formula calculates his or her current age:

```
=DATEDIF(Birthdate, TODAY(), "y")
```

### NETWORKDAYS(): Calculating the Number of Workdays Between Two Dates

If you calculate the difference in days between two days, Excel includes weekends and holidays. In many business situations, you need to know the number of workdays between two dates. For example, when calculating the number of days an invoice is past due, it's often best to exclude weekends and holidays.

This is easily done using the Analysis ToolPak's NETWORKDAYS() function (read the name as "net workdays"), which returns the number of working days between two dates:

```
NETWORKDAYS(start_date, end_date, [holidays])
```

| | |
|---|---|
| start_date | The starting date (or a string representation of the date). |
| end_date | The ending date (or a string representation of the date). |
| holidays | A list of dates to exclude from the calculation. This can be a range of dates or an array constant (that is, a series of date serial numbers or date strings, separated by commas and surrounded by braces, {}). |

For example, here's an expression that returns the number of workdays between December 1, 2003, and January 10, 2004, excluding December 25, 2003, and January 1, 2004:

```
=NETWORKDAYS("12/1/2003", "1/10/2004", {"12/25/2003","1/1/2004"})
```

Figure 10.4 shows an update to the accounts receivable worksheet that uses NETWORKDAYS() to calculate the number of workdays that each invoice is past due.

10

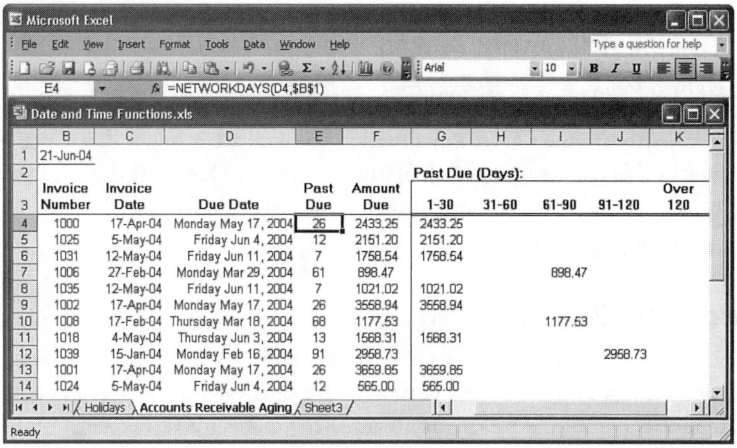

**Figure 10.4**
This worksheet calculates the number of workdays that each invoice is past due by using the NETWORKDAYS() function.

## DAYS360(): Calculating Date Differences Using a 360-Day Year

Many accounting systems operate using the principle of a 360-day year, which divides the year into 12 periods of uniform (30-day) lengths. Finding the number of days between dates in such a system isn't possible with the standard addition and subtraction of dates. However, Excel makes such calculations easy with its DAYS360() function, which returns the number of days between a starting date and an ending date based on a 360-day year:

DAYS360(*start_date*, *end_date*, [*method*])

| | |
|---|---|
| *start_date* | The starting date (or a string representation of the date) |
| *end_date* | The ending date (or a string representation of the date) |
| *method* | An integer that determines how DAYS360() performs certain calculations: |

| | |
|---|---|
| FALSE | If *start_date* is the 31st of the month, it is changed to the 30th of the same month. If *end_date* is the 31st of the month and *start_date* is less than the 30th of any month, the *end_date* is changed to the 1st of the next month. This is the North American method and it's the default. |
| TRUE | Any *start_date* or *end_date* value that falls on the 31st of a month is changed to the 30th of the same month. This is the European method. |

For example, the following expression returns the value 1:

DAYS360("3/30/2005", "4/1/2005")

### YEARFRAC(): **Returning the Fraction of a Year Between Two Dates**

Business worksheet models often need to know the fraction of a year that has elapsed between one date and another. For example, if an employee leaves after three months, you might need to pay out a quarter of a year's worth of benefits. This calculation can be complicated by the fact that your company might use a 360-day accounting year. However, the Analysis ToolPak's YEARFRAC() function can help you. This function converts the number of days between a start date and an end date into a fraction of a year:

YEARFRAC(*start_date*, *end_date*, [*basis*])

| | |
|---|---|
| *start_date* | The starting date (or a string representation of the date) |
| *end_date* | The ending date (or a string representation of the date) |
| *basis* | An integer that determines how YEARFRAC() performs certain calculations: |

| | |
|---|---|
| 0 | Uses a 360-day year divided into twelve 30-day months. This is the North American method, and it's the default. |
| 1 | Uses the actual number of days in the year and the actual number of days in each month. |
| 2 | Uses a 360-day year and the actual number of days in each month. |
| 3 | Uses a 365-day year and the actual number of days in each month. |
| 4 | Any *start_date* or *end_date* value that falls on the 31st of a month is changed to the 30th of the same month. This is the European method. |

For example, the following expression returns the value 0.25:

YEARFRAC("3/15/2005", "6/15/2005")

# Using Excel's Time Functions

Working with time values in Excel is not greatly different than working with date values, although there are some exceptions, as you'll see in this section. Here you'll work mostly with Excel's time functions, which work with or return time serial numbers. All of Excel's time-related functions are listed in Table 10.5. (For the *serial_number* arguments, you can use any valid Excel time.)

**Table 10.5    Excel's Time Functions**

| Function | Description |
| --- | --- |
| HOUR(*serial_number*) | Extracts the hour component from the time given by *serial_number* |
| MINUTE(*serial_number*) | Extracts the minute component from the time given by *serial_number* |
| NOW() | Returns the serial number of the current date and time |
| SECOND(*serial_number*) | Extracts the seconds component from the time given by *serial_number* |
| TIME(*hour, minute, second*) | Returns the serial number of a time, in which *hour* is a number between 0 and 23, and *minute* and *second* are numbers between 0 and 59 |
| TIMEVALUE(*time_text*) | Converts a time from text to a serial number |

## Returning a Time

If you need a time value to use in an expression or function, either you can enter it by hand if you have a specific date that you want to work with, or you can take advantage of the flexibility of three Excel functions: NOW(), TIME(), and TIME().

### NOW(): Returning the Current Time

When you need to use the current time in a formula, function, or expression, use the NOW() function, which doesn't take any arguments:

```
NOW()
```

This function returns the serial number of the current time, with the current date as the assumed date. For example, if it's noon and today's date is December 31, 2004, the NOW() function returns the following serial number:

```
38352.5
```

If you just want the time component of the serial number, subtract TODAY() from NOW():

```
NOW() - TODAY()
```

Just like the TODAY() function, remember that NOW() is a dynamic function that doesn't keep its initial value (that is, the time at which you entered the function). Each time you edit the formula, enter another formula, recalculate the worksheet, or reopen the workbook, NOW() uptimes its value to return the current system time.

### TIME(): **Returning Any Time**

A time consists of three components: the hour, the minute, and the second. It often happens that a worksheet generates one or more of these components and you need some way of building a proper time out of them. You can do that by using Excel's TIME() function:

TIME(*hour, minute, second*)

| | |
|---|---|
| *hour* | The hour component of the time (a number between 0 and 23) |
| *minute* | The minute component of the time (a number between 0 and 59) |
| *second* | The second component of the time (a number between 0 and 59) |

For example, the following expression returns the serial number of the time 2:45:30 p.m.:

TIME(14, 45, 30)

Like the DATE() function, TIME() adjusts for "wrong" hour, month, and second values. For example, the following expression returns the serial number for 3:00:30 p.m.:

TIME(14, 60, 30)

Here, TIME() takes the extra minute and "adds" 1 to the hour value.

### TIMEVALUE(): **Converting a String to a Time**

If you have a time value in string form, you can convert it to a time serial number by using the TIMEVALUE() function:

TIMEVALUE(*time_text*)

| | |
|---|---|
| *time_text* | The string containing the time |

For example, the following expression returns the time serial number for the string 2:45:00 PM:

TIMEVALUE("2:45:00 PM")

## Returning Parts of a Time

The three components of a time—hour, minute, and second—can also be extracted individually from a given time using Excel's HOUR(), MINUTE(), and SECOND() functions.

### The HOUR() **Function**

The HOUR() function returns a number between 0 and 23 that corresponds to the hour component of a specified time:

HOUR(*serial_number*)

| | |
|---|---|
| *serial_number* | The time (or a string representation of the time) you want to work with |

For example, the following expression returns 12:

HOUR(0.5)

10

### The MINUTE() **Function**

The MINUTE() function returns a number between 0 and 59 that corresponds to the minute component of a specified time:

MINUTE(*serial_number*)

> serial_number     The time (or a string representation of the time) you want to work with

For example, if it's currently 3:15 p.m., the following expression will return 15:

HOUR(NOW())

### The SECOND() **Function**

The SECOND() function returns a number between 0 and 59 that corresponds to the second component of a specified time:

SECOND(*serial_number*)

> serial_number     The time (or a string representation of the time) you want to work with

For example, the following expression returns 30:

SECOND("2:45:30 PM")

### Returning a Time *X* Hours, Minutes, or Seconds from Now

As I mentioned earlier, TIME() automatically adjusts "wrong" hour, minute, and second values. You can take advantage of this by applying formulas to one or more of the TIME() function's arguments. The most common use for this is to return a time that occurs *X* number of hours, minutes, or seconds from now (or from any time).

For example, the following expression returns the time 12 hours from now:

TIME(HOUR(NOW()) + 12, MINUTE(NOW()), SECOND(NOW()))

Unlike the DATE() function, the TIME() function doesn't enable you to simply add an hour, minute, or second to a specified time. For example, consider the following expression:

NOW() + 1

All this does is add one day to the current date and time.

If you want to add hours, minutes, and seconds to a time, you need to express the added time as a fraction of a day. For example, because there are 24 hours in a day, 1 hour is represented by the expression 1/24. Similarly, because there are 60 minutes in an hour, 1 minute is represented by the expression 1/24/60. Finally, because there are 60 seconds in a minute, 1 second is represented by the expression 1/24/60/60. Table 10.6 shows you how to use these expressions to add *n* hours, minutes, and seconds.

**Table 10.6  Adding Hours, Minutes, and Seconds**

| Operation | Expression | Example | Example Expression |
|---|---|---|---|
| Add *n* hours | `n*(1/24)` | Add 6 hours | `NOW()+6*(1/24)` |
| Add *n* minutes | `n*(1/24/60)` | Add 15 minutes | `NOW()+15*(1/24/60)` |
| Add *n* seconds | `n*(1/24/60/60)` | Add 30 seconds | `NOW()+30*(1/24/60/60)` |

### Summing Time Values

When working with time values in Excel, you need to be aware that there are two subtly different interpretations for the phrase "adding one time to another":

- Adding time values to get a future time. As you saw in the previous section, adding hours, minutes, or seconds to a time returns a value that represents a future time. For example, if the current time is 11:00 p.m. (23:00), adding two hours returns the time 1:00 a.m.

- Adding time values to get a total time. In this interpretation, time values are summed to get a total number of hours, minutes, and seconds. This is useful if you want to know how many hours an employee worked in a week, or how many hours to bill a client. In this case, for example, if the current total is 23 hours, adding 2 hours brings the total to 25 hours.

The problem is that adding time values to get a future time is Excel's default interpretation for added time values. So, if cell A1 contains 23:00 and cell A2 contains 2:00, the following formula will return `1:00:00 AM`:

```
=A1 + A2
```

The time value 25:00:00 is stored internally, but Excel adjusts the display so that you see the "correct" value `1:00:00 AM`. If you want to see 25:00:00 instead, apply the following custom format to the cell:

```
[h]:mm:ss
```

## Calculating the Difference Between Two Times

Excel treats time serial numbers as decimal expansions (numbers between 0 and 1) that represent fractions of a day. Because they're just numbers, there's nothing to stop you from subtracting one from another to determine the difference between them:

```
EndTime - StartTime
```

This expression works just fine, as long as *EndTime* is greater than *StartTime*. (I used the names *EndTime* and *StartTime* purposefully so you would remember to always subtract the later time from the earlier time.)

However, there's one scenario in which this expression will fail: If *EndTime* occurs after midnight the next day, there's a good chance that it will be less than *StartTime*. For example, if a person works from 11:00 p.m. to 7:00 a.m., the expression `7:00 AM - 11:00 PM` will result in an illegal negative time value. (Excel displays the result as a series of `#` symbols that fill the cell).

To ensure that you get the correct positive result in this situation, use the following generic expression:

```
IF(EndTime < StartTime, 1 + EndTime - StartTime, EndTime - StartTime)
```

The `IF()` function checks to see if ***`EndTime`*** is less than ***`StartTime`***. If it is, it adds 1 to the value ***`EndTime`*** – ***`StartTime`*** to get the correct result; otherwise, just ***`EndTime`*** – ***`StartTime`*** is returned.

**CASE STUDY**



## Building an Employee Time Sheet

In this case study, you'll put your new knowledge of time functions and calculations to good use building a time sheet that tracks the number of hours an employee works each week, takes into account hours worked on weekends and holidays, and calculates the total number of hours and the weekly pay. Figure 10.5 shows the completed time sheet.

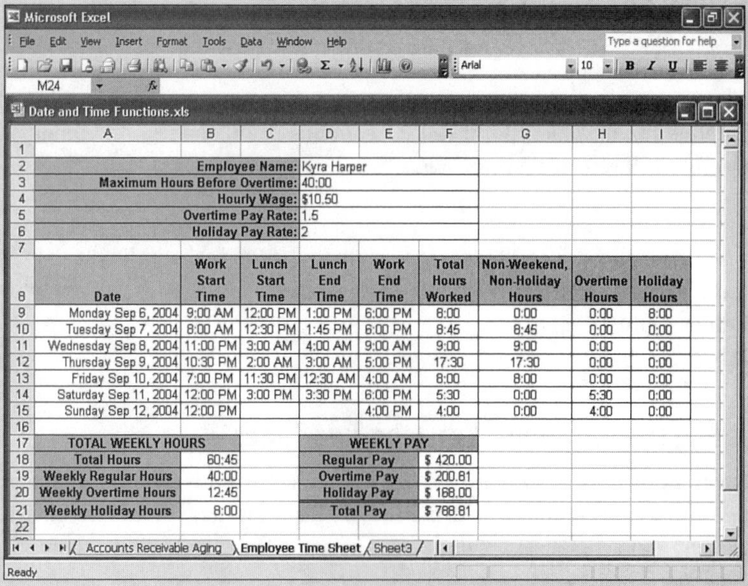

| | |
|---|---|
| Employee Name: | Kyra Harper |
| Maximum Hours Before Overtime: | 40:00 |
| Hourly Wage: | $10.50 |
| Overtime Pay Rate: | 1.5 |
| Holiday Pay Rate: | 2 |

| Date | Work Start Time | Lunch Start Time | Lunch End Time | Work End Time | Total Hours Worked | Non-Weekend, Non-Holiday Hours | Overtime Hours | Holiday Hours |
|---|---|---|---|---|---|---|---|---|
| Monday Sep 6, 2004 | 9:00 AM | 12:00 PM | 1:00 PM | 6:00 PM | 8:00 | 0:00 | 0:00 | 8:00 |
| Tuesday Sep 7, 2004 | 8:00 AM | 12:30 PM | 1:45 PM | 6:00 PM | 8:45 | 8:45 | 0:00 | 0:00 |
| Wednesday Sep 8, 2004 | 11:00 PM | 3:00 AM | 4:00 AM | 9:00 AM | 9:00 | 9:00 | 0:00 | 0:00 |
| Thursday Sep 9, 2004 | 10:30 PM | 2:00 AM | 3:00 AM | 5:00 PM | 17:30 | 17:30 | 0:00 | 0:00 |
| Friday Sep 10, 2004 | 7:00 PM | 11:30 PM | 12:30 AM | 4:00 AM | 8:00 | 8:00 | 0:00 | 0:00 |
| Saturday Sep 11, 2004 | 12:00 PM | 3:00 PM | 3:30 PM | 6:00 PM | 5:30 | 0:00 | 5:30 | 0:00 |
| Sunday Sep 12, 2004 | 12:00 PM | | | 4:00 PM | 4:00 | 0:00 | 4:00 | 0:00 |

| TOTAL WEEKLY HOURS | |
|---|---|
| Total Hours | 60:45 |
| Weekly Regular Hours | 40:00 |
| Weekly Overtime Hours | 12:45 |
| Weekly Holiday Hours | 8:00 |

| WEEKLY PAY | |
|---|---|
| Regular Pay | $ 420.00 |
| Overtime Pay | $ 200.81 |
| Holiday Pay | $ 168.00 |
| Total Pay | $ 788.81 |

**Figure 10.5** This employee time sheet tracks the daily hours, takes weekends and holidays into account, and calculates the employee's total working hours and pay.

Before starting, you need to understand three terms used in this case study:

- **Regular hours**—These are hours worked for regular pay.
- **Overtime hours**—These are hours worked beyond the maximum number of regular hours, as well as any hours worked on the weekend.
- **Holiday hours**—These are hours worked on a statutory holiday.

## Entering the Time Sheet Data

Let's begin at the top of the time sheet, where the following data is required:

- `Employee Name`—You'll create a separate sheet for each employee, so enter the person's name here. You might also want to augment this with the date the person started or other data about the employee.
- `Maximum Hours Before Overtime`—This is the number of regular hours an employee has to work in a week before overtime hours take effect. Enter the number using the hh:mm format. Cell D3 uses the [h]:mm custom format, to ensure that Excel displays the actual value.
- `Hourly Wage`—This is the amount the employee earns per regular hour of work.
- `Overtime Pay Rate`—This is the factor by which the employee's hourly rate is increased for overtime hours. For example, enter `1.5` if the employee earns time and a half for overtime.
- `Holiday Pay Rate`—This is the factor by which the employee's hourly rate is increased for holiday hours. For example, enter `2` if the employee earns double time for holidays.



## Calculating the Daily Hours Worked

Figure 10.6 shows the portion of the time sheet used to record the employee's daily hours worked. For each day, you enter five items:

- `Date`—Enter the date the employee worked. This is formatted to show the day of the week, which is useful for confirming overtime hours worked on weekends.
- `Work Start Time`—Enter the time of day the employee began working.
- `Lunch Start Time`—Enter the time of day the employee stopped for lunch.
- `Lunch End Time`—Enter the time of day the employee resumed working after lunch.
- `Work End Time`—Enter the time of day the employee stopped working.

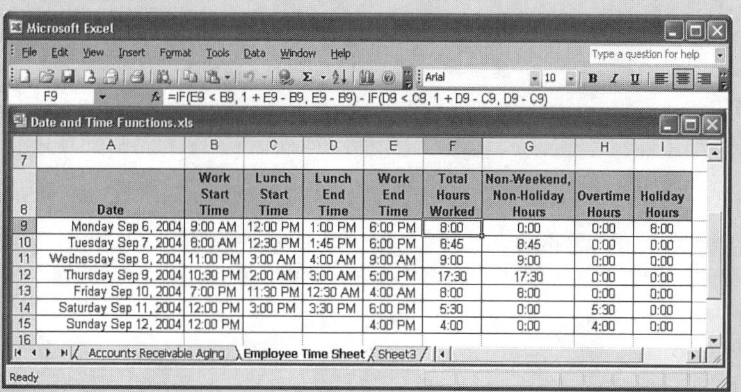


| | A | B | C | D | E | F | G | H | I |
|---|---|---|---|---|---|---|---|---|---|
| 7 | | | | | | | | | |
| 8 | Date | Work Start Time | Lunch Start Time | Lunch End Time | Work End Time | Total Hours Worked | Non-Weekend, Non-Holiday Hours | Overtime Hours | Holiday Hours |
| 9 | Monday Sep 6, 2004 | 9:00 AM | 12:00 PM | 1:00 PM | 6:00 PM | 8:00 | 0:00 | 0:00 | 8:00 |
| 10 | Tuesday Sep 7, 2004 | 8:00 AM | 12:30 PM | 1:45 PM | 6:00 PM | 8:45 | 8:45 | 0:00 | 0:00 |
| 11 | Wednesday Sep 8, 2004 | 11:00 PM | 3:00 AM | 4:00 AM | 9:00 AM | 9:00 | 9:00 | 0:00 | 0:00 |
| 12 | Thursday Sep 9, 2004 | 10:30 PM | 2:00 AM | 3:00 AM | 5:00 PM | 17:30 | 17:30 | 0:00 | 0:00 |
| 13 | Friday Sep 10, 2004 | 7:00 PM | 11:30 PM | 12:30 AM | 4:00 AM | 8:00 | 8:00 | 0:00 | 0:00 |
| 14 | Saturday Sep 11, 2004 | 12:00 PM | 3:00 PM | 3:30 PM | 6:00 PM | 5:30 | 0:00 | 5:30 | 0:00 |
| 15 | Sunday Sep 12, 2004 | 12:00 PM | | | 4:00 PM | 4:00 | 0:00 | 4:00 | 0:00 |
| 16 | | | | | | | | | |

**Figure 10.6**
The section of the employee time sheet in which you enter the hours worked and in which the total daily hours are calculated.

The first calculation occurs in the `Total Hours Worked` column (F). The idea here is to sum the total number of hours the employee worked in a given day. The first part of the calculation uses the time-difference formula from the previous section to derive the number of hours between the `Work Start Time` (column B) and the `Work End Time` (column E). Here's the expression for the first entry (row 9):

```
IF(E9 < B9, 1 + E9 - B9, E9 - B9)
```

However, we also have to subtract the time the employee took for lunch, which is the difference between the `Lunch Start Time` (column C) and the `Lunch End Time` (column D). Here's the expression for the first entry (row 9):

```
IF(D9 < C9, 1 + D9 - C9, D9 - C9)
```

Let's skip over the `Overtime Hours` calculation (column H). The idea behind this column is that if the employee worked on the weekend, all of the hours worked should be booked as overtime hours. So, the formula checks to see if the date is a Saturday or Sunday:

```
=IF(OR(WEEKDAY(A9) = 7, WEEKDAY(A9) = 1), F9, 0)
```

If the `OR()` function returns TRUE, the date is on the weekend, so the value from the `Total Hours Worked` column (F9, in the example) is entered into the `Overtime Hours` column; otherwise, 0 is returned.

Next up is the `Holiday Hours` calculation (column I). Here you want to see if the date is a statutory holiday. If it is, all of the hours worked that day should be booked as holiday hours. To that end, the formula checks to see if the date is part of the range of holiday dates calculated earlier in this chapter:

```
{=SUM(IF(A9 = Holidays!F4:F13, 1, 0)) * F9}
```

This is an array formula that compares the date with the dates in the holiday range (Holidays!F4:F13). If a match occurs, the `SUM()` function returns 1; otherwise, it returns 0. This result is multiplied by the value in the `Total Hours Worked` column (F9, in the example). So, if the date is a holiday, the hours for that day are entered as holiday hours.

Finally, the value in the `Non-Weekend, Non-Holiday Hours` column (G) is calculated by subtracting `Overtime Hours` and `Holiday Hours` from `Total Hours Worked`:

```
=F9 - H9 - I9
```

## Calculating the Weekly Hours Worked

Next up is the `Total Weekly Hours` section, which adds the various types of hours the employee worked during the week.

The `Total Hours` value is a straight sum of the values in the `Total Hours Worked` column (F):

```
=SUM(F9:F15)
```

To derive the `Weekly Regular Hours` value, the calculation has to check to see if the total in the `Non-Weekend, Non-Holiday Hours` column (G) exceeds the number in the `Maximum Hours Before Overtime` cell (D3):

```
=IF(SUM(G9:G15) > D3, D3, SUM(G9:G15))
```

If this is true, the value in D3 is entered as the `Regular Hours` value; otherwise, the sum is entered.

Calculating the `Weekly Overtime Hours` value is a two-step process, First you have to check to see if the sum in the Non-Weekend, Non-Holiday Hours column (G) exceeds the number in the `Maximum Hours Before Overtime` cell (D3). If so, the number of overtime hours is the difference between them; otherwise, it's 0:

```
IF(SUM(G9:G15) > D3, SUM(G9:G15) - D3, "0:00")
```

Second, you need to add the sum of the `Overtime Hours` column (H):

```
=IF(SUM(G9:G15) > D3, SUM(G9:G15) - D3, "0:00") + SUM(H9:H15)
```

Finally, the `Weekly Holiday Hours` value is a straight sum of the values in the `Holiday Hours` column (I):

```
=SUM(I9:I15)
```

### Calculating the Weekly Pay

The final section of the time sheet is the `Weekly Pay` calculation. The dollar amounts for `Regular Pay`, `Overtime Pay`, and `Holiday Pay` are calculated as follows:

```
Regular Pay = Weekly Regular Hours * Hourly Wage * 24
Overtime Pay = Weekly Overtime Hours * Hourly Wage * Overtime Pay Rate * 24
Holiday Pay = Weekly Holiday Hours * Hourly Wage * Holiday Pay Rate * 24
```

Note that you need to multiply by 24 to convert the time value to a real number. Finally, the `Total Pay` is the sum of these values.

10

## From Here

- For more information on formatting dates and times, **see** "Formatting Numbers, Dates, and Times," **p. 72**.

- For a general discussion of function syntax, **see** "The Structure of a Function," **p. 126**.

- `WEEKNUM()` is available only with the Analysis ToolPak loaded; **see** "Loading the Analysis ToolPak Functions," **p. 131**.

- To learn how to convert nonstandard date strings to dates, **see** "A Date-Conversion Formula," **p. 146**.

- To learn how to use `CHOOSE()` to convert the `WEEKDAY()` return value into a day name, **see** "Determining the Name of the Day of the Week," **p. 183**.

- It's possible to calculate the various holidays that occur within a year and place the dates within a range for use as the `WORKDAY()` function's *holidays* argument. **See** "Calculating Holiday Dates, **p. 213**.

# Working with Math Functions

**11**

Excel's mathematical underpinnings are revealed when you consider the long list of math-related functions that come with the program. Functions exist for basic mathematical operations such as absolute values, lowest and greatest common denominators, square roots, and sums. Plenty of high-end operations also are available for things such as matrix multiplication, multinomials, and sums of squares. Not all of Excel's math functions are useful in a business context, but a surprising number of them are. For example, operations such as rounding and generating random numbers have their business uses.

Table 11.1 lists the Excel math functions, but this chapter doesn't cover the entire list. Instead, I just focus on those functions that I think you'll find useful for your business formulas. Remember, too, that Excel comes with many statistical functions, covered in Chapter 12, "Working with Statistical Functions."

**11**

### Table 11.1   Excel's Math Functions

| Function | Description |
| --- | --- |
| ABS(*number*) | Returns the absolute value of *number* |
| CEILING(*number*,*significance*) | Rounds *number* up to the nearest integer |
| COMBIN(*number*,*number_chosen*) | Returns the number of possible ways that *number* objects can be combined in groups of *number_chosen* (this is an Analysis ToolPak function) |
| EVEN(*number*) | Rounds *number* up to the nearest even integer |
| EXP(*number*) | Returns *e* raised to the power of *number* |
| FACT(*number*) | Returns the factorial of *number* |
| FLOOR(*number*,*significance*) | Rounds *number* down to the nearest integer |
| GCD(*number1*,[*number2*,...]) | Returns the greatest common divisor of the specified numbers (this is an Analysis ToolPak function) |
| INT(*number*) | Rounds *number* down to the nearest integer |
| LCM(*number1*,[*number2*,...]) | Returns the least common multiple of the specified numbers (this is an Analysis ToolPak function) |
| LN(*number*) | Returns the natural logarithm of *number* |
| LOG(*number*,[*base*]) | Returns the logarithm of *number* in the specified *base* |
| LOG10(*number*) | Returns the base-10 logarithm of *number* |
| MDETERM(*array*) | Returns the matrix determinant of *array* |
| MINVERSE(*array*) | Returns the matrix inverse of *array* |
| MMULT(*array1*,*array2*) | Returns the matrix product of *array1* and *array2* |
| MOD(*number*,*divisor*) | Returns the remainder of *number* after dividing by *divisor* |
| MROUND(*number*,*multiple*) | Rounds *number* to the desired *multiple* (this is an Analysis ToolPak function) |
| MULTINOMIAL(*number1*,[*number2*]) | Returns the multinomial of the specified numbers (this is an Analysis ToolPak function) |
| ODD(*number*) | Rounds *number* up to the nearest odd integer |
| PI() | Returns the value pi |
| POWER(*number*,*power*) | Raises *number* to the specified *power* |
| PRODUCT(*number1*,[*number2*,...]) | Multiplies the specified numbers |

| Function | Description |
|---|---|
| QUOTIENT(*numerator*,*denominator*) | Returns the integer portion of the result obtained by dividing *numerator* by *denominator* (that is, the remainder is discarded from the result; this is an Analysis ToolPak function) |
| RAND() | Returns a random number between 0 and 1 |
| RANDBETWEEN(*bottom*,*top*) | Returns a random number between *bottom* and *top* (this is an Analysis ToolPak function) |
| ROMAN(*number*,[*form*]) | Converts the Arabic *number* to its Roman numeral equivalent (as text) |
| ROUND(*number*,*num_digits*) | Rounds *number* to a specified number of digits |
| ROUNDDOWN(*number*,*num_digits*) | Rounds *number* down, toward 0 |
| ROUNDUP(*number*,*num_digits*) | Rounds *number* up, away from 0 |
| SERIESSUM(*x*,*n*,*m*,*coefficients*) | Returns the sum of a power series (this is an Analysis ToolPak function) |
| SIGN(*number*) | Returns the sign of *number* (1 = positive, 0 = zero, -1 = negative) |
| SQRT(*number*) | Returns the positive square root of *number* |
| SQRTPI(*number*) | Returns the positive square root of the result of the expression *number * Pi* |
| SUBTOTAL(*function_num*,*ref1*,[*ref2*,...]) | Returns a subtotal from a list |
| SUM(*number1*,[*number2*,...]) | Adds the arguments |
| SUMIF(*range*,*criteria*,[*sum_range*]) | Adds only those cells in *range* that meet the *criteria* |
| SUMPRODUCT(*array1*,*array2*,[*array3*,...]) | Multiplies the corresponding elements in the specified arrays and then sums the resulting products |
| SUMSQ(*number1*,[*number2*,...]) | Returns the sum of the squares of the arguments |
| SUMX2MY2(*array_x*,*array_y*) | Squares the elements in the specified arrays and then sums the differences between the corresponding squares |
| SUMX2PY2(*array_x*,*array_y*) | Squares the elements in the specified arrays and then sums the corresponding squares |
| SUMXMY2(*array_x*,*array_y*) | Squares the differences between the corresponding elements in the specified arrays and then sums the squares |
| TRUNC(*number*,[*num_digits*]) | Truncates *number* to an integer |

11

Although I don't discuss Excel's trig functions in this book, Table 11.2 lists all of them. Here are some notes to keep in mind when you use these functions:

- In each function syntax, *number* is an angle expressed in radians.

- If you have an angle in degrees, you can convert it to radians by multiplying it by `PI()/180`. Alternatively, use the `RADIANS(angle)` function, which converts *angle* from degrees to radians.

- The trig functions return a value in radians. If you need to convert the result to degrees, multiply it by `180/PI()`. Alternatively, use the `DEGREES(angle)` function, which converts *angle* from radians to degrees.

**Table 11.2  Excel's Trigonometric Functions**

| Function | Description |
|---|---|
| ACOS(*number*) | Returns a value in radians between 0 and pi that represents the arccosine of *number* (which must be between –1 and 1) |
| ACOSH(*number*) | Returns a value in radians that represents the inverse hyperbolic cosine of *number* (which must be greater than or equal to 1) |
| ASIN(*number*) | Returns a value in radians between –pi/2 and pi/2 that represents the arcsine of *number* (which must be between –1 and 1) |
| ASINH(*number*) | Returns a value in radians that represents the inverse hyperbolic sine of *number* |
| ATAN(*number*) | Returns a value in radians between –pi/2 and pi/2 that represents the arctangent of *number* |
| ATAN2(*x_num, y_num*) | Returns a value in radians between (but not including) –pi and pi that represents the arctangent of the coordinates given by *x_num* and *y_num* |
| ATANH(*number*) | Returns a value in radians that represents the inverse hyperbolic tangent of *number* (which must be between –1 and 1) |
| COS(*number*) | Returns a value in radians that represents the cosine of *number* |
| COSH(*number*) | Returns a value in radians that represents the hyperbolic cosine of *number* |
| DEGREES(*angle*) | Converts *angle* from radians to degrees |
| SIN(*number*) | Returns a value in radians that represents the hyperbolic sine of *number* |
| SINH(*number*) | Returns a value in radians that represents the sine of *number* |
| TAN(*number*) | Returns a value in radians that represents the tangent of *number* |
| TANH(*number*) | Returns a value in radians that represents the hyperbolic tangent of *number* |

# Understanding Excel's Rounding Functions

Excel's rounding functions are useful in many situations, such as setting price points, adjusting billable time to the nearest 15 minutes, and ensuring that you're dealing with integer values for discrete numbers, such as inventory counts.

The problem is that Excel has so many rounding functions that it's difficult to know which one to use in a given situation. To help you, this section looks at the details of—and differences between—Excel's 10 rounding functions: ROUND(), ROUNDUP(), ROUNDDOWN(), MROUND(), CEILING(), FLOOR(), EVEN(), ODD(), INT(), and TRUNC().

## The ROUND() Function

The rounding function you'll use most often is ROUND():

ROUND(*number*, *num_digits*)

| | |
|---|---|
| *number* | The number you want to round |
| *num_digits* | An integer that specifies the number of digits you want *number* rounded to, as explained here: |

| num_digits | Description |
|---|---|
| > 0 | Rounds *number* to *num_digits* decimal places |
| 0 | Rounds *number* to the nearest integer |
| < 0 | Rounds *number* to *num_digits* to the left of the decimal point |

Table 11.3 demonstrates the effect of the *num_digits* argument on the results of the ROUND() function. Here, *number* is 1234.5678.

**Table 11.3    Effect of the num_digits Argument on the ROUND() Function Result**

| num_digits | Result of ROUND(1234.5678, num_digits) |
|---|---|
| 3 | 1234.568 |
| 2 | 1234.57 |
| 1 | 1234.6 |
| 0 | 1235 |
| −1 | 1230 |
| −2 | 1200 |
| −3 | 1000 |

**11**

## The MROUND() **Function**

MROUND() is an Analysis ToolPak function that rounds a number to a specified multiple:

MROUND(*number*, *multiple*)

| | |
|---|---|
| *number* | The number you want to round |
| *multiple* | The multiple to which you want *number* rounded |

Table 11.4 demonstrates MROUND() with a few examples.

| Table 11.4 | Examples of the MROUND() | **Function** |
|---|---|---|
| *number* | *multiple* | MROUND() **Result** |
| 5 | 2 | 6 |
| 11 | 5 | 10 |
| 13 | 5 | 15 |
| 5 | 5 | 5 |
| 7.31 | 0.5 | 7.5 |
| –11 | –5 | –10 |
| –11 | 5 | #NUM! |

## The ROUNDDOWN() **and** ROUNDUP() **Functions**

The Analysis ToolPak's ROUNDDOWN() and ROUNDUP() functions are very similar to ROUND(), except that they always round in a single direction: ROUNDDOWN() always rounds a number toward 0, and ROUNDUP() always rounds away from 0. Here are the syntaxes for these functions:

ROUNDDOWN(*number*, *num_digits*)

ROUNDUP(*number*, *num_digits*)

| | |
|---|---|
| *number* | The number you want to round |
| *num_digits* | An integer that specifies the number of digits you want *number* rounded to, as explained here: |

| *num_digits* | Description |
|---|---|
| > 0 | Rounds *number* down or up to *num_digits* decimal places |
| 0 | Rounds *number* down or up to the nearest integer |
| < 0 | Rounds *number* down or up to *num_digits* to the left of the decimal point |

Table 11.5 tries out ROUNDDOWN() and ROUNDUP() with a few examples.

**Table 11.5    Examples of the** ROUNDDOWN() **and** ROUNDUP() **Functions**

| number | num_digits | ROUNDDOWN() | ROUNDUP() |
|--------|------------|-------------|-----------|
| 1.1 | 0 | 1 | 2 |
| 1.678 | 2 | 1.67 | 1.68 |
| 1234 | −2 | 1200 | 1300 |
| −1.1 | 0 | −1 | −2 |
| −1234 | −2 | −1200 | −1300 |

## The CEILING() and FLOOR() Functions

The CEILING() and FLOOR() functions are an amalgam of the features found in MROUND(), ROUNDDOWN(), and ROUNDUP(). Here are the syntaxes:

CEILING(*number, significance*)

FLOOR(*number, significance*)

| | |
|---|---|
| *number* | The number you want to round |
| *significance* | The multiple to which you want *number* rounded |

Both functions round the value given by *number* to a multiple of the value given by *significance*, but they differ in how they perform this rounding:

- CEILING() rounds away from 0. For example, CEILING(1.56, 0.1) returns 1.6, and CEILING(-2.33, -0.5) returns -2.5.

- FLOOR() rounds *toward* 0. For example, FLOOR(1.56, 0.1) returns 1.5, and FLOOR(-2.33, -0.5) returns -2.0.

> **CAUTION**
>
> For the CEILING() and FLOOR() functions, both arguments must have the same sign, or they'll return the error value #NUM!. Also, if you enter 0 for the second argument of the FLOOR() function, you'll get the error #DIV/0!.

## Determining the Fiscal Quarter in Which a Date Falls

When working with budget-related or other financial worksheets, you often need to know the fiscal quarter in which a particular date falls. For example, a budget increase formula might need to alter the increase depending on the quarter.

You can use the CEILING() function combined with the DATEDIF() function from Chapter 10, "Working with Date and Time Functions," to calculate the quarter for a given date:

=CEILING((DATEDIF(*FiscalStart, MyDate,* "m") + 1) / 3, 1)

→ To learn about DATEDIF(), **see** "The DATEDIF() Function," **p. 216**.

Here, *FiscalStart* is the date on which the fiscal year begins, and *MyDate* is the date you want to work with. This formula uses DATEDIF() with the m parameter to return the number of months between the two dates. The formula adds 1 to the result (to avoid getting a "0th" quarter) and then divides by 3. Applying CEILING() to the result gives the quarter in which *MyDate* occurs.

## Calculating Easter Dates

If you live or work in the United States, you'll rarely have to calculate for business purposes when Easter Sunday falls because there is no statutory holiday associated with Easter. However, if Easter Monday is a statutory holiday where you live (as it is in Canada and Britain), or if you're responsible for businesses in such jurisdictions, it can be handy to calculate when Easter Sunday falls in a given year.

Unfortunately, there is no straightforward way of calculating Easter. The official formula is that Easter falls on the first Sunday after the first ecclesiastical full moon after the spring equinox. Mathematicians have tried for centuries to come up with a formula, and although some have succeeded (most notably, the famous mathematician Carl Friedrich Gauss), the resulting algorithms have been hideously complex.

Here's a relatively simple worksheet formula that employs the FLOOR() function and that works for the years 1900 to 2078 for date systems that use the mm/dd/yyyy format:

```
=FLOOR("5/" & DAY(MINUTE(B1 / 38) / 2 + 56) & "/" & B1, 7) - 34 + 1
```

For date systems that use the dd/mm/yyyy format, use this formula instead:

```
=FLOOR(DAY(MINUTE(B1 / 38) / 2 + 56) & "/5/" & B1, 7) - 34
```

## The EVEN() and ODD() Functions

The EVEN() and ODD() functions round a single numeric argument:

```
EVEN(number)
```

```
ODD(number)
```

>    *number*    The number you want to round

Both functions round the value given by *number* away from 0, as follows:

- EVEN() rounds to the next even number. For example, EVEN(14.2) returns 16, and EVEN(-23) returns -24.
- ODD() rounds it to the next odd number. For example, ODD(58.1) returns 59 and ODD(-6) returns -7.

## The `INT()` and `TRUNC()` Functions

The `INT()` and `TRUNC()` functions are similar, in that you can use both to convert a value to its integer portion:

`INT(number)`

`TRUNC(number,[num_digits])`

| | |
|---|---|
| *number* | The number you want to round |
| *num_digits* | An integer that specifies the number of digits you want *number* rounded to, as explained here: |

| num_digits | Description |
|---|---|
| > 0 | Truncates all but *num_digits* decimal places |
| 0 | Truncates all decimal places (this is the default) |
| < 0 | Converts *num_digits* to the left of the decimal point into zeroes |

For example, `INT(6.75)` returns 6, and `TRUNC(3.6)` returns 3. However, these functions have two major differences that you should keep in mind:

- For negative values, `INT()` returns the next number away from 0. For example, `INT(-3.42)` returns -4. If you just want to lop off the decimal part, you need to use `TRUNC()` instead.

- You can use the `TRUNC()` function's second argument—*num_digits*—to specify the number of decimal places to leave on. For example, `TRUNC(123.456, 2)` returns 123.45, and `TRUNC(123.456, -2)` returns 100.

## Using Rounding to Prevent Calculation Errors

Most of us are comfortable dealing with numbers in decimal—or base-10—format (the odd hexadecimal-loving computer pro notwithstanding). Computers, however, prefer to work in the simpler confines of the binary—or base-2— system. So when you plug a value into a cell or formula, Excel converts it from decimal to its binary equivalent, makes its calculations, and then converts the binary result back into decimal format.

This procedure is fine for integers because all decimal integer values have an exact binary equivalent. However, many noninteger values don't have an exact equivalent in the binary world. Excel can only approximate these numbers, and this approximation can lead to errors in your formulas. For example, try entering the following formula into any worksheet cell:

`=0.01 = (2.02 - 2.01)`

This formula compares the value `0.01` with the expression `2.02 - 2.01`. These should be equal, of course, but when you enter the formula, Excel returns a `FALSE` result. What gives?

11

The problem is that, in converting the expression 2.02 - 2.01 into binary and back again, Excel picks up a stray digit in its travels. To see it, enter the formula =2.02 - 2.01 in a cell and then format it to show 16 decimal places. You should see the following surprising result:

```
0.0100000000000002
```

That wanton 2 in the 16th decimal place is what threw off the original calculation. To fix the problem, use the TRUNC() function (or possibly the ROUND() function, depending on the situation) to lop off the extra digits to the right of the decimal point. For example, the following formula produces a TRUE result:

```
=0.01 = TRUNC(2.02 - 2.01, 2)
```

## Setting Price Points

One common worksheet task is to calculate a list price for a product based on the result of a formula that factors in production costs and profit margin. If the product will be sold at retail, you'll likely want the decimal (cents) portion of the price to be .95 or .99, or some other standard value. You can use the INT() function to help with this "rounding."

For example, the simplest case is to always round up the decimal part to .95. Here's a formula that does this:

```
=INT(RawPrice) + 0.95
```

Assuming that *RawPrice* is the result of the formula that factors in costs and profit, the formula simply adds 0.95 to the integer portion. (Note, too, that if the decimal portion of *RawPrice* is greater than .95, the formula rounds down to .95.)

Another case is to round up to .50 for decimal portions less than or equal to 0.5 and to round up to .95 for decimal portion greater than 0.5. Here's a formula that handles this scenario:

```
=VALUE(INT(RawPrice) & IF(RawPrice - INT(RawPrice) <= 0.5, ".50", ".95"))
```

Again, the integer portion is stripped from the *RawPrice*. Also, the IF() function checks to see if the decimal portion is less than or equal to 0.5. If so, the string .50 is returned; otherwise, the string .95 is returned. This result is concatenated to the integer portion, and the VALUE() function ensures that a numeric result is returned.

## CASE STUDY

### Rounding Billable Time

An ideal use of MROUND() is to round billable time to some multiple number of minutes. For example, it's common to round billable time to the nearest 15 minutes. You can do this with MROUND() by using the following generic form of the function:

```
MROUND(BillableTime, 0:15)
```

Here, *BillableTime* is the time value you want to round. For example, the following expression returns the time value 2:15:

```
MROUND(2:10, 0:15)
```

Using MROUND() to round billable time has one significant flaw: Many (perhaps even most) people who bill their time prefer to round up to the nearest 15 minutes (or whatever). If the minute component of the MROUND() function's *number* argument is less than half the *multiple* argument, MROUND() rounds *down* to the nearest multiple.

To fix this problem, use the CEILING() function instead because it always rounds away from 0. Here's the generic expression to use for rounding up to the next 15-minute multiple:

```
CEILING(BillableTime, 0:15)
```

Again, *BillableTime* is the time value you want to round. For example, the following expression returns the time value 2:15:

```
CEILING(2:05, 0:15)
```

# Summing Values

Summing values—whether it's a range of cells, function results, literal numeric values, or expression results—is perhaps the most common spreadsheet operation. Excel enables you to add values using the addition operator (+), but it's often more convenient to sum a number of values by using the SUM() function, which you'll learn more about in this section.

## The SUM() Function

Here's the syntax of the SUM() function:

```
SUM(number1,[number2,...])
```

> *number1, number2,...*    The values you want to add

You can enter up to 30 arguments into the SUM() function. For example, the following formula returns the sum of the values in three separate ranges:

```
=SUM(A2:A13, C2:C13, E2:E13)
```

## Calculating Cumulative Totals

Many worksheets need to calculate cumulative totals. Most budget worksheets, for example, show cumulative totals for sales and expenses over the course of the fiscal year. Similarly, loan amortizations often show the cumulative interest and principal paid over the life of the loan.

Calculating these cumulative totals is straightforward. For example, see the worksheet shown in Figure 11.1. Column F tracks the cumulative interest on the loan, and cell F6 contains the following SUM() formula:

```
=SUM($D$7:D7)
```

**Figure 11.1**
The SUM( ) formulas in
column F calculate the
cumulative interest paid
on a loan.

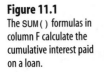

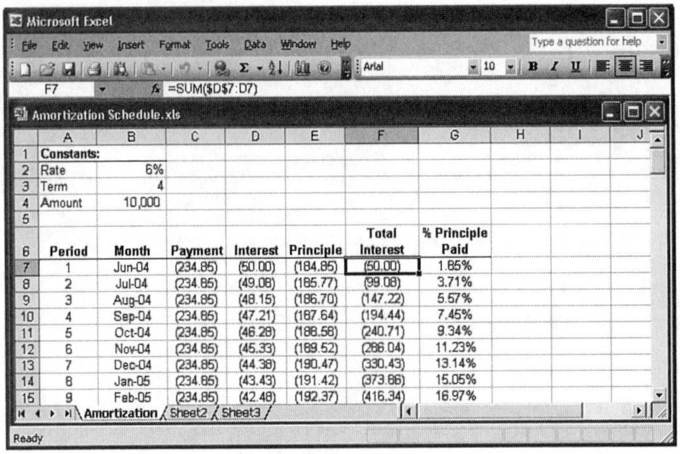

| | A | B | C | D | E | F | G | H | I | J |
|---|---|---|---|---|---|---|---|---|---|---|
| 1 | Constants: | | | | | | | | | |
| 2 | Rate | 6% | | | | | | | | |
| 3 | Term | 4 | | | | | | | | |
| 4 | Amount | 10,000 | | | | | | | | |
| 5 | | | | | | | | | | |
| 6 | Period | Month | Payment | Interest | Principle | Total Interest | % Principle Paid | | | |
| 7 | 1 | Jun-04 | (234.85) | (50.00) | (184.85) | (50.00) | 1.85% | | | |
| 8 | 2 | Jul-04 | (234.85) | (49.08) | (185.77) | (99.08) | 3.71% | | | |
| 9 | 3 | Aug-04 | (234.85) | (48.15) | (186.70) | (147.22) | 5.57% | | | |
| 10 | 4 | Sep-04 | (234.85) | (47.21) | (187.64) | (194.44) | 7.45% | | | |
| 11 | 5 | Oct-04 | (234.85) | (46.28) | (188.58) | (240.71) | 9.34% | | | |
| 12 | 6 | Nov-04 | (234.85) | (45.33) | (189.52) | (286.04) | 11.23% | | | |
| 13 | 7 | Dec-04 | (234.85) | (44.38) | (190.47) | (330.43) | 13.14% | | | |
| 14 | 8 | Jan-05 | (234.85) | (43.43) | (191.42) | (373.86) | 15.05% | | | |
| 15 | 9 | Feb-05 | (234.85) | (42.48) | (192.37) | (416.34) | 16.97% | | | |

**NOTE**
You can download the workbook that contains this chapter's examples here:
www.mcfedries.com/ExcelFormulas/

This formula just sums cell D7, which is no great feat. However, when you fill the range
F7:F54 with this formula, the left part of the SUM( ) range ($D$7) remains anchored; the
right side (D7) is relative and, therefore, changes. So, for example, the corresponding formula in cell F10 would be this:

```
=SUM($D$7:D10)
```

In case you're wondering, column G tracks the percentage of the total principal that has
been paid off so far. Here's the formula used in cell G7:

```
=SUM($E$7:E7) / $B$4 * -1
```

The SUM($E$7:E7) part calculates the cumulative principal paid. To get the percentage,
divide by the total principal (cell B4). The whole thing is multiplied by –1 to return a positive percentage.

## Summing Only the Positive or Negative Values in a Range

If you have a range of numbers that contains both positive and negative values, what do you
do if you need a total of only the negative values? Or only the positive ones? You could
enter the individual cells into a SUM( ) function, but there's an easier way that makes use of
arrays.

To sum the negative values in a range, you use the following array formula:

```
{=SUM((range < 0) * range)}
```

Here, *range* is a range reference or named range. The *range* < 0 test returns TRUE (the equivalent of 1) for those range values that are less than 0; otherwise, it returns FALSE (the equivalent of 0). Therefore, only negative values get included in the SUM().

Similarly, you use the following array formula to sum only the positive values in *range*:

`{=SUM((range > 0) * range)}`

➔ You can apply much more sophisticated criteria to your sums by using the SUMIF( ) function. **See** "Using SUMIF( )," **p. 307**.

# The MOD ( ) Function

The MOD() function calculates the remainder (or *modulus*) that results after dividing one number into another. Here's the syntax for this more-useful-than-you-think function:

MOD(*number, divisor*)

| | |
|---|---|
| *number* | The dividend (that is, the number to be divided) |
| *divisor* | The number by which you want to divide *number* |

For example, MOD(24, 10) equals 4 (that is, 24 ÷ 10 = 2, with remainder 4).

The MOD() function is well suited to values that are both sequential and cyclical. For example, the days of the week (as given by the WEEKDAY() function) run from 1 (Sunday) through 7 (Saturday) and then start over (the next Sunday is back to 1). So, the following formula always returns an integer that corresponds to a day of the week:

`=MOD(number, 7) + 1`

If *number* is any integer, the MOD() function returns integer values from 0 to 6, so adding 1 gives values from 1 to 7.

You can set up similar formulas using months (1 to 12), seconds or minutes (0 to 59), fiscal quarters (1 to 4), and more.

## A Better Formula for Time Differences

In Chapter 10, I told you that subtracting an earlier time from a later time is problematic if the earlier time is before midnight and the later time is after midnight. Here's the expression I showed you that overcomes this problem:

`IF(EndTime < StartTime, 1 + EndTime - StartTime, EndTime - StartTime)`

➔ For the details on the time-difference formula, **see** "Calculating the Difference Between Two Times," **p. 223**.

However, time values are sequential and cyclical: They're real numbers that run from 0 to 1 and then start over at midnight. Therefore, you can use MOD() to greatly simplify the formula for calculating the difference between two times:

`=MOD(EndTime - StartTime, 1)`

This works for any value of *EndTime* and *StartTime*, as long as *EndTime* comes later than *StartTime*.

## Summing Every *n*th Row

Depending on the structure of your worksheet, you might need to sum only every *n*th row, where *n* is some integer. For example, you might want to sum only every 5th or 10th cell to get a sampling of the data.

You can accomplish this by applying the MOD() function to the result of the ROW() function, as in this array formula:

`{=SUM(IF(MOD(ROW(Range), n) = 1, Range, 0))}`

For each cell in *Range*, MOD(ROW(*Range*), n) returns 1 for every *n*th value. In that case, the value of the cell is added to the sum; otherwise, 0 is added. In other words, this sums the values in the 1st row of *Range*, the n + 1st row of *Range*, and so on. If instead you want the 2nd row of *Range*, the n + 2nd row of *Range*, and so on, compare the MOD() result with 2, like so:

`{=SUM(IF(MOD(ROW(Range), n) = 2, Range, 0))}`

### Special Case No. 1: Summing Only Odd Rows

If you want to sum only the odd rows in a worksheet, use this straightforward variation in the formula:

`{=SUM(IF(MOD(ROW(Range), 2) = 1, Range, 0))}`

### Special Case No. 2: Summing Only Even Rows

To sum only the even rows, you need to sum those cells where MOD(ROW(*Range*), 2) returns 0:

`{=SUM(IF(MOD(ROW(Range), 2) = 0, Range, 0))}`

## Determining Whether a Year Is a Leap Year

If you need to determine whether a given year is a leap year, the MOD() function can help. Leap years (with some exceptions) are years divisible by 4. So, a year is (usually) a leap year if the following formula returns 0:

`=MOD(year, 4)`

In this case, *year* is a four-digit year number. This formula works for the years 1901 to 2099, which should take care of most people's needs. The formula doesn't work for 1900 and 2100 because, despite being divisible by 4, these years aren't leap years. The general rule is that a year is a leap year if it's divisible by 4 and it's not divisible by 100, *unless* it's also divisible by 400. Therefore, because 1900 and 2100 are divisible by 100 and not by 400, they aren't leap years. The year 2000, however, is a leap year. If you want a formula that takes the full rule into account, use the following formula:

`=(MOD(year, 4) = 0) - (MOD(year, 100) = 0) + (MOD(year, 400) = 0)`

The three parts of the formula that compare a MOD() result to 0 return 1 or 0. Therefore, the result of this formula always is 0 for leap years and nonzero for all other years.

# Creating Ledger Shading

*Ledger shading* is formatting in which rows alternate cell shading between a light color and a slightly darker color (for example, white and light gray). This type of shading is often seen in checkbook registers and account ledgers, but it's also useful in any worksheet that presents data in rows because it makes it easier to differentiate each row from its neighbors. Figure 11.2 shows an example.

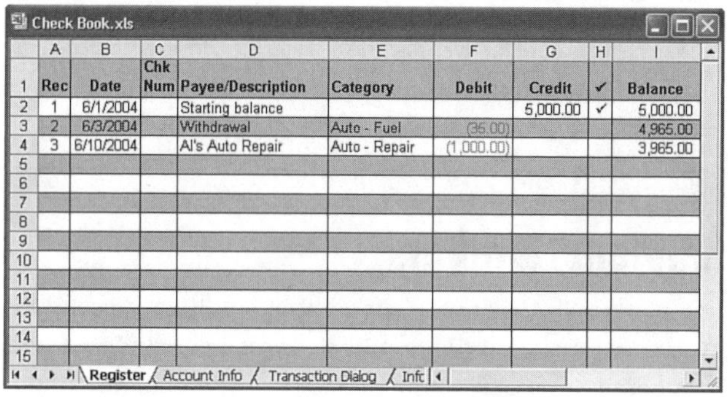

**Figure 11.2**
This worksheet uses ledger shading for a checkbook register.

However, ledger shading isn't easy to work with by hand:

- It can take a while to apply if you have a large range to format.
- If you insert or delete a row, you have to reapply the formatting.

To avoid these headaches, you can use a trick that combines the MOD() function and Excel's conditional formatting. Here's how it's done:

1. Select the area you want to format with ledger shading.
2. Choose Format, Conditional Formatting to display the Conditional Formatting dialog box.
3. In the Condition 1 drop-down list, select Formula Is.
4. In the text box, enter the following formula:
   =MOD(ROW(), 2)
5. Click Format to display the Format Cells dialog box.
6. Select the Patterns tab, click the color you want to use for the nonwhite ledger cells, and then click OK to return to the Conditional Formatting dialog box (see Figure 11.3).
7. Click OK.

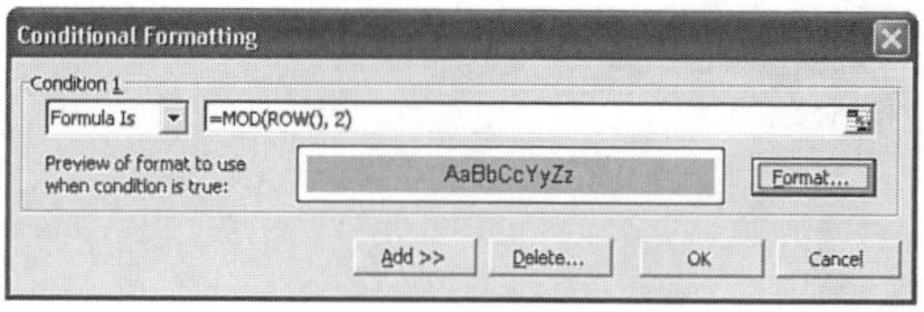

**Figure 11.3**
This MOD ( ) formula applies the cell shading to every second row (1, 3, 5, and so on).

The formula =MOD(ROW(), 2) returns 1 for odd-numbered rows and 0 for even-numbered rows. Because 1 is equivalent to TRUE, Excel applies the conditional formatting to the odd-numbered rows and leaves the even-numbered rows as they are.

> **TIP**
>
> If you prefer to alternate shading on columns, instead, use the following formula in the Conditional Formatting dialog box:
>
>     =MOD(COL(), 2)
>
> If you prefer to have the even rows shaded and the odd rows unshaded, use the following formula in the Conditional Formatting dialog box:
>
>     =MOD(ROW() + 1, 2)

# Generating Random Numbers

If you're using a worksheet to set up a simulation, you'll need realistic data on which to do your testing. You could make up the numbers, but it's possible that you might skew the data unconsciously. A better approach is to generate the numbers randomly using the worksheet functions RAND() and RANDBETWEEN().

→ Excel's Analysis ToolPak also comes with a tool for generating random numbers; **see** "Using the Random Number Generation Tool," **p. 275**.

## The RAND() Function

The RAND() function returns a random number that is greater than or equal to 0 and less than 1. RAND() is often useful by itself (for example, it's perfect for generating random time values). However, you'll most often use it in an expression to generate random numbers between two values.

In the simplest case, if you want to generate random numbers greater than or equal to 0 and less than $n$, use the following expression:

    RAND() * n

For example, the following formula generates a random number between 0 and 30:

    =RAND() * 30

The more complex case is when you want random numbers greater than or equal to some number $m$ and less than some number $n$. Here's the expression to use for this case:

    RAND() * (n - m) + m

For example, the following formula produces a random number greater than or equal to 100 and less than 200:

    =RAND() * (200 - 100) + 100

> **CAUTION**
>
> RAND() is a volatile function, meaning that its value changes each time you recalculate or reopen the worksheet, or edit any cell on the worksheet. To enter a static random number in a cell, type **=RAND()**, press F9 to evaluate the function and return a random number, and then press Enter to place the random number into the cell as a numeric literal.

## Generating Random *n*-Digit Numbers

It's often useful to create random numbers with a specific number of digits. For example, you might want to generate a random six-digit account number for new customers, or you might need a random eight-digit number for a temporary filename.

The procedure for this is to start with the general formula from the previous section and apply the INT() function to ensure an integer result:

```
INT(RAND() * (n - m) + m)
```

In this case, however, you set *n* equal to $10^n$, and you set *m* equal to $10^{n-1}$:

```
INT(RAND() * (10^n - 10^n-1) + 10^n-1)
```

For example, if you need a random eight-digit number, this formula becomes the following:

```
INT(RAND() * (100000000 - 10000000) + 10000000)
```

This generates random numbers greater than or equal to 10,000,000 and less than or equal to 99,999,999.

## Generating a Random Letter

You normally use RAND() to generate a random number, but it's also useful for text values. For example, suppose that you need to generate a random letter of the alphabet. There are 26 letters in the alphabet, so you start with an expression that generates random integers greater than or equal to 1 and less than or equal to 26:

```
INT(RAND() * 26 + 1)
```

Now you plug this into a CHOOSE() function that picks out a letter based on the result:

```
=CHOOSE(INT(RAND() * (26) + 1), "A", "B", "C", "D", "E", "F", "G", "H",
➥"I", "J", "K", "L", "M", "N", "O", "P", "Q", "R", "S", "T", "U", "V",
➥"W", "X", "Y", "Z")
```

## Sorting Values Randomly

If you have a set of values on a worksheet, you might need to sort them in random order. For example, if you want to perform an operation on a subset of data, sorting the table randomly removes any numeric biases that might be inherent if the data was sorted in any way.

11

Follow these steps to randomly sort a data table:

1. Assuming that the data is arranged in rows, select a range in the column immediately to the left or right of the table. Make sure that the selected range has the same number of rows as the table.
2. Enter `=RAND()`, and press Ctrl+Enter to add the `RAND()` formula to every selected cell.
3. Choose Tools, Options; select the Calculation tab; click Manual; and then click OK.
4. Select the range that includes the data and the column of `RAND()` values.
5. Choose Data, Sort to display the Sort dialog box.
6. In the Sort By list, select the column that contains the `RAND()` values.
7. Click OK.

This procedure tells Excel to sort the selected range according to the random values, thus sorting the data table randomly. Figure 11.4 shows an example. The data values are in column A, the `RAND()` values are in column B, and the range A2:B21 was sorted on column B.

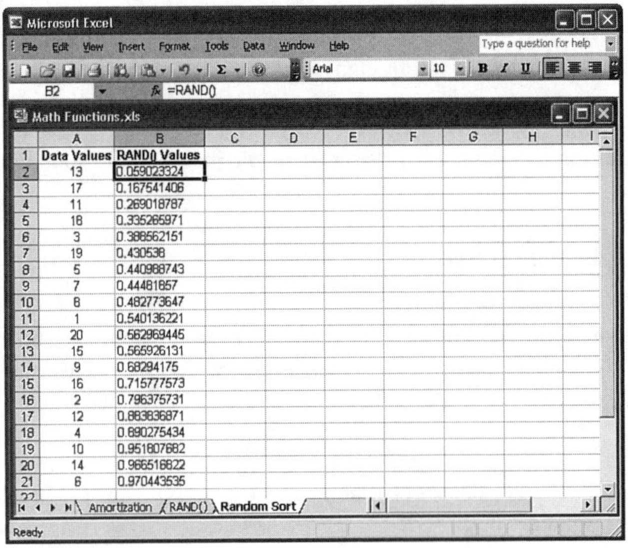


| | A | B |
|---|---|---|
| 1 | Data Values | RAND() Values |
| 2 | 13 | 0.059023324 |
| 3 | 17 | 0.167541406 |
| 4 | 11 | 0.269018787 |
| 5 | 18 | 0.335265971 |
| 6 | 3 | 0.388562151 |
| 7 | 19 | 0.430538 |
| 8 | 5 | 0.440988743 |
| 9 | 7 | 0.44481857 |
| 10 | 8 | 0.482773647 |
| 11 | 1 | 0.540136221 |
| 12 | 20 | 0.562969445 |
| 13 | 15 | 0.565926131 |
| 14 | 9 | 0.68294175 |
| 15 | 16 | 0.715777573 |
| 16 | 2 | 0.796375731 |
| 17 | 12 | 0.883836871 |
| 18 | 4 | 0.890275434 |
| 19 | 10 | 0.951807682 |
| 20 | 14 | 0.966516822 |
| 21 | 6 | 0.970443535 |

**Figure 11.4**
To randomly sort data values, add a column of =RAND() formulas and then sort the entire range on the random values.

11

## The RANDBETWEEN() Function

If you have access to the Analysis ToolPak, Excel offers the `RANDBETWEEN()` function, which can simplify working with certain sets of random numbers. `RANDBETWEEN()` lets you specify a lower bound and an upper bound, and then returns a random integer between them:

```
RANDBETWEEN(bottom, top)
```

|  |  |
|---|---|
| *bottom* | The smallest possible random integer. (That is, Excel generates a random number that is greater than or equal to *bottom*.) |
| *top* | The largest possible random integer. (That is, Excel generates a random number that is less than or equal to *top*.) |

For example, the following formula returns a random integer between 0 and 59:

```
=RANDBETWEEN(1, 59)
```

## From Here

- Excel also comes with a large collection of statistical functions for calculating averages, maximums and minimums, standard deviations, and more. **See** "Working with Statistical Functions," **p. 249**.

- To learn how to create sophisticated distributions of random numbers, **see** "Using the Random Number Generation Tool," **p. 275**.

- Excel can apply subtotals to list data automatically. To learn how, **see** "Creating Automatic Subtotals," **p. 301**.

- The SUMIF() function enables you to apply sophisticated criteria to sum operations. **See** "Using SUMIF()," **p. 307**.

11

# Working with Statistical Functions

Excel's statistical functions calculate all the standard statistical measures, such as average, maximum, minimum, and standard deviation. For most of the statistical functions, you supply a list of values (which could be an entire *population* or just a *sample* from a population). You can enter individual values or cells, or you can specify a range. Excel has dozens of statistical functions, many of which are rarely, if ever, used in business. Table 12.1 lists those statistical functions that have some utility in the business world.

# 12

**Table 12.1  Statistical Functions of Use in the Business World**

| Function | Description |
|---|---|
| AVERAGE(*number1*,[*number2*,...]) | Returns the average |
| CORREL(*array1*,*array2*) | Returns the correlation coefficient |
| COUNT(*value1*,[*value2*,...]) | Counts the numbers in the argument list |
| COUNTA(*value1*,[*value2*,...]) | Counts the values in the argument list |
| COVAR(*array1*,*array2*) | Returns the covariance, the average of the products of deviations for each data point pair |
| FORECAST(*x*,*known_y's*,*known_x's*) | Returns a forecast value for *x* based on a linear regression of the arrays *known_y's* and *known_x's* |
| FREQUENCY(*data_array*,*bins_array*) | Returns a frequency distribution |
| FTEST(*array1*, *array2*) | Returns an F-test result, the one-tailed probability that the variances in the two sets are not significantly different |
| GROWTH(*known_y's*, [*known_x's*,*new_x's*,*const*]) | Returns values along an exponential trend |
| INTERCEPT(*known_y's*,*known_x's*) | Returns the y-intercept of the linear regression trendline generated by the *known_y's* and *known_x's* |
| KURT(*number1*,[*number2*,...]) | Returns the kurtosis of a frequency distribution |
| LARGE(*array*,*k*) | Returns the *k*th largest value in *array* |
| LINEST(*known_y's*, [*known_x's*,*const*,*stats*]) | Uses the least squares method to calculate a straight-line regression fit through the *known_y's* and *known_x's* |
| LOGEST(*known_y's*, [*known_x's*,*const*,*stats*]) | Uses the least squares method to calculate an exponential regression fit through the *known_y's* and *known_x's* |
| MAX(*number1*,[*number2*,...]) | Returns the maximum value |
| MEDIAN(*number1*,[*number2*,...]) | Returns the median value |
| MIN(*number1*,[*number2*,...]) | Returns the minimum value |
| MODE(*number1*,[*number2*,...]) | Returns the most common value |
| PERCENTILE(*array*,*k*) | Returns the *k*th percentile of the values in *array* |
| RANK(*number*,*ref*,[*order*]) | Returns the rank of a number in a list |
| RSQ(*known_y's*,*known_x's*) | Returns the coefficient of determination that indicates how much of the variance in the *known_y's* is due to the *known_x's* |

| Function | Description |
|----------|-------------|
| SKEW(*number1*,[*number2*,...]) | Returns the skewness of a frequency distribution |
| SLOPE(*known_y's*,*known_x's*) | Returns the slope of the linear regression trendline generated by the *known_y's* and *known_x's* |
| SMALL(*array*,*k*) | Returns the *k*th smallest value in *array* |
| STDEV(*number1*,[*number2*,...]) | Returns the standard deviation based on a sample |
| STDEVP(*number1*,[*number2*,...]) | Returns the standard deviation based on an entire population |
| TREND(*known_y's*, [*known_x's*,*new_x's*,*const*]) | Returns values along a linear trend |
| TTEST(*array1*,*array2*,*tails*,*type*) | Returns the probability associated with a student's t-Test |
| VAR(*number1*,[*number2*,...]) | Returns the variance based on a sample |
| VARP(*number1*,[*number2*,...]) | Returns the variance based on an entire population |
| ZTEST(*array*,*x*,[*sigma*]) | Returns the P-value of a two-sample z-test for means with known variances |

→ For the details of the regression functions—FORECAST(),GROWTH(),INTERCEPT(),LINEST(),LOGEST(),RSQ(), SLOPE(),and TREND()—**see** "Using Regression to Track Trends and Make Forecasts," **p. 339**.

# Understanding Descriptive Statistics

One of the goals of this book is to show you how to use formulas and functions to turn a jumble of numbers and values into results and summaries that give you useful information about the data. Excel's statistical functions are particularly useful for extracting analytical sense out of data nonsense. Many of these functions might seem strange and obscure, but they reward a bit of patience and effort with striking new views of your data.

This is particularly true of the branch of statistics known casually as *descriptive statistics* (or *summary statistics*). As the name implies, descriptive statistics are used to describe various aspects of a data set, to give you a better overall picture of the phenomenon underlying the numbers. In Excel's statistical repertoire, 16 measures make up its descriptive statistics package: sum, count, mean, median, mode, maximum, minimum, range, *k*th largest, *k*th smallest, standard deviation, variance, standard error of the mean, confidence level, kurtosis, and skewness.

In this chapter, you'll learn how to wield all of these statistical measures (except sum, which you've already seen earlier in this book). The context will be the worksheet database of product defects shown in Figure 12.1.

12

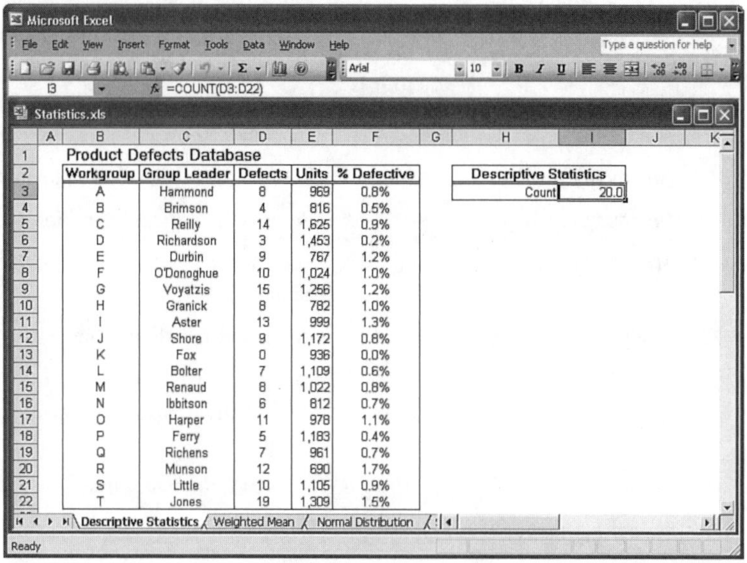

**Figure 12.1**

To demonstrate Excel's descriptive statistics capabilities, this case study uses the data shown here in a database of product defects.

| | A | B | C | D | E | F | G | H | I | J | K |
|---|---|---|---|---|---|---|---|---|---|---|---|
| 1 | | Product Defects Database | | | | | | | | | |
| 2 | | Workgroup | Group Leader | Defects | Units | % Defective | | Descriptive Statistics | | | |
| 3 | | A | Hammond | 8 | 969 | 0.8% | | Count | 20.0 | | |
| 4 | | B | Brimson | 4 | 816 | 0.5% | | | | | |
| 5 | | C | Reilly | 14 | 1,625 | 0.9% | | | | | |
| 6 | | D | Richardson | 3 | 1,453 | 0.2% | | | | | |
| 7 | | E | Durbin | 9 | 767 | 1.2% | | | | | |
| 8 | | F | O'Donoghue | 10 | 1,024 | 1.0% | | | | | |
| 9 | | G | Voyatzis | 15 | 1,256 | 1.2% | | | | | |
| 10 | | H | Granick | 8 | 782 | 1.0% | | | | | |
| 11 | | I | Aster | 13 | 999 | 1.3% | | | | | |
| 12 | | J | Shore | 9 | 1,172 | 0.8% | | | | | |
| 13 | | K | Fox | 0 | 936 | 0.0% | | | | | |
| 14 | | L | Bolter | 7 | 1,109 | 0.6% | | | | | |
| 15 | | M | Renaud | 8 | 1,022 | 0.8% | | | | | |
| 16 | | N | Ibbitson | 6 | 812 | 0.7% | | | | | |
| 17 | | O | Harper | 11 | 978 | 1.1% | | | | | |
| 18 | | P | Ferry | 5 | 1,183 | 0.4% | | | | | |
| 19 | | Q | Richens | 7 | 961 | 0.7% | | | | | |
| 20 | | R | Munson | 12 | 690 | 1.7% | | | | | |
| 21 | | S | Little | 10 | 1,105 | 0.9% | | | | | |
| 22 | | T | Jones | 19 | 1,309 | 1.5% | | | | | |

NOTE
You can download the workbook that contains this chapter's examples here:
www.mcfedries.com/ExcelFormulas/

# Counting Items with the COUNT() Function

The simplest of the descriptive statistics is the total number of values, which is given by the COUNT() function:

COUNT(*value1*,[*value2*,...])

> *value1, value2,...*     One or more ranges, arrays, function results, expressions, or literal values for which you want the count

The COUNT() function counts only the numeric values that appear in the list of arguments. Text values, dates, logical values, and errors are ignored. In the worksheet shown later in this chapter in Figure 12.5, the following formula is used to count the number of defect values in the database:

=COUNT(D3:D22)

TIP
To get a quick look at the count, select the range, right-click the Sum= indicator in the status bar, and then click Count Nums (or click Count to see the count of all the cells in the range).

# Calculating Averages

The most basic statistical analysis worthy of the name is probably the average, although you always need to ask yourself *which* average you need. There are three—mean, median, and mode. The next few sections show you the worksheet functions that calculate them.

## The AVERAGE() Function

The *mean* is what you probably think of when someone uses the term *average*. That is, it's the arithmetic mean of a set of numbers. In Excel, you calculate the mean using the AVERAGE() function:

```
AVERAGE(number1,[number2,...])
```

        *number1, number2,...*    A range, array, or list of values of which you want the mean

For example, to calculate the mean of the values in the defects database, you use the following formula:

```
=AVERAGE(D3:D22)
```

> **TIP**
>
> If you need just a quick glance at the mean value, select the range, right-click the Sum= indicator in the status bar, and then click <u>A</u>verage.

> **CAUTION**
>
> The AVERAGE() function (as well as the MEDIAN() and MODE() functions discussed in the next two sections) ignores text and logical values. It also ignores blank cells, but it does *not* ignore cells that contain the value 0.

**12**

## The MEDIAN() Function

The *median* is the value in a data set that falls in the middle when all the values are sorted in numeric order. That is, 50% of the values fall below the median, and 50% fall above it. The median is useful in data sets that have one or two extreme values that can throw off the mean result because the median is not affected by extremes.

You calculate the median using the MEDIAN() function:

```
MEDIAN(number1,[number2,...])
```

        *number1, number2,...*    A range, array, or list of values of which you want the median

For example, to calculate the median of the values in the defects database, you use the following formula:

```
=MEDIAN(D3:D22)
```

## The MODE() **Function**

The *mode* is the value in a data set that occurs most frequently. The mode is most useful when you're dealing with data that doesn't lend itself to being either added (necessary for calculating the mean) or sorted (necessary for calculating the median). For example, you might be tabulating the result of a poll that included a question about the respondent's favorite color. The mean and median don't make sense with such a question, but the mode will tell you which color was chosen the most.

You calculate the mode using the MODE() function:

```
MODE(number1,[number2,...])
```

> *number1, number2,...*    A range, array, or list of values of which you want the mode

For example, to calculate the mode of the values in the defects database, you use the following formula:

```
=MODE(D3:D22)
```

## Calculating the Weighted Mean

In some data sets, one value might be more "important" than another. For example, suppose that your company has several divisions, the biggest of which does $100 million in annual sales and the smallest of which does only $1 million in sales. If you want to calculate the average profit margin for the divisions, it doesn't make sense to treat the divisions equally because the largest is two orders of magnitude bigger than the smallest. You need some way of factoring the size of each division into your average profit margin calculation.

You can do this by calculating the *weighted mean*. This is an arithmetic mean in which each value is weighted according to its importance in the data set. Here's the procedure to follow to calculate the weighted mean:

1. For each value, multiply the value by its weight.
2. Sum the results from step 1.
3. Sum the weights.
4. Divide the sum from step 2 by the sum from step 3.

Let's make this more concrete by tying this into our database of product defects. Suppose you want to know the average percentage of product defects (the values in column F). Simply applying the AVERAGE() function to the range F3:F22 won't give an accurate answer because the number of units produced by each division is different (the maximum is 1,625 in division C, and the minimum is 690 in division R). To get an accurate result, you must give more weight to those divisions that produced more units. In other words, you need to calculate the weighted mean for the percentage of defective products.

In this case, the weights are the units produced by each division, so the weighted mean is calculated as follows:

1. Multiply the percentage defective values by the units. (The sharp-eyed reader will note that this just gives the number of defects. I'll ignore this for now for illustration purposes.)

2. Sum the results from step 1.

3. Sum the units.

4. Divide the sum from step 2 by the sum from step 3.

You can combine all of these steps into the following array formula, as shown in Figure 12.2:

`{=SUM(F3:F22 * E3:E22) / SUM(E3:E22))}`

**Figure 12.2**
This worksheet calculates the weighted mean of the percentage of defective products.

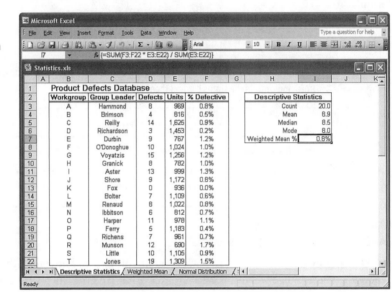

## Calculating Extreme Values

The average calculations tell you things about the "middle" of the data, but it can also be useful to know something about the "edges" of the data. For example, what's the biggest value and what's the smallest? The next two sections take you through the worksheet functions that return the extreme values of a sample or population.

### The MAX() and MIN() Functions

If you want to know the largest value in a data set, use the MAX() function:

`MAX(number1,[number2,...])`

       *number1, number2,...*      A range, array, or list of values of which you want the maximum

For example, to calculate the maximum value in the defects database, you use the following formula:

```
=MAX(D3:D22)
```

To get the smallest value in a data set, use the MIN() function:

```
MIN(number1,[number2,...])
```

> *number1, number2,...*     A range, array, or list of values of which you want the minimum

For example, to calculate the minimum value in the defects database, you use the following formula:

```
=MIN(D3:D22)
```

> **TIP**
>
> If you need just a quick glance at the maximum or minimum value, select the range, right-click the Sum= indicator in the status bar, and then click Max or Min.

> **NOTE**
>
> If you need to determine the maximum or minimum over a range or array that includes text values or logical values, use the MAXA() or MINA() functions instead. These functions ignore text values and treat logical values as either 1 (for TRUE) or 0 (for FALSE).

## The LARGE() and SMALL() Functions

Instead of knowing just the largest value, you might need to know the $k$th largest value, where $k$ is some integer. You can calculate this using Excel's LARGE() function:

```
LARGE(array, k)
```

> *array*     A range, array, or list of values.
>
> *k*     The position (beginning at the largest) within *array* that you want to return. (When $k$ equals 1, this function returns the same value as MAX().)

For example, the following formula returns 15, the second-largest defects value in the product defects database:

```
=LARGE(D3:D22, 2)
```

Similarly, instead of knowing just the smallest value, you might need to know the $k$th smallest value, where $k$ is some integer. You can determine this value using the SMALL() function:

```
SMALL(array, k)
```

> *array*     A range, array, or list of values.
>
> *k*     The position (beginning at the smallest) within *array* that you want to return. (When $k$ equals 1, this function returns the same value as MIN().)

For example, the following formula returns 4, the third-smallest defects value in the product defects database:

```
=SMALL(D3:D22, 3)
```

Figure 12.3 shows the defects database with the maximum, minimum, range, second-largest, and third-smallest values added to the descriptive statistics.

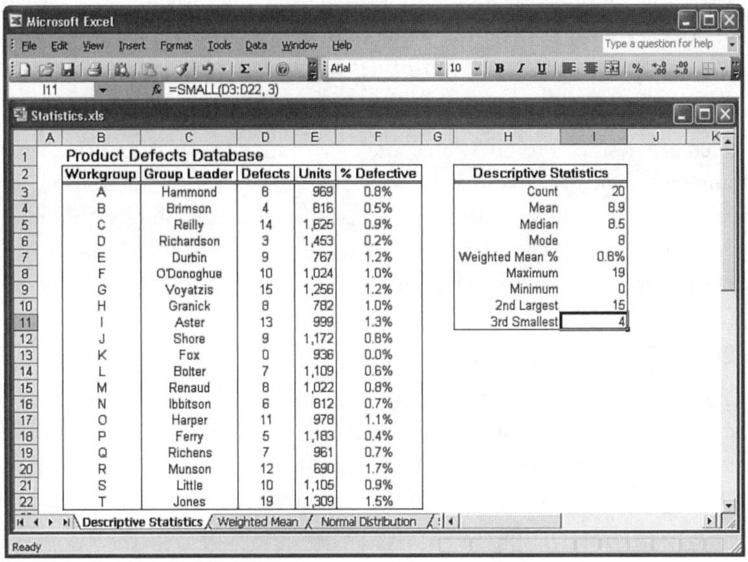


Product Defects Database

| Workgroup | Group Leader | Defects | Units | % Defective |
|---|---|---|---|---|
| A | Hammond | 8 | 969 | 0.8% |
| B | Brimson | 4 | 816 | 0.5% |
| C | Reilly | 14 | 1,625 | 0.9% |
| D | Richardson | 3 | 1,453 | 0.2% |
| E | Durbin | 9 | 767 | 1.2% |
| F | O'Donoghue | 10 | 1,024 | 1.0% |
| G | Voyatzis | 15 | 1,256 | 1.2% |
| H | Granick | 8 | 782 | 1.0% |
| I | Aster | 13 | 999 | 1.3% |
| J | Shore | 9 | 1,172 | 0.8% |
| K | Fox | 0 | 936 | 0.0% |
| L | Bolter | 7 | 1,109 | 0.6% |
| M | Renaud | 8 | 1,022 | 0.8% |
| N | Ibbitson | 6 | 812 | 0.7% |
| O | Harper | 11 | 978 | 1.1% |
| P | Ferry | 5 | 1,183 | 0.4% |
| Q | Richens | 7 | 961 | 0.7% |
| R | Munson | 12 | 690 | 1.7% |
| S | Little | 10 | 1,105 | 0.9% |
| T | Jones | 19 | 1,309 | 1.5% |

| Descriptive Statistics | |
|---|---|
| Count | 20 |
| Mean | 8.9 |
| Median | 8.5 |
| Mode | 8 |
| Weighted Mean % | 0.8% |
| Maximum | 19 |
| Minimum | 0 |
| 2nd Largest | 15 |
| 3rd Smallest | 4 |

**Figure 12.3**
The product defects database with calculations derived using the MAX(), MIN(), LARGE(), and SMALL() functions.

## Performing Calculations on the Top *k* Values

You might sometimes need to sum only the top 3 values in a data set, or take the average of the top 10 values. You can do this by combining the LARGE() function and the appropriate arithmetic function (such as SUM()) in an array formula. Here's the general formula:

```
{=FUNCTION(LARGE(range, {1,2,3,...,k}))}
```

Here, *FUNCTION*() is the arithmetic function, *range* is the array or range containing the data, and k is the number of values you want to work with. In other words, LARGE() applies the top k values from *range* to the *FUNCTION*().

For example, suppose that you want to find the mean of the top five values in the defects database. Here's an array formula that does this:

```
{=AVERAGE(LARGE(D3:D22,{1,2,3,4,5}))}
```

## Performing Calculations on the Bottom *k* Values

You can probably figure out that performing calculations on the smallest *k* values is similar. In fact, the only difference is that you substitute the SMALL() function for LARGE():

```
{=FUNCTION(SMALL(range, {1,2,3,...,k}))}
```

For example, the following array formula sums the smallest three defect values in the defects database:

```
{=SUM(SMALL(D3:D22,{1,2,3}))}
```

# Calculating Measures of Variation

Descriptive statistics such as the mean, median, and mode fall under what statisticians call *measures of central tendency* (or sometimes *measures of location*). These numbers are designed to give you some idea of what constitutes a "typical" value in the data set.

This is in contrast to the so-called *measures of variation* (or sometimes *measures of dispersion*), which are designed to give you some idea of how the values in the data set vary with respect to one another. For example, a data set in which all the values are the same would have no variability; in contrast, a data set with wildly different values would have high variability. Just what is meant by "wildly different" is what the statistical techniques in this section are designed to help you calculate.

## Calculating the Range

The simplest measure of variability is the *range* (also sometimes called the *spread*), which is defined as the difference between a data set's maximum and minimum values. Excel doesn't have a function that calculates the range directly. Instead, you first apply the MAX() and MIN() functions to the data set. Then, when you have these extreme values, you calculate the range by subtracting the minimum from the maximum.

For example, here's a formula that calculates the range for the defects database:

```
=MAX(D3:D22) - MIN(D3:D22)
```

Speaking generally, the range is a useful measure of variation only for small sample sizes. The larger the sample is, the more likely it becomes that an extreme maximum or minimum will occur, and the range will be skewed accordingly.

## Calculating the Variance with the VAR() Function

When computing the variability of a set of values, one straightforward approach would be to calculate how much each value deviates from the mean. You could then add those differences and divide by the number of values in the sample to get what might be called the "average difference." The problem, however, is that, by definition of the arithmetic mean, adding the differences (some of which are positive and some of which are negative) gives the result 0. To solve this problem, you need to add the *absolute values* of the deviations and then divide by the sample size. This is what statisticians call the *average deviation*.

Unfortunately, this simple state of affairs is still problematic because (for highly technical reasons) mathematicians tend to shudder at equations that require absolute values. To get around this, they instead use the *square* of each deviation from the mean, which always results in a positive number. They sum these squares and divide by the number of values

(I'm simplifying things considerably here), and the result is the called the *variance*. This is a common measure of variation, although interpreting it is hard because the result isn't in the units of the sample: It's in those units squared. What does it mean to speak of "defects squared," for example? This doesn't matter that much for our purposes because, as you'll see in the next section, the variance is used chiefly to get to the standard deviation.

In any case, variance is usually a standard part of a descriptive statistics package, so that's why I'm covering it. Excel calculates the variance using the VAR() function:

VARP(*number1*,[*number2*,...])

VAR(*number1*,[*number2*,...])

>   *number1, number2,...*    A range, array, or list of values of which you want the variance

You use the VARP() function if your data set represents the entire population (as it does, for example, in the product defects case); you use the VAR() function if your data set represents only a sample from the entire population.

For example, to calculate the variance of the values in the defects database, you use the following formula:

=VARP(D3:D22)

> ₪ **NOTE**   If you need to determine the variance over a range or array that includes text values or logical values, use the VARPA() or VARA() functions instead. These functions ignore text values and treat logical values as either 1 (for TRUE) or 0 (for FALSE).

## Calculating the Standard Deviation with the STDEVP() and STDEV() Functions

As I mentioned in the previous section, in real-world scenarios, the variance is really used only as an intermediate step for calculating the most important of the measures of variation, the *standard deviation*. This measure tells you how much the values in the data set vary with respect to the average (the arithmetic mean). What exactly this means won't become clear until you learn about frequency distributions in the next section. For now, however, it's enough to know that a low standard deviation means that the data values are clustered near the mean, and a high standard deviation means the values are spread out from the mean.

The standard deviation is defined as the square root of the variance. This is good because it means that the resulting units will be the same as those used by the data. For example, the variance of the product defects is expressed in the meaningless "defects squared" units, but the standard deviation is expressed in defects.

You could calculate the standard deviation by taking the square root of the VAR() result, but Excel offers a more direct route:

STDEVP(*number1*,[*number2*,...])

STDEV(*number1*,[*number2*,...])

> *number1, number2,...*      A range, array, or list of values of which you want the standard deviation

You use the STDEVP() function if your data set represents the entire population (as in the product defects case); you use the STDEV() function if your data set represents only a sample from the entire population.

For example, to calculate the standard deviation of the values in the defects database, you use the following formula (see Figure 12.4):

=STDEVP(D3:D22)

> **NOTE**
>
> If you need to determine the standard deviation over a range or array that includes text values or logical values, use the STDEVPA() or STDEVA() functions instead. These functions ignore text values and treat logical values as either 1 (for TRUE) or 0 (for FALSE).

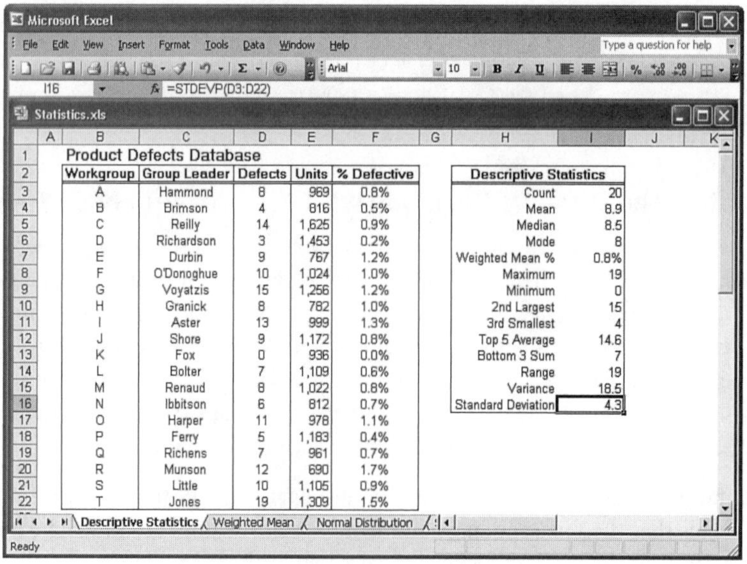

**Figure 12.4**
The product defects worksheet showing the results of the VARP() and STDEVP() functions.

# Working with Frequency Distributions

A *frequency distribution* is a data table that groups data values into *bins*—ranges of values—and shows how many values fall into each bin. For example, here's a possible frequency distribution for the product defects data:

| Bin (Defects) | Count |
|---|---|
| 0–3 | 2 |
| 4–7 | 5 |
| 8–11 | 8 |
| 12–15 | 4 |
| 16+ | 1 |

The size of each bin is called the *bin interval*. How many bins should you use? The answer usually depends on the data. If you want to calculate the frequency distribution for a set of student grades, for example, you'd probably set up six bins: 0–49, 50–59, 60–69, 70–79, 80–89, and 90+. For poll results, you might group the data by age into four bins: 18–34, 35–49, 50–64, and 65+.

If your data has no obvious bin intervals, you can use the following rule:

If *n* is the number of values in the data set, enclose *n* between two successive powers of 2, and take the higher exponent to be the number of bins.

For example, if *n* is 100, you would use 7 bins because 100 lies between $2^6$ (64) and $2^7$ (128). For the product defects, *n* is 20, so the number of bins should be 5 because 20 falls between $2^4$ (16) and $2^5$ (32).

> **TIP**
> Here's a worksheet formula that implements the bin-calculation rule:
>
> ```
> =CEILING(LOG(COUNT(input_range), 2), 1)
> ```

12

## The FREQUENCY() **Function**

To help you construct a frequency distribution, Excel offers the FREQUENCY() function:

FREQUENCY(*data_array, bins_array*)

| | |
|---|---|
| *data_array* | A range or array of data values |
| *bins_array* | A range or array of numbers representing the upper bounds of each bin |

Here are some things you need to know about this function:

- For the *bins_array*, you enter only the upper limit of each bin. If the last bin is open-ended (such as 16+), you don't include it in the *bins_array*. For example, here's the *bins_array* for the product defects frequency distribution shown earlier: {3, 7, 11, 15}.

---

- CAUTION ---

Make sure that you enter your bin values in ascending order.

---

- The FREQUENCY() function returns an array (the number of values that fall within each bin) that is one greater than the number of elements in *bins_array*. For example, if the *bins_array* contains four elements, FREQUENCY() returns five elements (the extra element is the number of values that fall in the open-ended bin).

- Because FREQUENCY() returns an array, it must be entered as an array formula. To do this, select the range in which you want the function results to appear (again, make this range one cell bigger than the *bins_array* range), type in the formula, and press Ctrl+Shift+Enter.

Figure 12.5 shows the product defects database with a frequency distribution added. The *bins_array* is the range K4:K7, and the FREQUENCY() results appear in the range L5:L8, with the following formula entered as an array in that range:

```
{=FREQUENCY(D3:D22, K4:K7)}
```

**Figure 12.5**
The product defects worksheet showing the results of the VARP() and STDEVP() functions.

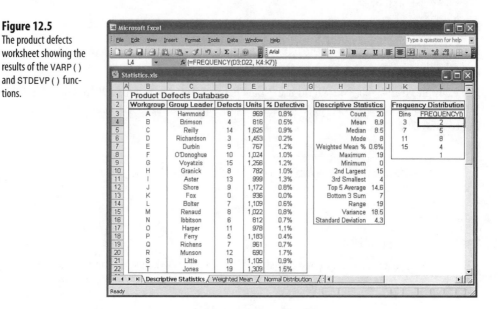

## Understanding the Normal Distribution and the NORMDIST() Function

The next few sections require some knowledge of perhaps the most famous object in the statistical world: the *normal distribution* (it's also called the *normal frequency curve*). This refers to a set of values that are symmetrically clustered around a central mean, with the frequencies of each value highest near the mean and falling off as you move farther from the mean (either to the left or to the right).

Figure 12.6 shows a chart that displays a typical normal distribution. In fact, this particular example is called the *standard normal distribution*, and it's defined as having mean 0 and standard deviation 1. The distinctive bell shape of this distribution is why it's often called the *bell curve*).

**Figure 12.6**
The standard normal distribution (mean 0 and standard deviation 1) generated by the NORMDIST() function.

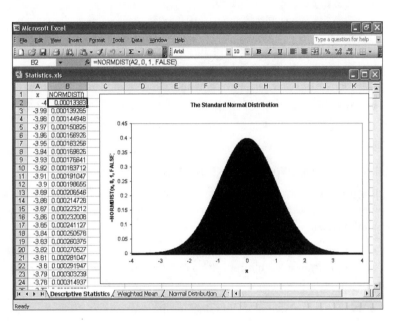

To generate this normal distribution, I used Excel's NORMDIST() function, which returns the probability that a given value exists within a population:

NORMDIST(*x, mean, standard_dev, cumulative*)

| | |
|---|---|
| *x* | The value you want to work with. |
| *mean* | The arithmetic mean of the distribution. |
| *standard_dev* | The standard deviation of the distribution. |
| *cumulative* | A logical value that determines how the function results are calculated. If *cumulative* is TRUE, the function returns the cumulative probabilities of the observations that occur at or below *x*; if *cumulative* is FALSE, the function returns the probability associated with *x*. |

For example, consider the following example that computes the standard normal distribution—mean 0 and standard deviation 1—for the value 0:

=NORMDIST(0, 0, 1, TRUE)

With the *cumulative* argument set to TRUE, this formula returns 0.5, which makes intuitive sense because, in this distribution, half of the values fall below 0. In other words, the probabilities of all the values below 0 add up to 0.5.

12

Now consider the same function, but this time with the *cumulative* argument set to FALSE:

```
=NORMDIST(0, 0, 1, FALSE)
```

This time, the result is 0.39894228. In other words, in this distribution, about 3.99% of all the values in the population are 0.

For our purposes, the key point about the normal distribution is that it has direct ties to the standard deviation:

- Approximately 68% of all the values fall within one standard deviation of the mean (that is, either one standard deviation above or one standard deviation below).

- Approximately 95% of all the values fall within two standard deviations of the mean.

- Approximately 99.7% of all the values fall within three standard deviations of the mean.

## The Shape of the Curve I: The SKEW( ) Function

How do you know if your frequency distribution is at or close to a normal distribution? In other words, does the shape of your data's frequency curve mirror that of the normal distribution's bell curve?

One way to find out is to consider how the values cluster around the mean. For a normal distribution, the values cluster symmetrically about the mean. Other distributions are asymmetric in one of two ways:

- **Negatively skewed**—The values are bunched above the mean and drop off quickly in a "tail" below the mean.

- **Positively skewed**—The values are bunched below the mean and drop off quickly in a "tail" above the mean.

Figure 12.7 shows two charts that display examples of negative and positive skewness.

In Excel, you calculate the *skewness* of a data set by using the SKEW( ) function:

```
SKEW(number1,[number2,...])
```

| | |
|---|---|
| *number1, number2,...* | A range, array, or list of values for which you want the skewness |

For example, the following formula returns the skewness of the product defects:

```
=SKEW(D3:D22)
```

The closer the SKEW( ) result is to 0, the more symmetric the distribution is, so the more like the normal distribution it is.

**Figure 12.7**
The distribution on the left is negatively skewed, while the distribution on the right is positively skewed.

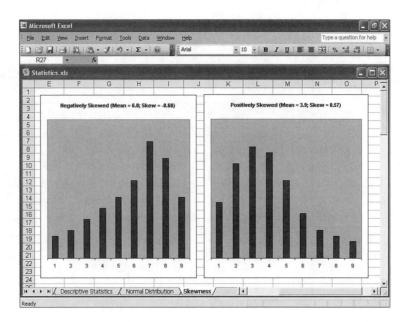

## The Shape of the Curve II: The KURT() **Function**

Another way to find out how close your frequency distribution is to a normal distribution is to consider the "flatness" of the curve:

- **Flat**—The values are distributed evenly across all or most of the bins.
- **Peaked**—The values are clustered around a narrow range of values.

Statisticians call the flatness of the frequency curve the *kurtosis*: a flat curve has a negative kurtosis, while a peaked curve has a positive kurtosis. The further these values are from 0, the less the frequency is like the normal distribution. Figure 12.8 shows two charts that display examples of negative and positive kurtosis.

In Excel, you calculate the kurtosis of a data set by using the KURT() function:

KURT(*number1*,[*number2*,...])

> *number1, number2,...*     A range, array, or list of values for which you want the
>                                          kurtosis

For example, the following formula returns the kurtosis of the product defects:

=KURT(D3:D22)

Figure 12.9 shows the final product defects worksheet, including values for the skewness and kurtosis.

→ Many of the descriptive statistics covered in this case study are available via the Analysis ToolPak; **see** "Using the Descriptive Statistics Tool," **p. 269**.

12

**Figure 12.8**
The distribution on the left is negative, while the distribution on the right is positive.

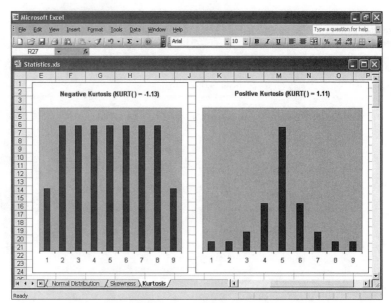

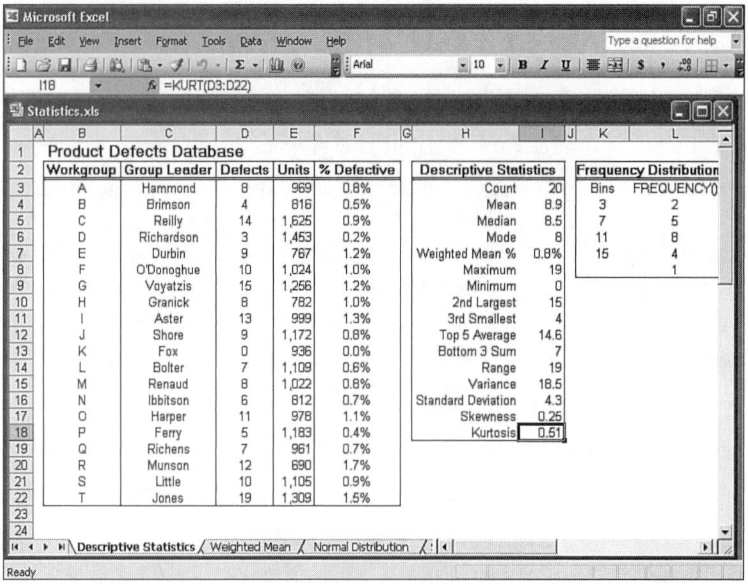

**Figure 12.9**
The final product defects worksheet, showing the values for the distribution's skewness and kurtosis.

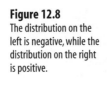

# Using the Analysis ToolPak Statistical Tools

When you load the Analysis ToolPak, the add-in inserts a new <u>D</u>ata Analysis command to Excel's <u>T</u>ools menu. This command displays the Data Analysis dialog box shown in Figure 12.10. This dialog box gives you access to 19 new statistical tools that handle everything from an analysis of variance (anova) to a z-test.

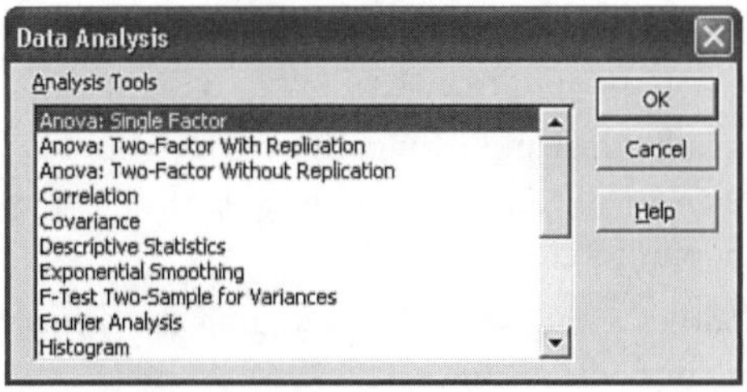

**Figure 12.10**
The Data Analysis dialog box contains 19 powerful statistical-analysis features.

Here's a summary of what each statistical tool can do for your data:

- **Anova: Single Factor**—A simple (that is, single-factor) analysis of variance. An analysis of variance (anova) tests the hypothesis that the means from several samples are equal.

- **Anova: Two-Factor with Replication**—An extension of the single-factor anova to include more than one sample for each group of data.

- **Anova: Two-Factor Without Replication**—A two-factor anova that doesn't include more than one sampling per group.

- **Correlation**—Returns the correlation coefficient: a measure of the relationship between two sets of data. This is also available via the following worksheet function:
  CORREL(*array1*, *array2*)

    *array1*    A reference, range name, or array of values for the first set of data

    *array2*    A reference, range name, or array of values for the second set of data

- **Covariance**—Returns the average of the products of deviations for each data point pair. Covariance is a measure of the relationship between two sets of data. This is also available via the following worksheet function:
  COVAR(*array1*, *array2*)

    *array1*    A reference, range name, or array of values for the first set of data

    *array2*    A reference, range name, or array of values for the second set of data

- **Descriptive Statistics**—Generates a report showing various statistics (such as median, mode, and standard deviation) for a set of data.

- **Exponential Smoothing**—Returns a predicted value based on the forecast for the previous period, adjusted for the error in that period.

- **F-Test Two-Sample for Variances**—Performs a two-sample F-test to compare two population variances. This tool returns the one-tailed probability that the variances in the two sets are not significantly different. This is also available via the following worksheet function:
  FTEST(*array1*, *array2*)

    *array1*    A reference, range name, or array of values for the first set of data

    *array2*    A reference, range name, or array of values for the second set of data

- **Fourier Analysis**—Performs a Fast Fourier Transform. You use Fourier Analysis to solve problems in linear systems and to analyze periodic data.

- **Histogram**—Calculates individual and cumulative frequencies for a range of data and a set of data bins. The FREQUENCY() function, discussed earlier in this chapter, is a simplified version of the Histogram tool.

- **Moving Average**—Smoothes a data series by averaging the series values over a specified number of preceding periods.

- **Random Number Generation**—Fills a range with independent random numbers.

- **Rank and Percentile**—Creates a table containing the ordinal and percentage rank of each value in a set. These are also available via the following worksheet functions:

  RANK(*number*, *ref*, [*order*])

  | | |
  |---|---|
  | *number* | The number for which you want to find the rank. |
  | *ref* | A reference, range name, or array that corresponds to the set of values in which *number* will be ranked. (Note that *ref* must include *number*.) |
  | *order* | An integer that specifies how *number* is ranked within the set. If *order* is 0 (this is the default), Excel treats the set as though it was ranked in descending order; if *order* is any nonzero value, Excel treats the set as though it was ranked in ascending order. |

  PERCENTILE(*array*, *k*)

  | | |
  |---|---|
  | *array* | A reference, range name, or array of values for the set of data. |
  | *k* | The percentile, expressed as a decimal value between 0 and 1. |

- **Regression**—Performs a linear regression analysis that fits a line through a set of values using the least-squares method.

- **Sampling**—Creates a sample from a population by treating the input range as a population.

- **t-Test: Paired Two-Sample for Means**—Performs a paired two-sample student's t-Test to determine whether a sample's means are distinct. This is also available via the following worksheet function (set *type* equal to 1):

  TTEST(*array1*, *array2*, *tails*, *type*)

  | | |
  |---|---|
  | *array1* | A reference, range name, or array of values for the first set of data |
  | *array2* | A reference, range name, or array of values for the second set of data |
  | *tails* | The number of distribution tails |
  | *type* | The type of t-Test you want to use: 1 = paired, 2 = two-sample equal variance (homoscedastic), 3 = two-sample unequal variance (heteroscedastic) |

- **t-Test: Two-Sample Assuming Equal Variances**—Performs a paired two-sample student's t-test, assuming that the variances of both data sets are equal. You can also use the TTEST() worksheet function with the *type* argument set to 2.

- **t-Test: Two-Sample Assuming Unequal Variances**—Performs a paired two-sample student's t-test, assuming that the variances of both data sets are unequal. You can also use the TTEST() worksheet function with the *type* argument set to 3.

- **z-Test: Two-Sample for Means**—Performs a two-sample z-test for means with known variances. This is also available via the following worksheet function:

  `ZTEST(array, x, [sigma])`

  | | |
  |---|---|
  | *array* | A reference, range name, or array of values for the data against which you want to text $x$. |
  | *x* | The value you want to test. |
  | *sigma* | The population (that is, the known) standard deviation. If you omit this argument, Excel uses the sample standard deviation. |

The next few sections look at five of these tools in more depth: Correlation, Descriptive Statistics, Histogram, Random Number Generation, and Rank and Percentile.

## Using the Descriptive Statistics Tool

You saw earlier in this chapter that Excel has separate statistical functions for calculating values such as the mean, maximum, minimum, and standard deviation values of a population or sample. If you need to derive all of these basic analysis stats, entering all those functions can be a pain. Instead, use the Analysis ToolPak's Descriptive Statistics tool. This tool automatically calculates 16 of the most common statistical functions and lays them all out in a table. Follow these steps to use this tool:

> **NOTE**
> Keep in mind that the Descriptive Statistics tool outputs only numbers, not formulas. Therefore, if your data changes, you'll have to repeat the following steps to run the tool again.

1. Select the range that includes the data you want to analyze (including the row and column headings, if any).
2. Choose <u>T</u>ools, <u>D</u>ata Analysis to display the Data Analysis dialog box.
3. Select the Descriptive Statistics option and click OK. Excel displays the Descriptive Statistics dialog box. Figure 12.11 shows the completed dialog box.
4. Use the Output Options group to select a location for the output. For each set of data included in the input range, Excel creates a table that is 2 columns wide and up to 18 rows high.
5. Choose the statistics you want to include in the output:
   - **<u>S</u>ummary Statistics**—Activate this option to include statistics such as the mean, median, mode, and standard deviation.
   - **Co<u>n</u>fidence Level for Mean**—Activate this option if your data set is a sample of a larger population and you want Excel to calculate the confidence interval for the population mean. A confidence level of 95% means that you can be 95% confident that the population mean will fall within the confidence interval. For example, if the sample mean is 10 and Excel calculates a confidence interval of 1.5, you can be 95% sure that the population mean will fall between 8.5 and 12.5.

- **Kth Largest**—Activate this option to add a row to the output that specifies the *k*th largest value in the sample. The default value for *k* is 1 (that is, the largest value), but if you want to see any other number, enter a value for *k* in the text box.
- **Kth Smallest**—Activate this option to include the sample's *k*th smallest value in the output. Again, if you want *k* to be something other than 1 (that is, the smallest value), enter a number in the text box.

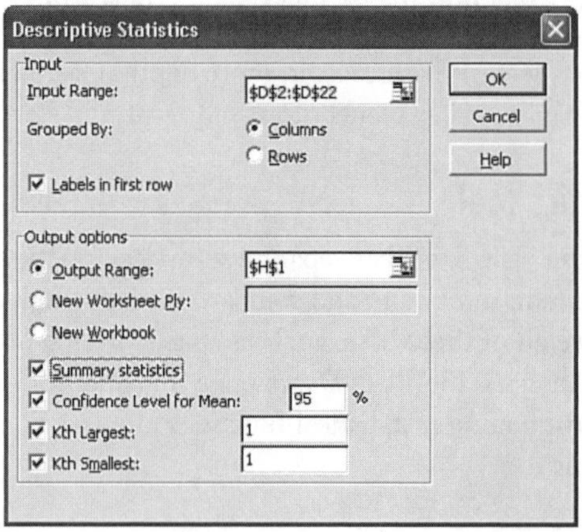


**Figure 12.11** Use the Descriptive Statistics dialog box to select the options you want to use for the analysis.

6. Click OK. Excel calculates the various statistics and displays the output table. (See Figure 12.12 for an example.)

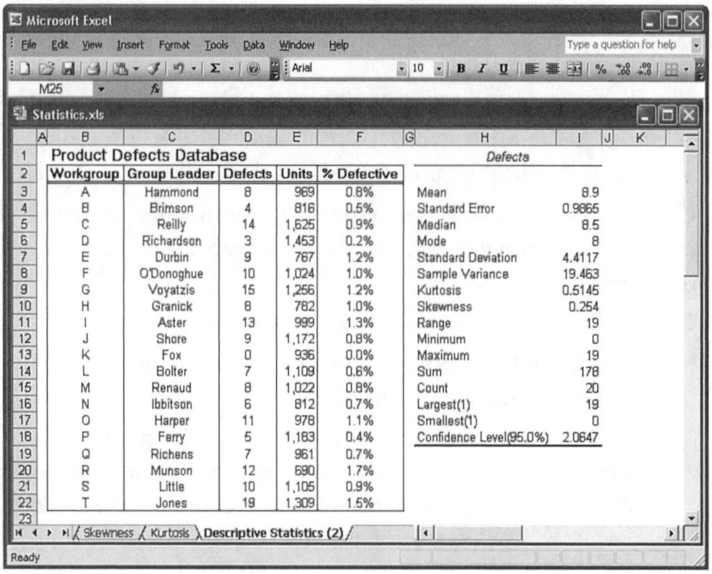


| Workgroup | Group Leader | Defects | Units | % Defective |
|---|---|---|---|---|
| A | Hammond | 8 | 969 | 0.8% |
| B | Brimson | 4 | 816 | 0.5% |
| C | Reilly | 14 | 1,625 | 0.9% |
| D | Richardson | 3 | 1,453 | 0.2% |
| E | Durbin | 9 | 767 | 1.2% |
| F | O'Donoghue | 10 | 1,024 | 1.0% |
| G | Voyatzis | 15 | 1,256 | 1.2% |
| H | Granick | 8 | 782 | 1.0% |
| I | Aster | 13 | 999 | 1.3% |
| J | Shore | 9 | 1,172 | 0.8% |
| K | Fox | 0 | 936 | 0.0% |
| L | Bolter | 7 | 1,109 | 0.6% |
| M | Renaud | 8 | 1,022 | 0.8% |
| N | Ibbitson | 6 | 812 | 0.7% |
| O | Harper | 11 | 978 | 1.1% |
| P | Ferry | 5 | 1,183 | 0.4% |
| Q | Richens | 7 | 961 | 0.7% |
| R | Munson | 12 | 690 | 1.7% |
| S | Little | 10 | 1,105 | 0.9% |
| T | Jones | 19 | 1,309 | 1.5% |

| Defects | |
|---|---|
| Mean | 8.9 |
| Standard Error | 0.9865 |
| Median | 8.5 |
| Mode | 8 |
| Standard Deviation | 4.4117 |
| Sample Variance | 19.463 |
| Kurtosis | 0.5145 |
| Skewness | 0.254 |
| Range | 19 |
| Minimum | 0 |
| Maximum | 19 |
| Sum | 178 |
| Count | 20 |
| Largest(1) | 19 |
| Smallest(1) | 0 |
| Confidence Level(95.0%) | 2.0647 |

**Figure 12.12** Use the Analysis ToolPak's Descriptive Statistics tool to generate the most common statistical measures for a sample.

## Determining the Correlation Between Data

*Correlation* is a measure of the relationship between two or more sets of data. For example, if you have monthly figures for advertising expenses and sales, you might wonder whether they're related. That is, do higher advertising expenses lead to more sales?

To determine this, you need to calculate the *correlation coefficient*. The coefficient is a number between –1 and 1 that has the following properties:

| Correlation Coefficient | Interpretation |
|---|---|
| 1 | The two sets of data are perfectly and positively correlated. For example, a 10% increase in advertising produces a 10% increase in sales. |
| Between 0 and 1 | The two sets of data are positively correlated (an increase in advertising leads to an increase in sales). The higher the number is, the higher the correlation is between the data. |
| 0 | There is no correlation between the data. |
| Between 0 and –1 | The two sets of data are negatively correlated (an increase in advertising leads to a *decrease* in sales). The lower the number is, the more negatively correlated the data is. |
| –1 | The data sets have a perfect negative correlation. For example, a 10% increase in advertising leads to a 10% decrease in sales (and, presumably, a new advertising department). |

To calculate the correlation between data sets, follow these steps:

1. Choose Tools, Data Analysis to display the Data Analysis dialog box.
2. Select the Correlation option and then click OK. The Correlation dialog box, shown in Figure 12.13, appears.

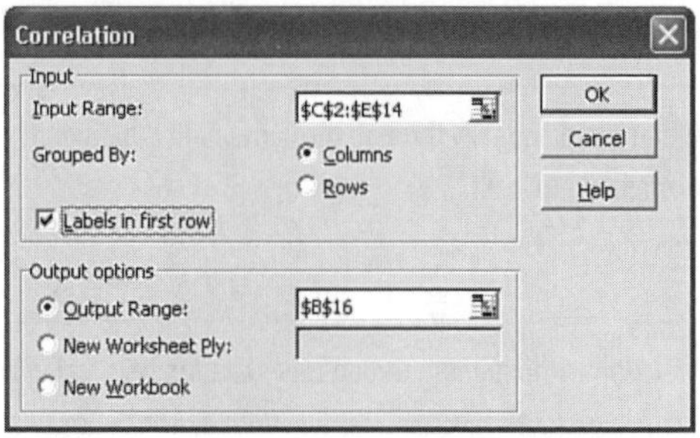

**Figure 12.13**
Use the Correlation dialog box to set up the correlation analysis.

3. Use the Input Range box to select the data range you want to analyze, including the row or column headings.
4. If you included labels in your range, activate the Labels in First Row check box. (If your data is arranged in rows, this check box reads Labels in First Column.)

5. Excel displays the correlation coefficients in a table, so use the Output Range box to enter a reference to the upper-left corner of the table. (If you're comparing two sets of data, the output range is three columns wide by three rows high.) You also can select a different sheet or workbook.
6. Click OK. Excel calculates the correlation and displays the table.

Figure 12.14 shows a worksheet that compares advertising expenses with sales. For a control, I've also included a column of random numbers. The Correlation table lists the various correlation coefficients. In this case, the high correlation between advertising and sales (0.74) means that these two factors are strongly (and positively) correlated. As you can see, there is (as you might expect) almost no correlation among advertising, sales data, and the random numbers.

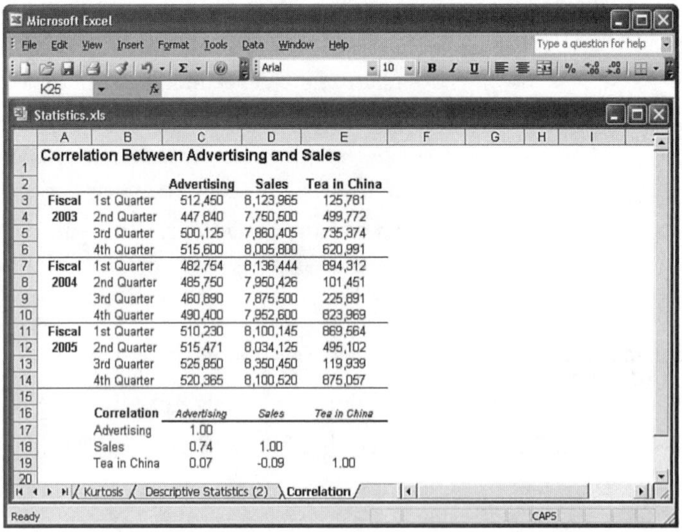

Correlation Between Advertising and Sales

| | | Advertising | Sales | Tea in China |
|---|---|---|---|---|
| Fiscal | 1st Quarter | 512,450 | 8,123,965 | 125,781 |
| 2003 | 2nd Quarter | 447,840 | 7,750,500 | 499,772 |
| | 3rd Quarter | 500,125 | 7,860,405 | 735,374 |
| | 4th Quarter | 515,600 | 8,005,800 | 620,991 |
| Fiscal | 1st Quarter | 482,754 | 8,136,444 | 894,312 |
| 2004 | 2nd Quarter | 485,750 | 7,950,426 | 101,451 |
| | 3rd Quarter | 460,890 | 7,875,500 | 225,891 |
| | 4th Quarter | 490,400 | 7,952,600 | 823,969 |
| Fiscal | 1st Quarter | 510,230 | 8,100,145 | 869,564 |
| 2005 | 2nd Quarter | 515,471 | 8,034,125 | 495,102 |
| | 3rd Quarter | 525,850 | 8,350,450 | 119,939 |
| | 4th Quarter | 520,365 | 8,100,520 | 875,057 |

| Correlation | Advertising | Sales | Tea in China |
|---|---|---|---|
| Advertising | 1.00 | | |
| Sales | 0.74 | 1.00 | |
| Tea in China | 0.07 | -0.09 | 1.00 |

**Figure 12.14**
The correlation among advertising expenses, sales, and a set of randomly generated numbers.

> **NOTE** The 1.00 values that run diagonally through the Correlation table signify that any set of data is always perfectly correlated to itself.

> **NOTE** To calculate a correlation without going through the Data Analysis dialog box, use the `CORREL(array1, array2)` function. This function returns the correlation coefficient for the data in the two ranges given by *array1* and *array2*. (You can use references, range names, numbers, or an array for the function arguments.)

## Working with Histograms

The Analysis ToolPak's Histogram tool calculates the frequency distribution of a range of data. It also calculates cumulative frequencies for your data and produces a bar chart that shows the distribution graphically.

Before you use the Histogram tool, you need to decide which groupings (or *bins*) you want Excel to use for the output. These bins are numeric ranges, and the Histogram tool works by counting the number of observations that fall into each bin. You enter the bins as a range of numbers, where each number defines a boundary of the bin.

For example, Figure 12.15 shows a worksheet with two ranges. One is a list of student grades. The second range is the bin range. For each number in the bin range, Histogram counts the number of observations that are greater than or equal to the bin value, and less than (but *not* equal to) the next higher bin value. Therefore, in Figure 12.15, the six bin values correspond to the following ranges:

```
 0 <= Grade < 50
50 <= Grade < 60
60 <= Grade < 70
70 <= Grade < 80
80 <= Grade < 90
90 <= Grade < 100
```

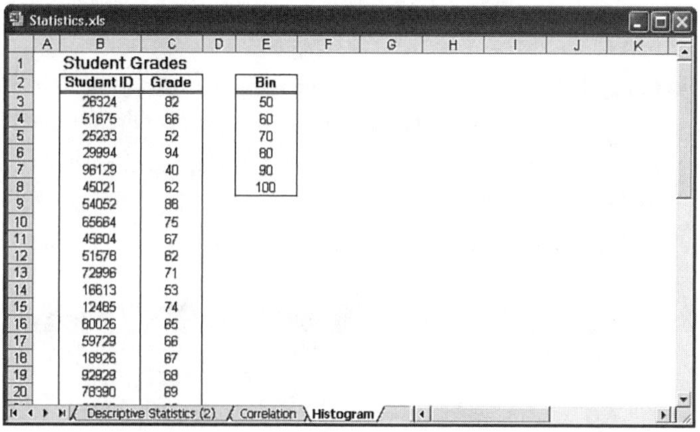


| Student ID | Grade | | Bin |
|---|---|---|---|
| 26324 | 82 | | 50 |
| 51675 | 66 | | 60 |
| 25233 | 52 | | 70 |
| 29994 | 94 | | 80 |
| 96129 | 40 | | 90 |
| 45021 | 62 | | 100 |
| 54052 | 88 | | |
| 65664 | 75 | | |
| 45604 | 67 | | |
| 51578 | 62 | | |
| 72996 | 71 | | |
| 16613 | 53 | | |
| 12485 | 74 | | |
| 80026 | 65 | | |
| 59729 | 66 | | |
| 18926 | 67 | | |
| 92929 | 68 | | |
| 78390 | 69 | | |

**Figure 12.15**
A worksheet set up to use the Histogram tool. Notice that you have to enter the bin range in ascending order.

> **CAUTION**
> Make sure that you enter your bin values in ascending order.

Follow these steps to use the Histogram tool:

1. Choose Tools, Data Analysis to display the Data Analysis dialog box.
2. Select the Histogram option and then click OK. Excel displays the Histogram dialog box. Figure 12.16 shows the dialog box already filled in.

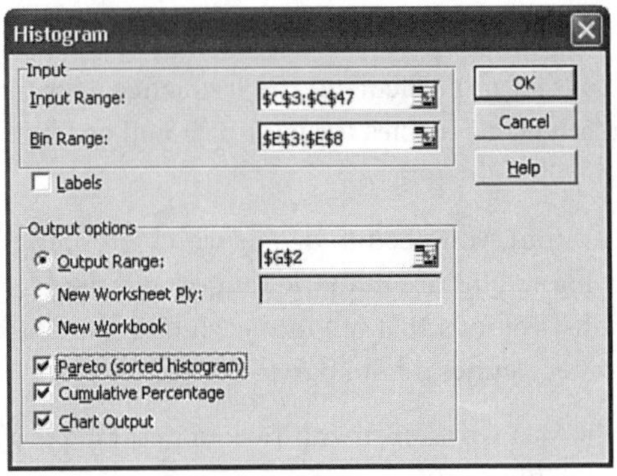

**Figure 12.16**
Use the Histogram dialog
box to select the options
you want to use for the
Histogram analysis.

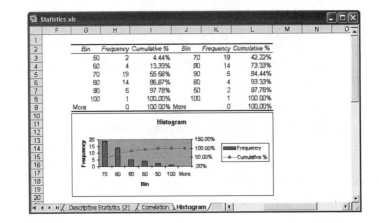

3. Use the Input Range and Bin Range text boxes to enter the ranges holding your data and bin values, respectively.

4. Use the Output Options group to select a location for the output. The output range will be one row taller than the bin range, and it could be up to six columns wide (depending on which of the following options you choose).

5. Select the other options you want to use for the frequency distribution:

   • **Pareto**—If you activate this check box, Excel displays a second output range with the bins sorted in order of descending frequency. (This is called a *Pareto distribution*.)

   • **Cumulative Percentage**—If you activate this option, Excel adds a new column to the output that tracks the cumulative percentage for each bin.

   • **Chart Output**—If you activate this option, Excel automatically generates a chart for the frequency distribution.

6. Click OK. Excel displays the histogram data, as shown in Figure 12.17.

**Figure 12.17**
The output of the
Histogram tool.

# Using the Random Number Generation Tool

Unlike the RAND() function that generates real numbers only between 0 and 1, the Analysis ToolPak's Random Number Generation tool can produce numbers in any range and can generate different distributions, depending on the application. Table 12.2 summarizes the seven available distribution types.

**Table 12.2    The Distributions Available with the Random Number Generation Tool**

| Distribution | Description |
|---|---|
| Uniform | Generates numbers with equal probability from the range of values you provide. Using the range 0 to 1 produces the same distribution as the RAND() function. |
| Normal | Produces numbers in a bell curve (normal) distribution based on the mean and standard deviation you enter. This is good for generating samples of things such as test scores and population heights. |
| Bernoulli | Generates a random series of 1s and 0s based on the probability of success on a single trial. A common example of a Bernoulli distribution is a coin toss (in which the probability of success is 50%; in this case, as in all Bernoulli distributions, you would have to assign either heads or tails to be 1 or 0). |
| Binomial | Generates random numbers characterized by the probability of success over a number of trials. For example, you could use this type of distribution to model the number of responses received for a direct-mail campaign. The probability of success would be the average (or projected) response rate, and the number of trials would be the number of mailings in the campaign. |
| Poisson | Generates random numbers based on the probability of a designated number of events occurring in a time frame. The distribution is governed by a value, Lambda, that represents the mean number of events known to occur over the time frame. |
| Patterned | Generates random numbers according to a pattern that's characterized by a lower and upper bound, a step value, and a repetition rate for each number and the entire sequence. |
| Discrete | Generates random numbers from a series of values and probabilities for these values (in which the sum of the probabilities equals 1). You could use this distribution to simulate the rolling of dice (where the values would be 1 through 6, each with a probability of 1/6; see the following example). |

Follow the steps outlined in the following procedure to use the Random Number Generation tool.

**NOTE** If you'll be using a Discrete distribution, be sure to enter the appropriate values and probabilities before starting the Random Number Generation tool.

1. Choose Tools, Data Analysis to display the Data Analysis dialog box.

2. Select the Random Number Generation option and then click OK. The Random Number Generation dialog box appears, as shown in Figure 12.18.

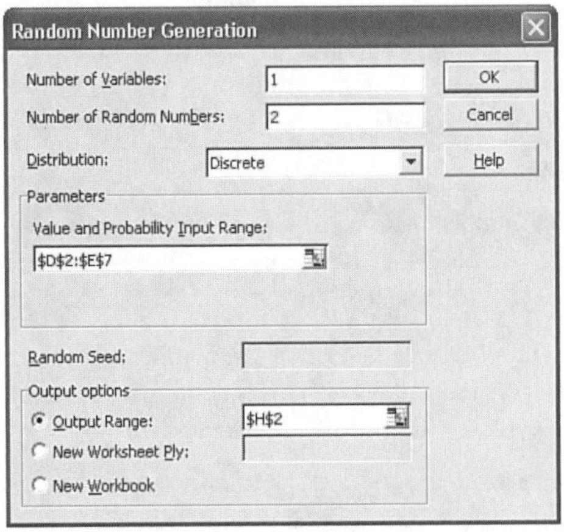

**Figure 12.18**
Use the Random Number Generation dialog box to set up the options for your random numbers.

3. If you want to generate more than one set of random numbers, enter the number of sets (or variables) you need in the Number of Variables box. Excel enters each set in a separate column. If you leave this box blank, Excel uses the number of columns in the Output Range.

4. Use the Number of Random Numbers text box to enter how many random numbers you need. Excel enters each number in a separate row. If you leave this box blank, Excel fills the Output Range.

5. Use the Distribution drop-down list to click the distribution you want to use.

6. In the Parameters group, enter the parameters for the distribution you selected. (The options you see depend on the selected distribution.)

7. The Random Seed number is the value Excel uses to generate the random numbers. If you leave this box blank, Excel generates a different set each time. If you enter a value (which must be an integer between 1 and 32,767), you can reuse the value later to reproduce the same set of numbers.

8. Use the Output Options group to select a location for the output.

9. Click OK. Excel calculates the random numbers and displays them in the worksheet.

As an example, Figure 12.19 shows a worksheet that is set up to simulate rolling two dice. The Probabilities box shows the values (the numbers 1 through 6) and their probabilities (=1/6 for each). A Discrete distribution is used to generate the two numbers in cells H2 and H3. The Discrete distribution's Value and Probability Input Range parameter is the range $D$2:$E$7. Figure 12.20 shows the formulas used to display Die #1. (The formulas for Die #2 are similar, except that $H$2 is replaced with $H$3.)

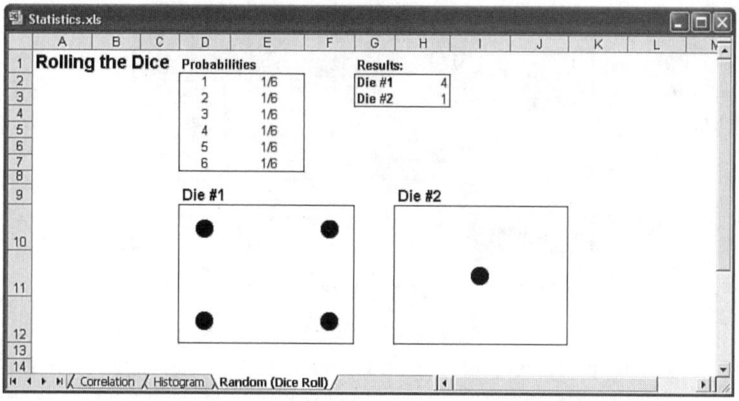

**Figure 12.19**
A worksheet that simulates the rolling of a pair of dice.

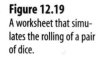
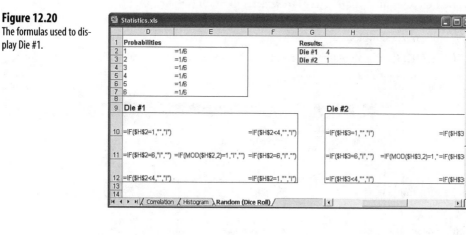

**Figure 12.20**
The formulas used to display Die #1.

> **NOTE**
> The die markers in Figure 12.19 were generated using a 24-point Wingdings font.

## Working with Rank and Percentile

If you need to rank data, use the Analysis ToolPak's Rank and Percentile tool. This command not only ranks your data from first to last, but it also calculates the percentile—the percentage of items in the sample that are at the same level or a lower level than a given value. Follow the steps in the following procedure to use the Rank and Percentile tool:

1. Choose Tools, Data Analysis to display the Data Analysis dialog box.
2. Select the Rank and Percentile option and then click OK. Excel displays the Rank and Percentile dialog box, shown in Figure 12.21.
3. Use the Input Range text box to enter a reference for the data you want to rank.
4. Click the appropriate Grouped By option (Columns or Rows).

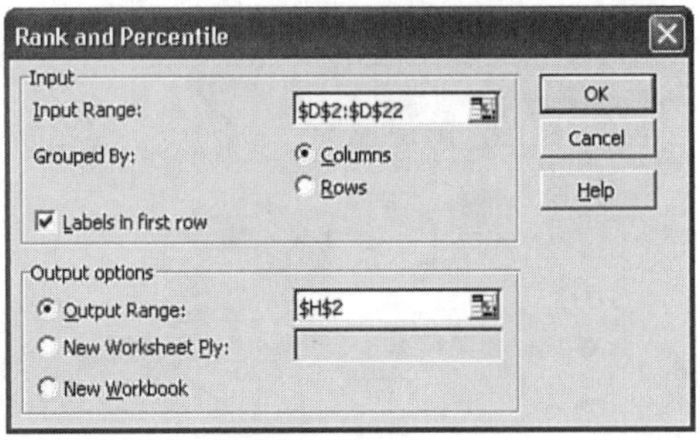

**Figure 12.21**

Use the Rank and Percentile dialog box to select the options you want to use for the analysis.

Rank and Percentile

Input
Input Range: `$D$2:$D$22`
Grouped By: ⦿ Columns
○ Rows
☑ Labels in first row

Output options
⦿ Output Range: `$H$2`
○ New Worksheet Ply:
○ New Workbook

OK
Cancel
Help

5. If you included row or column labels in your selection, activate the Labels in First Row check box. (If your data is in rows, the check box will read Labels in First Column.)

6. Use the Output options group to select a location for the output. For each sample, Excel displays a table that is four columns wide and the same height as the number of values in the sample.

7. Click OK. Excel calculates the results and displays them in a table similar to the one shown in Figure 12.22.

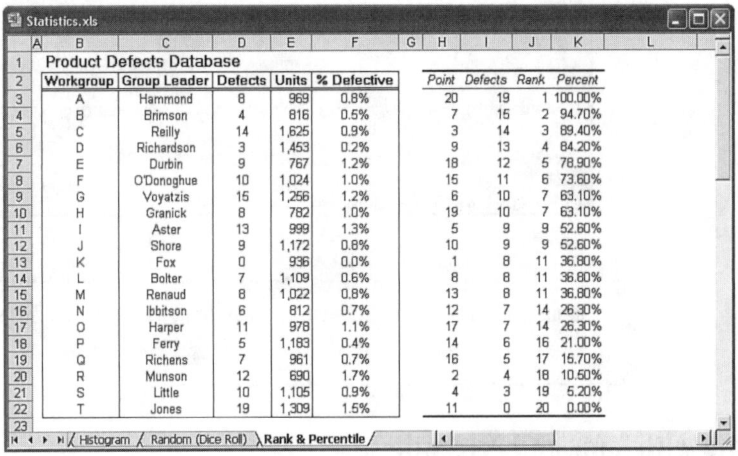

**Figure 12.22**

Sample output from the Rank and Percentile tool.

Statistics.xls

|  | B | C | D | E | F | G | H | I | J | K | L |
|---|---|---|---|---|---|---|---|---|---|---|---|
| 1 | **Product Defects Database** | | | | | | | | | | |
| 2 | Workgroup | Group Leader | Defects | Units | % Defective | | Point | Defects | Rank | Percent | |
| 3 | A | Hammond | 8 | 969 | 0.8% | | 20 | 19 | 1 | 100.00% | |
| 4 | B | Brimson | 4 | 816 | 0.5% | | 7 | 15 | 2 | 94.70% | |
| 5 | C | Reilly | 14 | 1,625 | 0.9% | | 3 | 14 | 3 | 89.40% | |
| 6 | D | Richardson | 3 | 1,453 | 0.2% | | 9 | 13 | 4 | 84.20% | |
| 7 | E | Durbin | 9 | 767 | 1.2% | | 18 | 12 | 5 | 78.90% | |
| 8 | F | O'Donoghue | 10 | 1,024 | 1.0% | | 15 | 11 | 6 | 73.60% | |
| 9 | G | Voyatzis | 15 | 1,256 | 1.2% | | 6 | 10 | 7 | 63.10% | |
| 10 | H | Granick | 8 | 782 | 1.0% | | 19 | 10 | 7 | 63.10% | |
| 11 | I | Aster | 13 | 999 | 1.3% | | 5 | 9 | 9 | 52.60% | |
| 12 | J | Shore | 9 | 1,172 | 0.8% | | 10 | 9 | 9 | 52.60% | |
| 13 | K | Fox | 0 | 936 | 0.0% | | 1 | 8 | 11 | 36.80% | |
| 14 | L | Bolter | 7 | 1,109 | 0.6% | | 8 | 8 | 11 | 36.80% | |
| 15 | M | Renaud | 8 | 1,022 | 0.8% | | 13 | 8 | 11 | 36.80% | |
| 16 | N | Ibbitson | 6 | 812 | 0.7% | | 12 | 7 | 14 | 26.30% | |
| 17 | O | Harper | 11 | 978 | 1.1% | | 17 | 7 | 14 | 26.30% | |
| 18 | P | Ferry | 5 | 1,183 | 0.4% | | 14 | 6 | 16 | 21.00% | |
| 19 | Q | Richens | 7 | 961 | 0.7% | | 16 | 5 | 17 | 15.70% | |
| 20 | R | Munson | 12 | 690 | 1.7% | | 2 | 4 | 18 | 10.50% | |
| 21 | S | Little | 10 | 1,105 | 0.9% | | 4 | 3 | 19 | 5.20% | |
| 22 | T | Jones | 19 | 1,309 | 1.5% | | 11 | 0 | 20 | 0.00% | |
| 23 | | | | | | | | | | | |

Histogram / Random (Dice Roll) ╲ Rank & Percentile /

**NOTE**

Use the RANK(`number`, `ref`, [`order`]) function to calculate the rank of a `number` in the range `ref`. If `order` is 0 or is omitted, Excel ranks `number` as though `ref` was sorted in descending order. If `order` is any nonzero value, Excel ranks `number` as though `ref` was sorted in ascending order.

For the percentile, use the PERCENTRANK(`range`, `x`, [`significance`]) function, where `range` is a range or array of values, `x` is the value of which you want to know the percentile, and `significance` is the number of significant digits in the returned percentage. (The default is 3.)

## From Here

- Many of the descriptive statistics functions are also available in a list (or database) version that enables you to apply criteria. **See** "List Functions That Require a Criteria Range," **p. 307**.

- Excel's `COUNTIF()` function counts the number of items in a range that meet your specified criteria. **See** "Using `COUNTIF()`," **p. 307**.

- Regression analysis is an important statistical method for business. To read all about it, **see** "Using Regression to Track Trends and Make Forecasts," **p. 339**.

# Building Business Models

III

# Analyzing Data with Lists

Excel's forte is spreadsheet work, of course, but its row-and-column layout also makes it a natural flat-file database manager. In Excel, a *list* is a collection of related information with an organizational structure that makes it easy to find or extract data from its contents. Specifically, a list is a worksheet range that has the following properties:

- **Field**—A single type of information, such as a name, an address, or a phone number. In Excel lists, each column is a field.

- **Field value**—A single item in a field. In an Excel list, the field values are the individual cells.

- **Field name**—A unique name you assign to every list field (worksheet column). These names are always found in the first row of the list.

- **Record**—A collection of associated field values. In Excel lists, each row is a record.

- **List range**—The worksheet range that includes all the records, fields, and field names of a list.

For example, suppose that you want to set up an accounts-receivable list. A simple system would include information such as the account name, account number, invoice number, invoice amount, due date, and date paid, as well as a calculation of the number of days overdue. Figure 13.1 shows how this system would be implemented as an Excel list.

> **NOTE** You can download this chapter's example workbooks here:
>
> `www.mcfedries.com/ExcelFormulas/`

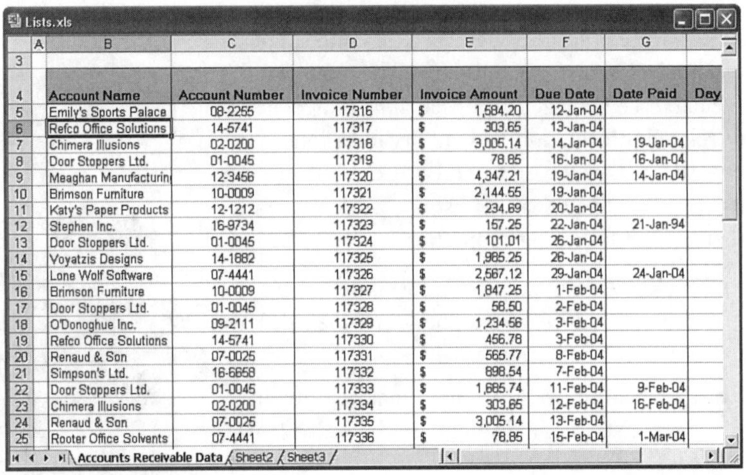


| | Account Name | Account Number | Invoice Number | Invoice Amount | Due Date | Date Paid | Day |
|---|---|---|---|---|---|---|---|
| 5 | Emily's Sports Palace | 08-2255 | 117316 | $ 1,584.20 | 12-Jan-04 | | |
| 6 | Refco Office Solutions | 14-5741 | 117317 | $ 303.65 | 13-Jan-04 | | |
| 7 | Chimera Illusions | 02-0200 | 117318 | $ 3,005.14 | 14-Jan-04 | 19-Jan-04 | |
| 8 | Door Stoppers Ltd. | 01-0045 | 117319 | $ 78.85 | 16-Jan-04 | 16-Jan-04 | |
| 9 | Meaghan Manufacturin | 12-3456 | 117320 | $ 4,347.21 | 19-Jan-04 | 14-Jan-04 | |
| 10 | Brimson Furniture | 10-0009 | 117321 | $ 2,144.55 | 19-Jan-04 | | |
| 11 | Katy's Paper Products | 12-1212 | 117322 | $ 234.69 | 20-Jan-04 | | |
| 12 | Stephen Inc. | 16-9734 | 117323 | $ 157.25 | 22-Jan-04 | 21-Jan-94 | |
| 13 | Door Stoppers Ltd. | 01-0045 | 117324 | $ 101.01 | 26-Jan-04 | | |
| 14 | Voyatzis Designs | 14-1882 | 117325 | $ 1,985.25 | 26-Jan-04 | | |
| 15 | Lone Wolf Software | 07-4441 | 117326 | $ 2,567.12 | 29-Jan-04 | 24-Jan-04 | |
| 16 | Brimson Furniture | 10-0009 | 117327 | $ 1,847.25 | 1-Feb-04 | | |
| 17 | Door Stoppers Ltd. | 01-0045 | 117328 | $ 58.50 | 2-Feb-04 | | |
| 18 | O'Donoghue Inc. | 09-2111 | 117329 | $ 1,234.56 | 3-Feb-04 | | |
| 19 | Refco Office Solutions | 14-5741 | 117330 | $ 456.78 | 3-Feb-04 | | |
| 20 | Renaud & Son | 07-0025 | 117331 | $ 565.77 | 8-Feb-04 | | |
| 21 | Simpson's Ltd. | 16-6658 | 117332 | $ 898.54 | 7-Feb-04 | | |
| 22 | Door Stoppers Ltd. | 01-0045 | 117333 | $ 1,685.74 | 11-Feb-04 | 9-Feb-04 | |
| 23 | Chimera Illusions | 02-0200 | 117334 | $ 303.65 | 12-Feb-04 | 16-Feb-04 | |
| 24 | Renaud & Son | 07-0025 | 117335 | $ 3,005.14 | 13-Feb-04 | | |
| 25 | Rooter Office Solvents | 07-4441 | 117336 | $ 78.85 | 15-Feb-04 | 1-Mar-04 | |

**Figure 13.1**
Accounts-receivable data in an Excel worksheet.

Excel lists don't require elaborate planning, but you should follow a few guidelines for best results. Here are some pointers:

- Always use the top row of the list for the column labels.
- Field names must be unique, and they must be text or text formulas. If you need to use numbers, format them as text.
- Some Excel commands can automatically identify the size and shape of a list. To avoid confusing such commands, try to use only one list per worksheet. If you have multiple related lists, include them in other worksheets in the same workbook.
- If you have nonlist data in the same worksheet, leave at least one blank row or column between the data and the list. This helps Excel to identify the list automatically.
- Excel has a command that enables you to filter your list data to show only records that match certain criteria. (See "Filtering List Data," later in this chapter, for details.) This command works by hiding rows of data. Therefore, if the same worksheet contains nonlist data that you need to see or work with, don't place this data to the left or right of the list.



## Converting a Range to a List

Excel has several commands that enable you to work efficiently with list data. To take advantage of these commands, you must convert your data from a normal range to a list. Here are the steps to follow:

1. Click any cell within the range that you want to convert to a list.

2. Choose Data, List, Create List (or press Ctrl+L). Excel displays the Create List dialog box.

3. The Where Is the Data for Your List? box should already show the correct range coordinates. If not, enter the range coordinates or select the range directly on the worksheet.

4. If your range has column headers in the top row (as it should), make sure the My List Has Headers check box is activated.

5. Click OK.

When you convert a range to a list, Excel makes three changes to the range, as shown in Figure 13.2:

- It displays a border around the list.
- It adds drop-down arrows to each field header.
- It displays the List toolbar whenever you select a cell within the list.

**Figure 13.2**
The accounts-receivable data converted to a list.

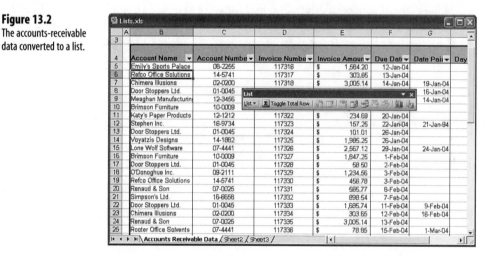

If you ever need to change the list back to a range, select a cell within the list and choose Data, List, Convert to Range.

# Basic List Operations

After you've converted the range to a list, you can start working with the data. Here's a quick look at some basic list operations:

■ **Adding a new record at the bottom of the list**—Below the last record in the list you'll see an asterisk (*) in the first field. This is the new record symbol, and it means that you can use this row to add a new record to the list.

> **NOTE**  As soon as you start entering data in the new record, Excel displays a dialog box to tell you that it has inserted a row. You can avoid being pestered by this obvious bit of news by clicking the Do Not Display This Dialog Again check box.

■ **Adding a new record anywhere in the list**—Select any cell in a record below which you want to add the new record. In the List toolbar, choose List, Insert, Row. Excel inserts a blank row above the selected cell into which you can enter the new data.

■ **Deleting a record**—Select any cell in the record you want to delete. In the List toolbar, choose List, Delete, Row.

■ **Working with a record using a data form**—Choose Data, Form (or, on the List toolbar, choose List, Form). This displays the list's *data form*, which is a dialog box that enables you to add, edit, delete, and find list records quickly (see Figure 13.3). To add a record to the list, click New and enter the data in the blank fields. To edit a record, use the scroll bar to select it and then edit the fields. To delete a record, use the scroll bar to select it, click Delete, and then click OK to confirm the deletion.

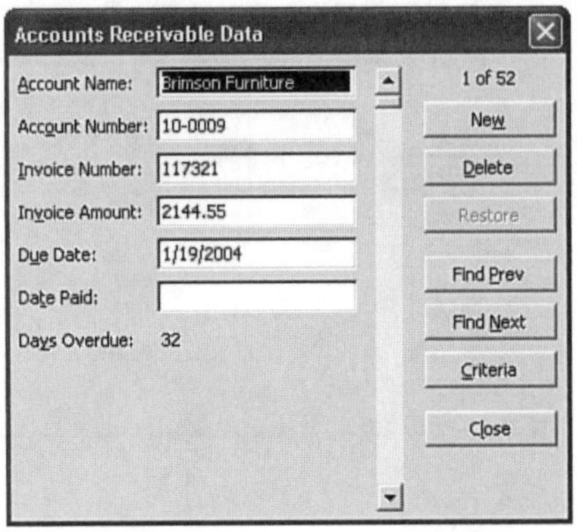

**Figure 13.3**
The data form for the accounts-receivable list.

■ **Finding a record using criteria**—Display the data form, click Criteria, and then enter the criteria you want to use in the corresponding field. For example, if you want to find a record where the Invoice Amount field is greater than $1,000, enter **>1000** in the data form's Invoice Amount box. Use the Find Prev and Find Next buttons to scroll through the records that match the criteria.

# Sorting a List

One of the advantages of a list is that you can rearrange the records so that they're sorted alphabetically or numerically. This feature enables you to view the data in order by customer name, account number, part number, or any other field. You even can sort on multiple fields, which would enable you, for example, to sort a client list by state and then by name within each state.

The following procedure shows you how to sort a list:

1. Select a cell inside the list.
2. Choose <u>D</u>ata, <u>S</u>ort (or choose <u>L</u>ist, <u>S</u>ort on the List toolbar). Excel displays the Sort dialog box, shown in Figure 13.4.

**Figure 13.4**
Use the Sort dialog box to sort the list on one or more fields.

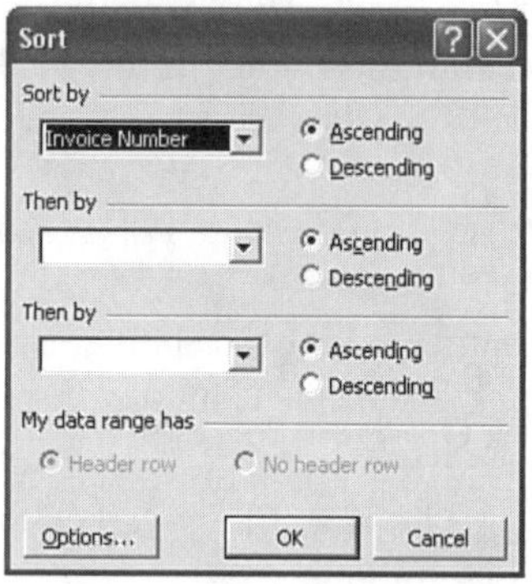

3. Use the Sort By list to select the field you want to use for the overall order for the sort.
4. (Optional) If you want to sort the data on more than one field, use one or both of the Then By lists to select the field or fields you want to use.

> **CAUTION**
>
> Be careful when you sort list records that contain formulas. If the formulas use relative addresses that refer to cells outside their own record, the new sort order might change the references and produce erroneous results. If your list formulas must refer to cells outside the list, be sure to use absolute addresses.

5. For each sort field, select either Ascending or Descending.

**13**

NOTE

How Excel sorts the list depends on the data. Here's the order Excel uses in an ascending sort:

| Type (in Order of Priority) | Order |
|---|---|
| Numbers | Largest negative to largest positive |
| Text | Space ! " # $ % & ' ( ) * + , - . / 0 through 9 (when formatted as text) : ; < = > ? @ A through Z (Excel ignores case) [ \ ] ^ _ ' {, } ~ |
| Logical | FALSE before TRUE |
| Error | All error values are equal |
| Blank | Always sorted last (ascending or descending) |

6. (Optional) Choose <u>O</u>ptions to specify one or more of the following sort controls:

- **First Key Sort Order**—Sets a custom sort order for the field you chose in the <u>S</u>ort By list. For example, to sort by the days of the week, select the Sun, Mon, Tue option.

→ The <u>F</u>irst Key Sort Order choices are the same as Excel's AutoFill lists, so you can create your own custom sort orders by setting up custom AutoFill lists. **See** "Creating a Custom AutoFill List," **p. 20**.

- **Case Sensitive**—Activate this option to have Excel differentiate between upper case and lower case during sorting. In an ascending sort, for example, lowercase letters are sorted before uppercase letters.

- **Orientation**—Excel normally sorts list rows (the Sort <u>T</u>op to Bottom option). To sort list columns, activate Sort <u>L</u>eft to Right.

7. Click OK. Excel sorts the range.

## Sorting on More Than Three Keys

You're not restricted to sorting on just three fields in an Excel list. By performing consecutive sorts, you can sort on any number of fields. For example, suppose that you want to sort a customer list by the following fields (in order of importance): Region, State, City, ZIP Code, and Name. To use five fields, you must perform two consecutive sorts. The first sort uses the three least important fields: City, ZIP Code, and Name. Of these three, City is the most important, so it's selected in the Sort By field; ZIP Code is selected in the first Then By field, and Name is selected in the second Then By field. When this sort is complete, you must run a second sort using the remaining keys, Region and State. Select Region in the Sort By list and State in the first Then By list.

By running multiple sorts and always using the least important fields first, you can sort on as many fields as you like.

13

## Sorting a List in Natural Order

It's often convenient to see the order in which records were entered into a list, or the *natural order* of the data. Normally, you can restore a list to its natural order by choosing Edit, Undo Sort immediately after a sort.

Unfortunately, after several sort operations, it's no longer possible to restore the natural order. The solution is to create a new field, called, say, Record, in which you assign consecutive numbers as you enter the data. The first record is 1, the second is 2, and so on. To restore the list to its natural order, you sort on the Record field.

> **CAUTION**
>
> The Record field works only if you add it either before you start inserting new records in the list or before you've irrevocably sorted the list. Therefore, when planning any list, consider always including a Record field, just in case you need it.

Follow these steps to add a new field to the list:

1. Select a cell in the field to the right of where you want the new field inserted.
2. In the List toolbar, choose List, Insert, Column. Excel inserts the column.
3. Rename the column header to the field name you want to use.

Figure 13.5 shows the accounts-receivable list with a Record field added and the record numbers inserted.

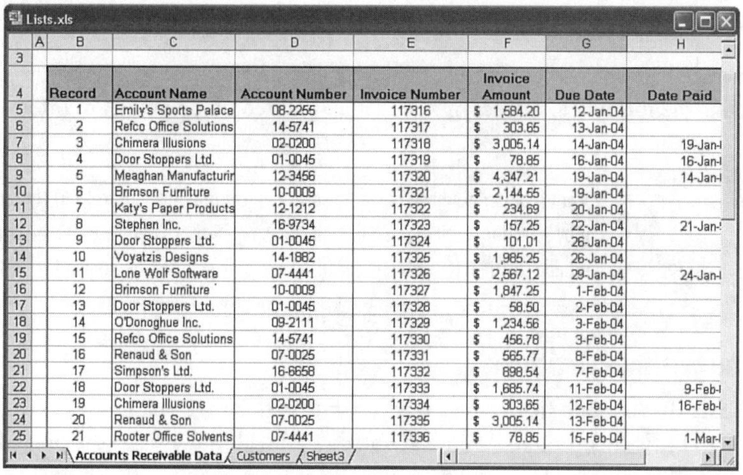

| Record | Account Name | Account Number | Invoice Number | Invoice Amount | Due Date | Date Paid |
|---|---|---|---|---|---|---|
| 1 | Emily's Sports Palace | 08-2255 | 117316 | $ 1,584.20 | 12-Jan-04 | |
| 2 | Refco Office Solutions | 14-5741 | 117317 | $ 303.65 | 13-Jan-04 | |
| 3 | Chimera Illusions | 02-0200 | 117318 | $ 3,005.14 | 14-Jan-04 | 19-Jan- |
| 4 | Door Stoppers Ltd. | 01-0045 | 117319 | $ 78.85 | 16-Jan-04 | 16-Jan- |
| 5 | Meaghan Manufacturin | 12-3456 | 117320 | $ 4,347.21 | 19-Jan-04 | 14-Jan- |
| 6 | Brimson Furniture | 10-0009 | 117321 | $ 2,144.55 | 19-Jan-04 | |
| 7 | Katy's Paper Products | 12-1212 | 117322 | $ 234.69 | 20-Jan-04 | |
| 8 | Stephen Inc. | 16-9734 | 117323 | $ 157.25 | 22-Jan-04 | 21-Jan- |
| 9 | Door Stoppers Ltd. | 01-0045 | 117324 | $ 101.01 | 26-Jan-04 | |
| 10 | Voyatzis Designs | 14-1882 | 117325 | $ 1,985.25 | 26-Jan-04 | |
| 11 | Lone Wolf Software | 07-4441 | 117326 | $ 2,567.12 | 29-Jan-04 | 24-Jan- |
| 12 | Brimson Furniture | 10-0009 | 117327 | $ 1,847.25 | 1-Feb-04 | |
| 13 | Door Stoppers Ltd. | 01-0045 | 117328 | $ 58.50 | 2-Feb-04 | |
| 14 | O'Donoghue Inc. | 09-2111 | 117329 | $ 1,234.56 | 3-Feb-04 | |
| 15 | Refco Office Solutions | 14-5741 | 117330 | $ 456.78 | 3-Feb-04 | |
| 16 | Renaud & Son | 07-0025 | 117331 | $ 565.77 | 8-Feb-04 | |
| 17 | Simpson's Ltd. | 16-6658 | 117332 | $ 898.54 | 7-Feb-04 | |
| 18 | Door Stoppers Ltd. | 01-0045 | 117333 | $ 1,685.74 | 11-Feb-04 | 9-Feb- |
| 19 | Chimera Illusions | 02-0200 | 117334 | $ 303.65 | 12-Feb-04 | 16-Feb- |
| 20 | Renaud & Son | 07-0025 | 117335 | $ 3,005.14 | 13-Feb-04 | |
| 21 | Rooter Office Solvents | 07-4441 | 117336 | $ 78.85 | 15-Feb-04 | 1-Mar- |



**Figure 13.5** The Record field tracks the order in which records are added to a list.

> **TIP** If you're not sure how many records are in the list, and if the list isn't sorted in natural order, you might not know which record number to use next. To avoid guessing or searching through the entire Record field, you can generate the record numbers automatically using the MAX() function. Click the formula bar and type (but don't confirm) the following:
>
> `=MAX(Column:Column)`
>
> Replace *Column* with the letter of the column that contains the record number (for example, MAX(B:B) for the list in Figure 13.4) Now highlight the formula and press F9. Excel displays the formula result that will be the highest record number used so far. Therefore, your next record number will be one more than the calculated value.

## Sorting on Part of a Field

Excel performs its sorting chores based on the entire contents of each cell in the field. This method is fine for most sorting tasks, but occasionally you need to sort on only part of a field. For example, your list might have a ContactName field that contains a first name and then a last name. Sorting on this field orders the list by each person's first name, which is probably not what you want. To sort on the last name, you need to create a new column that extracts the last name from the field. You can then use this new column for the sort.

Excel's text functions make it easy to extract substrings from a cell. In this case, assume that each cell in the ContactName field has a first name, followed by a space, followed by a last name. Your task is to extract everything after the space, and the following formula does the job (assuming that the name is in cell D2):

`=RIGHT(D2, LEN(D2) - FIND(" ", D2))`

→ For an explanation of how this formula works, **see** "Extracting a First Name or Last Name," **p. 148**.

Figure 13.6 shows this formula in action. Column D contains the names, and column A contains the formula to extract the last name. I sorted on column A to order the list by last name.

> **TIP** If you'd rather not have the extra sort field (column A in Figure 13.6) cluttering the list, you can hide it by selecting a cell in the field and choosing F̲ormat, C̲olumn, H̲ide. Fortunately, you don't have to unhide the field to sort on it because Excel still includes the field in the Sort By list.

## Sorting Without Articles

Lists that contain field values starting with articles (*A*, *An*, and *The*) can throw off your sorting. To fix this problem, you can borrow the technique from the preceding section and sort on a new field in which the leading articles have been removed. As before, you want to extract everything after the first space, but you can't just use the same formula because not all the titles have a leading article. You need to test for a leading article using the following OR() function:

`OR(LEFT(A2,2) = "A ", LEFT(A2,3) = "An ", LEFT(A2,4) = "The ")`

**Figure 13.6**
To sort on part of a field, use Excel's text functions to extract the string you need for the sort.

| | A | B | C | D | E | |
|---|---|---|---|---|---|---|
| 1 | Sort Field | CustomerID | CompanyName | ContactName | ContactTitle | Address |
| 2 | Accorti | FRANS | Franchi S.p.A. | Paolo Accorti | Sales Representative | Via Monte |
| 3 | Afonso | COMMI | Comércio Mineiro | Pedro Afonso | Sales Associate | Av. dos Lu |
| 4 | Anders | ALFKI | Alfreds Futterkiste | Maria Anders | Sales Representative | Obere Str. |
| 5 | Ashworth | BSBEV | B's Beverages | Victoria Ashworth | Sales Representative | Fauntleroy |
| 6 | Batista | QUEDE | Que Delícia | Bernardo Batista | Accounting Manager | Rua da Pa |
| 7 | Bennett | ISLAT | Island Trading | Helen Bennett | Marketing Manager | Garden Ho |
| 8 | Berglund | BERGS | Berglunds snabbköp | Christina Berglund | Order Administrator | Berguvsvä |
| 9 | Bergulfsen | SANTG | Santé Gourmet | Jonas Bergulfsen | Owner | Erling Ska |
| 10 | Bertrand | PARIS | Paris spécialités | Marie Bertrand | Owner | 265, boule |
| 11 | Braunschweig | SPLIR | Split Rail Beer & Ale | Art Braunschweiger | Sales Manager | P.O. Box £ |
| 12 | Brown | CONSH | Consolidated Holdings | Elizabeth Brown | Sales Representative | Berkeley G |
| 13 | Camino | ROMEY | Romero y tomillo | Alejandra Camino | Accounting Manager | Gran Vía, |
| 14 | Cartrain | SUPRD | Suprêmes délices | Pascale Cartrain | Accounting Manager | Boulevard |
| 15 | Carvalho | QUEEN | Queen Cozinha | Lúcia Carvalho | Marketing Assistant | Alameda d |
| 16 | Chang | CENTC | Centro comercial Moctezu | Francisco Chang | Marketing Manager | Sierras de |
| 17 | Citeaux | BLONP | Blondel père et fils | Frédérique Citeaux | Marketing Manager | 24, place I |
| 18 | Cramer | KOENE | Königlich Essen | Philip Cramer | Sales Associate | Maubelstr. |
| 19 | Crowther | NORTS | North/South | Simon Crowther | Sales Associate | South Hou |
| 20 | Cruz | FAMIA | Familia Arquibaldo | Aria Cruz | Marketing Assistant | Rua Orós, |
| 21 | de Castro | PRINI | Princesa Isabel Vinhos | Isabel de Castro | Sales Representative | Estrada da |
| 22 | Devon | EASTC | Eastern Connection | Ann Devon | Sales Agent | 35 King Ge |
| 23 | Dewey | MAISD | Maison Dewey | Catherine Dewey | Sales Agent | Rue Josep |
| 24 | Domingues | TRADH | Tradição Hipermercados | Anabela Domingues | Sales Representative | Av. Inês de |

Here I'm assuming that the text being tested is in cell A2. If the left two characters are A , or the left three characters are An , or the left four characters are The , this function returns TRUE (that is, you're dealing with a title that has a leading article).

Now you need to package this OR() function inside an IF() test. If the OR() function returns TRUE, the command should extract everything after the first space; otherwise, it should just return the entire title. Here it is (Figure 13.7 shows the formula in action):

```
=IF( OR(LEFT(A2,2) = "A ", LEFT(A2,3) = "An ", LEFT(A2,4) = "The "),
➡RIGHT(A2, LEN(A2) - FIND(" ", A2, 1)), A2)
```

**Figure 13.7**
A formula that removes leading articles for proper sorting.

| | A | B | C | E | F | G | H | I | |
|---|---|---|---|---|---|---|---|---|---|
| 1 | Title | Year | Director | In Stoc | Sort Field2 | | | | |
| 2 | Alien | 1979 | Ridley Scott | 3 | Alien | | | | |
| 3 | An Angel from Texas | 1940 | Ray Enright | 1 | Angel from Texas | | | | |
| 4 | Big | 1988 | Penny Marshall | 5 | Big | | | | |
| 5 | The Big Sleep | 1946 | Howard Hawks | 2 | Big Sleep | | | | |
| 6 | Blade Runner | 1982 | Ridley Scott | 4 | Blade Runner | | | | |
| 7 | A Christmas Carol | 1951 | Brian Hurst | 0 | Christmas Carol | | | | |
| 8 | Christmas In July | 1940 | Preston Sturges | 1 | Christmas In July | | | | |
| 9 | A Clockwork Orange | 1971 | Stanley Kubrick | 3 | Clockwork Orange | | | | |
| 10 | Die Hard | 1991 | John McTiernan | 6 | Die Hard | | | | |
| 11 | Old Ironsides | 1926 | James Cruze | 1 | Old Ironsides | | | | |
| 12 | An Old Spanish Custom | 1936 | Adrian Brunel | 1 | Old Spanish Custom | | | | |
| 13 | A Perfect World | 1993 | Clint Eastwood | 3 | Perfect World | | | | |
| 14 | Perfectly Normal | 1990 | Yves Simoneau | 2 | Perfectly Normal | | | | |
| 15 | The Shining | 1980 | Stanley Kubrick | 5 | Shining | | | | |
| 16 | The Terminator | 1984 | James Cameron | 7 | Terminator | | | | |

13

# Filtering List Data

One of the biggest problems with large lists is that it's often hard to find and extract the data you need. Sorting can help, but in the end, you're still working with the entire list. What you need is a way to define the data that you want to work with and then have Excel display only those records onscreen. This action is called *filtering* your data. Fortunately, Excel offers several techniques that get the job done.

## Using AutoFilter to Filter a List

Excel's AutoFilter feature makes filtering out subsets of your data as easy as selecting an option from a drop-down list. In fact, that's literally what happens. When you convert a range to a list, Excel automatically turns on AutoFilter, which is why you see drop-down arrows in the cells containing the list's column labels. (You can toggle AutoFilter off and on by choosing Data, Filter, AutoFilter.) Clicking on one of these arrows displays a list of all the unique entries in the column. Figure 13.8 shows the drop-down list for the Account Name field in an accounts-receivable database.

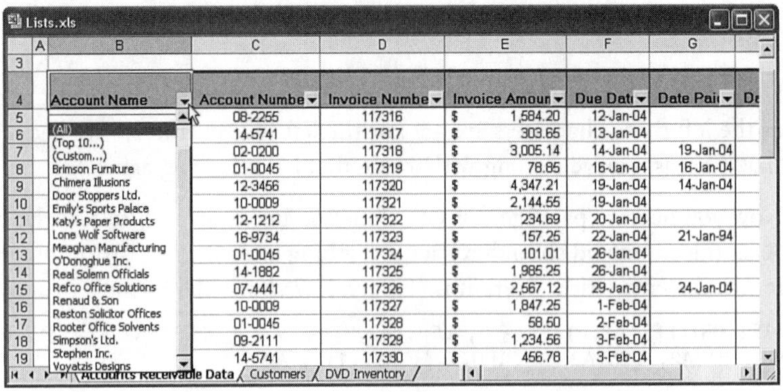

**Figure 13.8**
For each list field, AutoFilter adds drop-down lists that contain only the unique entries in the column.

If you click an item in one of these AutoFilter lists, Excel takes the following actions:

- It displays only those records that include the item in that field. For example, Figure 13.9 shows the resulting records when the item Brimson Furniture is selected from the list attached to the Account Name column. The other records are hidden and can be retrieved whenever you need them.

---

**CAUTION**

Because Excel hides the rows that don't meet the criteria, you shouldn't place any important data either to the left or to the right of the list.

---

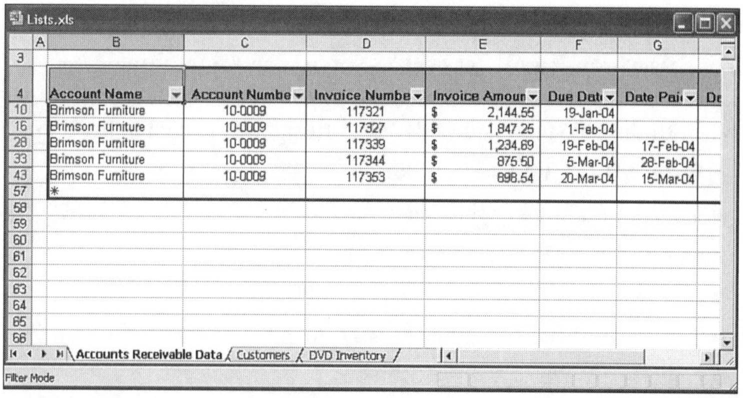

**Figure 13.9**
Clicking an item in an AutoFilter drop-down list displays only records that include the item in the field.

- It changes the color of the column's drop-down arrow. This indicates which column you used to filter the list.
- It displays `Filter Mode` in the status bar.

To continue filtering the data, you can select an item from one of the other lists. For example, you could choose a date from the Due Date list to see only those Brimson Furniture invoices due on that date.

## AutoFilter Criteria Options

The items you see in each drop-down list are called the *filter criteria*. Besides selecting specific criteria (such as an account name), you have the following choices in each drop-down list:

- **All**—Removes the filter criterion for the column. If you've selected multiple criteria, you can remove all the filter criteria and display the entire list by choosing Data, Filter, Show All.
- **Top 10**—In a numeric or date field, displays the Top 10 AutoFilter dialog box, as shown in Figure 13.10. The left drop-down list has two choices, Top or Bottom. The center spin box enables you to choose a number. The right drop-down list has two choices, Items and Percent. For example, if you choose the default choices (Top, 10, and Items), AutoFilter displays the records that have the 10 highest values in the current field.
- **Custom**—Enables you to enter more sophisticated criteria. For details, see the next section.

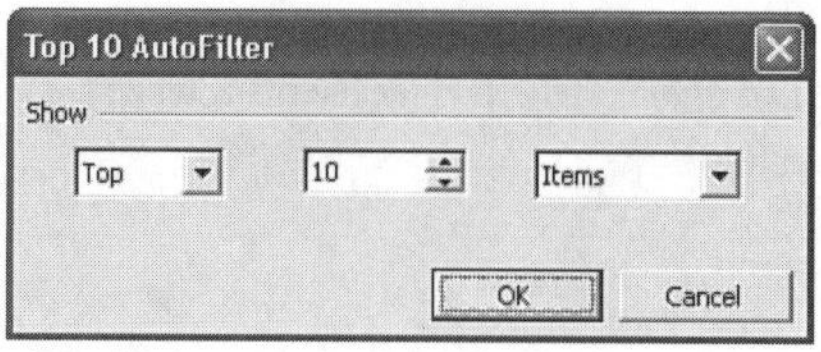

**Figure 13.10**
Use the Top 10 AutoFilter dialog box to filter your records based on values in the current field.

13

## Setting Up Custom AutoFilter Criteria

In its basic form, AutoFilter enables you to select only a single item from each column drop-down list. AutoFilter's *custom filter criteria*, however, give you a way to select multiple items. In the accounts-receivable list, for example, you could use custom criteria to display all the invoices with the following:

- An account number that begins with 07
- A due date in January
- An amount between $1,000 and $5,000
- An account name of either Refco Office Solutions or Brimson Furniture

Before you learn the steps required to create a custom AutoFilter criterion, let's go through an overview of what happens. When you click the Custom option in an AutoFilter drop-down list, Excel displays the Custom AutoFilter dialog box, shown in Figure 13.11.

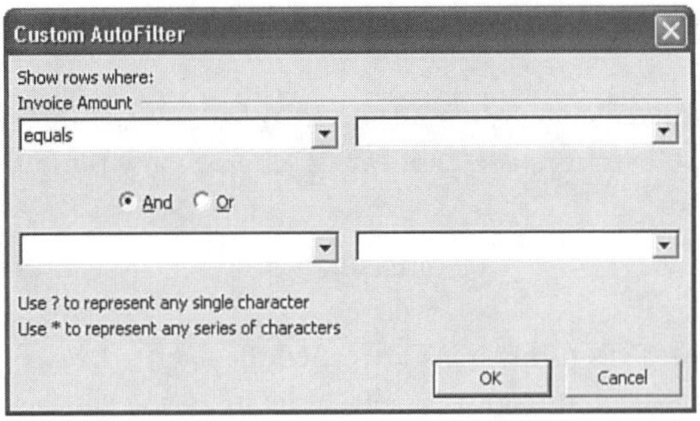

**Figure 13.11**
Use the Custom AutoFilter dialog box to enter your custom criteria.

You use the two drop-down lists across the top to set up the first part of your criterion. The list on the left contains a list of Excel's comparison operators (such as Equals and Is Greater Than). The combo box on the right enables you to select a unique item from the field or enter your own value. For example, if you want to display invoices with an amount greater than or equal to $1,000, click the Is Greater Than or Equal operator and enter **1000** in the text box.

For text fields, you also can use *wildcard characters* to substitute for one or more characters. Use the question mark (?) wildcard to substitute for a single character. For example, if you enter **sm?th**, Excel finds both Smith and Smyth. To substitute for groups of characters, use the asterisk (*). For example, if you enter **\*carolina**, Excel finds all the entries that end with "carolina."

> **TIP**
> To include a wildcard as part of the criteria, precede the character with a tilde (~). For example, to find OVERDUE?, enter **OVERDUE~?**.

You can create *compound criteria* by clicking the <u>A</u>nd or <u>O</u>r buttons and then entering another criterion in the bottom two drop-down lists. Use <u>A</u>nd when you want to display records that meet both criteria; use <u>O</u>r when you want to display records that meet at least one of the two criteria.

For example, to display invoices with an amount greater than or equal to $1,000 and less than or equal to $5,000, you fill in the dialog box as shown in Figure 13.12.

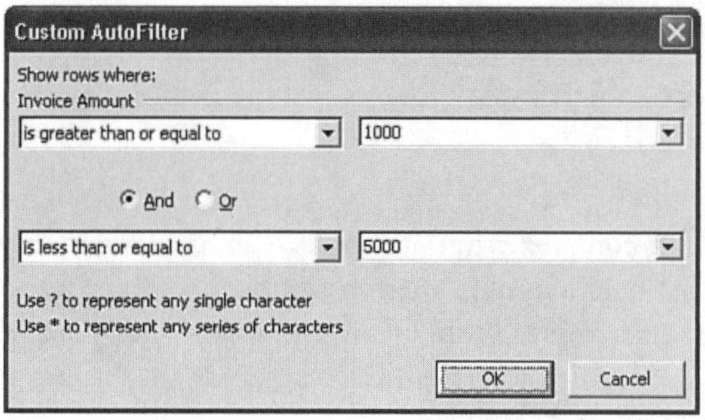

**Figure 13.12**
A compound criterion that displays the records with invoice amounts between $1,000 and $5,000.

The following procedure takes you through the official steps to set up a custom AutoFilter criterion:

1. Click Custom in the drop-down list attached to the column you want to work with. Excel displays the Custom AutoFilter dialog box.
2. Click a comparison operator and enter a value for the first part of the criterion. If you don't want to create a compound criterion, skip to step 5.
3. Click either the <u>A</u>nd option or the <u>O</u>r option, as appropriate.
4. Click a comparison operator and enter a value for the second part of the criterion.
5. Click OK. Excel filters the list.

## Showing Filtered Records

When you need to redisplay records that have been filtered via AutoFilter, use any of the following techniques:

- To display the entire list and remove AutoFilter's drop-down arrows, deactivate the <u>D</u>ata, <u>F</u>ilter, Auto<u>F</u>ilter command.
- To display the entire list without removing the AutoFilter drop-down arrows, choose <u>D</u>ata, <u>F</u>ilter, <u>S</u>how All.
- To remove the filter on a single field, display that field's AutoFilter drop-down list, and click the All option.

**13**

## Using Complex Criteria to Filter a List

The AutoFilter should take care of most of your filtering needs, but it's not designed for heavy-duty work. For example, AutoFilter can't handle the following accounts-receivable criteria:

- Invoice amounts greater than $100, less than $1,000, or greater than $10,000
- Account numbers that begin with 01, 05, or 12
- Days overdue greater than the value in cell J1

To work with these more sophisticated requests, you need to use *complex criteria*.

### Setting Up a Criteria Range

Before you can work with complex criteria, you must set up a *criteria range*. A criteria range has some or all of the list field names in the top row, with at least one blank row directly underneath. You enter your criteria in the blank row below the appropriate field name, and Excel searches the list for records with field values that satisfy the criteria. This setup gives you two major advantages over AutoFilter:

- By using either multiple rows or multiple columns for a single field, you can create compound criteria with as many terms as you like.
- Because you're entering your criteria in cells, you can use formulas to create *computed criteria*.

You can place the criteria range anywhere on the worksheet outside the list range. The most common position, however, is a couple of rows above the list range. Figure 13.13 shows the accounts-receivable list with a criteria range. As you can see, the criteria are entered in the cell below the field name. In this case, the displayed criteria will find all Brimson Furniture invoices that are greater than or equal to $1,000 and that are overdue (that is, invoices that have a value greater than 0 in the Days Overdue field).

**Figure 13.13**
Set up a separate criteria range (B1:D2, in this case) to enter complex criteria.

| | Account Name | Account Number | Invoice Number | Invoice Amount | Due Date | Date Paid | Days Overdue |
|---|---|---|---|---|---|---|---|
| 1 | Account Name | Account Number | Invoice Number | Invoice Amount | Due Date | Date Paid | Days Overdue |
| 2 | Brimson Furniture | | | >=1000 | | | >0 |
| 3 | | | | | | | |
| 4 | Account Name | Account Number | Invoice Number | Invoice Amount | Due Date | Date Paid | Days Overdue |
| 5 | Emily's Sports Palace | 08-2255 | 117316 | $ 1,584.20 | 12-Jan-04 | | 39 |
| 6 | Refco Office Solutions | 14-5741 | 117317 | $ 303.65 | 13-Jan-04 | | 38 |
| 7 | Chimera Illusions | 02-0200 | 117318 | $ 3,005.14 | 14-Jan-04 | 19-Jan-04 | |
| 8 | Door Stoppers Ltd. | 01-0045 | 117319 | $ 78.85 | 16-Jan-04 | 16-Jan-04 | |
| 9 | Meaghan Manufacturing | 12-3456 | 117320 | $ 4,347.21 | 19-Jan-04 | 14-Jan-04 | |
| 10 | Brimson Furniture | 10-0009 | 117321 | $ 2,144.55 | 19-Jan-04 | | 32 |
| 11 | Katy's Paper Products | 12-1212 | 117322 | $ 234.69 | 20-Jan-04 | | 31 |
| 12 | Stephen Inc. | 16-9734 | 117323 | $ 157.25 | 22-Jan-04 | 21-Jan-94 | |
| 13 | Door Stoppers Ltd. | 01-0045 | 117324 | $ 101.01 | 26-Jan-04 | | 25 |
| 14 | Voyatzis Designs | 14-1882 | 117325 | $ 1,965.25 | 26-Jan-04 | | 25 |
| 15 | Lone Wolf Software | 07-4441 | 117326 | $ 2,567.12 | 29-Jan-04 | 24-Jan-04 | |
| 16 | Brimson Furniture | 10-0009 | 117327 | $ 1,847.25 | 1-Feb-04 | | 19 |

Accounts Receivable Data / Customers / DVD Inventory /

## Filtering a List with a Criteria Range

After you've set up your criteria range, you can use it to filter the list. The following procedure takes you through the basic steps:

1. Copy the list field names that you want to use for the criteria, and paste them into the first row of the criteria range. If you'll be using different fields for different criteria, consider copying all your field names into the first row of the criteria range.

> **T I P**
>
> The only problem with copying the field names to the criteria range is that if you change a field name, you must change it in two places (that is, in the list and in the criteria). So, instead of just copying the names, you can make the field names in the criteria range dynamic by using a formula to set each criteria field name equal to its corresponding list field name. For example, you could enter =**B4** in cell B1 of Figure 13.13.

2. Below each field name in the criteria range, enter the criteria you want to use.

3. Select a cell in the list, and then choose <u>D</u>ata, <u>F</u>ilter, <u>A</u>dvanced Filter. Excel displays the Advanced Filter dialog box, shown in Figure 13.14.

**Figure 13.14**
Use the Advanced Filter dialog box to select your list and criteria ranges.

4. The <u>L</u>ist Range text box should contain the list range (if you selected a cell in the list beforehand). If it doesn't, activate the text box and select the list (including the field names).

5. In the <u>C</u>riteria Range text box, select the criteria range (again, including the field names you copied).

6. To avoid including duplicate records in the filter, activate the Unique <u>R</u>ecords Only check box.

7. Click OK. Excel filters the list to show only those records that match your criteria (see Figure 13.15).

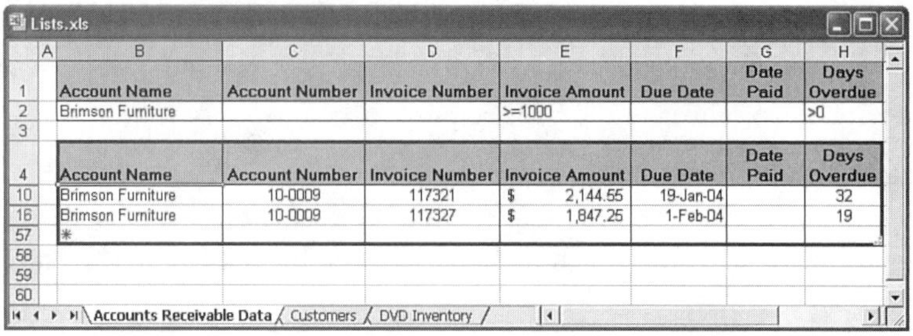

| | A | B | C | D | E | F | G | H |
|---|---|---|---|---|---|---|---|---|
| 1 | | Account Name | Account Number | Invoice Number | Invoice Amount | Due Date | Date Paid | Days Overdue |
| 2 | | Brimson Furniture | | | >=1000 | | | >0 |
| 3 | | | | | | | | |
| 4 | | Account Name | Account Number | Invoice Number | Invoice Amount | Due Date | Date Paid | Days Overdue |
| 10 | | Brimson Furniture | 10-0009 | 117321 | $ 2,144.55 | 19-Jan-04 | | 32 |
| 16 | | Brimson Furniture | 10-0009 | 117327 | $ 1,847.25 | 1-Feb-04 | | 19 |
| 57 | | * | | | | | | |
| 58 | | | | | | | | |
| 59 | | | | | | | | |
| 60 | | | | | | | | |

**Figure 13.15**
Set up a separate criteria range (B1:H2, in this case) to enter complex criteria.

## Entering Compound Criteria

To enter compound criteria in a criteria range, use the following guidelines:

- To find records that match all the criteria, enter the criteria on a single row.
- To find records that match one or more of the criteria, enter the criteria in separate rows.

Finding records that match all the criteria is equivalent to activating the And button in the Custom AutoFilter dialog box. The sample criteria shown earlier in Figure 13.13 match records with the account name Brimson Furniture *and* an invoice amount greater than $1,000 *and* a positive number in the Days Overdue field. To narrow the displayed records, you can enter criteria for as many fields as you like.

> **TIP** You can use the same field name more than once in compound criteria. To do this, you include the appropriate field multiple times in the criteria range and enter the appropriate criteria below each label.

Finding records that match at least one of several criteria is equivalent to activating the Or button in the Custom AutoFilter dialog box. In this case, you need to enter each criterion on a separate row. For example, to display all invoices with amounts greater than or equal to $10,000 or that are more than 30 days overdue, you would set up your criteria as shown in Figure 13.16.



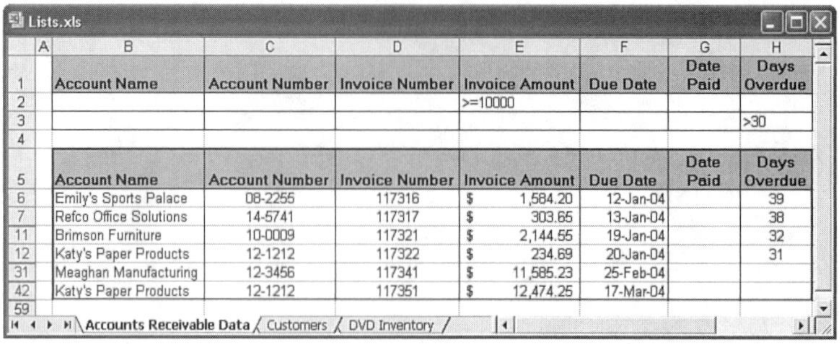

| | A | B | C | D | E | F | G | H |
|---|---|---|---|---|---|---|---|---|
| 1 | | Account Name | Account Number | Invoice Number | Invoice Amount | Due Date | Date Paid | Days Overdue |
| 2 | | | | | >=10000 | | | |
| 3 | | | | | | | | >30 |
| 4 | | | | | | | | |
| 5 | | Account Name | Account Number | Invoice Number | Invoice Amount | Due Date | Date Paid | Days Overdue |
| 6 | | Emily's Sports Palace | 08-2255 | 117316 | $ 1,584.20 | 12-Jan-04 | | 39 |
| 7 | | Refco Office Solutions | 14-5741 | 117317 | $ 303.65 | 13-Jan-04 | | 38 |
| 11 | | Brimson Furniture | 10-0009 | 117321 | $ 2,144.55 | 19-Jan-04 | | 32 |
| 12 | | Katy's Paper Products | 12-1212 | 117322 | $ 234.69 | 20-Jan-04 | | 31 |
| 31 | | Meaghan Manufacturing | 12-3456 | 117341 | $ 11,585.23 | 25-Feb-04 | | |
| 42 | | Katy's Paper Products | 12-1212 | 117351 | $ 12,474.25 | 17-Mar-04 | | |
| 59 | | | | | | | | |

**Figure 13.16**
To display records that match one or more of the criteria, enter the criteria in separate rows.

> **CAUTION**
>
> Don't include any blank rows in your criteria range because blank rows throw off Excel when it tries to match the criteria.

## Entering Computed Criteria

The fields in your criteria range aren't restricted to the list fields. You can create *computed criteria* that use a calculation to match records in the list. The calculation can refer to one or more list fields, or even to cells outside the list, and must return either TRUE or FALSE. Excel selects records that return TRUE.

To use computed criteria, add a column to the criteria range and enter the formula in the new field. Make sure that the name you give the criteria field is different from any field name in the list. When referencing the list cells in the formula, use the first row of the list. For example, to select all records in which the Date Paid is equal to the Due Date in the accounts-receivable list, enter the following formula:

```
=G5=F5
```

Note the use of relative addressing. If you want to reference cells outside the list, use absolute addressing.

> **TIP**
>
> Use Excel's AND, OR, and NOT functions to create compound computed criteria. For example, to select all records in which the Days Overdue value is less than 90 and greater than 31, type this:
>
> ```
> =AND(H5<90, H5>31)
> ```

Figure 13.17 shows a more complex example. The goal is to select all records whose invoices were paid after the due date. The new criterion—named Late Payers—contains the following formula:

```
=IF(ISBLANK(G5), FALSE(), G5 > F5)
```

If the Date Paid field (column G) is blank, the invoice hasn't been paid, so the formula returns FALSE. Otherwise, the logical expression G5 > F5 is evaluated. If the Date Paid (column G) is greater than the Due Date field (column F), the expression returns TRUE and Excel selects the record. In Figure 13.17, the Late Payers cell (B2) displays FALSE because the formula evaluates to FALSE for the first row in the list.

13

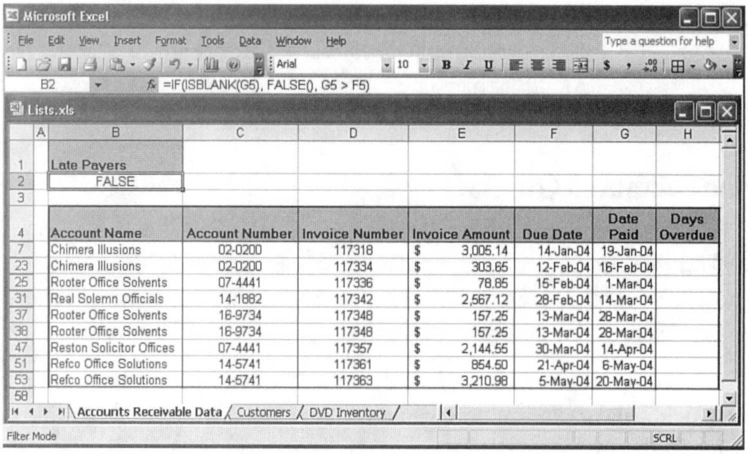

**Figure 13.17**
Use a separate criteria range column for calculated criteria.

| | B | C | D | E | F | G | H |
|---|---|---|---|---|---|---|---|
| 1 | Late Payers | | | | | | |
| 2 | FALSE | | | | | | |
| 3 | | | | | | | |
| 4 | Account Name | Account Number | Invoice Number | Invoice Amount | Due Date | Date Paid | Days Overdue |
| 7 | Chimera Illusions | 02-0200 | 117318 | $ 3,005.14 | 14-Jan-04 | 19-Jan-04 | |
| 23 | Chimera Illusions | 02-0200 | 117334 | $ 303.65 | 12-Feb-04 | 16-Feb-04 | |
| 25 | Rooter Office Solvents | 07-4441 | 117336 | $ 78.85 | 15-Feb-04 | 1-Mar-04 | |
| 31 | Real Solemn Officials | 14-1882 | 117342 | $ 2,567.12 | 28-Feb-04 | 14-Mar-04 | |
| 37 | Rooter Office Solvents | 16-9734 | 117348 | $ 157.25 | 13-Mar-04 | 28-Mar-04 | |
| 38 | Rooter Office Solvents | 16-9734 | 117348 | $ 157.25 | 13-Mar-04 | 28-Mar-04 | |
| 47 | Reston Solicitor Offices | 07-4441 | 117357 | $ 2,144.55 | 30-Mar-04 | 14-Apr-04 | |
| 51 | Refco Office Solutions | 14-5741 | 117361 | $ 854.50 | 21-Apr-04 | 6-May-04 | |
| 53 | Refco Office Solutions | 14-5741 | 117363 | $ 3,210.98 | 5-May-04 | 20-May-04 | |
| 58 | | | | | | | |

## Copying Filtered Data to a Different Range

If you want to work with the filtered data separately, you can copy it (or *extract* it) to a new location. Follow the steps in this procedure:

1. Set up the criteria you want to use to filter the list.

2. If you want to copy only certain columns from the list, copy the appropriate field names to the range you'll be using for the copy.

3. Choose Data, Filter, Advanced Filter to display the Advanced Filter dialog box.

4. Activate the Copy to Another Location option.

5. Enter your list and criteria ranges, if necessary.

6. Use the Copy To box to enter a reference for the copy location using the following guidelines (note that, in each case, you must select the cell or range in the same worksheet that contains the list):

   - To copy the entire filtered list, enter a single cell.

   - To copy only a specific number of rows, enter a range that contains the number of rows you want. If you have more data than fits in the range, Excel asks whether you want to paste the remaining data.

   - To copy only certain columns, select the column labels you copied in step 2.

   ___ CAUTION ___

   If you select a single cell in which to paste the entire filtered list, make sure that you won't be overwriting any data. Otherwise, Excel copies over the data without warning.

7. Click OK. Excel filters the list and copies the selected records to the location you specified.

Figure 13.18 shows the results of an extract in the accounts-receivable list. I've hidden rows 9–57 to show all three ranges onscreen.

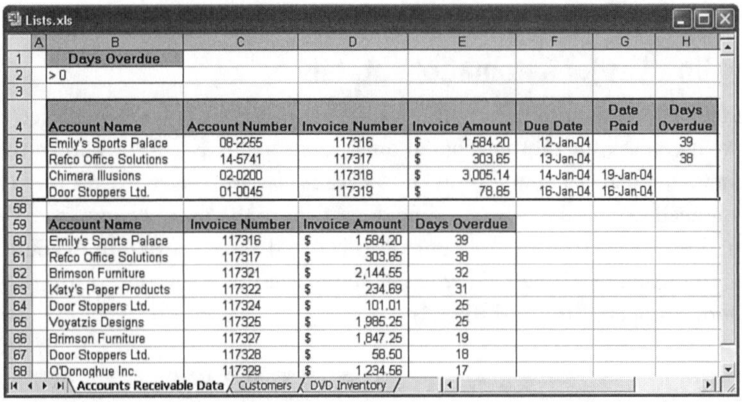

**Figure 13.18**
This filter operation selects those records in which the Days Overdue field is greater than 0 and then copies the results to a range below the list.

| | B | C | D | E | F | G | H |
|---|---|---|---|---|---|---|---|
| 1 | **Days Overdue** | | | | | | |
| 2 | > 0 | | | | | | |
| 3 | | | | | | | |
| 4 | Account Name | Account Number | Invoice Number | Invoice Amount | Due Date | Date Paid | Days Overdue |
| 5 | Emily's Sports Palace | 08-2255 | 117316 | $ 1,584.20 | 12-Jan-04 | | 39 |
| 6 | Refco Office Solutions | 14-5741 | 117317 | $ 303.65 | 13-Jan-04 | | 38 |
| 7 | Chimera Illusions | 02-0200 | 117318 | $ 3,005.14 | 14-Jan-04 | 19-Jan-04 | |
| 8 | Door Stoppers Ltd. | 01-0045 | 117319 | $ 78.85 | 16-Jan-04 | 16-Jan-04 | |
| 58 | | | | | | | |
| 59 | Account Name | Invoice Number | Invoice Amount | Days Overdue | | | |
| 60 | Emily's Sports Palace | 117316 | $ 1,584.20 | 39 | | | |
| 61 | Refco Office Solutions | 117317 | $ 303.65 | 38 | | | |
| 62 | Brimson Furniture | 117321 | $ 2,144.55 | 32 | | | |
| 63 | Katy's Paper Products | 117322 | $ 234.69 | 31 | | | |
| 64 | Door Stoppers Ltd. | 117324 | $ 101.01 | 25 | | | |
| 65 | Voyatzis Designs | 117325 | $ 1,985.25 | 25 | | | |
| 66 | Brimson Furniture | 117327 | $ 1,847.25 | 19 | | | |
| 67 | Door Stoppers Ltd. | 117328 | $ 58.50 | 18 | | | |
| 68 | O'Donoghue Inc. | 117329 | $ 1,234.56 | 17 | | | |

Accounts Receivable Data / Customers / DVD Inventory /

# Summarizing List Data

Because a list is just a special kind of worksheet range, you can analyze list data using many of the same methods you use for regular worksheet cells. Typically, this task involves using formulas and functions to answer questions and produce results. To make your analysis chores easier, Excel enables you to create *automatic subtotals* that can give you instant subtotals, averages, and more. Excel goes one step further by also offering many list-specific functions. These functions work with entire lists or subsets defined by a criteria range. The rest of this chapter shows you how to use all these tools to analyze and summarize your data.

# Creating Automatic Subtotals

Automatic subtotals enable you to summarize your sorted list data quickly. For example, if you have a list of invoices sorted by account name, you can use automatic subtotals to give you the following information for each account:

- The total number of invoices
- The sum of the invoice amounts
- The average invoice amount
- The maximum number of days an invoice is overdue

You can do all this and more without entering a single formula; Excel does the calculations and enters the results automatically. You also can just as easily create grand totals that apply to the entire list.

13

> NOTE
> The term *automatic subtotal* is somewhat of a misnomer because you can summarize more than just totals. For this topic, at least, think of a subtotal as any summary calculation.

## Setting Up a List for Automatic Subtotals

Excel calculates automatic subtotals based on data groupings in a selected field. For example, if you ask for subtotals based on account name, Excel runs down the account name column and creates a new subtotal *each time the name changes*. To get useful summaries, then, you need to sort the list on the field containing the data groupings you're interested in. Figure 13.19 shows the Accounts Receivable database sorted by account name. If you subtotal the Account Name field, you get summaries for Brimson Furniture, Chimera Illusions, Door Stoppers Ltd., and so on.

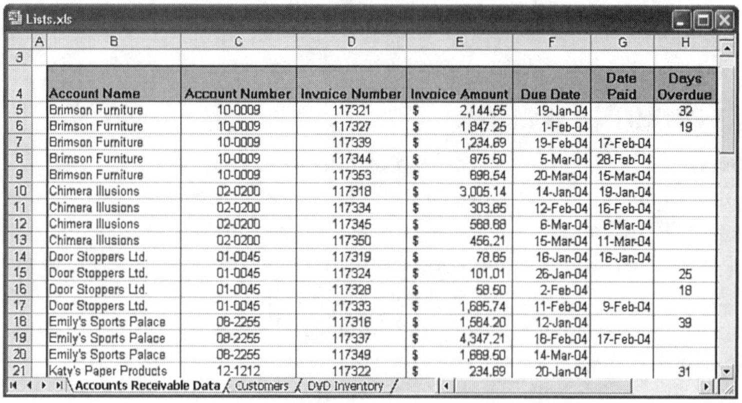

**Figure 13.19**
A sorted list ready for displaying subtotals.

| Account Name | Account Number | Invoice Number | Invoice Amount | Due Date | Date Paid | Days Overdue |
|---|---|---|---|---|---|---|
| Brimson Furniture | 10-0009 | 117321 | $ 2,144.55 | 19-Jan-04 | | 32 |
| Brimson Furniture | 10-0009 | 117327 | $ 1,847.25 | 1-Feb-04 | | 19 |
| Brimson Furniture | 10-0009 | 117339 | $ 1,234.69 | 19-Feb-04 | 17-Feb-04 | |
| Brimson Furniture | 10-0009 | 117344 | $ 875.50 | 5-Mar-04 | 28-Feb-04 | |
| Brimson Furniture | 10-0009 | 117353 | $ 698.54 | 20-Mar-04 | 15-Mar-04 | |
| Chimera Illusions | 02-0200 | 117318 | $ 3,005.14 | 14-Jan-04 | 19-Jan-04 | |
| Chimera Illusions | 02-0200 | 117334 | $ 303.65 | 12-Feb-04 | 16-Feb-04 | |
| Chimera Illusions | 02-0200 | 117345 | $ 588.88 | 6-Mar-04 | 6-Mar-04 | |
| Chimera Illusions | 02-0200 | 117350 | $ 456.21 | 15-Mar-04 | 11-Mar-04 | |
| Door Stoppers Ltd. | 01-0045 | 117319 | $ 78.85 | 16-Jan-04 | 16-Jan-04 | |
| Door Stoppers Ltd. | 01-0045 | 117324 | $ 101.01 | 26-Jan-04 | | 25 |
| Door Stoppers Ltd. | 01-0045 | 117328 | $ 58.50 | 2-Feb-04 | | 18 |
| Door Stoppers Ltd. | 01-0045 | 117333 | $ 1,685.74 | 11-Feb-04 | 9-Feb-04 | |
| Emily's Sports Palace | 08-2255 | 117316 | $ 1,584.20 | 12-Jan-04 | | 39 |
| Emily's Sports Palace | 08-2255 | 117337 | $ 4,347.21 | 18-Feb-04 | 17-Feb-04 | |
| Emily's Sports Palace | 08-2255 | 117349 | $ 1,689.50 | 14-Mar-04 | | |
| Katy's Paper Products | 12-1212 | 117322 | $ 234.69 | 20-Jan-04 | | 31 |

> NOTE
> If you want to display subtotals for a filtered list, be sure to filter the list before sorting it (as described earlier in this chapter).

## Displaying Subtotals

To subtotal a list, follow these steps:

1. If you haven't already done so, sort your list according to the groupings you want to use for the subtotals.

2. Convert the list to a normal range by choosing Data, List, Convert to Range, and then choosing Yes when Excel asks you to confirm.

3. Choose Data, Subtotals to display the Subtotal dialog box, shown in Figure 13.20.

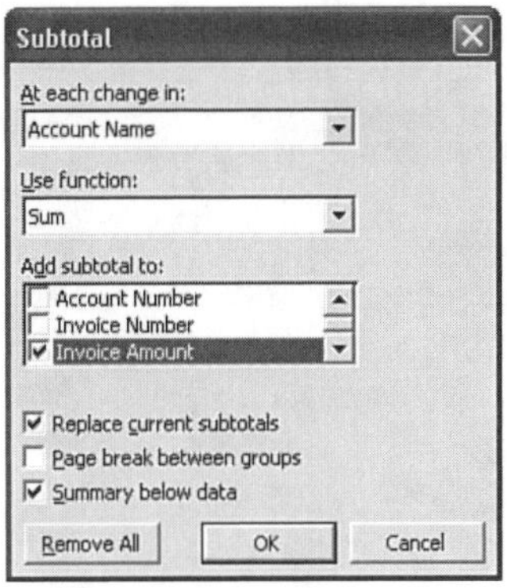

**Figure 13.20**
You use the Subtotal dialog box to create subtotals for your list.

4. Enter the options you want to use for the subtotals:

- **At Each Change In**—This box contains the field names for your list. Click the field you want to use to group the subtotals.

- **Use Function**—Select the function you want to use in the calculations. Excel gives you 11 choices, including Sum, Count, Average, Max, and Min.

- **Add Subtotal To**—This is a list of check boxes for each field. Activate the appropriate check boxes for the fields you want to subtotal.

- **Replace Current Subtotals**—Activate this check box to display new subtotal rows. To add to the existing rows, deactivate this option.

- **Page Break Between Groups**—If you intend to print the summary, activate this check box to insert a page break between each grouping.

- **Summary Below Data**—Deactivate this check box if you want the subtotal rows to appear above the groupings.

5. Click OK. Excel calculates the subtotals and enters them into the list.

Figure 13.21 shows the accounts-receivable list with the Invoice Amount field subtotaled.

## Adding More Subtotals

You can add any number of subtotals to the current summary. The following procedure shows you what to do:

1. Choose Data, Subtotals to display the Subtotal dialog box.

2. Enter the options you want to use for the new subtotal.

3. Deactivate the Replace Current Subtotals check box.

4. Click OK. Excel calculates the new subtotals and adds them to the list.

For example, Figure 13.22 shows the accounts-receivable list with two new subtotals that count the invoices and display the maximum number of days overdue.

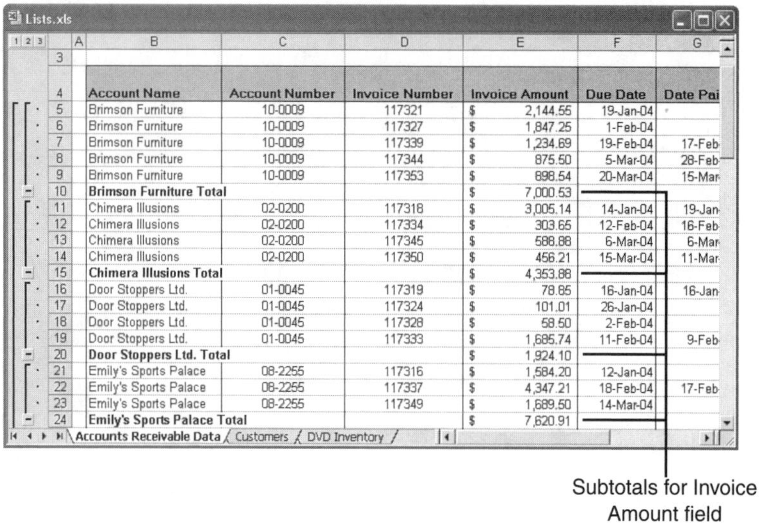

**Figure 13.21**
A list showing Invoice Amount subtotals for each Account Name.

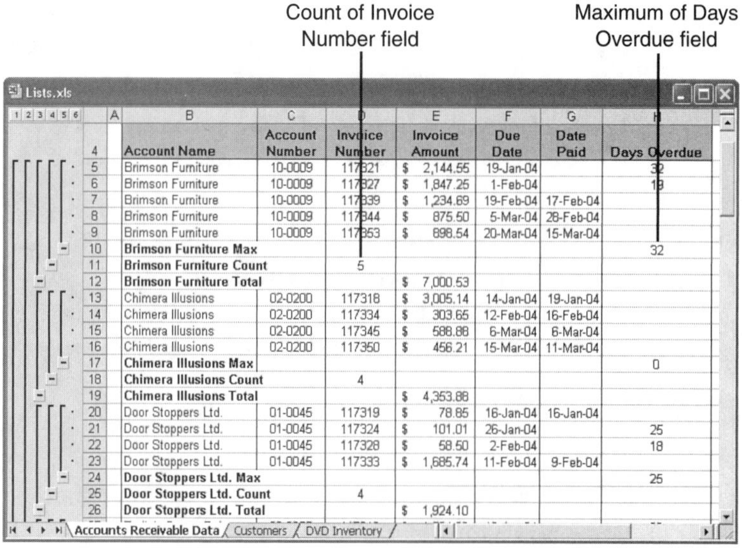

| | Account Name | Account Number | Invoice Number | Invoice Amount | Due Date | Date Pai |
|---|---|---|---|---|---|---|
| 5 | Brimson Furniture | 10-0009 | 117321 | $ 2,144.55 | 19-Jan-04 | |
| 6 | Brimson Furniture | 10-0009 | 117327 | $ 1,847.25 | 1-Feb-04 | |
| 7 | Brimson Furniture | 10-0009 | 117339 | $ 1,234.69 | 19-Feb-04 | 17-Feb |
| 8 | Brimson Furniture | 10-0009 | 117344 | $ 875.50 | 5-Mar-04 | 28-Feb |
| 9 | Brimson Furniture | 10-0009 | 117353 | $ 898.54 | 20-Mar-04 | 15-Mar |
| 10 | **Brimson Furniture Total** | | | $ 7,000.53 | | |
| 11 | Chimera Illusions | 02-0200 | 117318 | $ 3,005.14 | 14-Jan-04 | 19-Jan |
| 12 | Chimera Illusions | 02-0200 | 117334 | $ 303.65 | 12-Feb-04 | 16-Feb |
| 13 | Chimera Illusions | 02-0200 | 117345 | $ 586.88 | 6-Mar-04 | 6-Mar |
| 14 | Chimera Illusions | 02-0200 | 117350 | $ 456.21 | 15-Mar-04 | 11-Mar |
| 15 | **Chimera Illusions Total** | | | $ 4,353.88 | | |
| 16 | Door Stoppers Ltd. | 01-0045 | 117319 | $ 78.85 | 16-Jan-04 | 16-Jan |
| 17 | Door Stoppers Ltd. | 01-0045 | 117324 | $ 101.01 | 26-Jan-04 | |
| 18 | Door Stoppers Ltd. | 01-0045 | 117328 | $ 58.50 | 2-Feb-04 | |
| 19 | Door Stoppers Ltd. | 01-0045 | 117333 | $ 1,685.74 | 11-Feb-04 | 9-Feb |
| 20 | **Door Stoppers Ltd. Total** | | | $ 1,924.10 | | |
| 21 | Emily's Sports Palace | 08-2255 | 117316 | $ 1,584.20 | 12-Jan-04 | |
| 22 | Emily's Sports Palace | 08-2255 | 117337 | $ 4,347.21 | 18-Feb-04 | 17-Feb |
| 23 | Emily's Sports Palace | 08-2255 | 117349 | $ 1,689.50 | 14-Mar-04 | |
| 24 | **Emily's Sports Palace Total** | | | $ 7,620.91 | | |

Accounts Receivable Data / Customers / DVD Inventory

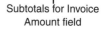

Subtotals for Invoice
Amount field

Count of Invoice
Number field

Maximum of Days
Overdue field

**Figure 13.22**
You can use multiple subtotals in a list.

| | Account Name | Account Number | Invoice Number | Invoice Amount | Due Date | Date Paid | Days Overdue |
|---|---|---|---|---|---|---|---|
| 5 | Brimson Furniture | 10-0009 | 117321 | $ 2,144.55 | 19-Jan-04 | | 32 |
| 6 | Brimson Furniture | 10-0009 | 117327 | $ 1,847.25 | 1-Feb-04 | | 18 |
| 7 | Brimson Furniture | 10-0009 | 117339 | $ 1,234.69 | 19-Feb-04 | 17-Feb-04 | |
| 8 | Brimson Furniture | 10-0009 | 117344 | $ 875.50 | 5-Mar-04 | 28-Feb-04 | |
| 9 | Brimson Furniture | 10-0009 | 117353 | $ 898.54 | 20-Mar-04 | 15-Mar-04 | |
| 10 | **Brimson Furniture Max** | | | | | | 32 |
| 11 | **Brimson Furniture Count** | | 5 | | | | |
| 12 | **Brimson Furniture Total** | | | $ 7,000.53 | | | |
| 13 | Chimera Illusions | 02-0200 | 117318 | $ 3,005.14 | 14-Jan-04 | 19-Jan-04 | |
| 14 | Chimera Illusions | 02-0200 | 117334 | $ 303.65 | 12-Feb-04 | 16-Feb-04 | |
| 15 | Chimera Illusions | 02-0200 | 117345 | $ 586.88 | 6-Mar-04 | 6-Mar-04 | |
| 16 | Chimera Illusions | 02-0200 | 117350 | $ 456.21 | 15-Mar-04 | 11-Mar-04 | |
| 17 | **Chimera Illusions Max** | | | | | | 0 |
| 18 | **Chimera Illusions Count** | | 4 | | | | |
| 19 | **Chimera Illusions Total** | | | $ 4,353.88 | | | |
| 20 | Door Stoppers Ltd. | 01-0045 | 117319 | $ 78.85 | 16-Jan-04 | 16-Jan-04 | |
| 21 | Door Stoppers Ltd. | 01-0045 | 117324 | $ 101.01 | 26-Jan-04 | | 25 |
| 22 | Door Stoppers Ltd. | 01-0045 | 117328 | $ 58.50 | 2-Feb-04 | | 18 |
| 23 | Door Stoppers Ltd. | 01-0045 | 117333 | $ 1,685.74 | 11-Feb-04 | 9-Feb-04 | |
| 24 | **Door Stoppers Ltd. Max** | | | | | | 25 |
| 25 | **Door Stoppers Ltd. Count** | | 4 | | | | |
| 26 | **Door Stoppers Ltd. Total** | | | $ 1,924.10 | | | |

Accounts Receivable Data / Customers / DVD Inventory

## Nesting Subtotals

If the existing subtotal groups don't show enough detail, you can insert a subtotal within a subtotal group (this is called *nesting* subtotals). Follow the steps in this procedure:

1. Choose Data, Subtotals to display the Subtotal dialog box.

2. In the At Each Change In list box, select the field you want to use for the new subtotal grouping.

3. Enter any other options you want to use for the new subtotal.

13

**4.** Deactivate the Replace Current Subtotals check box.

**5.** Click OK. Excel calculates the new subtotals and adds them to the list.

Figure 13.23 shows the original accounts-receivable subtotals (the ones shown in Figure 13.21), with nested subtotals for each month.

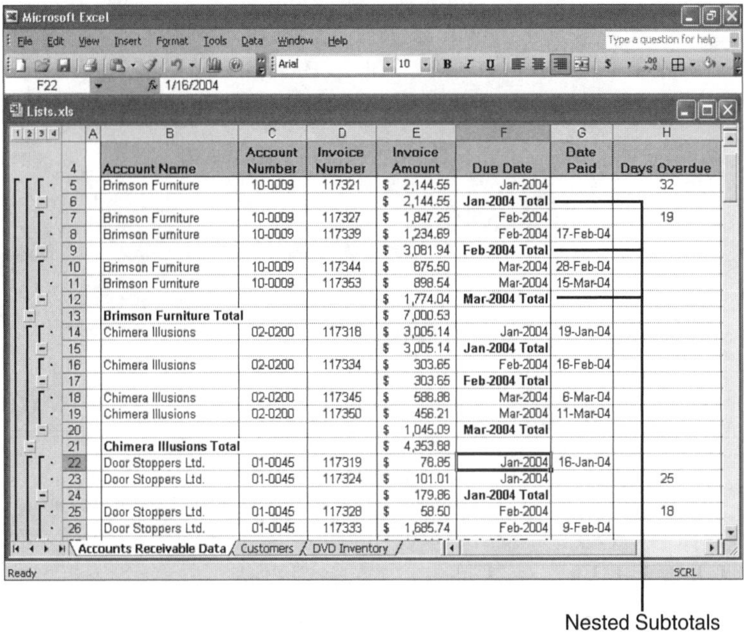

**Figure 13.23**
You also can nest subtotals inside existing subtotal groups.

Nested Subtotals

> **TIP**
>
> Because Excel uses the format of the data to decide on the subtotal groupings, you also can control the subtotals by formatting the data appropriately. In Figure 13.23, I formatted the Due Date field as mmm-yyyy. For example, this changes 1/16/2004 to Dec-2004 and enables Excel to group the invoices by month.

## Working with a Subtotal's Outline Symbols

When Excel creates a subtotal, it displays various *outline symbols* to the left of the worksheet. You can use these symbols to hide or show detail data in the subtotals. Outlines work by dividing your data into different *levels* that show different amounts of detail. The subtotaled data in Figure 13.24 has three levels:

■ **Level 1**—The list grand total, which appears at the bottom of the list. It can't be seen in Figure 13.24.

■ **Level 2**—The list subtotals.

■ **Level 3**—The entire list.

Level buttons

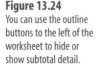

| | A | B | C | D | E | F | G | H | I |
|---|---|---|---|---|---|---|---|---|---|
| 3 | | | | | | | | | |
| 4 | | Account Name | Account Number | Invoice Number | Invoice Amount | Due Date | Date Paid | Days Overdue | |
| 5 | | Brimson Furniture | 10-0009 | 117321 | $ 2,144.55 | 19-Jan-04 | | 32 | |
| 6 | | Brimson Furniture | 10-0009 | 117327 | $ 1,847.25 | 1-Feb-04 | | 19 | |
| 7 | | Brimson Furniture | 10-0009 | 117339 | $ 1,234.69 | 19-Feb-04 | 17-Feb-04 | | |
| 8 | | Brimson Furniture | 10-0009 | 117344 | $ 875.50 | 5-Mar-04 | 28-Feb-04 | | |
| 9 | | Brimson Furniture | 10-0009 | 117353 | $ 898.54 | 20-Mar-04 | 15-Mar-04 | | |
| 10 | | **Brimson Furniture Total** | | | $ 7,000.53 | | | | |
| 15 | | **Chimera Illusions Total** | | | $ 4,353.88 | | | | |
| 20 | | **Door Stoppers Ltd. Total** | | | $ 1,924.10 | | | | |
| 21 | | Emily's Sports Palace | 08-2255 | 117316 | $ 1,584.20 | 12-Jan-04 | | 39 | |
| 22 | | Emily's Sports Palace | 08-2255 | 117337 | $ 4,347.21 | 18-Feb-04 | 17-Feb-04 | | |
| 23 | | Emily's Sports Palace | 08-2255 | 117349 | $ 1,689.50 | 14-Mar-04 | | | |
| 24 | | **Emily's Sports Palace Total** | | | $ 7,620.91 | | | | |
| 25 | | Katy's Paper Products | 12-1212 | 117322 | $ 234.69 | 20-Jan-04 | | 31 | |
| 26 | | Katy's Paper Products | 12-1212 | 117340 | $ 1,157.58 | 21-Feb-04 | | | |
| 27 | | Katy's Paper Products | 12-1212 | 117351 | $ 12,474.25 | 17-Mar-04 | | | |
| 28 | | Katy's Paper Products | 12-1212 | 117354 | $ 1,234.56 | 21-Mar-04 | | | |
| 29 | | Katy's Paper Products | 12-1212 | 117355 | $ 1,584.20 | 23-Mar-04 | | | |
| 30 | | **Katy's Paper Products Total** | | | $ 16,685.28 | | | | |

Accounts Receivable Data / Customers / DVD Inventory /

Expand button

Collapse button

Level bars

Here's a summary of the available outline tools:

- **Level bars**—These bars indicate the data included in the current level. Click a bar to hide the rows marked by a bar.

- **Collapse button**—Click this button to hide (or *collapse*) the rows marked by the attached level bar.

- **Expand button**—When you collapse a level, the collapse button changes to an expand button (+). Click an expand button to display the hidden rows.

- **Level buttons**—These buttons tell you which level each level bar is on. Click a level button to display all the detail data for that level.

In Figure 13.24, the detail data for Chimera Illusions and Door Stoppers Ltd. is collapsed, and the detail data for Brimson Furniture, Emily's Sports Palace, and Katy's Paper Products is expanded.

### Removing Subtotals

To remove the subtotals from a list, choose <u>D</u>ata, Su<u>b</u>totals to display the Subtotal dialog box, and then click <u>R</u>emove All.

## Excel's List Functions

To get more control over your list analysis, you can use Excel's *list functions*. These functions are the same as those used in subtotals, but they have the following advantages:

- You can enter the functions into any cell in the worksheet.
- You can specify the range the function uses to perform its calculations.
- You can enter criteria or reference a criteria range to perform calculations on subsets of the list.

## About List Functions

To illustrate the list functions, consider an example. If you want to, say, calculate the sum of a list field, you can enter SUM(*range*), and Excel produces the result. If you want to sum only a subset of the field, you must specify as arguments the particular cells to use. For lists containing hundreds of records, however, this process is impractical. (It's also illegal, for two reasons: Excel allows a maximum of 30 arguments in the SUM() function, and it allows a maximum of 255 characters in a cell entry.)

The solution is to use DSUM(), which is the list equivalent of the SUM() function. The DSUM() function takes three arguments: a list range, a field name, and a criteria range. DSUM() looks at the specified field in the list and sums only records that match the criteria in the criteria range.

The list functions come in two varieties: those that don't require a criteria range and those that do.

## List Functions That Don't Require a Criteria Range

Excel has two list functions that enable you to specify the criteria as an argument rather than a range: COUNTIF() and SUMIF().

### Using COUNTIF()

The COUNTIF() function counts the number of cells in a range that meet a single criterion:

COUNTIF(*range, criteria*)

| | |
|---|---|
| *range* | The range of cells to use for the count. |
| *criteria* | The criteria, entered as text, that determines which cells to count. Excel applies the criteria to *range*. |

For example, Figure 13.25 shows a COUNTIF() function that calculates the total number of invoices that are more than 30 days overdue.

### Using SUMIF()

The SUMIF() function is similar to COUNTIF(), except that it sums the range cells that meet its criterion:

SUMIF(*range, criteria, [sum_range]*)

| | |
|---|---|
| *range* | The range of cells to use for the criterion. |

**13**

*criteria*      The criteria, entered as text, that determines which cells to sum. Excel applies the criteria to *range*.

*sum_range*     The range from which the sum values are taken. Excel sums only those cells in *sum_range* that correspond to the cells in *range* and meet the criteria. If you omit *sum_range*, Excel uses *range* for the sum.

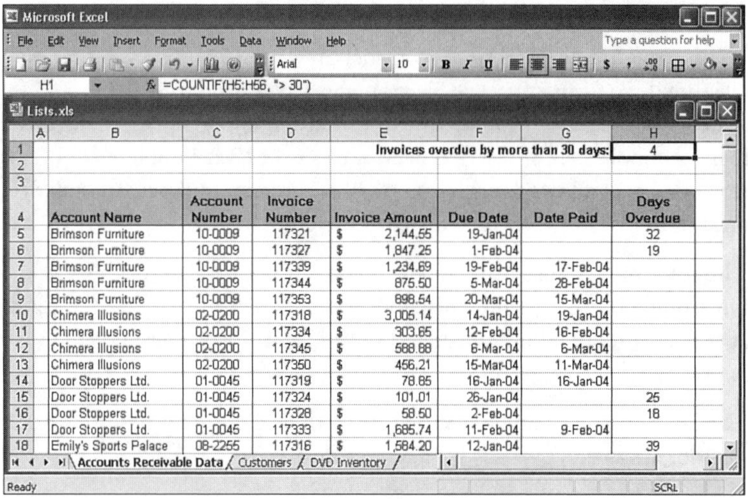

**Figure 13.25**
Use COUNTIF( ) to count the cells that meet a criterion.

Figure 13.26 shows a Parts database. The SUMIF( ) function in cell F16 sums the total cost (F7:F14) for the parts where Division (A7:A14) is equal to 3.

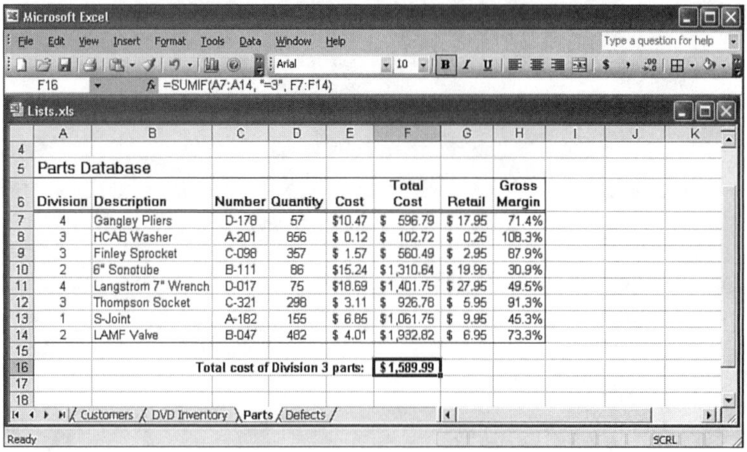

**Figure 13.26**
Use SUMIF( ) to sum cells that meet a criterion.

## List Functions That Require a Criteria Range

The remaining list functions require a criteria range. These functions take a little longer to set up, but the advantage is that you can enter compound and computed criteria.

All of these functions have the following format:

`Dfunction(database, field, criteria)`

| | |
|---|---|
| `Dfunction` | The function name, such as DSUM or DAVERAGE. |
| `database` | The range of cells that make up the list you want to work with. You can use either a range name, if one is defined, or the range address. |
| `field` | The name of the field on which you want to perform the operation. You can use either the field name or the field number as the argument (in which the leftmost field is field number 1, the next field is field number 2, and so on). If you use the field name, enclose it in quotation marks (for example, `"Total Cost"`). |
| `criteria` | The range of cells that hold the criteria you want to work with. You can use either a range name, if one is defined, or the range address. |

> **TIP**
>
> To perform an operation on every record in the list, leave all the `criteria` fields blank. This causes Excel to select every record in the list.

Table 13.1 summarizes the list functions.

**Table 13.1    Excel's List Functions**

| Function | Description |
|---|---|
| DAVERAGE() | Returns the average of the matching records in a specified field |
| DCOUNT() | Returns the count of the matching records |
| DCOUNTA() | Returns the count of the nonblank matching records |
| DGET() | Returns the value of a specified field for a single matching record |
| DMAX() | Returns the maximum value of a specified field for the matching records |
| DMIN() | Returns the minimum value of a specified field for the matching records |
| DPRODUCT() | Returns the product of the values of a specified field for the matching records |
| DSTDEV() | Returns the estimated standard deviation of the values in a specified field if the matching records are a sample of the population |
| DSTDEVP() | Returns the standard deviation of the values of a specified field if the matching records are the entire population |

*continues*

13

| Table 13.1 | Continued |
|---|---|
| **Function** | **Description** |
| DSUM() | Returns the sum of the values of a specified field for the matching records |
| DVAR() | Returns the estimated variance of the values of a specified field if the matching records are a sample of the population |
| DVARP() | Returns the variance of the values of a specified field if the matching records are the entire population |

➔ To learn about statistical operations such as standard deviation and variance, **see** "Working with Statistical Functions," **p. 249**.

You enter list functions the same way you enter any other Excel function. You type an equals sign (=) and then enter the function—either by itself or combined with other Excel operators in a formula. The following examples all show valid list functions:

=DSUM(A6:H14, "Total Cost", A1:H3)

=DSUM(List, "Total Cost", Criteria)

=DSUM(AR_List, 3, Criteria)

=DSUM(1993_Sales, "Sales", A1:H13)

The next two sections provide examples of the DAVERAGE() and DGET() list functions.

## Using DAVERAGE()

The DAVERAGE() function calculates the average *field* value in the *database* records that match the *criteria*. In the Parts database, for example, suppose that you want to calculate the average gross margin for all parts assigned to Division 2. You set up a criteria range for the Division field and enter **2**, as shown in Figure 13.27. You then enter the following DAVERAGE() function (see cell H3):

=DAVERAGE(A6:H14, "Gross Margin", A2:A3)

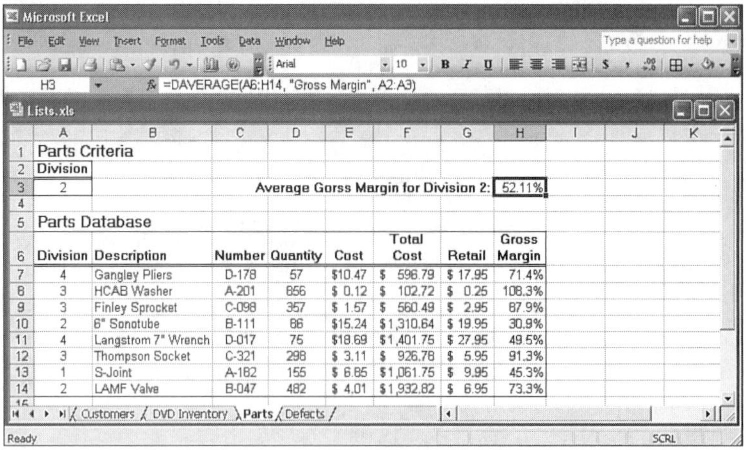

**Figure 13.27**

Use DAVERAGE() to calculate the field average in the matching records.

## Using DGET()

The DGET() function extracts the value of a single *field* in the *database* records that match the *criteria*. If there are no matching records, DGET() returns #VALUE!. If there is more than one matching record, DGET() returns #NUM!.

DGET() typically is used to query the list for a specific piece of information. For example, in the Parts list, you might want to know the cost of the Finley Sprocket. To extract this information, you would first set up a criteria range with the Description field and enter Finley Sprocket. You would then extract the information with the following formula (assuming that the list and criteria ranges are named Database and Criteria, respectively):

=DGET(Database, "Cost", Criteria)

A more interesting application of this function would be to extract the name of a part that satisfies a certain condition. For example, you might want to know the name of the part that has the highest gross margin. Creating this model requires two steps:

1. Set up the criteria to match the highest value in the Gross Margin field.
2. Add a DGET() function to extract the description of the matching record.

Figure 13.28 shows how this is done. For the criteria, a new field called Highest Margin is created. As the text box shows, this field uses the following computed criteria:

=H7 = MAX($H$7:$H$14)

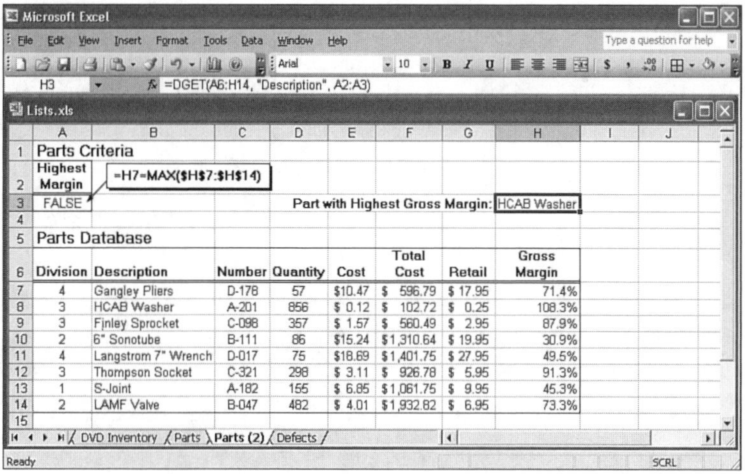

**Figure 13.28**
A DGET() function that extracts the name of the part with the highest margin.

The range $H$7:$H$14 is the Gross Margin field. (Note the use of absolute references.) Excel matches only the record that has the highest gross margin. The DGET() function in cell H3 is straightforward:

=DGET(A6:H14, "Description", A2:A3)

This formula returns the description of the part that has the highest gross margin.

CASE STUDY

## Applying Statistical List Functions to a Defects Database

Many list functions are most often used to analyze statistical populations. Figure 13.29 shows a list of defects found among 12 work groups in a manufacturing process. In this example, the list (B3:D15) is named Defects, and two criteria ranges are used—one for each of the group leaders, Johnson (G3:G4 is Criteria1) and Perkins (H3:H4 is Criteria2).

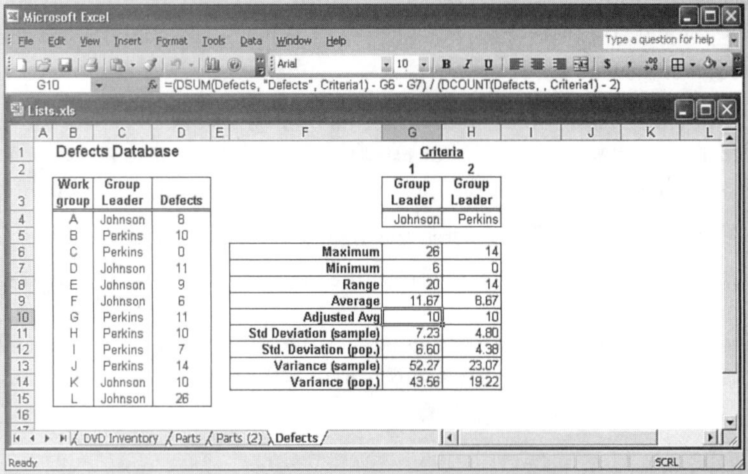


| Work group | Group Leader | Defects |
|---|---|---|
| A | Johnson | 8 |
| B | Perkins | 10 |
| C | Perkins | 0 |
| D | Johnson | 11 |
| E | Johnson | 9 |
| F | Johnson | 6 |
| G | Perkins | 11 |
| H | Perkins | 10 |
| I | Perkins | 7 |
| J | Perkins | 14 |
| K | Johnson | 10 |
| L | Johnson | 26 |

| | 1 Group Leader Johnson | 2 Group Leader Perkins |
|---|---|---|
| Maximum | 26 | 14 |
| Minimum | 6 | 0 |
| Range | 20 | 14 |
| Average | 11.67 | 8.67 |
| Adjusted Avg | 10 | 10 |
| Std Deviation (sample) | 7.23 | 4.80 |
| Std. Deviation (pop.) | 6.60 | 4.38 |
| Variance (sample) | 52.27 | 23.07 |
| Variance (pop.) | 43.56 | 19.22 |

**Figure 13.29**
Using statistical list functions to analyze a database of defects in a manufacturing process.

The table shows several calculations. First, DMAX() and DMIN() are calculated for each criteria. The *range* (a statistic that represents the difference between the largest and smallest numbers in the sample; it's a crude measure of the sample's variance) is then calculated using the following formula (Johnson's groups):

```
=DMAX(Defects, "Defects", Criteria1) - DMIN(Defects, "Defects", Criteria1)
```

Of course, instead of using DMAX() and DMIN() explicitly, you can simply refer to the cells containing the DMAX() and DMIN() results.

The next line uses DAVERAGE() to find the average number of defects for each group leader. Notice that the average for Johnson's groups (11.67) is significantly higher than that for Perkins's groups (8.67). However, Johnson's average is skewed higher by one anomalously large number (26), and Perkins's average is skewed lower by one anomalously small number (0).

To allow for this situation, the Adjusted Avg line uses DSUM(), DCOUNT(), and the DMAX() and DMIN() results to compute a new average without the largest and smallest number for each sample. As you can see, without the anomalies, the two leaders have the same average.

> **NOTE** As shown in cell G10 of Figure 13.29, if you don't include a *field* argument in the DCOUNT() function, it returns the total number of records in the list.

The rest of the calculations use the DSTDEV(), DSTDEVP(), DVAR(), and DVARP() functions.

## From Here

- To create custom sort orders, you need to create custom AutoFill lists. **See** "Creating a Custom AutoFill List," **p. 20**.

- For coverage of the regular SUM() function, **see** "The SUM() Function," **p. 239**.

- For coverage of the regular COUNT() function, **see** "Counting Items with the COUNT() Function," **p. 252**.

- For more detailed information on statistics such as standard deviation and variance, **see** "Working with Statistical Functions," **p. 249**.

**13**

# Using Excel's Business-Modeling Tools

# 14

At times it's not enough to simply enter data in a worksheet, build a few formulas, and add a little formatting to make things presentable. In the business world, you're often called on to divine some inner meaning from the jumble of numbers and formula results that litter your workbooks. In other words, you need to *analyze* your data to see what nuggets of understanding you can unearth. In Excel, analyzing business data means using the program's business-modeling tools. This chapter looks at a few of those tools and some analytic techniques that have a many uses. You'll learn how to use Excel's numerous methods for what-if analysis, how to wield Excel's useful Goal Seek tool, and how to create scenarios.

## Using What-If Analysis

*What-if analysis* is perhaps the most basic method for interrogating your worksheet data. With what-if analysis, you first calculate a formula D, based on the input from variables A, B, and C. You then say, "What if I change variable A? Or B or C? What happens to the result?"

For example, Figure 14.1 shows a worksheet that calculates the future value of an investment based on five variables: the interest rate, period, annual deposit, initial deposit, and deposit type. Cell C9 shows the result of the FV() function. Now the questions begin: What if the interest rate was 7%? What if you deposited $8,000 per year? Or $12,000? What if you reduced the initial deposit? Answering these questions is a straightforward matter of changing the appropriate variables and watching the effect on the result.

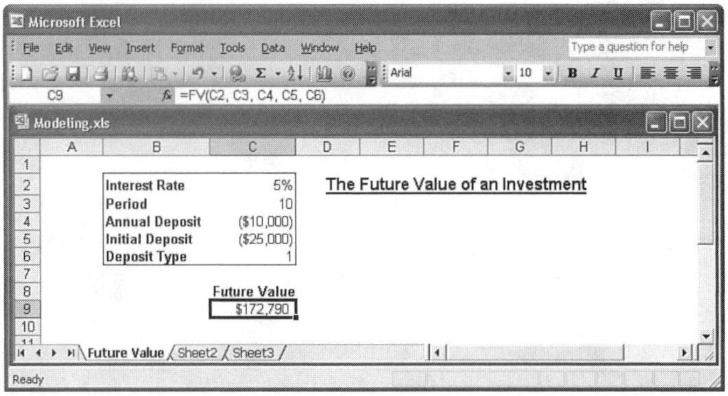


**Figure 14.1**
The simplest what-if analysis involves changing worksheet variables and watching the result.

> **NOTE**
> You can download the workbook that contains this chapter's examples here:
> `www.mcfedries.com/ExcelFormulas/`

## Setting Up a One-Input Data Table

The problem with modifying formula variables is that you see only a single result at one time. If you're interested in studying the effect a range of values has on the formula, you need to set up a *data table*. In the investment analysis worksheet, for example, suppose that you want to see the future value of the investment with the annual deposit varying between $7,000 and $13,000. You could just enter these values in a row or column and then create the appropriate formulas. Setting up a data table, however, is much easier, as the following procedure shows:

1. Add to the worksheet the values you want to input into the formula. You have two choices for the placement of these values:
   - If you want to enter the values in a row, start the row one cell up and one cell to the right of the formula.
   - If you want to enter the values in a column, start the column one cell down and one cell to the left of the cell containing the formula, as shown in Figure 14.2.
2. Select the range that includes the input values and the formula. (In Figure 14.2, this is B9:C16.)
3. Choose Data, Table. Excel displays the Table dialog box.
4. How you fill in this dialog box depends on how you set up your data table:
   - If you entered the input values in a row, use the Row Input Cell text box to enter the cell address of the input cell.
   - If the input values are in a column, enter the input cell's address in the Column Input Cell text box. In the investment analysis example, you enter `C4` in the Column Input Cell, as shown in Figure 14.3.

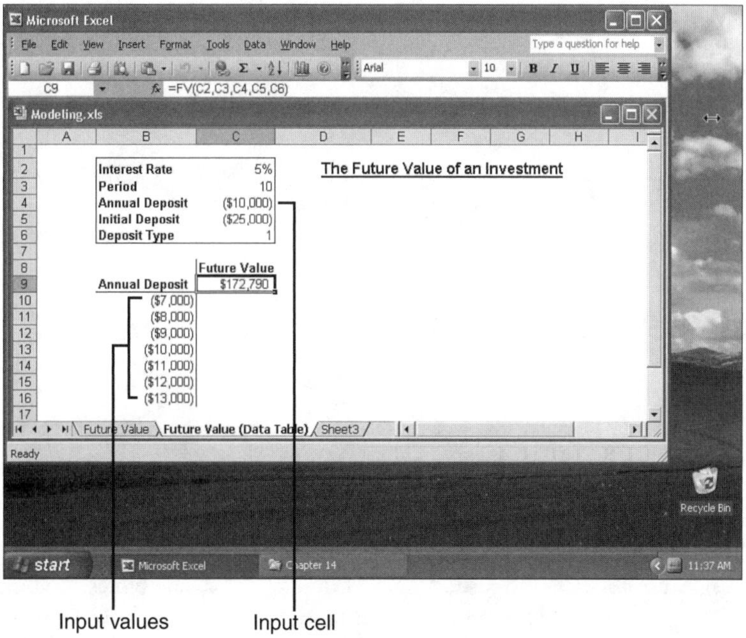

**Figure 14.2**
Enter the values you want to input into the formula.

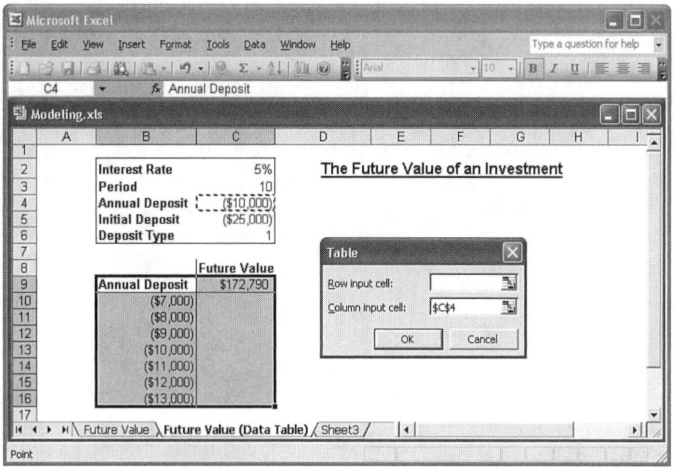

Input values          Input cell

**Figure 14.3**
In the Table dialog box, enter the input cell where you want Excel to substitute the input values.

5. Click OK. Excel places each of the input values in the input cell; Excel then displays the results in the data table, as shown in Figure 14.4.

14

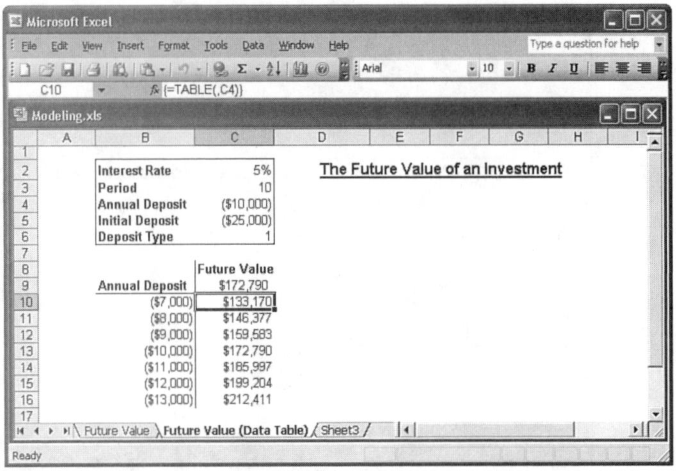

**Figure 14.4**
Excel substitutes each input value into the input cell and displays the results in the data table.

## Adding More Formulas to the Input Table

You're not restricted to just a single formula in your data tables. If you want to see the effect of the various input values on different formulas, you can easily add them to the data table. For example, in the future value worksheet, it would be interesting to factor inflation into the calculations to see how the investment appears in today's dollars. Figure 14.5 shows the revised worksheet with a new Inflation variable (cell C7) and a formula that converts the calculated future value into today's dollars (cell D9).

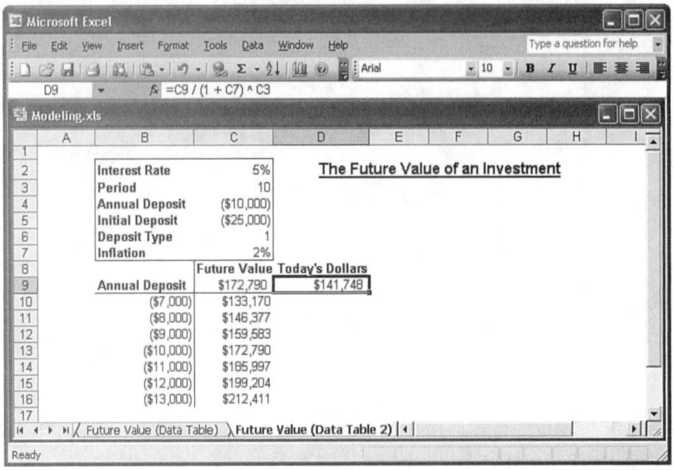

**Figure 14.5**
To add a formula to a data table, enter the new formula next to the existing one.

> **NOTE**
> This is the formula for converting a future value into today's dollars:
>
> $$Future\ Value\ /\ (1\ +\ Inflation\ Rate)\ \char`\^\ Period$$
>
> Here, `Period` is the number of years from now that the future value exists.

To create the new data table, follow the steps outlined previously. However, make sure that the range you select in step 2 includes the input values and *both* formulas (that is, the range B9:D16 in Figure 14.5). Figure 14.6 shows the results.

**Figure 14.6**
The results of the data table with multiple formulas.

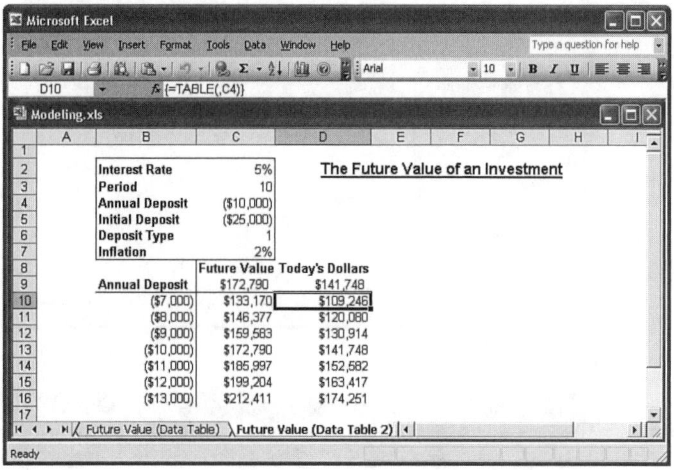


**NOTE** After you have a data table set up, you can do regular what-if analysis by adjusting the other worksheet variables. Each time you make a change, Excel recalculates every formula in the table.

## Setting Up a Two-Input Table

You also can set up data tables that take two input variables. This option enables you to see the effect on an investment's future value when you enter different values for, say, the annual deposit and the interest rate. The following steps show you how to set up a two-input data table:

1. Enter one set of values in a column below the formula and the second set of values to the right of the formula in the same row, as shown in Figure 14.7.
2. Select the range that includes the input values and the formula (B8:G15 in Figure 14.7).
3. Choose Data, Table to display the Table dialog box.
4. In the Row Input Cell text box, enter the cell address of the input cell that corresponds to the row values you entered (C2 in Figure 14.7—the Interest Rate variable).
5. In the Column Input Cell text box, enter the cell address of the input cell you want to use for the column values (C4 in Figure 14.7—the Annual Deposit variable).
6. Click OK. Excel runs through the various input combinations and then displays the results in the data table, as shown in Figure 14.8.

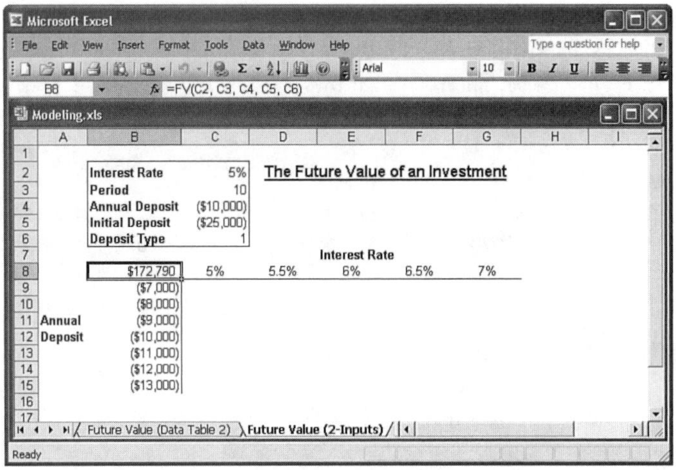

**Figure 14.7**
Enter the two sets of values that you want to input into the formula.

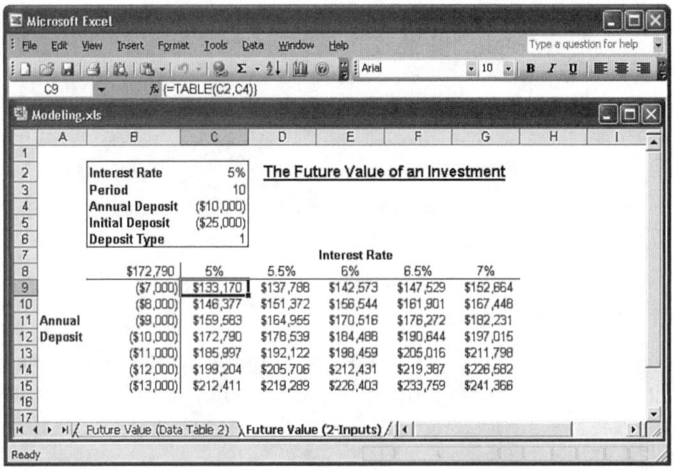

**Figure 14.8**
Excel substitutes each input value into the input cell and displays the results in the data table.

**TIP**

As mentioned earlier, if you make changes to any of the variables in a table formula, Excel recalculates the entire table. This isn't a problem in small tables, but large ones can take a very long time to calculate. If you prefer to control the table recalculation, choose Tools, Options; select the Calculation tab; and then activate the Automatic Except Tables check box. This tells Excel not to include data tables when it recalculates a worksheet. To recalculate a table, press F9 (or Shift+F9 to recalculate the current worksheet only).

## Editing a Data Table

If you want to make changes to the data table, you can edit the formula (or formulas) as well as the input value. However, the data table results are a different matter. When you run the <u>D</u>ata, <u>T</u>able command, Excel enters an array formula in the interior of the data table. This formula is a TABLE() function (a special function available only by using the <u>D</u>ata, <u>T</u>able command) with the following syntax:

```
{=TABLE(row_input_ref, column_input_ref)}
```

Here, `row_input_ref` and `column_input_ref` are the cell references you entered in the Table dialog box. The braces ({ }) indicate that this is an array, which means that you can't change or delete individual elements of the array. If you want to change the results, you need to select the entire data table and then run the <u>D</u>ata, <u>T</u>able command again. If you just want to delete the results, you must first select the entire array and then delete it.

→ To learn more about arrays, **see** "Working with Arrays," **p. 85**.

# Working with Goal Seek

Here's a what-if question for you: What if you already know the result you want? For example, you might know that you want to have $50,000 saved to purchase new equipment five years from now, or that you have to achieve a 30% gross margin in your next budget. If you need to manipulate only a single variable to achieve these results, you can use Excel's Goal Seek feature. You tell Goal Seek the final value you need and which variable to change, and it finds a solution for you (if one exists).

→ For more complicated scenarios with multiple variables and constraints, you need to use Excel's Solver feature. **See** "Solving Complex Problems with Solver," **p. 377**.

## How Does Goal Seek Work?

When you set up a worksheet to use Goal Seek, you usually have a formula in one cell and the formula's variable—with an initial value—in another. (Your formula can have multiple variables, but Goal Seek enables you to manipulate only one variable at a time.) Goal Seek operates by using an *iterative method* to find a solution. That is, Goal Seek first tries the variable's initial value to see whether that produces the result you want. If it doesn't, Goal Seek tries different values until it converges on a solution.

→ To learn more about iterative methods, **see** "Using Iteration and Circular References," **p. 90**.

## Running Goal Seek

Before you run Goal Seek, you need to set up your worksheet in a particular way. This means doing three things:

- Set up one cell as the *changing cell*. This is the value that Goal Seek will iteratively manipulate to attempt to reach the goal. Enter an initial value (such as 0) into the cell.
- Set up the other input values for the formula and give them proper initial values.
- Create a formula for Goal Seek to use to try to reach the goal.

For example, suppose you're a small-business owner looking to purchase new equipment worth $50,000 five years from now. Assuming that your investments earn 5% annual interest, how much will you need to set aside every year to reach this goal? Figure 14.9 shows a worksheet set up to use Goal Seek:

- Cell C6 is the changing cell: the annual deposit into the fund (with an initial value of 0).
- The other cells (C4 and C5) are used as constants for the FV() function.
- Cell C8 contains the FV() function that calculates the future value of the equipment fund. When Goal Seek is done, this cell's value should be $50,000.

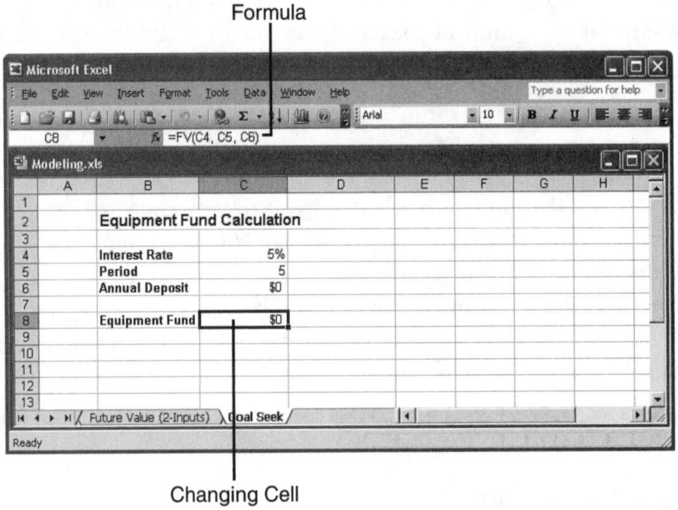

**Figure 14.9**
A worksheet set up to use Goal Seek to find out how much to set aside each year to end up with a $50,000 equipment fund in five years.

Formula

Changing Cell

With your worksheet ready to go, follow these steps to use Goal Seek:

1. Choose Tools, Goal Seek. Excel displays the Goal Seek dialog box.
2. Use the Set Cell text box to enter a reference to the cell that contains the formula you want Goal Seek to manipulate. (Cell C8 in Figure 14.9.)
3. Use the To Value text box to enter the final value you want for the goal cell (such as 50000).
4. Use the By Changing Cell text box to enter a reference to the changing cell. (This is cell C6 in Figure 14.9.) Figure 14.10 shows a completed Goal Seek dialog box.
5. Click OK. Excel begins the iteration and displays the Goal Seek Status dialog box. When finished, the dialog box tells you whether Goal Seek found a solution (see Figure 14.11).

> **NOTE** Most of the time, Goal Seek finds a solution relatively quickly, and the Goal Seek Status dialog box appears on the screen for just a second or two. For longer operations, you can choose Pause in the Goal Seek Status dialog box to stop Goal Seek. To walk through the process one iteration at a time, click the Step button. To resume Goal Seek, click Continue.

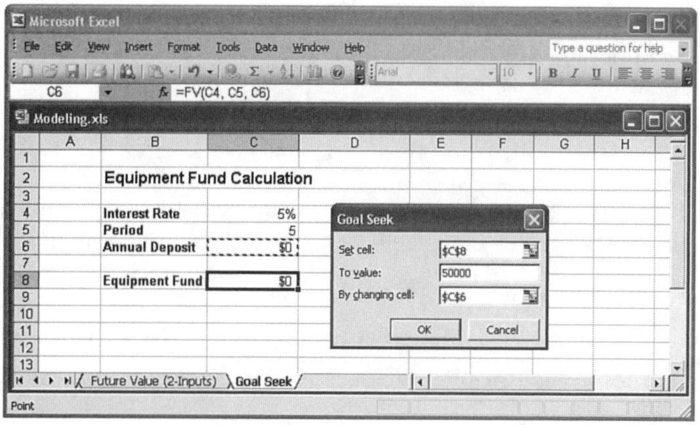

**Figure 14.10**
The completed Goal Seek dialog box.

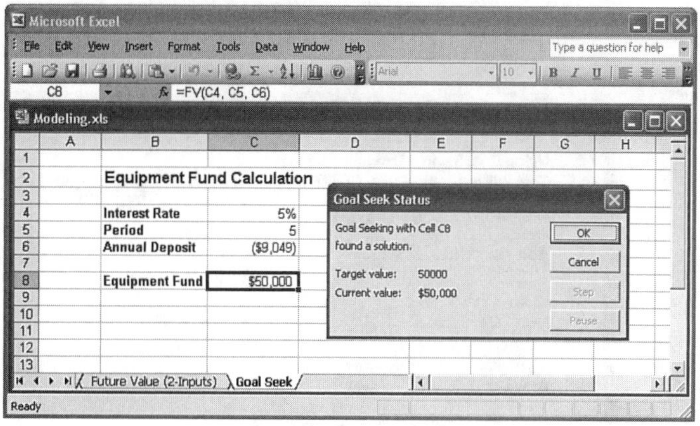

**Figure 14.11**
The Goal Seek Status dialog box shows you the solution (if one was found).

**6.** If Goal Seek found a solution, you can accept the solution by clicking OK. To ignore the solution, click Cancel.

## Optimizing Product Margin

Many businesses use product margin as a measure of fiscal health. A strong margin usually means that expenses are under control and that the market is satisfied with your price points. Product margin depends on many factors, of course, but you can use Goal Seek to find the optimum margin based on a single variable.

For example, suppose that you want to introduce a new product line, and you want the product to return a margin of 30% during the first year. Suppose, too, that you're operating under the following assumptions:

- The sales during the year will be 100,000 units.
- The average discount to your customers will be 40%.

**14**

- The total fixed costs will be $750,000.
- The cost per unit will be $12.63.

Given all this information, you want to know what price point will produce the 30% margin.

Figure 14.12 shows a worksheet set up to handle this situation. An initial value of $1.00 is entered into the Price Per Unit cell (C4), and Goal Seek is set up in the following way:

- The Set Cell reference is C14, the Margin calculation.
- A value of 0.3 (the 30% Margin goal) is entered in the To Value text box.
- A reference to the Price Per Unit cell (C4) is entered into the By Changing Cell text box.

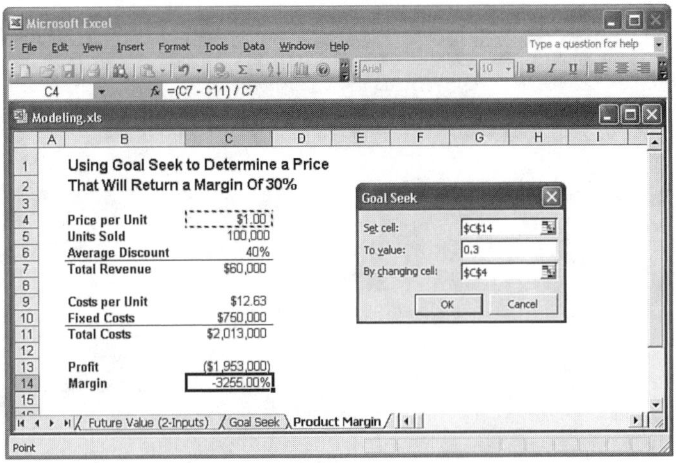

**Figure 14.12**
A worksheet set up to calculate a price point that will optimize gross margin.

When you run Goal Seek, it produces a solution of $47.87 for the price, as shown in Figure 14.13. This solution can be rounded up to $47.95.

## A Note About Goal Seek's Approximations

Notice that the solution in Figure 14.13 is an approximate figure. That is, the margin value is 29.92%, not the 30% we were looking for. That's pretty close (it's off by only 0.0008), but it's not exact. Why didn't Goal Seek find the exact solution?

The answer lies in one of the options Excel uses to control iterative calculations. Some iterations can take an extremely long time to find an exact solution, so Excel compromises by setting certain limits on iterative processes. To see these limits, choose Tools, Options, and select the Calculation tab in the Options dialog box that appears (see Figure 14.14). Two options control iterative processes:

- **Maximum Iterations**—The value in this text box controls the maximum number of iterations. In Goal Seek, this value represents the maximum number of values that Excel plugs into the changing cell.

- **Maximum Change**—The value in this text box is the threshold that Excel uses to determine whether it has converged on a solution. If the difference between the current solution and the desired goal is within this value, Excel stops iterating.

**Figure 14.13**
The result of Goal Seek's labors.

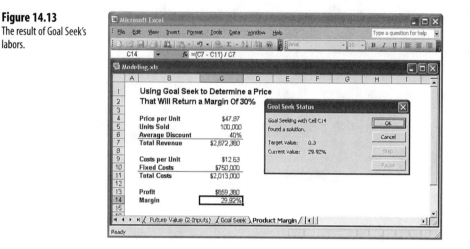

**Figure 14.14**
The text boxes in the Iteration group place limits on iterative calculations.

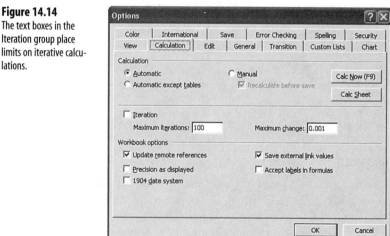

The Maximum Change value prevented us from getting an exact solution for the profit margin calculation. On a particular iteration, Goal Seek found the solution .2992, which put us within 0.0008 of our goal of 0.3. However, 0.0008 is less than the default value of 0.001 in the Maximum Change text box, so Excel called a halt to the procedure.

To get an exact solution, you would need to adjust the Maximum Change value to 0.0001.

## Performing a Break-Even Analysis

In a *break-even analysis,* you determine the number of units you have to sell of a product so that your total profits are 0 (that is, the product revenue equals the product costs). Setting up a profit equation with a goal of 0 and varying the units sold is perfect for Goal Seek.

To try this, we'll extend the example used in the "Optimizing Product Margin" section. In this case, assume a unit price of $47.95 (the solution found to optimize product margin, rounded up to the nearest 95¢). Figure 14.15 shows the Goal Seek dialog box filled out as detailed here:

- The <u>S</u>et Cell reference is set to C13, the profit calculation.
- A value of 0 (the profit goal) is entered in the To <u>V</u>alue text box.
- A reference to the Units Sold cell (C5) is entered into the By <u>C</u>hanging Cell text box.

**Figure 14.15**
A worksheet set up to calculate a price point that optimizes gross margin.

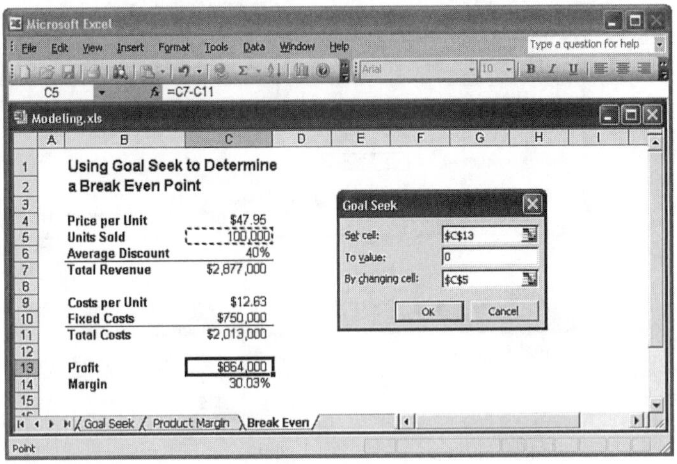

Figure 14.16 shows the solution: A total of 46,468 units must be sold to break even.

## Solving Algebraic Equations

Algebraic equations don't come up all that often in a business context, but they do appear occasionally in complex models. Fortunately, Goal Seek also is useful for solving complex algebraic equations of one variable. For example, suppose that you need to find the value of *x* to solve the rather nasty equation displayed in Figure 14.17. Although this equation is too complex for the quadratic formula, it can be easily rendered in Excel. The left side of the equation can be represented with the following formula:

```
=(((3 * A2 - 8) ^ 2) * (A2 - 1)) / (4 * A2 ^ 2 - 5)
```

Cell A2 represents the variable *x*. You can solve this equation in Goal Seek by setting the goal for this equation to 1 (the right side of the equation) and by varying cell A2. Figure 14.17 shows a worksheet and the Goal Seek dialog box.

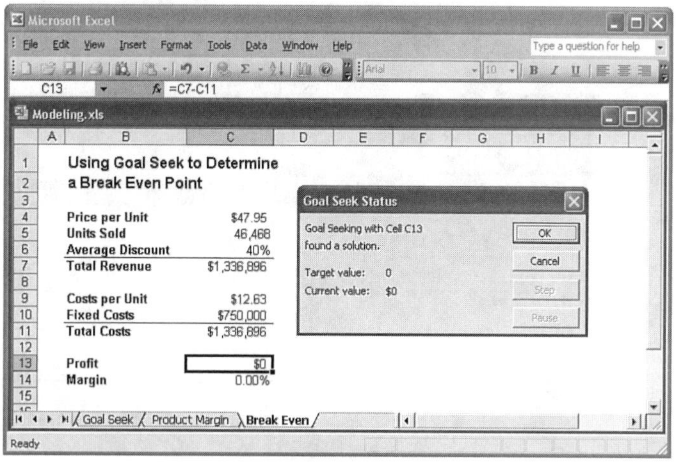

**Figure 14.16**
The break-even solution.

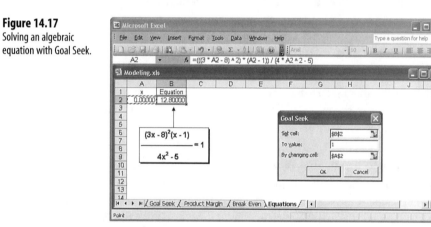

**Figure 14.17**
Solving an algebraic equation with Goal Seek.

Figure 14.18 shows the result. The value in cell A2 is the solution $x$ that satisfies the equation. Notice that the equation result (cell B2) is not quite 1. As mentioned earlier in this chapter, if you need higher accuracy, you must change Excel's convergence threshold. In this example, choose Tools, Options, and in the Calculation tab, type **0.000001** in the Maximum Change text box.

## Goal Seeking with Charts

If you have your data graphed in a 2D bar, column, line, or XY chart, you can run Goal Seek by using the mouse to drag a data marker to a new position. If the data marker represents a formula, Excel uses Goal Seek to work backward and derive the appropriate formula input values.

14

**Figure 14.18**
Cell A2 holds the solution
for the equation in
cell A1.

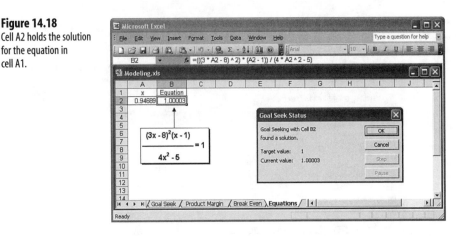

The following example helps explain this process. Suppose that you want to invest some money every year so that in 10 years, you'll have $150,000. Assuming a constant interest rate, how much do you need to set aside annually to reach your goal? The solution is to adjust the chart data marker at 10 years so that it has the value $150,000. The following procedure shows you the steps to follow:

1. Activate the chart and select the specific data marker you want to adjust. Excel adds selection handles to the marker. For the example, select the data marker corresponding to 10 years on the category axis.

2. Drag the black selection handle to the desired value. As you drag the handle, the current value appears in a pop-up, as shown in Figure 14.19.

3. Release the mouse button. If the marker references a number in a cell, Excel changes the number and redraws the chart. If the marker references a formula, as in the example, Excel displays the Goal Seek dialog box, shown in Figure 14.20. The Set Cell text box shows the cell referenced by the data marker, and the To Value text box shows the new number to which you dragged the marker.

4. Enter the appropriate reference in the By Changing Cell text box. For the example, you enter **B2** to calculate the required annual deposit.

5. Click OK. The Goal Seek Status dialog box appears while Excel derives the solution for the new number.

6. When the iteration is complete, click OK. Excel redraws the chart.

14

**Figure 14.19**
Drag the data marker to
the desired value.

Current value

Drag the chart data
marker to the value you want

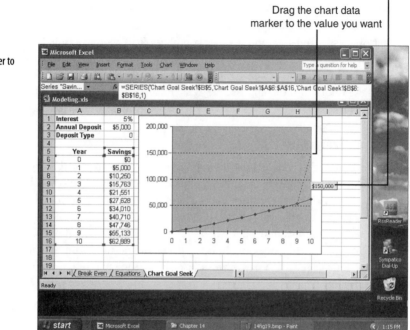

**Figure 14.20**
If the data marker is
derived from a formula,
Excel runs Goal Seek.

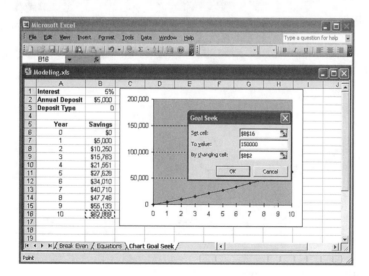

14

# Working with Scenarios

By definition, what-if analysis is not an exact science. All what-if models make guesses and assumptions based on history, expected events, or whatever voodoo comes to mind. A particular set of guesses and assumptions that you plug into a model is called a *scenario*. Because most what-if worksheets can take a wide range of input values, you usually end up with a large number of scenarios to examine. Instead of going through the tedious chore of inserting all these values into the appropriate cells, Excel has a Scenario Manager feature that can handle the process for you. This section shows you how to wield this useful tool.

## Understanding Scenarios

As you've seen in this chapter, Excel has powerful features that enable you to build sophisticated models that can answer complex questions. The problem, though, isn't in *answering* questions, but in *asking* them. For example, Figure 14.21 shows a worksheet model that analyzes a mortgage. You use this model to decide how much of a down payment to make, how long the term should be, and whether to include an extra principal paydown every month. The Results section compares the monthly payment and total paid for the regular mortgage and for the mortgage with a paydown. It also shows the savings and reduced term that result from the paydown.

→ The formula shown in Figure 14.21 uses the PMT ( ) function, which is covered later in the book; **see** "Calculating the Loan Payment," **p. 400**.

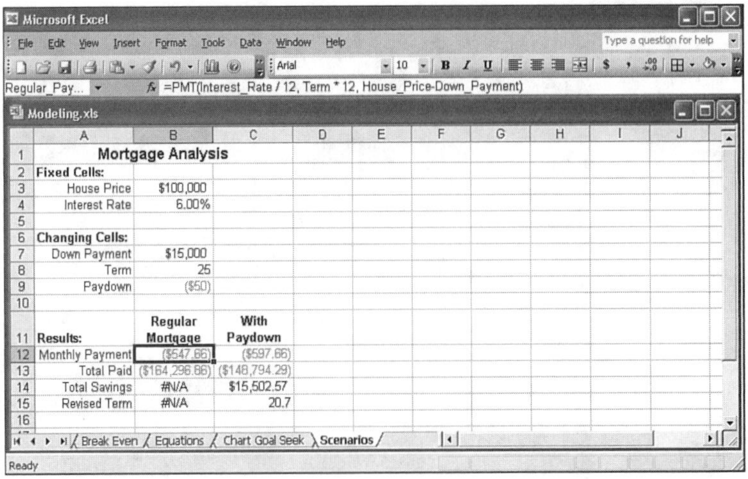

**Figure 14.21**
A mortgage-analysis worksheet.

Here are some possible questions to ask this model:

- How much will I save over the term of the mortgage if I use a shorter term and a larger down payment and include a monthly paydown?
- How much more will I end up paying if I extend the term, reduce the down payment, and forego the paydown?

These are examples of *scenarios* that you would plug into the appropriate cells in the model. Excel's Scenario Manager helps by letting you define a scenario separately from the worksheet. You can save specific values for any or all of the model's input cells, give the scenario a name, and then recall the name (and all the input values it contains) from a list.

## Setting Up Your Worksheet for Scenarios

Before creating a scenario, you need to decide which cells in your model will be the input cells. These will be the worksheet variables—the cells that, when you change them, change the results of the model. (Not surprisingly, Excel calls these the *changing cells*.) You can have as many as 32 changing cells in a scenario. For best results, follow these guidelines when setting up your worksheet for scenarios:

- The changing cells should be constants. Formulas can be affected by other cells, and that can throw off the entire scenario.

- To make it easier to set up each scenario, and to make your worksheet easier to understand, group the changing cells and label them. (See Figure 14.21.)

- For even greater clarity, assign a range name to each changing cell.

## Adding a Scenario

To work with scenarios, you use Excel's Scenario Manager tool. This feature enables you to add, edit, display, and delete scenarios as well as create summary scenario reports.

When your worksheet is set up the way you want it, you can add a scenario to the sheet by following these steps:

1. Choose Tools, Scenarios. Excel displays the Scenario Manager dialog box, shown in Figure 14.22.

**Figure 14.22**
Excel's Scenario Manager enables you to create and work with worksheet scenarios.

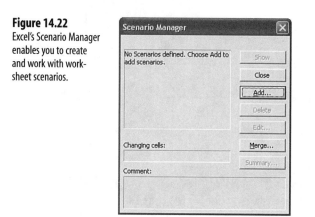

2. Choose Add. The Add Scenario dialog box appears. Figure 14.23 shows a completed version of this dialog box.

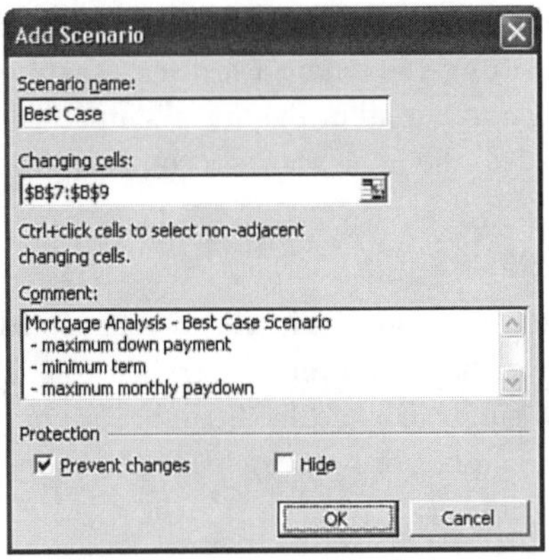

**Figure 14.23**
Use the Add Scenario
dialog box to define a
scenario.

3. Use the Scenario <u>N</u>ame text box to enter a name for the scenario.

4. Use the Changing <u>C</u>ells box to enter references to your worksheet's changing cells. You
   can type in the references (be sure to separate noncontiguous cells with commas) or
   select the cells directly on the worksheet.

5. Use the <u>C</u>omment box to enter a description for the scenario. This appears in the
   Comment section of the Scenario Manager dialog box.

6. Click OK. Excel displays the Scenario Values dialog box, shown in Figure 14.24.

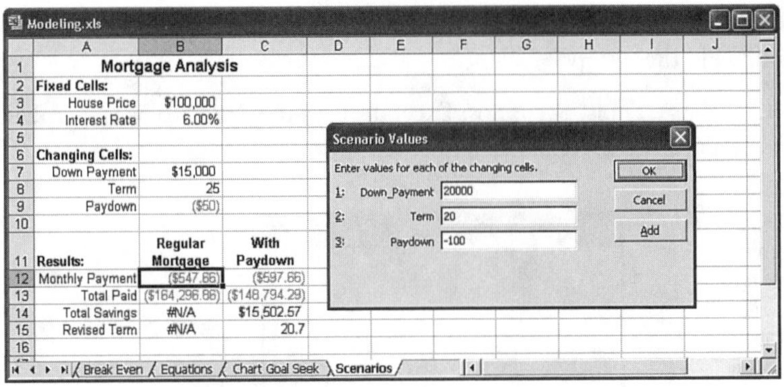

**Figure 14.24**
Use the Scenario Values
dialog box to enter the
values you want to use
for the scenario's chang-
ing cells.

7. Use the text boxes to enter values for the changing cells.

> **NOTE**
> You'll notice in Figure 14.24 that Excel displays the range name for each changing cell, which makes
> it easier to enter your numbers correctly. If your changing cells aren't named, Excel just displays the
> cell addresses instead.

**14**

**8.** To add more scenarios, click <u>A</u>dd to return to the Add Scenario dialog box and repeat steps 3–7. Otherwise, click OK to return to the Scenario Manager dialog box.

**9.** Click Close to return to the worksheet.

## Displaying a Scenario

After you define a scenario, you can enter its values into the changing cells by displaying the scenario from the Scenario Manager dialog box. The following steps give you the details:

**1.** Choose <u>T</u>ools, Sc<u>e</u>narios to display the Scenario Manager.

**2.** In the S<u>c</u>enarios list, click the scenario you want to display.

**3.** Click <u>S</u>how. Excel enters the scenario values into the changing cells. Figure 14.25 shows an example.

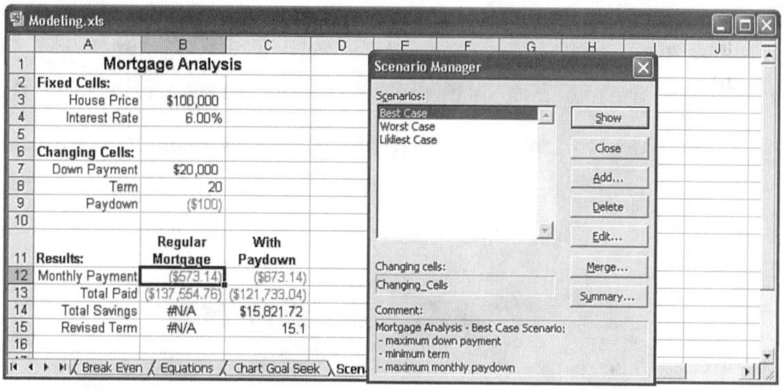

**Figure 14.25**
When you click Show, Excel enters the values for the highlighted scenario into the changing cells.

**4.** Repeat steps 2 and 3 to display other scenarios.

**5.** Click Close to return to the worksheet.

> **TIP**
> Displaying a scenario isn't hard, but it does require having the Scenario Manager onscreen. You can bypass the Scenario Manager by adding the Scenario list to any toolbar. Right-click a toolbar and click <u>C</u>ustomize to display the Customize dialog box. In the Comman<u>d</u>s tab, click Tools in the Categories list. In the Comman<u>d</u>s list, click and drag the Scenario list and drop it on a toolbar. (One caveat, though: If you select the same scenario twice in succession, Excel asks whether you want to redefine the scenario. Click <u>N</u>o to keep the current scenario definition.)

## Editing a Scenario

If you need to make changes to a scenario—whether to change the scenario's name, select different changing cells, or enter new values—follow these steps:

14

1. Choose Tools, Scenarios to display the Scenario Manager.

2. In the Scenarios list, click the scenario you want to edit.

3. Click Edit. Excel displays the Edit Scenario dialog box (which is identical to the Add Scenario dialog box, shown in Figure 14.23).

4. Make your changes, if necessary, and click OK. The Scenario Values dialog box appears (see Figure 14.24).

5. Enter the new values, if necessary, and then click OK to return to the Scenario Manager dialog box.

6. Repeat steps 2 through 5 to edit other scenarios.

7. Click Close to return to the worksheet.

## Merging Scenarios

The scenarios you create are stored with each worksheet in a workbook. If you have similar models in different sheets (for example, budget models for different divisions), you can create separate scenarios for each sheet and then merge them later. Here are the steps to follow:

1. Activate the worksheet in which you want to store the merged scenarios.

2. Choose Tools, Scenarios to display the Scenario Manager.

3. Click Merge. Excel displays the Merge Scenarios dialog box, shown in Figure 14.26.

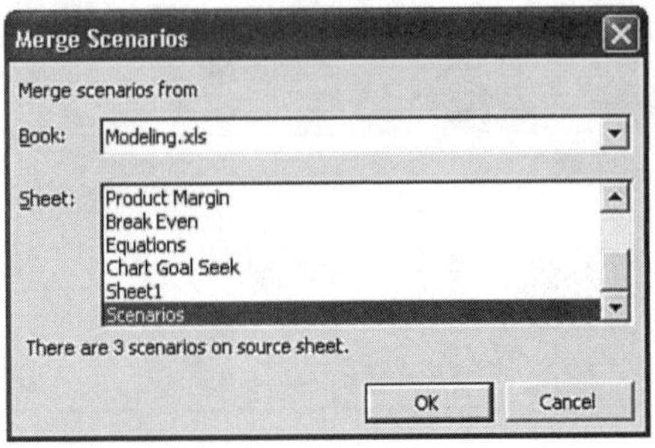

**Figure 14.26**
Use the Merge Scenarios dialog box to select the scenarios you want to merge.

4. Use the Book drop-down list to click the workbook that contains the scenario sheet.

5. Use the Sheet list to click the worksheet that contains the scenario.

6. Click OK to return to the Scenario Manager.

7. Click Close to return to the worksheet.

## Generating a Summary Report

You can create a summary report that shows the changing cells in each of your scenarios along with selected result cells. This is a handy way to compare different scenarios. You can try it by following these steps:

> **NOTE** When Excel sets up the scenario summary, it uses either the cell addresses or defined names of the individual changing cells and results cells, as well as the entire range of changing cells. Your reports will be more readable if you name the cells you'll be using before generating the summary.

1. Choose Tools, Scenarios to display the Scenario Manager.

2. Click Summary. Excel displays the Scenario Summary dialog box.

3. In the Report Type group, click either Scenario Summary or Scenario PivotTable Report.

4. In the Result Cells box, enter references to the result cells that you want to appear in the report (see Figure 14.27). You can select the cells directly on the sheet or type in the references. (Remember to separate noncontiguous cells with commas.)

**Figure 14.27**
Use the Scenario Summary dialog box to select the report type and result cells.

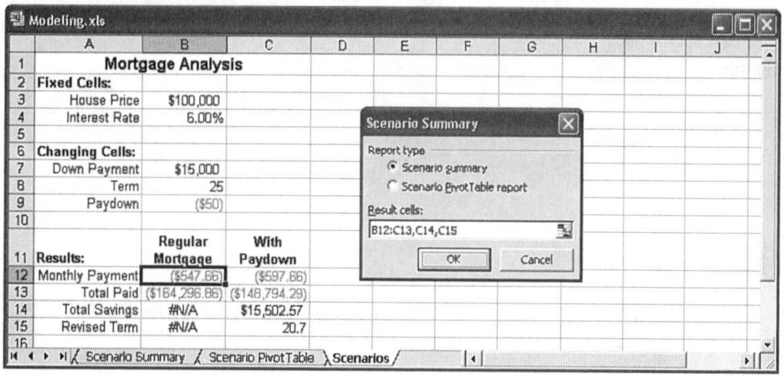

5. Click OK. Excel displays the report.

Figure 14.28 shows the Scenario Summary report for the Mortgage Analysis worksheet. The names shown in column C (Down_Payment, Term, and so on) are the names I assigned to each of the changing cells and result cells.

Figure 14.29 shows the Scenario PivotTable report for the Mortgage Analysis worksheet.

> **NOTE** The PivotTable's page field—labeled Changing Cells By—enables you to switch between scenarios created by different users. If no other users have access to this workbook, you'll see only your name in this field's list.

14

**Figure 14.28**
The Scenario Summary report for the Mortgage Analysis worksheet.

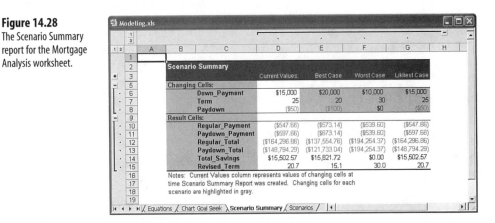

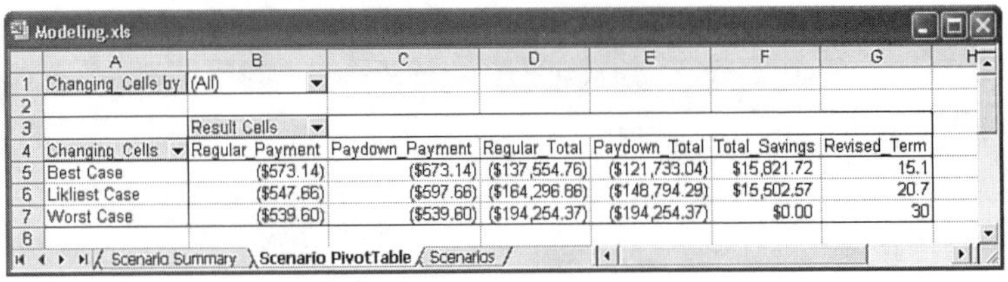

**Figure 14.29**
The Scenario PivotTable report for the Mortgage Analysis worksheet.

## Deleting a Scenario

If you have scenarios that you no longer need, you can delete them by following these steps:

1. Choose <u>T</u>ools, Sc<u>e</u>narios to display the Scenario Manager.
2. Use the S<u>c</u>enarios list to click the scenario you want to delete.

> **CAUTION**
>
> Excel doesn't ask you to confirm the deletion, and there's no way to retrieve a scenario that was deleted accidentally, so be sure that the scenario you highlighted is one you can live without.

3. Click <u>D</u>elete. Excel deletes the scenario.
4. Click Close to return to the worksheet.

## From Here

- To understand and use iterative methods, **see** "Using Iteration and Circular References," **p. 90**.
- Consolidating data is useful for analyzing models that have similar data spread out over multiple sheets. To learn how this is done, **see** "Consolidating Multisheet Data," **p. 92**.

- Goal Seek's "big brother" is the Solver tool. **See** "Solving Complex Problems with Solver," **p. 377**.

- Excel's Solver tool enables you to save its solutions as scenarios. **See** "Saving a Solution as a Scenario," **p. 384**.

- For the details of the `PMT()` function, **see** "Calculating the Loan Payment," **p. 400**.

# Using Regression to Track Trends and Make Forecasts

In these complex and uncertain times, forecasting business performance is increasingly important. Today, more than ever, managers at all levels need to make intelligent predictions of future sales and profit trends as part of their overall business strategy. By forecasting sales six months, a year, or even three years down the road, managers can anticipate related needs such as employee acquisitions, warehouse space, and raw material requirements. Similarly, a profit forecast enables the planning of the future expansion of a company.

Business forecasting has been around for many years, and various methods have been developed—some more successful than others. The most common forecasting method is the qualitative "seat of the pants" approach, in which a manager (or a group of managers) estimates future trends based on experience and knowledge of the market. This method, however, suffers from an inherent subjectivity and a short-term focus because many managers tend to extrapolate from recent experience and ignore the long-term trend. Other methods (such as averaging past results) are more objective but generally are useful for forecasting only a few months in advance.

This chapter presents a technique called *regression analysis*. Regression is a powerful statistical procedure that has become a popular business tool. In its general form, you use regression analysis to determine the relationship between one phenomenon that depends on another. For example, car sales might be dependent on interest rates, and units sold might be dependent on the amount spent on advertising. The dependent phenomenon is called the *dependent variable* or the *y-value*, and the phenomenon upon which it's dependent is called the *independent variable* or the *x-value*. (Think of a chart or

# 15

graph on which the independent variable is plotted along the horizontal [x] axis and the dependent variable is plotted along the vertical [y] axis.)

Given these variables, you can do two things with regression analysis:

- Determine the relationship between the known x- and y-values, and use the results to calculate and visualize the overall trend of the data.
- Use the existing trend to forecast new y-values.

As you'll see in this chapter, Excel is well stocked with tools that enable you to both calculate the current trend and make forecasts no matter what type of data you're dealing with.

## Choosing a Regression Method

Three methods of regression analysis are used most often in business:

- **Simple regression**—Use this type of regression when you're dealing with only one independent variable. For example, if the dependent variable is car sales, the independent variable might be interest rates. You also need to decide whether your data is linear or nonlinear:
  - *Linear* means that if you plot the data on a chart, the resulting data points resemble (roughly) a line.
  - *Nonlinear* means that if you plot the data on a chart, the resulting data points form a curve.
- **Polynomial regression**—Use this type of regression when you're dealing with only one independent variable, but the data fluctuates in such a way that the pattern in the data doesn't resemble either a straight line or a simple curve.
- **Multiple regression**—Use this type of regression when you're dealing with more than one independent variable. For example, if the dependent variable is car sales, the independent variables might be interest rates and disposable income.

You'll learn about all three methods in this chapter.

## Using Simple Regression on Linear Data

With linear data, the dependent variable is related to the independent variable by some constant factor. For example, you might find that car sales (the dependent variable) increase by one million units whenever interest rates (the independent variable) decrease by 1%. Similarly, you might find that division revenue (the dependent variable) increases by $100,000 for every $10,000 you spend on advertising (the independent variable).

## Analyzing Trends Using Best-Fit Lines

You make these sorts of determinations by examining the trend underlying the current data you have for the dependent variable. In linear regression, you analyze the current trend by calculating the *line of best-fit*, or the *trendline*. This is a line through the data points for which the differences between the points above and below the line cancel each other out (more or less).

### Plotting a Best-Fit Trendline

The easiest way to see the best-fit line is to use a chart. Note, however, that this works only if your data is plotted using an XY (scatter) chart. For example, Figure 15.1 shows a worksheet with quarterly sales figures plotted on an XY chart. Here, the quarterly sales is the dependent variable and the period is the independent variable. (In this example, the independent variable is just time, represented, in this case, by fiscal quarters.) I'll add a trendline through the plotted points.

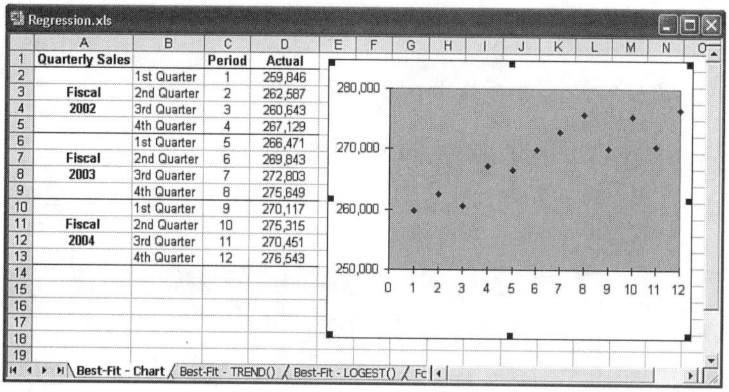


**Figure 15.1**
To see a trendline through your data, first make sure the data is plotted using an XY chart.

> **NOTE** You can download the workbook that contains this chapter's examples here:
> `www.mcfedries.com/ExcelFormulas/`

The following steps show you how to add a trendline to a chart:

1. Activate the chart and, if more than one data series is plotted, click the series you want to work with.
2. Choose Chart, Add Trendline. Excel displays the Add Trendline dialog box, shown in Figure 15.2.
3. On the Type tab, click Linear.
4. Select the Options tab.
5. Activate the Display Equation on Chart check box. (See "Understanding the Regression Equation," later in this chapter.)

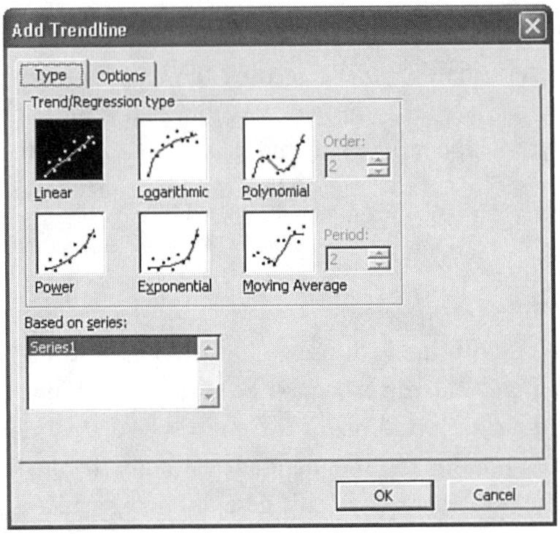

**Figure 15.2**
In the Add Trendline dialog box, use the Type tab to click the type of trendline you want to see.

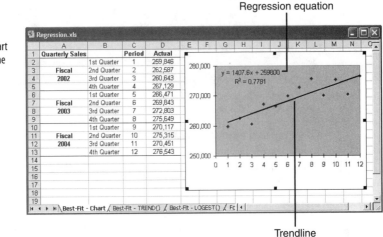

6. Activate the Display R-Squared Value on Chart check box. (See "Understanding $R^2$," later in this chapter.)
7. Click OK. Excel inserts the trendline.

Figure 15.3 shows the best-fit trendline added to the chart.

| Quarterly Sales | | Period | Actual |
|---|---|---|---|
| | 1st Quarter | 1 | 259,846 |
| Fiscal | 2nd Quarter | 2 | 262,587 |
| 2002 | 3rd Quarter | 3 | 260,643 |
| | 4th Quarter | 4 | 267,129 |
| | 1st Quarter | 5 | 266,471 |
| Fiscal | 2nd Quarter | 6 | 269,843 |
| 2003 | 3rd Quarter | 7 | 272,803 |
| | 4th Quarter | 8 | 275,649 |
| | 1st Quarter | 9 | 270,117 |
| Fiscal | 2nd Quarter | 10 | 275,315 |
| 2004 | 3rd Quarter | 11 | 270,451 |
| | 4th Quarter | 12 | 276,543 |

**Figure 15.3**
The quarterly sales chart with a best-fit trendline added.

## Understanding the Regression Equation

In the steps outlined in the previous section, I instructed you to activate the Display Equation on Chart check box. Doing this displays the *regression equation* on the chart, as pointed out in Figure 15.3. This equation is crucial to regression analysis because it gives you a specific formula for the relationship between the dependent variable and the independent variable.

For linear regression, the best-fit trendline is a straight line with an equation that takes the following form:

`y = mx + b`

Here's how you can interpret this equation with respect to the quarterly sales data:

y          This is the dependent variable, so it represents the trendline value (quarterly sales) for a specific period.

x          This is the independent variable, which, in this example, is the period (quarter) you're working with.

m          This is the slope of the trendline. In other words, it's the amount by which the sales increase per period, according to the trendline.

b          This is the y-intercept, which means that it's the starting value for the trend.

Here's the regression equation for the example (see Figure 15.3):

`y = 1407.6x + 259800`

To determine the first point on the trendline, substitute 1 for *x*:

`y = 1407.6 * 1 + 259800`

The result is `261,207.6`.

---

**CAUTION**

It's important not to view the trendline values as somehow trying to predict or estimate the actual y-values (sales). The trendline simply gives you an overall picture of how the y-values change when the x-values change.

---

## Understanding $R^2$

When you click the Display R-Squared Value on Chart check box when adding a trendline, Excel places the following on the chart:

`R² = n`

Here, *n* is called the *coefficient of determination* (statisticians abbreviate it as $r^2$, but Excel uses $R^2$). This is actually the square of the correlation; as you learned in Chapter 12, "Working with Statistical Functions," the correlation tells you something about how well two things are related to each other. In this context, $R^2$ gives you some idea of how well the trendline fits the data. Roughly, it tells you the proportion of the variance in the dependent variable that is associated with the independent variable. Generally, the closer the result is to 1, the better the fit is. Values below about 0.7 mean that the trendline is not a very good fit for the data.

→ To learn about more correlation, **see** "Determining the Correlation Between Data," **p. 271.**

> **TIP**  If you don't get a good fit with the linear trendline, your data might not be linear. Try using a different trendline type to see if you can increase the value of $R^2$.

You'll see in the next section that it's possible to calculate values for the best-fit trendline. Having those values enables you to calculate the correlation between the known y-values and the generated trend values using the CORREL() function:

```
=CORREL(known_y's, trend_values)
```

Here, *known_y's* is a range reference to the dependent variable values that you know (such as the sales figures in D2:D13 in Figure 15.3), and *trend_values* is a range or array containing the calculated trend points. Note that squaring the CORREL() result gives you the value of $R^2$.

### Calculating Best-Fit Values Using TREND()

The problem with using a chart best-fit trendline is that you don't get actual values to work with. If you want to get some values on the worksheet, you can calculate individual trendline values using the regression equation. However, what if the underlying data changes? For example, those values might be estimates, or they might change as more accurate data comes in. In that case, you need to delete the existing trendline, add a new one, and then recalculate the trend values based on the new equation.

If you need to work with worksheet trend values, you can avoid having to perform repeated trendline analyses by calculating the values using Excel's TREND() function:

```
TREND(known_y's, [known_x's], [new_x's], [const])
```

| | |
|---|---|
| *known_y's* | A range reference or array of the known y-values—such as the historical values—from which you want to calculate the trend. |
| *known_x's* | A range reference or array of the x-values associated with the known y-values. If you omit this argument, the known x's are assumed to be the array {1,2,3,...,n}, where n is the number of known y's. |
| *new_x's* | A range reference or array of the new x-values for which you want corresponding y-values. |
| *const* | A logical value that determines where Excel places the y-intercept. If you use FALSE, the y-intercept is placed at 0; if you use TRUE (this is the default), Excel calculates the y-intercept based on the known y's. |

To generate the best-fit trend values, you need to specify the only *known_y's* argument and, optionally, the *known_x's* argument. In the quarterly sales example, the known y-values are the actual sales numbers, which lie in the range D2:D13. The known x-values are the period numbers in the range C2:C13. Therefore, to calculate the best-fit trend values, you select a range that is the same size as the known values and enter the following formula as an array:

```
{=TREND(D2:D13, C2:C13)}
```

Figure 15.4 shows the results of this `TREND()` array formula in column F. For comparison purposes, the sheet also includes the trend values generated using the regression equation from the chart trendline shown in Figure 15.3. (Note that some of the values are slightly off. That's because the values for the slope and intercept shown in the regression equation have been rounded off for display in the chart.)

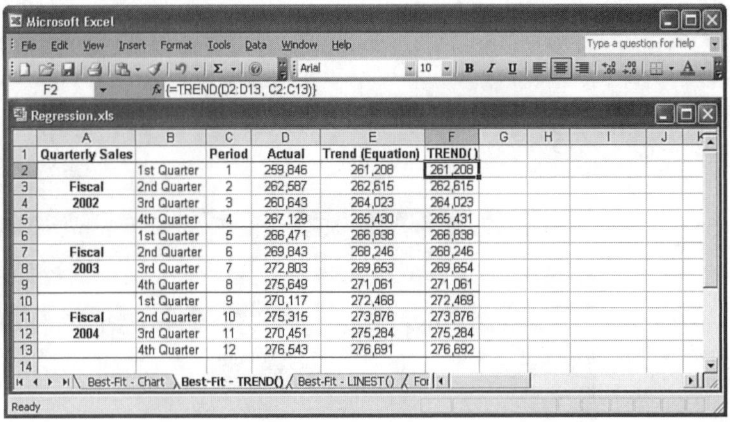

| | A | B | C | D | E | F |
|---|---|---|---|---|---|---|
| 1 | **Quarterly Sales** | | **Period** | **Actual** | **Trend (Equation)** | **TREND()** |
| 2 | | 1st Quarter | 1 | 259,846 | 261,208 | 261,208 |
| 3 | **Fiscal** | 2nd Quarter | 2 | 262,587 | 262,615 | 262,615 |
| 4 | **2002** | 3rd Quarter | 3 | 260,643 | 264,023 | 264,023 |
| 5 | | 4th Quarter | 4 | 267,129 | 265,430 | 265,431 |
| 6 | | 1st Quarter | 5 | 266,471 | 266,838 | 266,838 |
| 7 | **Fiscal** | 2nd Quarter | 6 | 269,843 | 268,246 | 268,246 |
| 8 | **2003** | 3rd Quarter | 7 | 272,803 | 269,653 | 269,654 |
| 9 | | 4th Quarter | 8 | 275,649 | 271,061 | 271,061 |
| 10 | | 1st Quarter | 9 | 270,117 | 272,468 | 272,469 |
| 11 | **Fiscal** | 2nd Quarter | 10 | 275,315 | 273,876 | 273,876 |
| 12 | **2004** | 3rd Quarter | 11 | 270,451 | 275,284 | 275,284 |
| 13 | | 4th Quarter | 12 | 276,543 | 276,691 | 276,692 |



**Figure 15.4**
Best-fit trend values (F2:F13) created with the `TREND()` function.

> **TIP**
> In the previous section, I mentioned that you can determine the correlation between the known dependent values and the calculated trend values by using the `CORREL()` function. Here's an array formula that provides a shorthand method for returning the correlation:
>
> `{=CORREL(known_y's, TREND(known_y's, known_x's)}`

## Calculating Best-Fit Values Using `LINEST()`

`TREND()` is the most direct route for calculating trend values, but Excel offers a second method that calculates the trendline's slope and y-intercept. You can then plug these values into the general linear regression equation—y = mx + b—as *m* and *b*, respectively. You calculate the slope and y-intercept using the `LINEST()` function:

`LINEST(known_y's, [known_x's], [const], [stats])`

*`known_y's`* — A range reference or array of the known y-values from which you want to calculate the trend.

*`known_x's`* — A range reference or array of the x-values associated with the known y-values. If you omit this argument, the known *x*'s are assumed to be the array {1,2,3,...,*n*}, where *n* is the number of known *y*'s.

*`const`* — A logical value that determines where Excel places the y-intercept. If you use `FALSE`, the y-intercept is placed at 0; if you use `TRUE` (this is the default), Excel calculates the y-intercept based on the known *y*'s.

*`stats`* — A logical value that determines whether `LINEST()` returns additional regression statistics besides the slope and intercept. The default is `FALSE`.

When you use LINEST() without the *stats* argument, the function returns a 1×2 array, where the value in the first column is the slope of the trendline and the value in the second column is the intercept. For example, the following formula, entered as a 1×2 array, returns the slope and intercept of the quarterly sales trendline:

```
{=LINEST(D2:D13, C2:C13)}
```

In Figure 15.5, the returned array values are shown in cells H2 and I2. This worksheet also uses these values to compute the trendline values by substituting $H$2 for *m* and $I$2 for *b* in the linear regression equation. For example, the following formula calculates the trend value for period 1:

```
=$H$2 * C2 + $I$2
```

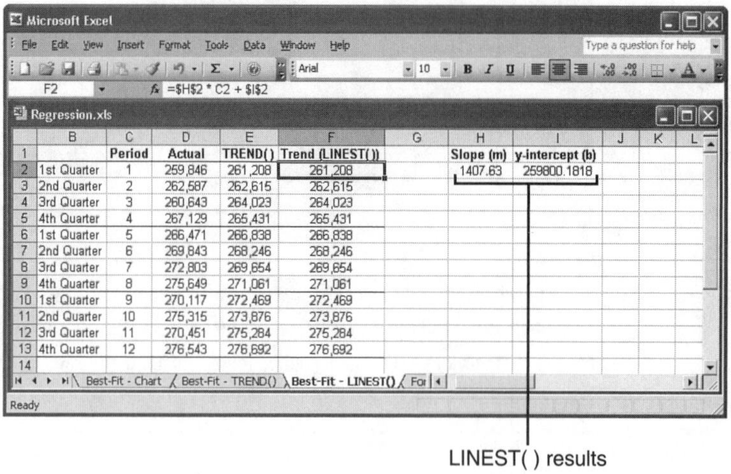

**Figure 15.5**
Best-fit trend values (F2:F13) created with the results of the LINEST() function (H2:I2) plugged into the linear regression equation.

LINEST() results

If you set the *stats* argument to TRUE, the LINEST() function returns 10 regression statistics in a 5×2 array. The returned statistics are listed in Table 5.1, and Figure 15.6 shows an example of the returned array.

**Table 5.1  Regression Statistics Returned by LINEST() When the *stats* Argument Is Set to TRUE**

| Array Location | Statistic | Description |
| --- | --- | --- |
| Row 1 Column 1 | m | The slope of the trendline. |
| Row 1 Column 2 | b | The y-intercept of the trendline. |
| Row 2 Column 2 | se | The standard error value for *m*. |
| Row 2 Column 2 | seb | The standard error value for *b*. |
| Row 3 Column 1 | $R^2$ | The coefficient of determination. |
| Row 3 Column 2 | sey | The standard error value for the *y* estimate. |

| Array Location | Statistic | Description |
|---|---|---|
| Row 4 Column 1 | F | The $F$ statistic. |
| Row 4 Column 2 | df | The degrees of freedom. |
| Row 5 Column 1 | ssreg | The regression sum of squares. |
| Row 5 Column 2 | ssresid | The residual sum of squares. |

**15**

> **NOTE**
>
> These and other regression statistics are available via the Analysis ToolPak's Regression tool. Assuming that the Analysis ToolPak add-in is installed, choose Tools, Data Analysis; select Regression; and then click OK. Use the Regression dialog box to specify the ranges for the y-values and x-values, and to choose which statistics you want to see in the output.

**Figure 15.6**
The range H5:I9 contains the array of regression statistics returned by LINEST() when its stats argument is set to TRUE.

Most of these values are beyond the scope of this book. However, notice that one of the returned values is $R^2$, the coefficient of determination that tells how well the trendline fits the data. If you want just this value from the LINEST() array, use this formula (see cell I11 in Figure 15.6):

```
=INDEX(LINEST(known_y's, known_x's, , TRUE), 3, 1)
```

> **NOTE**
>
> You can also calculate the slope, intercept, and $R^2$ value directly by using the following functions:
>
> ```
> SLOPE(known_y's, known_x's)
> INTERCEPT(known_y's, known_x's)
> RSQ(known_y's, known_x's)
> ```
>
> The syntax for these functions is the same as that of the first two arguments of the TREND() function, except that the known_x's argument is required. Here's an example:
>
> ```
> =RSQ(D2:D13, C2:C13)
> ```

**15**

## Analyzing the Sales Versus Advertising Trend

We tend to think of trend analysis as having a time component. That is, when we think about looking for a trend, we usually think about finding a pattern over a period of time. But regression analysis is more versatile than that. You can use it to compare any two phenomena, as long as one is dependent on the other in some way.

For example, it's reasonable to assume that there is some relationship between how much you spend on advertising and how much you sell. In this case, the advertising costs are the independent variable and the sales revenues are the dependent variable. We can apply regression analysis to investigate the exact nature of the relationship.

Figure 5.7 shows a worksheet that does this. The advertising costs are in A2:A13, and the sales revenues over the same period (these could be monthly numbers, quarterly numbers, and so on—the time period doesn't matter) are in B2:B13. The rest of the worksheet applies the same trend-analysis techniques that you learned over the past few sections.

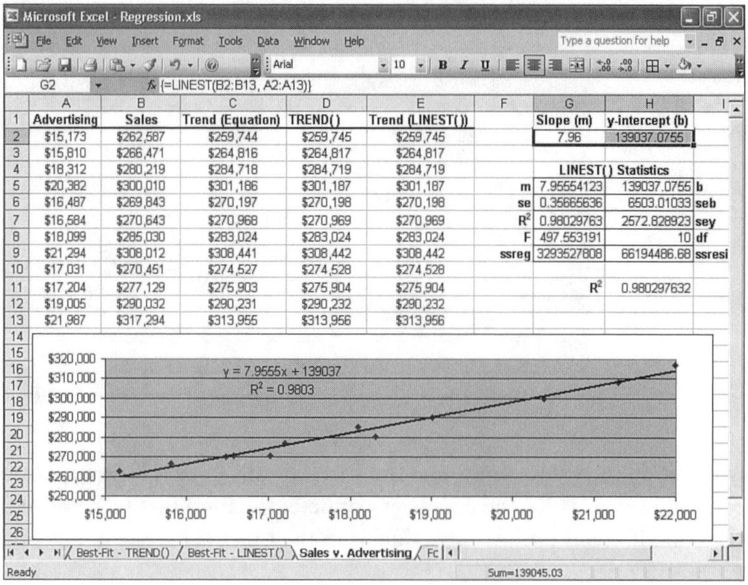

**Figure 15.7**
A trend analysis for advertising costs versus sales revenues.

## Making Forecasts

Knowing the overall trend exhibited by a data set is useful because it tells you the broad direction that sales or costs or employee acquisitions is going, and it gives you a good idea of how related the dependent variable is on the independent variable. But a trend is also useful for making forecasts in which you extend the trendline into the future (what will sales be in the first quarter of next year?) or calculate the trend value given some new independent value (if we spend $25,000 on advertising, what will the corresponding sales be?).

How accurate is such a prediction? A projection based on historical data assumes that the factors influencing the data over the historical period will remain constant. If this is a reasonable assumption in your case, the projection will be a reasonable one. Of course, the longer you extend the line, the more likely it is that some of the factors will change or that new ones will arise. As a result, best-fit extensions should be used only for short-term projections.

## Plotting Forecasted Values

If you want just a visual idea of the forecasted trend, you can extend the chart trendline that you created earlier. The following steps show you how to add a forecasting trendline to a chart:

1. Activate the chart and, if more than one data series is plotted, click the series you want to work with.

2. Choose Chart, Add Trendline to display the Add Trendline dialog box.

3. On the Type tab, click Linear.

4. Select the Options tab.

5. Activate the Display Equation on Chart check box. (See "Understanding the Regression Equation," previously in this chapter.)

6. Activate the Display R-Squared Value on Chart check box. (See "Understanding $R^2$," previously in this chapter.)

7. Use the Forward spinner to select the number of units you want to project the trendline into the future. (For example, to extend the quarterly sales number into the next year, you set Forward to 4 to extend the trendline by four quarters.)

8. Click OK. Excel inserts the trendline and extends it into the future.

Figure 15.8 shows the quarterly sales trendline extended by four quarters.

**Figure 15.8**
The trendline has been extended four quarters into the future.

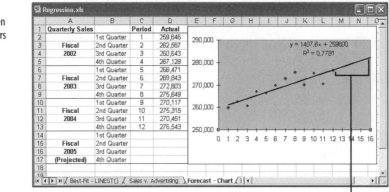

Extended trendline

**15**

## Extending a Linear Trend with the Fill Handle

If you prefer to see exact data points in your forecast, you can use the fill handle to project a best-fit line into the future. Here are the steps to follow:

1. Select the historical data on the worksheet.

2. Click and drag the fill handle to extend the selection. Excel calculates the best-fit line from the existing data, projects this line into the new data, and calculates the appropriate values.

Figure 15.9 shows an example. Here, I've used the fill handle to project the period numbers and quarterly sales figures over the next fiscal year. The accompanying chart clearly shows the extended best-fit line.

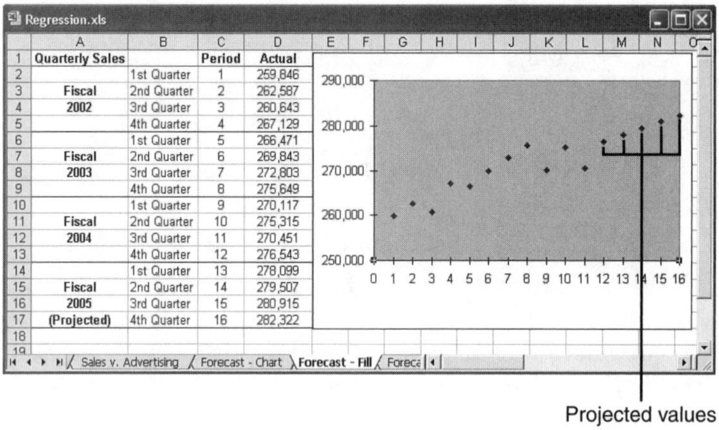

**Figure 15.9**
When you use the fill handle to extend historical data into the future, Excel uses a linear projection to calculate the new values.

Projected values

## Extending a Linear Trend Using the Series Command

You also can use the Series command to project a best-fit line. The following steps show you how it's done:

1. Select the range that includes both the historical data and the cells that will contain the projections (make sure that the projection cells are blank).

2. Choose Edit, Fill, Series. Excel displays the Series dialog box.

3. Activate AutoFill.

4. Click OK. Excel fills in the blank cells with the best-fit projection.

The Series command is also useful for producing the data that defines the full best-fit line so that you can see the actual trendline values. The following steps show you how it's done:

1. Copy the historical data into an adjacent row or column.

2. Select the range that includes both the copied historical data and the cells that will contain the projections (again, make sure that the projection cells are blank).

3. Choose <u>E</u>dit, F<u>i</u>ll, <u>S</u>eries. Excel displays the Series dialog box.

4. Activate the <u>T</u>rend check box.

5. Select the <u>L</u>inear option.

6. Click OK. Excel replaces the copied historical data with the best-fit numbers and projects the trend onto the blank cells.

In Figure 15.10, the trend values created by the Series command are in E2:E13 and are plotted on the chart with the best-fit line on top of the historical data.

**Figure 15.10**
A best-fit trendline created with the Series command.

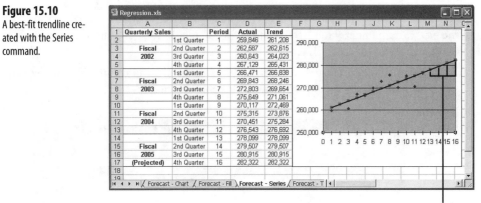

Trend values

## Forecasting with the Regression Equation

You can also forecast individual dependent values by using the regression equation returned when you add the chart trendline. (Remember that you must click the Display <u>E</u>quation on Chart check box when adding the trendline.) Recall the general regression equation for a linear model:

```
y = mx + b
```

The regression equation displayed by the trendline feature gives you the *m* and *b* values, so to determine a new value for *y*, just plug in a new value for *x*.

For example, in the quarterly sales model, Excel calculated the following regression equation:

```
y = 1407.6x + 259800
```

To find the trend value for the 13th period, you substitute 13 for x:

```
y = 1407.6 * 13 + 259800
```

The result is 278,099, the projected sales for the 13th period (first quarter 2005).

## Forecasting with TREND()

The TREND() function is also capable of forecasting new values. To extend the trend and generate new values, you need to add the *new_x's* argument to the TREND() function. Here's the basic procedure for setting this up on the worksheet:

1. Add the new x-values to the worksheet. For example, to extend the quarterly sales trend into the next fiscal year, you'd add the values 13 through 16 to the Period column.

2. Select a range large enough to hold all the new values. For example, if you're adding four new values, select four cells in a column or row, depending on the structure of your data.

3. Enter the TREND() function as an array formula, specifying the range of new x-value as the *new_x's* argument. Here's the formula for the quarterly sales example:

   `{=TREND(D2:D13, C2:C13, C14:C17)}`

Figure 15.11 shows the forecasted values in F14:F17. The values in column E were derived using the regression equation and are included for comparison.

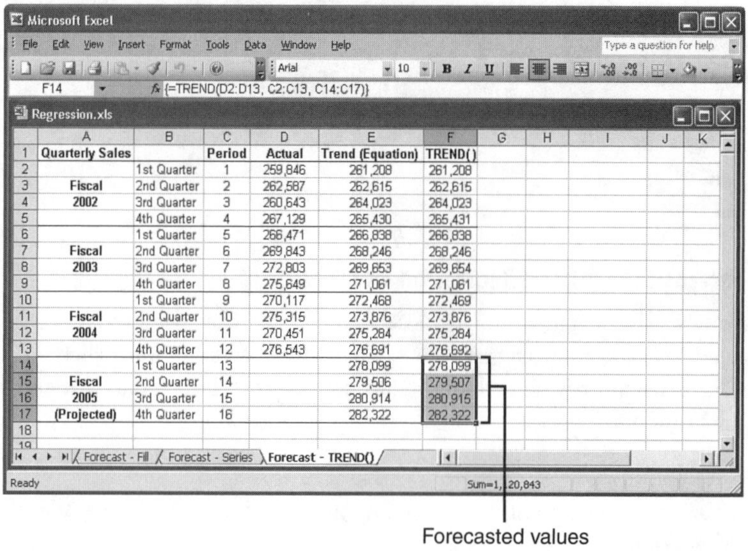

**Figure 15.11**
The range F14:F17 contains the forecasted values calculated by the TREND() function.

Forecasted values

## Forecasting with LINEST()

Recall that the LINEST() function returns the slope and y-intercept of the trendline. When you know these numbers, forecasting new values is a straightforward matter of plugging them into the linear regression equation along with a new value of *x*. For example, if the slope is in cell H2, the intercept is in I2, and the new x-value is in C13, the following formula will return the forecasted value:

`=H2 * C14 + I2`

Figure 15.12 shows a worksheet that uses this method to forecast the Fiscal 2005 sales figures.

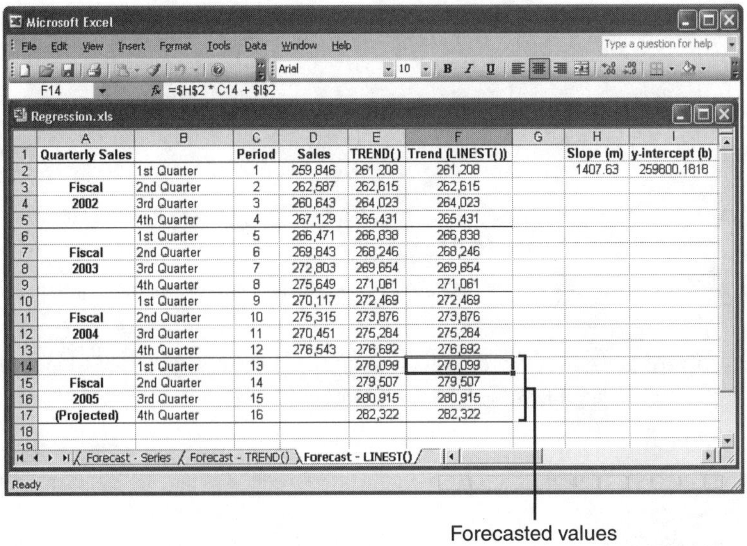

**Figure 15.12**
The range F14:F17 contains the forecasted values calculated by the regression equation using the slope (H2) and intercept (I2) returned by the LINEST() function.

Forecasted values

> **NOTE**
>
> You can also calculate a forecasted value for *x* by using the FORECAST() function:
>
>     FORECAST(*x*, *known_y's*, *known_x's*)
>
> Here, *x* is the new x-value that you want to work with, and *known_y*'s and *known_x*'s are the same as with the TREND() function (except that the *known_x*'s argument is required). Here's an example:
>
>     =FORECAST(13, D2:D13, C2:C13)

## CASE STUDY

# Trend Analysis and Forecasting for a Seasonal Sales Model

This case study applies some of the forecasting techniques from the previous sections to a more sophisticated sales model. The worksheets you'll see explore two different cases:

- Sales as a function of time. Essentially, this case determines the trend over time of past sales and extrapolates the trend in a straight line to determine future sales.

- Sales as a function of the season (in a business sense). Many businesses are seasonal—that is, their sales are traditionally higher or lower during certain periods of the fiscal year. Retailers, for example, usually have higher sales in the fall leading up to Christmas. If the sales for your business are a function of the season, you need to remove these seasonal biases to calculate the true underlying trend.

## About the Forecast Workbook

The Forecast workbook contains the following eight worksheets:

- **Monthly Data**—Use this worksheet to enter up to 10 years of monthly historical data. This worksheet also calculates the 12-month moving averages used by the Monthly Seasonal Index worksheet. Note that the data in column C—specifically, the range C2:C121—is a range named Actual.

- **Monthly Seasonal Index**—Calculates the seasonal adjustment factors (the seasonal indexes) for the monthly data.

- **Monthly Trend**—Calculates the trend of the monthly historical data. Both a normal trend and a seasonally adjusted trend are computed.

- **Monthly Forecast**—Derives a three-year monthly forecast based on both the normal trend and the seasonally adjusted trend.

- **Quarterly Data**—Consolidates the monthly actuals into quarterly data and calculates the four-quarter moving average (used by the Quarterly Seasonal Index worksheet).

- **Quarterly Seasonal Index**—Calculates the seasonal indexes for the quarterly data.

- **Quarterly Trend**—Calculates the trend of the quarterly historical data. Both a normal trend and a seasonally adjusted trend are computed.

- **Quarterly Forecast**—Derives a three-year quarterly forecast based on both the normal trend and the seasonally adjusted trend.

> **TIP**
>
> The Forecast workbook contains dozens of formulas. You'll probably want to switch to manual calculation mode when working with this file.

The sales forecast workbook is driven entirely by the historical data entered into the Monthly Data worksheet, shown in Figure 15.13.

## Calculating a Normal Trend

As mentioned earlier, you can calculate either a normal trend that treats all sales as a simple function of time or a deseasoned trend that takes seasonal factors into account. This section covers the normal trend.

All the trend calculations in the workbook use a variation of the TREND() function. Recall that the TREND() function's *known_x's* argument is optional; if you omit it, Excel uses the array $\{1, 2, 3, ...n\}$, where $n$ is the number of values in the *known_y's* argument. When the independent variable is time related, you can usually get away with omitting the *known_x's* argument because the values are just the period numbers.

In this case study, the independent variable is in terms of months, so you can leave out the *known_x's* argument. The *known_y's* argument is the data in the Actual column, which, as I pointed out earlier, has been given the range name Actual. Therefore, the following array formula generates the best-fit trend values for the existing data:

```
{=TREND(Actual)}
```

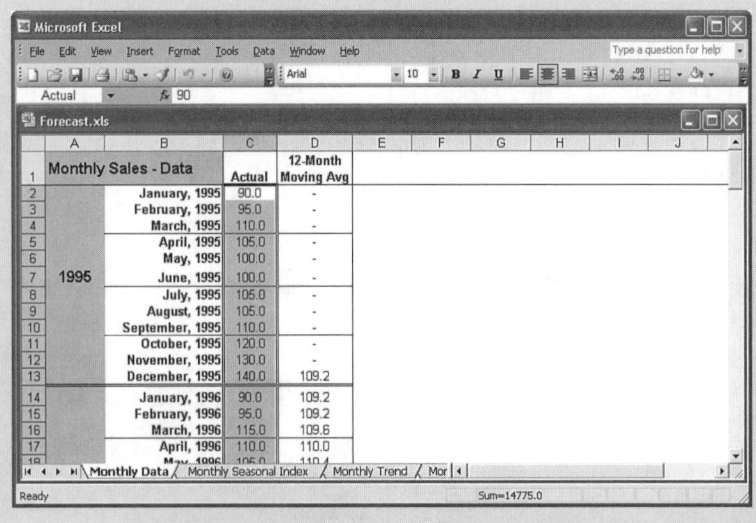

**Figure 15.13**
The Monthly Data worksheet contains the historical sales data.

This formula generates the values in the Normal Trend column of the Monthly Trend worksheet, shown in Figure 15.14.

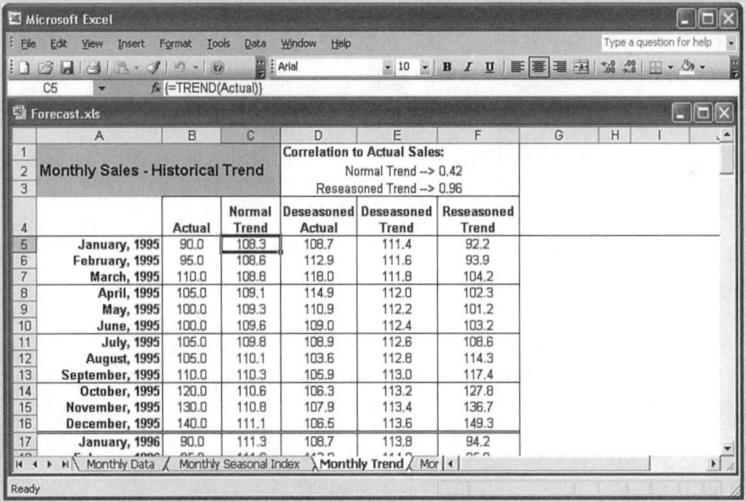

**Figure 15.14**
The Normal Trend column uses the TREND( ) function to return the best-fit trend values for the data in the Actual range.

**NOTE**
The values in column B of the Monthly Trend sheet are linked to the values in the Actual column of the Monthly Data worksheet. You use the values in the Monthly Data worksheet to calculate the trend, so, technically, you don't need the figures in column B. I included them, however, to make it easier to compare the trend and the actuals. Including the Actual values is also handy if you want to create a chart that includes these values.

15

To get some idea of whether the trend is close to your data, cell F2 calculates the correlation between the trend values and the actual sales figures:

```
{=CORREL(Actual, TREND(Actual))}
```

The correlation value of 0.42—and its corresponding value of $R^2$ of about 0.17—shows that the normal trend doesn't fit this data very well. We'll fix that later by taking the seasonal nature of the historical data into account.

## Calculating the Forecast Trend

As you saw earlier in this chapter, to get a sales forecast, you extend the historical trendline into the future. This is the job of the Monthly Forecast worksheet, shown in Figure 15.15.

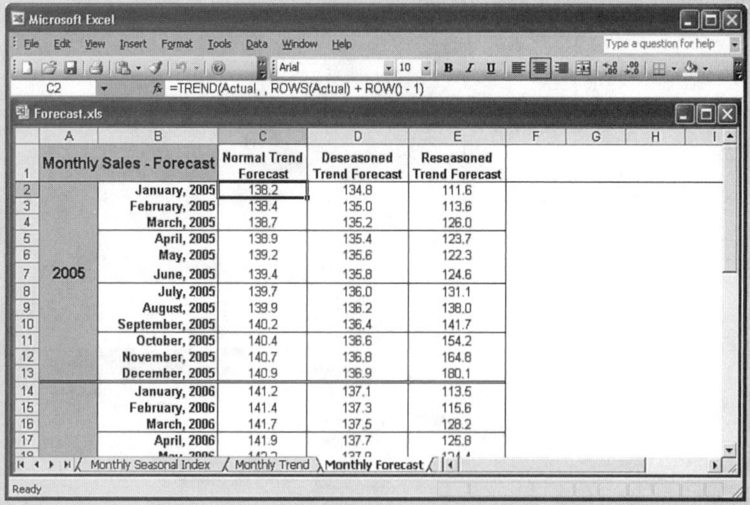


| | A | B | C | D | E |
|---|---|---|---|---|---|
| 1 | Monthly Sales - Forecast | | Normal Trend Forecast | Deseasoned Trend Forecast | Reseasoned Trend Forecast |
| 2 | 2005 | January, 2005 | 138.2 | 134.8 | 111.6 |
| 3 | | February, 2005 | 138.4 | 135.0 | 113.6 |
| 4 | | March, 2005 | 138.7 | 135.2 | 126.0 |
| 5 | | April, 2005 | 138.9 | 135.4 | 123.7 |
| 6 | | May, 2005 | 139.2 | 135.6 | 122.3 |
| 7 | | June, 2005 | 139.4 | 135.8 | 124.6 |
| 8 | | July, 2005 | 139.7 | 136.0 | 131.1 |
| 9 | | August, 2005 | 139.9 | 136.2 | 138.0 |
| 10 | | September, 2005 | 140.2 | 136.4 | 141.7 |
| 11 | | October, 2005 | 140.4 | 136.6 | 154.2 |
| 12 | | November, 2005 | 140.7 | 136.8 | 164.8 |
| 13 | | December, 2005 | 140.9 | 136.9 | 180.1 |
| 14 | | January, 2006 | 141.2 | 137.1 | 113.5 |
| 15 | | February, 2006 | 141.4 | 137.3 | 115.6 |
| 16 | | March, 2006 | 141.7 | 137.5 | 128.2 |
| 17 | | April, 2006 | 141.9 | 137.7 | 125.8 |

**Figure 15.15**
The Monthly Forecast worksheet calculates a sales forecast by extending the historical trend data.

Calculating a forecast trend requires that you specify the *new_x's* argument for the `TREND()` function. In this case, the *new_x's* are the sales periods in the forecast interval. For example, suppose that you have a 10-year period of monthly data from January 1995 to December 2004. This involves 120 periods of data. Therefore, to calculate the trend for January 2005 (the 121st period), you use the following formula:

```
=TREND(Actual, , 121)
```

You use `122` as the *new_x's* argument for February 2005, `123` for March 2005, and so on.

The Monthly Forecast worksheet uses the following formula to calculate these *new_x's* values:

```
ROWS(Actual) + ROW() - 1
```

`ROWS(Actual)` returns the number of sales periods in the Actual range in the Monthly Data worksheet. `ROW() - 1` is a trick that returns the number you need to add to get the forecast sales period. For example, the January 2005 forecast is in cell C2; therefore, `ROW() - 1` returns 1.

## Calculating the Seasonal Trend

Many businesses experience predictable fluctuations in sales throughout their fiscal year. Resort operators see most of their sales during the summer months; retailers look forward to the Christmas season for the revenue that will carry them through the rest of the year. Figure 15.16 shows a sales chart for a company that experiences a large increase in sales during the fall.

**Figure 15.16**
A chart for a company showing seasonal sales variations.

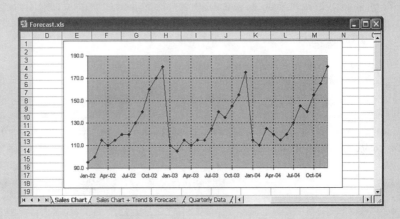

Because of the nature of the sales in companies that see seasonal fluctuations, the normal trend calculation won't give an accurate forecast. You need to include seasonal variations in your analysis, which involves four steps:

1.  For each month (or quarter), calculate a *seasonal index* that identifies seasonal influences.
2.  Use these indexes to calculate seasonally adjusted (or *deseasoned*) values for each month.
3.  Calculate the trend based on these deseasoned values.
4.  Compute the true trend by adding the seasonal indexes to the calculated trend (from step 3).

The next few sections show how the Forecast workbook implements each step.

## Computing the Monthly Seasonal Indexes

A *seasonal index* is a measure of how the average sales in a given month compare to a "normal" value. For example, if January has an index of 90, January's sales are (on average) only 90% of what they are in a normal month.

Therefore, you must first define what "normal" signifies. Because you're dealing with monthly data, you define normal as the 12-month moving average. (An *n*-month moving average is the average taken over the past *n* months.) The 12-Month Moving Avg column in the Monthly Data sheet (see column D in Figure 15.13) uses a formula named `TwelveMonthMovingAvg` to handle this calculation. This is a relative range name, so its definition changes with each cell in the column.

For example, here's the formula that's used in cell D13:

```
=AVERAGE(C13:C2)
```

In other words, this formula calculates the average for the range C2:C13, which is the preceding 12 months.

This moving average defines the "normal" value for any given month. The next step is to compare each month to the moving average. This is done by dividing each monthly sales figure by its corresponding moving-average calculation and multiplying by 100—which equals the sales *ratio* for the month. For example, the sales in December 1995 (cell C13) were 140.0, and the moving average is 109.2 (D13). Dividing C13 by D13 and multiplying by 100 returns a ratio of about 128. You can loosely interpret this to mean that the sales in December were 28% higher than the sales in a normal month.

To get an accurate seasonal index for December (or any month), however, you must calculate ratios for every December that you have historical data. Take an average of all these ratios to reach a true seasonal index (except for a slight adjustment, as you'll see).

The purpose of the Monthly Seasonal Index worksheet, shown in Figure 15.17, is to derive a seasonal index for each month. The worksheet's table calculates the ratios for every month over the span of the historical data. The Avg Ratio column then calculates the average for each month. To get the final values for the seasonal indexes, however, you need to make a small adjustment. The indexes should add up to 1,200 (100 per month, on average) to be true percentages. As you can see in cell B15, however, the sum is 1,214.0. This means that you have to reduce each average by a factor of 1.0116 (1,214/1,200). The Seasonal Index column does that, thereby producing the true seasonal indexes for each month.

**Figure 15.17**

The Monthly Seasonal Index worksheet calculates the seasonal index for each month based on the monthly historical data.

| | | Avg. Ratio | Seasonal Index | 1995 Ratios* | 1996 Ratios | 1997 Ratios | 1998 Ratios | 1999 Ratios | 2000 Ratios | 2001 Ratios | 2002 Ratios | 2003 Ratios | 2004 Ratios |
|---|---|---|---|---|---|---|---|---|---|---|---|---|---|
| 3 | Jan | 83.7 | 82.8 | - | 82.4 | 83.2 | 64.6 | 85.1 | 68.3 | 78.4 | 78.1 | 84.1 | 89.0 |
| 4 | Feb | 85.1 | 84.2 | - | 87.0 | 87.3 | 88.7 | 88.9 | 84.6 | 82.4 | 82.5 | 80.0 | 84.9 |
| 5 | Mar | 94.3 | 93.2 | - | 104.9 | 104.3 | 93.6 | 92.6 | 88.9 | 86.3 | 94.5 | 87.6 | 95.8 |
| 6 | Apr | 92.4 | 91.4 | - | 100.0 | 107.5 | 98.6 | 85.1 | 92.3 | 82.9 | 90.1 | 83.8 | 91.4 |
| 7 | May | 91.2 | 90.2 | - | 95.1 | 94.3 | 94.3 | 85.4 | 95.4 | 87.4 | 93.9 | 87.6 | 87.6 |
| 8 | Jun | 92.8 | 91.8 | - | 94.7 | 90.0 | 97.9 | 89.8 | 91.1 | 95.0 | 98.0 | 87.9 | 91.1 |
| 9 | Jul | 97.6 | 96.4 | - | 98.9 | 94.3 | 97.5 | 97.6 | 98.7 | 99.0 | 98.3 | 95.2 | 98.4 |
| 10 | Aug | 102.5 | 101.4 | - | 102.6 | 94.6 | 101.1 | 101.4 | 102.3 | 99.3 | 106.1 | 106.0 | 109.4 |
| 11 | Sep | 105.1 | 103.9 | - | 102.2 | 98.9 | 108.3 | 105.4 | 105.9 | 103.7 | 113.5 | 102.5 | 105.3 |
| 12 | Oct | 114.2 | 112.9 | - | 110.7 | 111.4 | 115.9 | 113.5 | 113.4 | 108.4 | 127.6 | 111.2 | 115.9 |
| 13 | Nov | 121.9 | 120.5 | - | 119.1 | 119.6 | 123.3 | 125.3 | 121.2 | 113.5 | 132.9 | 120.0 | 122.6 |
| 14 | Dec | 133.0 | 131.5 | 128.2 | 127.5 | 127.7 | 134.2 | 136.9 | 136.4 | 131.1 | 138.9 | 135.9 | 133.3 |
| 15 | Total | 1214.0 | 1200.0 | | | | | | | | | | |
| 16 | Adj | 1.0116 | | *Each Ratio = Monthly Actual ÷ 12-Month Moving Average | | | | | | | | | |

## Calculating the Deseasoned Monthly Values

When you have the seasonal indexes, you need to put them to work to "level the playing field." Basically, you divide the actual sales figures for each month by the appropriate monthly index (and also multiply them by 100 to keep the units the same). This effectively removes the seasonal factors from the data (this process is called *deseasoning* or *seasonally adjusting* the data).

The Deseasoned Actual column in the Monthly Trend worksheet performs these calculations (see Figure 15.18). Following is a typical formula (from cell D5):

```
=100 * B5 / INDEX(MonthlyIndexTable, MONTH(A5), 3)
```

B5 refers to the sales figure in the Actual column, and `MonthlyIndexTable` is the range A3:C14 in the Monthly Seasonal Index worksheet. The `INDEX()` function finds the appropriate seasonal index for the month (given by the `MONTH(A5)` function).

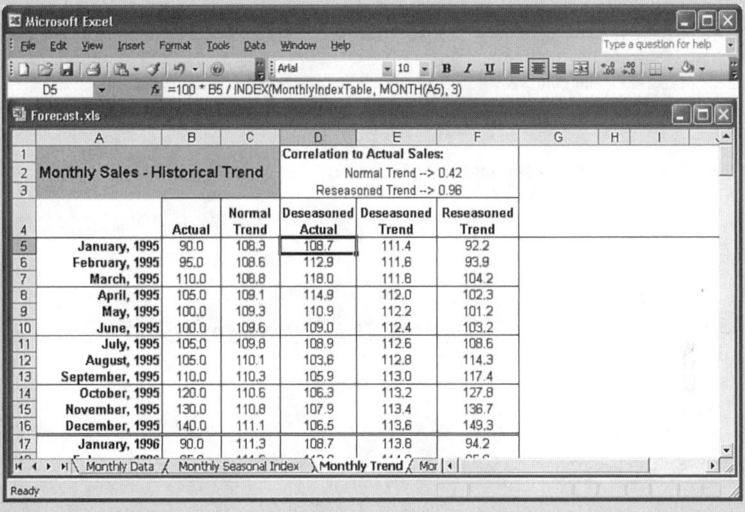


| | A | B | C | D | E | F |
|---|---|---|---|---|---|---|
| 1 | | | | Correlation to Actual Sales: | | |
| 2 | Monthly Sales - Historical Trend | | | Normal Trend --> 0.42 | | |
| 3 | | | | Reseasoned Trend --> 0.96 | | |
| 4 | | Actual | Normal Trend | Deseasoned Actual | Deseasoned Trend | Reseasoned Trend |
| 5 | January, 1995 | 90.0 | 108.3 | 108.7 | 111.4 | 92.2 |
| 6 | February, 1995 | 95.0 | 108.6 | 112.9 | 111.6 | 93.9 |
| 7 | March, 1995 | 110.0 | 108.8 | 118.0 | 111.8 | 104.2 |
| 8 | April, 1995 | 105.0 | 109.1 | 114.9 | 112.0 | 102.3 |
| 9 | May, 1995 | 100.0 | 109.3 | 110.9 | 112.2 | 101.2 |
| 10 | June, 1995 | 100.0 | 109.6 | 109.0 | 112.4 | 103.2 |
| 11 | July, 1995 | 105.0 | 109.8 | 108.9 | 112.6 | 108.6 |
| 12 | August, 1995 | 105.0 | 110.1 | 103.6 | 112.8 | 114.3 |
| 13 | September, 1995 | 110.0 | 110.3 | 105.9 | 113.0 | 117.4 |
| 14 | October, 1995 | 120.0 | 110.6 | 106.3 | 113.2 | 127.8 |
| 15 | November, 1995 | 130.0 | 110.8 | 107.9 | 113.4 | 136.7 |
| 16 | December, 1995 | 140.0 | 111.1 | 106.5 | 113.6 | 149.3 |
| 17 | January, 1996 | 90.0 | 111.3 | 108.7 | 113.8 | 94.2 |

**Figure 15.18**
The Deseasoned Actual column calculates seasonally adjusted values for the actual data.

## Calculating the Deseasoned Trend

The next step is to calculate the historical trend based on the new deseasoned values. The Deseasoned Trend column uses the following array formula to accomplish this task:

```
{=TREND(DeseasonedActual)}
```

The name `DeseasonedActual` refers to the values in the Deseasoned Actual column (E5:E124).

## Calculating the Reseasoned Trend

By itself, the deseasoned trend doesn't amount to much. To get the true historical trend, you need to add the seasonal factor back into the deseasoned trend (this process is called *reseasoning* the data). The Reseasoned Trend column does the job with a formula similar to the one used in the Deseasoned Actual column:

```
=E5 * INDEX(MonthlyIndexTable, MONTH(A5), 3) /100
```

Cell F3 uses `CORREL()` to determine the correlation between the Actual data and the Reseasoned Trend data:

```
=CORREL(Actual, ReseasonedTrend)
```

Here, `ReseasonedTrend` is the name applied to the data in the Reseasoned Trend column (F5:F124). As you can see, the correlation of 0.96 is extremely high, indicating that the new trend "line" is an excellent match for the historical data.

## Calculating the Seasonal Forecast

To derive a forecast based on seasonal factors, combine the techniques you used to calculate a normal trend forecast and a reseasoned historical trend. In the Monthly Forecast worksheet (see Figure 15.15), the Deseasoned Trend Forecast column computes the forecast for the deseasoned trend:

```
=TREND(DeseasonedTrend, , ROWS(Deseasoned Trend) + ROW() - 1)
```

The Reseasoned Trend Forecast column adds the seasonal factors back into the deseasoned trend forecast:

```
=D2 * Index(MonthlyIndexTable, MONTH(B2), 3) / 100
```

D2 is the value from the Deseasoned Trend Forecast column, and B2 is the forecast month.

Figure 15.19 shows a chart comparing the actual sales and the reseasoned trend for the last three years of the sample data. The chart also shows two years of the reseasoned forecast.

**Figure 15.19**
A chart of the sample data, which compares actual sales, the reasea-soned trend, and the reseasoned forecast.

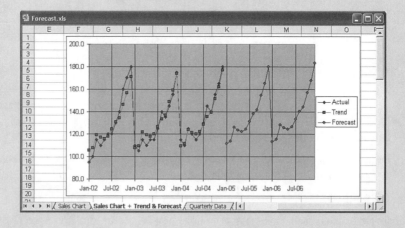

## Working with Quarterly Data

If you prefer to work with quarterly data, the Quarterly Data, Quarterly Seasonal Index, Quarterly Trend, and Quarterly Forecast worksheets perform the same functions as their monthly counterparts. You don't have to re-enter the data because the Quarterly Data worksheet consolidates the monthly numbers by quarter.

# Using Simple Regression on Nonlinear Data

As you saw in the case study, the data you work with doesn't always fit a linear pattern. If the data shows seasonal variations, you can compute the trend and forecast values by working with seasonally adjusted numbers, as you also saw in the case study. But many business scenarios aren't either linear or seasonal. The data might look more like a curve, or it might fluctuate without any apparent pattern.

These nonlinear patterns might seem more complex, but Excel offers a number of useful tools for performing regression analysis on this type of data.

## Working with an Exponential Trend

An *exponential* trend is one that rises or falls at an increasingly higher rate. Fads often exhibit this kind of behavior. A product might sell steadily but unspectacularly for a while, but then word starts getting around—perhaps because of a mention in the newspaper or on television—and sales start to rise. If these new customers enjoy the product, they tell their friends about it, and those people purchase the product, too. They tell *their* friends, the media notice that everyone's talking about this product, and a bona fide fad ensues.

This is called an exponential trend because, as a graph, it looks much like a number being raised to successively higher values of an exponent (for example, $10^1$, $10^2$, $10^3$, and so on). This is often modeled using the constant $e$ (approximately 2.71828), which is the base of the natural logarithm. Figure 15.20 shows a worksheet that uses the EXP() function in column B to return $e$ raised to the successive powers in column A. The chart shows the results as a classic exponential curve.

**Figure 15.20**
Raising the constant e to successive powers produces a classic exponential trend pattern.

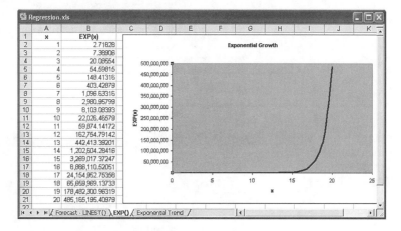

Figure 15.21 shows a worksheet that contains weekly data for the number of units sold of a product. As you can see, the unit sales hold steady for the first eight or nine weeks and then climb rapidly. As the accompanying chart illustrates, the sales curve is very much like an exponential growth curve. The next couple sections show you how to track the trend and make forecasts based on such a model.

### Plotting an Exponential Trendline

The easiest way to see the trend and forecast is to add a trendline—specifically, an exponential trendline—to the chart. Here are the steps to follow:

1. Activate the chart and, if more than one data series is plotted, click the series you want to work with.
2. Choose <u>C</u>hart, Add T<u>r</u>endline to display the Add Trendline dialog box.
3. On the Type tab, click E<u>x</u>ponential.

**4.** Select the Options tab and activate the Display Equation on Chart and Display R-Squared Value on Chart check boxes.

**5.** Click OK. Excel inserts the trendline.

Figure 15.22 shows the exponential trendline added to the chart.

**Figure 15.21**
The weekly unit sales show a definite exponential pattern.

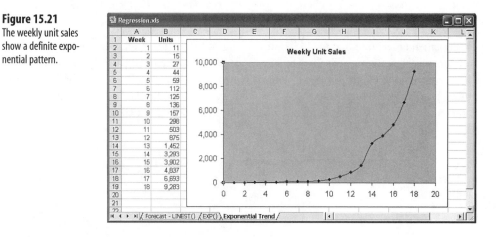

Regression equation

**Figure 15.22**
The weekly unit sales chart with an exponential trendline added.

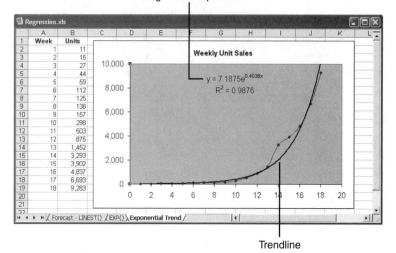

Trendline

## Calculating Exponential Trend and Forecast Values

In Figure 15.22, notice that the regression equation for an exponential trendline takes the following general form:

$$y = be^{mx}$$

Here, $b$ and $m$ are constants. So, knowing these values, given an independent value $x$, you can compute its corresponding point on the trendline using the following formula:

```
=b * EXP(m * x)
```

In the trendline of Figure 15.22, these constant values are 7.1875 and 0.4038, respectively. So, the formula for trend values becomes this:

```
=7.1875 * EXP(0.4038 * x)
```

If $x$ is a value between 1 and 18, you get a trend point for the existing data. To get a forecast, you use a value higher than 18. For example, using $x$ equal to 19 gives a forecast value of 15,437 units:

```
=7.1875 * EXP(0.4038 * 19)
```

## Exponential Trending and Forecasting Using the GROWTH() Function

As you learned with linear regression, it's often useful to work with actual trend values instead of just visualizing the trendline. With a linear model, you use the TREND() function to generate actual values. The exponential equivalent is the GROWTH() function:

```
GROWTH(known_y's, [known_x's], [new_x's], [const])
```

| | |
|---|---|
| *known_y's* | A range reference or array of the known y-values. |
| *known_x's* | A range reference or array of the x-values associated with the known y-values. If you omit this argument, the known $x$'s are assumed to be the array {1,2,3,...,$n$}, where $n$ is the number of known $y$'s. |
| *new_x's* | A range reference or array of the new x-values for which you want corresponding y-values. |
| *const* | A logical value that determines the value of the b constant in the exponential regression equation. If you use FALSE, $b$ is set to 1; if you use TRUE (this is the default), Excel calculates $b$ based on the known $y$'s. |

With the exception of a small difference in the *const* argument, the GROWTH() function syntax is identical to that of TREND().You use the two functions in the same way as well. For example, to return the exponential trend values for the known values, you specify the *known_y's* argument and, optionally, the *known_x's* argument. Here's the formula for the weekly units example, which is entered as an array:

```
{=GROWTH(B2:B19, A2:A19)}
```

To forecast values using GROWTH(), add the *new_x's* argument. For example, to forecast the weekly sales for weeks 19 and 20, assuming that these x-values are in A20:A21, you use the following array formula:

```
{=GROWTH(B2:B19, A2:A19, A20:A21)}
```

Figure 15.23 shows the GROWTH() formulas at work. The numbers in C2:C19 are the existing trend values, and the numbers in C20 and C21 are the forecast values.

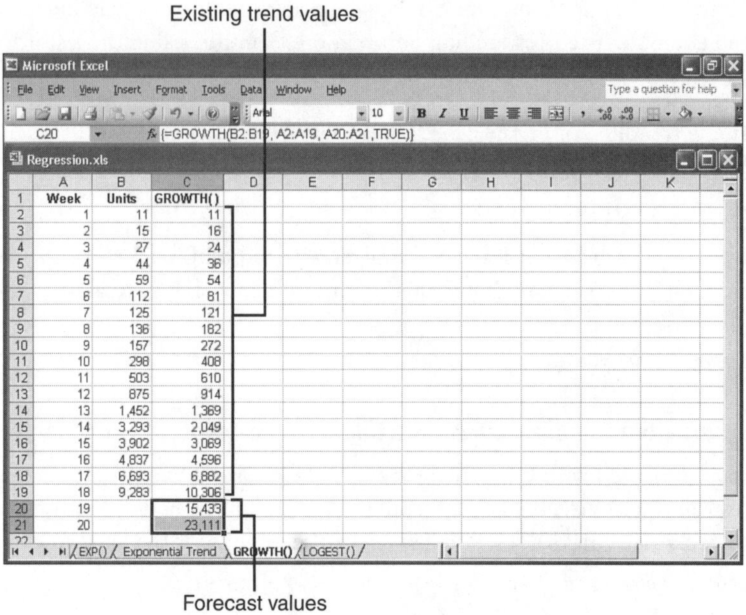

Existing trend values

**Figure 15.23**
The weekly unit sales with existing trend and forecast values calculated by the GROWTH() function.

Forecast values

What if you want to calculate the constants $b$ and $m$? You can do that by using the exponential equivalent of LINEST(), which is LOGEST():

LOGEST(*known_y's*, [*known_x's*], [*const*], [*stats*])

| | |
|---|---|
| *known_y's* | A range reference or array of the known y-values from which you want to calculate the trend. |
| *known_x's* | A range reference or array of the x-values associated with the known y-values. If you omit this argument, the known $x$'s are assumed to be the array $\{1,2,3,...,n\}$, where $n$ is the number of known $y$'s. |
| *const* | A logical value that determines the value of the $b$ constant in the exponential regression equation. If you use FALSE, $b$ is set to 1; if you use TRUE (this is the default), Excel calculates $b$ based on the known $y$'s. |
| *stats* | A logical value that determines whether LOGEST() returns additional regression statistics besides $b$ and $m$. The default is FALSE. If you use TRUE, LOGEST() returns the extra stats, which are (except for $b$ and $m$) the same as those returned by LINEST(). |

Actually, LOGEST() doesn't return the value for $m$ directly. That's because LOGEST() is designed for the following regression formula:

y = bm$_1$$^x$

However, this is equivalent to the following:

y = b * EXP(LN(m$_1$) * x)

This is the same as our exponential regression equation, except that we have `LN(m₁)` instead of just $m$. Therefore, to derive $m$, you need to use `LN(m₁)` to take the natural logarithm of the $m_1$ value returned by `LOGEST()`.



As with `LINEST()`, if you set *`stats`* to `FALSE`, `LOGEST()` returns a 1×2 array, with $m$ (actually $m_1$) in the first cell and $b$ in the second cell. Figure 15.24 shows a worksheet that puts `LOGEST()` through its paces:

- The value of $b$ is in cell H2. The value of $m_1$ is in cell G2, and cell I2 uses `LN()` to get the value of $m$.
- The values in column D are calculated using the exponential regression equation, with the values for $b$ and $m$ plugged in.
- The values in column E are calculated using the `LOGEST()` regression equation, with the values for $b$ and $m_1$ plugged in.

**Figure 15.24**
The weekly unit sales with data generated by the `LOGEST()` function.

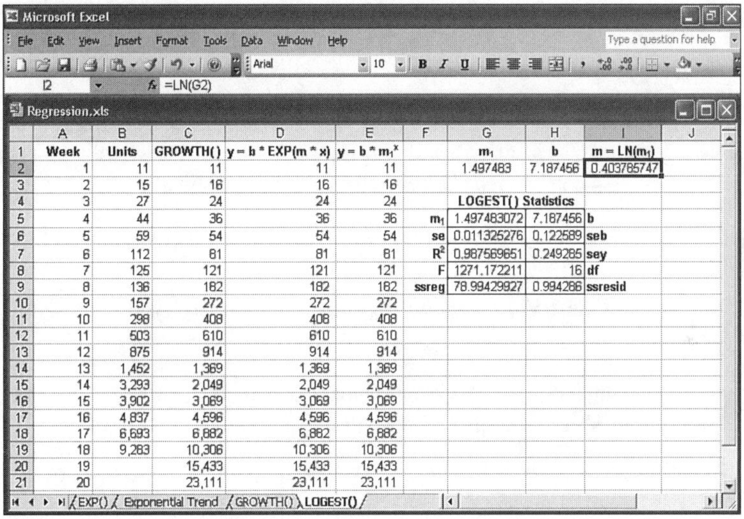


| | A | B | C | D | E | F | G | H | I |
|---|---|---|---|---|---|---|---|---|---|
| 1 | Week | Units | GROWTH() | y = b * EXP(m * x) | $y = b * m_1^x$ | | $m_1$ | b | $m = LN(m_1)$ |
| 2 | 1 | 11 | 11 | 11 | 11 | | 1.497483 | 7.187456 | 0.403785747 |
| 3 | 2 | 15 | 16 | 16 | 16 | | | | |
| 4 | 3 | 27 | 24 | 24 | 24 | | LOGEST() Statistics | | |
| 5 | 4 | 44 | 36 | 36 | 36 | $m_1$ | 1.497483072 | 7.187456 | b |
| 6 | 5 | 59 | 54 | 54 | 54 | se | 0.011325276 | 0.122589 | seb |
| 7 | 6 | 112 | 81 | 81 | 81 | $R^2$ | 0.987569651 | 0.249285 | sey |
| 8 | 7 | 125 | 121 | 121 | 121 | F | 1271.172211 | 16 | df |
| 9 | 8 | 136 | 182 | 182 | 182 | ssreg | 78.99429927 | 0.994286 | ssresid |
| 10 | 9 | 157 | 272 | 272 | 272 | | | | |
| 11 | 10 | 298 | 408 | 408 | 408 | | | | |
| 12 | 11 | 503 | 610 | 610 | 610 | | | | |
| 13 | 12 | 875 | 914 | 914 | 914 | | | | |
| 14 | 13 | 1,452 | 1,369 | 1,369 | 1,369 | | | | |
| 15 | 14 | 3,293 | 2,049 | 2,049 | 2,049 | | | | |
| 16 | 15 | 3,902 | 3,069 | 3,069 | 3,069 | | | | |
| 17 | 16 | 4,837 | 4,596 | 4,596 | 4,596 | | | | |
| 18 | 17 | 6,693 | 6,882 | 6,882 | 6,882 | | | | |
| 19 | 18 | 9,283 | 10,306 | 10,306 | 10,306 | | | | |
| 20 | 19 | | 15,433 | 15,433 | 15,433 | | | | |
| 21 | 20 | | 23,111 | 23,111 | 23,111 | | | | |



## Working with a Logarithmic Trend

A *logarithmic* trend is one that is the inverse of an exponential trend: The values rise (or fall) quickly in the beginning and then level off. This is a common pattern in business. For example, a new company hires many people up front, and then hiring slows over time. A new product often sells many units soon after it's launched, and then sales level off.

This pattern is described as logarithmic because it's typified by the shape of the curve made by the natural logarithm. Figure 15.25 shows a chart that plots the value `LN(x)` function for various values of $x$.

**Figure 15.25**
The natural logarithm produces a classic logarithmic trend pattern.

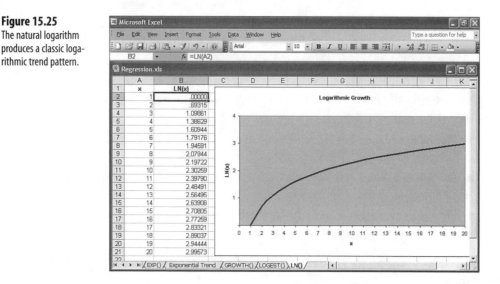

## Plotting a Logarithmic Trendline

The easiest way to see the trend and forecast is to add a trendline—specifically, an exponential trendline—to the chart. Here are the steps to follow:

1. Activate the chart and, if more than one data series is plotted, click the series you want to work with.
2. Choose Chart, Add Trendline to display the Add Trendline dialog box.
3. On the Type tab, click Logarithmic.
4. Select the Options tab and activate the Display Equation on Chart and Display R-Squared Value on Chart check boxes.
5. Click OK. Excel inserts the trendline.

Figure 15.26 shows a worksheet that tracks the total number of employees at a new company. The chart shows the employee growth and a logarithmic trendline fitted to the data.

## Calculating Logarithmic Trend and Forecast Values

The regression equation for a logarithmic trendline takes the following general form:

```
y = m * LN(x) + b
```

As usual, b and m are constants. So, knowing these values, given an independent value x, you can use this formula to compute its corresponding point on the trendline. In the trendline of Figure 15.26, these constant values are 182.85 and 157.04, respectively. So the formula for trend values become this:

```
=182.85 * LN(x) + 157.04
```

Trendline

**Figure 15.26**
Total employee growth,
with a logarithmic trend-
line added.

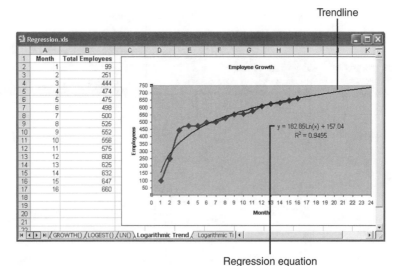

Regression equation

If $x$ is a value between 1 and 16, you get a trend point for the existing data. To get a fore-cast, you use a value higher than 16. For example, using $x$ equal to 17 gives a forecast value of 675 employees:

```
=182.85 * LN(17) + 157.04
```

Excel doesn't have a function that enables you to calculate the values of $b$ and $m$ yourself. However, it's possible to use the LINEST() function if you transform the pattern so that it becomes linear. When you have a logarithmic curve, you "straighten it out" by changing the scale of the x-axis to a logarithmic scale. Therefore, we can turn our logarithmic regression into a linear one by applying the LN() function to the *known_x's* argument:

```
=LINEST(known_y's, LN(known_x's))
```

For example, the following array formula returns the values of $m$ and $b$ for the Total Employees data:

```
{=LINEST(B2:B17, LN(A2:A17))}
```

Figure 15.27 shows a worksheet that calculates $m$ (cell E2) and $b$ (cell F2), and uses the results to derive values for the current trend and the forecasts (column C).

## Working with a Power Trend

The exponential and logarithmic trendlines are both "extreme" in the sense that they have radically different velocities at different parts of the curve. The exponential trendline begins slowly and then takes off at an ever-increasing pace; the logarithmic trendline shoots off the mark and then levels off.

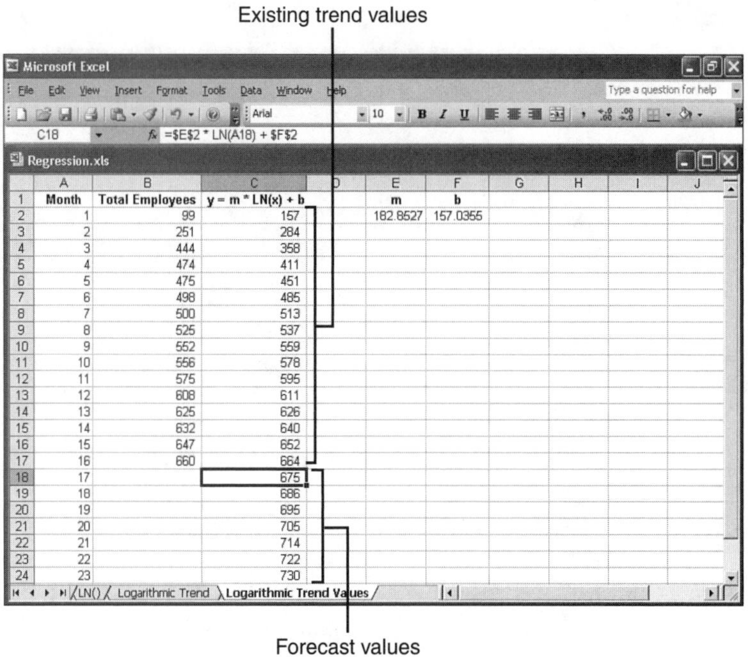

**Figure 15.27**
The Total Employees worksheet, with existing trend and forecast values calculated by the logarithmic regression equation and values returned by the LINEST() function.

Existing trend values

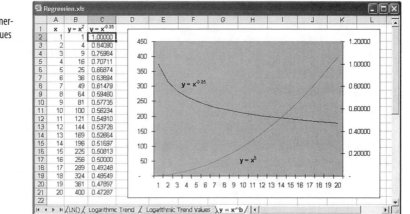

Forecast values

Most measurable business scenarios don't exhibit such extreme behavior. Revenues, profits, margins, and employee head count often tend to increase steadily over time (in successful companies, anyway). If you're analyzing a dependent variable that increases (or decreases) steadily with respect to some independent variable, but the linear trendline doesn't give a good fit, you should try a *power* trendline. This is a pattern that curves steadily in one direction. To give you a flavor of a power curve, consider the graphs of the equations $y = x^2$ and $y = x^{-0.25}$ in Figure 15.28. The $y = x^2$ curve shows a steady increase, while the $y = x^{-0.25}$ curve shows a steady decrease.

**Figure 15.28**
Power curves are generated by raising x-values to some power.

## Plotting a Power Trendline

If you think that your data fits the power pattern, you can quickly check by adding a power trendline to the chart. Here are the steps to follow:

1. Activate the chart and, if more than one data series is plotted, click the series you want to work with.

2. Choose Chart, Add Trendline to display the Add Trendline dialog box.

3. On the Type tab, click Power.

4. Select the Options tab and activate the Display Equation on Chart and Display R-Squared Value on Chart check boxes.

5. Click OK. Excel inserts the trendline.

Figure 15.29 shows a worksheet that compares the list price of a product (the independent variable) with the number of units sold (the dependent variable). As the chart shows, this relationship plots as a steadily declining curve, so a power trendline has been added. Note, too, that the trendline has been extended back to the $5.99 price point and forward to the $15.99 price point.

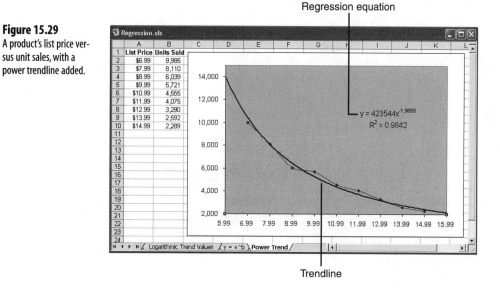

**Figure 15.29**
A product's list price versus unit sales, with a power trendline added.

## Calculating Power Trend and Forecast Values

The regression equation for a power trendline takes the following general form:

$$y = mx^b$$

As usual, $b$ and $m$ are constants. Given these values and an independent value $x$, you can use this formula to compute its corresponding point on the trendline. In the trendline of

Figure 15.29, these constant values are 423544 and -1.9055, respectively. Plugging these into the general equation for a power trend gives the following:

```
=423544 * x ^ -1.9055
```

If $x$ is a value between 6.99 and 14.99, you get a trend point for the existing data. To get a forecast, you use a value lower than 6.99 or higher than 14.99. For example, using $x$ equal to 15.99 gives a forecast value of 2,153 units sold:

```
=423544 * 15.99 ^ -1.9055
```

As with the logarithmic trend, Excel doesn't have functions that enable you to directly calculate the values of $b$ and $m$. However, you can "straighten" a power curve by changing the scale of *both* the y-axis and the x-axis to a logarithmic scale. Therefore, you can transform the power regression into a linear regression by applying the natural logarithm—the LN() function—to both the *known_y's* and *known_x's* arguments:

```
=LINEST(LN(known_y's), LN(known_x's))
```

Here's how the array formula looks for the list price versus units sold data:

```
{=LINEST(LN(B2:B10, LN(A2:A10))}
```

The first cell of the array holds the value of $b$. Because it's used as an exponent in the regression equation, you don't need to "undo" the logarithmic transform. However, the second cell in the array—let's call it m$_1$—holds the value of $m$ in its logarithmic form. Therefore, you need to "undo" the transform by applying the EXP() function to the result.

Figure 15.30 shows a worksheet performing these calculations. The LINEST() array is in E2:F2, and E2 holds the value of $b$ (cell E2). To get $m$, cell G2 uses the formula =EXP(F2). The worksheet uses these results to derive values for the current trend and the forecasts (column C).

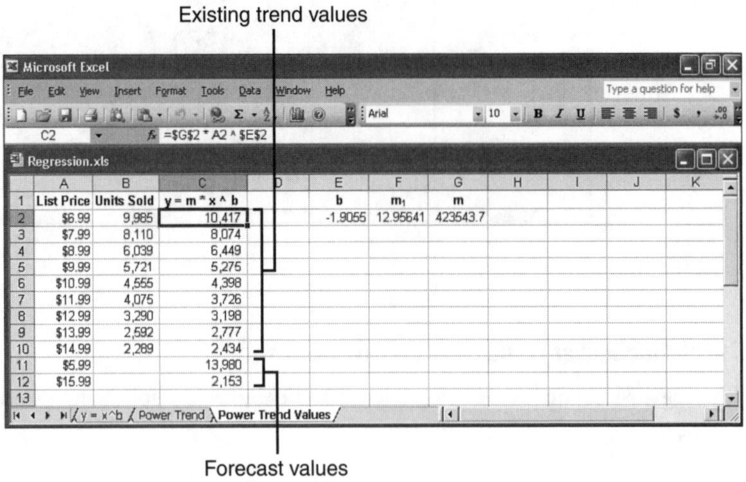

**Figure 15.30**
The worksheet of list price versus units, with existing trend and forecast values calculated by the power regression equation and values returned by the LINEST() function.

Existing trend values

Forecast values

## Using Polynomial Regression Analysis

The trendlines you've seen so far have all been unidirectional. That's fine if the curve formed by the dependent variable values is also unidirectional, but that's often not the case in a business environment. Sales fluctuate, profits rise and fall, and costs move up and down, thanks to varying factors such as inflation, interest rates, exchange rates, and commodity prices. For these more complex curves, the trendlines covered so far might not give either a good fit or good forecasts.

If that's the case, you might need to turn to a *polynomial* trendline, which is a curve constructed out of an equation that uses multiple powers of *x*. For example, a *second-order* polynomial regression equation takes the following general form:

$$y = m_2x^2 + m_1x + b$$

The values $m_2$, $m_1$, and *b* are constants. Similarly, a *third-order* polynomial regression equation takes the following form:

$$y = m_2x^2 + m_2x^2 + m_1x + b$$

These equations can go as high as a sixth-order polynomial.

### Plotting a Polynomial Trendline

Here are the steps to follow to add a polynomial trendline to a chart:

1. Activate the chart and, if more than one data series is plotted, click the series you want to work with.
2. Choose Chart, Add Trendline to display the Add Trendline dialog box.
3. On the Type tab, click Polynomial.
4. Use the Order spin box to choose the order of the polynomial equation you want.
5. Select the Options tab and activate the Display Equation on Chart and Display R-Squared Value on Chart check boxes.
6. Click OK. Excel inserts the trendline.

Figure 15.31 displays a simple worksheet that shows annual profits over 10 years, with accompanying charts showing two different polynomial trendlines.

Generally, the higher the order you use, the tighter the curve will fit your existing data, but the more unpredictable will be your forecasted values. In Figure 15.31, the top chart shows a third-order polynomial trendline, and the bottom chart shows a fifth-order polynomial trendline. The fifth-order curve ($R^2 = 0.6236$) gives a better fit than the third-order curve ($R^2 = 0.3048$). However, the forecasted profit for the 11th year seems more realistic in the third-order case (about 17) than in the fifth-order case (about 26).

In other words, you'll often have to try different polynomial orders to get a fit that you are comfortable with and forecasted values that seem realistic.

**Figure 15.31**
Annual profits with two charts showing different polynomial trendlines.

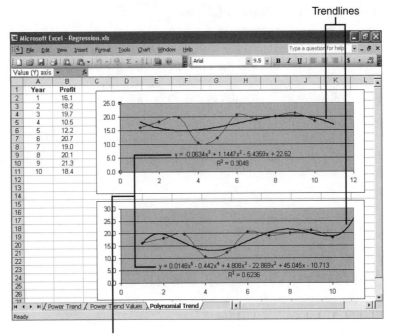

Trendlines

Regression equations

## Calculating Polynomial Trend and Forecast Values

You've seen that the regression equation for an $n$th-order polynomial curve takes the following general form:

$$y = m_nx^n + \ldots + m_2x^2 + m_1x + b$$

So, as with the other regression equations, if you know the value of the constants, then for any independent value $x$, you can use this formula to compute its corresponding point on the trendline. For example, the top trendline in Figure 15.31 is a third-order polynomial, so we need the values of $m_3$, $m_2$, and $m_1$, as well as $b$. From the regression equation displayed on the chart, we know that these values are, respectively, `-0.0634`, `1.1447`, `-5.4359`, and `22.62`. Plugging these into the general equation for a third-order polynomial trend gives the following:

```
=-0.0634 * x ^ 3 + 1.1447 * x ^ 2  + -5.4359 * x + 22.62
```

If $x$ is a value between 1 and 10, you get a trend point for the existing data. To get a forecast, you use a value higher than 10. For example, using $x$ equal to 11 gives a forecast profit value of 17.0:

```
=-0.0634 * 11 ^ 3 + 1.1447 * 11 ^ 2  + -5.4359 * 11 + 22.62
```

The trick here is to raise each of the known_x's values to the powers from 1 to n for an nth-order polynomial:

However, you don't need to put yourself through these intense calculations because the TREND() function can do it for you. The trick here is to raise each of the *known_x's* values to the powers from 1 to *n* for an *n*th-order polynomial:

`{=TREND(known_y's, known_x's ^ {1,2,...,n})}`

For example, here's the formula to use to get the existing trend values for a third-order polynomial using the year and profit ranges from the worksheet in Figure 15.31:

`{=TREND(B2:B11, A2:A11 ^ {1,2,3})}`

To get a forecast value, you raise each of the *new_x's* values to the powers from 1 to *n* for an *n*th-order polynomial:

`{=TREND(known_y's, known_x's ^ {1,2,...,n}, new_x's ^ {1,2,...,n})}`

For the profits forecast, if A12 contains 11, then the following array formula returns the predicted value.

`{=TREND(B2:B11, A2:A11 ^ {1,2,3}, A12 ^ {1,2,3})}`

Figure 15.32 shows a worksheet that uses this TREND() technique to compute both the trend values for years 1 through 10 and a forecast value for year 11 for all the second-order through sixth-order polynomials.

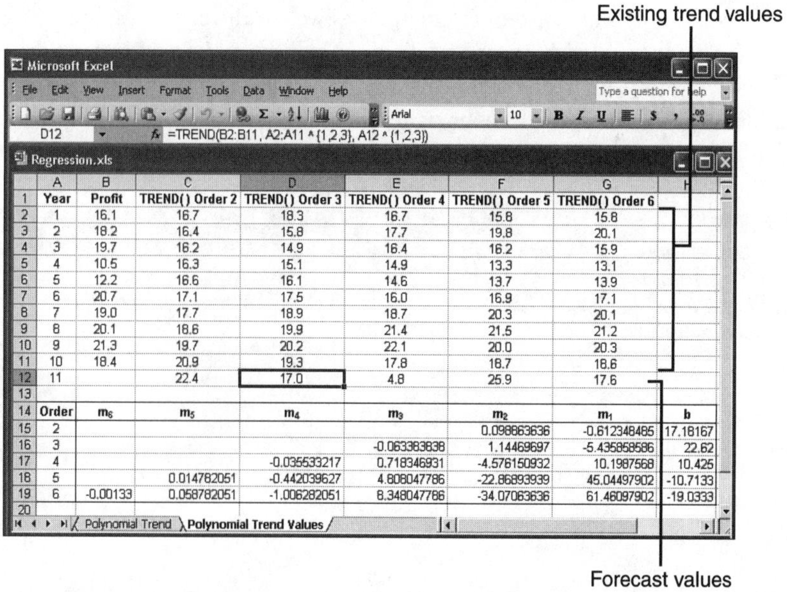

Existing trend values

**Figure 15.32**
The profits worksheet, with existing trend and forecast values calculated by the TREND() function.

Forecast values

Note, too, that Figure 15.32 also calculates the $m_n$ values and $b$ for each order of polynomial. This is done using LINEST() by again raising each of the *known_x's* values to the powers from 1 to *n*, for an *n*th-order polynomial:

`{=LINEST(known_y's, known_x's ^ {1,2,...,n})}`

**15**

The formula returns an $n + 1 \times 1$ array in which the first $n$ cells contain the constants $m_n$ through $m_1$, and then the $n+1$st cell contains $b$. For example, the following formula returns a $3 \times 1$ array of the constant values for a third-order polynomial using the year and profit ranges:

```
{=LINEST(B2:B11, A2:A11 ^ {1,2,3})}
```

# Using Multiple Regression Analysis

Focusing on a single independent variable is a useful exercise because it can tell you a great deal about the relationship between the independent variable and the dependent variable. However, in the real world of business, the variation that you see in most phenomena is a product of multiple influences. The movement of car sales isn't solely a function of interest rates; it's also affected by internal factors such as price, advertising, warranties, and factory-dealer incentives, as well as external factors such as total consumer disposable income and the employment rate.

The good news is that the linear regression techniques you learned earlier in this chapter are easily adapted to multiple independent variables.

As a simple example, let's consider a sales model in which the units sold—the dependent variable—is a function of two independent variables: advertising costs and list price. The worksheet in Figure 15.33 shows data for 10 products, each with its own advertising costs (column A) and list price (column B), as well as the corresponding unit sales (column C). The upper chart shows the relationship between units sold and list price, while the lower chart shows the relationship between units sold and advertising costs. As you can see, the individual trends look about right: Units sold go down as the list price goes up; units sold go up, and advertising costs go up.

**Figure 15.33**

This worksheet shows raw data and trendlines for units sold versus advertising costs and list price.

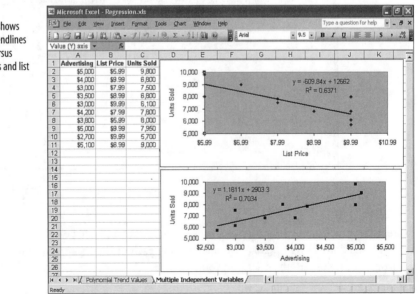

However, the individual trends don't tell us much about how advertising and price *together* affect sales. Clearly, a low advertising budget combined with a high price will result in lower sales; conversely, a high advertising budget combined with a low price should increase sales. What we really want, of course, is to attach some hard numbers to these seat-of-the-pants speculations. You can get those numbers using that linear regression workhorse, the TREND() function.

To use TREND() when you have multiple independent variables, you expand the *known_x's* argument so that it includes the entire range of independent data. In Figure 15.33, for example, the independent data resides in the range A2:B11, so that's the reference you plug into the TREND() function. Here's the array formula for computing the existing trend values:

```
{=TREND(C2:C11, A2:B11)}
```

In multiple regression analysis, you're most often interested in what-if scenarios. What if you spend $6,000 in advertising on a $5.99 product? What if you spend $1,000 on a $9.99 product?

To answer these questions, you plug the values into the *new_x's* argument as an array. For example, the following formula returns the predicted number of units that will sell if you spend $6,000 in advertising on a $5.99 product:

```
{=TREND(C2:C11, A2:B11, {6000, 5.99})}
```

Figure 15.34 shows a worksheet that puts the multiple regression form of TREND() to work. The values in D2:D11 are for the existing trend, and values in D12:D13 are forecasts.

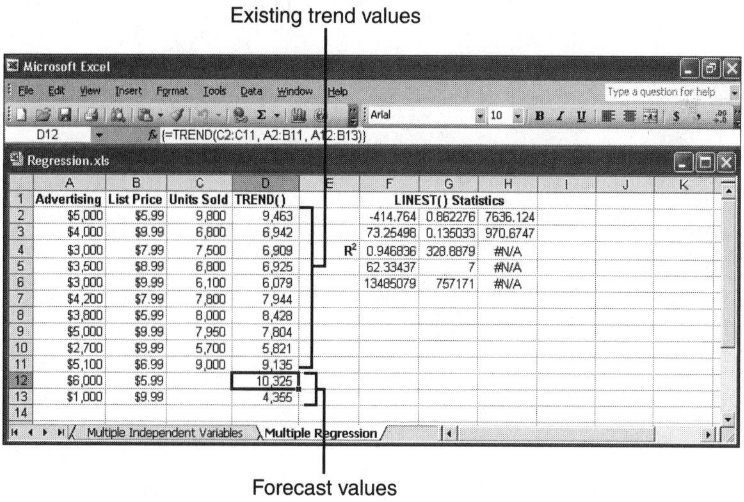

**Figure 15.34**
Trend and forecast values calculated by the multiple regression form of the TREND() function.

Notice, too, that the worksheet in Figure 15.34 also includes the statistics generated by the LINEST() function. The returned array is *three* columns wide because you're dealing with three variables (two independent and one dependent). Of particular interest is the value for

$R^2$ (cell F4)—0.946836. It tells us that the fit between unit sales and the combination of advertising and price is an excellent one, which gives us some confidence about the validity of the predicted values.

## From Here

- For detailed coverage of arrays, **see** "Working with Arrays," **p. 84**.

- You can use INDEX() to return results for the LINEST() and LOGEST() arrays directly. **See** "The MATCH() and INDEX() Functions," **p. 192**.

- To learn more about correlation, **see** "Determining the Correlation Between Data," **p. 271**.

- For coverage of many of Excel's other statistical functions, **see** "Working with Statistical Functions," **p. 249**.

# Solving Complex Problems with Solver

# 16

In Chapter 14, "Using Excel's Business-Modeling Tools," you learned how to use Goal Seek to find solutions to formulas by changing a single variable. Unfortunately, most problems in business aren't so easy. You'll usually face formulas with at least two and sometimes dozens of variables. Often a problem will have more than one solution, and your challenge will be to find the *optimal* solution (that is, the one that maximizes profit, or minimizes costs, or matches other criteria). For these bigger challenges, you need a more muscular tool. Excel has just the answer: Solver. Solver is a sophisticated optimization program that enables you to find the solutions to complex problems that would otherwise require high-level mathematical analysis. This chapter introduces you to Solver (a complete discussion would require a book in itself) and takes you through a few examples.

## Some Background on Solver

Problems such as "What product mix will maximize profit?" or "What transportation routes will minimize shipping costs while meeting demand?" traditionally have been solved by numerical methods such as *linear programming* and *nonlinear programming*. An entire mathematical field known as *operations research* has been developed to handle such problems, which are found in all kinds of disciplines. The drawback to linear and nonlinear programming is that solving even the simplest problem by hand is a complicated, arcane, and time-consuming business. In other words, it's a perfect job to slough off on a computer.

This is where Solver comes in. Solver incorporates many of the algorithms from operations research, but it keeps the sordid details in the background. All you do is fill out a dialog box or two, and Solver does the rest.

## The Advantages of Solver

Solver, like Goal Seek, uses an iterative method to perform its magic. This means that Solver tries a solution, analyzes the results, tries another solution, and so on. However, this cyclic iteration isn't just guesswork on Solver's part. The program looks at how the results change with each new iteration and, through some sophisticated mathematical trickery, can tell (usually) in what direction it should head for the solution.

However, the fact that Goal Seek and Solver are both iterative doesn't make them equal. In fact, Solver brings a number of advantages to the table:

- Solver enables you to specify multiple adjustable cells. You can use up to 200 adjustable cells in all.

- Solver enables you to set up *constraints* on the adjustable cells. For example, you can tell Solver to find a solution that not only maximizes profit, but also satisfies certain conditions, such as achieving a gross margin between 20% and 30%, or keeping expenses less than $100,000. These conditions are said to be *constraints* on the solution.

- Solver seeks not only a desired result (the "goal" in Goal Seek), but also the optimal one. This means that you can find a solution that is the maximum or minimum possible.

- For complex problems, Solver can generate multiple solutions. You then can save these different solutions under different scenarios, as described later in this chapter.

## When Do You Use Solver?

Solver is a powerful tool that most Excel users don't need. It would be overkill, for example, to use Solver to compute net profit given fixed revenue and cost figures. Many problems, however, require nothing less than the Solver approach. These problems cover many different fields and situations, but they all have the following characteristics in common:

- They have a single *target cell* that contains a formula you want to maximize, minimize, or set to a specific value. This formula could be a calculation, such as total transportation expenses or net profit.

- The target cell formula contains references to one or more *changing cells* (also called *unknowns* or *decision variables*). Solver adjusts these cells to find the optimal solution for the target cell formula. These changing cells might include items such as units sold, shipping costs, or advertising expenses.

- Optionally, there are one or more *constraint cells* that must satisfy certain criteria. For example, you might require that advertising be less than 10% of total expenses, or that the discount to customers be a number between 40% and 60%.

What types of problems exhibit these kinds of characteristics? A surprisingly broad range, as the following list shows:

- **The transportation problem**—This problem involves minimizing shipping costs from multiple manufacturing plants to multiple warehouses, while meeting demand.

- **The allocation problem**—This problem requires minimizing employee costs, while maintaining appropriate staffing requirements.

- **The product mix problem**—This problem requires generating the maximum profit with a mix of products, while still meeting customer requirements. You solve this problem when you sell multiple products with different cost structures, profit margins, and demand curves.

- **The blending problem**—This problem involves manipulating the materials used for one or more products to minimize production costs, meet consumer demand, and maintain a minimum level of quality.

- **Linear algebra**—This problem involves solving sets of linear equations.

## Loading Solver

Solver is an add-in to Microsoft Excel, so you'll need to load Solver before you can use it. Follow these steps to load Solver:

1. Choose Tools, Add-Ins. Excel displays the Add-Ins dialog box.
2. In the Add-Ins Available list, activate the Solver Add-In check box.

> **NOTE** If you don't see a Solver Add-In check box in the Add-Ins Available list, you didn't install Solver when you installed Excel. You need to run the Excel setup program and use it to install the Solver add-in.

3. Click OK. Excel installs the add-in and adds a Solver command to the Tools menu.

## Using Solver

So that you can see how Solver works, I'll show you an example. In Chapter 14, you used Goal Seek to compute the break-even point for a new product. (Recall that the break-even point is the number of units that need to be sold to produce a profit of 0.) I'll extend this analysis by computing the break-even point for two products: a Finley sprocket and a Langstrom wrench. The goal is to compute the number of units to sell for both products so that the total profit is 0.

The most obvious way to proceed is to use Goal Seek to determine the break-even points for each product separately. Figure 16.1 shows the results.

| | A | B | C |
|---|---|---|---|
| 1 | | | |
| 2 | | Finley Sprocket | Langstrom Wrench |
| 3 | Price | $24.95 | $19.95 |
| 4 | Units | 8032 | 7177 |
| 5 | Revenue | $200,402 | $143,182 |
| 6 | | | |
| 7 | Unit Cost | $12.50 | $9.50 |
| 8 | Variable Costs | $100,402 | $68,182 |
| 9 | Fixed Costs | $100,000 | $75,000 |
| 10 | Total Costs | $200,402 | $143,182 |
| 11 | | | |
| 12 | Product Profit | $0 | $0 |
| 13 | | | |
| 14 | Total Profit | $0 | |

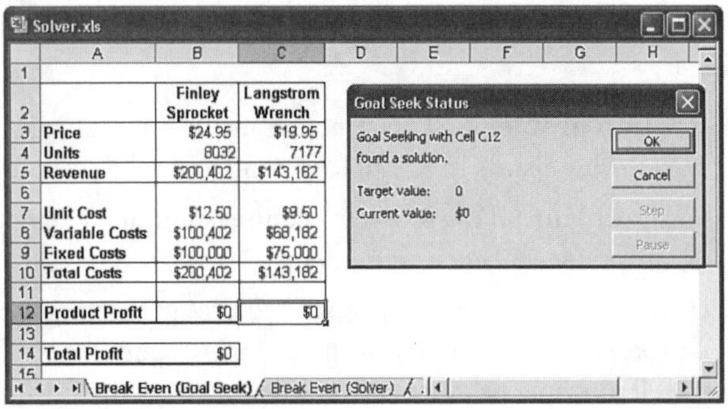

**Figure 16.1**
The break-even points for two products (using separate Goal Seek calculations on the Product Profit cells).

**NOTE** You can download the workbook that contains this chapter's examples here:

`www.mcfedries.com/ExcelFormulas/`

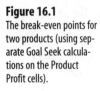

This method works, but the problem is that the two products don't exist in a vacuum. For example, there will be cost savings associated with each product because of joint advertising campaigns, combined shipments to customers (larger shipments usually mean better freight rates), and so on. To allow for this, you need to reduce the cost for each product by a factor related to the number of units sold by the other product. In practice, this would be difficult to estimate, but to keep things simple, I'll use the following assumption: The costs for each product are reduced by $1 for every unit sold of the other product. For instance, if the Langstrom wrench sells 10,000 units, the costs for the Finley sprocket are reduced by $10,000. I'll make this adjustment in the Variable Costs formula. For example, the formula that calculates variable costs for the Finley sprocket (cell B8) becomes the following:

```
=B4 * B7 - C4
```

Similarly, the formula that calculates variable costs for the Langstrom wrench (cell C8) becomes the following:

```
=C4 * C7 - B4
```

By making this change, you move out of Goal Seek's territory. The Variable Costs formulas now have two variables: the units sold for the Finley sprocket and the units sold for the Langstrom wrench. I've changed the problem from one of two single-variable formulas, which Goal Seek can easily handle (individually), to a single formula with two variables, which is the terrain of Solver.

To see how Solver handles such a problem, follow these steps:

1. Choose Tools, Solver. Excel displays the Solver Parameters dialog box.
2. In the Set Target Cell text box, enter a reference to the target cell—that is, the cell with the formula you want to optimize. In the example, you enter **B14**.

3. In the Equal To section, select the appropriate option button: Select M̲ax to maximize the target cell, select Mi̲n to minimize it, or select V̲alue Of to solve for a particular value (in which case, you also need to enter the value in the text box provided). In the example, you activate V̲alue Of and enter **0** in the text box.

4. Use the B̲y Changing Cells box to enter the cells you want Solver to change while it looks for a solution. In the example, you enter **B4,C4**. Figure 16.2 shows the completed Solver Parameters dialog box for the example (note that Solver changes all cell address to the absolute reference format).

**16**

**Figure 16.2**
Use the Solver Parameters dialog box to set up the problem for Solver.

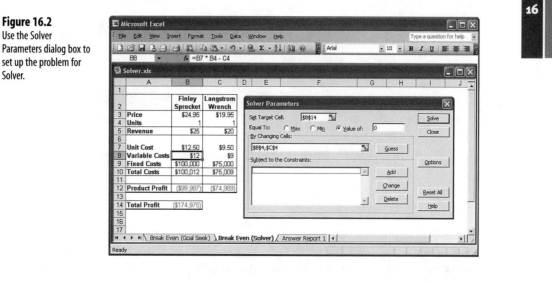

---

**NOTE**  You can enter a maximum of 200 cells in the B̲y Changing Cells box. Also, the G̲uess button enters into the B̲y Changing Cells text box all the nonformula cells that are directly or indirectly referenced by the target cell's formula.

---

5. Click S̲olve. (I discuss constraints and other Solver options in the next few sections.) Solver works on the problem and then displays the Solver Results dialog box, which tells you whether it found a solution. (See the section later in this chapter entitled "Making Sense of Solver's Messages.")

6. If Solver found a solution that you want to use, click the K̲eep Solver Solution option and then click OK. If you don't want to accept the new numbers, click Restore O̲riginal Values and click OK, or just click Cancel. (To learn how to save a solution as a scenario, see the section later in this chapter titled "Saving a Solution as a Scenario.")

Figure 16.3 shows the results for the example. As you can see, Solver has produced a total profit of 0 by running one product (the Langstrom wrench) at a slight loss and the other at a slight profit. Although this is certainly a solution, it's not really the one you want. Ideally, for a true break-even analysis, both products should end up with a product profit of 0. The problem is that you didn't tell Solver that was the way you wanted the problem solved. In other words, you didn't set up any *constraints*.

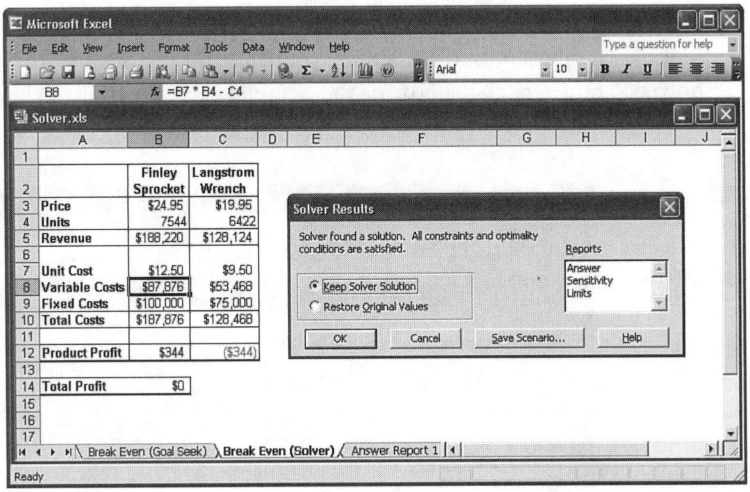

**Figure 16.3**
When Solver finishes its calculations, it displays the Solver Results dialog box and enters the solution (if it found one) into the worksheet cells.

## Adding Constraints

The real world puts restrictions and conditions on formulas. A factory might have a maximum capacity of 10,000 units a day, the number of employees in a company has to be a number greater than or equal to zero (negative employees would really reduce staff costs, but nobody has been able to figure out how to do it yet), and your advertising costs might be restricted to 10% of total expenses. All these are examples of what Solver calls *constraints*. Adding constraints tells Solver to find a solution so that these conditions are not violated.

To find the best solution for the break-even analysis, you need to tell Solver to optimize both Product Profit formulas to 0. The following steps show you how to do this:

> **NOTE**
> If Solver's completion message is still onscreen from the last section, select Cancel to return to the worksheet without saving the solution.

1. Choose Tools, Solver to display the Solver Parameters dialog box. Solver reinstates the options you entered the last time you used Solver.
2. To add a constraint, click Add. Excel displays the Add Constraint dialog box.
3. In the Cell Reference box, enter the cell you want to constrain. For the example, you enter cell **B12** (the Product Profit formula for the Finley sprocket).

4. Use the drop-down list in the middle of the dialog box to select the operator you want to use. The list contains several comparison operators for the constraint—less than or equal to (<=), equal to (=), and greater than or equal to (>=)—as well as two other data type operators—integer (int) and binary (bin). For the example, select the equal to operator (=).

> **NOTE** Use the int (integer) operator when you need a constraint, such as total employees, to be an integer value instead of a real number. Use the bin (binary) operator when you have a constraint that must be either TRUE or FALSE (or 1 or 0).

5. If you chose a comparison operator in step 4, use the Constraint box to enter the value by which you want to restrict the cell. For the example, enter 0. Figure 16.4 shows the completed dialog box for the example.

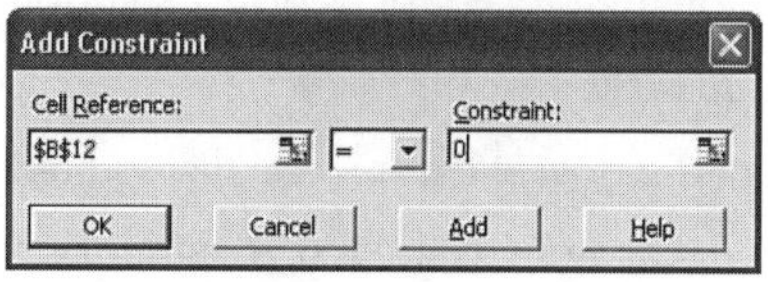

**Figure 16.4**
Use the Add Constraint dialog box to specify the constraints you want to place on the solution.

6. If you want to enter more constraints, click Add and repeat steps 3–5. For the example, you also need to constrain cell C12 (the Product Profit formula for the Langstrom wrench) so that it, too, equals 0.

7. When you're done, click OK to return to the Solver Parameters dialog box. Excel displays your constraints in the Subject to the Constraints list box.

> **NOTE** You can add a maximum of 100 constraints. Also, if you need to make a change to a constraint before you begin solving, click the constraint in the Subject to the Constraints list box, click Change, and then make your adjustments in the Change Constraint dialog box that appears. If you want to delete a constraint that you no longer need, click it and then click the Delete button.

8. Click Solve. Solver again tries to find a solution, but this time it uses your constraints as guidelines.

Figure 16.5 shows the results of the break-even analysis after adding the constraints. As you can see, Solver was able to find a solution in which both product margins are 0.

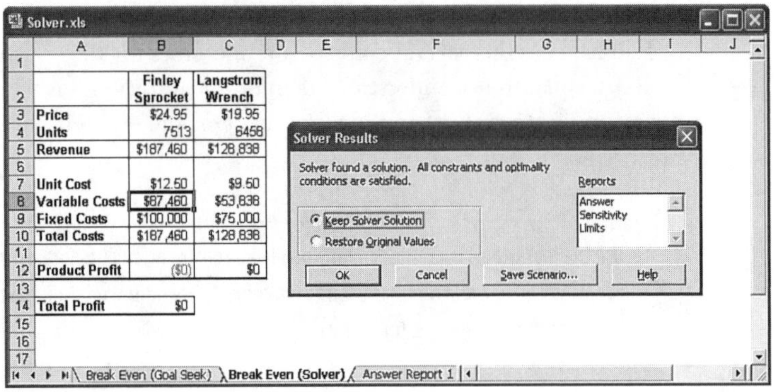

**Figure 16.5**
The solution to the break-even analysis after adding the constraints.

Saving a Solution as a Scenario
---

# Saving a Solution as a Scenario

If Solver finds a solution, you can save the changing cells as a scenario that you can display at any time. Use the steps in the following procedure to save a solution as a scenario:

→ To learn about scenarios, **see** "Working with Scenarios," **p. 330**.

1. Choose Tools, Solver to display the Solver Parameters dialog box.

2. Enter the appropriate target cell, changing cells, and constraints, if necessary.

3. Click Solve to begin solving.

4. If Solver finds a solution, click Save Scenario in the Solver Results dialog box. Excel displays the Save Scenario dialog box, shown in Figure 16.6.

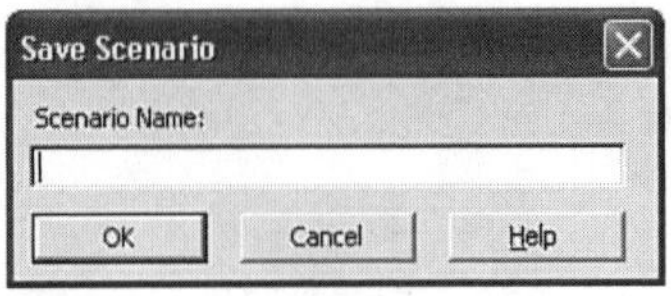

**Figure 16.6**
Use the Save Scenario dialog box to save the current Solver solution as a scenario.

5. Use the Scenario Name text box to enter a name for the scenario.

6. Click OK. Excel returns you to the Solver Results dialog box.

7. Keep or discard the solution, as appropriate.

# Setting Other Solver Options

Most Solver problems should respond to the basic target cell/changing cell/constraint cell model you've looked at so far. However, if you're having trouble getting a solution for a particular model, Solver has a number of options that might help. Start Solver and, in the Solver Parameters dialog box, click Options to display the Solver Options dialog box, shown in Figure 16.7.

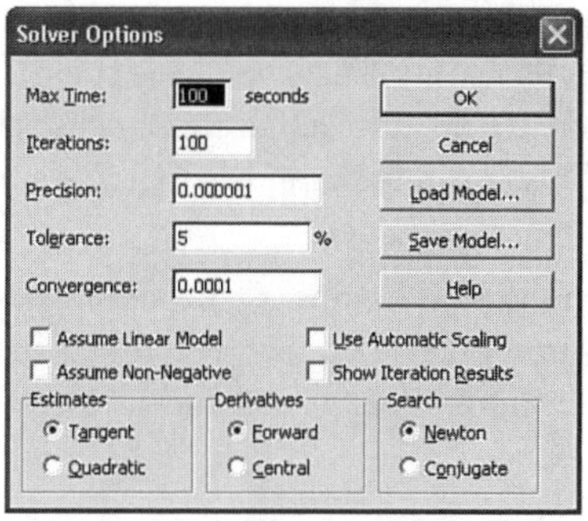

**Figure 16.7**
The Solver Options dialog box controls how Solver solves a problem.

## Controlling Solver

The following options control how Solver works:

- **Max Time**—The amount of time Solver takes is a function of the size and complexity of the model, the number of changing cells and constraint cells, and the other Solver options you've chosen. If you find that Solver runs out of time before finding a solution, increase the number in this text box.

> **CAUTION**
>
> Integer programming (in which you have integer constraints) can take a long time because of the complexity involved in finding solutions that satisfy exact integer constraints. If you find your models taking an abnormally long time to solve, increase the value in the Tolerance box to get an approximate solution. (See the Tolerance item later in this list.)

- **Iterations**—This box controls the number of iterations Solver tries before giving up on a problem. Increasing this number gives Solver more of a chance to solve the problem, but it takes correspondingly longer.

- **Precision**—This number determines how close a constraint cell must be to the constraint value you entered before Solver declares the constraint satisfied. The higher the precision is (that is, the lower the number is), the more accurate the solution is, but the longer it takes Solver to find it.

- **Tolerance**—If you have integer constraints, this box determines what percentage of the integer Solver has to be within before declaring the constraint satisfied. For example, if the integer tolerance is set to 0.05%, Solver will declare a cell with the value 99.95 to be close enough to 100 to declare it an integer.

- **Assume Linear Model**—In the simplest possible terms, a linear model is one in which the variables are not raised to any powers and none of the so-called transcendent functions—such as SIN() and COS()—is used. A linear model is so named because it can be charted as straight lines. If your formulas are linear, be sure to activate this check box because this will greatly speed up the solution process.

- **Assume Non-Negative**—Activate this check box to force Solver to assume that the cells listed in the <u>B</u>y Changing Cells list must have values greater than or equal to 0. This is the same as adding >=0 constraints for each of those cells, so it operates as a kind of implicit constraint on them. This is handy in models that use quite a few changing cells, none of which should have negative values.

- **<u>U</u>se Automatic Scaling**—Activate this check box if your model has changing cells that are significantly different in magnitude. For example, you might have a changing cell that controls customer discount (a number between 0 and 1) and sales (a number that might be in the millions).

- **Show Iteration <u>R</u>esults**—Activate this option to have Solver pause and show you its trial solutions, as shown in Figure 16.8. To resume, click Continue from the Show Trial Solution dialog box.

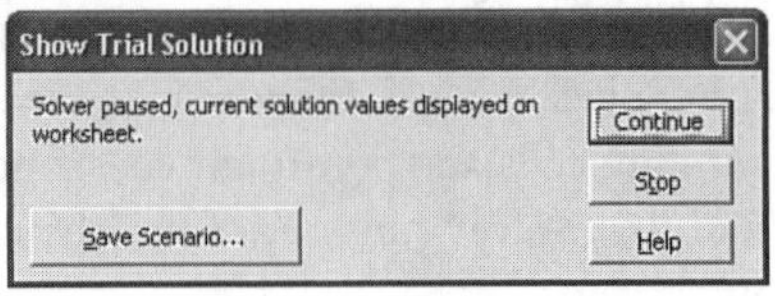

**Figure 16.8**
When the Show Iteration <u>R</u>esults option is activated, Solver displays the Show Trial Solution dialog box so that you can view each intermediate solution.

## Selecting the Method Solver Uses

The options in the Estimates, Derivatives, and Search groups at the bottom of the dialog box control the method Solver uses. The default options perform the job in the vast majority of cases. However, here's a quick rundown of the options, in case you need them:

- **Estimates**—These two options determine how Solver obtains its initial estimates of the model variables. The T<u>a</u>ngent option is the default. You need to select <u>Q</u>uadratic only if your model is highly nonlinear.

- **Derivatives**—Some models require Solver to calculate partial derivatives. These two options specify the method Solver uses to do this. <u>F</u>orward differencing is the default method. The <u>C</u>entral differencing method takes longer than forward differencing, but you might want to try it when Solver reports that it can't improve a solution. (See the section later in this chapter entitled "Making Sense of Solver's Messages.")

- **Search**—When finding a solution, Solver starts with the initial values in the model and then must decide which direction to take to adjust the variables. These options determine the method Solver uses to make this decision. The default <u>N</u>ewton option tells Solver to use a quasi-Newton search method. This method uses more memory, but it's faster than the C<u>o</u>njugate method, which uses a conjugate gradient search. Usually, you'll need to select C<u>o</u>njugate only for large models in which memory is at a premium.

## Working with Solver Models

Excel attaches your most recent Solver parameters to the worksheet when you save it. If you want to save different sets of parameters, you can do so by following these steps:

1. Choose Tools, Solver to display the Solver Parameters dialog box.

2. Enter the parameters you want to save.

3. Click Options to display the Solver Options dialog box.

4. Enter the options you want to save.

5. Click Save Model. Solver displays the Save Model dialog box to prompt you to enter a range in which to store the model.

6. Enter the range in the Select Model Area box. Note that you don't need to specify the entire area—just the first cell. Keep in mind that Solver displays the data in a column, so pick a cell with enough empty space below it to hold all the data. You'll need one cell for the target cell reference, one for the changing cells, one for each constraint, and one to hold the array of Solver options.

7. Click OK. Solver gathers the data, enters it into your selected range, and then returns you to the Solver Options dialog box.

Figure 16.9 shows an example of a saved model (the range F4:F8). I've changed the worksheet view to show formulas, and I've added some explanatory text so you can see exactly how Solver saves the model. Notice that the formula for the target cell (F4) includes both the target (B14) and the target value (=0).

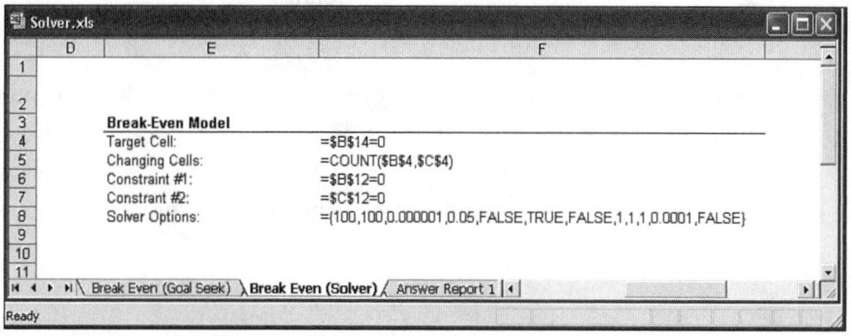

**Figure 16.9**
A saved Solver model with formulas turned on so that you can see what Solver saves to the sheet.

To use your saved settings, follow these steps:

1. Choose Tools, Solver to display the Solver Parameters dialog box.

2. Click Options to display the Solver Options dialog box.

3. Click Load Model. Solver displays the Load Model dialog box.

4. Select the entire range that contains the saved model, and then click OK. Excel asks if you want to reset the previous (that is, the saved) cell selections.

5. Click OK to use the saved model cells, or click Cancel to use the currently selected cells.

6. Click OK to return to the Solver Parameters dialog box.

# Making Sense of Solver's Messages

When Solver finishes its calculations, it displays the Solver dialog box and a message that tells you what happened. Some of these messages are straightforward, but others are more than a little cryptic. This section looks at the most common messages and gives their translations.

If Solver found a solution successfully, you'll see one of the following messages:

- `Solver found a solution. All constraints and optimality conditions are satisfied.`—This is the message you hope to see. It means that the value you wanted for the target cell has been found, and Solver was able to find the solution while meeting your constraints within the precision and integer tolerance levels you set.

- `Solver has converged to the current solution. All constraints are satisfied.`—Solver normally assumes that it has a solution if the value of the target cell formula remains virtually unchanged during a few iterations. This is called *converging to a solution*. Such is the case with this message, but it doesn't necessarily mean that Solver has found a solution. The iterative process might just be taking a long time, or the initial values in the changing cells might have been set too far from the solution. You should try rerunning Solver with different values. You also can try using a higher precision setting (that is, entering a smaller number in the <u>P</u>recision text box).

- `Solver cannot improve the current solution. All constraints are satisfied.`—This message tells you that Solver has found a solution, but it might not be the optimal one. Try setting the precision to a smaller number, or try using the central differencing method for partial derivatives.

If Solver didn't find a solution, you'll see one of the following messages telling you why:

- `The Set Cell values do not converge.`—This means that the value of the target cell formula has no finite limit. For example, if you're trying to maximize profit based on product price and unit costs, Solver won't find a solution; the reason is that continually higher prices and lower costs lead to higher profit. You need to add (or change) constraints in your model, such as setting a maximum price or minimum cost level (for example, the amount of fixed costs).

- `Solver could not find a feasible solution.`—Solver couldn't find a solution that satisfied all your constraints. Check your constraints to make sure that they're realistic and consistent.

- `Stop chosen when the maximum x limit was reached.`—This message appears when Solver bumps up against either the maximum time limit or the maximum iteration limit. If it appears that Solver is heading toward a solution, click <u>K</u>eep Solver Solution and try again.

- `The conditions for Assume Linear Model are not satisfied.`—Solver based its iterative process on a linear model, but when the results are put into the worksheet, they don't conform to the linear model. You need to clear the Assume Linear <u>M</u>odel check box and try again.

## CASE STUDY

# Solving the Transportation Problem

The best way to learn how to use a complex tool such as Solver is to get your hands dirty with some examples. Thoughtfully, Excel comes with several sample worksheets that use simplified models to demonstrate the various problems Solver can handle. This case study looks at one of these worksheets in detail.

The *transportation problem* is the classic model for solving linear programming problems. The basic goal is to minimize the costs of shipping goods from several production plants to various warehouses scattered around the country. Your constraints are as follows:

1. The amount shipped to each warehouse must meet the warehouse's demand for goods.

2. The amount shipped from each plant must be greater than or equal to 0.

3. The amount shipped from each plant can't exceed the plant's supply of goods.

Figure 16.10 shows the model for solving the transportation problem.

**Figure 16.10**
A worksheet for solving the transportation problem.

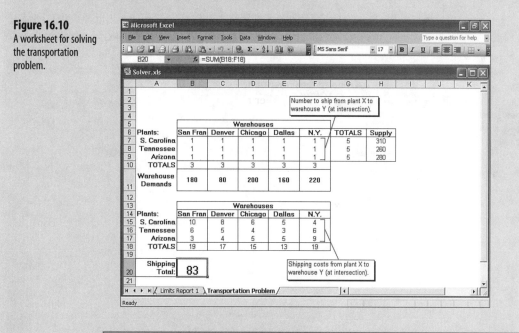

> **TIP**
>
> The worksheet in Figure 16.10 is a slightly modified version of the Shipping Routes worksheet in the Solvsamp.xls workbook. You'll find this workbook in the SAMPLES subfolder of your Office folder. Several other excellent example worksheets there are well worth studying.

The top table (A6:F10) lists the three plants (A7:A9) and the five warehouses (B6:F6). This table holds the number of units shipped from each plant to each warehouse. In the Solver model, these are the changing cells. The total shipped to each warehouse (B10:F10) must match the warehouse demands (B11:F11) to satisfy constraint no. 1. The amount shipped from each plant (B7:F9) must be greater than or equal to 0 to satisfy constraint no. 2. The total shipped from each plant (G7:G9) must be less than or equal to the available supply for each plant (H7:H9) to satisfy constraint no. 3.

> **NOTE** When you need to use a range of values in a constraint, you don't need to set up a separate constraint for each cell. Instead, you can compare entire ranges. For example, the constraint that the total shipped from each plant must be less than or equal to the plant supply can be entered as follows:
>
>     G7:G9 <= H7:H9

The bottom table (A14:F18) holds the corresponding shipping costs from each plant to each warehouse. The total shipping cost (cell B20) is the target cell you want to minimize.

Figure 16.11 shows the final Solver Parameters dialog box that you'll use to solve this problem. (Note also that I activated the Assume Linear Model check box in the Solver Options dialog box as well.) Figure 16.12 shows the solution that Solver found.

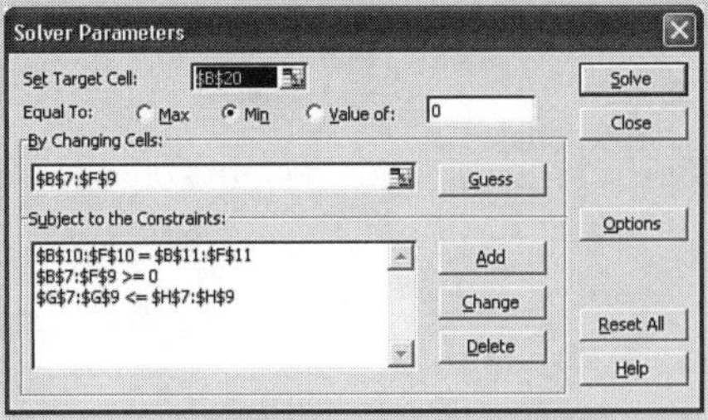

**Figure 16.11**
The Solver Parameters dialog box filled in for the transportation problem.

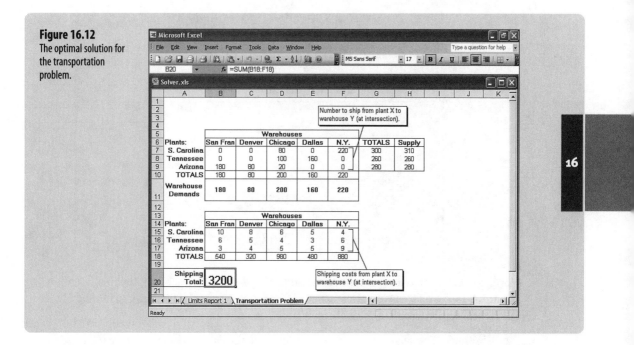

**Figure 16.12**
The optimal solution for the transportation problem.

16

## Displaying Solver's Reports

When Solver finds a solution, the Solver dialog box gives you the option of generating three reports: the Answer report, the Sensitivity report, and the Limits report. Click the reports you want to see in the <u>R</u>eports list box, and then click OK. Excel displays each report on its own worksheet.

> **TIP**
> If you've named the cells in your model, Solver uses these names to make its reports easier to read. If you haven't already done so, you should define names for the target cell, changing cells, and constraint cells before creating a report.

### The Answer Report

The Answer report displays information about the model's target cell, changing (adjustable) cells, and constraints. For the target cell and changing cells, Solver shows the original and final values. For example, Figure 16.13 shows this portion of the answer report for the transportation problem solution.

**Figure 16.13**
The Target Cell and Adjustable Cells sections of Solver's Answer report.

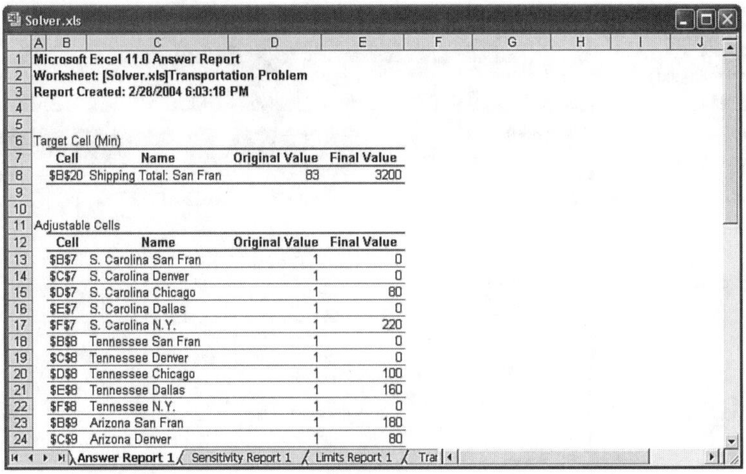
Solver.xls

Microsoft Excel 11.0 Answer Report
Worksheet: [Solver.xls]Transportation Problem
Report Created: 2/28/2004 6:03:18 PM

Target Cell (Min)

| Cell | Name | Original Value | Final Value |
|---|---|---|---|
| $B$20 | Shipping Total: San Fran | 83 | 3200 |

Adjustable Cells

| Cell | Name | Original Value | Final Value |
|---|---|---|---|
| $B$7 | S. Carolina San Fran | 1 | 0 |
| $C$7 | S. Carolina Denver | 1 | 0 |
| $D$7 | S. Carolina Chicago | 1 | 80 |
| $E$7 | S. Carolina Dallas | 1 | 0 |
| $F$7 | S. Carolina N.Y. | 1 | 220 |
| $B$8 | Tennessee San Fran | 1 | 0 |
| $C$8 | Tennessee Denver | 1 | 0 |
| $D$8 | Tennessee Chicago | 1 | 100 |
| $E$8 | Tennessee Dallas | 1 | 160 |
| $F$8 | Tennessee N.Y. | 1 | 0 |
| $B$9 | Arizona San Fran | 1 | 180 |
| $C$9 | Arizona Denver | 1 | 80 |



For the constraints, the report shows the address and name for each cell, the final value, the formulas, and two values called the *status* and the *slack*. Figure 16.14 shows an example from the transportation problem. The status can take one of three values:

- **Binding**—The final value in the constraint cell equals the constraint value (or the constraint boundary, if the constraint is an inequality).
- **Not Binding**—The constraint cell value satisfied the constraint, but it doesn't equal the constraint boundary.
- **Not Satisfied**—The constraint was not satisfied.

The slack is the difference between the final constraint cell value and the value of the original constraint (or its boundary). In the optimal solution for the transportation problem, for example, the total shipped from the South Carolina plant is 300, but the constraint on this total was 310 (the total supply). Therefore, the slack value is 10 (or close enough to it). If the status is binding, the slack value is always 0.

## The Sensitivity Report

The Sensitivity report attempts to show how sensitive a solution is to changes in the model's formulas. The layout of the Sensitivity report depends on the type of model you're using. For a linear model (that is, a model in which you clicked the Assume Linear Model check box in the Solver Options dialog box), you'll see a report similar to the one shown in Figure 16.15.

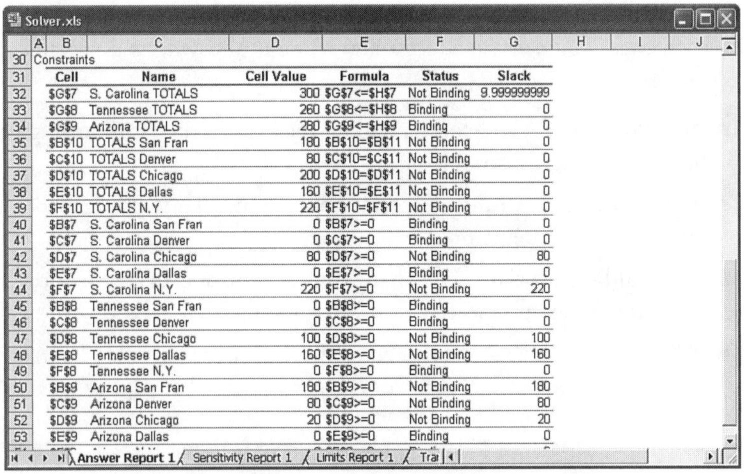

**Figure 16.14**
The Constraints section of Solver's Answer report.

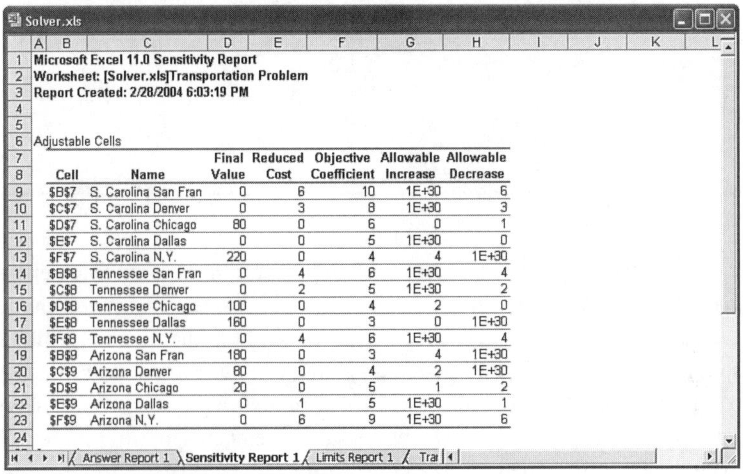

| Cell | Name | Cell Value | Formula | Status | Slack |
|---|---|---|---|---|---|
| | Constraints | | | | |
| $G$7 | S. Carolina TOTALS | 300 | $G$7<=$H$7 | Not Binding | 9.999999999 |
| $G$8 | Tennessee TOTALS | 260 | $G$8<=$H$8 | Binding | 0 |
| $G$9 | Arizona TOTALS | 260 | $G$9<=$H$9 | Binding | 0 |
| $B$10 | TOTALS San Fran | 180 | $B$10=$B$11 | Not Binding | 0 |
| $C$10 | TOTALS Denver | 80 | $C$10=$C$11 | Not Binding | 0 |
| $D$10 | TOTALS Chicago | 200 | $D$10=$D$11 | Not Binding | 0 |
| $E$10 | TOTALS Dallas | 160 | $E$10=$E$11 | Not Binding | 0 |
| $F$10 | TOTALS N.Y. | 220 | $F$10=$F$11 | Not Binding | 0 |
| $B$7 | S. Carolina San Fran | 0 | $B$7>=0 | Binding | 0 |
| $C$7 | S. Carolina Denver | 0 | $C$7>=0 | Binding | 0 |
| $D$7 | S. Carolina Chicago | 80 | $D$7>=0 | Not Binding | 80 |
| $E$7 | S. Carolina Dallas | 0 | $E$7>=0 | Binding | 0 |
| $F$7 | S. Carolina N.Y. | 220 | $F$7>=0 | Not Binding | 220 |
| $B$8 | Tennessee San Fran | 0 | $B$8>=0 | Binding | 0 |
| $C$8 | Tennessee Denver | 0 | $C$8>=0 | Binding | 0 |
| $D$8 | Tennessee Chicago | 100 | $D$8>=0 | Not Binding | 100 |
| $E$8 | Tennessee Dallas | 160 | $E$8>=0 | Not Binding | 160 |
| $F$8 | Tennessee N.Y. | 0 | $F$8>=0 | Binding | 0 |
| $B$9 | Arizona San Fran | 180 | $B$9>=0 | Not Binding | 180 |
| $C$9 | Arizona Denver | 80 | $C$9>=0 | Not Binding | 80 |
| $D$9 | Arizona Chicago | 20 | $D$9>=0 | Not Binding | 20 |
| $E$9 | Arizona Dallas | 0 | $E$9>=0 | Binding | 0 |

Answer Report 1 / Sensitivity Report 1 / Limits Report 1 / Tra

**Figure 16.15**
The Changing Cells section of Solver's Sensitivity report.

Microsoft Excel 11.0 Sensitivity Report
Worksheet: [Solver.xls]Transportation Problem
Report Created: 2/28/2004 6:03:19 PM

Adjustable Cells

| Cell | Name | Final Value | Reduced Cost | Objective Coefficient | Allowable Increase | Allowable Decrease |
|---|---|---|---|---|---|---|
| $B$7 | S. Carolina San Fran | 0 | 6 | 10 | 1E+30 | 6 |
| $C$7 | S. Carolina Denver | 0 | 3 | 8 | 1E+30 | 3 |
| $D$7 | S. Carolina Chicago | 80 | 0 | 6 | 0 | 1 |
| $E$7 | S. Carolina Dallas | 0 | 0 | 5 | 1E+30 | 0 |
| $F$7 | S. Carolina N.Y. | 220 | 0 | 4 | 4 | 1E+30 |
| $B$8 | Tennessee San Fran | 0 | 4 | 6 | 1E+30 | 4 |
| $C$8 | Tennessee Denver | 0 | 2 | 5 | 1E+30 | 2 |
| $D$8 | Tennessee Chicago | 100 | 0 | 4 | 2 | 0 |
| $E$8 | Tennessee Dallas | 160 | 0 | 3 | 0 | 1E+30 |
| $F$8 | Tennessee N.Y. | 0 | 4 | 6 | 1E+30 | 4 |
| $B$9 | Arizona San Fran | 180 | 0 | 3 | 4 | 1E+30 |
| $C$9 | Arizona Denver | 80 | 0 | 4 | 2 | 1E+30 |
| $D$9 | Arizona Chicago | 20 | 0 | 5 | 1 | 2 |
| $E$9 | Arizona Dallas | 0 | 1 | 5 | 1E+30 | 1 |
| $F$9 | Arizona N.Y. | 0 | 6 | 9 | 1E+30 | 6 |

Answer Report 1 / Sensitivity Report 1 / Limits Report 1 / Tra

Actually, this report is divided into two sections. The top section, called Adjustable Cells, shows for each cell the address and name of the cell, its final value, and the following measures:

- **Reduced Cost**—The corresponding increase in the target cell, given a one-unit increase in the changing cell
- **Objective Coefficient**—The relative relationship between the changing cell and the target cell
- **Allowable Increase**—The change in the objective coefficient before there would be an increase in the optimal value of the changing cell
- **Allowable Decrease**—The change in the objective coefficient before there would be a decrease in the optimal value of the changing cell

The bottom section of the Sensitivity report, called Constraints (see Figure 16.16), shows for each constraint cell the address and name of the cell, its final value, and the following values:

- **Shadow Price**—The corresponding increase in the target cell, given a one-unit increase in the constraint value
- **Constraint R.H. Side**—The constraint value that you specified (that is, the right side of the constraint equation)
- **Allowable Increase**—The change in the constraint value before there would be an increase in the optimal value of the changing cell
- **Allowable Decrease**—The change in the constraint value before there would be a decrease in the optimal value of the changing cell



**Figure 16.16**
The Constraints section of Solver's Sensitivity report.

Solver.xls

Constraints

| Cell | Name | Final Value | Shadow Price | Constraint R.H. Side | Allowable Increase | Allowable Decrease |
|---|---|---|---|---|---|---|
| $G$7 | S. Carolina TOTALS | 300 | 0 | 310 | 1E+30 | 10 |
| $G$8 | Tennessee TOTALS | 260 | -2 | 260 | 80 | 10 |
| $G$9 | Arizona TOTALS | 280 | -1 | 280 | 80 | 10 |
| $B$10 | TOTALS San Fran | 180 | 4 | 180 | 10 | 80 |
| $C$10 | TOTALS Denver | 80 | 5 | 80 | 10 | 80 |
| $D$10 | TOTALS Chicago | 200 | 6 | 200 | 10 | 80 |
| $E$10 | TOTALS Dallas | 160 | 5 | 160 | 10 | 80 |
| $F$10 | TOTALS N.Y. | 220 | 4 | 220 | 10 | 220 |

Answer Report 1 | Sensitivity Report 1 | Limits Report 1 | Trai

The Sensitivity report for a nonlinear model shows the changing cells and the constraint cells. For each cell, the report displays the address, the name, and the final value. The Changing Cells section also shows the Reduced Gradient value, which measures the corresponding increase in the target cell, given a one-unit increase in the changing cell (similar to the Reduced Cost measure for a linear model). The Constraints section also shows the Lagrange Multiplier value, which measures the corresponding increase in the target cell, given a one-unit increase in the constraint value (similar to the Shadow Price in the linear report).

## The Limits Report

The Limits report, shown in Figure 16.17, displays the target cell and its value, as well as the changing cells and their addresses, names, values, and the following measures:

- **Lower Limit**—The minimum value that the changing cell can assume while keeping the other changing cells fixed and still satisfying the constraints
- **Upper Limit**—The maximum value that the changing cell can assume while keeping the other changing cells fixed and still satisfying the constraints
- **Target Result**—The target cell's value when the changing cell is at the lower limit or upper limit

**Figure 16.17**
Solver's Limits report.

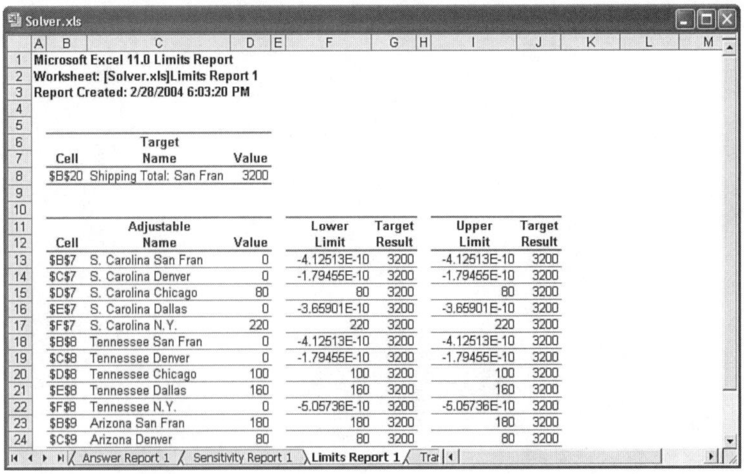

Microsoft Excel 11.0 Limits Report
Worksheet: [Solver.xls]Limits Report 1
Report Created: 2/28/2004 6:03:20 PM

| Cell | Target Name | Value |
|---|---|---|
| $B$20 | Shipping Total: San Fran | 3200 |

| Cell | Adjustable Name | Value | Lower Limit | Target Result | Upper Limit | Target Result |
|---|---|---|---|---|---|---|
| $B$7 | S. Carolina San Fran | 0 | -4.12513E-10 | 3200 | -4.12513E-10 | 3200 |
| $C$7 | S. Carolina Denver | 0 | -1.79455E-10 | 3200 | -1.79455E-10 | 3200 |
| $D$7 | S. Carolina Chicago | 80 | 80 | 3200 | 80 | 3200 |
| $E$7 | S. Carolina Dallas | 0 | -3.65901E-10 | 3200 | -3.65901E-10 | 3200 |
| $F$7 | S. Carolina N.Y. | 220 | 220 | 3200 | 220 | 3200 |
| $B$8 | Tennessee San Fran | 0 | -4.12513E-10 | 3200 | -4.12513E-10 | 3200 |
| $C$8 | Tennessee Denver | 0 | -1.79455E-10 | 3200 | -1.79455E-10 | 3200 |
| $D$8 | Tennessee Chicago | 100 | 100 | 3200 | 100 | 3200 |
| $E$8 | Tennessee Dallas | 160 | 160 | 3200 | 160 | 3200 |
| $F$8 | Tennessee N.Y. | 0 | -5.05736E-10 | 3200 | -5.05736E-10 | 3200 |
| $B$9 | Arizona San Fran | 180 | 180 | 3200 | 180 | 3200 |
| $C$9 | Arizona Denver | 80 | 80 | 3200 | 80 | 3200 |



## From Here

- To learn about using iteration to solve problems, **see** "Using Iteration and Circular References," **p. 90**
- For simple models, the Goal Seek tool might be all you need. **See** "Working with Goal Seek," **p. 321**
- To learn about scenarios, **see** "Working with Scenarios," **p. 330**

# Building Financial Formulas

**IV**

# Building Loan Formulas

# 17

Excel is loaded with financial features that give you powerful tools for building models that manage both business and personal finances. You can use these functions to calculate such things as the monthly payment on a loan, the future value of an annuity, the internal rate of return of an investment, or the yearly depreciation of an asset. The final four chapters of this book cover these and many other uses for Excel's financial formulas.

This chapter begins with formulas and functions related to loans and mortgages. You'll learn about the time value of money; how to calculate loan payments, loan periods, the principal and interest components of a payment, and the interest rate; and how to build an amortization schedule.

## Understanding the Time Value of Money

The *time value of money* means that a dollar in hand now is worth more than a dollar promised at some future date. This seemingly simple idea underlies not only the concepts and techniques you learn in this chapter, but also the investment formulas in Chapter 18, "Building Investment Formulas," and the discount formulas in Chapter 20, "Building Discount Formulas." A dollar now is worth more than a dollar promised in the future for two reasons:

- You can invest a dollar now. If you earn a positive return, the sum of the dollar and interest earned will be worth more than the future dollar.

- You might never see the future dollar. Due to bankruptcy, cash-flow problems, or any number of reasons, there's a risk that the company or person promising you the future dollar might not be able to deliver it.

These two factors—interest and risk—are at the heart of most financial formulas and models. Or, more realistically, these factors really mean that you're mostly comparing the benefits of investing a dollar now versus getting a dollar in the future *plus* some *risk premium*—an amount that compensates for the risk you're taking in waiting for the dollar to be delivered.

You compare these by looking at the *present value* (the amount something is worth now) and the *future value* (the amount something is worth in the future). They're related as follows:

**A.** Future value = Present value + Interest

**B.** Present value = Future value – discount

Much financial analysis boils down to comparing these formulas. If the present value in A is greater than the present value in B, then A is the better investment; conversely, if the future value in B is better than the future value in A, then B is the better investment.

Most of the formulas you'll work with over the next three chapters will involve these three factors—the present value, the future value, and the interest rate (or the discount rate)—plus two related factors: the *periods*, the number of payments or deposits over the term of the loan or investment, and the *payment*, the amount of money paid out or invested in each period.

When building your financial formulas, you need to ask yourself the following questions:

- Who or what is the subject of the formula? On a mortgage analysis, for example, are you performing the analysis on behalf of yourself or the bank?

- Which way is the money flowing with respect to the subject? For the present value, future value, and payment, enter money that the subject receives as a positive quantity, and enter money that the subject pays out as a negative quantity. For example, if you're the subject of a mortgage analysis, the loan principal (the present value) is a positive number because it's money that you receive from the bank; the payment and the remaining principal (the future value) are negative because they're amounts that you pay to the bank.

- What is the time unit? The underlying unit of both the interest rate and the period must be the same. For example, if you're working with the annual interest rate, you must express the period in years. Similarly, if you're working with monthly periods, you must use a monthly interest rate.

- When are the payments made? Excel differentiates between payments made at the end of each period and those made at the beginning.

# Calculating the Loan Payment

When negotiating a loan to purchase equipment or a mortgage for your house, the first concern that comes up is almost always the size of the payment you'll need to make each period. This is just basic cash-flow management because the monthly (or whatever) payment must fit within your budget.

To return the periodic payment for a loan, use the PMT() function:

PMT(*rate*, *nper*, *pv*, [*fv*], [*type*])

| | |
|---|---|
| *rate* | The fixed rate of interest over the term of the loan. |
| *nper* | The number of payments over the term of the loan. |
| *pv* | The loan principal. |
| *fv* | The future value of the loan. |
| *type* | The type of payment. Use 0 (the default) for end-of-period payments; use 1 for beginning-of-period payments. |

For example, the following formula returns the monthly payment of a $10,000 loan with an annual interest rate of 6% (0.5% per month) over 5 years (60 months):

=PMT(0.005, 60, 10000)

## Loan Payment Analysis

Financial formulas rarely use hard-coded function arguments. Instead, you almost always are better off placing the argument values in separate cells and then referring to those cells in the formula. This enables you to do a rudimentary form of loan analysis by plugging in different argument values and seeing the effects they have on the formula result.

Figure 17.1 shows an example of a worksheet set up to perform such an analysis. The PMT() formula is in cell B5, and the functions arguments are stored in B2 (*rate*), B3 (*nper*), and B4 (*pv*).

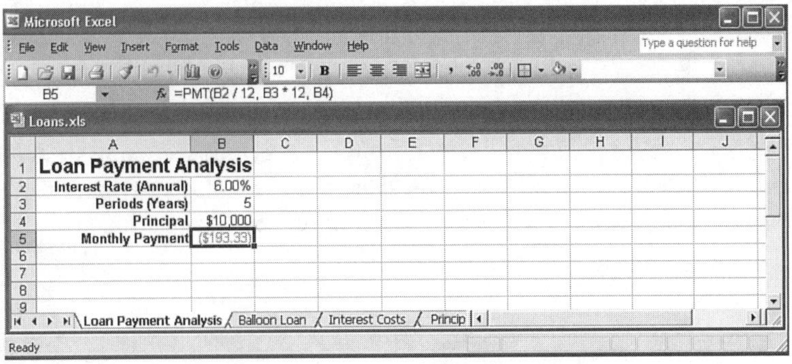

**Figure 17.1**
To perform a simple loan analysis, place the PMT() function arguments in separate cells, and then change those cell values to see the effect on the formula.

**NOTE**
You can download the workbook that contains this chapter's examples here:
www.mcfedries.com/ExcelFormulas/

Note two things about the formula and result in cell B5:

- The interest rate is an annual value and the periods are expressed in years, so to get a monthly payment, you must convert these values to their monthly equivalents. This means that the interest rate is divided by 12 and the number of periods is multiplied by 12:

```
=PMT(B2 / 12, B3 * 12, B4)
```

- The PMT() function returns a negative value, which is correct because this worksheet is set up from the point of view of the person receiving the loan, and the payment is money that flows away from that person.

## Working with a Balloon Loan

Many loans are set up so that the payments take care of only a portion of the principal, with the remainder due as an end-of-loan balloon payment. This balloon payment is the future value of the loan, so you need to factor it into the PMT() function as the *fv* argument.

You might think that the *pv* argument should be the partial principal—that is, the original loan principal minus the balloon amount. This seems right because the loan term is designed to pay off the partial principal. That's not the case, however. In a balloon loan, you also pay interest on the balloon part of the principal. That is, each payment in a balloon loan has three components:

- A paydown of the partial principal
- Interest on the partial principal
- Interest on the balloon portion of the principal

Therefore, the PMT() function's *pv* argument must be the entire principal, with the balloon portion as the (negative) *fv* argument.

For example, suppose that the loan from the previous section has a $3,000 balloon payment. Figure 17.2 shows a new worksheet that adds the balloon payment to the model and then calculates the payment using the following revised formula:

```
=PMT(B2 / 12, B3 * 12, B4, -B5)
```

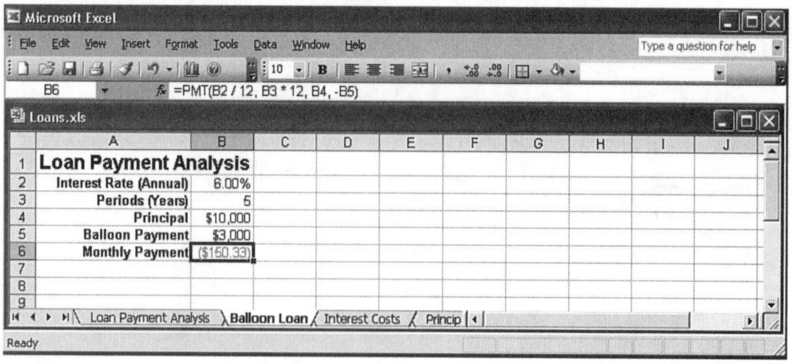

**Figure 17.2**
To allow for an end-of-loan balloon payment, add the *fv* argument to the PMT () function.

Note that the balloon payment is entered into the worksheet as a positive value, so (because it represents, in this model, money going out), the negation operation is used in the formula (–B5) to convert it to a negative value.

## Calculating Interest Costs

When you know the payment, you can calculate the total interest costs of the loan by first figuring the total of all the payments and then subtracting the principal. The remainder is the total interest paid over the life of the loan.

Figure 17.3 shows a worksheet that performs this calculation. In column B, cell B7 contains the total amount paid (the monthly payment multiplied by the number of months), and cell B8 takes the difference. Column C performs the same calculations on the loan with a balloon payment. As you can see, in the balloon payment scenario, the payment total is about $2,600 smaller, but the total interest is about $400 higher.

**Figure 17.3**

To calculate total interest paid out over the life of a loan, multiply the periodic payment by the number of periods, and then subtract the principal paid.

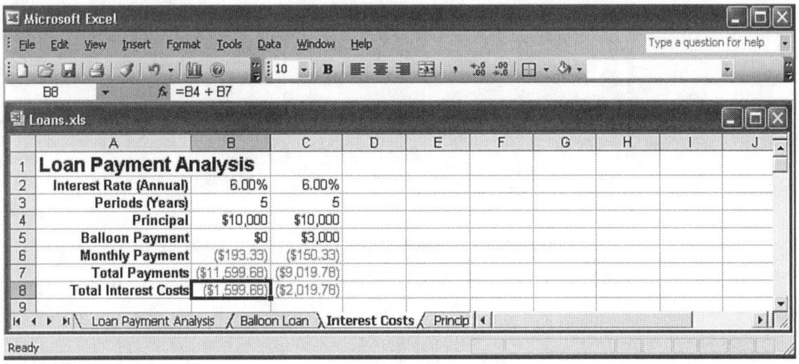

| | A | B | C |
|---|---|---|---|
| 1 | **Loan Payment Analysis** | | |
| 2 | Interest Rate (Annual) | 6.00% | 6.00% |
| 3 | Periods (Years) | 5 | 5 |
| 4 | Principal | $10,000 | $10,000 |
| 5 | Balloon Payment | $0 | $3,000 |
| 6 | Monthly Payment | ($193.33) | ($150.33) |
| 7 | Total Payments | ($11,599.68) | ($9,019.78) |
| 8 | Total Interest Costs | ($1,599.68) | ($2,019.78) |

Formula bar: B8 = =B4 + B7

## Calculating the Principal and Interest

Any loan payment has two components: principal repayment and interest charged. Interest charges are almost always *front-loaded*, which means that the interest component is highest at the beginning of the loan and gradually decreases with each payment. This means, conversely, that the principal component increases gradually with each payment.

To calculate the principal and interest components of a loan payment, use the PPMT() and IPMT() functions, respectively:

```
PPMT(rate, per, nper, pv, [fv], [type])
```

```
IPMT(rate, per, nper, pv, [fv], [type])
```

| | |
|---|---|
| *rate* | The fixed rate of interest over the term of the loan. |
| *per* | The number of the payment period (where the first payment is 1 and the last payment is the same as *nper*). |
| *nper* | The number of payments over the term of the loan. |
| *pv* | The loan principal. |

fv The future value of the loan (the default is 0).

type The type of payment. Use 0 (the default) for end-of-period payments; use 1 for beginning-of-period payments.

Figure 17.4 shows a worksheet that applies these functions to the loan. The data table shows the principal (column E) and interest (column F) components of the loan for the first 10 periods and for the final period. Note that with each period, the principal portion increases and the interest portion decreases. However, the total remains the same (as confirmed by the Total column), which is as it should be because the payment remains constant through the life of the loan.

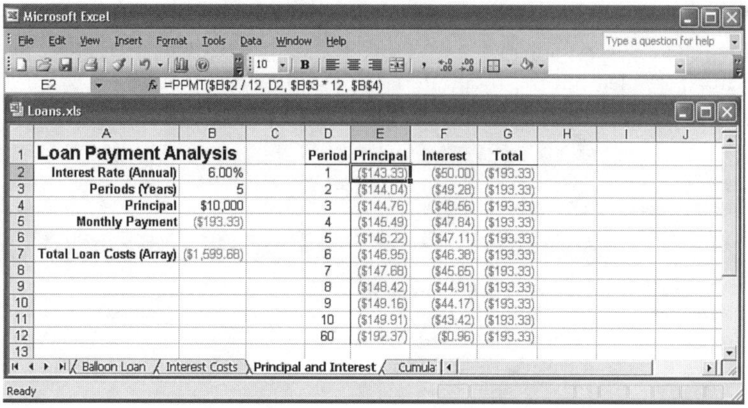

**Figure 17.4**
This worksheet uses the
PPMT() and IPMT()
functions to break out
the principal and inter-
est components of a
loan payment.

## Calculating Interest Costs, Part 2

Another way to calculate the total interest paid on a loan is to sum the various IPMT() values over the life of the line. You can do that by using an array formula that generates the values of the IPMT() function's *per* argument. Here's the general formula:

```
{=IPMT(rate, ROW(INDIRECT("A1:A" & nper)), nper, pv, [fv], [type])}
```

The array of *per* values is generated by the following expression:

```
ROW(INDIRECT("A1:A" & nper))
```

The INDIRECT() function converts a string range reference into an actual range reference, and then the ROW() function returns the row numbers from that range. By starting the range at A1, this expression generates integer values from 1 to *nper*, which covers the life of the loan.

For example, here's a formula that calculates the total interest cost of the loan model shown earlier in Figure 17.4:

```
{=SUM(IPMT(B2 / 12, ROW(INDIRECT("A1:A" & B3 * 12)), B3 * 12, B4))}
```

┌─ C A U T I O N ──────────────────────────────────────────────┐

The array formula doesn't work if the loan includes a balloon payment.

└───────────────────────────────────────────────────────────────┘

## Calculating Cumulative Principal and Interest

Knowing how much principal and interest you pay each period is useful, but it's usually more often handy to know how much principal or interest you've paid in total up to a given period. For example, if you sign up for a mortgage with a five-year term, how much principal will you have paid off by the end of the term? Similarly, a business might need to know the total interest payments a loan requires in the first year so that it can factor the result into its expense budgeting.

You could solve these kinds of problems by building a model that uses the PPMT() and IPMT() functions over the time frame you're dealing with and then summing the results. However, Excel's Analysis ToolPak has two functions that offer a more direct route:

```
CIMPRINC(rate, nper, pv, start_period, end_period, type)
```

```
CUMIPMT(rate, nper, pv, start_period, end_period, type)
```

| | |
|---|---|
| *rate* | The fixed rate of interest over the term of the loan. |
| *nper* | The number of payments over the term of the loan. |
| *pv* | The loan principal. |
| *start_period* | The first period to include in the calculation. |
| *end_period* | The last period to include in the calculation. |
| *type* | The type of payment. Use 0 for end-of-period payments; use 1 for beginning-of-period payments. |

┌─ C A U T I O N ──────────────────────────────────────────────┐

In both CUMPRINC() and CUMIPMT(), *all* of the arguments are required. If you omit the *type* argument (which is optional in most other financial functions), Excel returns the #N/A error.

└───────────────────────────────────────────────────────────────┘

The main difference between CUMPRINC() and CUMIPMT(), and PPMT() and IPMT() is the *start_period* and *end_period* arguments. For example, to find the cumulative principal or interest in the first year of a loan, you set *start_period* to 1 and *end_period* to 12; for the second year, you set *start_period* to 13 and *end_period* to 24. Here are a couple of formulas that calculate these values for any year, assuming that the year value (1, 2, and so on) is in cell D2:

*start_period*: (D2 - 1) * 12 + 1

*end_period*: D2 * 12

Figure 17.5 shows a worksheet that returns the cumulative principal and interest paid in each year of a loan, as well as the total principal and interest for all five years.

**17**

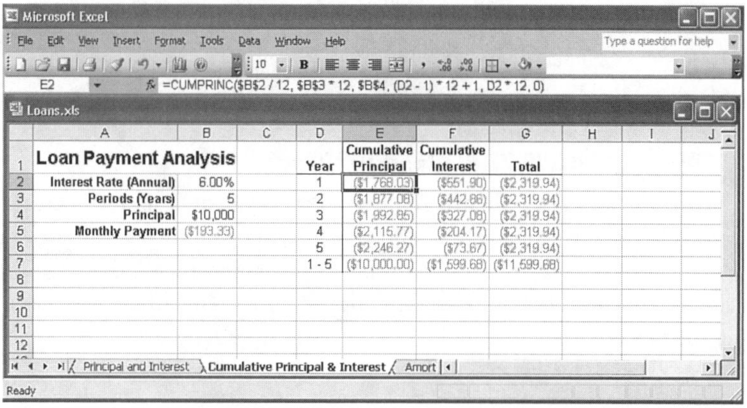

**Figure 17.5**
This worksheet uses the Analysis ToolPak's CUMPRINC() and CUMIPMT() functions to return the cumulative principal and interest for each year of a loan.

> **NOTE**
> Note that the CUMIPMT() function gives you an easier way to calculate the total interest costs for a loan. Just set the *start_period* to 1 and the *end_period* to the number of periods (the value of *nper*).

> **CAUTION**
> Although the CUMPRINC() function works as advertised if the loan includes a balloon payment, the CUMIPMT() function does not.

# Building a Loan Amortization Schedule

A loan *amortization schedule* is a table that shows a sequence of calculations over the life of a loan. For each period, the schedule shows figures such as the payment, the principal and interest components of the payment, the cumulative principal and interest, and the remaining principal. The next few sections take you through various amortization schedules designed for different scenarios.

## Building a Fixed-Rate Amortization Schedule

The simplest amortization schedule is just a straightforward application of three of the payment functions you've seen so far: PMT(), PPMT(), and IPMT(). Figure 17.6 shows the result, which has the following features:

- The values for the five main arguments of the payment functions are stored in the range B2:B6.
- The amortization schedule is shown in A9:G24. Column A contains the period, and subsequent columns calculate the payment (column B), principal component (C), interest component (D), cumulative principal (E), and cumulative interest (F). The Remaining Principal column shows the original principle amount (B4) minus the cumulative principal for each period.

- The cumulative principal and interest values are calculated by adding the running totals of the principal and interest components. You need to do this because the `CUMPRINC()` and `CUMIPMT()` functions don't work with balloon payments. If you never use balloon payments, you can convert the worksheet to use these functions.
- This schedule uses a yearly time frame, so no adjustments are applied to the *`rate`* and *`nper`* arguments.

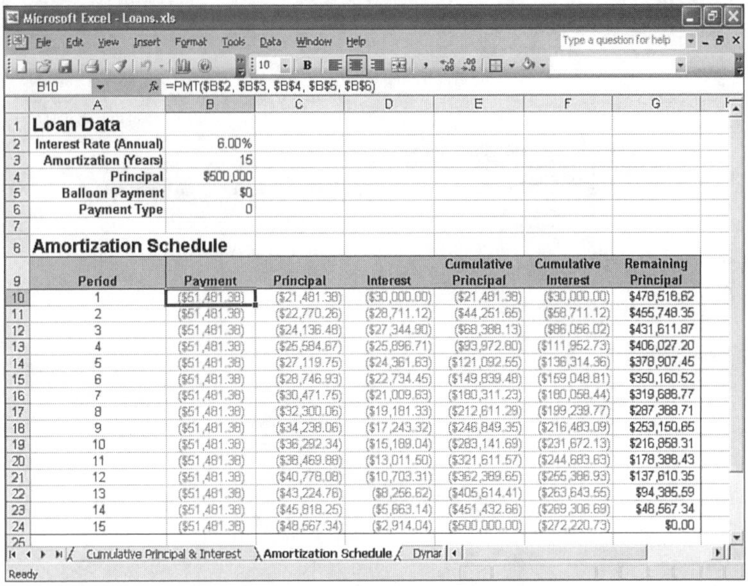


| | A | B | C | D | E | F | G |
|---|---|---|---|---|---|---|---|
| 1 | Loan Data | | | | | | |
| 2 | Interest Rate (Annual) | 6.00% | | | | | |
| 3 | Amortization (Years) | 15 | | | | | |
| 4 | Principal | $500,000 | | | | | |
| 5 | Balloon Payment | $0 | | | | | |
| 6 | Payment Type | 0 | | | | | |
| 7 | | | | | | | |
| 8 | Amortization Schedule | | | | | | |
| 9 | Period | Payment | Principal | Interest | Cumulative Principal | Cumulative Interest | Remaining Principal |
| 10 | 1 | ($51,481.38) | ($21,481.38) | ($30,000.00) | ($21,481.38) | ($30,000.00) | $478,518.62 |
| 11 | 2 | ($51,481.38) | ($22,770.26) | ($28,711.12) | ($44,251.65) | ($58,711.12) | $455,748.35 |
| 12 | 3 | ($51,481.38) | ($24,136.48) | ($27,344.90) | ($68,388.13) | ($86,056.02) | $431,611.87 |
| 13 | 4 | ($51,481.38) | ($25,584.67) | ($25,896.71) | ($93,972.80) | ($111,952.73) | $406,027.20 |
| 14 | 5 | ($51,481.38) | ($27,119.75) | ($24,361.63) | ($121,092.55) | ($136,314.36) | $378,907.45 |
| 15 | 6 | ($51,481.38) | ($28,746.93) | ($22,734.45) | ($149,839.48) | ($159,048.81) | $350,160.52 |
| 16 | 7 | ($51,481.38) | ($30,471.75) | ($21,009.63) | ($180,311.23) | ($180,058.44) | $319,688.77 |
| 17 | 8 | ($51,481.38) | ($32,300.06) | ($19,181.33) | ($212,611.29) | ($199,239.77) | $287,388.71 |
| 18 | 9 | ($51,481.38) | ($34,238.06) | ($17,243.32) | ($246,849.35) | ($216,483.09) | $253,150.65 |
| 19 | 10 | ($51,481.38) | ($36,292.34) | ($15,189.04) | ($283,141.69) | ($231,672.13) | $216,858.31 |
| 20 | 11 | ($51,481.38) | ($38,469.88) | ($13,011.50) | ($321,611.57) | ($244,683.63) | $178,388.43 |
| 21 | 12 | ($51,481.38) | ($40,778.08) | ($10,703.31) | ($362,389.65) | ($255,386.93) | $137,610.35 |
| 22 | 13 | ($51,481.38) | ($43,224.76) | ($8,256.62) | ($405,614.41) | ($263,643.55) | $94,385.59 |
| 23 | 14 | ($51,481.38) | ($45,818.25) | ($5,663.14) | ($451,432.66) | ($269,306.69) | $48,567.34 |
| 24 | 15 | ($51,481.38) | ($48,567.34) | ($2,914.04) | ($500,000.00) | ($272,220.73) | $0.00 |

**Figure 17.6**
This worksheet shows a basic amortization schedule for a fixed-rate loan.



➔ The amortization in Figure 17.6 assumes that the interest rate remains fixed throughout the life of the loan. To learn how to build an amortization for a variable-rate loan, **see** "Building a Variable-Rate Mortgage Amortization Schedule," **p. 413**.

## Building a Dynamic Amortization Schedule

The problem with the amortization schedule in Figure 17.6 is that it's static. It works well if you change the interest rate or the principal, but it doesn't handle other types of changes very well:

- If you want to use a different time basis—for example, monthly instead of annual—you need to edit the initial formulas for payment, principal, interest, cumulative principal, and cumulative interest, and then refill the schedule.
- If you want to use a different number of periods, you need to either extend the schedule (for a longer term) or shorten the schedule and delete the extraneous periods (for a shorter term).

Both operations are tedious and time consuming enough that they greatly reduce the value of the amortization schedule. To make the schedule truly useful, you need to reconfigure it so that the schedule formulas and the schedule itself adjust automatically to any change in the time basis or the length of the term.

Figure 17.7 shows a worksheet that implements such a dynamic amortization schedule.

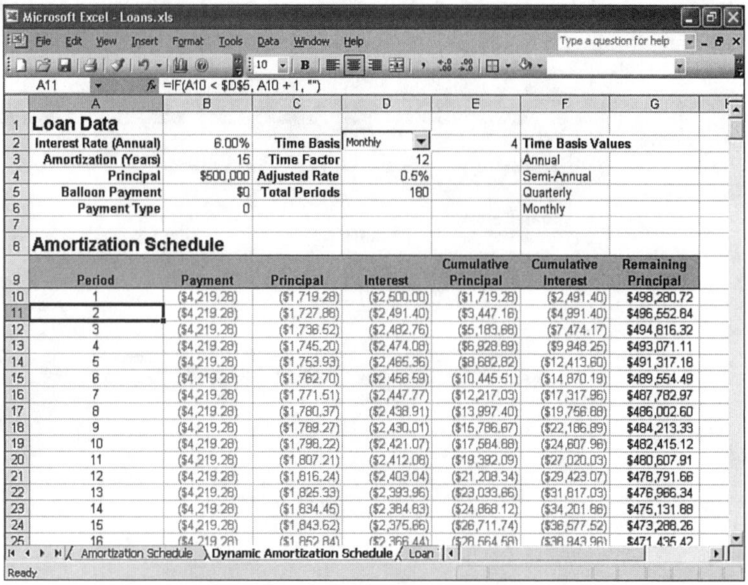

**Figure 17.7**
This worksheet uses a dynamic amortization schedule that adjusts automatically to changing the time basis or the length of the term.

Here's a summary of the changes I made to create this schedule's dynamic behavior:

- To change the time basis, select a value—Annual, Semiannual, Quarterly, or Monthly—in the Time Basis drop-down list. These values come from the text literals in the range F3:F6. The value of the chosen option is stored in cell E2.

→ To learn how to add a list box to a worksheet, **see** "Using Dialog Box Controls on a Worksheet," **p. 100**.

- The time basis determines the *time factor*, the amount by which you have to adjust the rate and the term. For example, if the time basis is Monthly, the time factor is 12. This means that you divide the annual interest rate (B2) by 12, and you multiply the term (B3) by 12. These new values are stored in the Adjusted Rate (D4) and Total Periods (D5) cells. The Time Factor cell (D3) uses the following formula:

```
=CHOOSE(E2, 1, 2, 4, 12)
```

- Given the adjusted rate (D4) and the total periods (D5), the schedule formulas can reference these cells directly and always return the correct value for any selected time basis. For example, here's the expression that calculates the payment:

```
PMT(D4, D5, B4, B5, B6)
```

- The schedule adjusts its size automatically, depending on the Total Periods value (D5). If Total Periods is 15, the schedule contains 15 rows (not including the headers); if Total Periods is 180, the schedule contains 180 rows.

- Dynamically adjusting the size of the schedule is a function of the Total Periods value (D5). The first period (A10) is always 1; each subsequent period checks the previous value to see if it's less than Total Periods. Here's the formula in cell A11:

```
=IF(A10 < D5, A10 + 1, "")
```

If the period value of the cell above the current cell is less than Total Periods, the current cell is still within the schedule, so calculate the current period (the value from the cell above, plus 1) and display the result; otherwise, you've gone past the end of the schedule, so write a blank.

- The various payment columns check the period value. If it's not blank, calculate and display the result; otherwise, display a blank. Here's the formula for the Payment value in B11:

```
=IF(A11 <> "", PMT($D$4, $D$5, $B$4, $B$5, $B$6), "")
```

These changes result in a totally dynamic schedule that adjusts automatically as you change the time basis or the term.

> **NOTE** The formulas in the amortization schedule have been filled down to row 500, which should be enough room for just about any schedule (up to about 40 years, using the monthly basis). If you require a longer schedule, you'll have to fill in the schedule formulas past the last row that will appear in your schedule.

# Calculating the Term of the Loan

In some loan scenarios, you need to borrow a certain amount at the current interest rates, but you can spend only so much on each payment. If the other loan factors are fixed, the only way to adjust the payment is to adjust the term of the loan: A longer term means smaller payments; a shorter term means larger payments.

You could figure this out by adjusting the *nper* argument of the PMT() function until you get the payment you want. However, Excel offers a more direct solution in the form of the NPER() function, which returns the number of periods of a loan:

```
NPER(rate, pmt, pv, [fv], [type])
```

| | |
|---|---|
| *rate* | The fixed rate of interest over the term of the loan. |
| *pmt* | The periodic payment. |
| *pv* | The loan principal. |
| *fv* | The future value of the loan (the default is 0). |
| *type* | The type of payment. Use 0 (the default) for end-of-period payments; use 1 for beginning-of-period payments. |

For example, suppose that you want to borrow $10,000 at 6% interest with no balloon payment, and the most you can spend is $750 per month. What term should you get? Figure

17.8 shows a worksheet that uses `NPER()` to calculate the answer: 13.8 months. Here are some things to note about this model:

- The interest rate is an annual value, so the `NPER()` function's *`rate`* argument divides the rate by 12.
- The payment is already a monthly number, so no adjustment is necessary for the *`pmt`* attribute.
- The payment is negative because it's money that you pay to the lender.

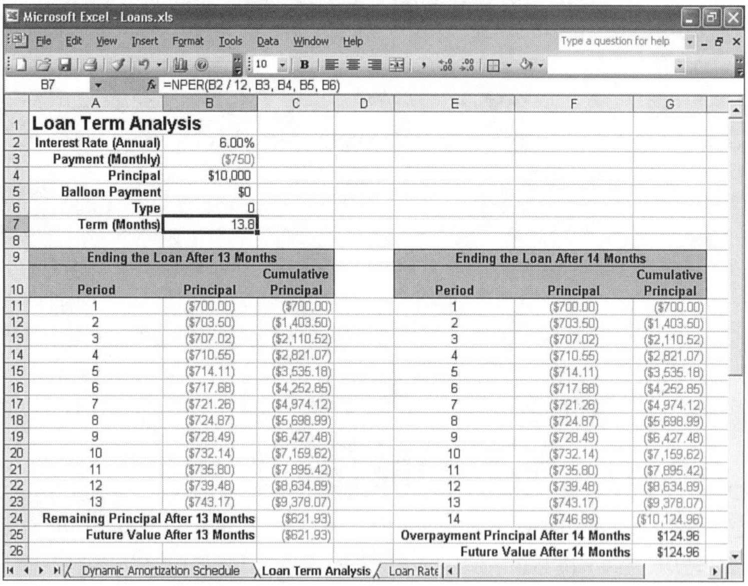


| | A | B | C | D | E | F | G |
|---|---|---|---|---|---|---|---|
| 1 | Loan Term Analysis | | | | | | |
| 2 | Interest Rate (Annual) | 6.00% | | | | | |
| 3 | Payment (Monthly) | ($750) | | | | | |
| 4 | Principal | $10,000 | | | | | |
| 5 | Balloon Payment | $0 | | | | | |
| 6 | Type | 0 | | | | | |
| 7 | Term (Months) | 13.8 | | | | | |
| 8 | | | | | | | |
| 9 | Ending the Loan After 13 Months | | | | Ending the Loan After 14 Months | | |
| 10 | Period | Principal | Cumulative Principal | | Period | Principal | Cumulative Principal |
| 11 | 1 | ($700.00) | ($700.00) | | 1 | ($700.00) | ($700.00) |
| 12 | 2 | ($703.50) | ($1,403.50) | | 2 | ($703.50) | ($1,403.50) |
| 13 | 3 | ($707.02) | ($2,110.52) | | 3 | ($707.02) | ($2,110.52) |
| 14 | 4 | ($710.55) | ($2,821.07) | | 4 | ($710.55) | ($2,821.07) |
| 15 | 5 | ($714.11) | ($3,535.18) | | 5 | ($714.11) | ($3,535.18) |
| 16 | 6 | ($717.68) | ($4,252.85) | | 6 | ($717.68) | ($4,252.85) |
| 17 | 7 | ($721.26) | ($4,974.12) | | 7 | ($721.26) | ($4,974.12) |
| 18 | 8 | ($724.87) | ($5,698.99) | | 8 | ($724.87) | ($5,698.99) |
| 19 | 9 | ($728.49) | ($6,427.48) | | 9 | ($728.49) | ($6,427.48) |
| 20 | 10 | ($732.14) | ($7,159.62) | | 10 | ($732.14) | ($7,159.62) |
| 21 | 11 | ($735.80) | ($7,895.42) | | 11 | ($735.80) | ($7,895.42) |
| 22 | 12 | ($739.48) | ($8,634.89) | | 12 | ($739.48) | ($8,634.89) |
| 23 | 13 | ($743.17) | ($9,378.07) | | 13 | ($743.17) | ($9,378.07) |
| 24 | Remaining Principal After 13 Months | | ($621.93) | | 14 | ($746.89) | ($10,124.96) |
| 25 | Future Value After 13 Months | | ($621.93) | | Overpayment Principal After 14 Months | | $124.96 |
| 26 | | | | | | Future Value After 14 Months | $124.96 |

**Figure 17.8**
This worksheet uses `NPER()` to determine the number of months that a $10,000 loan should be taken out at 6% interest to ensure a monthly payment of $750.

Of course, in the real world, although it's not unusual to have a noninteger term, the last payment must occur at the beginning or end of the last loan period. In the example, the bank uses the term of 13.8 months to calculate the payment, principal, and interest, but it rightly insists that the last payment be made at either the 13th period or the 14th period. The tables after the `NPER()` formula in Figure 17.8 investigate both scenarios.

If you elect to end the loan after the 13th period, you'll still have a bit of principal left over. To see why, the amortization table shows the period (column A) as well as the principal paid each period (column B), as returned by the `PPMT()` function. The Cumulative Principal column (column C) shows a running total of the principal. As you can see, after 13 months, the total principal paid is only $9,378.07, which leaves $621.93 remaining (cell C24). Therefore, the 13th payment will be $1,371.93 (the usual $750 payment, plus the remaining $621.93 principal).

> **NOTE** The cumulative principal values are calculated using the SUM() function. You can't use the CUMPRINC() function in this case because CUMPRINC() truncates the *nper* argument to an integer value.

If you elect to end the loan after the 14th period instead, you'll end up overpaying the principal. To see why, the second amortization table shows the Period (column E), Principal (column F), and Cumulative Principal (column G) columns. After 14 months the total principal paid is $10,124.96, which is $124.96 more than the original $10,000 principal. Therefore, the 14th payment will be $625.04 (the usual $750 payment minus the $124.96 principal overpayment).

> **NOTE** Another way to calculate the principal that is left over or overpaid is to use the FV() function, which returns the future value of a series of payments. For the 13-month scenario, you run FV() with the *nper* argument set to 13 (see cell C25 in Figure 17.8); for the 14-month scenario, you run FV() with the *nper* argument set to 14 (see cell G26). You'll learn about FV() in detail in Chapter 18.

## Calculating the Interest Rate Required for a Loan

A slightly less common loan scenario arises when you know the loan term, payment, and principal, and you need to know what interest rate will satisfy these parameters. This is useful in a number of circumstances:

- You might decide to wait until interest rates fall to the value you want.
- You might regard the calculated interest rate as a maximum rate that you can pay, knowing that anything less will enable you to reduce either the payment or the term.
- You could use the calculated interest rate as a negotiating tool with your lender by asking for that rate and walking away from the deal if you don't get it.

To determine the interest rate given the other loan factors, use the RATE() functions:

RATE(*nper, pmt, pv, [fv], [type], [guess]*)

| | |
|---|---|
| *nper* | The number of payments over the term of the loan. |
| *pmt* | The periodic payment. |
| *pv* | The loan principal. |
| *fv* | The future value of the loan (the default is 0). |
| *type* | The type of payment. Use 0 (the default) for end-of-period payments; use 1 for beginning-of-period payments. |
| *guess* | A percentage value that Excel uses as a starting point for calculating the interest rate (the default is 10%). |

→ The RATE ( ) function's *guess* parameter indicates that this function uses iteration to determine the answer. To learn more about iteration, **see** "Using Iteration and Circular References," **p. 90**.

For example, suppose that you want to borrow $10,000 over 5 years with no balloon payment and a monthly payout of $200. What rate will satisfy these criteria? The worksheet in Figure 17.9 uses RATE() to derive the result of 7.4%. Here are some notes about this model:

- The term is in years, so the RATE ( ) function's *nper* argument multiplies the term by 12.
- The payment is already a monthly number, so no adjustment is necessary for the *pmt* attribute.
- The payment is negative because it's money that you pay to the lender.
- The result of the RATE ( ) function is multiplied by 12 to get the annual interest rate.

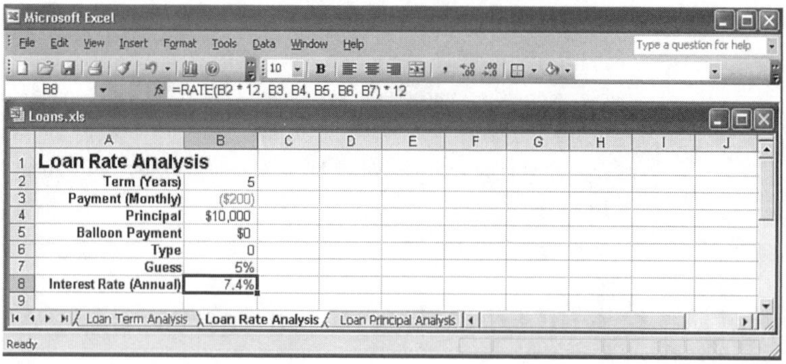

**Figure 17.9**
This worksheet uses RATE ( ) to determine the interest rate required to pay a $10,000 loan over 5 years at $200 per month.

# Calculating How Much You Can Borrow

If you know the current interest rate that your bank is offering for loans, when you want to have the loan paid off, and how much you can afford each month for the payments, you might then wonder what is the maximum amount you can borrow under those terms. To figure this out, you need to solve for the principal—that is, present value. You do that in Excel by using the PV() function:

PV(*rate, nper, pmt,* [*fv*], [*type*])

| | |
|---|---|
| *rate* | The fixed rate of interest over the term of the loan. |
| *nper* | The number of payments over the term of the loan. |
| *pmt* | The periodic payment. |
| *fv* | The future value of the loan (the default is 0). |
| *type* | The type of payment. Use 0 (the default) for end-of-period payments; use 1 for beginning-of-period payments. |

For example, suppose that the current loan rate is 6%, you want the loan paid off in 5 years, and you can afford payments of $500 per month. Figure 17.10 shows a worksheet that calculates the maximum amount that you can borrow—$25,862.78—using the following formula:

```
=PV(B2 / 12, B3 * 12, B4, B5, B6)
```

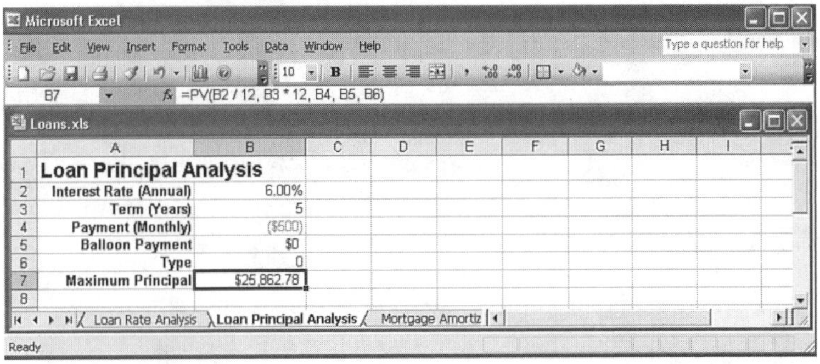

**Figure 17.10**
This worksheet uses PV ( ) to calculate the maximum principal that you can borrow, given a fixed interest rate, term, and monthly payment.

# CASE STUDY

## Working with Mortgages

For both businesses and people, a mortgage is almost always the largest financial transaction. Whether it's millions of dollars for a new building or hundreds of thousands of dollars for a house, a mortgage is serious business. It pays to know exactly what you're getting into, both in terms of long-term cash flow and in terms of making good decisions up front about the type of mortgage so that you minimize your interest costs. This case study takes a look at mortgages from both points of view.

## Building a Variable-Rate Mortgage Amortization Schedule

For simplicity's sake, it's possible to build a mortgage amortization schedule like the ones shown earlier in this chapter. However, these aren't realistic because a mortgage rarely uses the same interest rate over the full amortization period. Instead, you usually have a fixed rate over a specific *term* (usually 1–5 years), and you then renegotiate the mortgage for a new term. This renegotiation involves changing three things:

■ The interest rate over the coming term, which will reflect current market rates.

■ The amortization period, which will now be shorter by the length of the previous term. For example, a 25-year amortization will drop to a 20-year amortization after a 5-year term.

■ The present value of the mortgage, which will be the remaining principal at the end of the term.

Figure 17.11 shows an amortization schedule that takes these mortgage realities into account.

**Figure 17.11**
A mortgage amortization that reflects the changing interest rates, amortization periods, and present value at each new term.

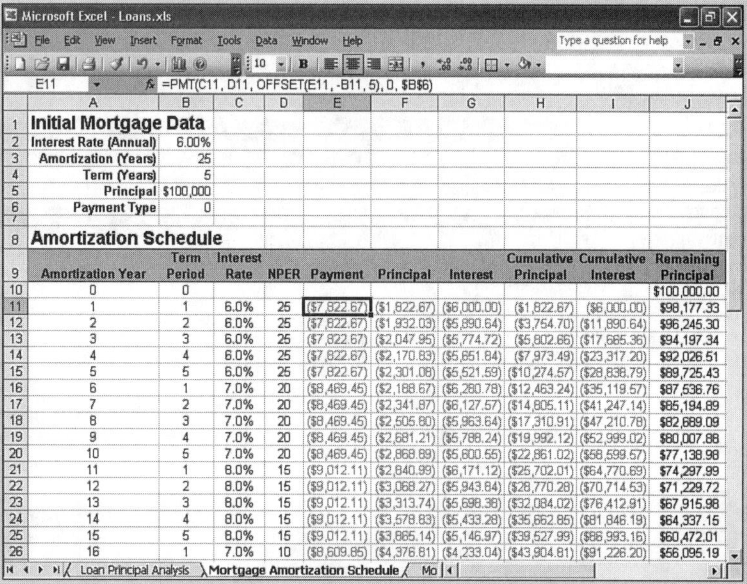


**Initial Mortgage Data**

| | |
|---|---|
| Interest Rate (Annual) | 6.00% |
| Amortization (Years) | 25 |
| Term (Years) | 5 |
| Principal | $100,000 |
| Payment Type | 0 |

**Amortization Schedule**

| Amortization Year | Term Period | Interest Rate | NPER | Payment | Principal | Interest | Cumulative Principal | Cumulative Interest | Remaining Principal |
|---|---|---|---|---|---|---|---|---|---|
| 0 | 0 | | | | | | | | $100,000.00 |
| 1 | 1 | 6.0% | 25 | ($7,822.67) | ($1,822.67) | ($6,000.00) | ($1,822.67) | ($6,000.00) | $98,177.33 |
| 2 | 2 | 6.0% | 25 | ($7,822.67) | ($1,932.03) | ($5,890.64) | ($3,754.70) | ($11,890.64) | $96,245.30 |
| 3 | 3 | 6.0% | 25 | ($7,822.67) | ($2,047.95) | ($5,774.72) | ($5,802.66) | ($17,665.36) | $94,197.34 |
| 4 | 4 | 6.0% | 25 | ($7,822.67) | ($2,170.83) | ($5,651.84) | ($7,973.49) | ($23,317.20) | $92,026.51 |
| 5 | 5 | 6.0% | 25 | ($7,822.67) | ($2,301.08) | ($5,521.59) | ($10,274.57) | ($28,838.79) | $89,725.43 |
| 6 | 1 | 7.0% | 20 | ($8,469.45) | ($2,188.67) | ($6,280.78) | ($12,463.24) | ($35,119.57) | $87,536.76 |
| 7 | 2 | 7.0% | 20 | ($8,469.45) | ($2,341.87) | ($6,127.57) | ($14,805.11) | ($41,247.14) | $85,194.89 |
| 8 | 3 | 7.0% | 20 | ($8,469.45) | ($2,505.80) | ($5,963.64) | ($17,310.91) | ($47,210.78) | $82,689.09 |
| 9 | 4 | 7.0% | 20 | ($8,469.45) | ($2,681.21) | ($5,788.24) | ($19,992.12) | ($52,999.02) | $80,007.88 |
| 10 | 5 | 7.0% | 20 | ($8,469.45) | ($2,868.89) | ($5,600.55) | ($22,861.02) | ($58,599.57) | $77,138.98 |
| 11 | 1 | 8.0% | 15 | ($9,012.11) | ($2,840.99) | ($6,171.12) | ($25,702.01) | ($64,770.69) | $74,297.99 |
| 12 | 2 | 8.0% | 15 | ($9,012.11) | ($3,068.27) | ($5,943.84) | ($28,770.28) | ($70,714.53) | $71,229.72 |
| 13 | 3 | 8.0% | 15 | ($9,012.11) | ($3,313.74) | ($5,698.38) | ($32,084.02) | ($76,412.91) | $67,915.98 |
| 14 | 4 | 8.0% | 15 | ($9,012.11) | ($3,578.83) | ($5,433.28) | ($35,662.85) | ($81,846.19) | $64,337.15 |
| 15 | 5 | 8.0% | 15 | ($9,012.11) | ($3,865.14) | ($5,146.97) | ($39,527.99) | ($86,993.16) | $60,472.01 |
| 16 | 1 | 7.0% | 10 | ($8,609.85) | ($4,376.81) | ($4,233.04) | ($43,904.81) | ($91,226.20) | $56,095.19 |

Here's a summary of what's happening with each column in the amortization:

- **Amortization Year**—This column gives the year of the overall amortization. This is mainly used to help calculate the Term Period values. Note that the values in this column are generated automatically based on the value in the Amortization (Years) cell (B3).
- **Term Period**—This column gives the year of the current term. This is a calculated value (it uses the `MOD()` function) based on the value in the Amortization Year column and the value in the Term (Years) cell (B4).
- **Interest Rate**—This is the interest rate applied to each term. You enter these rates by hand.
- **NPER**—This is the amortization period applied to each term. It's used as the *`nper`* argument for the `PMT()`, `PPMT()`, and `IPMT()` functions. You enter these values by hand.
- **Payment**—This is the monthly payment for the current term. The `PMT()` function uses the Interest Rate column value for the *`rate`* argument and the NPER column value for the *`nper`* argument. For the *`pv`* argument, the function grabs the remaining balance at the end of the previous term by using the `OFFSET()` function in the following general form:

  ```
  OFFSET(current_cell, -Term_Period, 5)
  ```

  Here, *`current_cell`* is a reference to the cell containing the formula, and *`Term_Period`* is a reference to the corresponding cell in Term Period column. For example, here's the formula in E11:

  ```
  OFFSET(E11, -B11, 5)
  ```

  Because the value in B11 is `1`, the function goes up one row and right five columns, which returns the value in J10 (in this case, the original principal).
- **Principal and Interest**—These columns calculate the principal and interest components of the payment, and they use the same techniques as the Payment column does.

■ **Cumulative Principal and Cumulative Interest**—These columns calculate the total principal and interest paid through the end of each year. Because the interest rate isn't constant over the life of the loan, you can't use `CUMPRINC()` and `CUMIPMT()`. Instead, these columns use running `SUM()` functions.

■ **Remaining Principal**—This column calculates the principal left on the loan by subtracting the value in the Principal column for each year. At the end of each term, the Remaining Principal value is used as the $pv$ argument in the `PMT()`, `PPMT()`, and `IPMT()` functions over the next term. In Figure 17.11, for example, at the end of the first 5-year term, the remaining principal is $89,725.43, so that's the present value used throughout the second 5-year term.

## Allowing for Mortgage Principal Paydowns

Many mortgages today allow you to include in each payment an extra amount that goes directly to paying down the mortgage principal. Before you decide to take on the financial burden of these extra paydowns, you probably want two questions answered:

■ How much quicker will I pay off the mortgage?

■ How much money will I save over the amortization period?

Both questions are easily answered using Excel's financial functions. Consider the mortgage-analysis model I've set up in Figure 17.12. The Initial Mortgage Data area shows the basic numbers needed for the calculations: the annual interest rate (cell B2), the amortization period (B3), the principal (B4), and the paydown that is to be added to each payment (B5— notice that this is a negative number because it represents a monetary outflow).

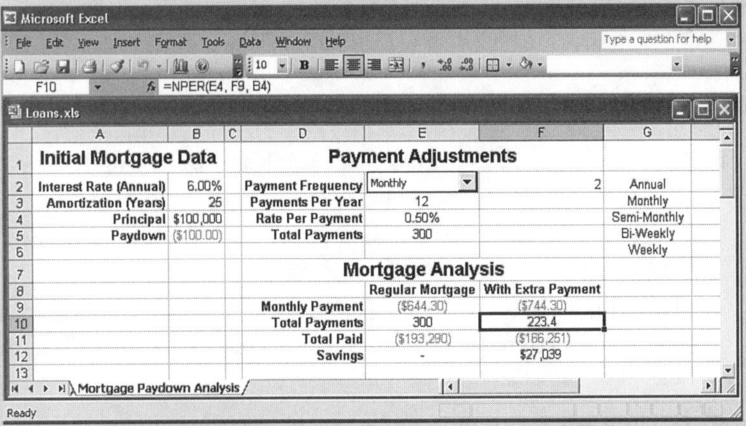

**Figure 17.12**
A mortgage-analysis worksheet that calculates the effect of making extra monthly paydowns toward the principal.

The Payment Adjustments area contains four values:

■ **Payment Frequency**—Use this drop-down list to specify how often you make your mortgage payments. The available values—Annual, Monthly, Semimonthly, Biweekly, and Weekly—come from the range G2:G6; the number of the selected list item is stored in cell F2.

- **Payments Per Year (D3)**—This is the number of payments per year, as given by the following formula:
  `=CHOOSE(E2, 1, 12, 24, 26, 52)`
- **Rate Per Payment**—This is the annual rate divided by the number of payments per year.
- **Total Payments**—This is the amortization value multiplied by the number of payments per year.

The Mortgage Analysis area shows the results of various calculations:

- *Frequency* **Payment**—(*Frequency* is the selected item in the drop-down list.) The Regular Mortgage payment (E9) is calculated using the `PMT()` function, where the *rate* argument is the Rate Per Payment value (E4) and the *nper* argument is the Total Payments value (E5):
  `=PMT(E4, E5, B4, 0, 0)`
  The With Extra Payment value (F9) is the sum of the Paydown (B5) and the Regular Mortgage payment (E9).
- **Total Payments**—For the Regular Mortgage (E10), this is the same as the Total Payments value (E5). It's copied here to make it easy for you to compare this value with the With Extra Payment value (F10), which calculates the revised term with the extra paydown included. It does this with the `NPER()` function, where the *rate* argument is the Rate Per Payment value (E4) and the *pmt* argument is the payment in the With Extra Payment column (F9).
- **Total Paid**—These values multiply the Payment value by the Total Payments value for each column.
- **Savings**—This value (cell F12) takes the difference between the Total Paid values, to show how much money you save by including the paydown in each payment.

In the example shown in Figure 17.12, paying an extra $100 per month toward the mortgage principal reduces the term on a $100,000 mortgage from 300 months (25 years) to 223.4 months (about 18 1/2 years), and reduces the total amount paid from $193,290 to $166,251, a savings of $27,039.

## From Here

- To learn how to add a list box to a worksheet, **see** "Using Dialog Box Controls on a Worksheet," **p. 100**.
- The `RATE()` function uses iteration to calculate its value. To learn more about iteration, **see** "Using Iteration and Circular References," **p. 90**.
- Many of the functions you learned in this chapter—including `PMT()`, `RATE()`, and `NPER()`—can also be used with investment calculations. **See** "Building Investment Formulas," **p. 417**.
- The `PV()` function is most often used in discount calculations. **See** "Calculating the Present Value," **p. 448**.

# Building Investment Formulas

The time value of money concepts introduced in Chapter 17, "Building Loan Formulas," apply equally well to investments. The only difference is that you need to reverse the signs of the cash values. That's because loans generally involve receiving a principal amount (positive cash flow) and paying it back over time (negative cash flow). An investment, on the other hand, involves depositing money into the investment (negative cash flow) and then receiving interest payments (or whatever) in return (positive cash flow).

With this sign change in mind, this chapter takes you through some Excel tools for building investment formulas. You'll learn about the wonders of compound interest; how to convert between nominal and effective interest rates; how to calculate the future value of an investment; ways to work toward an investment goal by calculating the required interest rate, term, and deposits; and how to build an investment schedule.

# 18

## Working with Interest Rates

As I mentioned in Chapter 17, the interest rate is the mechanism that transforms a present value into a future value. (Or, operating as a discount rate, it's what transforms a future value into a present value.) Therefore, when working with financial formulas, it's important to know how to work with interest rates and to be comfortable with certain terminology. You've already seen (again, in Chapter 17) that it's crucial for the interest rate, term, and payment to use the same time basis. The next sections show you a few other interest rate techniques you should know.

## Understanding Compound Interest

An interest rate is described as *simple* if it pays the same amount each period. For example, if you have $1,000 in an investment that pays a simple interest rate of 10% per year, you'll receive $100 each year.

Suppose, however, that you were able to add the interest payments to the investment. At the end of the first year, you would have $1,100 in the account, which means that you would earn $110 in interest (10% of $1,100) the second year. Being able to add interest earned to an investment is called *compounding*, and the total interest earned (the normal interest plus the extra interest on the reinvested interest—the extra $10, in the example) is called *compound interest*.

## Nominal Versus Effective Interest

Interest can also be compounded within the year. For example, suppose that your $1,000 investment earns 10% compounded semiannually. At the end of the first 6 months, you receive $50 in interest (5% of the original investment). This $50 is reinvested, and for the second half of the year, you earn 5% of $1,050, or $52.50. Therefore, the total interest earned in the first year is $102.50. In other words, the interest rate appears to actually be 10.25%. So which is the correct interest rate, 10% or 10.25%?

To answer that question, you need to know about the two ways that most interest rates are most often quoted:

- **The nominal rate**—This is the annual rate before compounding (the 10% rate, in the example). The nominal rate is always quoted along with the compounding frequency— for example, 10% compounded semiannually.

> **NOTE**  The nominal annual interest rate is often shortened to APR, or the annual percentage rate.

- **The effective rate**—This is the annual rate that an investment actually earns in the year after the compounding is applied (the 10.25%, in the example).

In other words, both rates are "correct," except that, with the nominal rate, you also need to know the compounding frequency.

If you know the nominal rate and the number of compounding periods per year (for example, semiannually means two compounding periods per year, and monthly means 12 compounding periods per year), you get the effective rate per period by dividing the nominal rate by the number of periods:

```
=nominal_rate / npery
```

Here, *npery* is the number of compounding periods per year. To convert the nominal annual rate into the effective annual rate, you use the following formula:

```
=((1 + nominal_rate / npery) ^ npery) - 1
```

Conversely, if you know the effective rate per period, you can derive the nominal rate by multiplying the effective rate by the number of periods:

```
=effective_rate * npery
```

To convert the effective annual rate to the nominal annual rate, you use the following formula:

```
npery * (effective_rate + 1) ^ (1 / npery) - npery
```

Fortunately, the next section shows you two functions that can handle the conversion between the nominal and effective annual rates for you.

## Converting Between the Nominal Rate and the Effective Rate

To convert a nominal annual interest rate to the effective annual rate, use the Analysis ToolPak's `EFFECT()` function:

```
EFFECT(nominal_rate, npery)
```

| | |
|---|---|
| *nominal_rate* | The nominal annual interest rate |
| *npery* | The number of compounding periods in the year |



For example, the following formula returns the effective annual interest rate for an investment with a nominal annual rate of 10% that compounds semiannually:

```
=EFFECT(0.1, 2)
```

Figure 18.1 shows a worksheet that applies the `EFFECT()` function to a 10% nominal annual rate using various compounding frequencies.

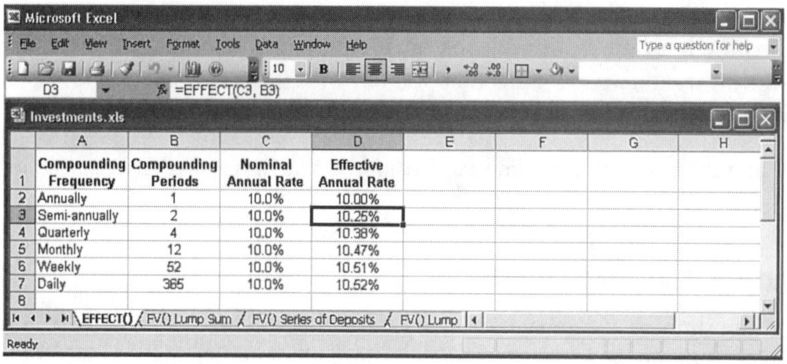


**Figure 18.1**
The formulas in column D use the `EFFECT()` function to convert the nominal rates in column C to effective rates based on the compounding periods in column B.

> **NOTE** You can download the workbook that contains this chapter's examples here:
> `www.mcfedries.com/ExcelFormulas/`

If you already know the effective annual interest rate and the number of compounding periods, you can convert the rate to the nominal annual interest rate by using the Analysis ToolPak's NOMINAL() function:

```
NOMINAL(effect_rate, npery)
```

> *effect_rate*    The effective annual interest rate
>
> *npery*    The number of compounding periods in the year

For example, the following formula returns the nominal annual interest rate for an investment with an effective annual rate of 10.52% that compounds daily:

```
=NOMINAL(0.1052, 365)
```

# Calculating the Future Value

Just as the payment is usually the most important value for a loan calculation, the future value is usually the most important value for an investment calculation. After all, the purpose of an investment is to place a sum of money (the present value) and in some instrument for a time, after which you end up with some new (and, hopefully, greater) amount: the future value.

To calculate the future value of an investment, Excel offers the FV() function:

```
FV(rate, nper, [pmt], [pv], [type])
```

> *rate*    The fixed rate of interest over the term of the investment.
>
> *nper*    The number of periods in the term of the investment.
>
> *pmt*    The amount deposited in the investment each period (the default is 0).
>
> *pv*    The initial deposit (the default is 0).
>
> *type*    The type of deposit. Use 0 (the default) for end-of-period deposits; use 1 for beginning-of-period deposits.

Because both the amount deposited per period (the *pmt* argument) and the initial deposit (the *pv* argument) are sums that you pay out, these must be entered as negative values in the FV() function.

The next few sections take you through various investment scenarios using the FV() function.

## The Future Value of a Lump Sum

In the simplest future value scenario, you invest a lump sum and let it grow according to the specified interest rate and term, without adding any deposits along the way. In this case, you use the FV() function with the *pmt* argument set to 0:

```
FV(rate, nper, 0, pv, type)
```

For example, Figure 18.2 shows the future value of $10,000 invested at 5% over 10 years.

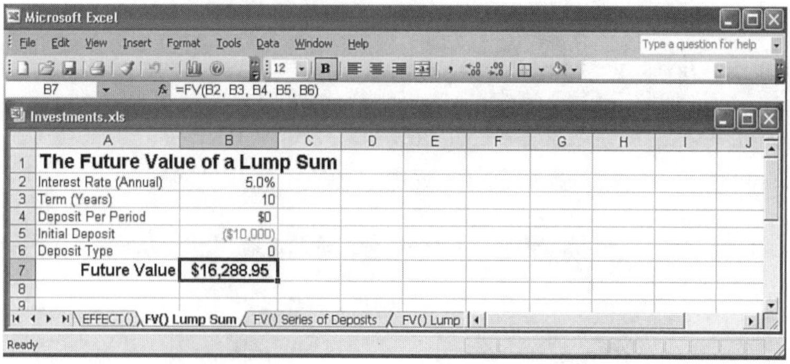

**Figure 18.2**
When calculating the
future value of an initial
lump sum deposit, set the
FV() function's *pmt*
argument to 0.

**TIP**

Excel's FV() function doesn't work with continuous compounding. Instead, you need to use a worksheet formula that takes the following general form:

```
=pv * e ^ (rate * nper)
```

For example, the following formula calculates the future value of $10,000 invested at 5% over 10
years compounded continuously (and returns a value of $16,487.21):

```
=10000 * EXP(0.05 * 10)
```

## The Future Value of a Series of Deposits

Another common investment scenario is to make a series of deposits over the term of the
investment, without depositing an initial sum. In this case, you use the FV() function with
the *pv* argument set to 0:

FV(*rate, nper, pmt,* 0, *type*)

For example, Figure 18.3 shows the future value of $100 invested each month at 5% over
10 years. Notice that the interest rate and term are both converted to monthly amounts
because the deposit occurs monthly.

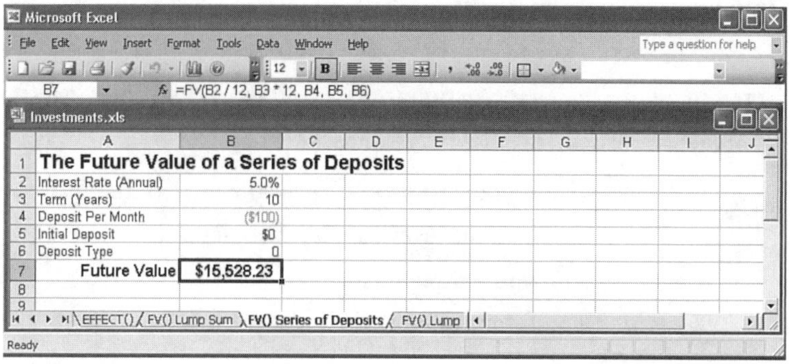

**Figure 18.3**
When calculating the
future value of a series of
deposits, set the FV()
function's *pv*
argument to 0.

## The Future Value of a Lump Sum Plus Deposits

For best investment results, you should invest an initial amount and then add to it with regular deposits. In this scenario, you need to specify all the FV() function arguments (except *type*). For example, Figure 18.4 shows the future value of an investment with a $10,000 initial deposit and 100 monthly deposits at 5% over 10 years.

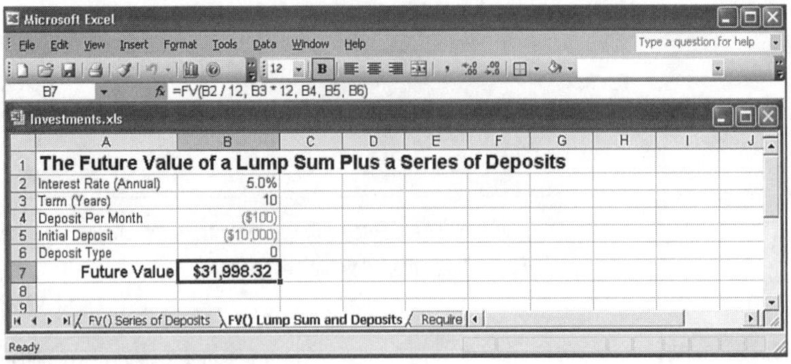

**Figure 18.4**
This worksheet uses the full FV() function syntax to calculate the future value of a lump sum plus a series of deposits.

# Working Toward an Investment Goal

Instead of just seeing where an investment will end up, it's often desirable to have a specific monetary goal in mind and then ask yourself, "What will it take to get me there?"

Answering that question means solving for one of the four main future value parameters—interest rate, number of periods, regular deposit, and initial deposit—while holding the other parameters (and, of course, your future value goal) constant. The next four sections take you through this process.

## Calculating the Required Interest Rate

If you know the future value that you want, when you want it, and the initial deposit and periodic deposits you can afford, what interest rate do you require to meet your goal? You answer that question using the RATE() function, which you first encountered in Chapter 17.

→ To work with the RATE() function in a loan context, **see** "Calculating the Interest Rate Required for a Loan," **p. 411**.

Here's the syntax for that function from the point of view of an investment:

RATE(*nper*, *pmt*, *pv*, *fv*, [*type*], [*guess*])

| | |
|---|---|
| *nper* | The number of deposits over the term of the investment. |
| *pmt* | The amount invested with each deposit. |
| *pv* | The initial investment. |
| *fv* | The future value of the investment. |

| type | The type of deposit. Use ø (the default) for end-of-period deposits; use 1 for beginning-of-period deposits. |
|---|---|
| guess | A percentage value that Excel uses as a starting point for calculating the interest rate (the default is 10%). |

For example, if you need $100,000 ten years from now, are starting with $10,000, and can deposit $500 per month, what interest rate is required to meet your goal? Figure 18.5 shows a worksheet that comes up with the answer: 6%.

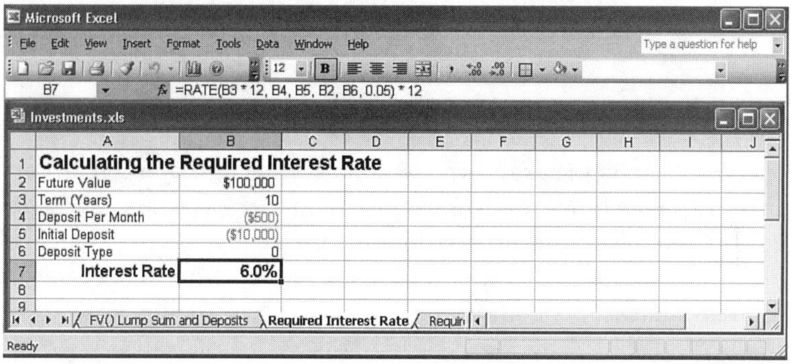

**Figure 18.5**
Use the RATE() function to work out the interest rate required to reach a future value given a fixed term, a periodic deposit, and an initial deposit.

## Calculating the Required Number of Periods

Given your investment goal, if you have an initial deposit and an amount that you can afford to deposit periodically, how long will it take to reach your goal at the prevailing market interest rate? You answer this question by using the NPER() function (which was introduced in Chapter 17). Here's the NPER() syntax from the point of view of an investment:

NPER(rate, pmt, pv, fv, [type])

| rate | The fixed rate of interest over the term of the investment. |
|---|---|
| pmt | The amount invested with each deposit. |
| pv | The initial investment. |
| fv | The future value of the investment. |
| type | The type of deposit. Use ø (the default) for end-of-period deposits; use 1 for beginning-of-period deposits. |

→ To work with the NPER() function in a loan context, **see** "Calculating the Term of the Loan," **p. 409**.

For example, suppose that you want to retire with $1,000,000. You have $50,000 to invest, you can afford to deposit $1,000 per month, and you expect to earn 5% interest. How long will it take to reach your goal? The worksheet in Figure 18.6 answers this question: 349.4 months, or 29.1 years.

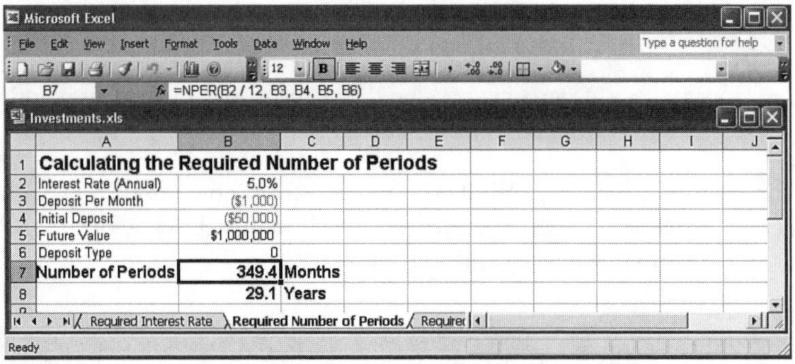

**Figure 18.6**
Use the NPER( ) function to calculate how long it will take to reach a future value, given a fixed interest rate, a periodic deposit, and an initial deposit.

## Calculating the Required Regular Deposit

Suppose that you want to reach your future value goal by a certain date and that you have an initial amount to invest. Given current interest rates, how much extra do you have to deposit into the investment periodically to achieve your goal? The answer here lies in the PMT( ) function from Chapter 17. Here are the PMT( ) function details from the point of view of an investment:

PMT(*rate, nper, pv, fv, [type]*)

| | |
|---|---|
| *rate* | The fixed rate of interest over the term of the investment. |
| *nper* | The number of deposits over the term of the investment. |
| *pv* | The initial investment. |
| *fv* | The future value of the investment. |
| *type* | The type of deposit. Use 0 (the default) for end-of-period deposits; use 1 for beginning-of-period deposits. |

→  To work with the PMT ( ) function in a loan context, **see** "Calculating the Loan Payment," **p. 400**.

For example, suppose that you want to end up with $50,000 in 15 years to finance your child's college education. If you have no initial deposit and you expect to get 7.5% interest over the term of the investment, how much do you need to deposit each month to reach your target? Figure 18.7 shows a worksheet that calculates the result using PMT( ): $151.01 per month.

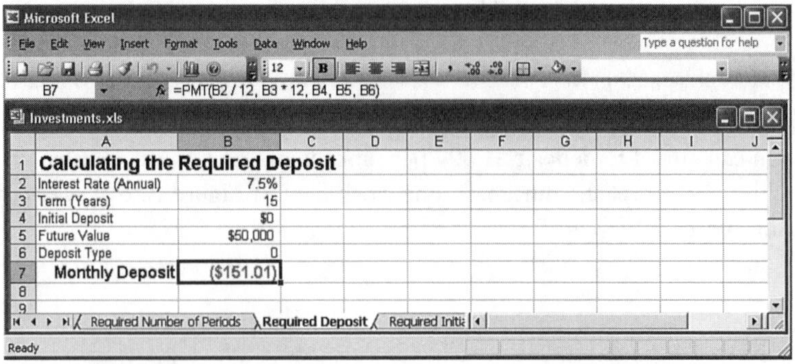

**Figure 18.7**
Use the PMT ( ) function to derive how much you need to deposit periodically to reach a future value, given a fixed interest rate, a number of deposits, and an initial deposit.

## Calculating the Required Initial Deposit

For the final standard future value calculation, suppose that you know when you want to reach your goal, how much you can deposit each period, and how much the interest rate will be. What, then, do you need to deposit initially to achieve your future value target? To find the answer, you use the PV() function, which uses the following syntax from the point of view of an investment:

PV(*rate, nper, pmt, fv, [type]*)

| | |
|---|---|
| *rate* | The fixed rate of interest over the term of the investment. |
| *nper* | The number of deposits over the term of the investment. |
| *pmt* | The amount invested with each deposit. |
| *fv* | The future value of the investment. |
| *type* | The type of deposit. Use 0 (the default) for end-of-period deposits; use 1 for beginning-of-period deposits. |

→ To work with the PV() function in a discount context, **see** "Calculating the Present Value," **p. 448**.

For example, suppose that your goal is to end up with $100,000 in 3 years to purchase new equipment. If you expect to earn 6% interest and can deposit $2,000 monthly, what does your initial deposit have to be to make your goal? The worksheet in Figure 18.8 uses PV() to calculate the answer: $17,822.46.

**Figure 18.8**
Use the PV() function to find out how much you need to deposit initially to reach a future value, given a fixed interest rate, a number of deposits, and a periodic deposit.

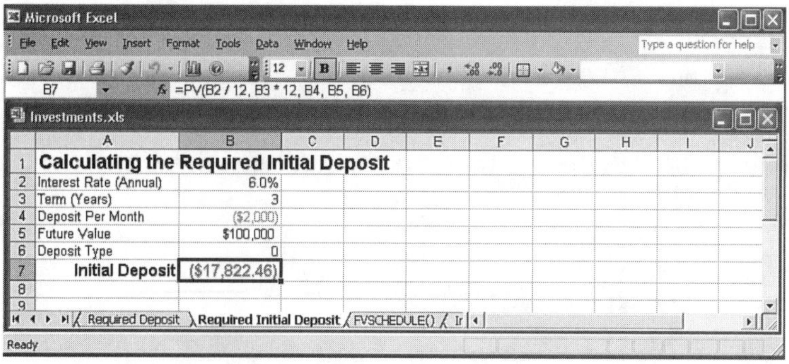

## Calculating the Future Value with Varying Interest Rates

The future value examples that you've worked with so far have all assumed that the interest rate remained constant over the term of the investment. This will always be true for fixed-rate investments, but for other investments, such as mutual funds, stocks, and bonds, using a fixed rate of interest is, at best, a guess about what the average rate will be over the term.

For investments that offer a variable rate over the term, or when the rate fluctuates over the term, Excel's Analysis ToolPak offers the FVSCHEDULE() function, which returns the future value of some initial amount, given a schedule of interest rates:

FVSCEDULE(*principal*, *schedule*)

    *principal*    The initial investment

    *schedule*    A range or array containing the interest rates

For example, the following formula returns the future value of an initial $10,000 deposit that makes 5%, 6%, and 7% over 3 years:

=FVSCHEDULE(10000, {0.5, 0.6, 0.7})

Similarly, Figure 18.9 shows a worksheet that calculates the future value of an initial deposit of $100,000 into an investment that earns 5%, 5.5%, 6%, 7%, and 6% over 5 years.

> **NOTE**
>
> If you want to know the average rate earned on the investment, use the RATE() function, where *nper* is the number of values in the interest rate schedule, *pmt* is 0, *pv* is the initial deposit, and *fv* is the negative of the FVSCHEDULE() result. Here's the general syntax:
>
> RATE(ROWS(*schedule*), 0, *principle*, -FVSCHEDULE(*principal*, *schedule*))

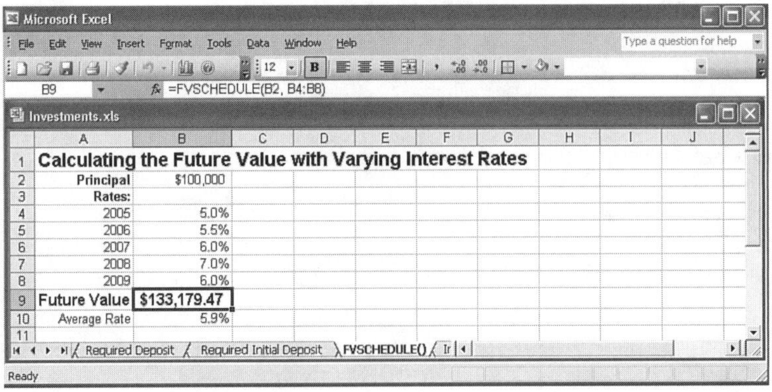

**Figure 18.9**
Use the FVSCHEDULE() function to return the future value of an initial deposit in an investment that earns varying rates of interest.

## CASE STUDY

### Building an Investment Schedule

If you're planning future cash-flow requirements or future retirement needs, it's often not enough just to know how much money you'll have at the end of an investment. You might need to also know how much money is in the investment account or fund at each period throughout the life of the investment.

To do this, you need to build an *investment schedule*. This is similar to an amortization schedule, except that it shows the future value of an investment at each period in the term of the investment.

→ To learn about amortization schedules, **see** "Building a Loan Amortization Schedule," **p. 406**.

In a typical investment schedule, you need to take two things into account:

- The periodic deposits put into the investment, particularly the amount deposited and the frequency of the deposits. The frequency of the deposits determines the total number of periods in the investment. For example, a 10-year investment with semiannual deposits has 20 periods.
- The compounding frequency of the investment (annually, semiannually, and so on). Assuming that you know the APR (that is, nominal annual interest rate), you can use the compounding frequency to determine the effect rate.

Note, however, that you can't simply use the `EFFECT()` function to convert the known nominal rate into the effective rate. That's because you're going to calculate the future value at the end of each period, which might or might not correspond to the compounding frequency. (For example, if the investment compounds monthly and you deposit semiannually, there will be 6 months of compounding to factor into the future value at the end of each period.)

Getting the proper effective rate for each period requires three steps:

1. Use the `EFFECT()` function to convert the nominal annual rate into the effective annual rate, based on the compounding frequency.
2. Use the `NOMINAL()` function to convert the effective rate from step 1 into the nominal rate, based on the deposit frequency.
3. Divide the nominal rate from step 2 by the deposit frequency to get the effective rate per period. This is the value that you'll plug into the `FV()` function.

Figure 18.10 shows a worksheet that implements an investment schedule using this technique.

18

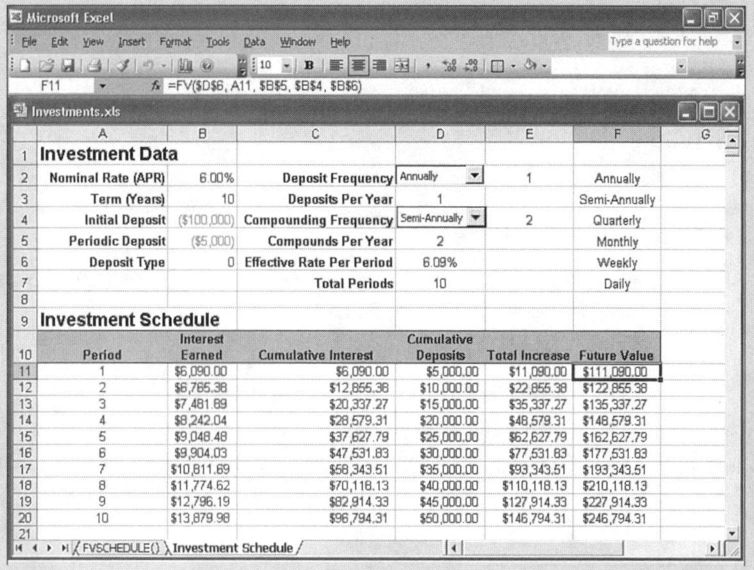


| | A | B | C | D | E | F |
|---|---|---|---|---|---|---|
| 1 | Investment Data | | | | | |
| 2 | Nominal Rate (APR) | 6.00% | Deposit Frequency | Annually | 1 | Annually |
| 3 | Term (Years) | 10 | Deposits Per Year | 1 | | Semi-Annually |
| 4 | Initial Deposit | ($100,000) | Compounding Frequency | Semi-Annually | 2 | Quarterly |
| 5 | Periodic Deposit | ($5,000) | Compounds Per Year | 2 | | Monthly |
| 6 | Deposit Type | 0 | Effective Rate Per Period | 6.09% | | Weekly |
| 7 | | | Total Periods | 10 | | Daily |
| 8 | | | | | | |
| 9 | Investment Schedule | | | | | |
| 10 | Period | Interest Earned | Cumulative Interest | Cumulative Deposits | Total Increase | Future Value |
| 11 | 1 | $6,090.00 | $6,090.00 | $5,000.00 | $11,090.00 | $111,090.00 |
| 12 | 2 | $6,765.38 | $12,855.38 | $10,000.00 | $22,855.38 | $122,855.38 |
| 13 | 3 | $7,481.89 | $20,337.27 | $15,000.00 | $35,337.27 | $135,337.27 |
| 14 | 4 | $8,242.04 | $28,579.31 | $20,000.00 | $48,579.31 | $148,579.31 |
| 15 | 5 | $9,048.48 | $37,627.79 | $25,000.00 | $62,627.79 | $162,627.79 |
| 16 | 6 | $9,904.03 | $47,531.83 | $30,000.00 | $77,531.83 | $177,531.83 |
| 17 | 7 | $10,811.69 | $58,343.51 | $35,000.00 | $93,343.51 | $193,343.51 |
| 18 | 8 | $11,774.62 | $70,118.13 | $40,000.00 | $110,118.13 | $210,118.13 |
| 19 | 9 | $12,796.19 | $82,914.33 | $45,000.00 | $127,914.33 | $227,914.33 |
| 20 | 10 | $13,879.98 | $96,794.31 | $50,000.00 | $146,794.31 | $246,794.31 |
| 21 | | | | | | |

**Figure 18.10**
An investment schedule that takes into account deposit frequency and compounding frequency to return the future value of an investment at the end of each deposit period.

Here's a summary of the items in the Investment Data portion of the worksheet:

- **Nominal Rate (APR) (B2)**—This is the nominal annual rate of interest for the investment.
- **Term (Years) (B3)**—This is the length of the investment, in years.
- **Initial Deposit (B4)**—This is the amount deposited at the start of the investment. Enter this as a negative number (because it's money that you're paying out).
- **Periodic Deposit (B5)**—This is the amount deposited at each period of the investment. (Again, this number must be negative.)
- **Deposit Type (B6)**—This is the `type` argument of the `FV()` function.
- **Deposit Frequency**—Use this drop-down list to specify how often the periodic deposits are made. The available values—Annually, Semiannually, Quarterly, Monthly, Weekly, and Daily—come from the range F2:F7; the number of the selected list item is stored in cell E2.
- **Deposits Per Year (D3)**—This is the number of periods per year, as given by the following formula:
  `=CHOOSE(E2, 1, 2, 4, 12, 52, 365)`
- **Compounding Frequency**—Use this drop-down list to specify how often the investment compounds. You get the same options as in the Deposit Frequency list. The number of the selected list item is stored in cell E4.
- **Compounds Per Year (D5)**—This is the number of compounding periods per year, as given by the following formula:
  `=CHOOSE(E4, 1, 2, 4, 12, 52, 365)`
- **Effective Rate Per Period (D6)**—This is the effective interest rate per period, as calculated using the three-step algorithm outlined earlier in this section. Here's the formula:
  `=NOMINAL(EFFECT(B2, D5), D3) / D3`
- **Total Periods (D7)**—This is the total number of deposit periods in the loan, which is just the term multiplied by the number of deposits per year.

Here's a summary of the columns in the Investment Schedule portion of the worksheet:

- **Period (column A)**—This is the period number of the investment. The Period values are generated automatically based on the Total Periods value (D7).

→ The dynamic features used in the investment schedule are similar to those used in the dynamic amortization schedule; **see** "Building a Dynamic Amortization Schedule," **p. 407**.

- **Interest Earned (column B)**—This is the interest earned during the period. It's calculated by multiplying the future value from the previous period by the Effective Rate Per Period (D6).
- **Cumulative Interest (column C)**—This is the total interest earned in the investment at the end of each period. It's calculated by using a running sum of the values in the Interest Earned column.
- **Cumulative Deposits (column D)**—This is the total amount of the deposits added to the investment at the end of each period. It's calculated by multiplying the Periodic Deposit (B5) by the current period number (column A).

- **Total Increase (column E)**—This is the total amount by which the investment has increased over the Initial Deposit at the end of each period. It's calculated by adding the Cumulative Interest and the Cumulative Deposits.

- **Future Value (column F)**—This is the value of the investment at the end of each period. Here's the FV() formula for cell A11:

```
=FV($D$6, A11, $B$5, $B$4, $B$6)
```

## From Here

- To get the details on the concept of the time value of money, **see** "Understanding the Time Value of Money," **p. 399**.

- To work with the RATE() function in a loan context, **see** "Calculating the Interest Rate Required for a Loan," **p. 411**.

- To work with the NPER() function in a loan context, **see** "Calculating the Term of the Loan," **p. 409**. (

- To work with the PMT() function in a loan context, **see** "Calculating the Loan Payment," **p. 400**.

- To work with the PV() function in a discount context, **see** "Calculating Present Value Using PV()," **p. 449**.

- To learn about amortization schedules, **see** "Building a Loan Amortization Schedule," **p. 406**.

18

# Working with Bonds

# 19

A *bond* is a debt instrument by which companies and governments raise money by borrowing it from investors. The bond is a promise to pay back at some future date the amount borrowed and to pay interest periodically throughout the term. This chapter takes you through a few formulas and functions that enable you as an investor to work with bonds.

## Glossary of Bond Terms

Before beginning, here are a few bond terms that you'll see throughout the next few sections and that you should be familiar with:

- **Coupon**—The interest rate paid by the bond.

- **Coupon dates**—The dates on which the bond pays the coupon interest. Most bonds have two coupon dates each year: One is usually the anniversary of either the issue date or the first coupon date, and the other is the date 6 months later.

- **Discount bond**—A bond with a market price below its par value.

- **Face value**—The amount borrowed, which is usually $1,000 per bond. Also called the *par value*.

- **First coupon date**—The date on which the first coupon interest payment is made.

- **Issue date**—The date the bond is made available to the public.

- **Issuer**—The company or government borrowing the money.

- **Last coupon date**—The date on which the last coupon interest payment is made.

- **Maturity date**—The date on which the bond expires and the issuer agrees to repay the amount borrowed, as well as any accrued interest.
- **Premium bond**—A bond with a market price above its par value.
- **Settlement date**—The date on which the bond is purchased.
- **Yield**—The rate of return the investor gets from the purchase date to the maturity date. Also called the *yield-to-maturity*, or *YTD*.)
- **Zero-coupon bond**—A bond that doesn't pay interest but that is sold at a deep discount. Also called *zeros*.

# Calculating Bond Yields

If you plan to hold a bond to maturity, the most important investment measure is the yield, which tells you what your return on investment will be. You might think that this is just the coupon rate compounded from the settlement date to the maturity date, but that's not the case. Instead, the yield depends on the current price of the bond, with more expensively priced bonds producing lower yields than cheaper bonds (assuming that the other factors are equal).

## The YIELD() Function

To avoid complex yield calculations, the Analysis ToolPak offers the YIELD() function:

```
YIELD(settlement, maturity, rate, pr, redemption, frequency, [basis])
```

| | |
|---|---|
| *settlement* | The settlement date of the bond, entered as a string or a date serial number. |
| *maturity* | The maturity date of the bond, entered as a string or a date serial number. |
| *rate* | The bond's coupon (interest rate). |
| *pr* | The bond's price per $100 of face value. |
| *redemption* | The bond's redemption value per $100 of face value. This is almost always 100. |
| *frequency* | The number of coupon payments made each year. Use 1 for annual payments, use 2 for semiannual payments, and use 4 for quarterly payments. |
| *basis* | An integer that specifies the assumed number of days in the month and year: |

| basis | Type | Description |
|---|---|---|
| 0 | US (NASD) 30/360 | Uses a 360-day year divided in twelve 30-day months. This is the North American method and is the default. |

| | | |
|---|---|---|
| 1 | Actual/actual | Uses the actual number of days in the year and the actual number of days in each month. |
| 2 | Actual/360 | Uses a 360-day year and the actual number of days in each month. |
| 3 | Actual/365 | Uses a 365-day year and the actual number of days in each month. |
| 4 | European 30/360 | Any date that falls on the 31st of a month is changed to the 30th of the same month. This is the European method. |

For example, if you're looking to purchase on August 23, 2004, a bond that matures on April 12, 2011, with a semiannual coupon of 6.3% and a current market price (per $100 of face value) of $102.21, the following formula returns the yield value of 5.89%:

```
=YIELD("August 23, 2004", "April 12, 2011", 0.063, 102.21, 100, 2)
```

Figure 19.1 shows a worksheet that runs several yield calculations.

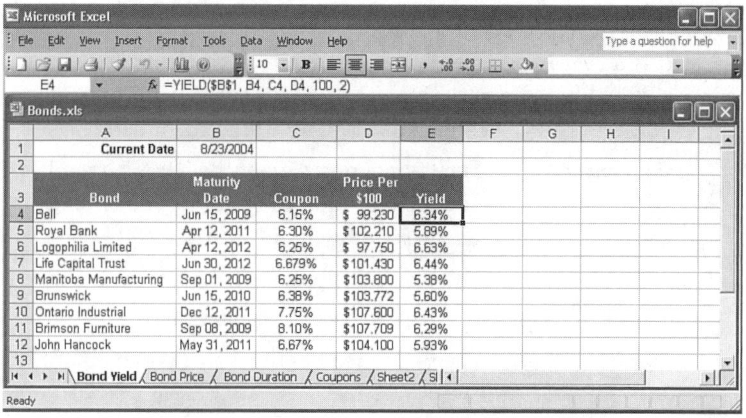


| | Bond | Maturity Date | Coupon | Price Per $100 | Yield |
|---|---|---|---|---|---|
| 1 | Current Date | 8/23/2004 | | | |
| 4 | Bell | Jun 15, 2009 | 6.15% | $ 99.230 | 6.34% |
| 5 | Royal Bank | Apr 12, 2011 | 6.30% | $102.210 | 5.89% |
| 6 | Logophilia Limited | Apr 12, 2012 | 6.25% | $ 97.750 | 6.63% |
| 7 | Life Capital Trust | Jun 30, 2012 | 6.679% | $101.430 | 6.44% |
| 8 | Manitoba Manufacturing | Sep 01, 2009 | 6.25% | $103.800 | 5.38% |
| 9 | Brunswick | Jun 15, 2010 | 6.38% | $103.772 | 5.60% |
| 10 | Ontario Industrial | Dec 12, 2011 | 7.75% | $107.600 | 6.43% |
| 11 | Brimson Furniture | Sep 08, 2009 | 8.10% | $107.709 | 6.29% |
| 12 | John Hancock | May 31, 2011 | 6.67% | $104.100 | 5.93% |

**Figure 19.1**
This worksheet uses the `YIELD()` function to calculate the yield to maturity of several bonds from the current date (cell B1).



## The `ODDFYIELD()` and `ODDLYIELD()` Functions

Some bonds have a first period that is *odd*, meaning that it's either shorter or longer than the standard coupon period. Consider a bond that pays semiannual coupon interest, which therefore has 6-month coupon periods. For example, a bond issued on January 15, 2001, would pay interest on July 15, 2001; January 15, 2002; and so on. However, an odd first period is one that's shorter or longer than 6 months. For example, suppose that you're considering purchasing a bond issued on January 15, 2001, and you see that the next interest payment occurs on April 15, 2004. Based on the issue date, you would expect the payment to have come on July 15, 2004, so this bond has an odd first coupon. (Here, "first" means the first coupon you receive.)

Similarly, some bonds have an odd last coupon period. For example, suppose that you're looking at a bond that pays semiannual interest and matures on January 15, 2011, and you see that it last paid interest on August 15, 2004. Based on the maturity date, you would have expected the payment to occur on July 15, 2004, so this bond has an odd last coupon. (Here, "last" means the last coupon that was paid.)

All of this complicates the yield calculation further, but the Analysis ToolPak offers two functions that can help: Use ODDFYIELD() to calculate the yield for a bond with an odd first coupon period, and use ODDLYIELD() to calculate the yield for a bond with an odd last coupon period:

ODDFYIELD(*settlement, maturity, issue, first_coupon, rate, pr, redemption, frequency, [basis]*)

ODDLYIELD(*settlement, maturity, last_coupon, rate, pr, redemption, frequency, [basis]*)

| | |
|---|---|
| *settlement* | The settlement date of the bond, entered as a string or a date serial number. |
| *maturity* | The maturity date of the bond, entered as a string or a date serial number. |
| *issue* | The issue date of the bond, entered as a string or a date serial number. |
| *first_coupon* | The first coupon date of the bond, entered as a string or a date serial number. Note that the date you enter must be the first coupon date *after* the settlement date. |
| *last_coupon* | The last coupon date of the bond, entered as a string or a date serial number. Note that the date you enter must be the last coupon date *before* the settlement date. |
| *rate* | The bond's coupon (interest rate). |
| *pr* | The bond's price per $100 of face value. |
| *redemption* | The bond's redemption value per $100 of face value. This is almost always 100. |
| *frequency* | The number of coupon payments made each year. Use 1 for annual payments, use 2 for semiannual payments, and use 4 for quarterly payments. |
| *basis* | An integer that specifies the assumed number of days in the month and year. 0 = US (NASD) 30/360 (the default), 1 = Actual/actual, 2 = Actual/360, 3 = Actual/365, and 4 = European 30/360. |

For example, suppose that you want to purchase on August 23, 2004, a semiannual coupon bond that matures on April 12, 2011; was issued on February 1, 2001; and has a first coupon date of October 12, 2004. Based on the issue date, you would expect the first coupon to be paid on February 1, 2005. This means that you're dealing with a bond with an odd first coupon, so you use the ODDFYIELD() function, like this (assume a 6.3% coupon and a price of $102.21):

```
=ODDFYIELD("8/23/2004", "4/12/2011", "2/1/2001", "10/12/2004",
0.063, 102.21, 100, 2, 0)
```

The result is 5.86%.

Similarly, suppose that you want to purchase on August 23, 2004, a semiannual coupon bond that matures on April 12, 2011, and that had a last coupon date of July 12, 2004. Based on the maturity date, you would expect the last coupon to have been paid on April 12, 2004. This means that you're dealing with a bond with an odd last coupon, so you use the ODDLYIELD() function (assume a 6.3% coupon and a price of $102.21):

```
=ODDLYIELD("8/23/2004", "4/12/2011", "7/12/2004", 0.063, 102.21, 100, 2, 0)
```

The result is 5.73%.

# Calculating Bond Prices

If you're a bond investor and have a particular goal in mind, you might need to earn a minimum yield to meet that goal. For example, you might need a bond to return 6% on your investment. You've seen that bond yields and prices have an inverse relationship. When prices fall, yields rise; when prices rise, yields fall. So if a particular bond's yield is too low, you need to wait for the price to fall far enough that you meet your yield target. The question is, however, how far is "enough"? In other words, what price will produce the yield you're looking for?

## The PRICE() Function

To answer that question, use the Analysis ToolPak's PRICE() function, which returns the price per $100 of a bond's face value:

PRICE(*settlement, maturity, rate, yld, redemption, frequency, [basis]*)

| | |
|---|---|
| *settlement* | The settlement date of the bond, entered as a string or a date serial number. |
| *maturity* | The maturity date of the bond, entered as a string or a date serial number. |
| *rate* | The bond's coupon (interest rate). |
| *yld* | The bond's yield. |
| *redemption* | The bond's redemption value per $100 of face value. This is almost always 100. |
| *frequency* | The number of coupon payments made each year. Use 1 for annual payments, use 2 for semiannual payments, and use 4 for quarterly payments. |
| *basis* | An integer that specifies the assumed number of days in the month and year. 0 = US (NASD) 30/360 (the default), 1 = Actual/actual, 2 = Actual/360, 3 = Actual/365, and 4 = European 30/360. |

19

For example, suppose that you're looking at a bond that matures on April 12, 2011; has a semiannual coupon of 6.3%; and has a current market price of $102.21. You know from the previous section that this bond has a yield of 5.89%. What lower price will produce at least a 6% yield? The worksheet in Figure 19.2 uses the PRICE() function to answer this question: $101.61.

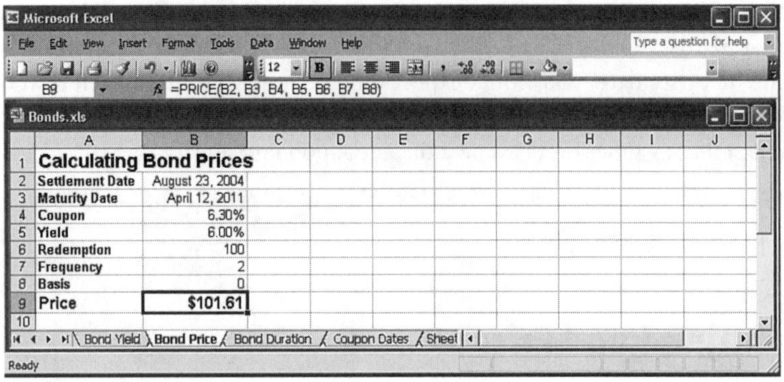

**Figure 19.2**
This worksheet uses the PRICE() function to calculate the market price required to return a 6% yield on a bond.

## The ODDFPRICE() and ODDLPRICE() Functions

If you're dealing with a bond that has an odd first or last period, as explained earlier, the Analysis ToolPak offers two functions that can calculate the prices: Use ODDFPRICE() to calculate the price for a bond with an odd first coupon period, and use ODDLPRICE() to calculate the price for a bond with an odd last coupon period:

ODDFPRICE(settlement, maturity, issue, first_coupon, rate, yld, redemption, frequency, [basis])

ODDLPRICE(settlement, maturity, last_coupon, rate, yld, redemption, frequency, [basis])

| | |
|---|---|
| settlement | The settlement date of the bond, entered as a string or a date serial number. |
| maturity | The maturity date of the bond, entered as a string or a date serial number. |
| issue | The issue date of the bond, entered as a string or a date serial number. |
| first_coupon | The first coupon date of the bond, entered as a string or a date serial number. Note that the date you enter must be the first coupon date *after* the settlement date. |
| last_coupon | The last coupon date of the bond, entered as a string or a date serial number. Note that the date you enter must be the last coupon date *before* the settlement date. |
| rate | The bond's coupon (interest rate). |

| *yld* | The bond's yield. |
|---|---|
| *redemption* | The bond's redemption value per $100 of face value. This is almost always 100. |
| *frequency* | The number of coupon payments made each year. Use 1 for annual payments, use 2 for semiannual payments, and use 4 for quarterly payments. |
| *basis* | An integer that specifies the assumed number of days in the month and year. 0 = US (NASD) 30/360 (the default), 1 = Actual/actual, 2 = Actual/360, 3 = Actual/365, and 4 = European 30/360. |

For example, suppose that you want to purchase on August 23, 2004, a semiannual coupon bond that matures on April 12, 2011; was issued on February 1, 2001; and has a first coupon date of October 12, 2004. Based on the issue date, you would expect the first coupon to be paid on February 1, 2005. This means that you're dealing with a bond with an odd first coupon, so you use the ODDFPRICE() function, like so (assume a 6.3% coupon and a yield of 6%):

```
=ODDFPRICE("8/23/2004", "4/12/2011", "2/1/2001", "10/12/2004",
0.063, 0.06, 100, 2, 0)
```

The result is $101.45.

Similarly, suppose that you want to purchase on August 23, 2004, a semiannual coupon bond that matures on April 12, 2011, and had a last coupon date of July 12, 2004. Based on the maturity date, you would expect the last coupon to have been paid on April 12, 2004. This means that you're dealing with a bond with an odd last coupon, so you use the ODDLPRICE() function (assume a 6.3% coupon and a yield of 6%):

```
=ODDLPRICE("8/23/2004", "4/12/2011", "7/12/2004", 0.063, 0.06, 100, 2, 0)
```

The result is $101.22.

# Calculating Bond Duration

If you hold a bond to maturity, the only risk you run is that the issuer will default and you will lose the principal plus any future interest. That's relatively rare (unless you invest in so-called *junk bonds*, high-risk bonds issued by companies with very low credit ratings), so bonds held to maturity represent a generally safe investment.

However, that's not the case if you intend to make money by buying and selling bonds. In general (and *very* simplistically), bond prices rise as interest rates fall (because the bond's coupon becomes relatively more attractive); conversely, bond prices fall as interest rates rise (because the coupon becomes relatively less attractive). Also, bond prices tend to converge toward the par value as the maturity date nears.

Therefore, buying and selling bonds for profit is a risky venture. It helps if you know how much risk is inherent in a particular bond. You can find out by calculating a bond's *duration*,

**19**

which gives you a rough idea of how sensitive the bond is to interest rate changes. The duration is expressed in years, but it really tells you what percentage the bond's price will change for every 1% change in interest rates. For example, if a bond has a duration of 5, for every 1% increase in interest rates, you can expect the bond's price to fall by 5%.

You calculate duration by using the Analysis ToolPak's DURATION() function:

```
DURATION(settlement, maturity, rate, yld, frequency, [basis])
```

| | |
|---|---|
| *settlement* | The settlement date of the bond, entered as a string or a date serial number. |
| *maturity* | The maturity date of the bond, entered as a string or a date serial number. |
| *rate* | The bond's coupon (interest rate). |
| *yld* | The bond's yield. |
| *frequency* | The number of coupon payments made each year. Use 1 for annual payments, use 2 for semiannual payments, and use 4 for quarterly payments. |
| *basis* | An integer that specifies the assumed number of days in the month and year. 0 = US (NASD) 30/360 (the default), 1 = Actual/actual, 2 = Actual/360, 3 = Actual/365, and 4 = European 30/360. |

For example, suppose that you want to purchase on August 23, 2004, a semiannual coupon bond with a maturity date of April 12, 2011; a coupon of 6.3%; and a yield of 6%. Figure 19.3 shows a worksheet that calculates the duration of 5.4 years.

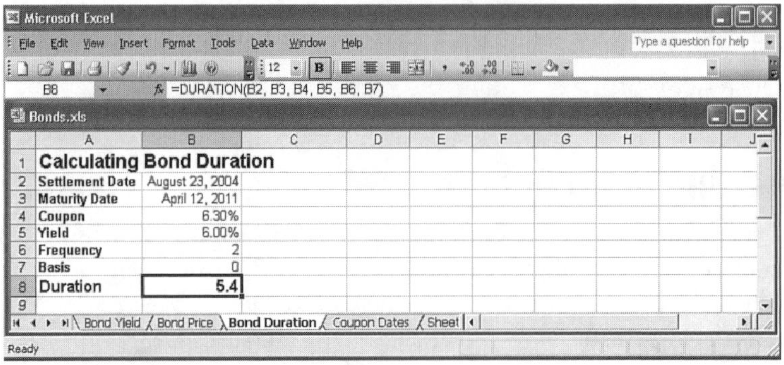

**Figure 19.3**
This worksheet uses the DURATION() function to calculate the duration of a bond.

# Calculating Bond Principal at Maturity

If you use bonds as a buy-and-hold investment, you're probably aware of the investing maxim that you need to spread your maturity dates over a number of years. For example, if you're investing for retirement at age 55, don't buy bonds that mature only in the year you turn 55. Instead, buy some bonds that mature at 55, some at 56, some at 57, and so on.

The strategy is easy to monitor if you have just a few bonds, but most heavy bond buyers end up with dozens of bonds that mature at various dates over a number of years. Calculating the total bond principal that matures each year can be a daunting task. However, with the help of a worksheet and a few array formulas, you can get Excel to handle this chore for you.

Figure 19.4 shows a worksheet with some basic data for a few bonds, including the maturity date, face value, number of units of each bond, and total face value. The table in G1:H5 shows the four different maturity years (2009–2012) in column G and the total face value of the bonds that mature in each year in column H. To calculate the latter, I constructed an array formula that uses IF() to check the year value in the corresponding cell in column G with the YEAR() function applied to the various maturity dates in column B. For those bonds in which the years matched, the SUM() function returns the total face value. Here's the formula in cell H2:

```
{=SUM(IF(G2 = YEAR(B2:B10), E2:E10, 0))}
```

→ To learn about arrays, **see** "Working with Arrays," **p. 85**.

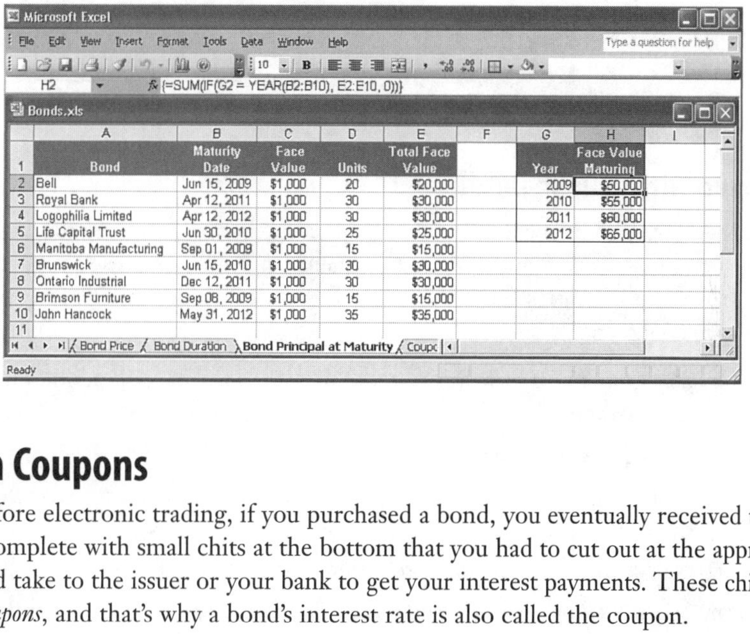

**Figure 19.4**
This worksheet uses an array formula to calculate the total face value of the bonds that mature in each year.

## Working with Coupons

In the days before electronic trading, if you purchased a bond, you eventually received the actual bond, complete with small chits at the bottom that you had to cut out at the appropriate time and take to the issuer or your bank to get your interest payments. These chits were called *coupons*, and that's why a bond's interest rate is also called the coupon.

The electronic revolution has not only enabled bondholders to put away their scissors, but it has also given them many tools to work more easily with coupons and coupon dates. You'll learn about a few of these tools in this section.

### Calculating the Coupon Payment

If you're an income investor, you'll want to know how much interest your investments earn each year. For your bonds, you'll want to know not only how much interest you make each year, but also how much interest you earn each coupon period. This is important not only so that you can monitor and plan for your clash-flow needs, but also because you probably want to reinvest the interest to get the compounding effect.

Fortunately, calculating the interest paid in each coupon period is simple:

```
rate * redemption / frequency
```

Here, `rate` is the bond's coupon, `redemption` is the bond's face value, and `frequency` is the number of coupon periods each year. Figure 19.5 shows a worksheet that calculates the coupon payment for a bond with a semiannual coupon of 5% and a face value of $1,000.

**Figure 19.5**
To calculate the coupon payment, multiply the coupon by the face value and divide by the payment frequency.

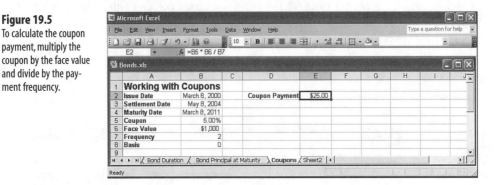

## Working with Coupon Dates

If you want to calculate values such as the number of days since the last coupon payment or the number of days until the next payment, you can always use Excel's data functions. However, the Analysis ToolPak also offers a few functions designed specifically to work with coupon dates:

- `COUPDAYS()`—Returns the number of days in the coupon period that includes the settlement date

- `COUPPCD()`—Returns the date of the most recent coupon payment

- `COUPDAYBS()`—Returns the number of days from the most recent coupon payment to the settlement date

- `COUPNCD()`—Returns the date of the next coupon payment

- `COUPDAYSNC()`—Returns the number of days from the settlement date to the next coupon payment

These five functions all use the same syntax:

```
COUPDAYS(settlement, maturity, frequency, [basis])
COUPPCD(settlement, maturity, frequency, [basis])
COUPDAYBS(settlement, maturity, frequency, [basis])
```

```
COUPNCD(settlement, maturity, frequency, [basis])

COUPDAYSNC(settlement, maturity, frequency, [basis])
```

| | |
|---|---|
| *settlement* | The settlement date of the bond, entered as a string or a date serial number. |
| *maturity* | The maturity date of the bond, entered as a string or a date serial number. |
| *frequency* | The number of coupon payments made each year. Use 1 for annual payments, use 2 for semiannual payments, and use 4 for quarterly payments. |
| *basis* | An integer that specifies the assumed number of days in the month and year. 0 = US (NASD) 30/360 (the default), 1 = Actual/actual, 2 = Actual/360, 3 = Actual/365, and 4 = European 30/360. |

Figure 19.6 shows a worksheet that puts each of these functions through its paces. The formulas used in column E are shown as text in column F.

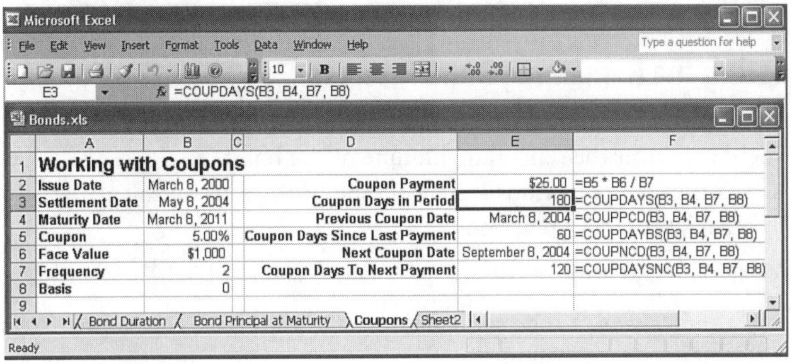

**Figure 19.6**
To calculate the coupon payment, multiply the coupon by the face value and divide by the payment frequency.

## Calculating the Accrued Bond Interest

When you purchase a bond, the total cost isn't just the price of the bond multiplied by the number of bonds. Your broker might charge a fee, of course, but you need to consider another charge: the *accrued interest*. This is the portion of the next coupon payment that you owe to the previous bondholder. For example, suppose that a $1,000 face value bond has a 10% coupon with semiannual payments, which means that each payment is worth $50. If you purchase the bond halfway through the current coupon period, you owe the previous bondholder half the interest payment, or $25.

To calculate the accrued interest, you divide the number of days since the previous coupon payment—the COUPDAYSBS() calculation—by the number of coupon days in the current period—the COUPDAYS() calculation—and multiply the result by the coupon payment:

```
Payment * COUPDAYSBS() / COUPDAYS()
```

Figure 19.7 shows the Coupons worksheet with the accrued interest calculation added.

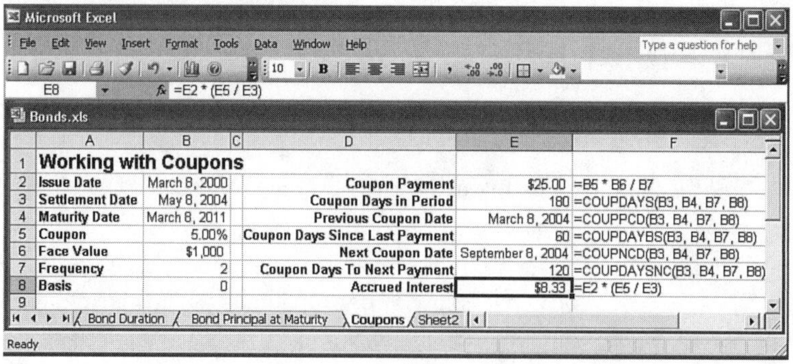

**Figure 19.7**
To calculate the accrued interest, divide the number of days in the current period by the number of days since the previous coupon payment, and multiply the result by the coupon payment.

> **NOTE**
>
> The Analysis ToolPak also comes with a function named ACCRINT(), which is supposed to return the accrued interest. However, either by design or by flaw, the function actually returns the accrued interest not from the previous coupon date, but from the bond's issue date. This calculation is not particularly useful, so I suggest avoiding the ACCRINT() function.

## Calculating the Remaining Bond Interest

If you plan to hold the bond to maturity, you probably want to know how much interest you'll earn over the remaining lifetime of the bond. To figure that, you first need to know how many coupon periods are left on the bond. You can calculate that by using the Analysis ToolPak's COUPNUM() function:

COUPNUM(*settlement*, *maturity*, *frequency*, [*basis*])

| | |
|---|---|
| *settlement* | The settlement date of the bond, entered as a string or a date serial number. |
| *maturity* | The maturity date of the bond, entered as a string or a date serial number. |
| *frequency* | The number of coupon payments made each year. Use 1 for annual payments, use 2 for semiannual payments, and use 4 for quarterly payments. |
| *basis* | An integer that specifies the assumed number of days in the month and year. 0 = US (NASD) 30/360 (the default), 1 = Actual/actual, 2 = Actual/360, 3 = Actual/365, and 4 = European 30/360. |

For example, if you purchase a semiannual coupon bond on May 8, 2004, and the bond matures on March 8, 2011, you can use the following formula to return the number of coupon payments remaining:

=COUPNUM("5/8/2004", "3/8/2011", 2, 0)

When you know the number of coupon periods remaining, calculating the remaining interest is a straightforward matter of multiplying by the coupon payment and then subtracting the accrued interest:

```
Coupon Periods * Coupon Payment - Accrued Interest
```

Figure 19.8 shows the final version of the Coupon worksheet showing the COUPNUM() calculation in E9 and the interest remaining formula in E10.

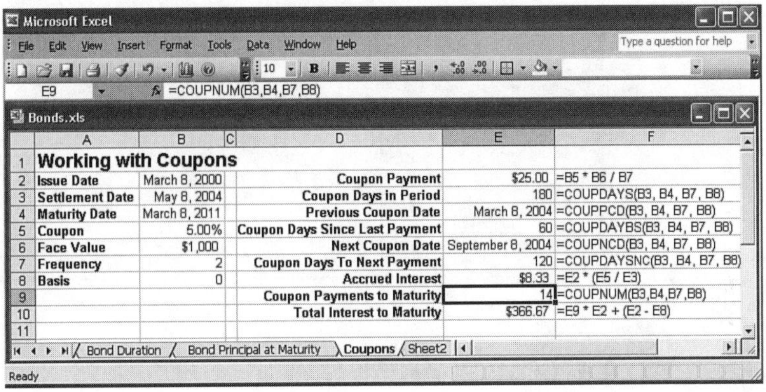

**Figure 19.8**
To calculate the interest remaining to be paid on the bond, multiply the number of remaining coupon periods by the coupon payment and subtract the accrued interest.

# Working with Zero-Coupon Bonds

A zero-coupon bond is one in which all the coupons have been "clipped" so that there are no interest payments. This might sound like a bad thing, but zeroes (as they're often called) are always sold at a deep discount from the face value, so the "interest" you earn is the difference between the discounted price and the face value you get at maturity. The big advantage of zeroes is that you have no *reinvestment risk*, which is the risk associated with reinvesting coupon payments with an ordinary bond. For example, if bond yields have gone down, your reinvested interest won't earn as much as you would like. That's not a problem with zeroes because there is no interest to reinvest: You simply watch the bond's value grow from the discounted price to the face value. (There are some downsides to zeroes: You must still pay taxes on the "income" you earn each year; zeroes are exceptionally volatile, so if you're forced to sell before maturity, it might be at a substantial loss; and the investment doesn't pay until maturity, so you run the risk of losing the entire investment if the issuer can't meet its obligations.)

Depending on how close the maturity date is, the yield on a zero-coupon bond is generated by purchasing the bond at a deep discount from the face value. For example, a zero-coupon bond that doesn't mature for another 20 years might sell for as little as $30 per $100 face value.

Fortunately, you don't need to do anything special to calculate either the yield or the price for a zero-coupon bond. Use the same YIELD() and PRICE() functions that you learned about earlier in this chapter, and set the *rate* argument to 0. Figure 19.9 shows a worksheet that uses YIELD() and PRICE() to perform these calculations on zero-coupon bonds.

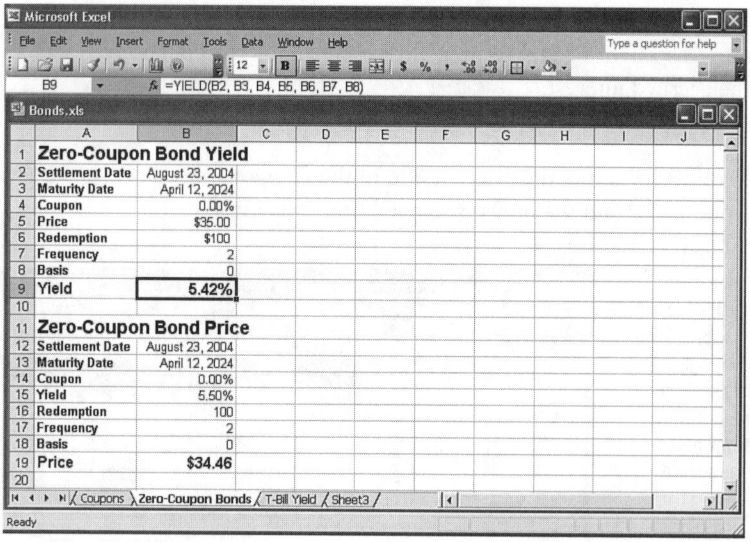

**Figure 19.9**
To calculate the yield and price for a zero-coupon bond, use the YIELD() and PRICE() functions with the rate argument set to 0.

# Working with Treasury Bills

U.S. Treasury bills (or T-bills) are short-term (up to a year) investments. Like zero-coupon bonds, they do not pay interest, but are sold at a discount from par. Excel offers several functions that enable you to perform calculations on these securities.

## Calculating the T-Bill Yield

To calculate the yield on a T-bill, use the Analysis ToolPak's TBILLYIELD() function:

TBILLYIELD(*settlement*, *maturity*, *pr*)

| | |
|---|---|
| *settlement* | The settlement date of the T-bill, entered as a string or a date serial number |
| *maturity* | The maturity date of the T-bill, entered as a string or a date serial number |
| *pr* | The T-bill's price per $100 of face value |

For example, Figure 19.10 shows a worksheet that calculates the yield on a T-bill that matures April 15, 2005, and is purchased August 23, 2004, for $98.75.

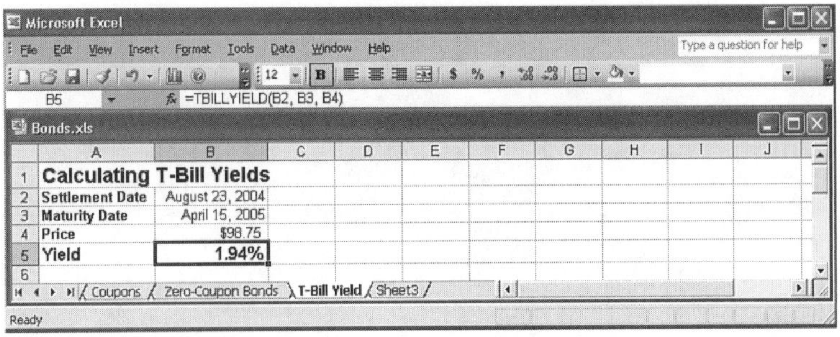

**Figure 19.10**
Use the
TBILLYIELD()
function to calculate the
yield on a Treasury bill.

## Calculating the T-Bill Price

To calculate the price of a T-bill, use the Analysis ToolPak's TBILLPRICE() function:

TBILLPRICE(*settlement*, *maturity*, *discount*)

| | |
|---|---|
| *settlement* | The settlement date of the T-bill, entered as a string or a date serial number |
| *maturity* | The maturity date of the T-bill, entered as a string or a date serial number |
| *discount* | The discount rate of the T-bill |

For example, Figure 19.11 shows a worksheet that calculates the price of a T-bill that matures April 15, 2005, and is purchased August 23, 2004, with a discount rate of 1.5%.

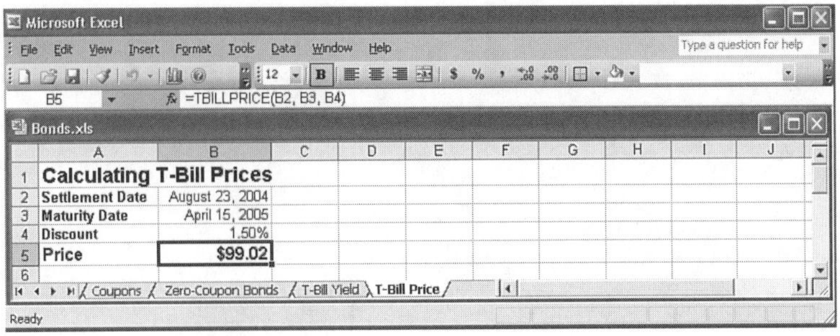

**Figure 19.11**
Use the
TBILLPRICE()
function to calculate the
price of a Treasury bill.

19

## From Here

■ To learn about arrays and array formulas, **see** "Working with Arrays," **p. 85**.

■ For information on using Excel for other types of investments, **see** "Building Investment Formulas," **p. 417**.

# Building Discount Formulas

## 20

In Chapter 18, "Building Investment Formulas," you saw that investment calculations largely use the same time-value-of-money concepts as the loan calculations that you learned about in Chapter 17, "Building Loan Formulas." The difference is the direction of the cash flows. For example, the present value of a loan is a positive cash flow because the money comes to you; the present value of an investment is a negative cash flow because the money goes out to the investment.

Discounting also fits into the time-value-of-money scheme, and you can see its relation to present value, future value, and interest earned in the following equations:

$$\text{Future value} = \text{Present value} + \text{interest}$$
$$\text{Present value} = \text{Future value} - \text{discount}$$

In Chapter 17, you learned about a form of discounting when you determined how much money you could borrow (the present value) when you know the current interest rate that your bank offers for loans, when you want to have the loan paid off, and how much you can afford each month for the payments.

→ See "Calculating How Much You Can Borrow," **p. 412**.

Similarly, in Chapter 18, you learned about another application of discounting when you calculated what initial deposit was required (the present value) to reach a future goal, knowing how much you can deposit each period and how much the interest rate will be.

→ See "Calculating the Required Initial Deposit," **p. 425**.

This chapter takes a closer look at Excel's discounting tools, including present value and profitability, and cash-flow analysis measures such as net present value and internal rate of return.

# Calculating the Present Value

The concept of the time value of money tells you that a dollar now is not the same as a dollar in the future. You can't compare them directly because it's like comparing apples and oranges. From a discounting perspective, the present value is important because it turns those future oranges into present apples. That is, it enables you to make a true comparison by restating the future value of an asset or investment in today's terms.

You know from Chapter 18 that calculating a future value relies on compounding. That is, a dollar today grows by applying interest on interest, like this:

Year 1: $1.00 × (1 + *rate*)

Year 2: $1.00 × (1 + *rate*) × (1 + *rate*)

Year 3: $1.00 × (1 + *rate*) × (1 + *rate*) × (1 + *rate*)

→ **See** "Understanding Compound Interest," **p. 418**

More generally, given an interest *rate* and a period *nper*, the future value of a dollar today is calculated as follows:

```
=$1.00 * (1 + rate) ^ nper
```

Calculating the present value uses the reverse process. That is, given some discount *rate*, a future dollar is expressed in today's dollars by dividing instead of multiplying:

Year 1: $1.00 ÷ (1 + *rate*)

Year 2: $1.00 ÷ (1 + *rate*) ÷ (1 + *rate*)

Year 3: $1.00 ÷ (1 + *rate*) ÷ (1 + *rate*) ÷ (1 + *rate*)

In general, given a discount *rate* and a period *nper*, the present value of a future dollar is calculated as follows:

```
=$1.00 / (1 + rate) ^ nper
```

The result of this formula is called the *discount factor*, and multiplying it by any future value restates that value in today's dollars.

## Taking Inflation into Account

The future value tells you how much money you'll end up with, but it doesn't tell you how much that money is *worth*. In other words, if an object costs $10,000 now and your investment's future value is $10,000, it's unlikely that you'll be able to use that future value to purchase the object because it will probably have gone up in price. That is, inflation erodes the purchasing power of any future value; to know what a future value is worth, you need to express it in today's dollars.

For example, suppose that you put $10,000 initially and $100 per month into an investment that pays 5% annual interest. After 10 years, the future value of that investment will be $31,998.32. Assuming that the inflation rate stays constant at 2% per year, what is the investment's future value worth in today's dollars?

Here, the discount rate is the inflation rate, so the discount factor is calculated as follows:

```
=1 / (1.02) ^ 10
```

This returns 0.82. Multiplying the future value by this discount factor gives the present value: $26,249.77.

## Calculating Present Value Using PV()

You're probably wondering what happened to Excel's PV() function. I've held off introducing it so that you could see how to calculate present value from first principles. Now that you know what's going on behind the scenes, you can make your life easier by calculating present values directly using the PV() function:

```
PV(rate, nper, pmt, [fv], [type])
```

| | |
|---|---|
| *rate* | The fixed rate over the term of the asset or investment. |
| *nper* | The number of periods in the term of the asset or investment. |
| *pmt* | The amount earned by the asset or deposited into the investment with each deposit. |
| *fv* | The future value of the asset or investment. |
| *type* | When the *pmt* occurs. Use 0 (the default) for the end of each period; use 1 for the beginning of each period. |

For example, to calculate the effect of inflation on a future value, you apply the PV() function to the future value, where the *rate* argument is the inflation rate:

```
PV(inflation rate, nper, 0, fv)
```

> **NOTE** Any time you set the PV() function's *pmt* argument to 0, you can ignore the *type* argument because it's meaningless without any payments.

Figure 20.1 shows a worksheet that uses PV() to derive the answer of $26,249.77 using the following formula:

```
=PV(B9, B3, 0, -B7)
```

Note that this is the same result that you derived using the discount factor, which is shown in Figure 20.1 in cell B10. (The table in D2:E13 shows the various discount factors for each year.)

The next few sections take you through some examples of using PV() in discounting scenarios.

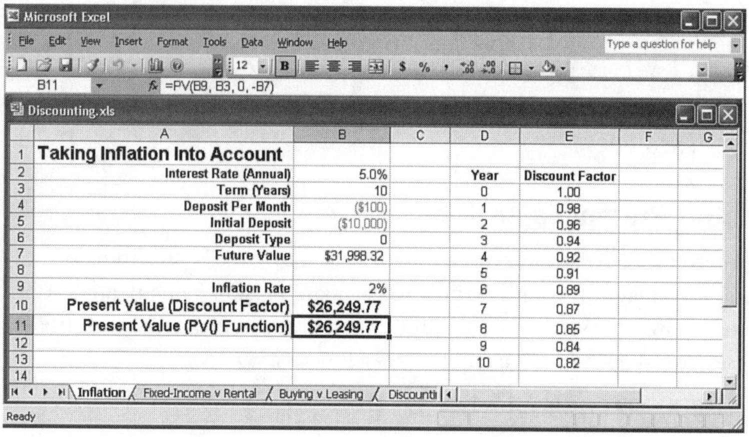

**Figure 20.1**
Using the PV( ) function to calculate the effects of inflation on a future value.

## Income Investing Versus Purchasing a Rental Property

If you have some cash to invest, one common scenario is to wonder whether the cash is better invested in a straight income-producing security (such as a bond or certificate) or in a rental property.

One way to analyze this is to gather the following data:

- On the fixed-income security side, find your best deal in the time frame you're looking at. For example, you might find that you can get a bond that matures in 10 years with a 5% yield.

- On the rental property side, find out what the property produces in annual rental income. Also, estimate what the rental property will be worth at the same future date that the fixed-income security matures. For example, you might be looking at a rental property that generates $24,000 a year and is estimated to be worth $1 million in 10 years.

Given this data (and ignoring complicating factors such as rental property expenses), you want to know the maximum that you should pay for the property to realize a better yield than with the fixed-income security.

To solve this problem, use the PV() function as follows:

```
=PV(fixed income yield, nper, rental income, future property value)
```

Figure 20.2 shows a worksheet model that uses this formula. The result of the PV() function is $799,235. You interpret this to mean that if you pay less than that amount for the property, the property is a better deal than the fixed-income security; if you pay more, you're better off going the fixed-income route.

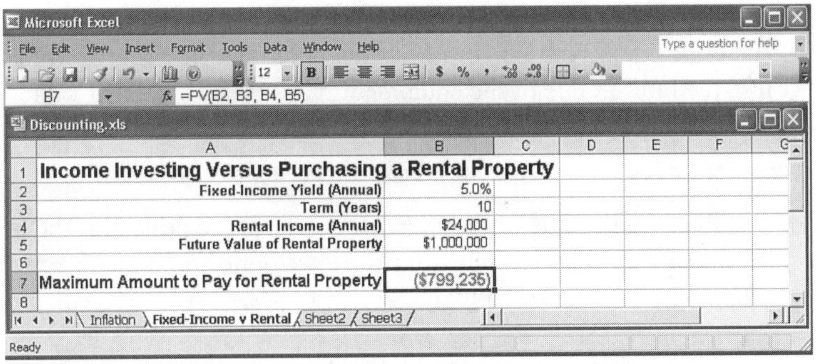

**Figure 20.2**

Using the PV ( ) function to compare investing in a fixed-income security versus purchasing a rental property.

**Buying Versus Leasing**

Another common business conundrum is whether to purchase equipment outright or to lease it. Again, you figure the present value of both sides to compare them, with the preferable option being the one that provides the lower present value. (This ignores complicating factors such as depreciation and taxes.)

Assume (for now) that the purchased equipment has no market value at the end of the term and that the leased equipment has no residual value at the end of the lease. In this case, the present value of the purchase option is simply the purchase price. For the lease option, you determine the present value using the following form of the PV() function:

```
=PV(discount rate, lease term, lease payment)
```

For the *discount rate*, you plug in a value that represents either a current investment rate or a current loan rate. For example, if you could invest the lease payment and get, say, 6% per year, you would plug 6% into the function as the *rate* argument.

For example, suppose that you can either purchase a piece of equipment for $5,000 now or lease the equipment for $240 a month over 2 years. Assuming a discount rate of 6%, what's the present value of the leasing option? Figure 20.3 shows a worksheet that calculates the answer: $5,415.09. This means that purchasing the equipment is the less costly choice.

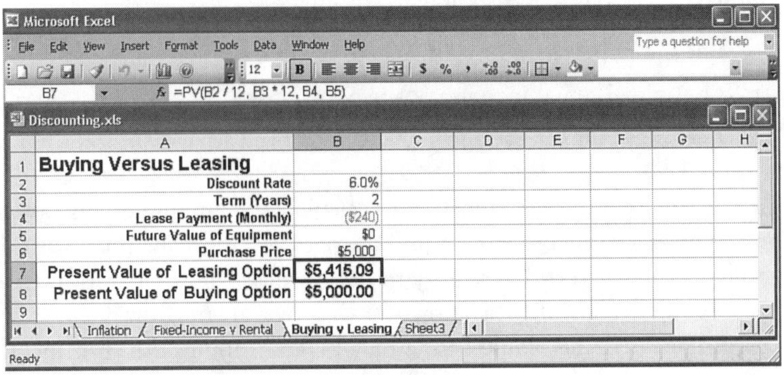

**Figure 20.3**

Using the PV ( ) function to compare buying versus leasing equipment.

20

What if the equipment has a future market value (on the purchase side) or a residual value (on the lease side)? This won't make much difference in terms of which option is better because the future value of the equipment raises the two present values by about the same amount. However, note how you calculate the present value for the purchase option:

```
=purchase price + PV(discount rate, term, 0, future value)
```

That is, the present value of the purchase option is the price plus the present value of the equipment's future market value. (For the lease option, you include the residual value as the PV() function's *fv* argument.) Figure 20.4 shows the worksheet with a future value added.

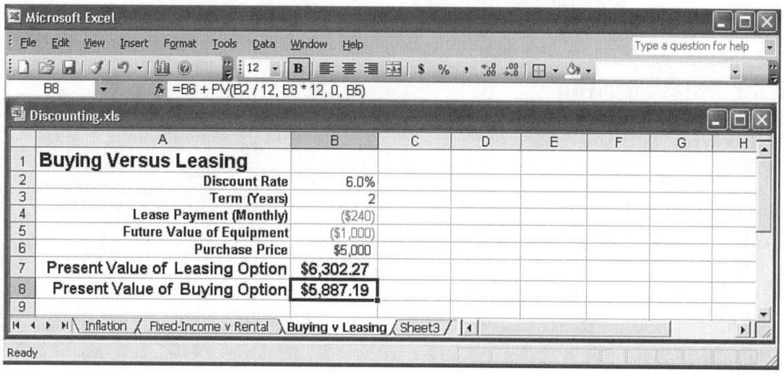

**Figure 20.4**
Using the PV() function to compare buying versus leasing equipment that has a future market or residual value.

# Discounting Cash Flows

One very common business scenario is to put some money into an asset or investment that generates income. By examining the cash flows—the negative cash flows for the original investment and any subsequent outlays required by the asset, and the positive cash flows for the income generated by the asset—you can figure out whether you've made a good investment.

For example, consider the situation discussed earlier in this chapter: You invest in a property that generates a regular cash flow of rental income. When analyzing this investment, you have three types of cash flow to consider:

- The initial purchase price (negative cash flow)
- The annual rental income (positive cash flow)
- The price you get by selling the property (positive cash flow)

Earlier you used the PV() function to calculate that an initial purchase price of $799,235 and an assumed sale price of $1 million gives you the same return as a 5% fixed-income security over 10 years. Let's verify this using a cash-flow analysis. Figure 20.5 shows a worksheet set up to show the cash flows for this investment. Row 3 shows the net cash flow each year (in practice, this would be the rental income minus the costs incurred while maintaining and repairing the property). Row 4 shows the cumulative cash flows. Note that columns

F through I (years 4–7) are hidden so that you can see the final cash flow: the rent in year 10 plus the sale price of the property.

| | A | B | C | D | E | J | K | L |
|---|---|---|---|---|---|---|---|---|
| 1 | Year | 0 | 1 | 2 | 3 | 8 | 9 | 10 |
| 2 | CASH FLOW | Purchase | | | | | | Sale |
| 3 | Net Cash Flow | ($799,235) | $24,000 | $24,000 | $24,000 | $24,000 | $24,000 | $1,024,000 |
| 4 | Cumulative Net Cash Flow | ($799,235) | ($775,235) | ($751,235) | ($727,235) | ($607,235) | ($583,235) | $440,765 |
| 5 | | | | | | | | |

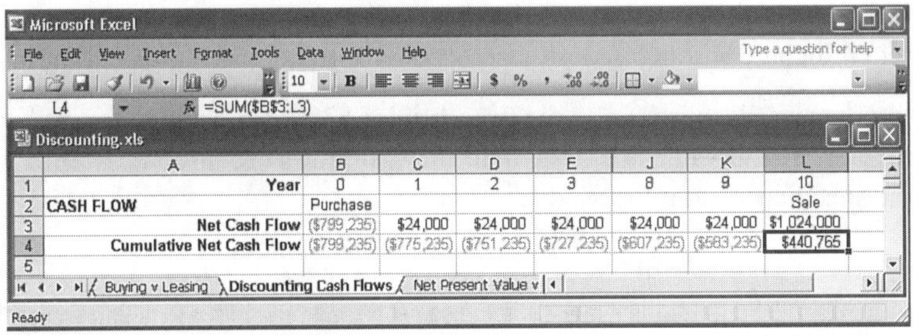

**Figure 20.5**
The yearly and cumulative cash flows for a rental property.

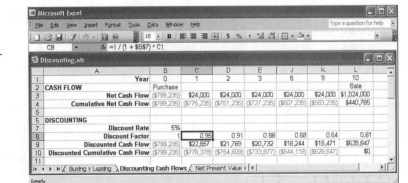

## Calculating the Net Present Value

The *net present value* is the sum of a series of net cash flows, each of which has been discounted to the present using a fixed discount rate. If all the cash flows are the same, you can use the `PV()` function to calculate the present value. But when you have a series of varying cash flows, as in the rental property example, you can apply the `PV()` function directly.

Excel has a direct route to calculating net present value, but let's take a second to examine a method that calculates this value from first principles. This will help you understand exactly what's happening in this kind of cash-flow analysis.

To get the net present value, you first have to discount each cash flow. You do that by multiplying the cash flow by the discount factor, which you calculate as described earlier in this chapter.

Figure 20.6 shows the rental property cash-flow worksheet with the discount factors (row 8) and the discounted cash flows (rows 9 and 10).

| | A | B | C | D | E | J | K | L |
|---|---|---|---|---|---|---|---|---|
| 1 | Year | 0 | 1 | 2 | 3 | 8 | 9 | 10 |
| 2 | CASH FLOW | Purchase | | | | | | Sale |
| 3 | Net Cash Flow | ($799,235) | $24,000 | $24,000 | $24,000 | $24,000 | $24,000 | $1,024,000 |
| 4 | Cumulative Net Cash Flow | ($799,235) | ($775,235) | ($751,235) | ($727,235) | ($607,235) | ($583,235) | $440,765 |
| 5 | | | | | | | | |
| 6 | DISCOUNTING | | | | | | | |
| 7 | Discount Rate | 5% | | | | | | |
| 8 | Discount Factor | 1 | 0.95 | 0.91 | 0.86 | 0.68 | 0.64 | 0.61 |
| 9 | Discounted Cash Flow | ($799,235) | $22,857 | $21,769 | $20,732 | $16,244 | $15,471 | $628,647 |
| 10 | Discounted Cumulative Cash Flow | ($799,235) | ($776,378) | ($754,609) | ($733,877) | ($644,118) | ($628,647) | $0 |
| 11 | | | | | | | | |

**Figure 20.6**
The discounted yearly and cumulative cash flows for a rental property.

20

The key number to notice in Figure 20.6 is the final Discounted Cumulative Cash Flow value in cell L10, which is $0. This is the net present value, the sum of the cumulative discounted cash flows at the end of year 10. This result makes sense because you already know that the initial cash flow—the purchase price of $799,235—was the present value of the rental income with a discount rate of 5% and a sale price of $1 million.

In other words, purchasing the property for $799,235 enables you to break even—that is, the net present value is 0—when all the cash flows are discounted into today's dollars using the specified discount rate.

> **NOTE** The discount rate that returns a net present value of 0 is sometimes called the *hurdle rate*. In other words, it's the rate that you must surpass to make the asset or investment worthwhile.

The net present value can also tell you whether an investment is positive or negative:

- If the net present value is negative, this can generally be interpreted in two ways: Either you paid too much for the asset or the income from the asset is too low. For example, if you plug –$900,000 into the rental property model as the initial cash flow (that is, the purchase price), the net present value works out to –$100,765, which is the loss on the property in today's dollars.

- If the net present value is positive, this can generally be interpreted in two ways: Either you got a good deal for the asset or the income makes the asset profitable. For example, if you plug –$700,000 into the rental property model as the initial cash flow (that is, the purchase price), the net present value works out to $99,235, which is the profit on the property in today's dollars.

## Calculating Net Present Value Using NPV()

The model built in the previous section was designed to show you the relationship between the present value and the net present value. Fortunately, you don't have to jump through all those worksheet hoops every time you need to calculate the net present value. Excel offers a much quicker method with the NPV() function:

NPV(*rate, values*)

    *rate*      The discount rate over the term of the asset or investment

    *values*   The cash flows over the term of the asset or investment

For example, to calculate the net present value of the cash flows in Figure 20.6, you use the following formula:

=NPV(B7, B3:L3)

That's markedly easier than figuring out discount factors and discounted cash flows. However, the NPV() function has one quirk that can seriously affect its results. NPV()

assumes that the initial cash flow occurs at the end of the first period. However, in most cases, the initial cash flow—usually a negative cash flow, indicating the purchase of an asset or a deposit into an investment—occurs at the beginning of the term. This is usually designated as period 0. The first cash flow resulting from the asset or investment is designated as period 1.

The upshot of this `NPV()` quirk is that the function result is usually understated by a factor of the discount rate. For example, if the discount rate is 5%, the `NPV()` result must be increased by 5% to factor in the first period and get the true net present value. Here's the general formula:

```
net present value = NPV() * (1 + discount rate)
```

Figure 20.7 shows a new worksheet that contains the rental property's net cash flows (B3:L3) as well as the discount rate (B5). The net present value is calculated using the following formula:

```
=NPV(B5, B3:L3) * (1 + B5)
```

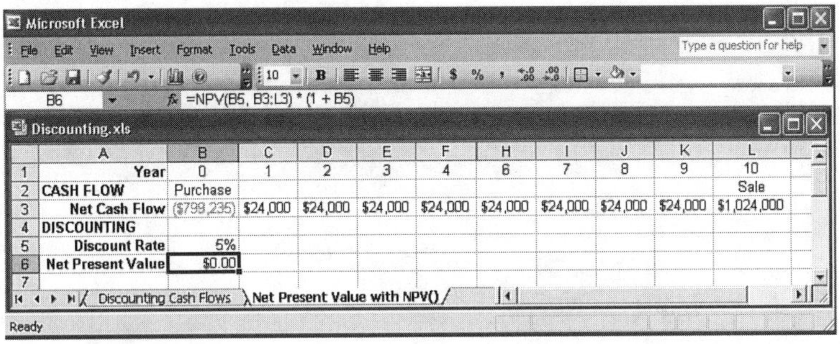


| | A | B | C | D | E | F | H | I | J | K | L |
|---|---|---|---|---|---|---|---|---|---|---|---|
| 1 | Year | 0 | 1 | 2 | 3 | 4 | 6 | 7 | 8 | 9 | 10 |
| 2 | CASH FLOW | Purchase | | | | | | | | | Sale |
| 3 | Net Cash Flow | ($799,235) | $24,000 | $24,000 | $24,000 | $24,000 | $24,000 | $24,000 | $24,000 | $24,000 | $1,024,000 |
| 4 | DISCOUNTING | | | | | | | | | | |
| 5 | Discount Rate | 5% | | | | | | | | | |
| 6 | Net Present Value | $0.00 | | | | | | | | | |
| 7 | | | | | | | | | | | |

**Figure 20.7**
The net present value calculated using the `NPV()` function plus an adjustment.

**CAUTION**

Make sure that you adjust the discount rate to reflect the frequency of the discounting periods. If the periods are annual, the discount rate must be an annual rate. If the periods are monthly, you need to divide the discount rate by 12 to get the monthly rate.



## Net Present Value with Varying Cash Flows

The major advantage to using `NPV()` over `PV()` is that `NPV()` can easily accommodate varying cash flows. You can use `PV()` directly to calculate the break-even purchase price, assuming that the asset or investment generates a constant cash flow each period. Alternatively, you can use `PV()` to help calculate the net present value for different cash flows if you build a complicated discounted cash flow model such as the one shown for the rental property in Figure 20.6.

You don't need to worry about either of these scenarios if you use `NPV()`. That's because you can simply enter the cash flows as the `NPV()` function's *`values`* argument.

For example, suppose that you're thinking of investing in a new piece of equipment that will generate income, but you don't want to make the investment unless the machine will generate a return of at least 10% in today's dollars over the first 5 years. Your cash-flow projection looks like this:

Year 0: $50,000 (purchase price)

Year 1: –$5,000

Year 2: $15,000

Year 3: $20,000

Year 4: $21,000

Year 5: $22,000

Figure 20.8 shows a worksheet that models this scenario with the cash flows in B4:G4. Using the target return of 10% as the discount rate (B6), the NPV() function returns $881 (B7). This amount is positive, which it means that the machine will make at least a 10% return in today's dollars over the first 5 years.

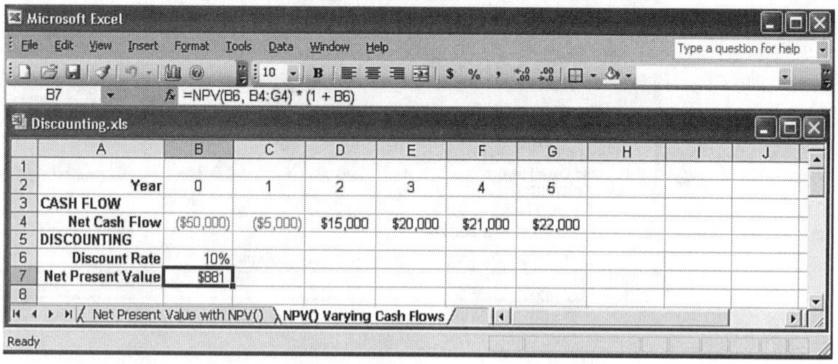

**Figure 20.8**

To see whether a series of cash flows meets a desired rate of return, use that rate as the discount rate in the NPV() function.

## Net Present Value with Nonperiodic Cash Flows

The examples you've seen so far have assumed that the cash flows were periodic, meaning that they occur with the same frequency throughout the term (such as yearly or monthly). In some investments, however, the cash flows occur sporadically. In this case, you can't use the NPV() function, which works only with periodic cash flows.

Happily, Excel's Analysis ToolPak offers the XNPV() function, which can handle nonperiodic cash flows:

XNPV(*rate, values, dates*)

| | |
|---|---|
| *rate* | The annual discount rate over the term of the asset or investment. |
| *values* | The cash flows over the term of the asset or investment. |
| *dates* | The dates on which each of the cash flows occurs. Make sure the first value in *dates* is the date of the initial cash flow. All the other dates must be later than this initial date, but they can be listed in any order. |

For example, Figure 20.9 shows a worksheet with a series of cash flows (B4:G4) and the dates on which they occur (B5:G5). Assuming a 10% discount rate (B7) the `XNPV()` function returns a value of $842 using the following formula (B8):

```
=XNPV(B7, B4:G5, B5:G5)
```

> **NOTE** Note that the `XNPV()` function doesn't have the "missing first period" quirk of the `NPV()` function. Therefore, you can use `XNPV()` straight up without adding a first period factor.

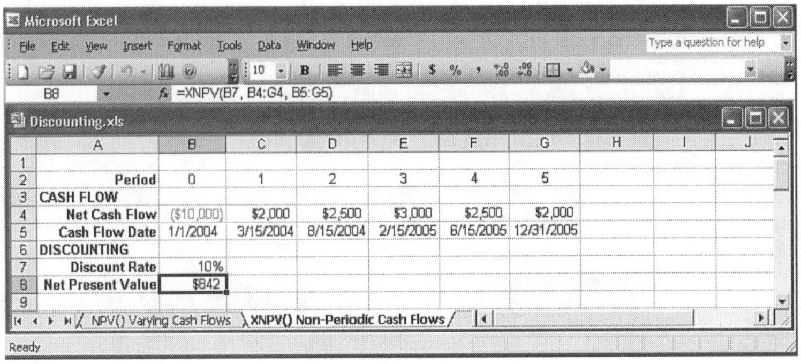


**Figure 20.9**
Use the `XNPV()` function to calculate the net present value for a series of nonperiodic cash flows.

# Calculating the Payback Period

If you purchase a store, a piece of equipment, or an investment, your hope always is to at least recoup your initial outlay through the positive cash flows generated by the asset. The point at which you recoup the initial outlay is called the *payback period*. When analyzing a business case, one of the most common concerns is when the payback period occurs: A short payback period is better than a long one.

## Simple Undiscounted Payback Period

Finding the undiscounted payback period is a matter of calculating the cumulative cash flows and watching when they turn from negative to positive. The period that shows the first positive cumulative cash flow is the payback period.

For example, suppose that you purchase a store for $500,000 and project the following cash flows:

| Year | Net Cash Flow | Cumulative Net Cash Flow |
|---|---|---|
| 0 | –$500,000 | –$500,000 |
| 1 | $55,000 | –$445,000 |
| 2 | $75,000 | –$370,000 |
| 3 | $80,000 | –$290,000 |

*continues*

*continued*

| Year | Net Cash Flow | Cumulative Net Cash Flow |
|------|---------------|--------------------------|
| 4 | $95,000 | –$195,000 |
| 5 | $105,000 | –$90,000 |
| 6 | $120,000 | $30,000 |

As you can see, the cumulative cash flow turns positive in year 6, so that's the payback period.

Instead of simply eyeballing the payback period, you can use a formula to calculate it. Figure 20.10 shows a worksheet that lists the cash flows and uses the following array formula to calculate the payback period (see cell B5):

```
{=SUM(IF(SIGN(C4:I4) <> SIGN(OFFSET(C4:I4, 0, -1)), C1:I1, 0))}
```

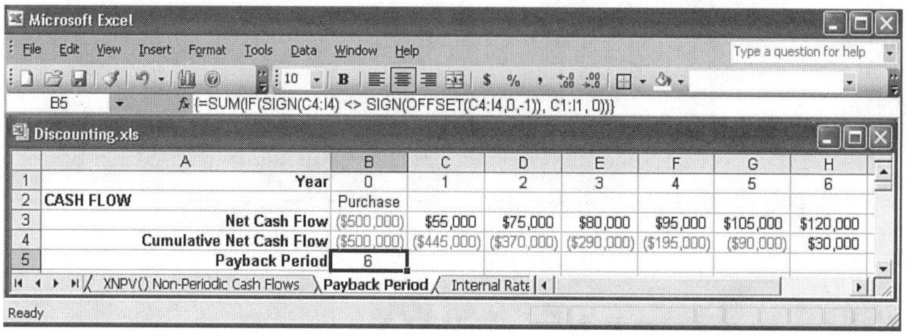

**Figure 20.10**
Using a formula to calculate the payback period.

The payback period occurs when the sign of the cumulative cash flows turns from negative to positive. Therefore, this formula uses IF() to compare each cumulative cash flow (C4:I4; you can ignore the first cash flow for this) with the cumulative cash flow from the previous period, as given by OFFSET(C4:I4, 0, -1). IF() returns 0 for all cases in which the signs are the same, and it returns the year value from row 1 (C1:I1) for the case in which the sign changes. Summing these values returns the year in which the sign changed, which is the payback period.

## Exact Undiscounted Payback Point

If the income generated by the asset is always received at the end of the period, your analysis of the payback period is done. However, many assets generate income throughout the period. In this case, the payback period tells you that some time within the period, the cumulative cash flows reaches 0. It might be useful to calculate exactly when during the period the payback occurs. Assuming that the income is received at regular intervals throughout the period, you can find the exact payback point by comparing how much is required to reach the payback with how much was earned during the payback period.

For example, suppose that the cumulative cash flow value was –$50,000 at the end of the previous period and that the asset generates $100,000 during the payback period. Assuming regular cash flow throughout the period, this means that the first $50,000 brought the cumulative cash flow to 0. Because this is half the amount earned in the payback period, you can say that the exact payback point occurred halfway through the period.

More generally, you can use the following formula to calculate the exact payback point:

```
=Payback Period - Cumulative Cash Flow at Payback / Cash Flow at Payback
```

For example, suppose you know that the store's payback period occurs in year 6, that the cumulative cash flow after year 6 is $30,000, and that the cash flow for year 6 was $120,000. Here's the formula:

```
=6 - 30,000 / 120,000
```

The answer is 5.75, meaning that the exact payback point occurs three quarters of the way through the fifth year.

To derive this in a worksheet, you first calculate the payback period and then use this number in the INDEX() function to return the values for the payback period's cumulative cash flow and net cash flow. Here's the formula used in Figure 20.11:

```
=B5 - INDEX(B4:H4, B5 + 1) / INDEX(B3:H3, B5 + 1)
```

**Figure 20.11**
Using a formula to calculate the exact payback point.

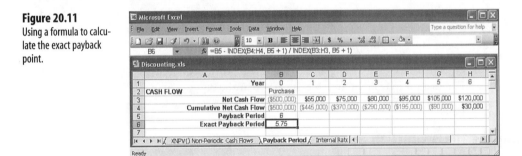

## Discounted Payback Period

Of course, the undiscounted payback period tells you only so much. To get a true measure of the payback, you need to apply these payback methods to the discounted cash flows. This tells you when the investment is paid back in today's dollars.

To do this, you need to set up a schedule of discounted net cash flow and cumulative cash flow for each period, and extend the periods until the cumulative discounted cash flow becomes positive. You can then use the formulas presented in the previous two sections (adjusted for the extra periods) to calculate the payback period and exact payback point (if applicable). Figure 20.12 shows the discounted payback values for the store's cash flows (columns D through F are hidden).

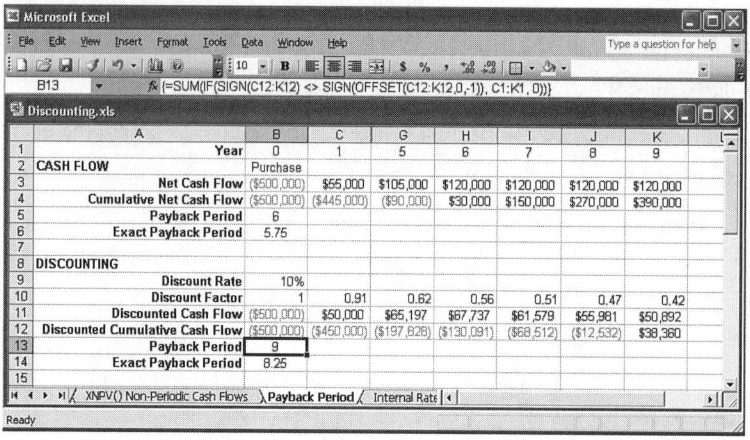


| | A | B | C | G | H | I | J | K |
|---|---|---|---|---|---|---|---|---|
| 1 | Year | 0 | 1 | 5 | 6 | 7 | 8 | 9 |
| 2 | CASH FLOW | Purchase | | | | | | |
| 3 | Net Cash Flow | ($500,000) | $55,000 | $105,000 | $120,000 | $120,000 | $120,000 | $120,000 |
| 4 | Cumulative Net Cash Flow | ($500,000) | ($445,000) | ($90,000) | $30,000 | $150,000 | $270,000 | $390,000 |
| 5 | Payback Period | 6 | | | | | | |
| 6 | Exact Payback Period | 5.75 | | | | | | |
| 7 | | | | | | | | |
| 8 | DISCOUNTING | | | | | | | |
| 9 | Discount Rate | 10% | | | | | | |
| 10 | Discount Factor | 1 | 0.91 | 0.62 | 0.56 | 0.51 | 0.47 | 0.42 |
| 11 | Discounted Cash Flow | ($500,000) | $50,000 | $65,197 | $67,737 | $61,579 | $55,981 | $50,892 |
| 12 | Discounted Cumulative Cash Flow | ($500,000) | ($450,000) | ($197,828) | ($130,091) | ($68,512) | ($12,532) | $38,360 |
| 13 | Payback Period | 9 | | | | | | |
| 14 | Exact Payback Period | 8.25 | | | | | | |
| 15 | | | | | | | | |

**Figure 20.12**
To derive the discounted payback values, create a schedule of discounted cash flows, extend the periods until the cumulative discounted cash flow turns positive, and then apply the payback formulas.

# Calculating the Internal Rate of Return

In the earlier example with varying cash flows, the discount rate was set to 10% because that was the minimum return required in today's dollars over the first 5 years after purchasing the equipment. This rate of return of an investment based on today's dollars is called the *internal rate of return*. It's actually defined as the discount rate required to get a net present value of $0.

In the equipment example, using a discount rate of 10% produced a net present value of $881. This is a positive amount, which means that the equipment actually produced an internal rate of return higher than 10%. What, then, was the actual internal rate of return?

## Using the `IRR()` Function

You could figure this out by adjusting the discount rate up (in this case) until the `NPV()` calculation returns `0`. However, Excel offers an easier method in the form of the `IRR()` function:

```
IRR(values, [guess])
```

| | |
|---|---|
| *values* | The cash flows over the term of the asset or investment |
| *guess* | An initial estimate of the internal rate of return (the default is `0.1`) |

20

**CAUTION**

**The `IRR()` function's *`values`* argument must contain at least one positive and one negative value. If all the values have the same sign, the function returns the `#NUM!` error.**

Figure 20.13 shows the cash flows generated by the equipment purchase and the resulting internal rate of return (cell B7) calculated by the `IRR()` function:

```
=IRR(B4:G4)
```

The calculated value of 10.51% means that plugging this value into the NPV() function as the discount rate would return a net present value of 0.

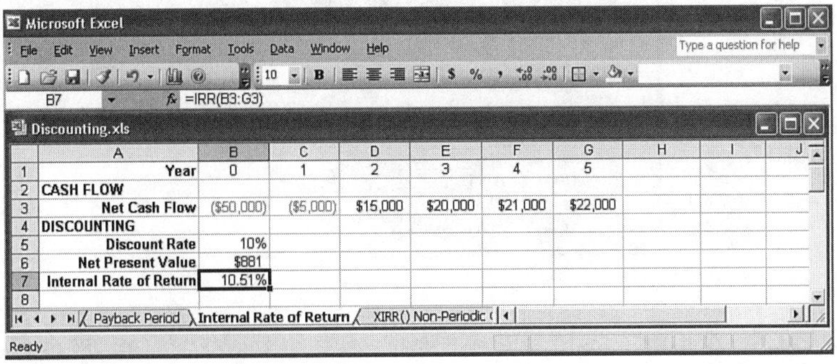

**Figure 20.13**
Use the IRR() function to calculate the internal rate of return for a series of periodic cash flows.

> **NOTE**
> The IRR() function uses iteration to find a solution that is accurate to within 0.00001%. If it can't find a solution within 20 iterations, it returns the #NUM! error. If this happens, try using a different value for the *guess* argument.

## Calculating the Internal Rate of Return for Nonperiodic Cash Flows

As with NPV(), the IRR() function works only with periodic cash flows. If your cash flows are nonperiodic, use the XIRR()function instead:

XIRR(*values*, *dates*, [*guess*])

| | |
|---|---|
| *values* | The cash flows over the term of the asset or investment. |
| *dates* | The dates on which each of the cash flows occur. Make sure that the first value in *dates* is the date of the initial cash flow. All the other dates must be later than this initial date, but they can be listed in any order. |
| *guess* | An initial estimate of the internal rate of return (the default is 0.1). |

Figure 20.14 shows a worksheet with nonperiodic cash flows and the resulting internal rate of return (cell B8) calculated using the XIRR() function:

=XIRR(B4:G4, B5:G5)

## Calculating Multiple Internal Rates of Return

Rarely does a business pay cash for major capital investments. Instead, some or all of the purchase price is usually borrowed from the bank. When calculating the internal rate of return, two assumptions are made:

■ The discount for negative cash flows is money paid to the bank to service borrowed money.

■ The discount for positive cash flows is money reinvested.

**20**

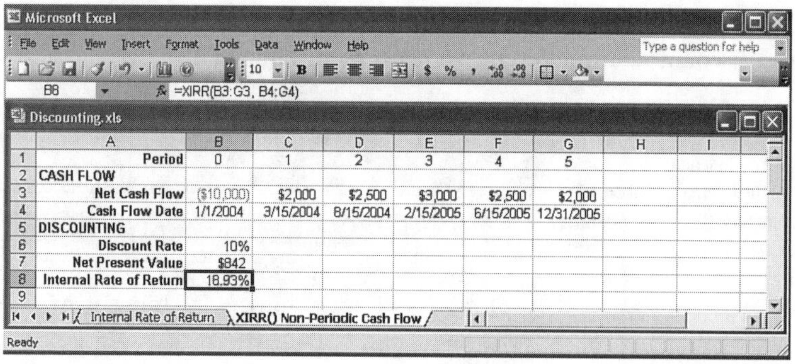

**Figure 20.14**
Use the XIRR ( ) function to calculate the internal rate of return for a series of nonperiodic cash flows.

However, a third assumption also is at work when you use the IRR ( ) function: The finance rate for negative cash flows and the reinvestment rate for positive cash flows are the same. In the real world, this is rarely true: Most banks charge interest for a loan that is 2 to 4 points higher than what you can usually get for an investment.

To handle the difference between the finance rate and the reinvestment rate, Excel enables you to calculate the *modified internal rate of return* using the MIRR ( ) function:

MIRR(*values, finance_rate, reinvest_rate*)

| | |
|---|---|
| *values* | The cash flows over the term of the asset or investment |
| *finance_rate* | The interest rate you pay for negative cash flows |
| *reinvest_rate* | The interest rate you get for positive cash flows that are reinvested |

For example, suppose that you're charged 8% for loans, and you can get 6% for investments. Figure 20.15 shows a worksheet that calculates the modified internal rate of return based on the cash flows in B3:G3 and these rates:

=MIRR(B3:G3, B5, B6)

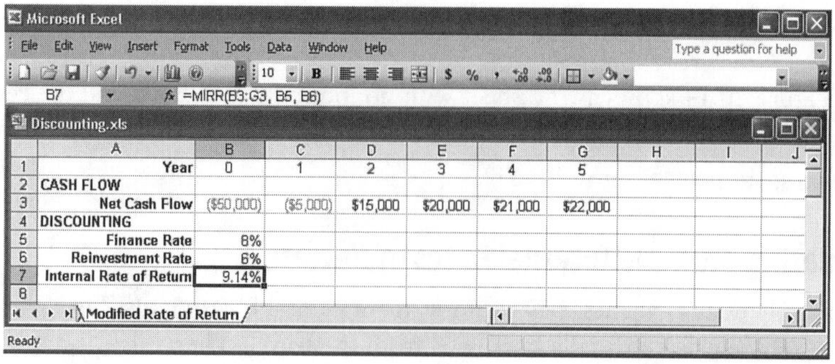

**Figure 20.15**
Use the MIRR ( ) function to calculate the modified internal rate of return when you're charged one rate for negative cash flows and a different rate for positive cash flows.

## Publishing a Book

Let's put some of this cash-flow analysis to work in an example that, although still simplified, is more realistically detailed than the ones you've seen so far in this chapter. Specifically, this case study looks at the business case of publishing a book, taking into account the costs involved (both up-front and ongoing) and the positive cash flow generated by the book. The cash-flow analysis will calculate the book's payback period (undiscounted and discounted), as well as the yearly values for the net present value and the internal rate of return.

### Per-Unit Constants

In publishing, many of the calculations involving both operating costs and sales are performed using per-unit (that is, per-book) constants. This case study uses the following six constants, as shown in Figure 20.16:

■ **List Price**—The suggested retail price of the book

■ **Average Customer Discount**—The amount taken off the retail price when selling the book to bookstores

■ **PP&B**—The per-unit costs for paper, printing, and binding

■ **Cost of Sales**—The per-unit costs of selling the book, including commissions, distribution, and so on

■ **Author Royalty**—The percentage of the list price that the author receives

■ **Margin**—The per-unit margin, which is the list price minus the customer discount, PP&B, cost of sales, and author royalty, divided by the list price

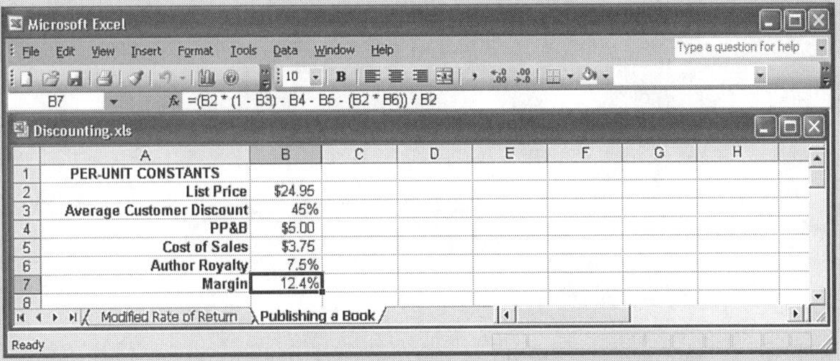

**Figure 20.16**
The per-unit constants used in the operating cost and sales calculations.

### Operating Costs and Sales

Figure 20.17 shows the annual operating costs and sales for the book over 10 years.

■ **Units Printed**—The number of books printed during the year.

■ **Units Sold**—The number of units sold during the year.

■ **New Title Costs**—Costs associated with producing the book, including acquiring, editing, indexing, and so on.

■ **Total PP&B**—The total paper, printing, and binding costs during the year. This is the year's Units Printed value (from row 10) multiplied by the PP&B value (B4).

- **Marketing**—The marketing and publicity costs during the year.
- **Total Cost of Sales**—The total cost of sales during the year. This is the year's Units Sold value (from row 11) multiplied by the Cost of Sales value (B5).
- **Author Advance**—The advance on royalties paid to the author, The assumption is that this value is paid at the beginning of the project, so it's placed in year 0.
- **Author Royalties**—The royalties paid to the author during the year. This is generally the year's Units Sold value (from row 11) multiplied by the List Price (B2) and the Author Royalty (B6). However, the formula also takes into account the Author Advance, and it doesn't pay royalties until the advance has earned out.
- **$ Sales**—The total sales, in dollars, during the year. This is the year's Unit Sales value (from row 11) multiplied by the List Price (B2) minus the Average Customer Discount (B3).
- **Translation Rights**—Payments for translation rights sold during the year.
- **Book Club Rights**—Payments for book club rights sold during the year.

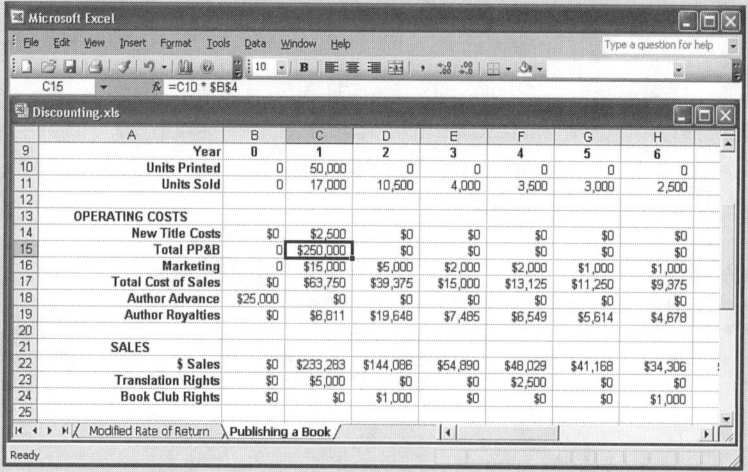

**Figure 20.17**
The operating costs and sales for each year.

## Cash Flow

With the operating costs and sales available, you can calculate the net cash flow for each year by subtracting the sum of the operating costs from the sum of the sales. Figure 20.18 shows the book's net cash flows in row 27, as well as its cumulative net cash flows (row 28). You also get the discounted net and cumulative cash flows using a discount rate of 12.4%. This is the same as the per-unit Margin value (B7), and it is the target rate of return for the book.

**Figure 20.18**
The yearly net and cumulative cash flows and their discounted versions.

| | A | B | C | D | E | F | G | H |
|---|---|---|---|---|---|---|---|---|
| 13 | OPERATING COSTS | | | | | | | |
| 14 | New Title Costs | $0 | $2,500 | $0 | $0 | $0 | $0 | $0 |
| 15 | Total PP&B | 0 | $250,000 | $0 | $0 | $0 | $0 | $0 |
| 16 | Marketing | 0 | $15,000 | $5,000 | $2,000 | $2,000 | $1,000 | $1,000 |
| 17 | Total Cost of Sales | $0 | $63,750 | $39,375 | $15,000 | $13,125 | $11,250 | $9,375 |
| 18 | Author Advance | $25,000 | $0 | $0 | $0 | $0 | $0 | $0 |
| 19 | Author Royalties | $0 | $6,811 | $19,648 | $7,485 | $6,549 | $5,614 | $4,678 |
| 20 | | | | | | | | |
| 21 | SALES | | | | | | | |
| 22 | $ Sales | $0 | $233,283 | $144,086 | $54,890 | $48,029 | $41,168 | $34,306 |
| 23 | Translation Rights | $0 | $5,000 | $0 | $0 | $2,500 | $0 | $0 |
| 24 | Book Club Rights | $0 | $0 | $1,000 | $0 | $0 | $0 | $1,000 |
| 25 | | | | | | | | |
| 26 | CASH FLOW | | | | | | | |
| 27 | Net | ($25,000) | ($99,779) | $81,063 | $30,405 | $28,854 | $23,304 | $20,253 |
| 28 | Cumulative | ($25,000) | ($124,779) | ($43,716) | ($13,311) | $15,544 | $38,848 | $59,101 |
| 29 | Discount Rate | 12.4% | | | | | | |
| 30 | Discount Factor | 1.00 | 0.89 | 0.79 | 0.70 | 0.63 | 0.56 | 0.50 |
| 31 | Discounted Net | ($25,000) | ($88,748) | $64,130 | $21,394 | $18,059 | $12,972 | $10,028 |
| 32 | Discounted Cumulative | ($25,000) | ($113,748) | ($49,618) | ($28,223) | ($10,165) | $2,808 | $12,835 |
| 33 | | | | | | | | |

## Cash-Flow Analysis

Finally, we're ready to analyze the cash flow, as shown in Figure 20.19. There are six values:

- **Undiscounted Payback Period**—The year in which the book's undiscounted cumulative cash flows turn positive.
- **Undiscounted Payback Point**—The exact point in the payback period at which the book's undiscounted cumulative cash flows turn positive.
- **Discounted Payback Period**—The year in which the book's discounted cumulative cash flows turn positive.
- **Discounted Payback Point**—The exact point in the payback period at which the book's discounted cumulative cash flows turn positive.
- **Net Present Value**—The net present value calculation at the end of each year, as returned by the NPV() function (with the fudge factor added, as explained earlier).
- **Internal Rate of Return**—The internal rate of return calculation at the end of each year, as returned by the IRR() function. Note that we don't start this calculation until year 2 because in year 1 there are nothing but negative cash flows.

> **NOTE**
> To get the internal rate of return for year 2, I had to use –0.1 as the *guess* argument for the IRR() function:
>
> ```
> =IRR($B$27:D27, -0.1)
> ```
>
> With this initial estimate, Excel can't complete the iteration and returns the #NUM! error.

20

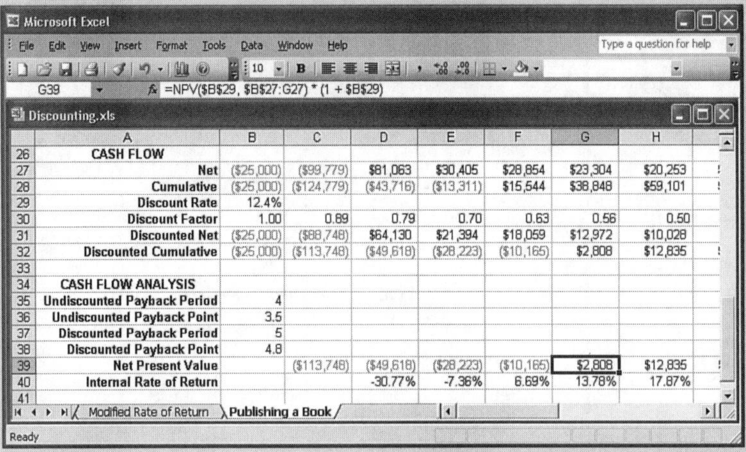

**Figure 20.19**
The cash-flow analysis for the book.

## From Here

- The IRR() and MIRR() functions use iteration to calculate their results. To learn more about iteration, **see** "Using Iteration and Circular References," **p. 90**.

- To get the details on the time value of money, **see** "Understanding the Time Value of Money," **p. 399**.

- To use the PV() function in a loan context, **see** "Calculating How Much You Can Borrow," **p. 412**.

- To use the PV() function in an investment context, **see** "Calculating the Required Initial Deposit," **p. 425**.

- For the details on compound interest, **see** "Understanding Compound Interest," **p. 418**.

20

# INDEX

## Symbols

+ (addition operator), 55

& (ampersand), 56

' (apostrophe), 64, 108

* (asterisk), 55, 77, 192, 286, 294

@ (at symbol), 77

\ (backslash), 77

{} (braces), 86-88, 321

, (comma), 34, 56, 76, 88

$ (dollar sign), 63

= (equals sign), 53-55, 310

> (greater than operator), 55

>= (greater than or equal to operator), 56

^ (exponentiation operator), 55

< (less than operator), 55

<= (less than or equal to operator), 56

<> (not equal to operator), 56

- (negation operator), 55

() (parentheses), 58-59, 112

% (percent sign), 55, 76

. (period), 76

# (pound sign), 76

? (question mark), 76, 294

; (semicolon), 33-34, 50, 56, 88

/ (slash), 55, 76

- (subtraction operator), 55

~ (tilde), 294

_ (underscore), 38, 43, 77

0 (zero), 76
- division by, 159
- hiding, 79
- rounding numbers toward/away from, 234-235

3D ranges, 12, 41-42

360-day year, 218

## A

ABS() function, 230

*The Absolute Beginner's Guide to VBA*, 100

absolute reference format, 63

account numbers
- generating, 147, 153
- looking up, 190

accounting formats, 73

accounts receivable aging worksheet, 168-171

ACCRINT() function, 442

accrued bond interest, 441

ACOS() function, 232

ACOSH() function, 232

Add Constraint dialog box, 382

Add Scenario dialog box, 331

Add Trendline command (Chart menu), 341

Add Trendline dialog box, 341-342

Add Watch dialog box, 121

add-ins, loading, 131-132

Add-Ins command (Tools menu), 131

Add-Ins dialog box, 131-132

adding values. *See* **summing values**

addition operator (+), 55

adjacent cells, selecting, 14

Advanced Filter dialog box, 300

advertising trends, 348

ages, calculating, 215-217

algebraic equations, 326-327

All criteria (AutoFilter), 293

allocation program, 379

Allowable Decrease option (Sensitivity reports), 393-394

Allowable Increase option (Sensitivity reports), 393-394

amortization schedules
- dynamic amortization schedules, 407-409
- fixed-rate amortization schedules, 406-407
- variable-rate mortgage amortization schedule, 413-415

ampersand (&), 56

Analysis ToolPak
- loading, 131-132
- statistical tools, 266-269
  - Anova: Single Factor tool, 267
  - Anova: Two-Factor with Replication tool, 267
  - Anova: Two-Factor Without Replication tool, 267
  - Correlation tool, 267, 271-272
  - Covariance tool, 267
  - Descriptive Statistics tool, 267-270
  - Exponential Smoothing tool, 267
  - F-Test Two-Sample for Variances tool, 267
  - Fourier Analysis tool, 268
  - Histogram tool, 268, 273-274
  - Moving Average tool, 268
  - Random Number Generation tool, 268, 275-276
  - Rank and Percentile tool, 268, 277-278
  - Regression tool, 268
  - Sampling tool, 268
  - t-Test: Paired Two-Sample for Means tool, 268